STAFFORDSHIRE PARISH REGIST

CU00780628

President

Col. I.S. Swinnerton

Chairman

Dr. P.D. Bloore

Hon.Secretary

Mr. I. Wallbank
82, Hillport Avenue,
Newcastle-under-Lyme,
Staffs
ST5 8QT
Email: secretary@sprs.org.uk

The Society has pleasure in placing in the hands of members a further volume of printed Staffordshire Parish Registers consisting of the Registers of the parish of Leigh

Enquiries concerning copies of registers already printed and still available for sale should be addressed to the Hon. Secretary

---

ISBN 978-0-9551159-8-1

British Library Cataloguing in Publication Data
A Catalogue record for this book is available from the British Library.

Acknowledgements

The register was transcribed by Marion Hall and indexed and prepared for printing by Robert Morton.

The Society would express its thanks to the PCC of All Saints Church Leigh, for permission to publish this register.

The Society is also indebted to Mrs Thea Randall, Head of Archives Service, Staffordshire County Record Office, for permission to use the microfiche for transcription purposes, for access to the original Register at Stafford and the Bishops Transcripts at the Lichfield Record Office. We would also like to thank Eve Proud for use of the photograph of All Saints Church and Eric Proud for the drawing outlining the location of the parish of Leigh on pages 3 and 5 respectively.

Transcribers Notes:-

Throughout this transcript the following abbreviations have been used:-

s/o	[the] son[ne] of
d/o	[the] daughter of
ux	uxoris eius
fa	filia
fs	filius
fi	filii

The Parish of Leigh

"Leigh is a parish divided into the townships of Leigh and Field, the former containing about 6800 acres of land, and 926 inhabitants, and the latter about 600 acres and 86 inhabitants. Lord Bagot is lord of the manor, and he and William Evans, Esq, own a great part of the parish.

Leigh township contains the hamlets of Church Leigh, Upper Leigh, and Lower Leigh, in the vale of the Blythe, and Leigh Railway Station, on the North Staffordshire line, five miles WNW of Uttoxeter. It also contains Dodsley, three quarters of a mile SW, Painley Hill, one and a half miles S, Middleton Green, two miles W by S, Upper & Lower Nobutt (or North-butt), one and a half miles ESE, and Withington, one mile E of Church Leigh.

Field township has a small village on the east side of the river Blythe, four and a half miles W of Uttoxeter. Field Hall, now a farmhouse, was formerly a seat of the Bagots. Field township passed from the Pipes to the Bagots, and was formerly thickly covered with wood, and was noted for a prodigious Witch Elm, cut down in 1680."

[From *History, Gazetteer and Directory of Staffordshire,* William White, Sheffield, 1851]

Church History

The Parish Church, dedicated to All Saints, was replaced at the expense of the Bagot family of Blithfield in 1845. The building was designed by a little-known architect, Thomas Johnson of Lichfield, and some say that it is the most perfect Victorian representation of Decorated architecture.   The Church is cruciform in shape and commands views to the south over the Blithe valley. Some of the medieval church survived the rebuilding, including the 14th century font and stained glass in the chancel.

The tiling of the chancel floor is reputed to have been designed by A.W.N. Pugin and supplied by the Stoke-on-Trent Pottery Manufacturer Herbert Minton. The Great West Window was designed by William Morris and (Sir) Edward Burne-Jones. An alabaster tomb of Sir John Ashenhurst (c1520) is in the south transcept.

'View of All Saints Church, Leigh, Staffordshire'
© Eve Proud; December 2008

Location of the Parish of Leigh

STAFFORDSHIRE

CHESHIRE

Longnor
Longnor

Rushton Spencer

Horton

Biddulph

Leek

Kidsgrove

Tunstall

Alstonfield
Grindon

Cheddleton

Burslem

Keele
Newcastle-u-Lyme

Hanley

STOKE ON TRENT

Blore

Oakamoor

Cheadle

Ellastone

Trentham

Alton

Maer

Tittensor

LEIGH

Rocester

Ashley

Loggerheads

Stone

Uttoxeter

Trent

Chartley

Adbaston

Eccleshall

Weston

Tutbury

Stowe

Rolleston

Seighford

Stafford

Abbots Bromley

Gnosall

Gt.Haywood

Burton on Trent

Church Eaton

Rugeley

Kings Bromley

Blymhill
Weston-u-Lizard

Lapley

Alrewas

Croxall

Penkridge

Cannock

Brewood

Lichfield

Codsall

Brownhills

Aldridge

Tamworth

SHROPSHIRE

Pattingham

WOLVERHAMPTON
Rushall

Willenhall

Bilston

Walsall

Sedgley

Wombourn

Tipton

Kingswinford

Dudley

West Bromwich

Brierley Hill

Kinver

WORCS

DERBYSHIRE

© Eric Proud - January 2009

Leigh, Staffordshire, Parish Register,
1541-1645

Regist baptizat, sepult et matrimonio regular infra poch de Leigh

MATRIMONIATA

1541
3 Jul   Margerye HYLL
30 Jul   Margerye CROMPTON
24 Sep   William PARKER
22 Nov   William AULTE
1542
5 Nov   Rogerus STATHAM
20 Jan   Willus SMYTHE
1543
8 Jul   Johes LOWE
22 Oct   Thomas CRUMPTON
22 Oct   Thomas BALLE
28 Oct   Johes RATCLYFFE
6 Nov   Richardus LEES
26 Nov   Johes WYTTERANS
26 Nov   Agneta MEDDLETON
3 Feb   Willus HYLL
1544
21 Oct   Johes AULTE
15 Jan   Thomas WARDE
22 Jan   Johes BAYLIE
22 Jan   Robertus WARDE
1545
.. May   B [or R?] *[damaged]*
.. Jul   *[damaged]*
.. Nov   *[damaged]* WYTHNALL
         [rest of page illegible & badly damaged]
1551
12 Oct   Thomas FOLDERINGE et Alicia ALLEN
19 Oct   Edvardus HOOE et Margeria TAYLIER
17 Jan   Johannes JOHNSON et Tomasina PEDLEY
24 Jan   Willus LYRCAM et Catherina BALL
1552
2 Jul   Johannes RUSSELL et Margeria AULTE
5 Jul   Thomas DRAKEFORDE et Ellena MELBORNE
29 Aug   Johannes WOODDE et Elizabetha CARTER
16 Jan   Willus BOTTE et Margareta GRENDON
1553
4 Jun   Willus ....NYALL et Elizabetha WYTTERANS
17 Sep   Johannes CROMPTON et Isabella TURNER
19 Sep   Johannes .... et Ellena STOANE
1 Nov   R......us .... et Elizabetha HARVEY
1554
10 Apr   Radulphus ADDERLEY [?] et Margareta BAGOTT [?]
18 Jun   Johannes B..... [et] ....

2 ... Willus [?] PEDLEY et Johanna [?] ...YLLES
28 ... Joh..... MY..... et .... BOTTE
13 Jan Johannes CARTER et ....
20 Jan Willus KYRCAM et Ellena ....
20 Jan Richardus TONKYNSON et Elizabetha COVELL
27 Jan Thomas CAN.... et ....
.. Feb Jo....... .... et ....
[rest of page illegible and badly damaged]

1561
28 Sep Henricus WALKER et Margeria BYLLINGE
23 Nov Edmundus PORTER et Elizabetha SHERRAT
30 Nov Johannes HOLLANDE et Isabella WYTTRYNS
1562
26 May Willus PROCTER et Catherina CHILDE
25 Oct Humfridus HYLL et Elizabetha FYTTON
7 Nov Robertus WOODE et Johanna BALL
10 Jan Robertus HORNEBYE et Felicia WALKER
21 Jan Thomas OWLEY et Margareta HODGESON
1563
24 Apr Johannes FORGE et Elizabetha PAYNE
8 Nov Edwardus ROYLEY et Agneta SHAWE
27 Jan Richardus BYRDE et ALICIA LEYES
14 Feb Johannes WALKER et Agneta HYDE
1564
1 Jul Richardus SHERRAT et Margareta CARTER
20 Aug Willus ASTBURYE et Dorothia COOKE
9 Sep Hugo OWLEY et Margareta SHERRAT
1565
7 Oct Thomas BYRCHE et Alicia SPOONER
1566
22 Apr Richardus FOORDE et Elizabetha MOSSE
21 Jul Franciscus MYDDLETON et Johanna WARDE
12 Oct Thomas BLAKEMAN et Johanna FOORDE
13 Oct Thomas BYRCHE et Elizabetha RUSSELL
10 Nov Robertus COVELL et Ellena BYRDE
18 Jan Willus BATE et Johanna CHYLDE
1567
14 Sep Richardus SHERRAT et Isabella ....
[2 more entries illegible]

1568
.. Nov .... HARVEY et Rosa F.......
14 Jan .... et Agneta ....
2 ... *[illegible]*
2 ... *[illegible]*
26 ... *[illegible]*
2. ... . et .... MYDDLETON
3 Feb *[illegible]*
[rest of page illegible & badly damaged]

1572
6 Jul Thomas AMERY et Agneta BEARDMORE
19 Nov Johannes HARVEY et Agneta SHERRAT
1 Jan Edwardus HOLTE et Franciscus KYRCAM

1 Jan   Franciscus SHERRAT et Elizabetha HARVEY
3 Feb   Johannes BLURTON et Elizabetha PORTER
6 Feb   Richardus CARTER et Agneta WARDE
1573
22 May   Johannes BAYLIE et Agneta BURGIS
26 Oct   Willmus TOMPKINSON et Elizabetha CARTER
22 Feb   Thomas KEELINGE et Johanna HARVEY
26 Feb   Johannes HYLL et Ellena DRAKEFORD
1574
1 Aug   Richardus SMYTHE et Margeria SHERRAT
4 Aug   Johannes HYDE et Agneta LEES
3 Nov   Humfridus MARGERUM et Isabella BYLLINGS
26 Jan   Johannes STUBBES et Cicellia STATHAM
1575
13 Aug   Georgius DEWBILL et Maria BLURTON
13 Feb   Christopherus HYDE et Ellena WALL
1576
25 Apr   Franciscus SMYTHE et Maria BATKYN
30 May   Franciscus KYRCAM et Anna WOODSALL
22 Jun   Johannes AULTE et Alicia CARTER
2 Jul   Humfridus MARGERAM et Johanna HARVEY
27 Nov   Henricus SMYTHE et Agneta COATES
26 Jan   Henricus HEATON et Margareta BOTTE
26 Jan   Hunfridus PEYDLEY et Margareta STONEEYARDE
1577
27 Jun   Johannes SAULTE et Ellena SHERRAT
4 Aug   Thomas MALKYN et Margareta RUSSON
14 Oct   Willmus CLUDDE et Johanna LEES
1578
27 Mar   Henricus SPOONER et Margareta SPENCER
14 …   Johannes WHYTEHURST et Esta SPENCER
1579
2 Aug   Thomas DYCHE [?] et Elizabetha OWLEY
1580
.. Sep   Thomas BENNET et Alicia A……. *[illegible]*
[1581]

Thomas C..KE et Elizabetha *[damaged]*
    et Ellena W.. *[damaged]*
[rest of page badly damaged – no dates or names have survived]
1584
9 Aug   Edwardus ROYLEY et Anthonissa WALLE
29 Nov   Johannes HURDMAN et Margareta SHERRAT
14 Jan   Willmus READE et Johanna ALLEN
1585
17 Jun   Thomas HURDE et Johanna EVES
21 Nov   Johannes HARVEY et Jana HYNCKS
14 Dec   Eliceus STATHAM et Francisca BYLLYNGES
1586
    [blank space]
1587
6 Jun   Johannes TILSTON et Dorothea BEETENSON

1588
23 Apr Georgius MALKYN et Margareta SHERRAT
Jul Johannes LEIGH et Alicia HARVEY
28 Jul Willmus SPOONER et Dorothea BYLANDE
26 Feb Richardus WOTTON et Elizabetha PEDLEY
30 Feb [stet] Hugo WALKER et Agneta COWAPE
7 Mar Johannes HARVIE et Anna HODGESON
1589
14 Jul Willmus KEENE et Jana BOWYER
17 Aug Eliceus BYRCHE et Catherina HODGESON
17 Aug Willmus SCOTTE et Ellena BYRCHE
3 Feb Willmus THACKER et Alicia RAWTON
2 Mar Willmus BYLLE et Francisca TURNER
1590
[blank space]
1591
24 Apr Richardus [?] SHERRAT et Alicia MASSYE
25 Oct [?Rog]….. HORDERNE et Margeria GREENEHOUGH
12 Dec ……… ……ARDE et Elizabetha CORKE
1592
9 … ………. BROWNE [?] et Ellena BL..SON [or BL..FO..?]
.. … ………. PHYLLIPPS et ……. ……..
.. Sep ……. ……… et Alicia B………
.. Nov *[illegible]*
1593
.. … Richardus *[illegible]*
.. … Joha….. *[illegible]*
.. … Joh…. *[illegible]*
.. … W……. *[illegible]*
[rest of page probably blank]
1594
12 May Radulphus HYDE et Jana WILKOPPE
22 Sep Lodovicus DYCHE et Anna LOWE
21 Dec Richardus PEDLEY et Elizabetha MOTTERAM
22 Dec Radulphus TAYLIER et Dorothea STUBBES
1595
2 Feb Franciscus WALL et Agneta WARDE
1596
24 Jan Willmus SHENTON et Dorothea TILSTON
1597
13 Jun Thomas BOWTH et Elizabetha KYNSON
9 Aug Anthonius LEES et Cicillia CANTRELL
18 Aug Willmus DRAKEFORDE et Gratia AWSTEN
10 Nov Johannes NEIDHAM et Agneta STATHAM
16 Nov Richardus PAKEMAN et Alicia BOWYER
1598
15 May Anthonius BLAKEMAN et Cicillia HODGESON
7 Aug Johannes CONWAYE et Anna MASSYE
14 Dec Franciscus MOORE et Margeria ROYLEY
1599
23 Sep Johes PHILLIPS et Maria MASSEY

6 Nov   Franciscus STATHAM et B...... WALKER
26 Dec   Helizeus HODGESON et Anna GALLIMORE p Licentium
14 Jan   Henricus HEATON et Johanna PEDLEY
1600
.. Apr   Willmus WOOD et Elizabetha WALL
.. Apr   Edwardus SHERRAT et Catherina HYDE
20 Apr   Willmus HOOFORDE et Anna MOTHERAM
22 ...   Henricus BOSWELL et Elizabetha ASTON
.. Jun   Stephanus WATSON et Helena TOWNSEND
26 Nov   Johes SUTTON par de Leeke et Alicia TRUSSILTE
         [rest of page damaged and illegible except 1601, 1602, 1603 written at left hand side]
1604
26 Nov   Thomam DUFFELT et Margeriam WARDE
1605
27 May   Radulphum CORKE et Isabellam TURNER
7 Jul   Anthonium HYDE et Katharina PEDLEY
30 Nov   Willmus SAMMSON et Katharina WILSON
10 Feb   Franciscus COTTON et Ellena TOMPKINSON
1606
6 Apr   Robertum POWELL et Anna COLLIER
22 Jun   Thomam SALTE et Elizabetha HOLLINS
30 Jun   Willmum BULLOCKE et Ellena BROWNE
5 Jul   Richardus DYCHE et Annam HODGESON
28 Jul   Willmum HODGESON et Ellenam DYCHE
1 Aug   Willmum HULME et Agnetam SPENSER
18 Aug   Thomam LOWE et Agnetam BILLINGE
4 Dec   Ricum CARTER et Ellenam DYCHE
1607
20 Jun   Henricum ATKINS et Elizabetham HYDE
3 Aug   Thomam PARKER et Dorotheam SMYTHE
1608
17 Feb   Thomam CROXTON et ....cam KEENE
26 Apr   Georgium FARMER et Elizabetham WALL
20 Oct   Willmum ......FORDE et Joanam WITTERING
1609
11 Nov   Thomam JOHNSON et Dorotheam BRASIER
1610
16 Apr   Willmum BELCHER et Ellenam NAYLOR
.. May   Willmum HILL et Marg.... ....SON
1 Nov   Willmum BLURTON et Annam DEGGE
29 Nov   Thomam COLLIER et Dorothea KEENE
1611
.. May   Ricum HODSON et Marg..... [?]NAR.....
         [illegible]
.. ...   Ricum [?] B.... et Anna SHERRAT
1612
20 Dec   .... et Margareta DYCHE
1613
.. ....   Willmum LECESTER et Elizabetha SMYTHE
15 Jan   Sampsona BOUGHIE et Jocosa ASTON
         Thomas COLLYER *[damaged]*

Arthur ...... *[damaged]*

1614

Nothinge done

1615

21 May	Willum MARTIN et Catherina ASTON
21 May	Johem WETTWOOD et Alicia SHEPPARD
5 Jul	Hugone PERSEVALL et Dorothea COTES

1616

24 Jul	Robertus SONT et Alicia WOOD
6 Sep	Willum GRUNDY et Margeria SAVAGE
30 Sep	Edvardum MANIFOLD et Dorothea LEES
17 Oct	Astone FOLDERING et Matheam HOADE
21 Oct	Michalum LATHEROPE et Jana SOAMS [?]
5 Nov	Radulpus LATHROPP et Margeriam ASTON
[ ]	Franciscus ATKINS et Cicilea HILL

1617

13 Jul	Willmum ALT et Saraa ENSWORTH
25 Oct	Georgius PY et Isabella TOMKINSON
3 Nov	Johes MIDDLETON et Agnes SHAWE
20 Nov	Johem TOOTH et Elizabetha SPENSER

1618

31 M..	Willmus AMBRE et Catherina HOUGHTON
13 Jun	Franciscus WILLIAMSON et Dithea [?] AMBRE
3 Aug	Robertu' TOWERS et Elizabetha SPOONER
13 Sep	Simones WARD et Margareta PROUDLOVE
20 Oct	Walteru' BLURTON et Anna WITTSNOLL [?]

1619

1 May	Johes STATHAM [?] et Jana ALT
.. Aug	Rich WHITALL et Margeria ....
8 Sep	Edwardus MERCER et Anna WOOD
8 Sep	Willmu' WHITHOUSE et Margareta WOLLOSON
6 Jan	..........us MILES et Jocosa GLOVER
7 Feb	Edwardus CARTER et Cicilia TOOTH

1620

14 Jun	Johannem [?] ROBINSON et Anna ALT
4 Sep	Thoma OSBORNE et Elizabetha MORE
2 Nov	Humphridus BAGNALL et Maria SMITH
14 May	Rogerus WOD et Margeria BOCKLEY
25 May	Henricus MAGIOR [?] et Katherina HOMES

1621

This yeare nothing ....

1622

27 Jan	Thoma *[illegible]*
29 Jan	Henri... GRUNDY et .... MALLOWE
3 Feb	W...... GLOVER et Anna ......

1623

24 May	Christopherum HILL et Jocosa BOWRING
24 Nov	..... NEVELL et ......eta BODEN [?]
3 Jan	Johannes PARKER et .... ROYER

1624

.. May	Rici SAVAGE et Elizabetham TALIER

.. Jun   .... BEARDSLEY et Anam POWELL
27 Jun   .... GILBERT
27 Sep   .... PRYER
.. Jan   .... Elizabetha ....
17 Jan   *[illegible]*

1625
.. Apr   Anthonius HYD et Dorothea WITTERINGE
17 Jul   Johes PEDLEY et Elizabetha SPENCER
23 Aug   Phillippus SHERWIN et Saram JOLLEY
20 Feb   Edvardus BARKER et Margareta ....

                                                           Johes Bakner [?] Rector

1626
12 Jun   Thomam WILSON et Saram HOLT
1 Dec   Edvardus HYDE et Jana WARD

1627
31 Mar   Johem CARTER et Margeria GRYNDY
15 Apr   Hugones WRIGHT et Elizabetha DAVIES
25 Feb   Thoma HYDE et Ellena SPENCER

1628
12 Jul   Amos HOLT et Susanna [ ]
2 Oct   Johan FLACKET et Maria DELKES
10 Nov   Sampsonem ALKIN et Johanna WITTERINGE
27 ...   Johem WHITBEY et Elizabetham HILL
3 Jan   Thomam SMITH et Margaretta SCOTT
4 May 1629   Thrustans LUEL et Ellena SPENCER

1629
14 Jan   Franciscus AMBERSLEY et Ana POWELL
23 Feb   Franciscus HAWKINS et Jana THACKER

1630
      Nothing done this year

1631
28 Apr   Richardus SPENSER et Margareta SPENSER
12 Jun   Johes KEELINGE et Margareta ALLEN
20 Jun   Robertus WHITALL et Jana SHERRAT
28 Nov   Richardus ALLEN et Maria PEDLEY
14 Jan   Willmus EDWARDS et Alicia AULT

1632
31 Jul   Franciscus BRADSHAW et Letticia CLARKE
22 Jan   Edvardus FORSTER et Anam WHITWICKE
14 Feb   Johem HODGSON et Elizabetha SPENCER

1633
4 Jan   Thoma GRIFFYN et Margareta WATTSON
1 Feb   Johes WHEATLEY et Jona PARMENTA

1634
19 Jun   Richardum PARKER et Philotes COVELL
25 Aug   Johem ALCOCK et Susana SONT
28 Oct   Willmum SHENTON et Elizabetha BROWNE
25 Nov   Johem GRATLEY et Jana KEENE

1635
30 Apr   Thomam WIGSON et Ellenam NORMANI
29 Aug   Willihelmus HARISON et Mariam HYDE

1636

19 Apr	Johem SHERRAT et Phelotis [ ]
7 Jun	Thomam ATKINS et Elizabetha STARKEY
20 Jun	Johnes SHERRAT et Elizabetha WARD
15 Sep	Robertus DEAKIN et Elizabetha COVELL
15 Nov	Johem FOLLOWES et Margareta NICKERSON
30 Jan	Thoma IPSON et Margareta DYCH

1637

26 Apr	Jacobus LEWIS et Anna SPENSER
.. …	Gulihelmum HARDEN et Anna GRIFFOLD
6 Jun	Johem INGRAMTHORP et Ellena BOTTE

1638

21 Jul	Johem PATE armiger et Letticia BRADSHAWE

1639

22 Apr	Thomam WAKLIN et Aliciam KORNE [?]
25 Jul	Johem AMERY et Dorothea ATKINS
4 …	Thomam SHERWINE et Elizabetham WITTERINGE
4 …	Gulihelmus COWAPP et Margareta SHERRAT
18 Nov	Radulphus GRAY et Francisca PHILLIPS
3 Dec	Henricus HANCOCKES et Elizabetham BIRD

1640

11 Dec	Gualterum SMYTH et Mariam DAVENPORT
16 Feb	Johannes CLARKE et Margarettam ROWLEY

Richard Chapman Rector

1641

3 May	Gulielmum BLURTON et Judith PARKER
4 May	Richardum AULT et Elizabetham MIDLETON
15 Jun	Thomam SPENSER et Margaretta GREATBATCH
5 Apr	Georgium RIKINS [?] et Brigit T……..
.. …	Thomam WRIGHT et Elizabetham ……….
22 Jan	Richardus [?]LOTON et Johannem COATE [?]

1642

Nothing done
The Parliament take arms against King Charles the first.

1643

Nothing done
Solemn League Covenant between Eng Scottish Parliaments.

1644

29 …	Johnes PEDLEY et Saram HAYWARD
26 …	Samuelem AUKINS et Annam YATES

1645

Nothing done
Archbishop Laud put to death
The King totally defeated at Nasby.

BAPTISMATA

1541

20 Aug	Elizabetha SHERRAT
2 Sep	Thomas DYCHE
12 Oct	John COVELDE

3 Dec	Izabell HERNE
2 Jan	Elizabeth KEY
8 Jan	Christopher BOWER
23 Jan	Frannces SHERRATT
8 Feb	Frannces WRIGHTE
18 Feb	Frannces MIDDLETON
20 Mar	Frannces KYRCAM

1542

1 Apr	Tomasyn KEELINGE in Ecc'lia Porciah de Leigh
2 Apr	Elena ALISANNDER
25 May	Frannciscus BYLLYNGE
27 Jun	Joanna SHERRATT
22 Aug	Christopher HYDE
19 Dec	Richardus WOOD
19 Dec	Elizabethe BYRCHE
16 Oct	Robertus COTE
10 Nov	Willus SPOONER
28 Jan	Thomas COVELDE
24? Feb	Richardus CARTER
27 Feb	Richardus SMYTHE

1543

10 May	Roberte SMYTHE
31 May	Roger SPRATTE
8 Jun	Thomas DYCHE
18 Jul	John HERVEY
31 Aug	Elizabetha BYRCHE
14 Sep	Elizabeth STATHAM
14 Oct	Margaret LEE
8 Nov	Frannces SPENCER
8 Nov	John BOWYER
20 Jan	Margerye TOMKYNSON
18 Feb	Alys BYRCHE
23 Feb	Thomas SHERRATT
23 Feb	Annes KEYLYNGE

1544

3 May	Ellen SPOONER
9 May	Annes WARDE
7 Jun	Margett WRIGHTE
15 Jun	Thomas HOLTE
8 Aug	Elizabetha DYCHE
6 Sep	Margaret COOTE
7 Jan	Margaret WOODE
9 Feb	Thomas HARVEY
16 Feb	Thomas MEDULTON
2 Mar	Margarett LOWE
12 Mar	William DYCHE

I Richard Chapman Parson of the Parish church of Lee alias Leigh in the County of Stafford haveing certaine intelligence of the …. [Eliz]abeth daughter of Edward and Hellena WRIGHT of Dodsley in the Parish aforesaid. And being also informed that it is the advise of her physician that flesh …….. and fytt meates dyett for the recovery of her health do herby (so farre fourth as in me lyeth) license the sayd Edward and Hellena to freshe meat in the .... for the eating of flesh for the use and sustenance of the said Elizabeth. And I do in lyke manner licence the said Elizabeth to eat flesh upon the sayd [day ?] continue during the sickness of the sayd Elizabeth and no longer. Dated the seaventh Day of March 1639

By me Richard Chapman
Rector of Leigh

1545

17 Apr	John HARVEY unlawfully bigotte
4 May	Frannces CARTER
25 Aug	Frannces ALTE
2 Sep	John BIRDE
30 Sep	William ALESANNDER
9 Oct	Joane HILL
24 Oct	John COVELL
30 Nov	Joane WETERYNS
12 Dec	Annes BOWER
12 Dec	Frannces PARKER
18 Dec	Joane WARDE
2 Jan	Alys LEE
20 Feb	James SUTTON

1546

1 Apr	Frannces KEELINGE
2 Apr	Roberte TOMKYNSON
16 Jun	Frannces SMYTHE
24 Jul	William STATHAM
20 Aug	Katherine WATSON
4 Nov	Frannces WOODE
20 Nov	Thomas WETERYNS
15 Dec	Frannces HARVEY
2 Jan	Agnes MEDULTON
18 Feb	Margarett DYCHE
18 Mar	Joane KEELINGE

1547

6 Apr	Frannces HOLTE
10 Apr	William LAPLONE
11 Apr	Richard WRIGHTE
23 Apr	Alys SHERRETT
17 May	John SPOONER
18 May	Frannces BYRCHE
5 Jul	Cicellie [ ]
4 Aug	Robert SHERRATT
6 Aug	Elizabeth LOWE
21 Sep	Roberte SMYTHE
15 Oct	John AULTE
20 Oct	Frannces WARDE
4 Nov	Joane CARTER
18 Dec	Roase MOLLERTE
15 Jan	Frannces HEYLE
6 Feb	Thomas KEELINGE

20 Feb   Roberte BOWER
1 Mar   Richarde SUTTON
18 Mar   Roger VENABLES
18 Mar   Alys CROMPTON
1548
30 Apr   Thomas STARKEY
25 May   Richarde PARKER
11 Jun   Agnes DYCHE
11 Jun   Margaret DYCHE
30 Jun   Margaret CAVNET
7 Jul   [ ] WOODE
9 Aug   Joane HARVEY
16 Sep   Ellen BYRCHE
20 Sep   Ellen ALEXANDER
2 Jan   John [ ]
23 Jan   Ellen HAUGHTON
22 Feb   Joane HOLTE
6 Mar   Catheryne MYDDLETON
6 Mar   Ellyn SMYTHE
1549
9 Apr   William SMYTHE
11 Apr   William HAWCHARDE
24 Apr   Frannces SHERRATT
19 May   Margerye HOLTE
9 Jun   Elizabethe BYRCHE
21 Jul   Thomas SPOONER
28 Jul   Walter BLURTON
31 Jul   Margaret CARTER
24 Aug   Thomas DYCHE
[no date]   Margaret [ ]
20 Oct   Marye HYLL
10 Nov   Joane WOLLASTON

R. Aston Rectoris ibid
Xpo [Christo] Hide ....
Willm Hodgeson

1549   remanent
20 Nov   Margaret SHERAT
21 Dec   John TOMKYNSON
25 Dec   Joyce WARDE
25 Jan   Edwarde HOOE
9 Feb   Margerye SUTTON
23 Feb   William VENABLES
28 Feb   [ ] WOODE
9 Mar   John WHYTTERYNS
13 Mar   Ellen HODGESON
1550
14 Apr   William AULTE
15 Apr   Ellen HARVEY
21 May   Margerye MYDDLETON
10 Jun   Margerye SHERAT
9 Jul   John HARVEY

16 Jul   William KEELINGE
20 Sep   [ ] BOWER
28 Sep   Joane ALLEYNE
5 Oct   Ellice SMYTHE s/o Henrye SMYTHE and Agnes his wife
5 Nov   Frannces CARTER d/o Tho: CARTER
23 Nov   John HILL s/o William HILL
1 Dec   Thomas SPENCER s/o Hugh SPENCER
23 Jan   Margerye CLEARKE d/o Wm CLEARKE
6 Feb   Thomas CARTER s/o Rich CARTER
20 Feb   Anthony HYLL s/o Humfrey HYLL
15 Mar   Frannces COVELL d/o William COVELL
20 Mar   William LOWE s/o John LOWE
20 Mar   Margerye SUTTON d/o George SUTTON

1551
2 Apr   Joane SHERAT d/o Raphe SHERAT
14 Apr   Thomas SMYTHE s/o William SMYTHE
9 May   Edwarde PARKER s/o Thomas PARKER
2 Jul   William ALLEYNE s/o Roberte ALLEYNE
19 Jul   John BLURTON s/o William BLURTON
31 Jul   Thomas ARCHARDE s/o Roger ARCHARDE
1 Aug   Elizabeth JONSON d/o John JONSON
10 Aug   Joane DYCHE d/o William DYCHE
.. Sep   William FALDERINGE s/o Tho: FALDERINGE
23 Sep   Frannces KEELINGE d/o James KEELINGE
12 Oct   Elizabeth WAYDE d/o Christopher WAYDE
22 Oct   Richarde HOLTE s/o Nicholasse HOLTE
2 Nov   Henrye VENABLES s/o Wm VENABLES
3 Nov   Richarde WAYDE s/o Roberte WAYDE
31 Jan   Margaret HOLASTON d/o Nic: HOLASTON
14 Feb   Henrye SPOONER s/o Tho: SPOONER
22 Feb   Katheryne DRAKEFORDE d/o Tho: DRAKEFORDE
3 Mar   Roger WOODE s/o Thomas WOODE

1552
1 May   Joane SHERRATT d/o William SHERRATT
2 May   Joane MYDDLETON d/o Thomas MYDDLETON
22 May   Joane ALYSANNDER d/o John ALYSANNDER
7 Jun   Richarde HARVEY s/o John HARVEY
23 Jul   Lewes BYRKE s/o William BYRKE
26 Aug   Frannces DYCHE d/o Tho: DYCHE
16 Sep   Margerye WOODE d/o John WOODE
3 Nov   William LOWE s/o John LOWE
20 Nov   Joane EVYS d/o Robte EVYS
26 Dec   Stephen SPENCER s/o Hugh SPENCER
15 Jan   Ellisse STATHAM s/o Roger STATHAM
22 Jan   Lewes DYCHE s/o Richarde DYCHE
20 Feb   Richarde SHERRATT s/o William SHERRATT
11 Mar   Anthone BLURTON s/o William BLURTON
11 Mar   Richarde BOTTE s/o William BOTTE

1553
11 Apr   Stephen SMYTHE s/o Will.....
7 Mar   William HYLL s/o ....

21 Mar Frannces KYRKAM s/o ....
9 Jul Margerye PARKER d/o Thomas ......
25 Jul Thomas RUSHTON s/o William RUSHTON
15 Aug William WARDE s/o Roberte WARDE
6 Sep Margret SHERRATT d/o Raphe ....
8 Sep John DYCHE s/o William DYCHE
8 Sep William WOODE s/o Th....
2 Nov Thomas HEAPE s/o R......
3 Nov William LEES s/o Nicholas ....
7 Nov Thomas WARDE s/o Christopher WARDE
20 Nov Mawde MYDDLETON d/o Tho: MYDDLETON
4 Dec Thomas JOHNSON s/o Richarde JONSON
19 Dec Cicellie HODGESON d/o Robte HODGESON
18 Jan John OLASTONE & Elizabeth children of Nicholas OLASTONE
17 Feb Jane COVELL d/o William COVELL
20 Feb Joane SUTTON d/o George SUTTON
27 Feb Elizabeth DRAKEFORDE d/o Tho: DRAKEFORD
1 Mar Ales CARTER d/o Richarde CARTER
7 Mar Alyce HOLTE d/o Nicholas HOLTE
18 Mar Margerye d/o Roger ORCHARDE
1554
26 May William KEELINGE s/o James KEELINGE
10 Jun Cicellie HYLL d/o Humfrey HYLL
23 Jul Joyce CLEARKE d/o William CLEARKE
24 Aug Isabell ALEXANDER d/o John ALEXANDER
13 Sep Ellyn HARVEY d/o John HARVEY
8 Oct William JOHNSON s/o John JOHNSON
24 Nov Frannces BEE d/o John BEE
10 Dec Marye BLURTON d/o William BLURTON
25 Dec Ellyn DYCHE d/o Richarde DYCHE
7 Jan Raphe CONWEY s/o William CONWEY
7 Feb Allys WYTHERYNGES d/o John WYTHERYNGES
9 Feb Katheryne SMYTHE d/o Thomas SMYTHE
24 Feb John CROMPTON s/o John CROMPTON
11 Mar Joane WARDE d/o Roberte WARDE
13 Mar Margarett SPENSER
1555
15 Jun Thomas LOWE s/o John LOWE
31 Jul Joane SMYTH d/o William SMYTHE
7 Aug Thomas ALLYN s/o Roberter ALLYN
16 Aug Richarde MYLNER s/o John MYLNER
25 Aug William SPOONER s/o Thomas SPOONER
20 Aug John KEELINGE s/o James KEELINGE
31 Aug John SPENSER s/o Hugh SPENSER
6 Oct Thomas HOOE s/o Edwarde HOOE
29 Nov Joane KYRCAM d/o William KYRCAM
20 Dec Alyce DRAKEFORDE d/o Thomas DRAKEFORDE
11 Jan Elizabeth BALL d/o John BALL
16 Jan Alyce PEYNE d/o Roberte PEYNE
19 Feb .... d/o Roger ORCHARDE
1 Mar Joane SHARRATT d/o William SHARRATT

4 Mar John SHARRATT s/o Raphe SHARRATT
13 Mar Isabell WARDE d/o Christopher WARDE
23 Mar Cicellye STATHAM d/o Roger STATHAM
1556
25 Apr James CLEARKE s/o William CLEARKE
7 Apr Humfrey FOLDERINGE s/o Thomas FOLDERINGE
14 May Joane MARTYN d/o Richarde MARTYN
4 Jun Joane CROMPTON d/o John CROMPTON
          Alse CARTER *[written in margin next to following entry]*
13 Jun Katheryne CARTER d/o John CARTER
4 Jul Roberte HYLL s/o Humfrey HYLL
28 Aug Richarde DYCHE s/o William DYCHE
2 Sep John LEE s/o Thomas LEE
2 Oct Jane BLURTON d/o William BLURTON
4 Oct Agnes PARKER d/o Thomas PARKER
13 Nov Raphe JOHNSON s/o Richarde JOHNSON
13 Sep Cicellye MOORE d/o Thomas MOORE
25 Sep Jane BLURTON d/o William BLURTON
23 Feb Nicholas LEES s/o Nicholas LEES
1 Mar Katheryne HARVEY d/o Phpi HARVEY
4 Mar William DYCHE s/o Thomas DYCHE
23 Mar Cicellye LEES d/o Nicholas LEES
1557
20 Apr William BALL s/o John BALL
20 Apr Isabell CARTER d/o Richarde CARTER
20[?] Apr Margarett BOTTE d/o William BOTTE
30 May Katheryne SUTTON d/o George SUTTON
3 Jun Joane HOLTE d/o Nicholas HOLTE
21 Jun Alice WOODE d/o John WOODE
6 Jul Richarde KYRCAM s/o William KYRCAM
20[?] Aug Austyne WATSON s/o Thomas WATSON
5 Sep Margerye WARDE d/o Roberte WARDE
23 Sep Nycholas HYLL s/o Humfrey HYLL
25 Sep Nycholas JOHNSON s/o John JOHNSON
2 Nov William and Elizabeth MORE children of Thomas MORE
13 Jan Richarde SMYTHE s/o William SMYTHE
18 Jan William DRAKEFORDE s/o Tho: DRAKEFORDE
23 Jan Cicellie ALLEN d/o Roberte ALLEYN
23 Jan Isabell CONWAY d/o William CONWAY

                                      R. Aston Rectoris ibid
                                         Xpo *[Christo]* Hide
                                          Willm Hodgson

1558
18 Apr Ellen SHERRATT d/o Raphe SHERRATT
27 May Joane ORCHARDE d/o Roger ORCHARDE
3 Jun Edmunde TYTLEY s/o John TYTLEY
11 Jun Margarett BYLLINGE d/o Thomas BYLLINGE
13 Jun Alyce WALCLATT d/o Thomas WALCLATTE
29 Jun John FOLDERINGE s/o Thomas FOLDERINGE
18 Jul Richarde SPENSER s/o Hugh SPENSER
19 Jul Elizabeth BLURTON d/o William BLURTON

15 Sep   Richarde WATSON s/o Thomas WATSON
13 Oct   William WALLE s/o Frances WALLE
25 Oct   Agnes LOWE & Katheryne the daughters of John LOWE
29 Oct   Joane HARRISON d/o Raphe HARRISON
6 Nov   Alyce WARDE d/o Roberte WARDE
8 Nov   Margaret WARDE d/o Christopher WARDE
16 Jan   Joane BYRKE d/o William BYRKE
21 Jan   Thomas BALL s/o John BALL
1 Mar   Margerye HARVEY d/o John HARVEY
12 Mar   Jane WALLTON d/o Hugh WALLTON
1559
2 Jun   Alice CROMPTON d/o John CROMPTON
24 Jul   James HYLL s/o Humfrey HYLL
22 Aug   Alyce KYRCAM d/o William KYRCAM
28 Aug   Elizabethe BOWYER d/o Tho: BOWYER
10 Sep   Cicellie THACKER d/o Roberte THACKER
21 Sep   Richarde PEDLEY s/o William PEDLEY
24 Sep   [Omitted] MOORE s/o Thomas MOORE
13 Oct   John BYLLINGE s/o Thomas BYLLINGE
11 Nov   Martyne LOWE & Henrye the sonnes of John LOWE
5 Feb   James JOHNSON s/o John JOHNSON
1560
31 Mar   Thomas FOORDE s/o Henrye FOORDE
6 Apr   Ellenor ORCHARDE d/o Roger ORCHARDE
20 Apr   Alyce ALLEYN d/o Roberte ALLEYN
8 Apr   Ellenor HEAPE d/o Raphe HEAPE
9 May   Ellen DYCHE d/o Thomas DYCHE
21 May   Ellen BLURTON d/o William BLURTON
21 May   Anthonye BALLE s/o John BALLE
.. ...   Agnes WATSON d/o Thomas WATSON
24 Jun   Christopher ...... s/o George SUTTON
31 Jul   Margerye SMYTHE d/o Thomas SMYTHE
18 Aug   William BOTTE s/o Richarde BOTTE
23 Aug   Edward FOLDERINGE s/o Thomas FOLDERINGE
24 Aug   Henrye HODGESON s/o William HODGESON
11 [?] Oct   Richard SYMONS s/o Richard SYMONS
3 Nov   Wenefreyd PEDLEY d/o William PEDLEY
25 Nov   Edwarde ASTON s/o Anthonye ASTON
18 Jan   Thomas CONWAYE s/o John CONWAYE
24 Jan   Cicellye HOLLTE d/o Nicholas HOLLTE
25 Jan   Elleyn LOWE d/o John LOWE
10 Feb   Elizabeth PEDLEY d/o Wm: PEDLEY
17 Feb   Anthonye BOWYER s/o William BOWYER
2 Mar   James DRAKEFORDE s/o Thomas DRAKEFORDE
1561
1 Jun   Frannces BYRDE s/o Anthonye BYRDE
28 Jun   Peeter SKYDMOORE s/o John SKYDMOORE
5 Jul   Randle HYDE s/o William HYDE
31 Aug   Lewes HYLLE s/o Humfrey HYLLE
20 Sep   Jane PHILLIPPES d/o Hugh PHILLIPPES
2 Nov   William CROMPTON s/o John CROMPTON

30 Nov Frannces LYNNALLES s/o Robte LYNNALLES
30 Nov Elleyn HODGESON d/o William HODGESON
19 Jan   Jane THACKER d/o Roberte THACKER
12 Feb   Cicellye ORCHARDE d/o Roberte ORCHARDE
21 Feb   Richarde FOLDERINGE s/o Thomas FOLDERINGE
20 Mar Elleyn KEY d/o William ...

1562

27 Mar Margerye BYLLINGE d/o Tho... ....
30 Apr   Alyce BOTTE d/o Richarde BOTTE
17 May John JOHNSON s/o John JOHNSON
21 May Peeter SHERRAT s/o Raphe SHERRAT
 1 Aug   John PROCTOR s/o William PROCTOR
10 Aug Elizabethe KYRCAM d/o William KYRCAM
22 Aug Joanne BALLE d/o John BALLE
 6 Sep   Stephan WATSON s/o Thom.. ......
29 Sep   Ellenor CLEARKE d/o ....
28 Oct   Elleyn WEYDGEWOOD d/o ....
28 Nov William BYRKES s/o W...... BYRKES
21 Dec   Alyce FOORDE d/o H........ FOORDE
23 Jan   Frannces PEYDLEY d/o William ....
30 Jan   Agnes WARDE d/o Roberte .....
 6 Mar   William HARRYSON s/o Nycholas HARRYSON
20 Mar Frannces HARVEY s/o John HARVEY

1563

18 Apr   William SUTTON s/o George SUTTON
 1 May Anthonye DYCHE s/o William DYCHE
15 May Elizabeth PARKER d/o Edwarde PARKER of the pishe of Ewgreve &
          Alyce ASCHETON of the same pishe Bastarde
29 May Alyce BLURTON d/o William BLURTON
24 Jul   Randle BYRDE s/o Anthonye BYRDE
24 Aug Bartholomewe CONWAYE s/o John CONWAYE
12 Sep   Thyomas MOORE s/o Thomas MOORE
10 Oct   Elleyn HEAPE d/o Raphe HEAPE
15 Oct   William OLEY s/o Roger OLEYE
 6 Nov   Roberte HYLL s/o Humfrey HYLL
 8 Jan   Jane WATSON d/o Thomas WATSON
26 Feb   Roberte ORCHARDE s/o Roger ORCHARDE
 4 Mar   Richarde PEYDLEY s/o William PEYDLEY

1564

28 Mar Anthonye THACKER s/o Roberte THACKER
25 Apr   Elleyn MYLNER d/o John MYLNER
26 Jul   Thomas DRAKEFORDE s/o Thomas DRAKEFORDE
18 Aug Elizabethe ROYLEY d/o Edwarde ROYLEY
23 Sep   Frannces SHERRAT d/o Richarde SHERRAT
25 Nov   Elizabethe LEES d/o Frannces LEES
21 Oct   Thomas HODGESON s/o William HODGESON
25 Dec   Marye HANSON d/o Richarde HANSON
 3 Jan   Agnes BOTTE d/o Richarde BOTTE
16 Jan   Frannces BYLLINGE s/o Frannces BYLLINGE
20 Jan   Agnes PEDLEY d/o William PEDLEY
20 Jan   Thomas RUMNEY s/o Roberte RUMNEY

1 Jan	Marye WARDE d/o Roberte WARDE
5 Feb	Thomas KEY s/o William KEY
18 Feb	Frannces LEEY s/o Thomas LEEY
18 Feb	Margerye BOWYER d/o William BOWYER
3 Mar	Agnes SHARRAT d/o Raphe SHARRAT
23 Mar	Agnes & Katheryne LOWE ds/o John LOWE

1565

1 May	Agnes COWAPPE d/o Thomas COWAPPE
5 May	William LYNNALLES s/o Roberte LYNNALLES
8 May	Elizabethe ASTON d/o Anthonye ASTON
28 May	Thomas COATES s/o Alexannder COATES
3 Jun	Frannces JOHNSON s/o John JOHNSON
3 Jun	Will... ...... [s/o] Henrye FOORDE
.. ....	Hugh HEAPE s/o Raphe HEAPE
11 Nov	Elleyn DYCHE d/o Wm: DYCHE
16 Dec	Ellyn OLEY d/o Hughe OLEY
13 Jan	Alyce WATSON d/o Thomas WATSON
19 Jan	Agnes BYLLINGE d/o Thomas BYLLINGE
7 Mar	Agnes HARRYSON d/o Nicholas HARRYSON

1566

4 Apr	Katheryne LEES d/o Frannces LEES
7 Apr	John PEYDLEY s/o William PEYDLEY
1 May	Frannces CONWAYE s/o John CONWAYE
25 Apr	Joane PEYDLEY d/o William PEYDLEY
5 May	Susanne BEE d/o John BEE
6 May	Frannces BEARDEMOORE s/o John BEARDEMOORE
24 Jul	William PHILLIPPES s/o Hugh PHILLIPPES
24 Jul	Margaret SPENSER d/o Hugh SPENSER
25 Jul	Cycellye ROYLEY d/o Edward ROYLEY
21 Sep	Frannces BYLLINGE d/o John BYLLINGE
10 Feb	Dorothye THACKER d/o Roberte THACKER
1 Mar	William GREENEHOUGH s/o Wm. GREENEHOUGH
1 Mar	Elizabeth MYLNER d/o John MYLNER
31 Aug	Elizabethe BYRCHE
14 Oct	Margarett LEE
8 Nov	Frannces SPENSER
20 Jan	Margerye TOMKYNSON
18 Feb	Alice BYRCHE
23 Feb	Thomas SHERRATT
23 Feb	Agnes KEELINGE

R. Aston Rectoris ibid
Xpo Hide
Willm Hodgeson ......

1567

25 Mar	John LEEY s/o Thomas LEEY
11 Jun	Frannces HARVYE d/o Stephen HARVYE
27 Jul	Frannces MYDDLETON d/o Frannces MYDDLETON
25 Jul	Ellen BYRCHE d/o Thomas BYRCHE
9 Aug	Roase HARRYSON d/o Nicholas HARRYSON
7 Sep	Raphe ORCHARDE s/o Roger ORCHARDE
12 Sep	Anthonye BLACKMAN s/o Tho: BLACKMAN

23 Sep William HODGESON s/o William HODGESON
28 Sep Frannces MOORE s/o Thomas MOORE
5 Oct Margery ROYLEY d/o Edward ROYLEY
12 Dec William BOTTE s/o Richarde BOTTE
9 Feb Frannces CATERBANKE d/o Raphe CATERBANKE
11 Feb Jane HEAPE d/o Raphe HEAPE
28 Feb John BEARDEMOORE s/o John BEARDEMOORE
7 Mar Cicellie BYLLINGES d/o Thomas BYLLINGES
12 Mar Thomas SHARRATT s/o Raphe SHARRATT
16 Mar Roase BYLLINGE d/o Roger BYLLINGES
1568
25 Mar Margerye SHARRATTE d/o Richarde SHARRATT
10 Apr Alyce LEEY d/o Thomas LEEY
30 May Isabell BOWYER d/o William BOWYER
30 Jun William OLEY s/o Hugh OLEY
23 Jul Agnes LEES d/o Frannces LEES
28 Jul Margaret COATE d/o Alexannder COATES
30 Jul William COVELL s/o Roberte COVELL
17 Sep George KEENE s/o Richarde KEENE
19 Sep Margaret HURTE d/o Roberte HURTE
27 Nov Ales CONWAYE d/o John CONWAYE
1569
17 Apr Elleyn CATERBANKE d/o Raphe CATERBANKE
22 May Frannces BYLLINGE s/o Thomas BYLLINGES
28 Jun Frannces NAYLLER s/o Roberte NAYLLER
6 Jul Elizabethe HARVEY d/o Stephen HARVEY
27 Jul Frannces RAWLYN
.. Sep Joane PEDLEY d/o William PEDLEY
20 Sep Thomas HEAPE s/o Raphe HEAPE
20 Sep Annys KEY d/o William KEYE
16 Nov Walter ASTON s/o Anthonye ASTON
27 Nov Thomas WALLEY s/o Hugh WALLEY
16 Jan Elizabethe BOTTE d/o Richarde BOTTE
3 Feb Margarett MYLLER
1570
22 Apr Jane COVELL d/o Roberte COVELL
15 Apr John HODGESON
29 Apr Thomas CHESSHIRE
15 Jun Margaret GREENEHOUGHE d/o William GREENEHOUGH
2 Sep John WARDE s/o Roberte WARDE
29 Sep Margarett ORCHARDE d/o Roger ORCHARDE
29 Sep Joane ROYLEY d/o Edwarde ROYLEY
30 Sep Anthonye LEES s/o Frannces LEES
15 Oct Thomas MYDDLETON s/o Frannces MYDDLETON
25 Sep William SHERRATT s/o Raphe SHERRATT
17 Oct Agnes SHERRATT d/o Richarde SHERRATT
17 Mar Jane LEA
20 Mar Anthonye HURTE
20 Mar Agnes BYLLINGE
10 Oct Cicellye TURNER d/o Roberte TURNER

1571

1 Sep	Roberte HARVYE
14 Nov	Frannces KEYNE s/o Richarde KYNE
6 Jan	Agnes HEAPE d/o Raphe HEAPE
8 Jan	Marye BYRCHE d/o Thomas BYRCHE
2 Feb	Roberte WOLLEY
26 Mar	Elizabeth LEA d/o Thomas LEA
26 Mar	Anthonye HURTE s/o Roberte HURTE
30 May	Agnes KEELINGE d/o Thomas KEELINGE
1 Oct	Roberte HARVEY s/o Stephen HARVEY
4 Feb	Roberte NAYLER s/o Roberte NAYLER

1572

[blank space]

1573

26 Mar	John ROYLEY s/o Edwarde ROYLEY
20 May	John HARVEY s/o William HARVEY

[blank space]

1574

5 Apr	Thomas SANCT fs Thoma SANCT
27 Apr	Chistopherus BYRCHE fs Thoma BYRCHE
30 May	Willus HILL fs Johis HILL
25 Jun	Agneta COKE fa Thoma COKE
28 Jul	Maria ASTON fa Anthonii ASTON
22 Sep	Willus LEES fs Frannsisci LEES
22 Sep	Margeria LEES fa Frannsisci LEES
18 Oct	Walterus BLURTON fs Johis BLURTON
26 Oct	Frannsiscus MOTTERAM filis Henrici MOTTERAM
12 Nov	Thomas HARVEY fs Thoma HARVEY
1 Jan	Johes KEELINGE fs Thoma KEELINGE
12 Jan	Agneta WOLLEY fa Hugonis WOLLEY
18 Jan	Fransiscus HARVEY
19 Jan	Robertus MARGEERAM fs Humfridi MARGERAM
27 Jan	Frannsiscus SALTE fili Fransisci SALTE
13 Mar	Robertus NAYLER fs Roberti NAYLER

1575

7 Apr	Margareta TOMKYNSON fa Roberti TOMKINSON
4 May	Thomas NORTHE filuus Nicholai NORTHE
21 Jul	Johes THACKER fs Roberti THACKER
22 Jul	Thomas SMYTHE fs Richardi SMYTHE
7 Aug	Elizabeth HEAPE fa Radi
20 Oct	Agneta BROWNE fa Henrici BROWNE
6 Nov	Johes MIDDETON fs Fransisci MIDDLETON
1 Dec	Dorothea fa Philippi DRAYCOT
6 Dec	Anna fa Stephani HARVEY
1 Jan	Fransiscus fs Thoma WARDE
10 Feb	Elena OSBOURNE
3 Mar	Jana fa Johis HYLL
6 Mar	Margareta COLLYER
18 Mar	Agneta COTES fil Fransisci

1576

6 May	Thomas LEES fs Fransisci LEES

6 Jun   Fransiscus fs Christopheri HEAPE
20 Jun   Ricus fs Thoma COWHOP
7 Jul   Johes fs Thoma LEES
11 Aug   Fransisca HYDE fa Xpi HYDE
18 Aug   Elliceus HODGESON fs Willmi HODGESON
27 Sep   Ellena COWELL fa Roberti COWELL
28 Nov   Katherina SHERRAT fa Rici SHERRAT
10 Jan   Susanna fa Philippi DRAYCOTTE
10 Mar   Elizabeth fa Johis BYRCHE
14 Mar   Nicholaus NORTHE fs Nicholai NORTHE

> R. Aston Rectoris ibid
> ... Hide ....
> William Hodgeson

1577
27 Mar   Ellena TOMKYNSON fa Roberti TOMKYNSON
6 Apr   Jane BLURTON fa Johis BLURTON
27 Apr   Margareta MOSELEY fa Willmi MOSELEY
5 Jun   Johes CARTER fs Richardi CARTER
20 Sep   SMYTHE fa Henrici SMYTHE
20 Sep   Joanna COATES fa Francisci COATES
22 Sep   Robertus SUNCTE fs Thoma SANCTE
23 Sep   Franciscus fili Thoma SANCT
5 Oct   Elizabetha fa Stephani HARVEY
5 Nov   Elizabetha fa Edwardi TUCKETT
23 Dec   Margeria fa Johis HARVEY
23 Feb   Johes fs Johis HYLL
27 Feb   Margareta fa Francisci AULTE
1578
9 Mar   Franciscus MARGERAM fs Humfridi MARGERAM
27 Mar   Anthonius CLUDDE fs Willmi CLUDDE
28 Mar   Robertus fs Francisci MYDDLETON
1 May   Joanna fa Thoma KEELINGE
1 May   Thomas fs Henrici SPOONER
5 Jun   Cicellia fa Willmi STATHAM
3 Oct   Georgius fs Michaelis FORSTER
1 Nov   Anthonius fs Philippi DRAYCOTTE
2 Nov   Robertus fs Francisci LEES
27 Nov   Robertus fs Roberti NAYLER
16 Dec   Edwardus HOWE fs Thoma HOWE
13 Jan   Joanna fa Johis GRUNDYE
16 Mar   Franciscus fs Johis AULTE
1579
1 Apr   .... SHARRAT fs Thoma SHARRATT
9 Apr   Agnes BOTTE fa Richardi BOTTE
12 May   Willus AULTE fs Francisci AULTE
15 May   Philippus CARTER fs Richardi CARTER
3 Jul   Willus BLURTON fs Johis BLURTON
6 Jul   Robertus NORTHE fs Nicholai NORTHE
4 Aug   Robertus COVELL fs Roberti COVELL
4 Oct   Thomas WOODE fs putat Robti KEELINGE et Elizabetha WOODE
11 Oct   Margareta fa Richardi SHARRAT

2 Nov	Radulphus JACKSON fs [ ] JACKSON
13 Dec	Oliverus fs Thoma LEA
1 Jan	Edwardus FORSTER fs Michaelis FORSTER
3 Jan	Isabella fa Thoma KEELINGE
11 Mar	Thomas fs Fransisci COATES
12 Mar	Henricus MOTTERAM fs Henrici MOTTERAM

1580

28 Mar	Agnes TOMPKINSON fa Roberti TOMPKYNSON
22 Apr	Agnes HYLL fa Johis HYLL
23 Apr	Jana MELLINGTON fa Willmi MELLINGTON
12 Jun	Francisca fa Johis GRUNDIE
17 Aug	Franciscus fs Francisci AULTE
25 Aug	Anthonius fs Magistra AMIS
23 Sep	Humfridus fs Francisci WARDE
22 Oct	Willus fs Willmi SALTE
29 Sep	Margareta fa Thoma SHARRAT
2 Jan	Johes fs Johis AULTE
13 Jan	Margareta fa Willmi HODGESON
17 Jan	Jana fa Willmi CLUDE
20 Jan	Franciscus fs Willmi STATHAM
9 Feb	Joanna fa Philippi DRAYCOTT

1581

7 Apr	Franciscus MASSIE fs Thoma MASSIE
25 Apr	Ellena DYCHE fa Thoma DYCHE
2 Jun	Johes MARGERAM fs Humfridi MARGERAM
30 Aug	Joanna NORTHE fa Nicholai NORTHE
2 Sep	Dorothea FORSTER fa Michaelis FORSTER
16 Oct	Thomas SPENSER fs Francisci SPENSER
21 Dec	Willimus SPOONER fs Henrici SPOONER
6 Jan	Willimus SHARRAT fs Richardi SHARRAT
21 Jan	Willimus KEELINGE fs Thoma KEELINGE
28 Jan	Isabella TOMPKYNSON fa Roberti TOMPKYNSON
29 Jan	Thomas KEELINGE fs Francisci KEELINGE
1 Feb	Catharina HOWE fa Thoma HOWE
10 Feb	Alicea BLURTON fa Johis

1582

2 Apr	Penelope ASTON fa Anthonii ASTON et Anne ux
9 Apr	Willus GRUNDIE fs Johis GRUNDIE et Elizabethe ux
20 Apr	Thomas SPOONER fs Henrici SPOONER et Margarete ux
3 Jun	Richardus BYRKE fs Lodovici BYRKE et Alicea RAWLEN
[ ] Jul	Agnes HYLL fa Johis HYLL et Ellena ux
[ ] Jul	[ ] NAYLER fa Roberti NAYLER et [ ] ux
20 Aug	Sara ASTON fa Richardi ASTON et Anna ux
23 Aug	Henricus SMYTHE fs Henrici SMYTHE et Agneta ux
30 Aug	Anthonius LEA fs Thoma LEA et Agneta ux
28 Oct	Johes COATES fs Francisci COATES et [ ] ux
2 Dec	Joanna LEES fa Francisci LEES et Margerie ux
9 Jan	Anna CLUDDE fa Willmi CLUDDE et Joanna ux
24 Dec	Richardus WYLDE fs [ ] WYLDE et [ ] ux
17 Feb	Thomas BYRD fs Randulphi BYRDE et Alicea WALKELAT
25 Feb	Richardus ALTE fs Francisci ALTE et [ ] ux

13 Mar	Richardus BOTTE fs Richardi BOTTE et M'garete ux
1583	
18 Apr	Elizabetha fa Thoma COLLYER et Katherina ux
15 May	Randulphus MARGERAM fs Sampsoni MARGERAM et [ ] HEAPE
[ ] May	Margareta RROWNE fa Henrici BROWNE et [ ] ux
6 Jul	Johes WARDE fs Symonis WARDE et Margareta ux
8 Sep	Anna AUTE fa Johes AUTE et Alicea ux
20 Oct	Ezra ASTON fa Richardi ASTON Rector de Leigh et Anna ux
1 Nov	Elizabeth SPENSER fa Willmi SPENSER et Anna ux
3 Nov	Anthonius HYDE fs Xpi [Christi] HYDE et Ellena ux
1 Dec	Jacobus KEELINGE fs Thoma KEELINGE et Joanna ux
9 Dec	Elizabeth NORTHE fa Nicholai NORTHE et M'gareta ux
24 Dec	Maria FORSTER fa Michaelis FORSTER et Isabella ux
7 Feb	Elizabeth SPENCER fa Francisci SPENCER et M'gareta ux
16 Feb	Willus SMYTHE fs Stephani SMYTHE et Elizabeth ux
1584	
30 Mar	Elizabeth ALLEN fa Willmi ALLEN et M'gerie ux
1 May	Humfridus BURNE fs Davidi BURNE et Jana ux
9 Jun	Maria BLURTON fa Johis BLURTON et Elizabeth ux
1 Oct	[ ] GRUNDIE fs Johis GRUNDIE et Elizabeth ux
14 Oct	Xpoferus WARDE fs Symonis WARD et Margareta ux
1 Nov	Catharina KEELINGE fa Francisci KEELINGE et Jana ux
10 Dec	Robertus ASTON fs Richardi ASTON et Anna ux
10 Dec	[ ] TOMPKINSON fa Roberti TOMPKINSON et Elizabeth ux
6 Jan	Elizabeth NORTHE fa Nicholai NORTHE et Margareta ux
27 Feb	[ ] KEELINGE fs Thoma KEELINGE et Joanna ux
20 Mar	[ ] HYLL [ ] Johis HYLL et Elena ux
21 Mar	[ ] AWTE fa Francisci AWTE et Margareta ux

R. Aston Rectoris ibid
Xpi Hide ….
Willm Hodgeson

1585	
21 May	Willmus SHARRAT fs Thoma SHARRAT et Joanna ux
29 Jun	[ ] COATES fili Francisci COATES et [ ] ux
8 Jul	[ ] ALLEN fs Willmi ALLEN et Marg ux
28 Aug	Thomas COLLYER fs Thoma COLLYER et Katheryna ux
14 Nov	Richardus CLUDDE fs Willmi CLUDDE et Joanna ux
16 Nov	Gracea SALSBURYE fa [ ] SALSBURYE et Margareta ux
23 Jan	Franciscus COOKE fs Thoma COOKE et Elizabetha ux
13 Mar	Michaell BLURTON fs Johis BLURTON et Elizabeth ux
13 Mar	Edwardus KEELINGE fs Thoma KEELINGE et Joanna ux
1586	
25 Mar	Ellena BOTTE fa Rici BOTTE et Ellena ux
7 Jul	Catherina HYDE fa Xpi [Christi] HYDE et Elena ux
24 Sep	Margeria HARVEY fa Johis et Jana ux
30 Sep	Richardus DYCHE fs Thoma DYCHE et Elizabetha ux
4 Nov	Johes ALLEN fs Willmi ALLEN et Margeria ux
10 Mar	Vernonus ASTON fs Rici ASTON C'lici et Anna ux
1587	
21 Oct	Maria NORTHE fa Nicholai NORTHE et M'gareta ux
31 Jan	Johannes CONWAYE fs Rici CONWAYE et Maria ux

 3 Feb   Anna TILSTON fa Johis TILSTON et Dorothea ux
18 Feb   Edwardus HYLL fs Johis HYLL et Ellena ux
24 Feb   Catherina ELSON fa Roberti ELSON et Ellena BENNET
1588
29 Mar   Richardus COLLYER fs Thoma COLLYER et Katherina ux
  [ ]   Thomas WYTHRINGE fs Thoma WYTHRINGE et Joanna ux
20 Apr   Dorothea KEELINGE fa Francisci KEELINGE et Jana ux
 9 May   Anna [?] TOMPKYNSON fa Roberti TOMPKYNSON et Elizabetha
12 May   Robertus GRUNDIE fs Johis GRUNDIE et Elizabetha ux
23 Jun   Richardus KEELINGE [fs] Thoma KEELINGE et Joanna ux
24 Jun   Elizabeth CLUDDE fa Willmi CLUDDE et Joanna ux
10 Aug   Alicea WARDE fa Symonis WARDE et Margareta ux
16 Aug   Dorothea COATES fa Francisci COATES et Margareta ux
 5 Jan   Thomas CORKE fs Thoma CORKE et Elizabetha ux
20 Feb   Anna ASTON fa Rici ASTON et Anna ux
20 Feb   Johes STATHAM fs Elicei STATHAM et Francisci ux
23 Jan   Catherina NORTHE fa Nicholai NORTHE et Margareta ux
 7 Mar   Margareta SPENSER fa Francisci SPENSER et [ ] ux
1589
11 Apr   Elizabeth SMYTHE fa Francisci SMYTHE et Maria ux
15 Apr   [ ] PARKER fa Richardi PARKER et [ ] ux
11 May   Franciscus LEIGH fs Johis LEIGH et Alicea uxorsi eius
28 Jun   Willus H[AR]VEY fs Johis HARVEY et Anna ux
14 Jul   Anna ALTE fa Johis ALTE et Alicea ux
14 Aug   [ ] ASTON fa Roberti A[STO]N et Jocosa ux
24 Aug   Auston FAWDRINGE fs Anthonii FAW[DRIN]GE et Dorothea
 4 Nov   Francisca DYCHEFEILD fa Thoma DYCHEFEILD et Margeria HARRISON
16 Nov   Willmus LEEKE fs Willmi LEEKE et Joanna ux
21 Dec   Robertus WALKER fs Hugonis WALKER et Agneti ux
28 Dec   Elizabeth KEELINGE fa Thoma KEELINGE et Joanna ux
25 Jan   Margeria BALL fa Johis BALL et Alicea ux
1590
24 Apr   Richardus RUSHTON fs Jacobi RUSHTON et [ ] ux
26 Apr   Elizabeth WARDE fa Xpi WARDE et Margareta ux
27 Jun   Ellena CONWAYE fa Richardi CONWAYE et Margareta ux
30 Jul   Willus MOORE fs Thoma MOORE et Ellena ux
 1 Jan   Thomas BLURTON fs Johis BLURTON et Elizabetha ux
 7 Feb   Thomas GRUNDIE fs Johis GRUNDYE et Elizabetha ux
21 Feb   Griffinus DAVYE fs Rici DAVIE et [ ] ux
26 Feb   Willus SPENCER fs Willmi SPENCER et Anna ux
 2 Mar   Joanna ALTE fa Francisci ALTE et Margareta ux
 3 Mar   Elizabeth TOMKINSON fa Roberti TONKINSON et [ ] ux
1591
18 Apr   Elizabeth PARKER fa Richardi PARKER et Margareta ux
10 May   Thomas HOWE fs Thoma HOWE et Margareta ux
27 Jun   Elizabeth CLUDDE fa Willmi CLUDDE et Joanna ux
27 Jul   Francisca ALLEN fa Willmi ALLEN et Margareta ux
 8 Aug   Alicea BYRCHE fa Elicei BYRCHE et Catherina ux
 2 Sep   Jocosa ASTON fa n'uri [?] Robti ASTON et Jocosa ux
 2 Sep   Robertus BYLL fs Willmi BYLL et Francisca ux
16 Sep   Jana WARNER fa Georgeii WARNER et Dorothea ux

3 Nov   Elizabeth HYLL fa Johis HYLL et Ellena ux
4 Nov   Elizabeth SPOONER fa Willmi SPOONER et Dorothea ux
20 Feb   Thomas STATHAM fs Elicei STATHAM et Francisca ux
21 Feb   Thomas WYTHRINS fs Thoma WYTHRINS et Jana ux
24 Feb   Jocosa ASTON fa Rici ASTON et Anna ux

1592
28 Mar   Elizabeth BOTTE fa Richardi BOTTE et Ellena ux
9 Apr   Maria ROYLEY fa Margeria ROYLEY et Sampsonis MARALL
15 Apr   Martha BLURTON fa Johis BLURTON et Elizabeth ux
23 Apr   Dorothea LEE fa Johis LEE et Alicea ux
7 May   Walterus NORTHE fs Nicholai NORTHE et Margareta ux
29 Jun   Willus ALLEN fs Willmi ALLEN et Margeria ux
3 Aug   Agneta et Dorothea RUSHTON fi Jacobi RUSHTON et Isabella ux
4 Aug   Catherina WALKELATE fa Alicea WALKELATE
16 Sep   Johes BACON fs Rogeri BACON Cleri et Alicea MOUNTFORDE
         de [ ] in Com War.
14 Oct   Joanna MORE fa Thoma MORE et Ellena ux
26 Nov   Humfridus KEELINGE fs Thoma KEELINGE et [ ] ux
24 Dec   Joanna BYLL fa Willmi BYLL et Francisca ux
2 Feb   Richardus fs cuiusdam mendici et [ ] ux
2 Feb   Alicea ALTE fa Johis ALTE et ux

1593
25 Mar   Franciscus PAKEMAN fs Richardi PAKEMAN et Custancia ux
25 Mar   Elizabeth BROWNE fa Henrici BROWNE et Ellena ux
8 Apr   Willus SPOONER fs Willmi SPOONER et Dorothea ux
11 May   Franciscus PHILLIPPES fs Johis PHILLIPPES et Joana ux
22 Jul   Robertus ALLEN fs Johis ALLEN et Elizabeth ux
22 Aug   Richardus TILSTON fs Johis TILSTON et Dorothea ux
29 Sep   Herveus CONWAYE fs Rici CONWAYE et Margareta ux
30 Oct   Margareta ALLEN fa Willmi ALLEN et Margeria ux
1 Nov   Thomas BYRCHE fs Elicei BYRCHE et Cat[heri]na ux
11 Nov   Willus HEYLEY fs Henrici HEILEY et Elizabeth ux
11 Jan   Cicellia fa Johis MORRIS et ux
27 Jan   Franciscus WYTHERINGE fs Thoma WYTHERINGE et Joanna ux

1594
27 Mar   Cicelia NORTHE fa Nicholai NORTHE et Margareta ux
30 Apr   Margareta WARDE fa Johis WARDE et Agneta ux
21 May   Johes HARVEY fs Johis HARVEY et Anna ux
1 Jan   Franciscus ALLEN fs Willmi ALLEN et Margeria ux
18 Jan   Johes LAWRENCE fs Edwardi LAWRENCE et Joanna ux
6 Mar   Ellena WHITTELL fa Mathai WHITTELL et Anna ux
16 Mar   Margareta fa Simonis WARDE
         R. Aston ....
         ... .
         Wm. Hodgeson ....

1595
23 Apr   Elizabetha PEDLEY fa Richardi PEDLEY et Elizabetha ux
9 Jun   Ellena SHARRATT fa Rici SHARRATT
4 Jul   Elizabetha SHARRATT fa Johis SHARRATT et Francisca ux
27 Jul   Jacobus HYDE fs Xpi HYDE et Francisca ux
14 Dec   Hugo HELEY fs Henrici HELEY et Elizabetha ux

8 Jan   Johes PAKEMAN fs Richardi PAKEMAN et Susanna ux
11 Jan   Elizabetha fa Sampsonis MARALL et Joanna ux
1 Feb   Margeria BYRTCHE fa Elicei BYRTCHE et Catherina ux
9 Feb   Anthonius LEES fs Johis LEES et Elizab: ux
1596
11 Jun   Willmus BOTTE fs Richardi BOTTE et Ellena ux
24 Jun   Catherina PARKER fa Richardi PARKER et Margareta ux
18 Jul   Thomas PHILLIPPES fs Johis PHILLIPPES et Johanna ux
5 Aug   Georgius HEAPE fs Johis MASSYE et Anna HEAPE illegittima genit
7 Aug   Thomas MOORE fs Thoma MOORE et Ellena ux
17 Aug   [ ] SHERRAT fa Johis SHERRAT et Elizabetha ux
25 Aug   Johes WYTTERINS fs Thoma WYTTERINS
23 Dec   Eliseus STATHAM fs Elisei STATHAM et Francisca ux
20 Mar   Johes PEDLEY fs Rici PEDLEY et Elizabetha ux
1597
4 May   Maria et Johanna fi Willmi SPOONER et Dorothea ux
26 Jun   Anthonius WARDE fs Simonis WARDE et Marg'eta ux
26 Jun   Jocosa BLURTON fa Johis BLURTON et Elizabetha ux
13 Nov   Thomas RUSHTON fs Jacobi RUSHTON et Isabella ux
7 Dec   Margareta WYTTERINS fa Thoma WYTTERINS et Johanna ux
22 Jan   Johes HEALIE fs Henrici HEALIE et Elizabetha ux
5 Feb   Anna WHITTELL fa Mathei WHITTELL et Anna ux
19 Feb   Johanna MASSYE fa Johis MASSYE et Anna ux
24 Feb   Edwardus SHERRAT fs Johis SHERRAT et Francisca ux
12 Mar   ………. fs Sampsonis MARALL et Johanna ux
21 Mar   Richardus ALLEN fs Willmi ALLEN et Margeria ux
21 Mar   Elizabetha SHERRAT fa Richardi SHERRAT et Alicia ux
1598
25 Mar   Maria BROWNE fa Henrici BROWNE et Ellena ux
30 Apr   Agneta SPOONER fa Willmi SPOONER et Dorothea ux
8 Jun   Johes SMYTHE fs Thoma SMYTHE et Margareta ux
2 Jul   Randulphus HYDE fs Xpri HYDE et Francisca ux
9 Aug   Elizabetha HARVEY fa Johis HARVEY et Anna ux
10 Sep   Johes DRAKEFORDE fs Willmi DRAKEFORDE et Gratia ux
14 Nov   Agneta BYRCHE fa Elisei BYRCHE et Catherina ux
21 Jan   Jacobus COWAPE fs Michaelis COWAPE et ux
30 Jan   Dorothea COLLYER fa Rici COLLYER et Sarae ux
24 Feb   Henricus NORTHE fs Nicholai NORTHE et Catherina ux
1 Mar   Willmus DEGGE fs Edwardi DEGGE et Katherina ux
9 Mar   Prissilla DILWORTHE fa Georgii DILWORTHE et Felicia ux
1599
21 Apr   Margareta BLURTON fa Walteri BLURTON et Joanna ux
5 May   Richardus STATHAM fs Elicei STATHAM et Francisse ux
27 May   Willmus LEES fs Johis LEES et Elizabetha ux
3 May   Richardus PARKER fs Richardi PARKER et ux
3 May   Elizabetha MOORE fa Francisci MOORE et ux
11 Aug   Franciscus WARDE fs Simonis WARDE et Margareta ux
12 Aug   Thomas BLAKEMAN fs Anthonii BLAKEMAN et Cicilie ux
19 Aug   Johanna PEDLEY fa Richardi PEDLEY et Elizabetha ux
13 Sep   Katherina MOORE fa Thoma MOORE et ux
28 Oct   Edwardus LAWRENCE fs Edwardi LAWRENCE et ux

2 Feb   Eliceus BAILIE fs Henrici BAILIE et ux
2 Mar   Georgius MARRALL fs Sampsonis MARRALL et ux
20 Mar   Anna SMYTHE fa Thoma SMYTHE et ux

1600
16 Apr   Stephanus SPENCER fs illegitimus Rici SPENCER et Margareta ATKINS
17 Apr   Margareta HELEY fa Henrici HELEY et ux
13 May   Willus BLURTON fs Anthonii BLURTON et ux
18 May   Thomas SHERRAT et Johes SHERRAT fi Johis SHERRAT ux
23 May   Johanna HOOFORDE fa Willmi HOOFORDE et ux
1 Jun   Dorothea WITHRINGE fa Thoma WITHRINGE et ux
1 Jun   Jacobus RUSHTON fs Jacobi RUSHTON et ux
10 Jun   Johes CONWAYE fs Johis CONWAYE et ux
6 Aug   Edmundus BEARDMORE fs Johis BEARDMORE et ux
11 Aug   Willus SHERRAT fs Rici SHERRAT et ux
15 Aug   Johanna PAKEMAN fa Rici PAKEMAN et ux
29 Aug   Edwardus DAVYE fs Rici DAVYE et ux
31 Aug   Anna ASTON fa Johis ASTON et ux
1 Oct   Willus BILLE fs Willmi BILLE et ux porcia de Seighford
23 Oct   Dorothea RAWNSDALE fa Thoma RAWNSDALE et ux
25 Oct   Dorothea ALLEN fa Willmi ALLEN et ux
23 Nov   Richardus CONWAY fs Michaeli CONWAY et ux
2 Dec   Robtus HEATON fs Henrici HEATON et ux
[part of page blank]

1601
9 Aug   Joana fil Elicea BIRCH
4 Sep   Walterus fil Johis MASSIE
8 Sep   Richus fil illimus Jocosa BROWNE
29 Nov   Margareta fil Antonii BLAKMAN
5 Jan   Francisca fil Willmi HYDE
7 Feb   Dorothea fil Thoma WALL
17 Feb   Judith fil Richi PARKER
18 Mar   Henricus fil Edwardi LAWRENCE

1602
25 Mar   Winifreda fil Richi PEDLEY
14 Apr   Anthonius fil illimus Dorothea HILLE et Willmi PHILIPS
15 Apr   Anna fil Willmi ALTE
10 May   Anna fil Johis HALL
30 May   Agnes fil Thoma MORE
6 Jun   Margareta fil Henrici BROWNE
14 Jun   Thomas fil Henrici LEESE

Johes Palmer)   churchw....... [?] Thomas
Rector ibid   )   [illegible]   Tunstal

1602
16 Sep   Maria fa Johannis ASTON et Dorothea ux
19 Sep   Ellena et Dorothea gemelli fa Gulielmi LOWE et Elizabetha ux
25 Sep   Johanes et Joanna gemelli fil Johanis DYCHE de Fole
9 Dec   Elizabetha fa Willi PHILLIPPES
11 Dec   Joanna fa Henrici HEALEY
26 Dec   Dorothea fa Willi HYDE de Checkley Banke
21 Jan   Anna fa Joannis KEELINGE de Doddesley
25 Jan   Judith fa Anthonii ATKINS de Feilde

27 Feb   Johanes fs Richardi SPENSER et Anna ux
3 Mar   Margareta fa Eduardi SHERRARDE et Katharina ux
1603
13 Apr   Gulielmus fs Johanis CONWAIE
14 Apr   Joanna fa Thoma WITTERANS et Joanna ux
6 May   Anna fa Jacobi RUSHTON
6 May   Anna fa Stepani WATSON et Ellena ux
29 May   Matheus fs Sampsonis MARRALL et ux
9 Jun   Katharina fa Willi DRAKEFORDE et ux
23 Jun   Emma fa Johanis JACKSON et ux
21 Jul   Thomas fs Henrici BAYLIE et ux
24 Jul   Franciscus fs Johanis SHERRARDE et ux
10 Oct   Anthonius fs Ranulphi BIRDE et ux
12 Oct   Johanes fs Arthuris BLURTON et ux
27 Oct   Franciscus fs Johanis DYCHE de Fole
6 Jan   Joanna fa Rici SHERRARD et ux
19 Feb   Jocosa fa illigitima Katharina ASTON et Thoma FELLONER
1 Mar   Willimus fs Helizei BIRCH et ux
2 Mar   Elizabetha fa Johanis BEARDMORE et ux
4 Mar   Eduardus fs Eduardi BARKER et ux
18 Mar   Anna fa Richardi PARKER et ux
20 Mar   Johanes fs Willmi SALTE et ux
1604
15 Apr   Elizabetha fa Anthonii BLAKEMAN et ux
16 Apr   Johanes fs Thoma HILL et ux
29 Apr   Ellena fa Richardi WULLASTON et ux
22 May   Katharina [?] [fa] Thoma [?] [?]AWREMEERE et ux
22 Jul   Jocosa fa Richardi BOWRINGE et ux
22 Jul   Willimus fs Richardi PEDLEY et ux
12 Aug   Ellena fa Thoma MASSIE et ux
12 Aug   Thomas fs Thoma WALL et ux
22 Sep   Pholotis fa Johanis COVELL et ux
27 Sep   Elizabetha fa Richardi SPENSER et ux
27 Sep   Elizabetha fa Johanis RODES et ux
22 Oct   Katharina fa Johanis LEES et ux
4 Nov   Hugo fs Willmi LOWE et ux
8 Jan   Katharina fa Johanis KEELINGE et ux
29 Jan   Maria fa Willmi BILL et ux
7 Feb   Judeth fa Mathei GREATBATCH et ux
17 Feb   Franciscus fs Richardi GILBERDE et ux
1605
28 Mar   Anna fa Anthonii DUTTON et Margareta ux
20 May   Eduardus fs Richardi COWOPPE et ux
4 Jul   Thomas fs Johanis HALL et ux
17 Aug   [ ] fa Willmi HYDE et ux
19 Oct   Elizabetha fa Ranulphi BIRDE et ux
12 Nov   Willimus fs Thoma BAYLIE poch: Yoxall et Dorothea ux
27 Jan   Anna fa illigitima Sara ASTON
11 Feb   Robertus fs Henrici HEALEY et ux
22 Feb   Johanes fs Willmi SHERRARD et ux
9 Mar   Anna fa Anthonii BLAKEMAN et ux

11 Mar Mercie fa Thoma HILL et ux
13 Mar Margareta fa Willi DRAKEFORDE et ux
17 Mar Hugo fs Eduardi BARKER et ux
21 Mar Dorothea fa Willmi PHILLIPPES et ux
1606
21 Apr Anna fa Johanis SHERRARDE et ux
1 May Anna fa Robti POWELL et ux
22 May Willus fs Willmi LOWE et ux

Johes Palmer)   Tho: Cowoppe (ibm
Rector ibm   )   Xpofer Hyde (

26 Jul Margi [?] fa Richardi SHERRAT et ux
17 Aug Thomas fs Stephani WATSON et ux
2 Nov Ellena fa Richardi SPENSER et ux
28 Nov Margeria fa Rici GILBERTE et ux
1 Dec Georgius fs Richardi PARKER et ux
3 Dec Katharina fa Richardi PEDLEY et ux
8 Dec Gracea fa illegitima Roberti SONTE et Ellena DYCHE
1 Jan Joanna fa Johis KEELINGE et ux
1 Jan Anthonius fs Henrici BAYLIE et ux
8 Mar Francisca fa illegitima Johis HYDE et Emma
1607
20 Apr Joanna fa Thoma SHERRAT et ux
26 Apr Issabella fa Richardi THROWER et ux
25 Jul Franciscus fs Francisci WARDE et ux
16 Aug Margeria fa Johis DYCHE et ux
3 Sep Henricus fs Mathai GREATBATCH et ux
27 Sep Thomas fs Henrici ATKINS et ux
11 Oct Johanes fs Johis RODES et ux
12 Nov Jana fa Johanis COVELL et ux
9 Dec Elizabetha fa Rici COWOPPE et ux
3 Jan Eduardus fs Anthonii HYDE et ux
14 Jan Allicea fa Eduardi BARKER et ux
4 Feb Johanis fs Johis WARDE et ux
4 Feb Eduardus fs Robti NORTHE et ux
6 Mar Johannes fs Thoma LOWE et ux
1608
1 May Willimus fs Willmi PHILLIPPES et ux
27 May Elizabetha fa Thoma WALL et ux
29 May Sampson fs Rici SPENSER et ux
9 Jun Joanna fa Francisci WARDE et ux
2 Jul Johes fs Anthonii BLAKEMAN et ux
14 Jul Maria fa Robti POWELL et ux
24 Jul Katharena fa Willmi HODGESON et ux
14 Aug Georgius fs Willi SHERRAT et ux
21 Aug Martha fa Willi SALTE et ux
14 Sep Jana fa Roberti THACKER et Judith ux
20 Sep Willus fs Johis HALL et ux
15 Oct Franciscus fs Richardi PEDLEY et ux
30 Nov Hugo fs Roberti SONTE et ux
3 Dec Margareta fa Richardi DYCHE et ux
27 Dec Ellena fa Arthuris BLURTON et ux

19 Jan   Jana fa Johanis KEELINGE et ux
3 Mar   Ranulphus fs Rici PARKER et ux
19 Mar   Elizabetha fa Willi DRAKEFORDE et ux
1609
21 Apr   Elizabetha fa Richardi GILBERTE et ux
9 May   Elizabetha fa Thoma SPENSER et ux
6 Jun   Willus fs illimus Willi CARTER et Ellena GILLER
22 Jun   Willus fs Stephani WATSON et ux
20 Oct   Elizabetha fa Helizei BIRCH et ux
26 Nov   Willus fs Ranulphi BIRDE et ux
30 Dec   Ellena fa Willi NORMAN et ux
1 Jan   Jana fa Johanis WARDE et ux
11 Jan   Juditha fa Eduardi BARKER et ux
30 Jan   Joanna fa Richardi WOOLLASTON et ux
2 Feb   Susan fa Roberti SONTE et ux
1610
30 Apr   Jana fa Willi HYDE et ux
4 May   Eduardus fs Johis RODES et ux
7 Jun   Johannes fs Willi HILL et ux
27 Jun   Robertus fs Roberti THACKER et ux
.2 Jul   Margareta fa Johanis COVELL et ux
21 Aug   Johanes fs Thoma JOHNSON et ux
11 Sep   Thoma fs Eduardi HOOWE et ux
22 Sep   Margareta fa Mathei GREATBATCHE et ux
6 Oct   Thomas fs Thoma SONTE et ux
29 Nov   Anna fa Thoma PYBUS et ux
4 Dec   Thomas fs Francisci WARDE et ux
6 Jan   Georgius fs illegitimus Richardi FOWALL et Elizabetha CHAWLNER
6 Jan   Thomas fs Thoma WETTON et ux
3 Feb   Maria fa Richardi PEDLEY et ux
17 Feb   Johannes fs Willi HODGESON et ux
21 Mar   Margareta fa Richardi SPENSER et ux
1611
4 Apr   Anna fa Willi SALTE et ux
7 Apr   Johanes fs Eduardi SHERRAT et ux
1 Jun   Elizabetha fa Thoma SHERRAT et ux
29 Sep   Abigail fa Francisci WHITCOME et Jana ux
8 Nov   Elizabetha fa Thoma COLIER et Dorothea ux
8 Nov   Margareta fa Stephani WATSON et Hellena ux
10 Nov   Johannes COWAP fs Richardi et ux
21 Nov   Margerea SMYTH fa Johis SMYTH et Hellena ux
15 Dec   Thomas JOHNSON fs Thoma JOHNSON et Dorothea ux
26 Dec   Jocosa HIDE fa Anthonii HIDE et Katarina ux
25 Jan   Johes NORMAN fs Gulielmi NORMAN et ux
27 Feb   Anna SPENSER fa Thoma SPENSER et ux
29 Feb   Katerina BARKER fa Eduardi et ux
1 Mar   Thomas SHERRAT fs Guliel SHERRAT et ux
18 Mar   Jana WALL fa Thoma WALL et ux
1612
22 Jul   Christopherus fs Roberti THACKER
29 Jul   Elizabetha fa Henrici MANNERING

18 Sep   Thoma HILL fs Willi HILL
18 Sep   Jana fa Anthonii BLAKEMAN
16 Oct   Catherina HOWE fa Eduardi HOWE et ux
5 Nov   Elizabetha COVELL fa Johis COVELL et ux
22 Nov   Anthonius MIDDLETON fs Johis MIDDLETON et ux
20 Dec   Anna WETTON fa Roberti WETTON et Margreta ux
8 Jan   Maria SMITH fa Johis SMITH et Hellena ux
1 Feb   Franciscus STATHAM fs Cislea STATHAM (elegittumus natus)
5 Feb   [ ] COVELL fa Roberti COVELL et Anna ux
28 Feb   Johes GREATBATCH fs Mathea GREATBATCH et Anna ux
7 Mar   ……… WARD fa Johis WARD et Francisca ux
8 Mar   Thomas ALLEN fs Georgei ALLEN et [ ] ux
8 Mar   Franciscus ROODE fs Johis ROODE et Elizabetha ux

1613
6 May   Catherina WARD fa Francisci WARD et Johana ux
10 May   [ ] WOLLASTON fa Richardi WOLLASTON et Margareta
17 May   Willimus KEELING fs Johis KEELING et Isabella ux
27 Jun   Hellena DYCHE fa Francisci DYCHE et Anna ux
29 Jun   Willmus HODGSON fs Willmi HODGSON et Hellena ux
2 Sep   [ ] ATKINS fs Henrici ATKINS et Elizabetha ux
17 Sep   Thomas BOTT fs Rici BOT et Anna ux
28 Oct   Elizabetha FORSTER fa Edwardi FORSTER et Sibilla ux
21 Nov   Thomas PROKTER fs Radulphi PROCTER et Hellena ux
1 Jan   Francis JOHNSON fs Tho: JOHNSON et ux
4 Jan   Thomas KEENE fs Francisci KEENE et Susan ux
30 Jan   Stephen WATTSON fs Stepha WATSON et Hellena ux
20 Feb   Maria PIBUS fa Thoma PIBUS et Catherina ux

1614
7 Apr   Georgius THACKER fs Roberti THACKER et Judith ux
8 May   Tho: WAKLET fs Catherina WAKLETT (singlewoman)
3 Jul   Agnes SPENSER fa Rici SPENSER et ux
15 Jul   Willus SONT fs Thoma SANT et Hellena ux
23 Jul   Willus MIDDLETON fs Tho MIDDLETON et ux
28 Jul   Johes SPENSER fs Johis SPENSER et ux
25 Sep   Elizabetha ASTON fa Johis ASTON et ux
2 Oct   Willm SHERET fs Thoma SHERET et ux
15 Jan   Johes RUSHON fs Rici RUSHON et Francisca ux
27 Jan   Elizabetha HILL fa Willm HILL et ux
20 Feb   Willm SHERETT fs Tho: SHERETT
11 Mar   Agnes BOTT fa Rici BOTT et Anna ux
2 Mar   Elizabetha PHILLIPS fa Willmi PHILLIPS

1615
11 Apr   Elizabetha THACKER fs* Roberti THACKER et Judith ux [*sic]
13 Apr   Elizabetha [erased] SMITH fa ~~Thoma~~ Willmi SMITH et ux
16 May   Margareta JOHNSON fa Johis JOHNSON et ux
25 May   Hellena COVELL fa Johis COVELL et ux
15 Jul   Willimus BOUGHY fs Sampsonis BOUGHY et Jocosa ux
25 Jul   Dorothea KEELINGE fa Johis KEELINGE et Izabella ux
23 Jul   Elizabeth MIDDLETON fa Thoma MIDDLETON et ux
8 Oct   Elizabetha ASTON fa Johis ASTON et ux
30 Oct   Catherina HYD fa Johis HYD et ux

15 Dec   Anna SMITH fa Johis SMITH et Hellena ux
18 Dec   Elizabetha DYCH fa Rici DYCH et ux
21 Jan   Franciscus WATSON fs Stepheni WATSON et ux
6 Feb   Willimus GRUNDY fs Thoma GRUNDY et ux
15 Feb   Thomas CAWAPP fs Rici CAWAP et ux
24 Feb   Dorothea LEES fa Francisci LEES et ux
6 Mar   Franciscus WARD fs Francisci WARD et Jana ux
18 Mar   Robertus PROCKTOR fs Xphori PROCKTOR et ux
22 Mar   Agnes WAKLET fa Caterina WAKLET (ellegitimus nata)
1616
26 Mar   Willimus SPENCER fs Johis SPENCER et ux
13 Jun   Maria WOLLASTON fa Rici WOLLASTON et ux
27 Jun   Agnes SHERET fa Edvardi SHERRET et Catherina ux
7 Jul   Richardus PHILLIPS fs Roberti PHILLIPS et Gracia ux
17 Jul   Constancia GREATBATCH fa Mathei GREATBATCH et ux
8 Sep   Alicia MORRY fa Thoma MORRY et Dorothea ux
30 Sep   Jana ASTON fa Johis ASTON et Margeria ux
17 Sep   Robertus BROWNE fs Johis BROWNE et Elizabetha ux
16 Nov   Breerton ASTON fs Jocosa ASTON (illigitima nata)
[ ]   Willimus GOODWAINE fs Samueli GOODWAINE et Elizabetha *[Jana written above Elizabetha]* ux
13 Feb   Gulihelmus BOTT fs Rici BOTT et Anna ux
13 Feb   Cicylea HODSON fa Gulihel HODSON et ux
13 Feb   Jocosa SLACK fa Thoma SLACK et Anna ux
1617
30 Mar   Elizabetha SHERRAT fa Willmi SHERRAT et Jana ux
15 Apr   Franciscus COLLES [?] fs Thoma COLES [?] et Margeria ux
8 May   Thomas CAWAP fs Rici CAWAP et Ana ux
7 Jun   Gracia WAKLET fa Catherina WAKLET
8 Jun   Margeria SONT fa Roberti SONT et Alicia ux
8 Jun   Tabitha HILL fa Willmi HILL et Margreta ux
9 Jun   Tho THACKER fs Robti THACKER et Judith ux
18 Jun   Wilimus SMITH fs Johis SMITH et Hellena ux
25 Jun   Johes GRUNDIE fs Thoma GRUNDIE et Agnes ux
23 Oct   Francisca fa Willmi PHILLIPS et Johanna ux
23 Nov   Elizabetha fa Johis HYDE et Francisca ux
9 Nov   Elizabetha SWYNSHED fa Francisci SWYNSHED decici
10 Nov   Juditha SWYNSHED fa Francisci SWYNSHED decici
13 Nov   Edvardus SHENTON fs Rogeri SHENTON et ux
23 Nov   Elizabetha WITTERINGE fa Francisci WITTERINGE et Agnes ux
8 Feb   Christopherus BLURTON fs Roberti BLURTON et ux
14 Feb   Willmus WALKER fs Thoma WALKER et ux
5 Mar   Alicia LEA fa Oliveri LEA et Alicia ux
5 Mar   Elizabetha GOODWYNE fa Samuelis GOODWYNE et ~~Elizabetha~~ Jana ux
19 Mar   Johes WARD fs Francisci WARD et Jona ux
1618
25 May   Richardus ALT fs Francisci ALT et Elizabetha ux
6 Jul   Willmus DYCH filus Rici DYCH et Anna ux
30 Aug   Elisius WATTSON fs Stephani WATTSON et ux
4 Oct   Elizabetha PY fa Georgii PY et Izabella ux
7 Nov   Thomas et Johis COVILL (gemelli) fi Johis COVILL et ux

12 Dec   Elizabetha BULLOCK fa Henrici BULLOCK et ux
 1 Jan   Dorithea SHERAT fa Thoma SHERAT et ux
13 Jan   Elizabetha FOLDERING Astonis FOLDERING Mathea ux
21 Jan   Edvardus LOE fs Francisci LOE et ux
 7 Mar   Robertus LATHEROPP fs Radulphi LATHEROP et Margeria ux
1619
11 Apr   Willihelmus SMITH fs Johis SMITH et Hellena ux
29 Apr   Willihelmus THACKER fs Roberti THACKER
30 May   [ ] WARD fa Johis WARD et ux
11 Jul   Robertus SHERAT fs Roberti SHERAT et Alicia ux
22 Aug   Francis GOODWYNE fs Samuelis GOODWYNE et ux
27 Aug   Johes KEELING fs Johis KEELING et ux
 9 Sep   Jona GREATBATCH fa Mathea GREATBATCH et Ana ux
 9 Sep   Maria TOWERS fa Roberti TOWERS et ux
 1 Feb   Anna STATHA' fa Johis STATHA' et ux
1620
25 Mar   Maria ALT fa Francisci ALT et ux
 9 May   Anna PHILLIPS fa Robti PHILLIPS et ux
17 May   Willimus RISHON fs Rici RISHON et ux
21 May   Sampsonis PY fs Georgii PY et ux
 8 Jun   Margeria NAYLOR fa Henrici NAYLOR et ux
19 Jun   Franciscus LEA fs Oliveri LEA et ux
19 Jun   Hellena BOTT fa Randulphi BOT et ux
27 Jul   Johes SMITH fs Johis SMITH et ux
13 Oct   Thomas HODSON fs Willi HODSON et ux
10 Sep   Thomas WITTERINGE fs Francisci WITTERINGE et ux
 1 Nov   Johis SMITH fs Jona SMITH (singlewoman)
14 Dec   Jona COTES fa Thoma COTHES et ux
26 Dec   Hellena HEALY fa Jona HEALY (singlewoman)
 3 Jan   Sampsonis GOODWYN fs Sami GOODWYNE et ux
 8 Jan   Edwardus BAGNALL fs Humphridi BAGNALL et ux
21 Jan   Walterus BLURTON fs Walteri BLURTON et ux
13 Feb   Anna COVELL fa Johis COVELL et ux
27 Feb   Anna WOOD fa Rogeri WOOD et ux
21 Sep   [blank – "Gualterus" written in margin] BAGOTT fs Harvy BAGOT
         (armiger) et ux
1621
14 Apr   Anna BARKER fa Edvardi BARKER et ux
21 Apr   [ ] ASTON fa Anna ASTON (singlewoman)
17 Jun   Margareta SHERAT fa Willimi SHERAT
 1 Jul   Wilimus LATHEROPP fs Radulphi LATHEROP et ux
 7 Sep   Margareta BOTT fa Rici BOTT et ux
 1 Nov   Alicia FOLDERING fa Astonis FOLDERINGE et ux
 9 Nov   Johes STATHA fs Johis STATHAM et ux
13 Nov   Johes ROBINSON fs Johis ROBINSON et ux
26 Nov   Thomas FROST fs Thoma FROST et ux
 2 Dec   Franciscus WALKER fs Thoma WALKER et ux
 9 Dec   Maria SWYNSHED fa Francisci SWYNSHED et ux
12 Jan   Radulphi GOLD fs Francisci GOLD et ux
 3 Feb   Symon THACKER fs Robti THACKER et ux

1622

21 Apr	Margareta PHILLIPS fa Robti PHILLIPS et ux
12 Jun	Johes OSBORNE fs Thomas OSBORNE et ux
16 Jun	Dorothea HILL fa Willi HILL et ux
9 Jun	~~Johes OSBORNE fs Thoma OSBORNE et Elizabetha ux~~
18 Aug	Tho: GOODWYNE fs Samuelis GOODWYNE et ux
10 Sep	Elizabetha DAVIES fa Griphinus DAVIES et ux
20 Oct	Edvardus LATHEROPP fs Radulphi LATHROPP et ux
2 Nov	Franciscus ATKINS fs Henrici ATKINS et ux
24 Nov	Catherina ALT fa Francisci ALT et ux
30 Nov	Thomas WALKER fs Thoma WALKER et ux
22 Dec	Catherina LEE fa Francisci LEE et ux
17 Nov	Hellena ROBINSON fa Johis ROBINSON et ux
12 Jan	Margareta DYCH fa Rici DYCH et ux
16 Jan	Elizabetha BAGOTT fa Harvii BAGOTT et ux
5 Mar	Richardus WATTSON fs Stephani WATSON et ux

1623

18 May	Franciscus SHERRAT fs Thoma SHERRAT et ux
1 Jun	Willmus HARVIE fs Willi HARVY et ux
12 Jun	Wilmus WARD fs Francisci WARD et ux
15 Jun	Edvardus BLURTON fs Walteri BLURTON et ux
22 Jun	Robertus BAGNOLD fs Humphridi BAGNOLD et ux
20 Jul	Franciscus COVELL fs Johis COVELL et ux
14 Aug	Anna COTES fa Thoma COTES et ux
23 Aug	Ana HELY fa Henrici HELY et ux
19 Sep	Thomas MORE fs Willmi MORE et ux
24 Sep	[ ] WITTERINGE fili Francisci WITTERING et ux
26 Dec	Edwardus WOOD fs Rogeri WOOD et ux
1 Feb	Anna ASHE fa Oliveri ASHE et ux
5 Feb	Catherina SWYNSHED fa Francisci SWYNSHED et ux
8 Feb	Franciscus SONT fs Robti SONT et ux

1624

9 May	Hellena HILL fs *[sic]* Willi HILL et ux
24 May	Samueli GOODWYN fs Samuelis GOODWYNE
30 May	Willimus HILL fs Xpopher HILL ux
2 Jul	Lucus THACKER fs Robti THACKER et ux
24 Oct	Elizabetha BOTT fa Richardi BOTT et ux
30 Oct	Franciscus MOULTON fs Francisci MOULTON et Jocosa ux
30 Dec	Franciscus MIDDLETON fs Johis MIDDLETON et ux
20 Jan	Johes ATKINS fs Henrici ATKINS et ux
3 Feb	Franciscus SMITH fs Johis SMITH et ux
2 Mar	Jana RISHON fa Richardi RISHON et ux
6 Mar	Anna GOUGH fa Tho. GOUGH et ux
24 Mar	Anna MORE fa Willi MORE et ux

1625

10 Apr	Thomas LATHROPP fs Radulphi LATHROP et ux
1 Apr	Margareta WARD fa Francisci WARD et ux
30 May	Jona HEALEY (illegitt) fa Joh Jona HELEY singilwoman
17 Jul	Edwardus RISHON fs Rici RISHON et ux
25 Jul	Willmus HYD fs Anthonius HYD et ux
3 Aug	Anna ROBINSON fa Johis ROBINSON et ux

14 Aug	Jona BARKER fa Edwardi BARKER et ux
6 Oct	Georgius SALT fs Willi SALT et ux
30 Oct	Thomas BLURTON fs Walteri BLURTON et ux
3 Nov	Edvardus LICESTER fs Willmi LICESTER et ux
6 Nov	Johes TOWERS fs Robti TOWERS et ux
17 Nov	Elizabetha SHERRAT fa Edvardi SHERRAT et ux
2 Feb	Johes HYDE fs Jacobi HYD et ux
7 Mar	Jona WRIGHT fa Alica WRIGHT (illigittima nata)
21 Mar	Elizabetha RISHON fa Rici RISHON et ux

1626

26 Mar	Elizabetha LEA fa Francisci LEA et ux
30 Mar	Mabal ASTON fa Johis ASTON et ux
7 May	Thomas BAGNOLD fs Humphridi BAGNOLD et ux
9 May	Willimus SHERRAT filus Willimi SHERRAT et ux
17 May	Anna HOLT (illigittima nata) fa Sara HOLT
16 Feb	Margareta OSBORNE fa Thoma OSBORNE et ux
4 Mar	Elizabetha MOULTON fa Fra: MOULTON et ux

1627

31 Mar	Hellena SONT fa Robti SONT et ux
3 Apr	Willimus MORE fs Willi MORE et ux
21 May	Johis et Franciscus SWYNSHED fi Francisci SWYNSHED et Elizabetha eius
21 Jun	Anna SALT fa Willmi SALT et ux
16 Oct	Edvardus SHERRAT fs Edvardi SHERRAT Jun et Elizabetha
16 Oct	Willimus SHERRAT fs Willmi SHERRAT et ux
5 Nov	[ ] WITTERINGE fs Francisci WITTERINGE et ux
15 Nov	Radulphus et Catherina ATKINS fi Henrici ATKINS
1 Dec	Elizabeth GOUGH fa Rici GOUGH
25 Feb	Thomas HELEY fs Henrici HELY

1628

24 Apr	Elizabetha HILL fa Christopheri HILL
25 Apr	Josephus THACKER fs Robti THACKER
8 May	Jocosa ASTON fa Johis ASTON
8 May	Anna CHAPLIN fa Rici CHAPLIN
29 May	Elizabetha BLADON fa Johis BLADON
10 Aug	Johes SPENCER fs Samsonis SPENCER
9 Aug	Francisca ASTON fa Wilmi ASTON Armigeri
22 Aug	Franciscus HYD fs Jacobi HYDE
21 Sep	Constancia OSBORNE fa Thoma OSBORNE
16 Nov	Elizabetha SALT fa Wilimi SALT Jn
23 Nov	Anna PEDLEY fa Johis PEDLEY
5 Dec	Edvardus SWYNSHED fs Francisci SWYNSHED Clerici
13 Dec	Franciscus HYDE fs Edvardi HYD
14 Feb	Amy RISHON fa Richardi et ux
24 Mar	Franciscus BAGNOLD fs Humphridi BAGNOLD et ux
22 Mar	Ellena SMITH fa Johes SMITH et ux

1629

9 Apr	Margareta SONT fa Robti SONT et ux
11 Apr	Anna HOLT fa Amos HOLT et ux
30 Jun	Katherina WOOD fa Rogeri WOOD et ux
13 Aug	Edvardus THROWER fs Griphini THROWER et ux

25 Sep	Thomas UPPINGE fs Thomas UPPINGE et ux
27 Sep	Robertus MOULTON fs Francisci MOULTON et ux
4 Oct	Tabitha WHITBEY fa Johis WHITBEY et ux
[ ]	[ ] LEES fs Francisci LEES et ux
8 Nov	Dorothea MARRETT fa Johis MARRET et ux
29 Nov	Johes OSBURNE fs Thomas OSBURNE et ux
23 Jan	Maria GOUGH fa Rici GOUGH et ux
19 Feb	Maria GOLD fa ~~Francisci~~ Thoma GOLD et ux
25 Mar	Anna SHERRATT fa Edvardi SHERRAT et ux

1630

1 Apr	Margareta LOW fa Hugonis LEES et ux
30 May	Thomas HEALEY fs Willimi HEALEY et ux
15 Jul	Margareta SALT fa Wilmi SALT et uxo eius
25 Sep	Henricis BLADON fs Johis BLADON et uxo eius
24 Oct	Johes DAVIES fs Griphini DAVIES et ux eius
12 Nov	Franciscus AMBERSLEY fs Fra AMBERSLEY
13 Feb	Margareta WOOD fa Rogeri WOOD et ux

1631

11 Apr	Richardus PEDLEY fs Johis PEDLEY et uxo eius
12 Apr	Maria MARRETT fa Johis MARRETT et ux
24 Apr	Thomas HILL fs Xpopheri HILL et ux
19 Jun	Willimus WITTERINGE fs Fra: WITTERINGE et ux
17 Jul	Anna LOW fa Hugonis LOW et ux
21 Jul	Robertus HYD fs Edvardi HYDE et ux
18 Sep	Johes WHITBEY fs Johis WHITBEY et ux
3 Nov	Robertus HYD fs Jacobi HYDE et ux
4 Dec	Franciscus OSBURNE fs Tho: OSBURNE et ux
18 Dec	Jona CHAPLIN fa Richardi CHAPLIN et ux
29 Jan	Edvardus BLURTON fs Johis BLURTON et ux
18 Mar	Gulihelmus SALT fs Gulihelmi SALT et ux

1632

8 Apr	Richardus SPENCER fs Sampsonis SPENCER et ux
23 Apr	Margareta BIGGINS fa Henricus BIGINS et ux
22 Jul	Dorothea HOLT fa Amos HOLT et ux
2 Aug	Elizabetha PYBUS fa Thomas PYBUS et ux
24 Nov	Elizabetha JOHNSON fa Johis JOHNSON et ux
6 Jan	Thomas HYDE fs Edvardi HYDE et ux
17 Jan	Elizabetha BAGNOD fa Humfridi BAGNOD et ux
17 Jan	Alicea SHERRAT fa Willmi SHERRAT et ux
31 Jan	Robertus ASTON fs Johis ASTON et ux

1633

20 Apr	Edvardus MOULTON fs Francisci MOULTON et Jocosa ux
22 Apr	Willmus OSBORNE fs Thoma OSBORNE et Elizabetha ux
2 Jun	Johes SALT fs Willmi SALT et Isabella ux
9 Jun	Edvardus BOOKLEY fs Johis BOOKLEY et Dorothea ux
14 Jul	Martha ASTON fa Richardi ASTON et ux
4 Aug	Thomas GRIPHIN fs Thoma GRIPHIN et Margareta ux
16 Nov	Thomas HOWE fs Thoma HOW et ux
24 Nov	Johes CHAPLIN fs Richardi CHAPLIN et ux
23 Dec	Thomas LEES fs Francisci LEES et ux
9 Mar	Johes PEDLEY fs Johis PEDLEY et ux

1634

27 Apr Alicea BLURTON fa Johis BLURTON et Alicea ux
2 May Franciscus SHERRAT fs Edvardi SHERRAT et Elizabetha ux
5 Jun Alicea BIGGINS fa Henrici BIGGINS et Izabella ux
25 Jul Robertus SPOONER illegitt nat fs Anna SPOONER
12 Aug Richardus OSBURNE fs Thoma OSBURNE et ux
4 Nov Katherina HYDE fa Jacobi HYD et Elizabetha ux
2 Jan Anna GOODWYNDE fa Thoma GOODWIND et Anna ux

Johes Palmer Rector
Tho Spencer:
Will Hodgson: Church wardens

3 Feb Elizabeth HOLT fa Amos HOLT et ux
1635
16 Apr Jana SALT fs Willmi SALT et Izabella ux
1 May Maria BAGNOLD fa Humphridi BAGNOLD et ux
6 May Willmus EDWARDS fs Willmi EDWARDS et Alicea ux
6 May An'a AMBERSLEY fa Francisci AMBERSLEY et Anna ux
30 Jul Jacobus HYD fs Edvardi HYD et Jona ux
25 Oct Richardus HOW fs Thoma HOW et Margeria ux euis
9 Nov Richardus ASTON fs Johis ASTON clerici et Margeria ux
28 Jan Sampson SPENSER fs Sampsonis SPENSER et ux
2 Feb Judith BIGGINS fa Henrici BIGGINS et [ ] ux
22 Feb Willmus HODGSON fs Johis HODGSON et Elizabetha ux
22 Mar Willmus PHILLIPS fs Willimi PHILLIPS et [ ] ux
1636
30 May Maria PEDLEY fa Johis PEDLEY et Elizabetha ux
24 Apr Thomas WALL fs Thoma WALL et Elizabetha ux
28 Apr Sara SALT fa Willmi SALT et Izabella ux
16 May Tho: GOODWIND fs [ ] GOODWIND et ux
23 Jul Elizabetha OSBURNE fa Thoma OSBURNE et ux
23 Aug Anna LEES fa Francisci LEES et ux
30 Sep Ricus ALLEN fs Rici ALLEN et Maria ux
2 Oct Thomas WATSON fs Anna WATTSON
23 Oct Wilmus ASTON fs Rici ASTON et Mattha ux
8 Feb Margeria HEALEY fa Robti HEALEY et ux
9 Feb Edvardus BIRD fs Anthonii BIRD et ux
24 Feb Edvardus AMBERSLEY fs Francisci AMBERSLEY et Anna
12 Mar Willmus SHERRAT fs Johes SHERRAT et Phelis ux
1637
29 May Johis BLURTON fs Johis BLURTON et Alicea ux euis
29 Jun Richardus LOW fs Hugonis LOW et ux
2 Jul Gulhelmus SHERRAT fs Edvardi SHERAT et Elizabetha ux
13 Aug Alicea JOHNSON fa Johis JOHNSON et ux
20 Aug Gulihelmus JEFFERY fs Walteri JEFFERY et Elizabetha ux
3 Oct Alicea SALT fa Gulihelmi SALT et ux
8 Oct Sara SHERRAT fa Gulihelmi SHERRAT et ux
10 Dec Juditha OSBURNE fa Thoma OSBURNE et ux
24 Dec Edvardus HYD fs Edvardi HYDE et ux
1638
15 Apr Dorothea WHITHURST fa Johis WHITHURST et Dorothea ux
19 Aug Anna SPENCER fa Sampsonis SPENCER et Letticia ux

© Staffordshire Parish Registers Society

6 Sep   Maria LOWE fa Johis LOWE generosi et Katherina ux
23 Sep   Thomas CHAPLIN fs Richardi CHAPLIN et ux
21 Oct   Anna PHILLIPS fa Gulihelmi PHILLIPS et ux
21 Oct   Anna HODGSON fa Johis HODGSON et ux
23 Oct   Franciscus PEDLEY fs Johis PEDLEY et ux
2 Nov   Johes BAGNOLD fs Humphridi BAGNOLD et ux
2 Nov   Franciscus HOW fs Thoma HOW et ux
17 Nov   Katherina SHERRAT fa Johis SHERRAT et Elizabetha ux
15 Dec   Martinus JOHNSON alias SMITH (illegitimus natus)
23 Dec   Anna BIRD fa Anthonii BIRD et ux
3 Feb   Anna LOW fa Gulihelmi LOW et ux
12 Apr   ano p'dict Johes KEELING alias WARTON (illegitimus natus)
3 Mar   Jana SHERRAT fa Johis SHERRAT et Phelis ux
1639
28 Jul   Maria ELSMORE fa Henrici ELSMORE et Margareta ux
20 Aug   Johes LOWE fs Johis LOWE et Jdyth ux
25 Aug   Elizabetha ASTON fa Richardi ASTON et ux
1 Nov   Elizabetha HYD fa Jacobi HYDE et Elizabetha ux
11 Nov   Anna LOWE fa Johis LOW gen et Katherina eius ux
8 Dec   Richardus AMBERSLEY fs Francisci AMBERSLEY et Anna ux
22 Dec   Thomas JOHNSON fs Johis JOHNSON et [ ] ux
25 Dec   Maria MIDDLETON fa Johis MIDDLETON et Maria ux
23 Feb   Gulihelmus HOLLINS fs Gulihelmi HOLLINS et Saraa ux
6 Feb   Rogerus WALTON fs Jacobi WALTON (pegrini) et Jana ux
9 Feb   Constantia KEENE fa Gulihelmi KEENE et Dorothea ux
9 Feb   Thomas SHERRAT fs Edvardi SHERRAT et Elizabetha ux

Richardus Chapman Rectori

1640
- Apr   Richardus COWAP fs Richardi COWAP et Isabella ux
19 Apr   Eduardus SHERRAT fs .... et Helizabeth [?] ux
2 May   Francis WALL [?] fs .... et Elizabetha ux
8 Jun   Elizabetha .... fa .... ux
14 Jun   Elizabetha .... Margeria ux

Richardus Chapman

16 Jun   Gulielmus LOW fs Hugonis LOW et Francisca ux
20 Sep   Maria CHAPMAN fa Richardi et Murielis CHAPMAN
22 Oct   Helena SALT fa Gulielmi SALT et Isabella ux
5 Nov   Anthonius [?] BIRD fs Anthonii et Maria ux
29 Nov   Johannis HIDE fs Eduardi HYDE et Johanna ux
10 Jan   Johanna PHILLIPS fa Gulielmi PHILLIPS et Elizabetha ux
31 Jan   Henricus HELY fs Gulielmi et Elizabetha HELE ux
4 Feb   Johannis WARD alias PEAK fs ....Margariae WARD et Johannis PEAK
10 Feb   Elizabetha KEELING fa Gulielmi et Timisonis KEELING
21 Feb   Anna SHERRAT fa Johannis SHERRAT et Phelis uxoros eius
1641
4 Apr   Margaretta SHERRAT fa Johaniis SHERRAT et Elizab ux
11 Apr   Maria LOW fa Gulielmi LOW et Anna ux
1 May   Chapman MATH fs illegitimus Richardi CHAPMAN Agricola et Anna MATH
9 May   Gulielmus BAGNOLD fs Humfridi BAGNOLD et Maria ux

	Anna [?] BRADDOCK fa ante diem Johannis BRADDOCK et Johannis HODGSON illegitima et Anna BRADDOCK uxoris Johannis BRADDOCK
23 ...	Michael LOWE fs Johannis LOWE sen [?] et Catherina ux
6 Jun	Timisona CHAPLIN fa Richardi CHAPLIN et Hellena ux
10 Jun	Hellena HODGSON fa Johannis HODGSON et Elizabetha ux
1 Jun	Stephanus SPENSER fs Sampsonis SPENSER et [ ] ux
19 Aug	Gulielmus BRINDLEY fs Guliemi BRINDLEY et Jana ux
10 Oct	Elizabetha MIDLETON fa Johanni MIDLETON et Maria ux
24 Oct	Margaretta BLURTON fa Johanni BLURTON et Aliciae ux
27 [?] Dec	Gulielmus JOHNSON fs Johanni JOHNSON et [ ] ux
14 Feb	Johannis WALL fs Thoma et Elizabetha WALL ux
27 [?] Feb	Catharina SALT fa Gulielmi SALT et Isabella ux
27 Feb	Johanna AMBERSLEY fa Francisci AMBERSLEY et Anna ux
20 Feb	Maria ASTON fa Richardi ASTON et Margeria ux

1642

15 May	Franciscus et Gulielmus KEENE fi Gulielmi et Dorothea KEENE
20 May	Francisca HOLT fa Amos HOLT et Susanna ux
29 May	Francisca LOW fa Johanni LOW ... et Katherina [ux]
16 Oct	Dorothy HOLT [?] KEELING .... Gulielmi et Timisonis KEELING *[entry has been altered]*
13 Nov	Anna CHAPMAN fa Richardi CHAPMAN et Murielis ux
24 Nov	Jocosa BAYLY fa Jacobi BAYLY et [ ] ux
26 Dec	Edith WRIGHT fa Eduardi et Hellena WRIGHT ux

1643

9 Apr	Evereta BIRD fs Anthonii et Maria BIRD ux
5 May	Alicea DAVIES fa Edvardi et Anna DAVIES
14 [?] May	Thomas SPENCER fs Thoma SPENCER et Margareta ux
25 Jun	Elizabetha PHILLIPS fa Gulielmi PHILLIPS et Elizabetha
12 Jul	Anna SHARP fa Edvardi et Elizabetha SHARP ux
21 Sep	Jana KEENE fa Thoma et Anna KEENE ux
8 Oct	Elizabetha SHERRAT fa Johis et Philotis SHERRAT ux
11 Jun	Maria AMBERSLEY fa Francisca et Anna AMBERSLEY ux
18 Jun	Margareta FYNNEY fa Radulphi et Margerea FYNNEY ux
25 Jan	Nicholaus OSBURNE fs Thoma et Elizabetha OSBURNE ux
8 Feb	Francesca HEALY fa Roberti et Margerea HEALY ux
11 Feb	Walterus BLURTON fs Johis et Alicea BLURTON ux
18 Feb	Gulihelmus LEES fs Edvardi LEES et ux
10 Mar	Martini LOW fs Gulihelmi et Anna ux

1644

31 Mar	Johannes JOHNSON fs Johis JOHNSON et Margareta ux
14 Apr	Johanes SHERRAT fs Johis et Elizabetha SHERRAT ux
14 Apr	Robertus HOLLINS fs Gulihelmi et Saraa HOLLINS ux
18 Apr	Catherina WALL filiaThoma et Elizabetha WALL ux
18 Apr	Dorothea ATKINS fa Thoma et Elizabetha ATKINS ux
28 Apr	Bryan HEALEY fs Gulihelmi et Elizabetha HEALY ux
6 May	Elizabetha SPENCER fa Sampsonium et Lettice ux
30 Jun	Edvardus DAVIES fs Edvardi et Anna DAVIES ux
26 Sep	Johanes LOW fs Johis LOW generosi et Catherina ux
26 Sep	Gulihelmus KEELING fs Gulihelmi et Temison ux
2 Oct	Johes CHAPLIN fs Rici CHAPLIN et Hellena CHAPLIN ux

6 Oct	Cicelea WILSON fa Edvardi et Maria WILSON ux
6 Oct	Anna MARTIN fa Richardi et Catherina MARTIN ux
22 Oct	Jana LATHROP fa Samuelis et [ ] LATHROP ux
10 Nov	Gulihelmus WHITHURST fs Gulihelmi WHITHURST et Hellena
12 Jan	Johana PHILLIPS fa Gulihelmi PHILLIPS et Elizabetha ux
7 Feb	Franciscus TILL fs Gulihelmi TILL et Jana TILL ux
16 Feb	Gulihelmus HYD fs Edvardi HYDE et Johana ux
8 Mar	Johes EDWARDS fs Marganis EDWARDS et [ ] ux
5 May	Richardus SALT fs Gulihelmi et Isabella SALT ux

1645

5 May	Richardus SALT fs Gulihelmi et Isabella SALT ux
17 Jul [?]	Thomas COCLEHOUSE fs Thoma COCLEHOUSE et Alicia ux
9 Aug	Edvardus CHAPMAN fs Richardi CHAPMAN Rectoris Ecclesia et Murielis ux
21 Aug	Katherina BOLD fa Thoma BOLD et Katherina ux
30 Oct	Thomas WOTTON fs Gulihelmi WOTTON et Eem [?] ux
9 Nov	Elizabetha HOLLINS fa Gulihelmi HOLLINS et Sara ux
22 Dec	Robertus JOHNSON fs Johes JOHNSON et Margareta ux
23 Dec	Sara WARD fa Thoma WARD et Hellena ux
7 Jan	Robertus HEALEY fs Roberti HEALEY et Margeria ux
9 Feb	Elizabetha AMBERSLOW fa Francisci AMBERSLOW et Anna ux
15 Mar	Gulihelmus LOW fs Gulihelmi LOW et Anna ux

1646

12 Apr	Gulihelmus BIRD fs Anthonii BIRD et Maria ux
12 Apr	Johannes SHERRAT fs Johannis SHERRAT et Phelis ux
26 Apr	Elizabetha OSBURNE fa Thoma OSBURNE et ux
31 May	Elizabetha GOODWINE fa Gulielmi GOODWINE
4 Jun	Dorothea CHAPMAN fa Richardi CHAPMAN
7 Jun	Catherina LOW fa Johannes et Catherina ux
5 Oct	Michael fs Gulielmi et Tymisona KEELING ux
25 Dec	Franciscus fs Johanis et Elizab SHERRAT de Leigh
23 Jan	Elizabetha fa Mathai et Ellena LOW

SEPULTURA

1541

20 Oct	Johannes COVELL
30 Dec	Willimus STERKEY

1542

19 Apr	Johannes MYDDLETON
26 Apr	Hugo HARVEY de Feilde
6 May	Nicholaus BULLWANTE
30 May	Willimus KYRCAM
29 Jun	Robertus BYRDE
10 Jul	Johanna LEY
27 Oct	Richardus MYDDLETON
[ ] Feb	Mantilda PARKER

1543

28 Mar	Willimus SPOONER
29 Mar	Robertus COOTE
15 Apr	Thomas KEELYNGE

	4 Jul	Robertus KYRCAM
	4 Aug	Willimus SHERRATT
	12 Nov	Franciscus WRIGHTE
	7 Dec	Johanna WYTTERENS
≥	17 Jan	Mantilda GREENE
	19 Feb	Hugo HARVEY
	21 Feb	Willmus OWLY

1544

	.. ...	Thomas ....
	.. Apr	Georgius ....
—	6 May	Richardus WARDE
	16 Sep	Thomas SHERRAT
	21 Sep	Agneta WOODDE

1545

	7 May	Agneta KEELINGE
	17 May	Thomasina KEELINGE
	30 May	Johannes SHEPPARDE illegittima genit
	28 Jun	Johanna KYRCAM
	30 Jun	Agneta MYLNES
	10 Jul	Margareta WALLE
	23 Aug	Robertus RUSSELL
—	1 Sep	Katherina HEATHE
—	19 Oct	Parnella HODGESON
	24 Oct	Richardus HARVEY
	13 Dec	Thomas MYDDLETON
—	16 Dec	Agneta PARKER
—	11 Feb	Willmus LOWE
—	17 Mar	Agneta HODGESON
	20 Mar	Jocosa SPOONER

1546

—	19 Apr	Hugo HODGESON
	8 Jun	Tomasina KEELINGE
	25 Jul	Thomas ALLEYN
—	23 Sep	Agneta WARDE
	14 Oct	Elizabetha HEILEY
	10 Dec	Thomas SHERRAT
—	13 Dec	Johanna HODGESON
	19 Dec	Ellena BYRKES
	21 Jan	Johannes WATSON
	27 Jan	Richardus BALLE

1547

	12 Apr	Thomas CROMPTON
	13 Apr	Katherina WATSON
	17 Apr	Johannes BOTTE
	20 Apr	Jana SHERRAT
	22 Apr	Anna WATSON
	31 May	Willmus OWLEY
	15 Jun	Agneta ALEXANDER
	20 Jun	Franciscus BYRCHE
—	6 Sep	Elizabetha LOWE
	16 [Sep]	Elizabetha HOLLES

30 Sep   Johannes KEELINGE
4 Nov   [ ] ALTE
8 Dec   Thomas CARTER
17 Feb   Mantilda HALEY
Ult Feb   Johannes WOLLASTON
1 Mar   Jana WOLLASTON
1548
12 Apr   Elizabetha HIGGENS
26 Apr   Johannes HANLEY
20 Jun   Richardus WATSON
8 Jul   Ellena BOTTE
17 Sep   Johanna COVELL
26 Oct   Richardus PARKER
2 Nov   Johannes SPENCER
31 Dec   Georgius MYDDLETON
11 Mar   Isabella TYBPER
1549
8 May   Ellena SMYTHE
13 Jun   Agneta BAULLE
16 Jun   Johannes GREENEHOUGHE
28 Aug   Robertus HARVEY
31 Oct   Maria HYLL
10 Nov   Robertus SMYTHE
21 Nov   Elizabetha WATSON
18 Dec   Johannes COATES
17 Jan   Anthonius DYCHE
7 Feb   Edwardus HOOE
14 Feb   Franciscus KYNNERSLEY Rector de Leigh
Ult Feb   Johanna CARTER
18 Mar   Johannes COATES

R. Aston Rector ibid
Xpo Hide) ….
Willm Hodgeson)

1550
6 Apr   Cicellia HYLL
8 May   Margeria SUTTON
11 May   Margareta PARKER
13 Jun   Margeria SUTTON
30 Jun   Elizabetha PHILLIPPES
27 Jul   Johanna ALEXANDER
11 Aug   Johanna JOHNSON
21 Aug   Willmus KEELINGE
28 Sep   Johannes ALLEN
1551
25 Apr   Margeria LEE uxor Thoma LEE
20 Jun   Katherina SMYTHE
24 Jun   Johanna SALTE
25 Jun   Agneta SALTE
25 Jun   Johanna BYRDE fa Johis BIRDE
2 Jul   Gracia BERINGTON
4 Jul   Agneta MOLLARTE

6 Aug   Walterus BLURTON
19 Aug   Elizabetha BEARDMORE
26 Sep   Johanna STATHAM
3 Dec   Johannes EVES
— 2 Jan   Willmus LOOE
13 Jan   Margareta uxor Elicie BYRKE
— 7 Feb   Franciscus HODGESON fs Roberti HODGESON
3 Mar   Richardus HOLLIES
21 Mar   Katherina ALEXANDER
1552
31 Mar   Ellena PHILLIPPES
21 Jun   Johannes OWLEY
6 Aug   Johanna MYDDLETON
31 Aug   Thomas CHEDULTON
30 Sep   Johanna CATERBANKE
18 Oct   Jocosa WADE
19 Oct   Johanna AULTE uxor Johis AULTE
⇒ 7 Nov   Isabella COWPER vidua
5 Feb   Rogerus SHERRAT
1553
⌐ 15 Apr   Rogerus WOODE fs Thoma WOODDE
5 Jun   Elizabetha OWLEY uxor Henrici OWLEY
9 Jun   Henricus OWLEY
— 26 Aug   Robertus LEES
28 Aug   Willmus RUSHTON
24 Sep   Ellena BYRDE uxor Johis BYRDE
— 18 Oct   Richardus WRIGHTE
31 Dec   Elizabetha WADE fa Christoferi WADE
10 Feb   Rogerus WALL
11 Feb   Johanna WOLLASTON
— 17 Mar   Ellena SPENCER
18 Mar   Alicia DYCHE
1554
4 May   Franciscus SPOONER fs Thoma SPOONER
12 Jun   Elizabetha WOLLASTON fa Nicholai WOLLASTON
16 Jul   Willmus KEELINGE fs Jacobi KEELINGE
18 Sep   Margareta KYRCAM uxor Willmi KYRCAM
— 14 Jan   Agneta HYLL uxor Willmi HILL
⌐ 24 Jan   Ellena WOODDE uxor Thoma WOODDE
— 28 Jan   Thomas CLEARKE
17 Feb   Robertus EVYS
⌐ 17 Feb   Cicillia HODGESON fa Roberti HODGESON
✓ 19 Feb   Agneta ALLSOPPE
1555
— 19 May   Willmus HYLL
14 Jun   Willmus CROMPTON fs Johis CROMPTON
20 Mar   Johes KEELINGE fs Jacobi KEELINGE
1556
⌐ 2 Jul   Cicillia SMYTHE fa Henrici SMYTHE
7 Sep   Johanna uxor Willmi PEDLEY
6 Nov   Alicia ALLEN

```
    4 Dec   Cicillia fa Thoma MOORE
   30 Dec   Elizabetha ALLEN vidua
   31 Dec   Radulphus JOHNSON
    6 Jan   Agneta BYLLINGS fa Rogeri BYLLINGES
   11 Jan   Agneta MYDDLETON vidua
   22 Jan   Robertus PAYNE
   17 Feb   Thomas DRAKEFORDE
   23 Feb   Elizabetha PEYDLEY
  Ult Feb   Radulphus PEYDLEY
   11 Mar   Willmus FOLDRINGE
   13 Mar   Willmus SHERRATT
   15 Mar   Willmus AULTE
   17 Mar   Katherina OWLEY
   20 Mar   Willmus JOHNSON
   24 Mar   Thomas MYDDLETON
```
1557
```
   25 Mar   Thomas SPOONER
   28 Mar   Johannes LEES
   31 Mar   Margeria BYRDE fa Johis BYRDE
    5 Apr   Thomas fs Thoma SHERRAT
   21 Apr   Henricus SPENCER
   10 May   Robertus THACKER
   11 May   Agneta CARTER uxor Richardi CARTER
   14 May   Johannes CARTER
   27 May   Johannes WYTTRYNS de Foole
   28 May   Elizabetha uxor Thoma BOWYER
   10 Jun   Richardus CARTER
   16 Jun   Agneta OWLEY vidua
   17 Jun   Thomas BOWYER
   21 Jun   Francisca fa Johis BEE
    5 Jun   Agneta LOWE vidua
   26 Jul   Margeria uxor Johis BEE
    7 Sep   Agneta uxor Richardi DYCHE
   18 Sep   Thomas fs Alexandri COATES
    2 Oct   Richardus DYCHE
    9 Oct   Thomas CANTRELL
   18 Oct   Johannes SALTE peregrinus
```

R. Aston Rector ibid
Xpo Hid)
Willmi Hodgeson) ....

```
   11 Nov   Katherina SHERRAT
   13 Nov   Willus et Elizabetha fi Thoma MOORE
   23 Nov   Johanna uxor Alexandri COATES
   28 Dec   Thomas BRADSHAWE gen'osus
   18 Jan   Elizabetha EVYS vidua
   22 Jan   Thomas PARKER
   18 Mar   Thomas CARTER
```
1558
```
    8 Apr   Ellena WRIGHTE uxor Radulphi WRIGHTE
   25 May   Willus ALTE fs Johis ALTE
    1 Aug   Richardus BERDMORE et Ellena uxor eius
```

5 Aug Johannes CROMPTON
12 Aug Ellena SHERRAT fa Radulphi SHERRAT
2 Oct Agneta CADE
19 [Oct] Rogerus BYLLYNGE
27 Oct Agneta LOOE fa Johis LOOE
29 Oct Katherina LOOE fa Johis LOOE
12 Nov Alicia WARDE fa Roberti WARDE
15 Dec Franciscus SHERRAT fs Radi SHERRAT
16 Dec Margeria DRAKEFORDE uxor Thoma DRAKEFORDE
8 Feb Alicia KYRCAM vidua
1 Mar Thomas SHERRAT
19 Mar Margeria WALL
1559
28 Mar Elizabetha BOTTE uxor Richardi BOTTE
14 Apr Alicia GREENEHOUGH vidua
19 Apr Agneta PARKER fa Thoma PARKER
16 Jul Richardus SMYTHE
10 Sep Willus COVELL
21 Sep Richardus PEDLEY fs Willmi PEDLEY
3 Oct Agneta WALKER fa Humfridi WALKER
22 [?] Nov Henricus fs Johis ....
30 Nov Martynus LOOE fs Johis LOOE
22 Mar Franciscus HARVEY fs Johis HARVEY
1560
19 Apr Margeria HARVEY fa Johis HARVEY
7 Jun Richardus WATSON de Feeilde
3 Jul Jacobus HYLL fs Humfridi HYLL
24 Jul Ellenora HEAPE fa Radulphi HEAPE
12 Oct Henricus HODGESON fs Willmi HODGESON
17 Feb Johannes WOODDE
26 Feb Willmus BOTTE s/o Richarde BOTTE
1561
20 Apr Johannes HODGESON de Wythyngton
17 May Cicillia HOLTE fa Nicholai HOLTE
28 May Alicia FOORDE fa Thoma FOORDE
8 Jun Anthonius BOWYER fs Willmi BOWYER
27 Jul Johannes OWLEY fs Rogeri OWLEY
10 Sep Lodovicus HYLL fs Humfridi HYLL
30 Nov Franciscus LYMYALLES fs Roberti LYMYALLES
27 Jan Johannes HARVEY fs Johis HARVEY
14 Mar Cicillia THACKER fa Roberti THACKER
23 Mar Johannes COATES fs Alexandri COATES
1562
1 Apr Margeria COATES uxor Alexandri COATES
1 May Johanna OLLASON fa Nicholai OLLASON
31 May Willus KYRCAM
15 Jun Agneta HYLL uxor Humfridi HYLL
17 Jun Johannes CROMPTON de Leighe
31 Jul Richardus HARVEY fs Johis HARVEY
20 Aug Ellena WEYTTON fa Richardi WEYTTON
21 Aug Johannes LEES fs Francisci LEES

26 Aug   Alicia OWLEY uxor Thoma OWLEY
13 Sep   Johannes LEES fs Johis LEES de Nobolde
25 Nov   Franciscus PEDLEY fs Willmi PEDLEY
28 Dec   Jana MYNORS gen'os vidua
17 Jan   Richardus LEEY als WRIGHTE
1563
7 Mar   Petrus SHERRATT fs Radulphi SHERRATT
11 Apr   Jacobus KEELINGE
12 Apr   Johanna SHERRAT fa Radulphi SHERRATT
14 Apr   Francisca BOWYER fa Willmi BOWYER
24 Apr   Alicia SUTTON fa Georgii SUTTON
1 May   Georgius SUTTON
18 May   Johanna SHERRATT uxor Radulphi SHERRATT
18 May   Ellena PEDLEY de Leighe vidua
1 Jul   Johanna SUTTON fa Georgii SUTTON
14 Sep   Nicholaus BRADSHAWE cl'icus
24 Oct   Franciscus LEES fs Francisci LEES
8 Jan   Ellena HEAPE fa Radulphi HEAPE
6 Feb   Richardus WYTTRYNS de Leigh
Ult Feb   Radulphus WRIGHTE
1564
10 Apr   Johannes BALL fs Johis BALL
10 May   Ellena WYGGYN uxor Richardi WYGGYN
28 Oct   Thomas fs Johis LAWTON de Checkley
6 Dec   Franciscus BYLLYNGE fs Rogeri BYLLYNGE
31 Dec   Maria HANSSON fa Richardi HANSSON
2 Jan   Johannes BYLLYNGES fs Thoma BYLLYNGE
5 Feb   Thomas DRAKEFORDE cl'icus
6 Feb   Franciscus BYRKES fs Willmi BYRKES
19 Feb   Henricus FOORDE de Wythington
1565
28 Mar   Katherina LOOE fa Johis LOOE
3 Apr   Alicia FOORDE fa Henrici FOORDE
25 Jun   Thomas OLEY de Wythington
25 Jun   Francisca fa Stephani HARVEY
28 Nov   Margeria RUSSELL
4 Dec   Thomas SPENCER fs Stephani SPENCER
11 Dec   Elizabetha WRIGHTE
8 Jan   Willus PHILLIPPES de Leighe
26 Jan   Johannes JOHNSON de Doddisley
20 Feb   Robertus HARVEY de Feeilde
18 Mar   Maria WADE fa Roberti WADE
1566
[blank space]

1567

R. Aston Rector ibid
Xpo Hide Willmi Hodgeson) ....

1568
4 Aug   Willmus SHERRAT
12 Nov   Franciscus WRIGHTE
27 Nov   Johanna WYTTRYNS

17 Jan Mantilda GREENEHOUGH
19 Feb Hugo HARVEY
21 Feb Willmus OLEY
1569
[blank space]
1570 [1636 written above]
[blank space]
1571
↘15 Mar Johanna WOODDE
15 Mar Franciscus NAYLER
1572
8 Jul Franciscus NAYLER
9 Jul Alicia NAYLER uxor Roberti NAYLER
14 Jul Willmus HARVEY
24 Jul Agneta DRAKEFORDE
2 Aug Richardus BOTTE
6 Aug Willmus KYRCAM
26 Aug Mantilda OLEY
30 Aug Franciscus PEDLEY
18 Oct Agneta HICKCHOCK [?]
26 Oct Stephanus SPENCER
16 Nov Alexander COATES
30 Nov Agneta THACKER
1573
26 Mar Franciscus HARRISON
16 May Agneta ROYLEY uxor Edwardi ROYLEY
24 May Franciscus SALTE fs Francisci SALTE
6 Oct Elizabetha BAYLIE
20 Oct Ellena GREENEHOUGHE
10 Jan Johanna CARTER fa Johis CARTER
12 Jan Gracea ASTON fa m'ri Anthoni ASTON
17 Jan Robertus DAVYE
5 Feb Agneta BYLLYNGES
22 Feb Margeria SHAWE
1 Mar Margareta COWAPE
20 Mar Elizabetha HODGESON fa Roberti HODGESON
21 Mar Franciscus* HEAPE fa* Radi HEAPE [*sic]
1574
1 Jun Johannes FALDRINGE
19 Aug Ellena KAYE fa Willmi KAYE
17 Oct Anthonius THACKER fs Roberti THACKER
11 Jan Richardus BYRDE
11 Jan Ellena TOMPSON fa Roberti TOMPSON
18 Jan Franciscus HARVEY
27 Jan Agneta SALTE
1575
16 May Franciscus SALTE fs Willmi SALTE
1 Sep Isabella MARGERAM
4 Sep Agneta SMYTHE
10 Sep Richardus SMYTHE
24 Feb Alicia MARCHETT

1576
29 Mar Thomas SMYTHE
3 Apr Ellena TOMPKYNSON
6 May Johanna HARVEY
14 Sep Franciscus HARVEY
28 Nov Francisca HARVEY
6 Dec Michael HARRISON
2 Mar Alicia SHERRATT
1577
6 Jul Ellena DYCHE
7 Sep Alicia HARRISON
1 Feb Willmus SMYTHE
1578
17 Oct Johannes ALTE
25 Oct Willmus PEDLEY
7 Nov Margeria HARVEY uxor Stephani HARVEY
5 Dec Radulphus CATERBANKE
16 Feb Johanna GRUNDIE fa Johis GRUNDIE
1579
1 May Ellena SHERRAT uxor Francisci [?] SHERRAT
15 May Johannes WYTTRYNS
20 Jun Agneta ALTE fa Francisci ALTE
8 Jul Robertus WOODE
27 Jul Elizabetha ASTON uxor m're Anthonii ASTON
1 Aug Elliceus BYRCHE
27 Aug Willmus ALTE fs Francisci ALTE
28 Oct Elizabetha WOODE
20 Nov Francisca DRAYCOT fa Philippi DRAYCOT
16 Dec Amya GREENEHOUGH uxor Willmi GREENEHOUGHE
26 Dec Henricus MOTTERAM
1 Mar Franciscus BYRDE
1580
20 Jun Johannes HARVEY fs Johis HARVEY
17 Aug Francisca ALTE fa Francisci ALTE
27 Aug Anthonius fs m'ri AMIS
31 Aug Margaret OWLEY uxor Hugonis OWLEY
1581
26 Jul Hugo OWLEY
25 Jan Margareta HODGEKYNSON
1582
29 Mar Richardus SPENCER
27 Aug Margeria BYRKE
18 Oct Richardus BYRKE
21 Oct Katherina BROWNE
13 Nov Hugo PHILLIPPES
22 Nov Willmus TOMKINSON
2 Dec Robertus ALLEN
18 Dec Isabella WARDE fa Xpi WARDE

R. Aston Rector ibid
Xpo Hide) ....
Willm Hodgeson)

1583
26 Mar   Richardus HYDE
26 Oct   Ezra ASTON fa Rici ASTON cl'ici
11 Feb   Elizabetha NORTHE fa Nicholai NORTHE
1584
24 Apr   Thomas LEES
5 May   Elizabetha COWAPPE
25 Aug   Maria BLURTON fa Johis BLURTON et Eliz ux
26 Sep   Margareta DYCHE
25 Sep   [ ] HYLL pochie de Bromshall
31 Oct   Elizabetha BAULL als COOKE
17 Nov   Margeria HARVEY
7 Dec   Franciscus HARVEY fs Johis HARVEY et Agneta ux
8 Dec   Agneta HARVEY
8 Dec   [ ] PSULL
16 Jan   Johannes BAYLIE
17 Jan   Alicia HYDE
1585
12 May   Johanna WOODE
21 May   Nicholaus WOLLASTON
1 Jul   Willus SHERRAT
16 Jul   Rogerus ORCHARDE
8 Nov   Johanna WARDE
25 Nov   Jana BROWNE
6 Jan   Johannes COVELL
22 Mar   Johannes LOWE
1586
27 Mar   Ellena BOTTE
2 Jul   Thomas SPOONER
29 Aug   Margeria HARVEY
30 Sep   Margareta MYLNER
30 Sep   Jana HARVEY mater eiusdem Margareta
9 Nov   Richardus GARRAT
25 Nov   Margeria SPENCER
1587
21 Oct   [ ] SMYTHE
29 Oct   [ ] ORCHARDE
14 Nov   Margareta ORCHARDE
23 Nov   Willus WOLLEY
5 Mar   Maria NORTHE
1588
20 Apr   [ ] WYTTRINGES
21 Apr   Robertus SPENCER
26 May   Johannes ALLEXANDER
29 May   Katherina KYRCAM
9 Jun   Thomas WALKELATE
28 Feb   Ellena AMES fa Thoma BENTELEY et Margareta AMES
10 Jan   Margareta MORGAN genosa
13 Jan   Lawrencius UTTWARDE als HATTOWE
24 Jan   Katherina KEELYNGE
25 Jan   Rogerus BYLLYNGE

1589
9 Apr   Francisca MOORE
16 Aug   Elizabetha SMYTHE
23 Nov   Willus LEEKE
28 Nov   Ellena MYLNER
5 Feb   Elizabetha KEELYNGE
23 Feb   Johanna KEELYNGE
21 Mar   Edwardus KEELYNGE
1590
3 May   Isabella HARVEY
11 May   Johannes HARVEY
21 May   Isabella RAWLEN
2 Jun   Robertus HODGESON
4 Jun   Margareta LEE
11 Jun   Agneta PEDLEY
29 Jul   Hugo SPENCER
3 Aug   Richardus BYRDE
8 Aug   Johanna SHERRAT
9 Aug   Johannes SHERRAT
15 Aug   Francisca HOLTE
17 Aug   Thomas WATSON
28 Sep   Ellena WOLLASTON
16 Nov   Agneta RYDER
25 Nov   Alicia LEES
14 Dec   Isabella FORSTER
23 Dec   Ellena GENNYES
25 Jan   Thomas BLURTON
3 Feb   Rogerus PARKER
20 Feb   Margareta SHERATT
23 Feb   Jana KAYE
26 Feb   Robertus ORCHARDE
4 Mar   Elizabetha SMYTHE
9 Mar   Margeria SMYTHE
10 Mar   Margeria ALLEN
1591
9 Apr   Franciscus SMYTHE
9 Apr   Radus SHERRAT
15 Apr   Isabella LEE
9 May   Alicia BLURTON
10 Jun   Anthonius DYCHE
25 Jun   Fra WOOD
15 Jul   Alicia CLEARKE
12 Aug   Francisca ALLEN
3 Nov   Henricus [ ]
2 Dec   Johannes BYLLYNGE
3 Jan   Thomas HOWE
9 Jan   Alicea WATSON
18 Jan   [ ] BROWNE
27 Feb   Franciscus HORDORNE
10 Mar   Alicea WOOD
23 Mar   Willus SHERRAT

1592

30 Mar Richardus ASTON fs Richardi ASTON Rcoris de Leigh qui quidem Ricus
transmigravitham vitam apud Bettley xxvii die eiusdem mensis

7 Apr [ ] RAVONSDALE

18 Apr Edmundus HOLTE

28 Apr Agneta BLACKMAN

3 May Agneta ALTE

8 May Johannes COATES

22 Jun Rosa HOLTE

R. Aston Rector ibid
Xpo Hide) ....
Willm Hodgeson)

18 Jul Thomas BYRCHE senior

12 Sep Agneta RUSHTON

14 Sep Walterus NORTHE

9 Oct Ellena DRAKEFORDE

18 Oct Dorothea RUSHTON

6 Dec Elizabetha BERWEEKE

24 Dec Franciscus COATES

13 Feb Johanna HODGESON

1593

9 Jun Thomas MASSYE

24 Jun Johannes WEBBE

16 Sep Alicia LYMER

1594

30 May [ ] SHERRAT fa Johis SHERRAT

8 Aug Agneta SPENCER

10 Aug Alicia KEELINGE

20 Oct Thomas LEE

10 Nov Johanna HYLL

26 Nov Johannes TILSTON

9 Dec Henricus SMYTHE

18 Dec Agneta MOORE

4 Jan Thomas WARDE

6 Jan Alicia HARDINGE

19 Jan Anna PARKER

3 Feb Johannes LAWRENCE

19 Feb Franciscus PHILLIPPES

27 Feb Anna PHILLIPPES

1595

30 Mar Willus CONWAYE

7 Apr Johannes WARDE

17 Apr Willus WOODE

23 Apr Margareta NORTHE

24 Jun Ellena CROMPTON

29 Jun Alicia PHILLIPPES

21 Sep Nicholaus HOLTE

17 Dec Humfridus ROWLEYN

26 Dec Anna ASTON fa Anthonii ASTON

1596

16 Apr Agneta BOTTE fa Georgii BOTTE et Eliz: SHERBROKE famila sua

17 Jun   Anthonius LEES
24 Jun   Johannes PAKEMAN
7 Aug   Willus BOTTE fs Richardi BOTTE
11 Sep   Johannes WYTTERINS fs Thoe WYTTERINS
11 Sep   Anna SPOONER fa Willmi SPOONER
13 Oct   Georgius HEAPE fs Johis MASSYE et Anna HEAPE
2 Nov   Thomas PHILLIPPES fs Johis PHILLIPPES
13 Nov   Richardus DEGGE fs Edwardi DEGGE
2 Dec   Ellena BYRCHE uxor Thoe BYRCHE
13 Feb   Thomas KEELYNGE
4 Mar   Radus HEAPE
20 Mar   Willmus STATHAM
1597
8 Apr   Robertus TOMPKINSON
8 Apr   Margeria ALEXANDER
3 May   Christopherus WARDE
6 May   Maria et Johanna SPOONER
8 Jun   Johannes HYDE
15 Jun   Humfridus BROWNE
15 Jun   Maria STANLEY
1 Feb   Isabella HARRISON de Myddleton greene
7 Feb   Rosa FLYNTE uxor Johis FLYNTE
8 Feb   Willmus SALTE
1598
8 Apr   Maria SHERRAT
10 Apr   Robertus HORDERNE
20 Apr   Humfridus WARDE
23 Apr   Anna LAYTHROPPE
5 Sep   Henricus SPOONER
28 Sep   Johannes HARVEY
3 Nov   Margareta HEATON
14 Nov   Franciscus DYCHE
17 Nov   Thomas WOLLE
13 Dec   Agneta STATHAM
1 Jan   Elizabetha BOTTE
23 Jan   Johannes MYLNER
14 Feb   Anna DAVID
1599
22 May   Robertus WARDE
13 Jun   Alicia BYRCHE
11 Jul   Johanna MARGERISON
11 Nov   Nicholaus NORTHE
13 Nov   Franciscus COTE fs Margareta COTE Vidua
13 Dec   Johanna WILLOWES famula Katherina NORTHE
17 Dec   Johanna BURTON pauper
28 Dec   Franciscus SHERRATT
4 Feb   Margareta LOWE uxor Willmi LOW
1600
20 Apr   Richardus WALKER fs Willmi WALKER et ux

                                          Civitatis Lich

9 Jun   Johanna HOOFORD fa Willmi HOOFORD et ux

19 Jul	Franciscus WALLE huius pochia sepult erat apud Checkley
13 Jul	Edwardus LAWRENCE fs Edwardi LAWRENCE
16 Aug	Anna HOOFORD uxor Willmi HOOFORDE decius
8 Nov	Margareta HODGESON uxor Robti HODGESON
4 Mar	Jona BLURTON ux Walteri BLURTON
10 Mar	M'geria BLURTON wid

> Hugo Weare Curatus de Leighe scdo die
> Mensis Juny Ano Dni Millimo sixcentisimo scdo

1601

3 Sep	Elizabetha fa Willmi HYLLE [?]
16 Oct	Richus fil illimus Jocosa BROWN
23 Oct	Margareta WRIGHT
28 Oct	Alicia ROYLEY ux Edwardi ROYLEY
21 Nov	Helena ux Johis STANLEY
12 Dec	Willmus DICHE
16 Dec	Richus BOTTE
12 Jan	Raffus COVILL
14 Jan	Francisca fil Willmi HYDE
22 Mar	Jana fil vid COVILL

1602

15 Apr	Michaell COWAP
21 Apr	Panil [?] fil illimi Katherine NORTHE
26 Jul	Johannes BEARDMOORE
10 Aug	Richardus HAMBLETON
11 Sep	Walterus MASSEY infans fs Johanis MASSEY et Agneta ux

> Johes Palmer Rcoris ibid
> Michaell Forster) Gard
> Thomas Rawnsdon [?])

26 Sep	Johanes et Johanna gemelli fil Johis DYCHE de Fole
29 Sep	Dorothea fa Willi LOWE et Elizabetha ux
1 Oct	Gulielmus SPENSER de Feilde
28 Oct	Queda fa Willmi BLURTON et ux
3 Dec	Elizabetha COWAPPE
11 Dec	Katherina LOWE vid
11 Dec	Margareta fa Johis BEARDMORE de Checkley
19 Feb	Margareta BEARDMORE vid
23 Feb	Henricus BROWNE
8 Mar	Margareta DYCHE vid

1603

4 Apr	Agneta JACKSON
24 Apr	Agneta HYDE vid
24 Jun	Allicea fa Richardi WULLASTON et ux
28 Jul	Agneta uxor Johanis NITUM [?]
11 Aug	Willimus SPOONER
11 Oct	Joanna fa Rici COWAPPE et ux
3 Jan	Elizabetha EAVES vid
10 Jan	Wynnefrida fa Rici PEDLEY

1604

26 Mar	Katharina uxor Helizei BIRCH
9 Apr	Willimus PEDLEY
5 Aug	Richardus fs Richardi KEENE

5 Dec   Ricus DYCHE
1605
29 Mar   Allicea MASSEY
14 Apr   Ellena HOULTE
— 25 Dec   Willimus SPENSER
8 Mar   Agnes RAWNSDALE vid
1606
28 Sep   Ellena fa Thoma MASSIE et ux
6 Oct   Thomas KIRCOME
10 Oct   Wmi KEY
24 Oct   Francisca uxor Johis SHERRAT
— 1 Nov   Ellena uxor Johanis HILL
14 Nov   Thoma WALL
25 Nov   Katharena WALL
13 Jan   Allicea PEDLEY vid
19 Mar   Allicea KENDRICKE vid
1607
— 28 Mar   Elizabetha PARKER vid
19 Apr   Robtus NAYLOR
26 Jul   Robertus HEAPE
— 27 Jul   Franciscus fs Francisci WARDE et ux
9 Aug   Johanes fs Richardi DYCHE et ux
— 30 Oct   Christopherum WARDE fs Simoni WARDE et ux
25 Jan   Dorothea fa Richardi CARTER et ux
— 15 Feb   Robertus JACKSON
20 Feb   Thomas BROWER [?]
1608
— 14 Apr   Nicholaus TURNER et Thomas WITTERINGE de Fole
— 24 Apr   Margeria uxor Francisci LEES
— 28 Jun   Katharena fa Johanis LEES et ux
20 Sep   Richardus STOCKWELL
9 Oct   Thomas STEWARD paup
13 Oct   Reppingtonus fs Thoma LATHROPPE et Maria ux
11 Oct   Radus BOWYER
2 Dec   Hugo fs Roberti SONTE et ux
25 Dec   Margareta uxor Thoma JOHNSON
10 Mar   Johes BIRDE
1609
15 May   Franciscus MIDDLETON
— 21 May   Joanna SMYTH paupcula
11 Jun   Allicea uxor Robti THACKER
13 Jun   Willus fs illegitimus Willi CARTER et Ellena GILLER
— 30 Jun   Thomas MOORE
10 Jul   Johannes ALLIN
— 4 Nov   Ellena FORSTER
28 Nov   Elizabetha uxor Anthonii CLUD
— 15 Dec   Margareta uxor Rogeri WOOLLEY
8 Dec   Franciscus PHILLIPPES
27 Dec   Thomas BALL
— 25 Feb   Thomas WRIGHTE

1610
30 Mar   Rogerus WOOLLEY
6 Apr   Willus HODGESON
9 Apr   Margeria ORCHARDE
5 May   Elizabetha uxor Anthonii BIRDE
20 May   Johanes BLURTON
22 Jul   Agnes DYCHE
10 Nov   Susanna uxor Willi FARMER als GRUNDIE
7 Jan   Thomas SONTE
.. Jan   Willus fs Willi DRAKEFORDE et ux
7 Mar   Agnes fa Thoma HOOWE et ux
1611
4 Jun   Joanna fa Michaelis FORSTER
3 Aug   Margeria PARKER vide
9 Aug   Margareta NAYLOR vide
27 Oct   Anna ARME
31 Dec   Johes HIDE
31 Dec   Jocosa HIDE
2 Feb   Radulphus HIDE fs Christopheri HIDE
15 Feb   Franciscus ALTE fs Johis ALTE
1 Mar   Robertus THACKER
2 Mar   Agnes SPENSER fa Thoma SPENSER et ux
1612
16 Apr   Agnes CLEARKE
2 Jun   Elizabetha DOUGHTIE vid
14 Dec   Thomas SHERRETT
27 Dec   quada ignata
28 Jan   Edvardus COOKE
4 Feb   Gulihelmus fs Richardi PEDLEY
5 Feb   Henricus HEATON
21 Feb   Francisca HIDE fa Johis HYDE
22 Feb   Alicea ILEM uxor Rowlandi ILEM
1613
22 Apr   Elizabetha PHILLIPS fa Willmi PHILLIPS
12 Nov   Agnes MASSY vid
1614
7 Feb   Thomas JOHNSON
26 Mar   Dorothea TYLSTONS vide
16 Apr   Willmi BURCKES
1 Jun   Maria PYBUS fa Thoma PYBUS
8 Jun   Cycilea STATHAM
7 Aug   Ricus KEENE
15 Aug   Franciscus MARGERISON
21 Sep   Margareta BLURTON
9 Oct   Ricus WOOD
7 Dec   Humphridus WRIGHTE
12 Dec   Franciscus WARD
9 Mar   Catherina WAKLETT
1615
6 Aug   [ ] MIDDLETON
25 Dec   Thomas LATHEROPP

10 Jan Ricus HALLOM
17 Feb Gracia DRAKEFORD
13 Mar Elizabetha WATSON
1616
10 May Johes GRUNDY
22 Nov Franncies BIRCH fa Heliz BYRCH
27 Dec Elizabetha TILL
5 [?] Jan Willmus SMITH
1617
31 Mar Johanna SHERRAT vidua
6 Apr Johana HILL
7 May Thomas BLAKEMAN
16 May Maria WOLLOSON
20 May …………. MARGERISON
7 Jun Catherina WAKLAT
30 Oct Margareta SPOONER vidua
5 Jan Margareta KOTES vidua
2 Mar Hellena COVELL vidua
1618
13 Apr Agnes BAYLY vidua
20 Apr Ricus WOLLOSTON
5 Jun Robertus HARVY
6 Aug Elizeus STATHAM
9 Sep Arthur BLURTON
1 Dec Catherina WARD vidua
12 Dec Robertus SHERRAT
5 Jan Dorothea MORREY
19 Jan Maria BARKER
24 Feb Jona BLAKMAN vidua
3 Mar [ ] BAGNOLL uxor Humphridi BAGNOLL
1619
31 Mar Jona FISHER
.. Jun Franciscus HOLT
15 Jul Jona WARD vidua
13 Aug Michaell FORSTER
12 Oct Abigall BATCOMBE
31 Dec Anthonius BIRD et Franciscus SPENSER
17 Jan Franciscus YATES
1 Feb Jana STATHAM
1620
25 Mar Willus DRAKFORD
23 Apr Anna HOOMES vidua
8 May Tho. BIRCH
24 Aug Elizabetha PY
2 Nov Eastera HOLT
29 Dec Jona KEENE
29 Jan Jona ADERLEY et Willus SMITH
15 Feb Elizabetha SHERRAT
15 Feb Thomas HARVY
17 Feb Anna GREATBATCH
12 [?] Feb Johis RODE

18 [?] Feb   Johes HERVY [?]
.. Feb   Sampson PY
24 Feb   Simon WARD
28 Feb   Catherina FALLOWES
4 Mar   Henricus NAYLOR
31 Jul   Elizabetha HEALY
16 Aug   Mathea GREATBATCH

1621
8 May   Jona CHALLENNER
7 Jun   Jona SHORT vidua
1 Jul   Elizabetha HEALY
29 Nov   Johes ROBINSON
14 Dec   Jona CLUD
17 Dec   Elizabetha GRUNDY
18 Dec   Catherina PIBUS
20 Dec   Margareta BOYER

1622
20 Jun   Hellena HALLEN
14 Nov   Elizabetha SHERRAT
17 Jan   Walterus BAGOTT
16 Feb   Jona MIDLETON widdow

1623
29 Mar   Robertus BLURTON
2 Jul   Johes STATHAM
4 Jul   Catherina COLLIER
18 Sep   Ricus SPENSER
18 Oct   Fra: BOYER
3 Nov   Elizabetha CHY [?]
22 Nov   Maria HILL
29 Nov   Robertus ASTON armigeri
13 Mar   Johes SHERRAT
21 Mar   quida pegrinus

1624
29 May   Samuellis GOODWYND
14 Jul   Richardus BOWRING
17 Jul   Richardus BANN
5 Nov   Thomas SPENCORE
6 Dec   Thomas DYCH
14 Feb   Willmus GRYNDY
16 Feb   Lucus THACKAR

1625
4 Apr   Jana RISHON
9 Apr   Xpherus HYD
10 Apr   Margareta WARD
17 Jun   Thomas LATHROPP
27 Jun   Johes THACKAR
28 Aug   Cicylea BARKER
6 Sep   Stephen SPENCER

This Stephen Spencer was the founder of the Free School.

L. Bagot Rector

2 Oct   Elizabetha DAVIES

8 Oct   Astonus FOLDERING
10 Jan   Margareta COVILL
1626
24 May   Elizabetha LICESTER
24 May   Willmus SHERRAT
15 May   Anna ASTON vid
2 Aug   Margeria WHITALL
17 Aug   Gulihelmus LOWE
29 Oct   Edvardus LAWRENCE
21 Nov   Elizabetha LICESTER uxor Willi LICESTER
27 Jan   Catherina BARKER
13 Mar   Margareta NORTH
1627
6 May   Johana MORE
16 Jul   Elizabetha PARKER
12 Aug   Richardus BARBER sen
16 Feb   Katherina HYD
11 Feb   Johes SWYNSHED
1628
9 Aug   [ ] OSBORNE
20 Jan   Ellena SONT
12 Feb   Thomas COVELL
9 Mar   Isabella RISHON
23 Mar   Jona HYDE
1629
7 Apr   Johana LAWRENCE vidua
21 May   Thomas LOW
17 Jul   Stephanus WATTSON
5 Oct   Sandra BROOKES
23 Jan   Symon THACKER
8 Mar   Jacobus RISHON
14 Mar   Margeria CARTER
1630
9 Apr   Francisca SONT
2 May   Elizabetha BOOT
30 Jun   Thomas HARVY
18 Sep   Willmus PHILLIPPES
9 Nov   Hellena SALT
10 Feb   Cicylea ORCHARGE
14 Mar   Maria LATHROPP
1631
29 Sep   Elizabetha FORSTER
8 Oct   Izablla KEELING
25 Feb   Elizabetha PERSEVALL
1632
29 Sep   Elizabetha TOMKINSON
2 Oct   Xpherus HILL
7 Sep   Anna LOWE
28 Nov   Thomas THACKER
24 Feb   Francisca HYDE
6 Mar   Dorothea SPOONER

15 Mar	Robertus THACKER
1633	
13 May	Johes SHERRATT
5 Jun	Constancia GAYWOOD
26 Jul	Willmus ALLEN
2 Aug	Jona WARD
15 Aug	Ellena GOUGH
18 Dec	Edvardus MERCER
24 Jan	Richardus DYCH
1634	
2 Oct	Katherina HYDE
18 Nov	Willmus ASTON Armig
22 Nov	Jona PARTON
25 Nov	Anna CARTER
29 Nov	Phillipus HODGSON
15 Jan	Johes HILL junior
16 Jan	Anna GOODWYNE
25 Jan	Johes HILL junior
15 Feb	Jocosa ~~ASTON~~ WILSON
1635	
1 Apr	Elizabetha BLURTON
8 Aug	Jana SALT fa Willi SALT
27 Sep	Katherina HYDE
2 Oct	Elizabetha SMITH
31 Dec	Elizabetha AULT
19 Mar	Anna ORDIMORE
1636	
12 Jun	[ ] EDWARDS fs Willmi EDWARDS
15 Jun	Margareta COVELL
18 Jul	Anna DAVIES vid
10 Jul	[ ] HEALEY
3 Dec	Richardus HODGSON
7 Jan	Constancia KEENS
26 Jan	Johes LEES
24 Feb	Juditha BIGINGS
25 Mar	Anna COWAP
1637	

Johes Palmer Rector

4 Apr	*[illegible]*
20 Apr	Franciscus AULT
5 …	*[illegible]*
.. Sep	*[illegible]*
10 Oct	Johes ………
28 Jan	Richardus MOORE
21 Mar	Thoma [?] LEES [?]
1638	
26 Apr	Elizabetha SHERRAT
14 Jul	Margreta SPENCER
7 Jan	Jocosa ASTON fa Johes ASTON gen
19 Jan	Anna BIRD
6 Feb	………. PHILLIPS

1639

.. ...	Margeria ALLEN vidua
17 Aug	Edwardus HOW
23 Jan	Anna LOWE
8 Feb	Maria WILSON
22 Feb	Johannis LOW
22 Feb	Johanna PHILLIPS vidua
8 Mar	Anna PEDLEY fa Johannis PEDLEY
	Franciscus SHERRAT *[incomplete entry – erased]*

Richardus Chapman Rector de Legh

1640

1 Apr	Franciscus SHERRAT Sen [?]
8 Apr	Christopherus THACKER
24 Apr	Randulphus BIRD
30 Sep	Christopherus HIDE
4 Oct	Thoma LO.. [?]
28 Oct	Margaretta PARKER
3 Nov	[ ] WILSON
27 Nov	Elizabetha PEDLEY
28 Nov	Johannis ASTON generosus
19 Dec	Fran [?] ATHERLY
9 Jan	Margaretta HILL
10 Jan	Maria BAYLY
13 Jan	Margaretta BOTT
26 Jan	Francisca SHERRAT
28 Jan	Johanna Th......... DAVIS [?]

1641

12 Jun	*[illegible]*
26 Jul	...... R....SON
30 Oct	Maria CHARLTON [?]
27 Nov	Elizabetha MIDLETON
2 Dec	Edvardus ...HEAD
.. ...	Richardus COWAP
19 Feb	Johanna MARGERAM
.. ...	Elizabetha ....

1642

.. ...	Helena SALT
2. ...	*[illegible]*
30 Apr	.... LOW
	[the next three entries are illegible]
	Anna [?] ....
2 Aug	Johanna [?] AMBERSLEY
17 Nov	Johann [es?] ....HILL [?]
24 Nov	Johannes S... [?]
.. Jan	*[illegible]*
11 Jan	*[illegible]*
23 Jan	*[illegible]*
2 Feb	Franciscus HEALY
6 Mar	Gulihelmus HASSALL
	Elizabetha COLLIER *[incomplete entry – erased see below]*

1643

20 Apr	Elizabetha COLLIER
6 May	Dorothea SHERRAT
21 May	Thomas SPENSER
22 Jun	fa Edvardi DAVIES
11 Jul	Richardus AULT
6 Aug	Johanna WHITHURST
25 Aug	Alicea HEATON
29 Aug	Elizabetha AULT
18 Sep	Margareta HUDSON
9 Nov	Anna KEENE
18 Nov	Margareta PARKER
4 Feb	Elizabetha WHITHURST
9 Feb	Franciscus HEALY
28 Feb	Edvardus BARKER
1 Mar	Rogerus ROSTER

1644

25 Mar	Anthonius HYDE
17 Jul	Elizabetha LEES
29 Jul	Elizabetha PHILLIPS
3 Aug	Catherina LEES
6 Sep	Henricus HEALY
8 Oct	Thomas ASTON
21 Oct	Anna HILL
13 Jan	Vidua NEEDHAM
4 Feb	Hellena MARTIN
19 Mar	Gulihelmus BULLOCK

1645

23 Apr	Johes COVELL
21 May	Johes HYD
17 Jun	Johes PHILLIPS
25 Jun	Gulihelmus HYD
1 Jul	Gulihelmus ASTON
18 Jul	Johana PHILLIPS fa Gulihelmi PHILLIPS
4 Aug	Katherina NAYLOR

Leigh, Staffordshire, Parish Register
1646-1704

[Transcriber's note..]
Many entries in this register are partly or completely illegible, or missing due to damage. From the start of the Bishops Transcripts in 1660 the damaged or missing entries have been added from the BT's, as have dates or names which differ from those in the register. The years 1664 to 1669 inclusive were omitted from the BT's. For some years there is a second BT which differs in some details from the register and/or the other-BT. Information added from the BT's is shown in *italics*.

The order in which entries were made in the register is somewhat erratic. All the register pages are divided into two columns of entries with the page number in the top outer corner.

The entries are to be found on the following -		Register page(s)
Marriages	1646-1672	1-2
	1672-1685	19
	1686-1687	20
	1687-1693	22
	1693-1698 & 1704	24
	1699-1703	30
	1703-1704	24
Baptisms	1646-1672	5-11
	1672-1681	17
	1682-1685 & 1686-1688	20
	1688-1689	21
	1690-1693	23
	1694-1695	24
	1696-1700	27-28
	1700-1703	31-33
	1703-1704	29
Births	1695-1700	2-4
	1700-1701	12
	1701-1704	34*
	1703-1704	29
Burials	1646-1672	13-16
	1673-1683	18
	1683-1687	19
	1687-1690	21
	1690-1693	22
	1694-1699	25
	1699-1701	30-31
	1701-1704	26

*On the microfiche copy of the original register page 34 is at the start of the fiche, before page 1.

BIRTHS
1701/2
-	Elizabeth fa *[damaged]* uxoris qui nata
2[-] Jan	Johannes fs Joh[anni]s COA[PE] *[damaged]* uxoris qui natus
24 Jan	Sara fa Johan et Sara LI[NY] *[damaged]* qui nata
19 Feb	Martha fa Richardi et Maria MORECROFT nata fuit
3 Mar	Helena fa Thoma & Maria WRIGHT nata fuit
14 Mar	Franciscus fs Francisci & Maria OSBORNE natus fuit
20 Mar	Johannes fs Thoma & Elizabetha COLLIER natus est

1702
25 Mar	Ricardus fs Ricardi & Anna DAVIS natus fuit
25 Mar	Gulielmus fs Johannis & Elizabetha PHILLIPS natus fuit
25 Mar	Ricardus fs Ricardi & Gratia BAYLIE natus fuit
5 Apr	Maria fa Philippi & Dorothea HOLLINS nata fuit
5 May	Maria fa Georgii & Maria TOOTH nata fuit
31 May	Anna fa Johannis & Maria EDWARDS nata fuit
14 Jun	Gulielmus fs Gulielmi & Maria STANLY natus fuit
.. Jul	Thomas [fs] [Gulie]lmi & Hanna TUNSTALL nata fuit
.. ..	Hanna [?] *[damaged]* Maria [?] DAVIS nata fuit
	[rest of page badly damaged & illegible]
12 Sep	*[illegible]*
.. Oct	Sara fa Thoma & Maria WRIGHT nata fuit
5 Oct	Johannes fs Roberti & Dorothea WOOD nata fuit
15 Oct	Margareta fa Johannis & Margareta SHERRAT nata fuit
19 Oct	Hanna fa Georgii & Hanna VERNON nata fuit
9 Nov	Helena fa Ricardi & Dorothea HOLLAND nata fuit
19 Nov	Francisca fa Johannis & Sara ARNOLD nata fuit
14 Dec	Thomas fs Thoma & Elizabetha COLECLOUGH nata fuit
.. ...	Brigeta fa Johannis & Elizabetha CARTWRIGHT nata fuit
17 Feb	Johannis fs Ricardi & Maria MORECROFT de Midleton Green nata fuit
17 Feb	Francisca fa Francisci & Anna LAKIN nata fuit
8 Mar	Francisca [?] fa Francisci & Maria [?] [HARVY] nata fuit
20 Mar	Sara fa Georgii & Maria RUSHTON nata fuit 1702/1703 [?]

1703
2 Apr	Catherina fa Ricardi & Elizabetha [SHERRAT] nata fuit
.. Apr	Anna fa Edwardi & .... [BLURTON]
.8 May	*[illegible]* HEALY
.. Jun	Johannis fs Henrici & Susanna HEATON ....
14 Jun	Thoma fs Thoma & Joanna KNIGHT nata fuit
13 Jun	Edwardus fs Thomas & Maria SHERRAT nata fuit
23 Jun	Gulielmus fs Ricardi & Ann [a] DAVIS natus fuit
23 ...	Margeria fa Guliel [mi &] *[damaged]*thea [?] BAILIE nata fuit
5 ...	Elizabetha *[damaged & illegible]* PHILLIPS
	[rest of page damaged & illegible]

Registerium ....tus [de] Parochia de Leigh P Deliver [antius] Fennihouse
Rectorem Anno Millessimo Sexcentessimo quaduagessimo Sexto.

[Written in different handwriting below the page heading]
Anno ...... ad 1704

MATRIMONI

1646
26 Dec   Georgius SHERRAT et Maria ALLEN
2 Feb   Robertus MIDLETON et Juditha SWINSHEAD
1647
19 Apr   Gulielmus PHILLIPS et Dorothea BAGGELIE
28 Apr   Johes WHITEALL generosus et Francisca ASTON
30 Nov   Robertus HEATON et Elizabetha TONKS
1648

> During this year King Charles the first remained in imprisonment
> and in the beginning of this week he was put to death.

1662   In the 2nd year after the Restoration
4 Feb*   Wilhelmum PENSEL *[Pensill-BT]* et Ellenoram SONT *[*1661BT]*
6 Aug   Johannis SONT et Elizabetham ABBERLY
5 Feb   Franciscum OSBURNE et Margeriam BRIGED
1663
7 Nov   Johannem GREATBATCH et Ellenam WHITEHALL
28 Dec   Ricardi CARTHWR[IGHT] & *Ellenam SONT [BT]*
[1664]
9 May   Gul…….. *[badly damaged]*
         [badly damaged]   Mariam
1666
17 Apr   Robertum BELCHER et Mariam PARKER
18 Jun   Thomam JOHNSON et Annam HEILDRICH
1667
29 Apr   Thomam SALT et Janam BEASTON
1668
29 Oct   Robertum BELCHER et Margarettam WAKEFIELD
1669
10 May   Henricum BALL et Elizabetham BLURTON
         [1664 – 1669 entries omitted from-BT]
1670
4 Apr   Wilhelmum PYOT *[Pyatt-BT]* et Jonam RUSHTON
29 May   Thomam PHILLIPS et Elizabetham LOWE
1671
25 May   Ricardus BANNISTER & Alicia ALLEN
27 May   Thomam READ & Aliciam BRADBURY
31 Jul   Johannem GILBERT de Marchington et Elizab[etham] [S]HERRAT de
         Leigh Paroch
[1672]
26 Apr   Johem *[damaged]* [et] [Eliz]abetham LAKIN *[entry missing from BT]*
         [rest of page badly damaged but appears to be blank]

BIRTHS of children anno 1695

[register pages damaged – entries completed where possible by reference to baptism entries]
2 May   Moses & Aaron twin sons of Thom HEIRS & Mary his wife born
4 May   William s/o Will RUSHTON & Elizab his wife born
28 May   John s/o [Thomas] OSBORNE & Katherine his wife born
11 Jun   Anne d/o Joh. BAYLIE & Margaret his wife born
8 Jun   Ellen d/o Francis SHERRATT & Margaret his wife born
4 Jul   Mary d/o Francis LAKIN & Margaret his wife born

27 Sep   Willm s/o Wm & Dorothy BAILEY born
27 Sep   Ruth d/o Francis & [Anna] IBSON born
24 Oct   Mary d/o Richard [PRICE & his] wife Angela born
2 Nov   Robert s/o Wm & Susana TUNSTALL born
3 Nov   Dorothy d/o Francis & [Maria] MIDDLETON born
14 Nov   Elizabeth d/o Thomas & [Sara] PARKER born
18 Nov   Martha Bastard child of [Elizabeth LAKYN] Born
27 Dec   Mary d/o Francis & Dorothy LEES born
1 Jan   Samuel s/o Robert & Margaret BELCHER born
8 Jan   Rebecca d/o Tho & Catharine BAYLY born
27 Jan   Hannah d/o Francis & Hannah SWINSHEAD born
24 Jan   Annam d/o Thomas & Mary WITTERANCE born
28 Jan   William s/o John & Margaret SHERRAT born
3 Feb   [D]orath[y] [dau]ghter of John & Frances WRIGH[T]
.. Feb   Edwa[rd] [son] of Edward & Anna LAWRENCE born
.. Feb   [Robert s/o Ricard &] Elizabeth JUMP
.. Feb   [Ann d/o Tho: & Ma]garet [ASBURY]
1696
9 Apr   Thomas s/o Henry HEATON & Susanna his wife born
7 May   Thomas s/o William & Mary ETHRINGTON born
10 May   Hannah d/o John & Sara BARKER born
4 Jun   Elizabeth d/o Francis & Jana DITCH born
12 Jun   William s/o William & Margaret BLURTON born
7 Jul   John fs Richardi et Maria SNAPE born
30 Jul   Elizabeth d/o Thomas & Mary SHERRAT born
14 Aug   Elizabeth d/o John & Sara WARDLE born
1 Aug   John s/o John & Jane DONE born
18 Aug   Sarah d/o Richard & Elizabeth SHERRAT born
27 Aug   Ralph s/o Francis & Margaret LAKIN born
17 Sep   Mary d/o John & Elizabeth TILL born
5 Oct   Elizabeth d/o John & Sarah ARNET born
17 Oct   William s/o Edward & Ann BLURTON born
19 Nov   Thomas s/o William & Joane HOLLINS born
21 Dec   Richard s/o Samuel & Dorothy STEEL born
[ ]   [ ] d/o Henry & Mary CHEL born
31 Dec   Will s/o Richard & Grace BAILY born
12 Jan   Thos s/o Francis & Anne WITTERANCE born
17 Jan   Sara d/o Edward & Mary DAVIS born
2 Feb   Elizabeth d/o Thomas & Susanna RUSHTON born
24 Feb   John s/o Rich & Mary DITCH born
1697
.. ...   Johnathan s/o William & Joanna TUNSTALL born
.. ...   Anne d/o J [ohn & Anna] STANLY bo [rn]
[next entry struck through & partly illegible]
.. ...   ~~Anne daug~~ [illegible] ~~born~~
9 Apr [?]   Anne da[ughter of] .....hen [?] & Anne HARVY born
17 May   Edward s/o Edward & Jane HOUGH born
23 Jun   Elizabeth d/o Francis & Jane DITCH born
4 Jul   Mary d/o Francis & Margaret SHERRAT born
18 Jul   Joseph s/o Joseph & Edith HEALY born
24 Jul   Edward s/o Thomas & Dorothy BOURNE born

9 Aug   William s/o John & [ ] COLLIER born
14 Aug Hannah d/o John & Hannah COAPE born
15 Aug Sam fs Sam et Maria POTS born
2 Sep   Anne d/o Richard & Ann WILKS born
8 Sep   William s/o Phillip & Dorothy HOLLINS born
16 Sep Elizabeth d/o Thomas & Catherine OSBORN born
14 Oct Liddia d/o Francis & Anne WALL born
15 Oct Catharine d/o William & Anne PHILLIPS born
21 Oct Anne d/o John & Mary THROWER born
7 Nov   Mary d/o Tho: & Mary HART born
25 Nov William s/o Thomas & Sara PARKER born
7 Jan   Elizabeth d/o Thomas & Sarah JOHNSON born
17 Jan John s/o Henry & [Susanna HEA]TON [born]
.. ...   Elizabeth d[aughter of Francis &] Han[na] SWINSH[EA]D
10 Mar Thomas s/o Thomas [& Mary] SHERRATT born
22 Mar John s/o Francis & Dorothy LEES born

1698

31 Mar Anne d/o Robert & Dorothy WOOD born
10 May William s/o William JOHNSON & Mary his wife born
16 May Lidia d/o Thomas & Mary WITTERANCE born
12 May Sarah d/o Thomas & Susanna RUSHTON born
8 Jul   Elizabeth d/o John SAUNDERS Rector of Leigh & Elizabeth his wife born
9 Aug   John s/o Willm & Margarett BLURTON born
19 Aug Elizabeth d/o John & Hanna HYDE born
19 Aug Thomas s/o John & Jane DONE born
9 Sep   Lewis illegitimate s/o Mary HILL & the supposed s/o Lewis BURGES born
22 Sep Jone d/o Rich & Mary DYTCH born
16 Oct Mary d/o Thomas & Dorothy BOURNE born
16 Oct William s/o Rich & Mary WHISTONS born
25 Nov [Isa]ac s/o [Thoma]s & Catherine BAYLEY born
.. Jan   [Ann] dau[ghter of John] & Elizabeth TILL born
2. Jan   Jos[eph] s/o [Edward & Mary PEDLEY] born
.. ...   John s/o P[hilip & Dorothy HOLLINS]
5 ...   Ellen daughter [of John & Mary SHIPLEY]
.. ...   John son
25 Feb Elizabeth d/o Henry & Mary CHELL
16 Mar Thomas s/o Thomas & Frances JOHNSON born

1699

21 Apr Dorothy d/o Edward & Anne LAWRENCE born
20 Apr Edward s/o George & his wife TOOTH born
14 May Ralph s/o John & Sara BARKER born
10 Jun Samuel s/o Edward & Jane HOUGH born
3 Jun   Gratiana BAYLY fa Richardi et Gratiana BAYLEY nata fuit intra Horas
        quartam et quintam pomeridinianas
21 Jun Anna fa Anna HALL erratrundea mulieris nata est Horaderima vespertina
8 Jul   Hanna fa Francisci et Anna HARVEY nata est
25 Sep Richard s/o Thomas & Mary SHERRAT born
23 Oct Mary d/o Samuel & Mary POTS born
25 Oct Thomas fs Francisci et Jana DIKE de Nobot natus est
9 Nov   Willielmus fs Edvardi et Maria THROWER natus est
2 Nov   Maria fa Francisci et Margareta LAKIN nata fuit

— 16 Dec   Anna fa Ricardi et Jana BULLOCK nata fuit
18 Dec   Edvardus fs Johannis et Magareta SHERRATT de Middleton Green in Parochia Lee natus fuit
24 Dec   Thomas fs Josephi et Editha HEELEY natus erat
1 Jan   Robertus fs Henrici et Susanna HEATON natus erat
— 4 Jan   Dorothea fa Roberti et Dorothea WOOD nata fuit
.. Jan   ~~Maria HEATH de Lee church Ancilla baptizata~~
22 Jan   [Mari]a fa [Jo]hannis et Elizabetha SAUNDERS de … h Churc. fuit …panio [?] a…. ….tam horam matulinam *[entry damaged]*
2 Feb   [Marg]areta [fa] Edv[ardi] et Maria PEDLEY de Withing[ton] [nata] [Johanna fa Gilielmi BLURTONet ux]oris eius de Checkley- [blank]
1700
2. …   *[damaged]*   natus est

BAPTISMATA in Parochia de Leigh
1646
5 Oct   Michael fs Gulielmi et Timisonis KEELING ux
— 15 Oct   Eduardus fs Richardi et Anna WALKER ux
25 Dec   Franciscus fs Johannis et Elizabetha SHERRAT ux
26 Dec   Richardus fs Eduardi et Anna DAVIES
— 23 Jan   Elizabetha fa Matthai et Ellena LOWE
1 Apr   Gulielmi fs Antonii et Maria BYRD
1647
14 Feb   Dorothea fa Johannis et Maria MIDLETON
10 Aug   Maria fa Samuelis et Elizabetha LATHROP
— 7 Nov   Jana fa Eduardi et Margeria LEES
14 Oct   Georgius fs Georgii et Maria SHERRAT
6 Sep   Robertus fs Roberti et Elizabetha HEATON
      turn four leaves forward for the Births of the p'sent year 1700 where they are written over again
      [four birth entries follow, these have been crossed out and are not transcribed here]
1648
9 Jan   Robertus fs Roberti et Anna THACKER ux
— 16 Jan   Ellena et Elizabeth Gemelli fa Thoma et Ellena WARD ux
23 Jan   Phillippus fs Gulielmi et Alicia CLAYTON ux
20 Feb   Jacobus fs Johis et Margareta JOHNSON ux
2 Mar   Elinora fa Mri Johis et Elizabetha SKRIMSHER ux
8 Mar   Elizabetha fa Gulielmi et Amolis WETTON ux
19 Mar   Joanna fa Thoma et Anna SHERRAT ux
7 May   Margareta fa Stephani et Elizabetha HARRISON ux
6 Apr   Maria fa Johis et Francisca WHITEALL generosi
16 Jul   [ ] fs Gulielmi et Elizabetha RUSHTON ux
25 Jul   Franciscus fs Francisci et Hana COATES ux
14 Aug   Sarah fa Deliveranti et Margareta FENNYHOUSE ux
9 Nov   Ricus fs Gul[ie]l[mi] et Timis[onis] KEELING ux
21 …   Johes fs [damaged] Margeria ux
.. Sep   *[damaged]*   et Mar…..
       [damaged]   et Dorothea
       [damaged]   LOWE ux
       [damaged]   Thomas
2 Dec   ~~Jana fa Robti THACKER baptisat~~

3 Dec   Margarita fa Rici WALKER
16 Dec   Thomas fs Georgii et Maria SHERRAT
~~22 Feb   Anna fa Thoma et Joana PHILLIPS~~
1649
22 Feb   Anna fa Thoma et Joana PHILLIPS
12 Apr   Anna fa Gulielmi HOLLINS
1 May   Mrs Elizabetha SKRIMSHER
17 May   Margarita fa Thoma & Maria HILL
18 May   Elizabetha fa Roberti & Juditha MIDDLETON
7 Aug   Joanna fa Francisci OMBERSLEY
30 Sep   Anna DAVIES fa Eduardi et Anna ux
9 Oct   Ellena fa Johis et Elizabth BLAKEMAN
11 Nov   Franciscus fs Johis BARTLE
2 Dec   ....a fa Robti THACKER
3 Dec   [Mar]garita fa Rici WALKER
7 Sep   …….. fs Thoma PERCIVALL
[1650]
.. Mar   Maria fa G *[damaged]*
.. Apr   Margarita fa *[damaged]*
        …… fa J *[damaged]*
        Maria fa *[damaged]*
1650   Baptismata
28 Mar   Maria fa Gulielmi et Maria GELLY
24 Aug   Richardus fs Thoma et Mar DYCH
26 Aug   Elizabetha fa Johis & Francisca WHITEALL
1 Sep   Gilbertus CLAYTON fs Gulielmi et Alicia ux
3 Oct   Ricus fs Francisci et Ellena ux [no surname]
14 Nov   Elizabetha fa Roberti et Ellena HEATON
17 Nov   Juditha fa Edw & Katherina BARTLE
1 Dec   Maria fa Gulielmi et Dorothea PHILLIPS
26 Dec   Joanna fa Eduardi et Joanna KEEN
1 Dec   Thomas fs Eduardi et Anna THROER
1651   Baptismata
2 Jan   fs Gulielmi et Elizab RUSHTON
11 Apr   Elizaba fa Gulielmi et Maria ATKIN
18 Apr   Meria fa Johis et Margaret JOHNSON
1 May   Isabella fa Guliel et Timison KEELING
3 Nov   Elizabeth fa Johis et Elizaba BLAKEMAN
5 Dec   Marger' fa Francisci et Jana COTES
29 Dec   Thomas fs Johis et An'e SHERRAT
1652   Baptismata
11 Mar   Thomas fs Thoma et Maria DYCH
23 Mar   Gulielmus fs Rici et Alicie WALKER
1 Apr   Maria fa Rici et Joha WOOD
6 May   Katherina fa Robti et Juditha MIDDLETON
13 May   Hesther fa Thom et Ellen WARD
7 Jun   Maria fa Thom et Elizaba ATKIN
17 Jun   Gulielmus fs Georgii et Maria SHERRAT
20 Jun   Katherina fa Rici et Anna RUSHTON
24 Jun   Kather' fa Thoma et Maria HILL
5 Aug   Johis fs Gulielmi et Maria GELLY

31 Aug   Johis fs Francisci et Ellena SHERRAT
3 Nov   Isabela fa Mathii et Ellena LOW
10 [?] Nov   Eduardus fs Eduardi et Ell SHARP
3 Dec   Elizaba fa Thoma et [ ] PERCIVALL
9 Dec   Francisca [fa] [Jo]his et Fr WHITEALL
12 Dec   Franciscus [fs] ….. et Elizth HEATON [damaged]
3 Mar   Johis fs ……. BOLD [damaged]
15 Mar   …..ina fa ……….. COTES [damaged]
20 Mar   …hes ……….. et Elizabth BLAKEMAN [damaged]
28 Jun   [damaged]

1653
2 Feb   [Omitted] fs Gulielmi HOLLYNS
3 Mar   Johannes fs Johis et Eliz: BALD
15 Mar   Jana fa Francisci et Jana COATES
20 Mar   Johannes fs Johis et Elisabetha BLAKEMAN
20 Apr   Isabella fa Gulielmi et Eliz: RUSTON
22 …   Frances fa Roberti HEELYE
6 Jul   Thomas fs Gulielmi et Timison KEELING
7 Jul   Thomas fs Anna THACKER Vidua
21 Oct   Abel fs Francisci et Ellena WHITE
14 Nov   Maria fa Gulielmi et Maria ATKYN
3 Nov   Priscilla fa Eduardi et Anna THROER alias DAVIES
3 Dec   Johes fs Ricardi et Jana WOOD

1654
4 Jan   Johes fs Henrici et Elizab: KEELINGE
13 Jan   Johes fs Thoma CEACRAP [?]
6 Apr   Elizabetha fa Johis et Elizabetha SHERRAT
30 Apr   Philippus fs Thoma & Maria DYCH
7 May   Ricardus fs Willielmi & Margt SHERRAT
12 Jul   Gulielmus fs Wmi et Katherina BROMWALL
13 Jul   Franciscus fs Roberti et Judith MIDDLETON
17 Sep   Margaretta fa Thoma PERCIVAL
28 Sep   Elianora [?] fa Anthi et Maria [?] [PHILLIPS?]
25 Oct   Thomas fs Francisci et Jana COATES
26 Oct   Johes fs Mosis et Martha ASTON

1655
24 Feb   Elizabetha fa Eduardi et Anna BAYLEY
22 Feb   Jana fa Radulphi TILLSTON
2 Feb 1654   Thomas fs Thoma & Ezzard OSBORN
15 Apr   Ricardus fs Wmi: et Eliz: GRAT…. [?]
17 Apr   Ricardus fs Eduardi & Eliz: SHARP
19 Apr   Thomas fs Thoma et Ellen WARD
8 May   Sarah fa Wmi: et Emma WETTON
9 May   Thomas fs Thoma OSBORN
19 May   Ellen fa Matha et Ellen LOW
27 Jun   Elizabetha fa Wmi: et Katherina BROMWALL
2 Sep   Johannes fs Eduardi et Anna THROER
8 Sep   Timison fa Wmi: et Timison KEELING
20 Sep   Willielmus fs Thoma et Amey BOTT
30 Oct   Alicia fa Robti & El: EATON

1656
10 Apr   Johes fs Thoma & Mary DYCH
20 May   Franciscus fs Gulielmi et Maria ATKYNS
4 Sep   Anna fa Johannis et Frances WHITEHALL
24 Nov   Thomas fs Ricardi & Anna COLLIER
16 Nov   Maria fa Thoma et Sara HEELEY
4 Nov   Elisabetha fa Ric: PEDLEY
28 Dec   Anna fa Johis et Eliz SHERRAT
15 Dec   Johes fs Fost: et Anna CHELL
1657
1 Jan   Thomas fs Mosis et Martha HILL
1 Feb   Jacobus fs Johes et Maria [or Marg?] HYDE [?]
2 Feb   Joanna fa Thoma et Eliz: ......
.. Mar   Georgius fs Mathai et Ellen LOW
23 Apr   Joanna fa Francisci et ...... COATES
17 May   Agnes fa Thom et Anna OSBOURNE junioris
16 May   Elizabetha fa Henrici KEEL
.. Jul   Ruth fa Wmi et Emm WETTON
1 Oct   Thomas fs Robti et Judith MIDDLETON
13 Nov   [ ] fa Thoma BYRCH
23 Nov   Johes fs Eduardi & Elizab SHARP
8 Dec   Katherina fa Eduardi et Mercia LEES
10 Dec   Anna fa Wmi et Anna SHERRAT
28 Dec   Alicia fa Wmi et Timison KEELINGE
7 Oct   Ellena fa Thoma et Ann DYCH
1658
4 Mar   Isabella fa Radulphi TILSTON
11 Mar   Gulielmus fs Wmi et Maria GELLEY
8 Mar   Johis fa Wmi HOLLINS
10 Apr   Ellena fa Francis & Ellen SHERRAT
30 May   Robertus fs Robti ALLEN
20 Jun [?]   Franciscus fs Wmi et Margaretta SHERRAT
14 Sep   Anna fa Eduardi & Anna DAVIES
30 Sep [?]   Wmus fs Robti & Elizab HEATON
8 Oct   Richardus fs Eduardi et Eliz WOOD
2 Nov   Maria fa Thoma et Maria HILL
1659
.. ...   Johes fs Eduardi & Anna BAYLEY
20 ...   Henricus fs Lawrentii et Joana THORLY [?]
.. ...   Dorothea fa Ricardi et Anna COLLIER
.. ...   Eduardus fs Gualt et Anna HARD[ERN ?]
.. ...   Josephus fs Wmi et Emm WETTON
.. ...   Ricardus fs Wmi et Elizabetha RUSHTON
.. ...   Antonius fs Johis & Margaretta HYDE
.. ...   Ricardus fs .... et Anna LOE
11 Aug   Josephus fs Stephani & Elizab HARRISON
28 Aug   Sara fa Wmi et [ ] SHERRAT
1 Sep   Elizabetha fa Thoma et Eleanora HYDE
25 Oct   Margaretta fa Francisci et Ellen SHERRAT
3 Nov   Willielmus fs Anthonii et Jana BAILYE
20 Nov   Franciscus fs Thoma et Elizabetha LEES

4 Sep   Eduardus fs Fosteri et Anna CHELL
23 Feb 1659   Robertus fs Johis et Elizabetha SHERRAT
22 Mar   Sara fa Thoma et Maria BYRCH
22 Jun   Johes fs Ricardi PEDLEY
25 Mar   Josephus fs Gulielmi et Emm WETTON
20 Mar   Henricus fs Gulielmi et Maria ATKYN
1660
18 Oct   Anna fa Thoma et Lydia WITTERANS
18 Oct   Dorothea fa Henrici et Ellen BIGGEN
1 Nov   Margaretta fa Wmi et Katherina BROMHAL *[Bromhall-BT]*
16 Sep   Margaretta fa Thoma et Amye BOTT
25 Jun   Radulphus fs Johis SMYTH *[Smith-BT]*
22 Nov   Franciscus fs Francisci et Alicia SWINSHEAD
6 Dec   Elizabetha fa Thoma HEELEY *[Heely-BT]*
27 Dec   Moses fs Mosis et [ ] HILL
27 Dec   Johes fs Wmi et [ ] SHERRAT
3 Jan   Eduardus fs Thoma et Elleanora HYDE
1 Feb   Johannes fs Ricardi et Elizabetha SPENCER
7 Feb   Elizabetha fa Gualteri et Anna HORDERN
24 Feb   Elizabetha fa Eduardi et Elizabetha WOOD
5 Mar   Maria fa Anthonii et Maria PHILLIPPS
21 Mar   Maria fa Randolphi et Elizabetha SHERMAN
24 Mar   Thomas fs Roberti et Elizabetha EATON *[Heaton-BT]*
1661
5 May   [Omitted] fs Radulphi TILSTON *[Tilstone-BT]*
13 May   Willielmus fs Wilielmi SHERRAT
19 May   Isaacus fs Wmi et Emm WETTON
-    Dorothea fa Thoma et Anna COPE die Martii Pentecostes
5 Jul   Maria fa Wmi et Maria PUREFOYE *[Purifoy-BT]*
1 Aug   Willielmus fs Mathai et Emm LOWE
22 Aug   Samuel fs Robti et Sara POTT
4 Nov   Ellen fa Francisci et Ellen SHERRAT
9 Nov   Franciscus fs Thoma et Maria DYCH
21 Nov   Anna fa Ricardi et Anna COLLIER *[Colliar-BT]*
10 Dec   Sara fa Roberti et Ellena BELCHER
1662
16 Jan   Johes fs Henrici et Elizabetha BLADEN
17 Apr   Gulielmus fs Foster CHELL
24 Apr   Constantia fa Thoma et Elizab OSBURNE
30 Apr   Dorothea fa Caroli et Dorothea COLCLOUGH
15 May   Anna fa Eduardi et Anna BAILEY *[Bayley-BT]*
29 May   Thomas fs Thoma et Elleanora HYDE
20 Jul   Willielmus fs Elizabetha CLOWES: Nothuis [?]
10 Aug   Thomas fs Wmi et Elizab RUSHTON
28 Aug   Martha fa Roberti et Elizabetha LATHROP
20 Sep   Sara fa Ricardi RUSHTON senior et Elizabetha ux
2 Oct   Maria fa Ricardi & Maria PARKER
14 Nov   Thomas fs Thoma BYRCHE
2 Feb   Ricardus et Franciscus PEDLY Gemelli
5 Feb   Eliz: fa Thoma BOTT et ux *[Elizab:-BT]*
19 Feb   Antonius fs Gulielmi et Maria ATKYNS *[Atkins-BT]*

19 Feb   Jana fa Wmi et Maria PUREFOY
1663
29 Mar   Eduardus fs Francisci et Dorothea LAWRENCE
7 Apr   Anna fa Francisci SHERRAT et ux
1 Apr   Sara fa Roberti et Sara POTT
26 Apr   Margeria fa Antonii et Jo PHILLIPPS
17 May   Judith fa Thoma et Sara HEELEY
25 Jun   Sara fa Georgii et Maria SHERRAT
9 Jul   Hanna fa Thoma et Elleanora HYDE
12 Jul   Willielmus fs Thoma et Eliz LEES
2 Oct   Editha fa Eduardi WOOD et ux
15 Oct   Thomas fs Gualteri HORDERN
19 Nov   Johannes fs Gulielmi et Elizabetha TILL
19 Nov   Anna fa Gulielmi & Emma WETTON
19 Nov   Johannes fs Rowlandi et Ellen ASBURIE
10 Dec   Margaretta fa Gul: et Katherina BROMWALL
20 Dec   Elizabetha fa Francisci et Alicia SWINSHEAD
26 Dec   Francisca fa Francisci OSBURNE
28 Dec   [ ] fa SHERAT de Pansley *[Sherratt de Paynsley Hill-BT]*
10 Jan   Stephanus fs Antonii et Ellen BAILEY *[Bayley-BT]*
15 Jan   Editha fa Gulielmi et Timison KEELINGE *[Timason Keeling-BT]*
24 Jul   Thomas fs Thoma OSBURN
28 Jul 1664   Samuel fs Roberti et Elizabetha LATHROP
1664
25 Sep   Margaretta fa Eduardi et Elizabetha BLURTON
13 Oct   Maria fa Francisci et Elizabetha SHERRAT
27 Dec   Aron fs Mosis et M..... HILL
12 Jan   Johes fs Robti et Elizabetha HEATON
23 Jan   Thomas fs Johannis et Editha NORRIS
31 Jan   Henricus fs Foster et Anna CHELL
5 Feb   Margaretta fa Eduardi et Isabella SHERRAT
7 Mar   Katherina fa Gulielmi et Maria GELLY
1665
8 Apr   Thomas fs Thoma et Maria HILL
20 Apr   Elizabeth fa Wm et Katherina PHILLIPS
22 Jun   Johannes fs Thoma SHERRAT
22 Jun   Maria fa Wm et Emma WETTON
29 Jun   Willielmus fs Francisci KEENE
6 Aug   Susanna fa Anthonii BAYLEY
16 Aug   Katherina fa Hennrici et Eliz: BLADON
3 Sep   Thomas fs Thoma & Sara HEELEY
7 Sep   Thomas fs Thoma & Margeria HEELEY
23 Sep   Johannes fs Ricardi et Elizab: SPENCER
[ ]   Johannes fs Edvardi et Eliz: BLURTON
18 Oct   Thomas fs Thoma et Ellen HEELEY
8 Oct   Elizabetha fa Robti et Maria BOTT
8 ...   Thomas fs R et [ ] PEDLEY
.. ...   Ricardus fs Gualteri HORDERN
18 ...   Alicia fa illegitima Samsonis LAKYN et Alicia HIGGINS
14 Mar   Jana fa Roberti et Eliz: LATHROP

1666
29 Mar Elizabetha fa Johes et Maria KEELING
5 Apr Uria [?] fa erratisa mulueris
25 Mar [ ] fs Willielmi RUSHTON
10 May Maria fa Edvardi et Elizab: WOOD
5 Jun Dorothea fa Johes et Maria ADAMS
12 Jul Eleneanora fa Thoma et Elean: HYDE
21 Feb Sara fa Roberti BELCHER
10 May Anna fa Thoma et [ ] OSBURN
1667
7 Apr Elizabetha fa Francisci et Alicia SHERRAT
16 Apr Edvardus fs Edvardi & Eliz: BLURTON
24 Apr Katherina fa Roberti et Elizabetha HEATON
3 May Nathaniel fs Fosteri et Anna CHELL
20 Aug Johannes fs Ricardi et Eliz: COLLIER
8 Jul Jacobus fs Johannis et Francisci WHITEHAL de Parkehall
1 Aug Johannes fs Thoma BLOOD
25 ... Anna fa Ricardi et Ellena CARTHWRIGHT
.. Sep Willielmus fs Wm. & Eliz TILL
.. Sep Maria fa Solominis et Dorothea SHAWE
.. ... Prudentia fa Johis et ....
19 Sep Gulielmus fs Thoma & Anna JOHNSON
13 Oct Margaretta fa Thoma et Margaretta STRONGITHARM
20 Oct Gulielmus filis Samuelis & Anna LAKYN
23 Jan Elizabetha fa Samuelis et Elizab: TAYLOR
24 Jan Josephus fs Moses et Martha HILL
26 Jan Anna fa Thoma et Sara HEELY
8 Feb Thomas fs Edvardi et Isabella SHERRAT
8 Mar Ricardus fs Anthony et Susanna BAYLEY
1668
26 Mar Willielmus fs Gulielmi et Amol WETTON
16 Apr Anna fa Henrici et Elizabetha BLADON
15 May Elizabetha fa Gulielmi et .... SHERRAT
26 May Johannes fs Johis et Maria KEELING
4 Jun Franciscus fs Thoma et [ ] WITTERANS
24 Jul Elizabetha fa Stephani et Margaretta WATSON
3 Sep Thomas fs Edvardi et Elizabetha WOOD
12 Oct Maria fa Samuelis et Maria LAKYN
19 Nov Frances fa Franc: et Ellen SHERRAT
20 Dec Edvardus fs Ricardi et Elizab: PEDLEY
20 Dec Elizabetha fa Thoma et Timison JEFFRIES
14 Jan Anna fa Willielmi et [ ] LEES
6 Jan Elizabetha fa Thoma et Timison JEFFRIES
6 Feb Johannes fs Willielmi et Anna HANDY
1669
15 Apr Dorothea fa Roberti et Elizabetha LATHROP
18 Nov Middleton fs Solomonis et Dorothea SHAWE
30 Dec Margaretta fa Thoma et Elizabetha OSBORNE
3 Jan Franciscus fs Samuelis et Maria LAKYN
13 Jan Elizabetha fa Gulielmi et Elizabetha TILL
13 Jan Edmundus fs Edmundi et Elizab: STRONGITHARM

6 Mar   Elizabetha fa Wmi et Eliz: LEES
9 Sep   Gratia fa Thoma BAYLEY
16 Sep   Isabella fa Johannes et Margeria HYDE
4 Oct   Robertus fs Roberti et Margaretta BELCHER
8 Nov   Johannes fs Johannis et Editha NORRIS
14 Dec   Thomas fs Thoma et Elizabetha LEES
24 Jun   Bridgetta fa Johannis et Francis WHITEHAL
29 Jul   Rebecca fa Johannis et Maria KEELING
29 Jul   Anna fa Francisci et [ ] KEENE
15 Aug   Thomas fs Edvardi et Elizabetha BLURTON
19 Aug   Johannes fs Wmi et [ ] SHERRAT

1670
28 Apr   Henricus fs Henrici et Elizab: BLADON
8 May   Maria fa Thoma JEFFRIES *[Jeofferies-BT]*
13 Sep   Ricardus fs Ricardi et Ellen CARTWRIGHT
15 Sep   Frances fa Johannis et Francis WHITEHAL *[Whitehall-BT]*
3 Nov   Ricardus fs Fosteri et Anna CHELL
24 Nov   Willielmus fs Francisci et Ellen SHERRAT
4 Dec   Maria fa Henrici et [ ] BAYLEY
15 Dec   Thomas fs Thoma & Anna JOHNSON
31 Dec   Winifreda uxor Gulielmi BELCHER Bap
1 Jan   Maria fa Anthony & Sara SAUNDERS
5 Mar   Ricardus fs Anthony & Anna HOYLE

1671
24 Apr   Edvardus fs Edvardi et Isabella SHERRAT
22 Apr   Henricus fs Johannes BAYLEY
12 May   Gulilmus fs Gulielmi et Anna HANDY
29 May   Philotis fs Gulielmi et [ ] SHERRAT
6 Jul   Robertus fs Roberti et Elizabetha LATHROP
9 Nov   ~~Antonius~~ Nathaniel fs Roberti BELCHER
27 Nov   Ellena fa Thoma et Margeria HEALY *[Heeley-BT]*
5 Dec   Gulielmus fs Edvardi et Editha SHARP

1672
25 Mar   Thomas fs Antony et Sara SAUNDERS
17 Apr   Johannes fs Thoma PHILLIPS et Elizabetha ux
4 Jul   Elizab: fa Edvardi et Elizabetha BLURTON
11 Aug   Radulphus fs Radulphi et Sara WOOD

R……. NATES P **Anno 1700 [Births]**
25 Mar   Thomas fs Johannis et Maria EDWARDS natus est
29 Mar   Thomas fs Georgii et Maria MERRYDONE natus est
24 Apr   Thomas fs Johannis et Sara COLLIER de Field natus est
8 May   Anna fa Gulielmi et Anna PHILIPS de Leigh-town [?] nata fuit
21 May   Johannes fs Jacobi et Juditha BRIERYHURST de Withington natus
8 Jun   Gulielmus fs Isaaci et Anna RATCLIFF de Checkly-bank natus est
24 Jun   Dorothea fa Thoma et Sara PARKER de Withington nata est
20 Jul   Johannes fs Johannis et Elizabetha PHILIPS de Lee-town natus est
24 Jul   Elizabetha fa Ricardi et Maria DITCH de Nobott nata fuit
24 Jul   Josephus fs illegitimus Elizabetha LAKIN de Withington-green natus est
14 Aug   Maria fa Francisci et Margareta SHERRATT de Middleton-green nata est
12 Aug   Brigida SWINSHEAD fa Francisci et Hanna SWINSHEAD nata fuit

10 Aug   Gulielmus fs Gulielmi et Dorothea BAYLY natus fuit
22 Aug   Rutha fa illegitima Johanna LAKIN de Withington Green nata fuit
20 Oct   Dorothea fa Thoma et Dorothea BOURN de Nobott nata fuit
31 Oct   Johannes fs Thoma et Jana JOHNSON natus fuit
4 Nov   Thomas fs Ricardi et Elizabetha SHERRATT natus est
2 Jan   Johanna fa Johannis TILL de Checkley-bank/vestiary/ et Elizabetha ux nata est
.. ...   Jana fa Roberti LAKIN et Elizab.....................
19 Jan   Ricardus fs Ricardi WHISTON de Foal/Coloni/ et Maria ux natus est
4 Mar   Stephanus fs Francisci HARVEY de Field Agricola, et Anna ux natus est
12 Mar   Adeliza fa Thoma WITTERANCE de Foal, Coloni, et Maria ux nata est
17 Mar   Robertus fs Edvardi BLURTON de Park-hall, Lanii, et Anna ux, natus est
19 Mar   Thomas fs Thoma RUSHTON de Morrily-heath, pauperis, et Susanna ux natus est

1701

27 Mar   Thomas fs Gulielmi TUNSTALL de Morrily-heath, Sartoris, et Hanna ux natus est
11 Apr   Maria fa illegitima Elizabeth MOORECROFT de Middleton-green nata fuit
30 Mar   Sara fa Francisci LAKIN de Withingtongreen, pauperis, et Margareta ux nata fuit
6 Jun   Sampson fs Henrici CHELL et ux Maria natus fuit
6 Jul   Ellena fa Johannis DANE et Jana ux nata fuit
24 Jul   Ricardus fs Ricardi SNAPE et Maria ux natus fuit
6 Aug   Elizabetha fa Thoma HITCHCOCK et Elizab: ux nata fuit
4 Sep   Dorothea fa Johannis SHAW et Alicia ux nata fuit
22 Sep   Jana fa Edvardi PEDLEY et Maria ux nata
2 Oct   Elizabetha fa Tho: BAILY et Cath: ux nata fuit
21 Sep   Eaditha fa Josephi HEELY et Aditha ux nata fuit
30 Sep   (Dorothea fa Johannis SAUNDERS et Elizabeth ux nata fuit
         (Maria inter Horas 5th et 6th anno Dom 1701)
1 Oct   Gulielmus fs Thoma SHARRAT et [ ] ux natus fuit
14 Nov   Samuel fs Henrici HEATON et Susanna ux natus fuit
12 Jan   Thomas fs Hugonis LEES et Maria ux natus fuit

DE SEPULTUS

1646
3 Oct   An'a uxor Richardi WALKER sepult fuit
1647
30 Oct   Magistra ASTON de Parkhall sepult fuit
4 Nov   Franciscus WARD sepultus fuit
1648
19 Mar   [ ] uxor Gulielmi SHERRAT de Painlehill sepult fuit
1 Jul   Custance KEEN sepult fuit
6 Jul   Henricus BAYLIE sepult
13 Jul   Tho. KEELING sepult
14   Franciscus SHARRAT Vid. sepult
16 Jul   Elizabetha uxor Johis WOODWARDE sepult
20 Jul   Dorothea fa Gulielmi HILL sepult
22 Jul   Elizabetha uxoris Francisci SWINSHEAD sepulta fuit
26 Aug   Elizabetha uxor Samuelis LATHROP sepulta fuit
1 Nov   Elizabetha fa Gulielmi HILL sepulta fuit

1649

18 Apr [ ] uxor Gulielmi WHITEHURST sepulta fuit
28 Apr Gulielmus WHITEHURST sepultus
23 Jul Franciscus fs Fr. SHERRATT Vid.
28 Jul Jana fa Edvardi HYDE sepult
23 Aug [ ] fs Gulielmi KEEN sepultus
31 Sep Ricus PROCTER sepultus
30 Sep An'a fa Edvardi DAVIES sepult
22 Oct Magistra Margeria ASTON sepult
1650
1 Mar Franciscus OMBERSLEY sepultus
16 Mar Katherina PARKER sepult
16 Mar Edvardus SHERRAT jun sepult
18 Mar Vidua CORWAP sepult
27 Jun Johes BARTLE sepult
5 Oct Rogerus WOODE sepult
12 Oct Gulielmus CLAYTON sepultus
1651
26 Mar Thomas COTES sepultus
27 Mar Ricus PEDLEY Sen sepultus
15 May Gulielmus fs Elizabeth HODGSON sepultus
25 Oct [ ] uxor Thom MIDLETON Sen. sepult
25 Oct Vidua ATKINS sepult
1 Dec Thoms ALLEN de Nobott sepult
3 Dec Feles uxor Johis SHERRATT sepult
27 Dec Johes SHERRATT de Nobott sepult
12 Dec Thoms. COLLIER Jun sepultus
12 Mar Thoms. MIDLETON Sen sepultus
1652
13 Apr Gulielm's EDWDS sepultus
16 Apr Robert's THACKER sepultus
15 Apr Ellena uxor Stephani WATSON sepultus
.. May Franciscus fs Ellena WATSON sepultus
20 Jul Ricus WATSON fs Ellena sepultus
20 Aug Johes HYDE de Leigh sepultus
21 [?] Sep Margaretta uxor [?]mea dilecta sepulta
       [damaged & illegible] sepultus
1653
16 Feb Sepultus fuit Robertus THACKER
12 Mar Sepultus fuit Thomas MIDLETON de Dodsley
13 Mar Sepultus fuit Gulielmus EDWARDS de Middleton Green
9 Apr Sepulta fuit Anna HEELEY
10 May Sepultus fuit Richardus ASTON Generosus
18 May Sepultus fuit Thomas SANDERS
30 Jun Sepulta fuit Ellicia BYRCHE
4 Jul Sepulta fuit Jona uxor Edvardi HYDE
13 Nov Sepulta fuit Elizabetha fa Jona KORTON
14 Nov Sepulta fuit Margaretta fa Johis et Marg BAYLIE
3 Dec Sepulta fuit Priscilla fa Edvardi et Anna DAVIES
1654
24 Jan Sepulta fuit Maria WOOD

7 Mar   Sepultus fuit Katherina BARTLE
13 Mar   Sepulta fuit Elizabetha HEELEY
6 May   Sepultus fuit Johannes KEELINGE
22 Jun   Sepult Elizabetha EDWARDS
27 Jun   Sepulta fuit Joicia KORTON
10 Sep   Sepultus fuit Edvardus fs Anna OMBERSLEY
.. ....   Sepultus [illegible]..............ena uxor ....HE
.. Oct   [illegible & damaged]

1655

6 Feb   Sepulta fuit Frances fa Johis WHITEHAL Generosi
14 Feb   Sepult fuit Johannes KEY de Alton
16 Feb   Sepult Elizab. fa Edvardi SHARP
1 May   Sepultus fuit Johannes LEES de Withington
11 & 14 Nov   Johannes HYDE habuit tris filios qui sepulti erant Novemb 11 et 14
7 Jan 1655   Sepultus fuit Gulielmus ASTON de Fielde

1656

3 Apr   Sepultus fuit Johes TOWERS
5 Apr   [Blank] fa Johes JOHNSON sepulta
12 Apr   Sepult fuit Johes COAPE
30 Apr   Sepult Vidua ALLEN de Nobott
8 May   Sepulta fuit Domina BAGOT
15 May   Sepult fuit Edvardus WRIGHT
15 May   Sepult Johes GELLY
6 Jan   Sepult Thomas fs Robti et Anna THACKER

1657

2 Jul   Sepulta fuit Vidua DYCH de Nobott
7 Jul   Sepulta fuit Isabella SALT
8 Aug   Sepult Johes COLLIER
18 Aug   Sepultus fuit Franciscus WITTERANCE
25 Aug   Sepult fuit Margeria WOOD
30 Sep   Sepulta fuit Margaretta SAUNT
2 Oct   Sepultus fuit Ricardus WOOD

1658

10 Feb   Sepult fuit Frances uxor Hugonis LOWE
26 Feb   Sepulta fuit [ ] SPENCER de Leigh
23 Mar   Sepulta Katherina fa Edvardi LEES
8 Apr   Sepult Margeria HEELEY
25 May   Sepulta Dorothea WHITEHURST
24 Jul   Sepultus fuit Robertus MIDDLETON
6 Sep   Sepulta fuit Maria DAVIES
25 Oct   Sepulta fuit Frances uxor Edvardi RUSHTON senioris
2 Nov   Baptie Maria fa Gulielmi & Katherina BROWNE
11 Dec   Sepult Franciscus LEES
22 Dec   Sepulta fuit Ellen fa Francisci SHERRAT

1659

14 Feb   Sepulta fuit [ ] LEICESTER
19 Apr   Sepulta Maria fa Thomas et Maria DYCHE
15 Jul   Sepulta Joanna uxor Francisci SHERRAT
16 Jul   Sepult Thomas fs Juditha MIDDLETON
13 Sep   Sepultus Georgius PARKER
22 Nov   Sepulta erat Anna WITTERANES

9 Jan   Sepultus Gulielmus HILL de Withington
2 Jan   Sepultus Thomas SONT de Leigh
1 Jan   Sepultus Willielmus HYK
22 Mar   Sepulta Sara fa Thomas et Maria BYRCH
19 May   Sepultus Gulielmus GRATELEYE
26 May   Sepultus Felicia PARKER
4 Jun   Sepulta Ellena SMYTH
1660
18 Feb   Sepulta Frances uxor Johis WHITEHAL de Parkhall
27 Mar   Sepultus fuit Johes LOWE de Withington
16 Apr   Sepulta Vidua COATES
12 May   Sepultus fa Gulielmi SHERRAT
16 May   Sepultus Willielmus LEICESTER senior
19 May   Sepult [ ] fs Willielmi GRATELEY
26 May   Sepulta Felicia PARKER
4 Jun   Sepulta Ellen SMITH
2 Mar   Sepulta Vidua ROE
1661
26 Feb   Sepultus Edvardus DAVIES
22 Aug   Sepulta Margaretta fa Wmi BRAMHALL
21 Aug   Sepulta Ellen uxor Thoma WOOD
12 Nov   Sepult fuit Margaretta OKES *[Oakes-BT]*
10 Dec   Sepulta Elizabetha uxor Roberti BELCHER
21 Dec   Sepulta Sara fa Roberti BELCHER
1662
3 Apr   Sepultus fuit Thomas OSBURN sen
12 Apr   Sepulta Dorothea fa Henrici BIGGIN
13 Apr   Sepulta Elizabetha DYCH
22 Apr   Sepulta fuit Elizabetha SHERRAT
2 Jun   Sepultus fuit Thomas fs Thoma et Elleneanora HYDE
5 Jun   Sepulta [ ] fa Samuelis SPENSER *junioris [BT]*
23 Jan   Sepultus Johannes BLADON
1663
23 Apr   Sepultus fuit Franciscus OSBURNE
27 Apr   Sepultus erat Johannes COVELL *[Covill-BT]*
28 Apr   Sepultus fuit Gulielmus LAKYN
1 May   Sepulta erat Anna GREATBACH *[Greatbatch-BT]*
4 May   Sepulta fuit Ellena OSBURNE
14 May   Sepultus fuit Thomas SHERRAT
30 Sep   Sepultus Ricardus WALKER
1 Oct   Sepulta fuit Ellena BIRD
5 Nov   Sepultus fuit Gulielmus PHILLIPPS
19 Nov   Sepultus Johannes HILL
24 Jan   Sepulta erat Anna MALLER *[Mallott-BT]*
31 Jan   Sepulta Anna fa Gulielmi WETTON
7 Feb   Sepulta Anna uxor Griffini DAVIES *[Davis-BT]*
17 Mar   Sepulta Dorothea uxor Francisci LAWRENCE
24 Mar   Sepultus Ricardus fs Ricardi PEDLEYE
9 Apr   Sepulta fuit [ ] fa Roberti PRETTYE
11 Apr   Sepultus Ricardus CHAPLAIN
19 Apr   Sepulta [ ] fa Anthonii BAILEYE

6 Nov   Sepult Margaretta fa Edvardi BLURTON
27 Nov   Sepulta Margaretta fa Franc: SHERRAT
6 Apr   Sepultus fuit Gulielmus BROWN
1664
29 Jan   Sepultus fuit Ricardus PARKER
13 Feb   Sepultus fuit Gulielmus HEELEYE
1665   *[Bottom of page damaged]*
         [Sepulta] fuit uxor Gulielmi ALLEN
         [Sepultus fuit Mar]garetta BLURTON
         [Sepulta fuit] uxor Gulielmi ALLEN
.. .... Sepulta fuit Vidua OSBURNE
.. Oct   Sepultus fuit Isabella uxor Henrici BIGGINS
1666
15 Jun   Sepultus fuit Thomas WATSON
1 Jul   Sepultus Edvardus fs Edvardi BLURTON
6 Jan   Sepulta Emm LOW
6 Jan   Sepultus Edvardus fs Johis HYDE
8 Jan   Sepulta erat Vidua HARVEY
16 Jan   Sepulta erat Vidua MANSFIELD
16 Mar   Sepulta fuit HATHERINGS Vidua
1667
7 Apr   Sepulta [ ] fa Johes et Margratt HYDE
23 Aug   Sepult fuit Gulielmus ALLEN
20 Jan   Sepultus erat Thomas BYRCH
1668
29 Mar   Sepulta erat Ellen HODGSON
10 Apr   Sepulta [ ] infans et fa Roberti BELCHER
15 Apr   Sepulta fuit Maria uxor Roberti BELCHER
29 Apr   Ellen uxor Willielmi SALT
10 May   Sepulta Hannah fa Thom. et Eleanna HYDE
19 Dec   Sepulta Anna uxor Ricardi COLLIER
3 Jan   Sepulta erat Isabella ALLEN
1669
3 Apr   Sepulta erat Isabella uxor eium marito
10 Apr   Sepult Jona SHARP
20 Jul   Sepulta Joanna uxor Thoma PHILLIPS
18 Nov   Sepult Johannes fs Johes et Editha NORRIS
19 Nov   Sepultus fuit Franciscus LAWRENCE
24 Dec   Sepultus fuit Thomas COLLIER
23 Dec   Sepult Dorothea THRAWR
29 Dec   Sepult Thomas HILL
1670
21 Jul   Sepulta erat [ ] fa Gulielmi SHERRAT de Painslowe Hill
15 Aug   Sepulta fuit Mater uxoris Gulielmi SALT *[Sault-BT]*
6 Aug   Sepultus Gulielmus HOLLYNS
27 Aug   Sepultus Edvardus COPE
3 Aug   Sepult Elizabetha uxor Johes SHERRAT
7 Sep   Sepultus erat Gulielmus BLURTON
31 Oct   Sepult Infans Gualteri HORDERN *[BT]*
1 Jan   Baptisata fuit Maria fa Anthony et Sara SAUNDERS
4 Jan   Sepultus erat Samuel SPENCER

16 Feb	Sepulta erat Judith BLURTON
1 Mar	Sepulta erat Isabella TILSTON [Tilstone-BT]
7 Mar	Sepultus fuit Thomas DYCH

1671

8 Apr	Sepulta fuit Anna fa Thoma WITTERANCE
12 Aug	Sepultus fuit Robertus HEATON
4 Aug	Sepultus fuit Thomas BOTT
30 Sep	Sepultus fuit Thomas HILL
23 Sep	Sepulta fuit fa Radulphi WOOD & Sara ux
30 Sep	Sepulta fuit Sara SHERRAT
25 Oct	Sepulta fuit Maria WILSON
4 Nov	Sepulta erat [ ] uxor GREATBACH [Greatbatch-BT]
14 Dec	Sepultus fuit Radulphus LATHROP senex

1672

21 Apr	Sepultus fuit Antonius BAYLEY
29 Apr	Sepultus fuit Moses HILL
7 Jul	Sepultus fuit Deliverantius FENNIHOUSE Rector de Leigh qui curam olim habuit Ammaram nune in Domino placido Requiescit
27* Jan	Sepultus fuit Gulielmus ~~Bayley senex~~ BEELAND [*17-BT]
23 Feb	Sepultus fuit Henricus BIGGINS Senex
21 Feb	Dorothea uxor Johannis GREATBATCH Sepult
15 Sep	Johanna WOOD Vidua sepulta fuit
11 Mar	Sepulta fuit Anna BIRCH Vidua

Register .... [Par]ochia de Leigh
Anno Domini
Millesimo Sexcencessimo Septagessimo tertio P Johannem Saunders
Regisr...

Joh fs Edvardi WOOD Baptis

BAPTISMATA 1672

19 Jan	Maria fa Gulilemi TILL Baptizata fuit
20 Jan	Joyce fa Gulielmi SHERRAT Baptizata fuit
18 Sep	Thoma fs Henrici BLADEN [Bladon-BT] Baptizatus fuit
21 Feb	Johannes fs Johannis GREATBATCH Baptiz fuit
23 Feb	Elizabetha fa Thoma LEES Baptizata fuit

1673

1 Apr	Dorothea fa Gulielmi HANDY Baptisata fuit
25 Mar	Elizabetha fa Anthonii SAUNDERS Baptiz
10 Apr	Gulielmus fs Johannis BLURTON Baptizata fuit
20 Apr	Gulielmus fs Johannis EDWARDS Baptizatus fuit
26 Jun	Thomas fs Georgii SHERRAT Baptizata fuit
10 Jul	Gulielmus fs Solominis SHAW Baptizatus fuit
20 Jul	Elizabetha fa Tho BLOOD Baptizata
24 Jul	Johannes fs Roberti BELCHER Baptizatus fuit
29 Jul	Thoma fs Thoma MOOR Baptizatus fuit
14 Aug	Thoma fs Francisci KEEN Baptizatus fuit
20 Aug	Thoma fs Martini LOW Baptizatus fuit
14 Dec	Isabella fa Edv SHERRAT Baptizata
25 Sep	Thomas fs Edvardi SHARPE Baptizata
2 Oct	Jonathan fil Johannis KEELING Baptiz
20 Nov	Johannes fil Samuelis LAKIN Baptiz [Lakein-BT]

— 23 Nov	Richardus fil Richardi RAYLINS Baptiz
[1674]	
21 May	Robertus fs Roberti THACKER Baptiz
21 May	Thoma fs Richardi CARTWRIGHT Baptiz
24 May	Alicia fa Gulielmi RUSHTON Baptiz
5 Apr	Thomas fs Thoma FARMER Baptiz
10 Sep	Gulielmus fs Roberti LATHROP Baptiz
— 24 Sep	Catherina fa Gulielmi HILL
8 Nov	Thoma fs Richardi DITCH *[Dych-BT]* Baptiz
26 Dec	Gulielmus fs Gulielmi SHERAT Baptiz
10 Jan	Adia *[Edia-BT]* fa Edvardi SHARPE Baptiz
— 11 Mar	Gulielmus fs Thom MOORE Baptiz
14 Mar	Martha fa Samuelis LAKIN *[Lakein-BT]* Baptiz
1675	
22 Apr	Georgius fs Georgii SHERRAT Baptiza
20 Jul	Hannah fa Gulielmi HANDY *[Handey-BT]* Baptiz
3 Sep	Gulielmus fs Roberti BELCHER Baptiz
18 Aug	Robertus fs Roberti HOLLINS Baptiz
28 Oct	Prudentia fa Edvardi BLURTON Baptiz
12 Nov	Rodulphus fs Roberti LATHROP Baptiz
18 Nov	Robertus fs Roberti JOHNSON Baptiz
1676	
4 Jan	Johannes fs Solomonis SHAW Baptiz
14 Jan	Gulielmus et Georgius fi BLOOD Baptiz
3 Feb	Johannes fs Richardi RAWLINS Baptiz
— 6 Feb	Johannes fs Thoma LEES Baptiz
6 Feb	Richardus fs Anthonii SAUNDERS Baptiz
— 19 Mar	Maria fa Gulielmi MOORE & Eliz ux: Baptiz
23 Mar	Edvardus fs Gulielmi TILL Baptizata fuit
17 Jul	Franciscus fs Francisci KEEN Baptiz
31 Aug	Johannes CARTWRIGHT fs Richardi CARTWRIGHT Baptiz
2 Nov	Alicia fa Johannis BLURTON Baptizata fuit
28 Nov	Thoma fs Johannis BROWNE Baptizatus fuit
5 Nov	Pauperis peregrina [?] sivemendici fs Baptizat
	[The child of a poor woman-BT2]
25 Dec	Elizabetha fa Edvardi SHERRAT Baptiz
28 Dec	Johannes fs Roberti THACKER Baptiz
— 1 Jan	Maria fa Gulielmi HILL Baptizata fuit
7 Jan	Maria fa Francisci WALL Babtizata fuit
1 Mar	Martha fa Gulielmi SHERRAT Baptizata
1 Mar	Jana fa Richardi DITCH *[Dych-BT]* Baptizata
— 4 Mar	Elizabetha fa Gulielmi MOOR *[Moore-BT]* Baptizata
17 Mar	Maria fa Thoma BLOOD Baptizata
1677	
— 29 Mar	Thoma fs Thoma MOORE Baptizata
— 1 Apr*	Henricus fs Henrici BAYLY Baptizata [*changed from Mar]
— 5 Apr	Tho. fs Tho. BAYLEY Baptizata fuit
— 19 Jul	Sara fa Gulielmi PARKER Baptizata fuit
1 Nov	Thomas fs Roberti BELCHER Baptizata fuit
30 Dec	Johannes fs Anthony SAUNDERS Baptizata fuit
1 Jan	Walterus fs Edvardi BLURTON Baptiz

 1 Jan   Robertus fs Samuelis LAKIN Baptizata
11 Feb   Dorothea fa Solomonis SHAW Baptizata fuit
21 Mar   Catherina fa Edvardi SHERRAT Baptizata
1678
29 Jun   Maria fa Walteri HIXON Baptizata
 8 Sep   Franciscus fs Roberti JOHNSON Baptizata
13 Nov   Johannes fs Gulielmi JOHNSON Baptiz
24 Nov   Thoma fs Johannis BOMFORD Baptiz
12 Dec   Thoma fs Gulielmi HANDY Bap….
31 Jan   Jana fa Francisci KEEN Baptizata
 9 Feb   Elizabetha fa Francisci WALL
16 Feb   Jana fa Thoma BAYLEY Baptizata fuit
 3 Mar   Valentinus fs Henrici BAYLEY Bap….
 8 Mar   Diana fa Gulielmi SHERRAT Bap…
1679
10 Apr   Eleonora fa Richardi CARTWRIGHT Bap…..
24 Jun   [ ] fs Gulielmi MOORE Baptiz
31 Jul   Maria fa Gulielmi BROUGH Baptiz
18 Aug   Johannes fs Edvardi SHERRAT Baptiz
 2 Feb   Anna fa Roberti HOLLINS Baptiz
18 Mar   Georgius fs [ ] RUSHTON Baptiz
1680
25 Apr   Josephus fs Roberti JOHNSON Baptiz
 2 May   Thomas fs Roberti THACKER Baptiz
23 May   Margareta fa Johannes BAYLEY Baptiz
 4 Jul   Johanna fa Samuelis LAKIN *[Lakein-BT]* Baptiz
29 Jul   Gulielmus fs Richardi CARTWRIGHT Bap
 5 Aug   Margareta fa Roberti BELCHER Baptiz
 3 Jan   [ ] fa Roberti STANLY *[Stanley-BT]* Baptiz
 6 Feb   Johannes fs Martini LOW Baptiz
14 Feb   Samuel fs Anthonii SAUNDERS Baptiz
1681
19 Apr   Elizabetha fa Gulilemi JOHNSON Baptiz
27 Apr   Johannis fs Edvardi BLURTON Ba….
28 Apr   Thomas fs Walteri HIXON Baptiz
23 May   Francisca fa Richardi RAWLINS Bap…
30 Jun   Felicia fa Johannes SAUNDERS et *Elizabetha [BT]* ux Baptiz
24 Jul   Anna fa Gulielmi HILL Baptiz
23 Oct   Maria fa Henrici HEATH Baptizata

1673   SEPULTUS
26 Apr   Gulielmus fs Johannis EDWARDS sepultus fuit
20 Aug   [ ] uxor Martini LOW sepulta fuit
25 Sep   Judith THACKER vidua sepult
12 Oct   Dorothea TILSTON vidua sepult
 8 Dec   Gulielmus SHERRAT Senex sepult
 1 Jan   Dorothea AMERY Senex sepult
11 Mar   Edvardus SHERRAT sepult
 7 Apr   Anna HORDERNE fa Gul: sepult
25 Dec   Gulielmus MOORE Senex sepult

1674
7 Sep Georgius SHERRAT sepultus fuit
25 Sep Johannes AMERY sepultus fuit
18 Oct Dorothea fa Gulielmi HANDY sepult
3 Nov Johannes ROBINSON Senex sepultus fuit
29 Nov Constantia LAWRENCE sepulta fuit
6 Feb Thoma fs Thoma MOORE sepultus
12 Feb Margery DIMOCK *[Dymmock-BT]* vid. Sepulta
1675
10 Jun Edy fa Edvardi WOOD sepult
28 Jun Jane LEES fa Edvardi LEES sepult
12 Aug Gulielmus HODGSON Senex sepult
18 Aug Johannes fs Henrici BLADON sepult
21 Aug Richardus RUSHTON Senex sepult
9 Sep Elizabetha fa Johannis HIDE *[Hyde-BT]* sepult
25 Oct ~~Margareta~~ Johanna fa Vid*. BOTT sepult *[*Amey- BT2]*
12 Nov Elizabetha OSBORNE fa Thoma OSBORNE et ux sepult
19 Nov Margaria uxor Johannis WOODWARD sepult
12 Nov Sara uxor Thoma SMITH sepulta fuit
7 Feb Maria GOFF sepults fuit
1676
11 Apr Maria fa Gulielmi MOORE sepulta fuit
17 Apr Vid: [ ] Senex pauperima sepulta fuit
24 Jun Gulielmus KEEN Senex sepultus fuit
1 Jul Amos HOLT Senex sepultus fuit
2 Nov Johannes BARKER Senex sepultus fuit
18 Dec Griffini THROWER Senex sepultus fuit
1677
4 Jan Elizabetha fa Gulielmi SHERRAT sepult
18 Jan Maria fa Francisci WALL sepulta
2 Feb Thoma fs Richardi CARTWRIGHT sep
2 Apr Franciscus fs Francisci KEEN sepult
9 Apr Arthurus LOW Senex pauper sepultus fuit
17 Apr Maria HILL vidua sepulta
18 Apr Franciscus SHERRAT Gen sep
3 Jun Thoma fs BAYLEY *[Bailey-BT]* sep
27 *[17 Jun]* Amab uxor [ ] *WETTON [BT]*
[1678]
19 Jan P*rudentia* fa *Johannis SAUNDERS [BT]* sen sepulta fuit
8 Sep Gulielmus SONT Senex sepult
17 Oct Filius Johannis BASFORD sepult
8 Dec Richardus COAPE sepultus fuit
13 Dec Eduardus SHARPE Senex sepultus fuit
21 Dec Gulielmus fs Thoma MOOR sepult
17 Jan Susanna HOLT vidua sepulta fuit
12 Mar Mr. Thoma PROCTER Senex sepultus fuit
1679
20 Apr Anna fa Gulielmi RUSHTON sepulta fuit
21 Apr Elizabetha fa Guleilmi RUSHTON sepulta fuit
23 Apr Franciscus fs Roberti JOHNSON sepult
28 Jun Ellianora fa Rich CARTWRIGHT sepult

8 Jul	Johannes fs Johannis GREATBATCH sepult
5 Sep	Maria DAVIS vid: sepult
13 Dec	Franciscus SHERRAT Senex sepult
22 Dec	Hugo LOW Senex sepultus fuit
12 Jan	Elizab uxor Henry KEELING sepult
7 Mar	Richardus HOMERSLEY sepultus fuit
28 Mar	Edward BARKER pauper sepultus fuit (Anno 1680)

1680

2 Apr	[ ] uxor Henrici HODGSON sepulta fuit
12 May	Johanna HEALY [Healey-BT] sepulta fuit
21 Jun	Elena fa Vid. BIRCH [Byrch-BT] sepulta fuit
29 Jul	Juditha uxor Richardi LOW sepults fuit
21 Jul	Catherina HODGSON sepults fuit
1 Sep	Anna fa Gulielmi WETTON sepulta fuit
4 Sep	Tabitha TAYLOR vid. sepulta fuit
26 Sep	Anna uxor Joh: ATKINS sepult
[blank*]	[ ] uxor Gulielmi SHERRAT [Sherratt-BT] sepult [*26 Oct-BT2]
7 Dec	Thoma WARD sepultus fuit
12 Dec	Eliz. uxor Richardi RUSHTON sepult
16 Dec	Henricus HODGSON Senex sepult
29 Dec	[ ] uxor Johannis JAMES sepult
13 Jan	Robertus STANLEY sepultus fuit
4 Mar	Johannes HEALY [Healey-BT] Senex sepult

1681

25 Jun	Gulielmus ASTON sepultus fuit
17 Jul	Sara fa Gulielmi PARKER sepult
3 Aug	Richardus SPENCER Sen sepult
10 Sep	Tho. SHERRAT Sen sepult
13 Oct	Samuel fs Anthonii SAUNDERS sepult
17 Oct	Tho. fs Vid BIRCH [Byrch-BT] sepultus fuit
3 Jan	Solomon SHAW sepultus fuit
5 Jan	Alicia BLURTON uxor Joh. BLURTON sepult
15 Jan	Elizab: BROMWELL vid: sepult
7 Nov	Elizabetha fa Tho WETTON Baptiz [sepult-BT]
4 Nov	Edw: HIDE fi Thom: HIDE sepult [BT2]

1682

26 Mar	Eliz. fa Gulielmi JOHNSON sepult
9 Apr	Henricus KEELING sepult
9 Jun	Jacobus fs Eduardi HIDE [Hyde-BT] sepult
26 Jun	Ellis BAYLY [Bayley-BT] sepult
8 Jan	Johannes GREATBATCH Senex sepult
21 Jan	Ellena CHAPLIN [Chaplaine-BT] vidua sepult
24 Mar	Maria fa Martini LOW sepult

1683

1 Apr	Valentinus fs Henrici BAYLY [Bayley-BT] sepult
22 May	Edvardus BOURNE sepultus fuit
26 May	Sara ASBURY sepulta fuit
28 Jun	Johannes SHERRAT Senex sepult
31 Jul	Gulielmus BELCHER Senex sepult
18 Aug	Anna uxor Anthonii HOYL [Hoyle-BT] sepult

1672 [Top of page damaged & illegible except for name Eleonora W]
       Marriages in BT
26 Apr   *Johannem GREATBATCH et Dorotheam LAKIN*
17 Jul   Georgius SHERRATT de Nobot Parochia Leigh et Eleonora WEBB de Coulton
1673 MATRIMONIUS
1 Apr   Gulielmus HILL et Maria WOOD parochia Leigh in matrimonio conjuncti
1 Apr   Josephus VERNON parochia de Myllwich et Elizabetha HOLLINS paroch de Leigh nupti erant
2 Apr   Richardus DYCH et Joanna LAKIN paroch de Leigh in matrimonio conjuncti
6 Jul   Richardus GREEN prochia de Bromly Abbots et Maria LEES poch de Leigh in matrimonio conjuncti erant
24 Nov   Thomas COLLIER de Dilorne & Elizabetha YATES de Colton vidua in matrimonio conjuncti fuere
1674
23*Apr Thoma JENKINS de Wirley et Catherina COPE de Cannock in matrimonio conjuncti fuere [*28-BT1, 24-BT2]
1675
6 Apr   Johannes HAYCOCK de Milwich et Jane BEECH de Stoke in matrimonio conjuncti fuere
1676
26 Dec   Johannes BOMFORD et Sara ROWLY [Rowley-BT] de paroch Lee in matrimonio conjuncti fuere
1680
14 Jul   Josephus OAKES de Checkly et Maria HILL de Leigh in matrimonio conjuncti fuere
9 Nov   Josephus PHILLIPS et Anna BAGGALY de Checkly in matrimonio conjuncti fuere
Jan   Henricus HEATH et Sara HORTON de Leigh in matrimonio conjuncti fuere
1681
19 Jan   Johannes ALLIN et Susanna BARNES de Dilhorne in mattrimonio conjuncti fuere
1682
21 May   Franciscus DITCH [Dytch-BT] et Jana BROUGH de paroch Leigh in matrimonio conjuncti fuerunt
30 Oct   Robertus HEATON et Maria MEAKIN de Lee in matrimonio conjuncti fuere
26 Dec   Eduardus GREEN de Abbots Bromly et Anna LOW de Leigh in matrimonio conjuncti fuerunt
5 Feb   Gulielmus SERGEANT de Chedleton et Elizabetha KEELING de Lee in matrimonio conjuncti fuere
1684
20 May   Thoma WHITHERINGS et Maria SHAW in matrimonio conjuncti fuere
13 Dec   Thomas HINLEY de Gratwich Jana MILLNES de Lee in matrimonio conjuncti fuere
9 Feb   Josephus ANSEL et Anna HARDEN de parochia Colwich in matrimonio conjuncti fuere

1685

30 Aug   Johannes BERISFORD poa Marston Montgomery et Dorothea COPE poa Norbury nupti fuere

27 Oct   Johannes STARTIN et Anna COOPER *[Cowper-BT]* paroch de Leigh in matrimonio conjuncti fuere

16 Feb   Johannes BARKER et Sara WILLOTT parochial de Leigh in matrimonio conjuncti fuere

1683   [BURIALS]

22 Dec   Stephanus WATSON sepulta fuit

28 Dec   Johannes fs Johannis LOW sepult

29 Dec   [ ] uxor Francisci COATES sen sepult

20 Jan   Anna uxor Gulielmi SALT sepulta fuit

1 Feb   Anna HOMERSLY vid sepult

1684

3 Apr   Thoma WITTERANCE Senex sepult

8 Apr   Thoma fs Vid SHERRAT sepultus fuit

12 Jun   Franciscus fs Thoma MOORE sepult

19 Jun   Henricus LAURENCE pauper sepult

19 Jul   Maria SHERRAT vidua sepulta fuit

26 Jul   Anna fa Sam. LAKIN sepulta fuit

7 Aug   Johannes fs Johannis SAUNDERS sepult

9 Aug   Anna COVELL vid sepulta fuit

11 Aug   Elizabetha uxor Johannis SAUNDERS Cler. Sepult

26 Aug   Margareta uxor Roberti BELCHER sepult

6 Nov   Thoma THROWER Senex sepultus fuit

12 Nov   Johannes MIDDLETON Senex sepultus fuit

11 Feb   Margaria fa Tho BAYLY sepult

17 Feb   Susanna BAYLY vid sepult

17 Feb   Sybilla HAILES mulier vagrans sepulta fuit

22 Feb   Rebecca fa Thoma BAYLY sepulta fuit

13 Mar   Jana fa Roberti HOLLINS sepult

23 Mar   Richardus fs Gulielmi RUSHTON sepult

1685

31 Mar   Mattheus fs Martini LOW sepult

31 May   Gulielmus RUSHTON Senex sepult

26 May   Tho WETTON fs Tho WETTON sepult

15 Jul   Maria WOOLLEY sepulta fuit

18 Jul   Ellena SHERRAT vid sepulta fuit

21 Aug   Gulielmus BROMALL *[Bromwell-BT]* sepultus fuit

30 Aug   [ ] WOODWARD Senex sepultus fuit

30 Aug   [ ] uxor Walteri BLURTON sepult

21 Sep   Sara uxor Joh HALL sepulta fuit

20 Nov   Robertus HEALY *[Healey-BT]* Senex sepultus fuit

25 Nov   Ellena JOHNSON vid sepulta fuit

19 Jan   Ellena SHERRAT vid sepulta fuit

Ult Feb   Johannes fil Hen BAYLY *[Bayley-BT]* sepult

17 Mar   Alicia uxor Guliel RAWBONE sepult

1686

29 Mar   Catherina JELLEY fa Guliel JELLEY *[Jolly-BT]* sepult

16 Apr   Franciscus fs Richardi SHERRAT sepult

9 May   Sara PEDLEY vidua sepulta fuit
25 May   Robertus HIDE *[Hyde-BT]* sepultus fuit
28 May   Anna uxor Edvardi BAYLY *[Bayley-BT]* sepult
27 Jun   Elizab. fa Thoma GEFFEREY *[Jeffery-BT]* sepult
29 Jun   Margareta fa Anthonii SAUNDERS sepult
3 Aug   Thoma SHERRAT sepultus fuit
1 Nov   Gulielmus PURIFOY Senex sepultus fuit
6 Dec   Tho fs Tho WITTERANCE sepult
          [bottom of page damaged]
7 Dec   *Maria [BT]* BAYLY *[Bayley-BT]* vid sepult
1687
4 Apr   *Ellena BLAKEMAN [BT]* vid sepult
5 Apr   Lettice SPENSER vid [BT]

1682   **BAPTISMATA**
9 Jul   Henricus fs Samuelis LAKIN Baptizatus fuit
13 Jul   Anna fa Edvardi WALKER Baptizata fuit
13 Jul   Franciscus fs Tho MOORE Baptizatus
17 Aug   Franciscus fs Francisci KEEN Baptizatus
31 Aug   Anna fa Anthonii SAUNDERS Baptizata fuit
8 Oct   Dorothea fa Francisci WALL Baptizata fuit
23 Nov   Thoma fs Eduardi BOURNE Baptizatus fuit
14 Dec   Gulielmus fs Gulielmi PARKER et Elizabetha ux Baptizatus
28 Dec   Gulielmus fs Johannis WRIGHT Bapt
11 Feb   Robertus fs Roberti HEATON Baptiz
14 Feb   Gulielmus fs Gulielmi JOHNSON Baptiz
1683
25 Mar   Maria fa Francisci DITCH *[Dych-BT]* Baptiz
22 Apr   Moses fs Roberti JOHNSON Baptiz
10 May Alicia fa Edvardi BLURTON Baptiz
10 Jun   Henricus fs Henrici BAYLY *[Bayley-BT]* Baptiz
17 Jul   Henricus fs Henrici HEATH Baptiz
27 Aug   Sara fa Gulielmi MOORE Baptizata fuit
23 Sep   Sara fa Tho BAYLY *[Bayley-BT]* Baptizata fuit
31 Oct   Johannes fs Joha LOWE Baptiz
1 Nov   Maria fa Gulielmi HILL Baptiz
10 Mar   Dorothea fa Richardi LOW Baptiz
1684
10 Apr   Elizabetha fa Edvardi WALKER Baptiz
21 May   Walterus fs Walteri HORDERNE Baptiz
29 May   Jana fa Roberti HOLLINS Baptiz
29 May   Isabella fa Henrici COAPE Baptiz
15 Jul   Ellena fa Thoma WARD et ux Ellena Bapt
26 Jul   Anna fa Samuelis LAKIN *[25 Jun- BT2]* Baptizata fuit
5 Aug   Johannes fs Johannis SAUNDERS Baptiz
28 Aug   Anna fa Thoma KEY Baptiz
15 Aug   Franciscus fs Richardi SHERRAT Baptiz *[28 Aug-BT2]*
2 Oct   Sara fa Simonis BLOOD Baptizata fuit
10 Oct   Margareta fa Anthonii SAUNDERS Baptizata fuit
26 Oct   Tho fs Thoma WETTON Baptiz
29 Oct   Johannes fs Joh. ALSOP Baptiz

21 Dec Elizabetha fa Walteri BLURTON Baptiz
— 29 Jan Anna fa Benjamini VERNON et Eliz ux Baptiz
— 8 Mar Robertus fs Gulielmi MOORE Baptiz *[28 Mar-BT2]*
— 22 Mar Waltarus fs Martini LOW Baptiz
1685
9 May Robertus fs Francisci MIDDLETON Baptiz
9 May Alicia fa Johannes PLANT Baptiz
11 Jun Thoma fs Thoma WITHERINGS Baptizatus
— 26 Jul Richardus fs Thoma BAYLY *[Bayley-BT]* Baptiz
2 Aug Elizabetha fa Roberti JOHNSON Baptiz
— 6 Sep Anna fa Johannis WRIGHT Baptiz
26 Sep Elizabetha SHERRAT fa Ricardi et Elizabatha
27 Sep Johannes fs Johannis JAQUES & Maria ux
        [bottom of page damaged]
--- 8 Nov Johannes fs Henrici *BAYLEY [BT]*
31 Dec *Tho fs Jacobi FENTON & Dor ux [BT]*
30 Jan *Tho: fs Tho: ASBURY [BT]*

[1686 MARRIAGES]
— 11 Mar Henricus WALKER De Dilhorne et Margarita PHILLIPS de Cheadle
        conjuncti fuere
27 Jun Richardus BLAKEMAN Parochia de Chebsy et Sara BELCHER Parochia
        de Leigh in matrimonio conjuncti fuere
1687
= 5 Jun Fransciscus LEES et Dorothea PORTER de Leigh in matrimonio
        conjuncta fuere
=> 20 Jul Thoma PYOT *[Pyott-BT]* de Leek et Elizabetha KEELING de Leigh in
        matrimonio conjuncti fuere
20 Jan Guliel fil. Walt BAGOT Generosi et Domina ux sua Baptiz fuit

1686 BAPTISMATA
10 Jun Johannes fs Tho GREENWOOD Bapt
15 Jun Eliz fa Roberti HEATON Baptiz
27 Jun Johannes fs Francisci DICH Baptiz
— 1 Aug Alicia fa Edvardi WALKER Baptiz
— 19 Aug Francisci fs Johannis LOW Baptiz
26 Aug Johan fs Fran PEDLY *[Pedley-BT]* Baptiz
28 Aug Christopherus fs Joh BARKER Baptiz
30 Sep Maria fa Josephi PHILLIPS Baptiz
10 Oct [ ] fil [ ] PHILIPS *[Phillips-BT]* Baptiz
— 14 Oct Margareta fa Joh HILL Baptiz
24 Oct Hingstans* fs Rich SHERRAT *[*Ilsley-BT]* Baptiz
✓ 9 Dec Jana fa Ben VERNON Baptiz
23 Jan Anna fa Franc WALL Baptiz
30 Jan Guliel fs Guliel BROUGH Bapt
7 Feb Sara fa Joh JAQES *[Jaques-BT]* et Maria ux Bapt
10 Mar Thoma fs Edvardi DAVIS *[Davies-BT]* Baptiz Baptiz
= 13 Mar Sara *PHILLIPS* fa *Guli SAULT et Elizab PHILIPS [BT]* illegitima nata Baptiz
1687
= 20 Mar *Jacobus fil Henrici BAYLEY [BT]* Baptiz
= 19 Apr .... SHERRAT Sepult

5 May   Sam fil Anth SAUNDERS Baptiz
8 May   Tho fil Hen COAPE Baptiz
29 May Tho fs Sam LAKIN Baptiz
10 Jun Gulielmus fs Tho PHILIPS et Margareta Baptiz
14 Jul Johannes fs Johan SAUNDERS cler et Sara ux Baptizatus
16 Oct Elizabetha fa Franc MIDDLETON Bapt
9 Jan   Eliz fa [ ] ROYLY *[Royley-BT]* Baptiz
15 Jan Eliz fa Jacobi FENTON et ux eius Dor. Bapt
19 Jan Gulielmus fs Simonis BLOOD et ux eius Marg Bap
22 Jan Thomas fs Franc PEDLY *[Pedley-BT]* Baptiz
9 Feb   Gulielm fs Anth HOYL *[Hoyle-BT]* Baptiz
12 Feb Jacobus fs Johan EDWARDS Baptiz
22 Mar Tho fs Guliel HILL jun Baptiz
1688
25 Mar Anna fa Franc LEES Baptiz
8 Apr   Jana fa Guliel MOOR *[Moore-BT]* Baptiz
15 May Difield fa Joh et Difield WRIGHT Baptiz

1687   SEPULTUS
19 Apr Isabella uxor Edvardi SHERRAT *[Sherratt-BT]* sepult
6 Jun   Elizabetha uxor Edvardi WOOD sepult
11 Jul Margareta PHILLIPS uxor Tho PHILLIPS sepult
13 Sep Tho fs Edvardi WOOD sepult
1 Oct   Tho fs Ric. PEDLY *[Pedley-BT]* sepult
18 Oct Franc HEALY [?] *[very feint entry in margin]* sepult
18 Nov Tho PHILLIPS Senex sepultus fuit
28 Nov Oliverus HILL sepultus fuit
12 Jan Margaria uxor Tho HOW sepult
12 Jan Eliz fa [ ] ROYLY *[Royley-BT]* sepult
4 Feb   Sara uxor Tho MOOR *[Moore-BT]* sepulta fuit
13 Feb Jacobus fs Johan EDWARDS sepult
25 Feb Johannes WRIGHT sepultus fuit
1688
26 Jun Tho COAPE Senex sepultus fuit
19 Jul Gulielmus fs Tho PHILLIPS sepult
2 Oct   Johannes JOHNSON Senex sepult
16 Oct Anna COAPE vid sepulta fuit
2 Dec   Gulielmus DITCH *[Dych-BT]* sepultus fuit
31 Dec Ellena BLAKEMAN vid sepulta fuit
2 Mar   Franciscus MIDDLETON Sen sepultus fuit
14 Mar Ellena fa Rich. SHERRAT et ux sepulta fuit
1689
13 May Anthonius BIRD *[Byrd-BT]* Senex sepultus fuit
19 May Dorothea uxor Gulielm CLARK sepulta fuit
4 Jun   Anna MILHOUSE vid sepulta fuit
8 Jul   Franciscus LEA sepultus fuit
6 Aug   Sara uxor Roberti POTTS sepults fuit
6 Aug   Anna fa illegitima [ ] sepulta fuit
20 Aug Joh fs Tho. OSBORNE *[Osburne-BT]* sepultus fuit
21 Jan Edith uxor Tho. MIDDLETON sepult
11 Feb Thomas HIDE *[Hyde-BT]* sepultus fuit

21 Feb Elianora uxor *[predict:-BT]* Tho HIDE *[Hyde-BT]* sepult
1690
21 Apr Steph. fs Vid WATSON sepult
1 May Margareta BAYLY vid sepult
4 May Margareta fa Marg. SHERRAT *[Sherratt-BT]* sepult
17 May Maria fa Francisci WALL sepult
21 May Franciscus MIDDLETON Sen sepult
5 Jun Joanna uxor Edvardi SMITH sepult
11 Jun Thoma OSBORNE *[Osburne-BT]* Sen sepultus fuit
15 Sep Tho SMITH sepultus fuit
15 Sep Elizabeth uxor Tho MIDDLETON sepult
29 Sep Anna MIDDLETON vidua sepults fuit
14 Nov Maria uxor Tho HOW jun sepult
2 Dec Margareta fa Franc COVEL sepult
21 Dec Gansela fs Will BAYLY *[Bayley-BT]* sepult
30 Dec Tho. SONT Senex sepultus fuit
31 Dec Robertus POTS *[Potts-BT]* Senex sepultus fuit

1688 BAPTISMATA
12 Jul Eliz. fa Tho WITTERANCE Bapt
12 Jul Eliz. fa Guliel PARKER Baptiz
22 Jul Georgius fs Georgii TURNER Baptiz
27 Jul Francisc. et Ellen gemelli Ric. SHERRAT Baptiz
26 Aug Sara fa Samuel STEEL *[Steell-BT]* et ux. Baptiz
26 Aug Johan fs Joh SHERRAT et ux. eius Baptiz
16 Sep Anna fa Fran. DITCH et ux Bapt
7 Sep Franc. fil Guliel ETHRINGTON *[Etherington-BT]* et Maria ux Bapt
21 Oct Eliz: fa Hen. HEATH et Susa ux Bapt
15 Nov Sara fa Sam: POTTS et Maria ux Bapt
18 Nov Nathaniel fs Edv. BLURTON et Eliz ux Bapt
9 Dec Gulielm fs Rob. HEATON et Maria ux Bapt
16 Dec Anna fa Edvardi THROWER et Maria ux Bapt
20 Dec Elizab. fa Tho. ASBURY et Marg ux Bapt
27 Dec Joh. fs Joh. BAILY et Margaret ux Bapt
3 Jan Georgius fil: Ben: VERNON et Eliz ux Bapt
14 Feb Samuel fil: Guliel JOHNSON et ux Bapt
21 Feb Maria fa Rogeri RUTCHISON *[Richardson-BT]* et Ellin ux
24 Feb Joseph fs Walt: HORDERN & ux Baptiz
10 Mar Margareta fil. Anth. PHILLIPS & ux Bapt
10 Mar Guliel fil: Fran. LEES et ux. Bapt
24 Mar Ruth fil Franc: IPSTO'S *[Ibson-BT]* et ux. Bapt
1689
1 Apr Jana fil: Hen: et Jana COAPE Baptz
16 May Benjamin fil Robt et Margr BELCHER Bapt
19 May Elizab. fa [ ] ROYLY *[Royley-BT]* et ux Bapt
23 May Rachel fa Joh et Sara BARKER Bapt
30 Jun Anna illegit fa Mullieris vaga Bapt
30 Jun Edvardus fil. illegittus [ ] Bapt
15 Aug Anna fa Joh CHELL et ux Baptiz
15 Aug Margareta fa Franc. SHERRAT et ux Bapt
25 Aug Margareta fa Robti JOHNSON et ux Bapt

12 Sep   Maria fa Tho PARKER et Sara ux Bapt
17 Sep   Maria fa Ric. SHERRAT et ux *[Eliza-BT]* Baptiz
 6 Oct   Susanna fa Hen BAYLY et Rosa ux Baptiz
17 Oct   Edvardus fs Joh SAUNDERS et Sara ux Baptiz
24 Oct   Anna fa George JOHNSON et ux Baptiz
29 Oct   Dorothea fa Franc & Maria COVEL Baptiz
 8 Dec   Joh fs Franc MIDDLETON et ux Bapt
10 Dec   Joh fs Joh JAQES et Maria ux Bapt *[Johan Jaques-BT]*
19 Dec   Maria fa Saml et Doroth STEEL Bapt
21 Jan   Maria fil Franc et Ann WALL Baptiz
10 Feb   Elizab fa Ric et Gra BAYLY *[Bayley-BT]* Baptiz
16 Feb   Guliel fs Guliel SALT *[Sault-BT]* et ux Baptiz
27 Feb   Guliel fs Guliel et Mar BATMAN Bap
16 Mar   Daniel fs Ric & Maria SNAPE Baptiz

1687   **MATRIMONIALIA**
22 Dec   Henricus HEATON de Leigh et Susanna MOSS de Leigh in matrimonio conjuncti fuere
 2 Feb   Rodulphus FOSTER er Maria MILNER *[Millner-BT]* paroch de Leigh in matrimonio conjuncti fuere

1688
22 Apr   Gulilelmus HENSHAW et Anna HOLLINS de Leigh in matrimonio conjuncti fuere

1689
 2 Apr   Johannes DAVIS *[Davies-BT]* et Maria HILL paroch de Leigh in matrimonio conjuncti fuere
11 Apr   James GEDLING de Shelton in comitat Notting*[ham-BT]* et Elizabetha SHERRAT *[Sherratt-BT]* de Lee in comitat Stafford in matrimonio conjuncti fuere
18 Apr   Guliel RAWBONE et Maria PHILLIPS de Leigh in matrimonio conjuncti fuere
17 Jan   Johannes HILTON de Stone et Anna BULLOCK de Leigh in comit Stafford in matrimonio conhuncti fuere

1691
 7 May   Thomas MIDDLETON et Margaret SHERRAT *[Sherratt-BT]* de Middleton Green in paroch de Leigh in matrimonio conjuncti fuere

1692
 7 Apr   Edvardus LAURENCE et Anna TILSTON in paroch de Leigh in matrimonio conjucti fuere

1693
27 Dec   Georgius HALL paroch de Leigh et Maria CHAMBERLIN paroch de Uttoxeter in matrimonio conjuncti fuere

1690   **SEPULTUS**
11 Jan   Guliel fs Anthonii HOYL *[Hoyle-BT]* sepult
18 Jan   Henry COAPE pauper sepult
19 Jan   Eliz HEATON vid sepulta fuit
19 Jan   Will fs Rob HEATON sepult
17 Feb   Johannes BLURTON Senex sepult
24 Feb   Will GELLY *[Gelley-BT]* Senex sepultus fuit

1691

18 Apr	Thomas STILSTON Senex sepultus fuit
14 Jun	Juditha MIDDLETON vid sepulta fuit
18 Jun	Carolus COLCLOUGH sepultus fuit
21 Jun	Anna fa Joh WRIGHT et ux sepult
4 Aug	Franciscus HYDE sepultus fuit
10 Aug	Edvardus fs Anna OSBORNE [Osburne-BT] sepult
28 Aug	Edvardus HYDE Senex sepultus fuit
16 Sep	Franciscus CHAPLIN [Chaplaine-BT] sepultus fuit
12 Nov	Gulielmus HIDE [Hyde-BT] sepultus fuit
12 Nov	Jacobus fs Jacobi FENTON sepult
28 Jan	Dorothea uxor Carol STEVENSON sepult
9 Feb	Anna fa Tho RUSHTON sepult
29 Feb	Cecilia uxor Nich. [Nicholae-BT] HILL sepult

1692

21 Apr	Maria IPSON [Ibson-BT] infans sepult
13 Jun	Sara HOLLINS vid sepult
2 Aug	Gulielm fs Sam. LAKIN sepult
24 Nov	Matth[eus-BT] LOW Senex sepult
30 Nov	Alicia uxor Fran SHERRAT sepult
21 Dec	Maria BIRD vidua sepulta fuit
4 Feb	Marga[reta-BT] fa Joh & Marg SHERRAT [Sherratt-BT] sepult

1693

29 Apr	Rebecca uxor Ric. HOW sepulta fuit
5 May	Richard fs Rich BAYLY sepult
12 Jun	Samuel fs Joh & Sara SAUNDERS sepult
4 Aug	Johannes fs Franc MIDDLETON sepult
31 Oct	Elizabetha SHAUKHURST [Shallcross-BT] sepulta fuit
14 Dec	Eduardus SHERRAT sepultus fuit
8 Feb	Richardus COLLIER sepultus fuit
26 Feb	Will fil Franc SHERRAT sepult
12 Mar	Sara fa Willi RUSHTON sepult

1690 BAPTISMATA

22 Apr	Esther fa illegit. Maria HAKINS Baptiz
9 May	Anna fa Thoma et Anna LEA Bapt
25 May	Fil. [ ] Anthonii HOYL [Hoyle-BT] et ux Baptiz
1 Jun	Margareta fa Edvardi DAVIES [Davis-BT] Baptiz
22 Sep	Rich fs Richardi et Eliz SHERRAT [Sherratt-BT] Baptiz
30 Oct	Robertus fs Sam & Maria POTTS [Pott-BT] Baptiz
20 Nov	Margareta fa Franc et Maria COVEL [Covell-BT] Baptiz
27 Nov	Dorothea fa Franc et Doroth LEES Bapt
29 Nov	Gulielmus fs Gulielmi et Eliza JACKSON Bapt
7 Dec	Catherina fa Henrici et Susan HEATON Bapt
9 Dec	Gansela fs Wm BAYLY et Maria ux Baptiz
14 Dec	Guliel fs Hen: HEATH et Sara ux Baptiz
27 Dec	Maria fa Tho: et Maria WITTERANCE Bapt
10 Jan	Gulielm fs Gulielmi et Maria ETHRINGTON [Etherington-BT] Bapt
11 Jan	Joh fs Edvardi DAVIES [Davis-BT] et ux Baptiz
27 Jan	Gulielmus fs Joh et Sara SAUNDERS Bapt
5 Feb	Josephus fs Joh et Margareta SHERRAT Bapt

15 Feb Johannes fs Joh et Sara BARKER Bapt
22 Feb Franciscus fs Francisci DITCH *[Dych-BT]* Baptiz
21 Mar Elizabetha fa Georgii TOOTH Baptiz
1691
2 Apr Francisc. fs Francisc et ux SHERRAT *[Sherratt-BT]* Baptiz
3 May Eliz fa Hen: et Eliz: COAPE Baptizata fuit
8 May Thoma fs Johes et Margareta BAYLY Baptiz
10 May Edvardus fs illegitimus Anna OSBORN *[Osburne-BT]* Baptizata fuit
14 May Anna fa Robti et Margareta BELCHER Baptizata fuit
11 Jun Gulielm fs Roberti et Mary HEATON Bapt
25 Jun Josephus fs Johann et Maria SIMSON Bapt
28 Jun Johannes fs Georgii JOHNSON et ux Baptiz
30 Aug Anna fa Tho RUSHTON & ux Baptiz
17 Sep Gulielm fs Johann TILL et ux Baptiz
24 Sep Edvard fs Joh et Hanna HYDE Baptiz
27 Sep Anna fa Tho et Sara PARKER ux Baptiz
4 Oct Gulielm fs Anthonii PHILLIPS Baptiz
5 Nov Jacobus fs Jacob & Dorothea FENTON Baptiz
8 Nov Sara fa Georgii TURNER et ux Baptiz
15 Nov Gulielm fs Tho HEIRS Baptiz
7 Dec Maria fa Carol et Doroth STIPSTON *[Stinston-BT]* Bapt
12 Dec Ellena fa Franc et Doroth LEES Baptiz
10 Jan Amos fs Ric. et Maria SNAPE Baptiz
21 Jan Samuel fs Sam et Doroth STEEL Baptiz
4 Feb Hanna fa Tho. BAYLY Baptiz
20 Mar Nathaniel fs Gulielm JOHNSON Baptiz
22 Mar Samuel fs Joh & Sara SANDERS Baptiz
24 Mar Jana fa Robti et Jana HOLLINS Baptiz
1692
7 Apr Maria fa Edvardi THROWER Baptiz
10 Apr Maria fa Franc IPSON *[Ibson-BT]* Baptiz
28 Apr Francisc. fs Franc COVEL
5 Jun Maria fa Tho & Maria ASBURY
7 Jun Thoma fs Johan & Maria JAQUESS
26 Jun Ric. fs Rich. BAYLY *[Bayley-BT]* Bapt
22 Aug Thoma fs Joh. COAPE et ux Bapt
2 Sep Rebeca fa illegit Sara RUSHTON
15 Sep Johan fs Richardi SHERRAT *[Sherratt-BT]* Bapt
17 Oct Elizabeth fa Willmi JACKSON
5 Nov Johan fs Joh. TOMLINSON
11 Nov Willmus fs Joh et Sara BARKER Bapt
20 Nov Alicia fa Hen. et Susa HEATON
18 Jan Edvardus fs Edvard & Maria SMITH Bapt
26 Jan Margaret fa Joh et Marg SHERRAT Bap
2 Feb Anna fa Edv. et Ann LAURENCE Bapt
23 Feb Steph. Fs Johan et Maria SIMSON Bapt
5 Mar Rich. fs Will TUNSTAL et ux Bapt
5 Mar Tho fs Wm BAYLY *[Bayley-BT]* et ux Bapt
16 Mar Tho. fs Ad: *[Adami-BT]* et Sara TURNER Bapt
1693
28 Mar Tho. fs Franc LEES et ux Bapt

9 Apr   Georg. fs Georgii JOHNSON et ux Bapt
20 Apr   Edvard. fs Hen: CHELL et ux Baptiz
20 Apr   Doroth. fa Tho. et Maria WITTERANCE Bapt
1 May   Maria fa Wmi et Maria .... Bapt *[missing from-BT]*
14 May   Willmus fs Franc SHERRAT et ux Bapt
1 Jun   Doroth. fa Franc. et Maria MIDDLETON Bapt
5 Jun   Willmus fs Tho. TOWNSEND et ux Bapt
25 Jun   Daniell fs Sam. STEELL Baptiz
31 Oct   Alicia fa Tho. RUSHTON et ux Bapt
2 Nov   Will. fs Franc. LAKIN et ux *[Margareta-BT]* Bapt
23 Nov   Joha. fa Tho. & Sara PARKER Bapt
9 Dec   Elizabetha fa Franc et ux *[Maria-BT]* COVEL Bapt *[Covill-BT]*
9 Dec   Gulielm fs HITCHCOCK et ux Bapt *[Thoma et Eliz-BT]*
11 Dec   Samuel fs Sam. POTTS et ux *[Maria-BT]* Bapt
1 Jan   Steph fs Rob et Margareta BELCHER Bapt
15 Feb   Anthon. fs [ ] *[Tho-BT]* BAYLY *[Bayley-BT]* et ux Bapt
15 Mar   Johan fs Robti et Maria HEATON Bapt

1693   MATRIMONIALIA
14 Feb   Thoma GRICE de Shefnal comit Salop et Anna CARTWRIGHT comit Stafford in matrimonio conjuncti fuere
1696
17 Jun   Richardus DITCH *[Dytch-BT]* et Maria WETTON de Nobot in paroch de Leigh in matrimonio conjuncti fuere
1697
26 Feb   Thomas FERNS de parochia Stone in Com Staffordis et Jana TILSTON de Leigh in matrimonio conjuncti fuere
1698
26 May   Thomas JOHNSON et Francessa SNAPE de parochial Leigh in Com Staffordia in matrimonio conjuncti fuere
1704
26 Aug   Gulielmus DEAKIN et Phebe PHRIDGLY huius parochial in matriminio conjuncti fuere
5 Sep   Robertus FRADLEY et Elizabetha MAUKIN huius parochia in matrimonio conjuncti fuere
27 Sep   Samuelis WOOLY & Helena SHAW in matrimonio conjuncti fuere

1694   BAPTISMATA
1 Apr   Frans fa Richar. SNAPE et ux *[Maria-BT]* Bapt
10 Apr   Margareta fa Willi et Margareta HYLL Bapt
26 Apr   Jonathan fs Tho. et Elizab. PIOT *[Piott-BT]* Bapt
18 May   Maria fa Joh & Maria JAKES ux Baptiz *[Jaquess-BT]*
20 May   Tho. fs Georgii TOOTH et [ ] *[Maria-BT]* ux Baptiz
24 Jun   Ellena fa Wm HILL et ux *[Ma:-BT]* Bap
21 Jul   Elizab. fa Rob. et ux *[Dorothea-BT]* WOOD Baptiz
26 Jul   Lyddia fa Joh. COAPE et ux *[Hanna-BT]* Baptiz
4 Aug   Elizab. fa Joh. et Elizab. TILL ux Baptiz
5 Aug   Johan fs Joh THROWER et ux *[Maria-BT]* Baptiz
14 Aug   Edvardus fs Eduardi et ux *[Anna-BT]* BLURTON Bapt
26 Aug   Eduard fs Eduardi THROWER et ux Bapt
26 Aug   Tho fs Thoa COLLIER et ux *[Eliza-BT]* Baptiz

30 Aug   Maria fa Hen. HEATON & Susa ux Bapt
13 Sep   Edvard fs Tho. BAYLY jun et ux Baptiz
20 Sep   Richardus fs Joh. et Sara SAUNDERS Bapt
14 Oct   Maria fa George JOHNSON et *[Anna-BT]* ux eius Bapt
8 Dec   Elizab. fa Francis LEES et *[Doro:-BT]* ux eius Bapt
2 Jan   Joh. fs Joh et Sara COLLIER Baptiz
29 Dec   Joh fs Gulielm & Margt *[Maria-BT]* BLURTON Baptiz
17 Jan   Henricus fs Henrici et Maria CHELL Bapt
7 Mar   Alicia fa Ada: et Sara TURNER Baptiz

1695
26 Apr   Anna fa Rich et Eliz: SHERRAT ux Bapt
          [2 entries erased]
13 May   Moses et Aaron fi Tho HEIRES *[Heirs-BT]* et ux Baptiz
16 May   Gulielm fs Guliel RUSHTON et ux Baptiz
7 Jun   Johan fs Tho. et Cath. OSBORN Baptiz
13 Jun   Ellen fa Franc et Margareta SHERRAT Baptiz
16 Jun   Anna fa Johan et Margareta BAYLY Baptiz
7 Jul   Maria fa Franc et Marget LAKIN *[Lakein-BT]* Bapt
2 Oct   Gulielm fs Gulielm & Doroth BAILY *[Bayley-BT]* Bap
6 Oct   Ruth fa Franc et Anna IPSO *[Ibson-BT]* Bap
29 Oct   Maria fa Ric. et Angel *[Angella-BT]* PRICE Bap
7 Nov   Robt fs Guliel et Hannah TUNSTLE *[Tunstall-BT]* Bapt
7 Nov   Doroth. fa Fracisc. et Maria MIDDLETON Bap
17 Nov   Elizab. fa Tho. et Sara PARKER Bapt
22 Nov   Martha fa illegit Elizab. LAKIN Bapt
3 Jan   Maria fa Franc. et Doroth LEES Bap
5 Jan   Samuel fs Rob et Margaret BELCHER Bap
12 Jan   Ribecca fa Tho & Cath. BAYLY Baptiz
28 Jan   Anna fa Tho. & Maria WITTERANCE Baptiz
31 Jan   Hannah fa Franc et Hanna SWINSHEAD Bap
2 Feb   Gulielm fs Johan et Margar. SHERRAT Bap
8 Feb   Doroth. Fa Johan. et Franc. WRIGHT Bap
18 Feb   Edvard fs Edvard et Anna LAURENCE Bap
23 Feb   Robt. fs Rich. et Eliz. JUMP Baptizatus
27 Feb   Anna fa Tho. et Margaret ASBURY Bapt
1 Mar   Maria fa Tho. et Anna TOWNSEND Bapt

1694   SEPULTUS
2 Jun   Anna MOORE sepulta fuit
10 Jun   Thomas PYOT sepultus fuit
3 Jul   Samuel fs Samuelis POTTS sepultus fuit
14 Jul   Joanna uxor Johan BLURTON sepulta fuit
9 Aug   Ellena BIRD uxor Nathaniel BIRD *[Byrd-BT]* sepult
27 Sep   Elizabetha fa Franc COVEL *[Covill-BT]* sepulta fuit
2 Oct   Franciscus fs Franc COVEL *[Covill-BT]* sepultus fuit
15 Oct   Sara uxor Johan. SAUNDERS sepulta fuit
29 Oct   Stephan fs Robti et Margareta BELCHER sepult
20 Nov   Tho. fs Tho. MOORE sepultus fuit
25 Nov   Ruth fa Franc. IBSON sepulta fuit
1 Dec   Gulielm fs Franc. LAKIN *[Lakyn-BT]* sepultus fuit
2 Dec   Gulielm fs Franc. KEEN sepultus fuit

16 Dec Elizab. fa Franc. LEES sepult
18 Dec Francisc. fs Franc. IBSON sepult
19 Dec Edvardus fs Tho BAILY *[Bayley-BT]* sepult
12 Jan Johan. fs Guleilmi BLURTON sepult
17 Jan Foster CHELL Senex sepultus fuit
25 Jan Anna uxor Tho JOHNSON sepult
4 Feb Ellena fa Guliel HILL sepult
21 Feb Amos fs Rich SNAPE sepult
1695
13 May Gulielm fs Henr. et Sara HEATH sepult
14 May Margareta uxor Gulielm HILL sepult
6 Jun Elizabetha fa Franc. et Anna WALL ux sepult
20 Jun Jana uxor Francisci DYTCH sepulta fuit
25 Jun Maria MIDDLETON vid sepulta fuit
31 Aug Maria JELLEY *[Jolley-BT]* vid sepulta fuit
13 Dec Eliz. fa Hen. et Susan HEATON sepult
6 Jan Franciscus fs Fran. DICH sepult
6 Feb Joanna uxor Rich DITCH sepult
11 Feb Christian [written over Christibel] uxor Simon BRINLY sepult
18 Feb Will fil Will BAYLY sepultus fuit
28 Feb Anna fil Constantia STATHAM vid sepult
2 Mar Richardus PEDLY Senex sepultus fuit
8 Mar Elizabetha uxor Ric JUMP sepulta fuit
19 Mar Margareta JOHNSON vid seplta fuit
1696
4 Apr Moses fs Thoma HEIRS sepult
22 Apr Gulielm fs Catharina BRAMMALL sepult
18 May Gulielm fs Simonis et Margaria BLOOD sepult
6 Jun Elizab. fa Franc. et Jana DITCH sepult
16 Jun Thomas HOW Senex sepultus fuit
31 Jul Thomas fs Wm ETHRINGTON *[Etherington-BT]* sepult
1 Nov Tho MIDDLETON Senex sepultus fuit
12 Nov Georgius fs Georg et Anna JOHNSON sepult
21 Nov Sara uxor Ludov BARNS sepulta fuit
8 Dec Maria fa Franc & Marg LAKIN *[Marga Lakein-BT]*
29 Dec Elizabetha RUSHTON vid sepulta
24 Feb Elizab fa Tho & Susanna RUSHTON
1697
17 Apr Tho. fs Anth. et Maria WORRILOW *[Wirrelo-BT]*
23 Apr Ellena fa Joh. & Hanna HIDE sepult
13 Jun Ellena fa Franc. et Marg. SHERRAT sep
23 Aug Maria fa Georg. et Maria TURNER sep
13 Sep Elizabetha uxor Willmi TILL sepulta fuit
26 Sep Willmus fs Philip & Doroth HOLLINS sepult
4 Dec Margareta WATSON vid sepulta fuit
6 Dec Thomas MOORE Senex sepultus fuit
24 Dec Thomas fs Edvardi et Gra'a HOW sepult
9 Jan Prudentia BLURTON spinster sepulta fuit
13 Jan Samuel SMITH pauper sepultus fuit
2 Feb Anna COPE spinster sepulta fuit
16 Feb Anna ASBURY fa Thoma et Margareta ASBURY sepulta fuit

7 Mar   Sara fa Richardi et Eliz: SHERRATT sepulta fuit
20 Mar   Eliabetha fa Francisci et Jana DYCH sepulta fuit

1698

9 Apr   Anna GOUGH paupercula sepulta fuit
1 May   Anna HEELEY spinster sepulta fuit
7 May   Edvardus fs Thoma et Dorothea BOURNE sepultus erat
4 Oct   Johannes fs Henrici et Susanna HEATON sepultus erat
16 Dec   Thoma fs Henrici et Susanna HEATON sepultus fuit
21 Feb   Rodolphus TILSTON Senex sepult
21 Feb   Anna DAVIS vid: sepulta fuit
2 Mar   Maria YARDLY sepulta fuit
23 Mar   Lidia WITTERANCE vid sepulta fuit
30 Mar   Tho. fs Tho. et Francess JOHNSON sepult

1699

~~5 Apr~~   ~~Georgius SHERRAT sepultus fuit~~
~~15 Apr~~   ~~Gulielmus fs Simonis et Margaria BLOOD sepultus fuit~~
~~16 Apr~~   ~~Francisca uxor Tho. JOHNSON sepulta fuit~~
~~9 May~~   ~~Tho. WARD sepultus fuit~~
~~19 Jun~~   ~~Elizabetha COAPE~~

1702

7 Apr   *Thomas [BT]* fs Hugonis & Maria LEES sepultus
24 Apr   Maria DITCH sepulta fuit
25 Apr   Jacobus BRIGETS *[Brieryhurst-BT]* sepultus fuit
14 May   Elizabetha uxor Johannis SAUNDERS (Rectoris de Leigh) sepulta fuit
26 May   Johannes FERNS de Hilderson in Parochia de Stone sepultus fuit
20 Jun   Anna fa Johannis & Maria EDWARDS sepulta fuit
10 Sep   Edvardus BLURTON Senex sepultus fuit
26 Oct   Richardus fs Richardi et Anna DAVIS sepultus fuit
28 Nov   Franciscus SWINSHEAD Senex sepultus fuit
24 Jan   Thomas RUSHTON sepultus fuit
26 Feb   Elizabetha uxor Thoma COLECLOUGH de Feild sepulta fuit
9 Mar   Elizabetha ROYLY vidua pauperima sepulta fuit

1703

2 Apr   *Mary [BT] fa* Henrici *BAILY [BT]* sepulta fuit
20 Apr   *Sarah d/o George [BT]* RUSHTON sepulta fuit
28 Apr   Thomas JOHNSON de Middleton Green sepultus fuit
28 Apr   Gulielmus PHILLIPS senex sepultus fuit
4 May   Gulielmus WETTON Senex sepultus fuit
18 May   Thomas BLURTON Senex sepultus fuit
22 Jun   *Thomas s/o Thomas KNIGHT [BT] sepultus fuit*
25 Feb   *Francis s/o Richard EMBERY [BT] sepult*
12 Mar   *Prudence d/o Robert LAKIN [BT] sepulta fuit*
20 Mar   *Mary MERIDEN [BT] buried*

1704

25 Mar   *Margret SPENCER [BT]*
13 Jul   *Amy BOTT [BT]*
9 Aug   Josephus fs Johannis COLLIER sepultus fuit
7 Nov   Reverendus Franciscus ASHENHURST Rector de Kingswinford &
       Archdeaconis de Derbia sepultus fuit
7 Nov   Sara BARKER uxoris Johannis BARKER de Withington sepulta fuit
12 Feb   *Margret & John EMBERY*

7 Mar   Ann late wife of Francis WALL
15 Mar   Thomas HEALY of Boxhedge

[1696]   BAPTISMATA
25 Mar   Maria fa Roberti et Dorothea WOOD Baptizata fuit
13 Apr   Tho. fs Henrici HEATON et Sus. ux Baptizata fuit
10 May   Tho. fs Gulielm et Maria ETHRINGTON *[Etherington-BT]* Baptizata fuit
15 May   Hanna fa Joh. BARKER et Sara ux Baptizata fuit
4 Jun   Elizabetha fa Francisci & Jana DITCH *[Dych-BT]* Baptizata fuit
25 Jun   Gulielm fs Gulielmi et Margareta BLURTON Baptizata fuit
12 Jul   Johannes fs Richardi et Maria SNAPE Bapt
6 Aug   Elizabetha fa Tho. et Maria SHERRAT Baptizata
16 Aug   Elizabetha fa Johan et Sara WARDLE Baptiz
16 Aug   Johan fs Joh. et Jana DONE Baptizata fuit
3 Sep   Sara fa Richardi et Elizab. SHERRAT Baptizata
3 Sep   Rodolph fs Franc. et Margareta LAKIN *[Lakein-BT]* Baptiz
10 Oct   Maria fa Joh. et Elizab. TILL Baptiz
12 Oct   Elizabetha fa Joh. et Sara ARNET *[Arnald-BT]* Baptiz
5 Nov   Gulielm fs Edvardi et Anna BLURTON Baptiz
23 Nov   Thomas fs Willielmi et Johanna HOLLINS Baptiz *[added in margin]*
29 Dec   Richardus fs Sam. et Dorothea STEEL Baptiz
6 Jan   Guleilm fs Rich. et Gra. BAILY *[Bayley-BT]* Baptiz
6 Jan   Maria fa Hen. & Maria CHEL *[Chell-BT]* Baptiz
16 Jan   Tho. fs Franc et Anna WITTERANCE Baptiz
18 Jan   Sara fa Edvardi et Maria DAVIES *[Davis-BT]* Baptiz
7 Feb   Elizabetha fa Tho. et Susanna RUSHTON B...
24 Feb   Joh. fs Rich. et Maria DITCH *[Dytch-BT]* Baptizatus fuit
1697
25 Apr   Jonathan fs Guliel. et Joanna TUNSTAL Baptiz
25 Apr   Anna fa Johan. et Anna STANLY Baptizata fuit
13 May   Anna fa Thom. et Elizabetha COLLIER Baptiz
25 May   Edvardus fs Edvardi & Jana HOUGH Baptizatus
27 Jun   Elizabetha fa Francisci et Jana DITCH *[Dytch-BT]* Baptizata fuit
4 Jul   Maria fa Francisci et Margareta SHERRAT Baptizata fuit
20 Jul   Josephus fs Joseph et Edith HEALY *[Heeley-BT]* Baptiz
19 Aug   Edvardus fs Tho. & Dorothy BOURNE Baptizatus fuit
21 Aug   Sam. fs Sam. et Maria POTS *[Potts-BT]* Baptiz
21 Aug   Hannah fa Johann et Hann COAP *[Cope-BT]* Baptiz
22 Aug   Willm fs Joh. et Sara COLLIER Baptiz
5 Sep   Anna fa Richardi et Anna WILKS Baptiz
8 Sep   Willm fs Philippi et Dorothea HOLLINS Baptizata fuit
14 Oct   Elizabetha fa Tho. et Katharina OSBORN Baptizata fuit
24 Oct   Liddia fa Franc. et Anna WALL
24 Oct   Anna fa Johan et Maria THROWER
28 Oct   Catharina fa Wmi et Anna PHILLIPS Bap
22 Nov   Maria fa Tho. et Maria HEIRS Baptizata
28 Nov   Will: fs Tho et Sara PARKER Baptizata
9 Jan   Elizabetha fa Thoma et Sara JOHNSON de Withington Baptizata fuit
17* Jan   Johannes fs Henrici et Susanna HEATON de With*[ington]* Baptizatus fuit
         *[*10-BT]*
1 Feb   Elizabetha fa Francisci et Hanna SWINSHEAD Baptizata fuit

12 Mar Thomas fs Thoma et Maria SHERRATT Baptizatus erat
15 Mar Anna fa Francisci et Margareta LAKEIN *[Lakyn-BT]* Baptizata fuit
20 Mar David fs Richardi et Maria SNAPE Baptizatus fuit
1698
— 27 Mar Johannis fs Francisci & Dorothea LEES Baptizatus fuit
29 Mar Willielmus fs Simonis et Margaria BLOOD Baptizatus erat
— 20 Apr Anna fa Roberti et Dorothea WOOD Baptizata fuit
12*May Willielmus fs Willielmi et Maria JOHNSON Baptizatus fuit *[*21-BT2]*
26*May Lidia fa Thoma et Maria WITTERANCE Baptizata fuit *[*29-BT but 26-BT2]*
29 May Sara fa Thoma et Susanna RUSHTON Baptizata fuit
ـ 21 Jul Elizabetha fa Johannis SAUNDERS Rectoris de [Leigh] et Elizabetha ux
Baptiz fuit
[bottom of page illegible & damaged]
20 Aug John s/o Will et Margery BLURTON [BT]
27 Aug Eliz d/o John & Hanny HIDE [BT]
— 28 Aug Thomas fs Johannis et Jana DONE Baptizatus erat
— 18 Sep Ludovicus fs illegitimus Maria HILL Baptizara erat
2 Oct Joanna fa Ricardi et Maria DYTCH Baptiz fuit
16 Oct Willialmus fs Ricardi et Maria WHISTON Baptiz erat
— 16 Oct Maria fa Thoma et Dorothea BOURN *[Burne-BT]* Baptizata fuit
— 4 Dec Isaacus fs Thoma et Catherina BAYLEY Baptiz fuit
3 Jan Anna fa Joh et Elizabetha TILL Baptizata fuit
28 Jan Josephus fs Edvardae et Maria PEDLY Baptizatus fuit
8 Feb Johan fs Phillipi et Dorothea HOLLINS Baptizatus fuit
16 Feb Ellena fa Johannis & Maria SHIPLEY Baptizata fuit
8 Mar Elizabetha fa Henrici et Maria CHELL Baptizata fuit
17 Mar Tho fs Thom JOHNSON et Francis ux Baptizata fuit
19 Mar Joha fs Edvardi et Anna BLURTON Baptizatus fuit
23 Apr Dorothea fa Edvardi et Anna LAWRENCE Baptizata fuit
1699
— 30 Apr Edvardus fs Georgii TOOTH et *[Mary-BT]* ux Baptizatus fuit
*29 May [BT] Rodol*phus fs Johan et Sara BARKER Baptizatus fuit
17 Jun [BT] Samuel fs Edvardi et Jana HOUGH Baptizatus fuit
— *16 Jun [BT] Grace fa Richardi et Gratiana BAYLY*
16 Jul Hanna fa Francisci et Anna HARVEY Baptizata fuit
25 Sep Richardus fs Tho et Maria SHERRAT Baptizatus fuit
29 Oct Thomas fs Francisci et Jana DIKE *[Dich-BT]* de Nobot publici Baptizatus
fuit
— 31 Oct Maria fa Samuelis et Maria POTT privatum Baptizata fuit
12 Nov Gulielmus fs Edvardi et Maria THROWER *[Davis-BT]* de Middleton-green
publici Baptizatus fuit
2 Dec Maria fa Francisci et Margareta LAKIN de parochia Leigh in Com: Staff:
Baptizata fuit publici
— 28 Dec Anna fa Ricardi et Jana BULLOCK Baptizata fuit
31 Dec Thomas fs Josephi et Editha HEELEY Baptizatus fuit
1 Jan Edvardus fs Johannis et Margareta SHERRATT de Middleton- green
Baptizatus fuit
— 3 Jan Maria HEATH de Lee-church Ancilla Baptizata erat
7 Jan Robertus fs Henrici et Susanna HEATON Baptizatus fuit
— 27 Jan Dorothea fa Roberti et Dorothea WOOD de Field Baptizata fuit privatim

---

8 Feb	Maria fa Johannis SAUNDERS Rectoris de Leigh et Elizabetha ux Baptizata fuit
24 Feb	Margareta fa Edvardi et Maria PEDLEY Baptizata fuit
16 Mar	Johanna fa Gulielmi BLURTON et ux de Checkly-bank Baptizata fuit
1700	
30*Mar	Thomas fs Johannis et Sara EDWARDS Baptizatus est [*31-BT]
27 Apr	Thomas fs Johannis et Sara COLLIER de Field in Parochia Lee Baptizatus est
23 May	Anna fa Guleilmi PHILIPS junioris et Ann IGI ux Baptizata fuit
23 May	Johannes ~~BRIERYHURST~~ fs Jacobi et Juditha BRIERYHURST [Brerehurst-BT] Baptizatus est
1703	**[BIRTHS]**
.. ….	Gulielmus fs ……………………..
1 [?] Dec	Catharina fa Thoma BAILY ….. ux eius nata fuit
27 Dec	Johannes fs Thoma et Maria WITTERANCE ………..
7 Jan	Anna fa Roberti & Elizabetha BAILY nata fuit
.. Feb	Franciscus fs illegitimus Ricardi EMBERY et Margareta HILL [?]
21 Jan [?]	Rebeca [?] fa illegitima Roberti FRADSLY [?] & Elizabetha M…
28 Feb	Johannes fs Henrici & Maria CHELL ………….
23 [?] Mar	Sara fa Ricardi NOWLS & Elizabetha nata fuit
1704	
.. …	Josephus fs Johannis & Sara COLLIER natus fuit
.. Apr	Gulielmus fs Will [ielmi] & Joanna HOLLINS natus fuit
.. …	Thomas fs ……………. TILL ………..
.. ….	Anna fa Richardi & Elizabetha HOILE [?]
7 May [?]	Johannes fs Richardi HODGESON ………
.. Jun	Robertus fs Ricardi BAILIE …………. uxoris
12 …	Anna fa Francisci OSBORN…………….
.. Aug	Elizabetha fa Edvardi COOKE & ux
.. …	Elizabetha fa Johannis & Elizabetha PHILIPS ….
27 …	Maria fa Simonis & Catherina WETTON ………
31 Aug	Jocosa fa Edvardi LAURENCE & ux nata fuit
.. …	Georgius fs Johannis & Margarita SHERRAT de ……..
.. Nov	Margareta fa Roberti & Dorothea WOOD de Field nata fuit
.. Nov	Thomas fs Johannis & Anna CARTER natus fuit
.. Dec	Dorothea fa Thoma …………………….
28 …	Prudentia fa Roberti LAKIN ………………
.. Dec	Anna [?] fa Phillipi & Dorothea [HOLLINS?]
	[top half of next page completely illegible]
	[Baptisms]
	[see list from-BT's at end of this transcription]
10 May	Thomas fs Edvardi & Dorothea TILL
18 May	Anna fa Ricardi & Maria HOILE Baptizata fuit
5 Jun	Johannis fs Ricardi HODGSON Baptizatus fuit
5 Jun	Thomas fs Gulielmi ……… Baptiz [not in-BT]
2 Jul [BT]	Robertus fs Ricardi BAILIE ……..
2 Jul	[A]nna fa Francisci OSBORN ………..
11 Aug	Elizabeth fa Edvardi COOKE ……
11 Aug	[Elizab]etha fa Johannis & Elizabetha PHILLIPS Baptizata fuit
17 Aug	Maria fa Simonis & Catherina WETTON Baptizata
3 Sep	Jocosa fa Edvardi LAWRENCE Baptizata fuit

.... & Margareta ....
Ma....... ....

30 *Nov [BT]* Thomas fs *John [BT]* . ... CARTER .... fuit.
[illegible & damaged]

1699 MATRIMONIALIA

3 Jan Edvardus FENNIMORE paroch de Uttoxeter et Jocosa SHERRAT proch: de Leigh in matrimonio confuncti fuere

5 Jan Christopherus TOMLINSON paroch de Ashbourne in Cmit Derby et Helena LEES paroch de Bromshulf in Comit Stafford in matrimonio Conjuncti fuere 1698/9

1699

21 May Johannes PHILLIPS de Leigh paroch et Elizabetha TILL de Leigh proch in matrimonio conjuncti fuere

1700

3 Nov Johannes CARTWRIGHT de Leigh et Elizabetha SHERRAT de Leigh in matriminio conjuncti fuere 1701

1702

11*May Ricardus DAVIS de Paroch de Leig..... & Anna *HARRISON [BT]* ... eadem in matrinonio conjuncti fuere *[*9-BT]*

8 Feb Henricus BRADSHAW et Dorothea LEADBEATER de parochia de Chedle in matrimonio sua conjuncti fuere

1703

27 Jul Thomas SNAPE de paroch de Tamoth *[BT]* et Maria HEATH huius parochia in matrimonio conjuncti fuere
[rest of page illegible]
[following entries taken from BTs]

21 Sep *Richard HOILE & Mary BULLOCK both of Leigh parish*

23 Sep *John BELCHER & Elizabeth MARLER both of Field in the parish of Leigh*

13 Feb *John CARTER of Stow Parish & Ann HEALEY of Leigh Parish*

1699 SEPULTUS

14 Jan Margareta FENTON sepulta fuit

9 Mar Tho. TOWNSEND sepultus fuit

5 Apr Georgius SHERRAT sepultus fuit

15 Apr Willielmus fs Simonis & Margeria BLOUD sepult

16 Apr Frances uxor Tho. JOHNSON sepulta fuit

9 May Thomas WARD sepultus fuit

21 May Thomas BLOUD sepultus fuit

21 May Dorothy uxor Franc. LEES sepulta fuit

31 May Elizabetha COPE vid. sepulta fuit

6 Jun Johannes HIDE Senex sulpultus fuit

8 Jun Anna LOW *[Loe-BT]* vidua sepulta fuit

9 Jun Johannes HOLLINS sepultus fuit

14 Jun Ellina uxor Richardi CARTWRIGHT sepult

19 Jun Elizabetha COAP de Middleton Green vidua sepulta fuit

1 Aug Thomas LEES de Middleton Green sepultus fuit

3 Aug Johannes HILL de Leigh Town sepultus fuit

18 Aug Jacobus EVELEY Paroch: de Leigh sepultus est

3 Oct Richardus LOW *[Loe-BT]* de Withington sepultus fuit

4 Nov Thomas CHAPLIN de Dodsley Paroch: de Leigh sepultus fuit

5 Nov Sara JOHNSON de Withington sepulta fuit

6 Nov   Elizabetha OSBOURN de Withington Paroch: p'dict: vidua sepulta fuit

23 Nov   Johannes BLURTON de Checkley-bank Paroch: de Lee, Colonas sepultus fuit

13*Dec   Johanna fa Ricardi et Maria DITCH de Nobott, in Paroch: Lee sepulta fuit [*14-BT]

14 Dec   Maria ADEN [Adin-BT] de Leigh inferiore vidua sepulta fuit

9 Jan   Eleonora HOW de Leigh sepulta fuit

20 Jan   Thomas OSBOURN de Withington sepultus fuit

24 Jan   Jana PEDLY vidua de Withington sepulta fuit

16 Feb   Anna fa Ricardi et Jana BULLOCK sepulta fuit

1700

24* Apr   Samuelis STEEL hujus Parochia Incola sepultus fuit [*altered in register – 24-BT]

2 Jun   Robertus BELCHER de Field sepultus fuit

9 Jun   Gulilemus fs Gulielmi et Maria JOHNSON de Leigh sepultus fuit

25 Jun   Thomas HOW junior de Lee-town sepultus est

11 Oct   Francisca SNAPE de Middleton-green sepulta fuit

6 Nov   Dorothea FENTON de Dodsley sepulta fuit

8 Dec   Dorothea COLECLOUGH de Field sepulta fuit

18 Dec   Edvardus WOOD de Leigh-town sepultus fuit

10 Jan   Maria PURFURY [Purify-BT] de Foal vidua sepulta fuit

13 Jan   Agatha HILL de Lee-town, infans, sepulta fuit

21 Jan   Margareta TAYLOR de Field, vidua gra'dava, sepulta fuit

23 Jan   Thomas COAP de Middleton-green, puer pauperium, sepultus fuit

28 Feb   Margareta BROMWELL de Nobott, virgo grandis, sepulta fuit

21 Mar   Edmundus fs Reverendi Domini Francisci ASHENHURST Rectoris de Kingswinford, et Anna ux sepultus fuit

1701

29 Apr   Maria PURFURY [Purify-BT] junior de Foal, virgo pauper, sepulta fuit

10 May   Maria fa illegitima Elizabetha MOORECROFT de Middleton-green, pauperis, sepulta fuit

27 May   Johannes SONT de Long-lease in parochial Bramshall sepultus fuit

28 Jun   Catherina OUFE [Woofe-BT] de Foale virgo sepulta fuit

21 Aug   Joanna fa Josephi HOROBBIN sepulta fuit

20 Dec   Thomas BAILY Senex sepultus fuit

1700   **BAPTISMATA**

23 Jun   Gulielmus RATCLIFF de Checkley-bank fs Isaaci et Anna RATCLIFF [Rallife-BT] Baptizata est

30 Jun   Dorothea fa Thoma et Sara PARKER de Withington Baptizata est

28 Jul   Elizabetha fili Ricardi et Maria DITCH de Nobott Baptizata fuit

30 Jul   Johannes fs Johannis et Elizabetha PHILIPS de Lee-town baptizatus est

19*Aug   Jacobus fs illegitimus Elizabetha LAKIN de Withington-green Baptizatus est [*15-BT]

25 Aug   Anna fa Francisci et Margareta SHERRATT de Middleton-green Baptizata fuit

29 Aug   Brigida SWINSHEAD fa Francisci et Hanna SWINSHEAD Baptizata fuit

30 Aug   Gulielmus fs Gulielmi et Dorothea BAYLY de Morrily-Heath Baptizatus fuit

13 Sep   Rutha fa illegitima Johanna LAKIN de Withington-green Baptizata fuit

15 Nov   Dorothea BOURN fa Thoma et Dorothea BOURN [Burne-BT] de Nobott Baptizata est

8*Nov   Thomas fs Ricardi et Elizabetha SHERRATT de Nobott Baptizatus est
       *[*16-BT]*
10*Nov   Johannes fs Thoma et Jana JOHNSON de ....ton-green Baptizatus est
       *[*19-BT]*
20 Jan   Ricardus fs Ricardi WHISTON de Foal Agricola et Maria ux Baptizatus est
25 Jan   Johanna fa Johannis TILL, sutoris, et Elizabetha ux Baptizata est
13 Mar   Stephanus fs Francisci HARVEY de Field Agricola et Anna ux Baptizatus
       est

1701
25 Mar   Adeliza *[Ales-BT]* fa Thoma WITTERANCE de Foal, cole..., et
       Maria ux Baptizata est
23 Mar   Robertus fs Edv BLURTON de Parkha[ll], Lanii, et Anna ux
       eius Baptizatus est
 3 Apr   Thomas fs Gulielmi TUNSTALL *[Tulston-BT]* de Morrilly [?]
       ....a ux *[page damaged – mother's name not in-BT]* Baptizat
 6 Apr   *Tho s/o Tho & Susanay RUSHTON [BT]*
 3 May   Sara fa Francisci et Margareta LAKIN de Withington-green,
       pauperum, Baptizata fuit
29 Jun   Sampson fs Henrici CHELL et Maria ux.... Baptizatus fuit
20 Jul   Ellena fa Johannes DONE et Jana ux Baptizata fuit
 3 Aug   Ricardus fs Ricardi SNAPE et Maria ux Baptizatus fuit
 4 Sep   Elizabetha fa Thoma HITCHCOCK *[Hidgcock-BT]* et Elizab... ux Baptizata
       fuit
14 Sep   Dorothea fa Johannes SHAW et Alicia uxor.. eius Baptizata fuit
 5 Oct   Elizabetha fa Thoma BAILY et ux Baptizata fuit
 5 Oct   Editha fa Josephi HEELY et Aditha ux Baptizata fuit
 5 Oct   Dorothea fa Johannis SAUNDERS et Elizabetha ux Baptizata fuit
16 *[BT]* Oct   Gulielmus fs Thoma SHERRAT & .... Baptizatus fuit *[wife's name*
       not in-BT]
    23 Oct   *Jana [BT]* fa Edvardi PEDLY et Ma *[damaged]* Baptizata fuit
 6 *[BT]* Nov   Samuel fs Henrici HEATON et .... ux Baptizatus fuit
20 *[BT]* Jan   Thomas fs Hugonis LEES et Maria [?] Baptizatus fuit
    24 *Jan*   *Jana [BT]* fa Roberti LAKIN et Elizabetha ux
26 *Jan [BT]*   Sara fa Johannis et Sara LINY Baptizatus fuit
29 *Jan [BT]*   Johannes fs Johannis COAPE et Eliza....
       [bottom of page damaged]
       [following entries from BT]
29 *Jan*   *Elizabeth d/o Robert WOOD*
19 *Feb*   *Martha d/o Richard MOORE*
1701/2
 7 *Mar*   Helena *[Ellen-BT]* fa Thomas et Maria WRIGHT Baptizata fuit
22 Mar   Franciscus fs Francisci et Maria OSBORNE Baptizatus
1702
25 Mar   Johannes fs Thoma & Elizabetha COLLIER Baptizatus fuit
28 Mar   Ricardus fs Ricardi & Anna DAVIS alias THROWER Baptizatus fuit
31 Mar   Gulielmus fs Johannis & Elizabetha PHILLIPS Baptizatus fuit
29 Mar   Ricardus fs Ricardi & Gratia BAYLIE Baptizatus fuit
12 Apr   Maria fa Philippi & Dorothea HOLLINS Baptizata fuit
10 May   Maria fa Georgii & Maria TOOTH Baptizata fuit
 7 Jun   Anna fa Johannis & Maria EDWARDS Baptizata fuit
15 Jun   Gulielmus fs Gulielmi & Maria STANDLY Baptizatus fuit

16 Jul   Thomas fs Gulielmi & Maria TUNSTALL Baptizatus fuit
9 Aug   *Hanna [BT] fa Edvardi & ……….. DAVIS Baptizata fuit*
— 23 Aug   *Jana [BT] fa Ricardi & Joanna BULLOCK*
13 Sep   Thomas fs Thoma TILL ………..
26 Sep   Maria [?] fa Francisci & Joanna DYTCH Baptiz….. [not in-BT]
24 Sep   *Richard s/o John COLLIER bap [BT entry not in parish register]*
7 Oct   Johannes fs Johannis & Elizabetha TILL Baptizata fuit
⌐ 11 Oct   Sara fa *Thoma [BT]* & …… PARKER Baptizata fuit
20 Oct   *Sara [BT] fa Johannis & Maria WINDLE [BT] Baptizata fuit*
.. Nov   ………………..is …………… [not in-BT]
— 23 [?] Oct   Johannes fs Roberti & Dorothea WOOD [not in-BT]
5 Nov   *Margareta fa Johannes SHERRAT [BT]*
⌐ 8 Nov   *Hanna fa Georgius VERNON [BT]*
29 Nov   *Ellen d/o Richard HOLLAND [BT] baptizata …..*
9 Dec   *Frances d/o John ARNOLD [BT]*
14 Jan   Thomas fs Thoma & Eliza *COLECLOUGH [BT]* Baptizatus fuit
4 Feb   Brigida fa Johannes & Elizabetha *CARTWRIGHT [BT]* Baptizata fuit
28 Feb   Johannis fs Ricardi & Maria MORECROFT Baptizatus fuit
18 Mar   Francisca fa Francisci & Anna LAKIN Baptizata fuit
1703
1 Apr   Franciscus fs Francisci & ……. *HARVY [BT]*
4 Apr   Catharina fa Ricardi & Elizabetha SHERRAT
10 Apr   Sara fa *Georgii [BT]* & Maria RUSHTON
18 Apr   *Anna [BT] fa Edvardi & ……… BLURTON*
25 Apr   *Hester fa Josephi HEALY [BT]*
6 Jun   *Johannes fs Henrici HEATON [BT]*
14 Jun   *Thoma [BT] fs* Thoma & Joanna KNIGHT Baptizatus
22 Jun   *Edvardus [BT] fs* Tho [ma] & Maria SHERRAT Baptiz….
4 Jul   *William [BT]* Thomas fs Ric….. DAVIS
— 11 Jul   *Margeria fa Gulielmi & ……… BAILIE [BT]*
15 Jul   *Elizabeth d/o William PHILLIPS [BT]*
21 Aug   *Thomas s/o Richard EMBERY [BT]*
7 Oct   *Anna fa Laurentis & ………. AUSTIN [BT]*
16 Oct   Franciscus fs Francisci & Hanna *SWINSHEAD [BT]*
⌐ 17 Oct   Jacobus fs Johannis & Jana DONE Baptizatus fuit
5 Nov   *Prudentia fa Roberti & Jana LAKIN [BT]*
7 Nov   *Gulielmus fs Gulielmi CLAY [BT]*
— 5 Dec   Catherina fa Thoma BAILY *[Bailie-BT]*……….
1 Jan   *Johannes fs Thoma WITTERANCE [BT]*
— 14 Jan   *Anna fa Roberti & Elizabetha BAILIE [BT]*
[Remainder of register is illegible – the following entries are in the Bishops Transcripts]
13 Feb   *Francis s/o Richard EMBERY*
1 Mar   *Rebecca d/o Robert FRADSLY*
12 Mar   *John s/o Henry CHELL*
   1704
2 Apr   *Sara d/o Richard NOWLS*
16 Apr   *Joseph s/o John COLLIER*
20 Apr   *William s/o William HOLLINS*
10 May   *Thomas s/o Edward TILL*
18 May   *Ann d/o Richard HOILE*
5 Jun   *John s/o Richard HODGSON*

2 Jul   Robert s/o Richard BAILIE
2 Jul   Anne d/o Francis OSBORNE
11 Aug   Elizabeth d/o Edward COOKE
11 Aug   Elizabeth d/o John PHILLIPS
17 Aug   Mary d/o Simon WETTON
3 Sep   Joyce d/o Edward LAURENCE
20 Oct   George s/o John SHERRAT
13 Nov   Margret d/o Robert WOOD
30 Nov   Thomas s/o John CARTER
26 Dec   Prudence d/o Robert LAKIN
7 Jan   Anne d/o Philip HOLLINS
25 Jan   Richard s/o Francis DITCH
27 Jan   John s/o Richard EMBERY
2 Feb   Sarah d/o Thomas SHERRAT
11 Feb   John s/o John CARTWRIGHT
11 Feb   Richard s/o Richard MOORE
23 Feb   Thomas s/o John TILL
1 Mar   Anne d/o Joseph HEALY
4 Mar   Richard s/o Richard DAVIS
8 Mar   John s/o Francis LAKIN
9 Mar   John s/o Richard WISTON
11 Mar   John s/o John HARRIS
18 Mar   John s/o John ARNOLD
18 Mar   Mary d/o Thomas COLLIER
18 Mar   John s/o Francis HARVY

Leigh, Staffordshire, Parish Register
1704 –1767

John SAUNDERS Rect'r de Leigh
Gulielmus SAUNDERS Curatus de Leigh
1714

Registerum pro Parochia de Leigh incoatum Anno Dom 1704

Baptism

1704

2 Feb	Sara fa Thoma & Maria SHERAT	Born 17 Jan
11 Feb	Johannes fs Johannis & Elizabetha CARTWRIGHT	Born 7 Feb
11 Feb	Ricardus fs Ricardi & Maria MORECROFT *[Moore BT]*	Born 27 Jan
23 Feb	Thomas fs Johannis & Elizabetha TILL	Born 4 Feb
1 Mar	Anna fa Josephi & Editha HEALY	Born 31 Jan
1 Mar	Anna fa Georgii & Maria TOOTH	Born 16 Feb
4 Mar	Ricardus fs Ricardi & Anna DAVIS alias THROWER	Born 26 Feb
8 Mar	Johannes fs Fransisci LAKIN	Born 17 Feb
9 Mar	Johannes fs Ricardi & Maria WISTON	Born 16 Feb
9*Mar	Johannes fs Johannis HARRIS & ux Joanna *[*11 BT]*	Born 20 Feb
18 Mar	Johannes fs Johannis ARNOLD & ux Sarah	Born 16 Feb
18 Mar	Maria fa Thoma COLLIER de Middleton Green	Born 20 Feb
18 Mar	Johannes fs Francisci HARVEY de Field	Born 5 Mar
30 Mar 1705	Franciscus fs Gulielmi & Hanna TUNSTALL	Born 17 Mar

1705

6 May	Elizabetha fa Johannis & Margareta BAILIE	Born 25 Apr
6 May	Martha fa Henrici BAILIE de Morrely-heath	Born 25 Apr
6 Jun	Maria fa Gulielmi & Dorothea WHILTON	Born 30 May
5 Jul	Elizabeth fa Henrici & Susanna HEATON	Born 5 Jul
26 Jul	Margareta fa Johannis & Elizabetha BELCHER	Born 10 Jul
12 Aug	Johannes fs Ricardi & Dorothea HOLLAND	Born 30 Jul
2 Sep	Elizabetha fa Johannis & Alicia SHAW	Born 1 Sep
18 Oct	Sara fa Gulielmi & Joanna HOOMS	Born 24 Sep
24 Oct	Franciscus fs Johannis & Jana DONE	Born 1 Oct
8 Nov	Elizabetha fa Edvardi & Anna BLURTON	Born 2 Nov
18 Nov	Catherina fa Thoma & Catherina BAILIE	Born 2 Nov
18 Nov	Maria fa Ricardi & Maria HOILE	Born 5 Nov
30 Nov	Johannes fs Thoma & Maria WRIGHT	Born 27 Nov
2 Dec	Josephus fs Ricardi DYTCH	Born 30 Nov
26 Dec	Thomas fs Roberti HOLLINS	Born 16 Dec
18 Jan	Ricardus fs Ricardi BAILIE	Born 2 Jan
22 Jan	Maria fa Edvardus & Dorothea TILL	Born 23 Dec
15 Feb	Robertus fs Roberti & Dorothea WOOD	Born 8 Feb
23 Feb	Gulielmus fs Ricardi & Elizabetha NOWLS	Born 20 Feb
17 Mar	Thomas fs Roberti & Elizabetha FRADSLY alias SMITH	Born 1 Mar
	exam P Joh Yapp …..	

1706

4 Aug	Sara fa Gulielmi & Joanna HOLLINS	Born 22 Jul
13 Aug	Ricardus fs Ricardi & Elizabetha JACKSON	Born 12 Aug
15 Aug	Thomas fa Thoma & Maria WHITTERANCE *[Whiterance-BT]*	Born 8 Aug

4 Nov   Francisca fa Ricardi & Elizabetha SHERRATT
24 Nov Benjaminus fs Josephi HEALY
1 Dec   Johannes fs Johannis LEES
15 Dec Johannes fs Thoma & Maria SHERRAT
26 Dec Richardus fs Francisci OSBOURNE *[Osborne-BT]*
23 Jan   Thomas fs Thoma SNAPE de Tamworth
27 Jan   Ricardus fs Rogeri RICHARDSON
16 Mar Ricardus fs Thoma TILL
1707
27 Mar Johannes fs Gulielmi & Dorothea WHILTON
14 Apr   Jana fa Roberti HOLLINS
16 Apr   Maria fa Edvardi COOKE
8 May   Sara fa Johannis TILL
11 May   Jocosa fa Roberti LAKIN
2 Jun   Gulielmus fs Ricardi MOORE
29 Jun   Thomas fs Simonis WETTON
29 Jun   Edvardus fs Ricardi DAVIS
3 Jul   Johannes fs Johannis WAKEFIELD
10 Jul   Johannes fs Johannis STARTIN
31 Jul   Maria fa Gulielmi & Anna PHILLIPS
24 Aug Elizabetha fa Johannis DONE
12 Oct   Georgius fs Georgii TOOTH
17 Oct   Isabella fa Joanna HARRIS
4 Nov   Thomas fs Johannis & Alicia SHAW
20 Nov Helena fa Johannis CARTWRIGHT
25 Nov Johannes fs Ricardi LYON de Ridware
13 Dec Johannes fs Johannis BELCHER
25 Dec Johanna fa Francisci SWINSHEAD
14 Jan   Hanna fa Gulielmi TUNSTAL
15 Jan   Elizabetha fa Edvardi TILL
12 Feb   Maria fa Edvardi BLURTON
22 Feb   Ricardus fs Francisci OSBORNE
23 Feb   Thomas fs Francisci HARVEY
24 Mar Gulielmus fs Roberti HOLLINS
1708
8 Apr   Thomas fs Ricardi KNOWLS
18 Apr   Thomas fs Henrici CHELL
18 Apr   Dorothea fa Phillippi HOLLINS
11 Jul   Aron fs Josephi HEELY
18 Jul   Thomas fs Thoma BAILIE *[Bealie-BT]*
7 Aug   Letitia HOLLINS fa Gulielmi
26 Aug Ricardus fs Francisci LACHIN
12 Sep   Elizabetha fa Johannis LEES
17 Oct   Elizabetha fa Johannis HAMSON
21 Oct   Hanna fa Johannis STARTIN
12 Nov   Francisca fa Thoma & Maria SHERRATT
26 Dec Henricus fs Henrici BAILIE
6 Jan   Prudentia fa Ricardi BAILIE
25 Feb   Rachaelis fs Francisci SWINSHEAD
27 Feb   Johannes fs Roberti BAILIE
6 Mar   Jana fil Johannis DONE

1709

26 Mar	Anna fa Thoma TILL
27 Mar	Sara fa Johannis COLLIER
20 Apr	Thomas fs Gulielmi HARVEY
26 Apr	Maria fa Roberti BELCHER
28 Apr	Elizabetha fa Roberti FRADSLEY
13 May	Margarita fa Johannis WAKEFIELD
19 May	Jana fa Thoma WOODRUFF *de Beamhurst [BT]*
20 May	Johannes fs Johannis LOW
26 May	Maria fa Roberti HOLLINS
8 Jun	Jana fa Josephi TURNER
11 Jun	Robertus fs Johannis ARNOLD
10 Jul	Dorothea fa Phillippi HOLLINS
1 Aug	Helena fa Georgii & Maria ATKINS
7 Aug	Lea fa Roberti LAKIN *[Lachin-BT]*
10 Oct	Thomas fs Moses VISE
23*Oct	Maria fa Georgii DEAKIN *[*13-BT]*
1 Nov	Edvardus fs Edvardi COOKE
6 Nov	Anna fa Josephi DEAKIN
17 Nov	Phillippus fs Thoma PARKER
20 Nov	Elizabetha fa Johannis CARTWRIGHT
26 Dec	Jana fa Francicsi DYTCH
17 Jan	Gulielmus fs Gulielmi WHILTON
5 Mar	Sara fa Ricardi HOILE
12 Mar	Anna fa illegitima Roberti MOORE

1710

10 Apr	Maria fa Thoma WHITTERANCE
20 Apr	Catherina fa Johannis WAKEFIELD
25 May	Gulielmus fs Johannis BELCHER
29 May	Gulielmus fs Johannis HAMSON
30 May	Elizabetha fa Samuelis B ARNFIELD
10 Jun	Catherina fa Thoma SHERRATT
14 Jun	Franciscus fs Ricardi KNOWLS
22 Jul	Johannes fs Josephi HEALY
18 Aug	Johannes fs Thoma TILL
31 Aug	Josephus fs Roberti HOLLINS
10 Sep	Maria fa Ricardi DYTCH
12 Oct	Maria fa Johannes STARTIN
30 Oct	Gulielmus fs Edvardi TILL
4 Nov	Gulielmus fs Francisci HARVEY
12 Nov	Elizabetha fa Mosis VISE
6 Dec	Maria fa Johannis TOMBLISON
14 Jan	Dorothea fa Johannis LEES
13 Mar	Maria fa Josephi DEAKIN

1711

2 Apr	Samuel fs Samuelis WOOLLY
2 Apr	Gulielmus fs Thoma HILL
5 Apr	Anna fa Gulielmi TAYLER
7 Jun	Maria fa Johannis HAMSON
10 Jun	Thomas fs Ricardi DAVIS
15 Jul	Maria fa Ricardi BAILIE

19 Jul	Johannes fs Johannis GARRETT
9 Aug	Moses fs Mosis JOHNSON
9 Aug	Marcus fs Henrici BAILIE
7 Oct	Maria fa Gulielmi HARVEY
21 Oct	Elizabetha fa Roberti HOLLINS
23 Oct	Helena fa Thoma SHERRATT
6 Nov	Gulielmus fs Jacobi MARSON
10 Nov	Susanna fa Johannis TILL
27 Dec	Johannes fs Thoma ARMISHAW
24 Dec	Anna fa Georgii DEAKIN
20 Jan	Gulielmus fs Sam: HOLLINS
30 Jan	Anna fa Thoma CARTER
2 Feb	Gualterus fs Edvardi BLURTON
3 Feb	Thomas fs Ricardi MOOR
18 Feb	Gulielmus fs illegitimus Eliz: LATHBURY
24 Feb	Dorothea fa Roberti BAILIE
28 Feb	Margareta fa Thoma RATFORD
13 Mar	Johannes fs Francisci PHILLIPS

1712

30 Mar	Maria & Sara gemelli fa Johannis & Jana DONE
10 Apr	Robertus fs Johannis BELCHER
26 Apr	Maria fa Johannis SHERRATT
12 Jun	Georgius fs Georgii ATKINS
24 Jul	Georgius fs illegitimus Hanna JOHNSON
17 Aug	Hannah fa John: et Elizabetha CARTWRIGHT
8 Sep	Anna fa Thoma & Anna TILL
17 Sep	Ric: fs Ric: & Anna SHERRATT
27 Sep	Eliz: fa Jobi & Elizabetha BIRD
28 Oct	Guliel: fs Gulielmi et Anna DANIEL
30 Oct	Robertus fs Roberti et [ ] BELCHER
20 Dec	Eliz. fa Anton. & Eliz. BROWN
27 Dec	Edwardus fs Edwar: et Doroth TILL

1713

23 Jan	Eliz: fa Roberti et Gratia HOLLINS de Dairy House
21 Feb	Eleanora fa Phillipi et Dodorthea HOLLINS
22 Feb	Gulielmus fs Thoma et Eliz: RATFORD
5 Mar	Thomas fs Johannis et [ ] TOMLINSON
31 Mar	Johannes fs Gulielm: et Joanna HOLLINS
22 Mar	Thomas fs Roberti et Eliz MIDDLETON
6 Apr	David fs Tho: BAYLY
6 Apr	Margareta fa Thoma et Martha HILL
26 Apr	Anna fa Simonis et [ ] BLUER
10 May	Jana HARVEY fa Francisci et Anna
10 Jun	Eliz et Lydia gemella fa Jacobi et Dorothea MARSON
17 Jun	Sarah fa Jons et Jana AMSON
25 Jun	Hannah fa Joh: et Anna STARTIN
27 Jun	Catherina fa Thoma et Maria SHERRATT
29 Jun	Thomas filis illegitimus Isabella LAKIN
9 Aug	Anna fa Johannis LEES
6 Sep	Thomas fs Thoma et Ann: ASTBURY *[Asbury-BT]*
12 Oct	Joseph et Anna fs et fa Gulil et Doroth WHILTON

5 [?] Nov Thomas fs illegitimus, natus et baptiz (post nuptias, anno quart parte) Eliz. olim FENTON, nunc

5 Nov *Tho: fs Tho: et Eliz: BLUER [BT]*

6 Dec Maria fa Gualt: et Maria HORDERN

20 Dec Maria fa Johs et Jana CADMAN *[Cadmon-BT]*

3 Jan Thomas fs Joh: et Ann: TUNSTALL

20 Jan Margareta fa Antonii et Eliz. BROWN

31 Jan Margareta fa Magsti Johes et Maria SHERRATT de Painsley Hill

16 Feb Josephs. JOHNSON fs Mos: et Sar:

23 Feb Ricards. fs Francisci et Maria PHILLIPS

7 Mar Elizab fa Ric: et Maria MOOR

8 Mar Maria fa Thoma SCILETO

1714

29 Mar *Rob. fs [ ] [BT]*

29 Mar Johannes fs Johns & Eliz TURNER

29 Mar Gratia fa Roberti et Gratia HOLLINS

4 Apr Maria fa Thom: et Eliz: RATFORD

7 Apr Ellena fa GUIL: et Eliz. DANIEL

9 May Thomas fs Thoma et Maria ARMISHAW

8 Jun Eliz fa Johns RUSHTON

1 Jul Rob: fs Robt. BAILEY

11 Jul Ann fa illeg: Ann CARTWRIGHT pauperis vagabondi

3 Jun Georgius fs Georgii DEAKIN

29 Jul Thom. fs Johns et Eliz. BELCHER

22 Aug Jana fa Josepi et Edith. HEALY

2 Sep Fran: fs Franc. KEEN

26 Sep John fs Tho: BUCKLEY de Checkley

17 Oct Johns MIDDLETON fs Roberti

21 Oct Josephus fs Josepi DEAKIN

1 Jan Maria fa Georgii ATKIN

3 Jan Guil. SHAWE fs Johns et Alicia

15 Jan Tho: fs Tho: et Martha HILL

13 Mar Simon fs Sim BLUER *[et Ellen-BT]*

1715

1 Apr Diana fa Guil: et Joanna HOLLINS

19 May Thomas fs Johannis & Margareta GERRATT

24 May Thomas fs Johannis et Elizabetha CARTWRIGHT

1 Jun Maria fa Radulphi & Lydia TURNER

12 Jun Elizabetha fa Maria PHILLIPS vid.

26 Jun Maria fa Johanis & Jana HAMPSON

3 Jul Johannes fs Thoma & Margaretta CARTAR

5 Jul Elizabetha fa Philippi & Dorothea HOLLINS

21 Jul Elizabetha fa Roberti & Ellena THACKER

29 Jul Johannes fs Jobi & Elizab: BYRD

11 Aug Nathaniel fs Johannis & Elizabeta BELCHER

18 Aug Ellena fa Joha'is & Ellena RAWLINS

27 Sep Hanna fa Edvardi & Elizabet. COOK

9 Oct Maria fa Johannis & Eliz. TURNER

31 Oct Johannes fs Johannis & Anna TOMLINSON

15 Nov Johannes fs Edvardi & Dorothea TILL

27 Nov Elizabetha fa Rogeri & Hannah RICHARDSON

2 Dec   Ellena fa Thoma & Elizab. RADFORD *[Ratford-BT]*
17 Dec   Elizabetha fa illegitima Hanna LOCKER
26 Jan   Thoma fs Johan & Ann: STARTIN
29 Jan   Johannes fs Antonii & Elizabetha BROWN
19 Feb   Thomas fs Thoma BUCKLEY de Checkley Bank
19 Feb   Maria fa Roberti & Ellena HEATON
23 Feb   Maria fa Gulielmi & Elizabetha HITCHCOCK
22 Mar   Diana fa Thoma & Martha HILL
1716
26 Apr   Juditha fa Roberti & Maria MIDDLETON
30 Apr   Franciscus fs Samuelis & Ellena WOOLEY
8 May   Richardus fs Mosis & Sara JOHNSON
22 May   Frianciscus & Thomas gemelli fi Jacobi & Doroth. MARSON
3 Jul   Jacobus fs Thoma & Maria SHERRATT
13 Sep   Jana fa Jacobi & Jana BAKER
30 Sep   Gulielmus fs Guliel & Anna DANIEL
21 Oct   Elizabetha fa Richardi & Maria MOOR
5 Nov   Amata fa Jacobi & Joanna BEALEY
11 Nov   Maria fa Thoma & Maria ARMISHAW
25 Nov   Samuel fs Roberti & Gratia HOLLINS
11 Dec   Elizabetha fa Georgii & Maria AYTKIN
3 Jan   Georgius fs Gul & Maria JOHNSON
13 Jan   Johannes fs illegitimus Maria HANSELL
17 Jan   Jodoca *[Joyce-BT]* fa Johannis & Maria SHERRATT
28 Feb   Josephus fs Francisci & Eliz. LOWE
5 Mar   Johannes fs Johannis & Ellena RAWLINS
23 Mar   Gulielmus fs Gulielmi & Anna SHENTON
23 Mar   Maria fa Ludovici & Jodoca *[Lewis & Joyce-BT]* THACKER
1717
31 Mar   Sara fa Georgii & Anna DEAKIN
27 Apr   Sara fa Radulphi & Lydia TURNER
17 May   Thomas fs Jobi & Sara BYRD
20 May   Anna fa Antonii & Sara GRETTON
22 May   Robertus fs Roberti & Jana BEALEY *[Bailey-BT]*
22 May   Anna fa Johannis & Elizabetha TURNER
24 May   Thomas fs Roberti & Ellena TRUNLY
6 Jun   Maria fa illegitima Sara BARLOUR
9 Jun   Jonathan fs Uria & [ ] NELSON
7 Jul   Johannes fs Johannis & Jana HAMPSON
8 Aug   Thomas fs Benjamin et Anna BELCHER
26 Aug   Johannis fs Rogeri & Hanna RICHARDSON
3 Sep   Elizabetha fa Johannis & Eliz. BELCHER
22 Sep   Jana fa Tho. & Eliz. RADFORD *[Ratford-BT]*
24 Sep   Anna fa Edwardi & Anna CHELL
3 Oct   Maria fa Thoma & Maria CLARK
12 Oct   Maria fa Johans & Martha LOW
23 Oct   Anna fa Gulielmi & Joanna HOLLINS
3 Nov   Catherina fa Roberti & Maria MIDDLETON
3 Nov   Elizabetha fa Antonii & Elizabetha BROWN
5 Nov   Simon s/o Simon & Ellen BLUER [BT]

[added at bottom of register page - see below]

16 Nov Margaretta fa Gulielmi & Elizabetha HICHCOCK
15 Dec Johannes fs Joanis & Alicia SHAW
2 Jan Elizabetha fa Francisci & Maria KEEN
4 Mar Jacobus & Dorothea gemelli Jacobi & Dorothea MARSON
24 Mar Thomas fs illegitimus Eliz. HARRIS
1718
31 Mar Aron fs Josephi & Editha HEALEY
22 Apr Richardus fs Edvardi & Dorothea TILL
28 Apr Hannah fa Josephi & Anna JOHNSON
1 Jun Gynar fa Roberti & Jana BEALEY
5 Nov 1717 Simon fs Simonis & Ellena BLUER
2 Jun Anna fa Joh: & Anna STARTIN
3 Jun Sara fa Francisci & Eliza. LOW
23 Jul Josephus fs Josephi & Sara TURNER
25 Jul Ellena fa Samuelis & Rachel HOLLINS
11 Sep Johannes fs Thoma & Marg. DAVIES
2 Oct Elizabetha fa Johannis & Eliza ARMISHAW
2 Oct Josephus fs Thoma & Eliza. BUCKLEY
8 Oct Elizabetha fa Gualteri & Maria HORDERN
14 Oct Gulielmus fs Job & Sara BYRD
6 Nov Elizabetha fa Thoma & Alicia HALL
11 Nov Samuel fs Josephi & Johanna DEAKIN
20 Nov Johannes fs Benjamini & Anna BELCHER
27 Nov Lydia fa Johannis & Lyda. BASSET
11 Dec Gulielmus fs Thoma & Maria CLARK
17 Dec Elizabetha fa Johans. & Eliz. TURNER
21 Dec Thomas fs Johans. & Jana HAMPSON
6 Jan Gulielmus fs Mosos & Sara JOHNSON
16 Jan Johannes fs Thoma & Maria HORN
30 Jan Maria fa Gul. & Anna DANIEL
12 Feb Anna fa Johans. & Eliz. CARTWRIGHT
1 Mar Jacobus fs Jacobi & Johanna BEALEY
3 Mar Elizabetha fa Thoma & Maria ARMISHAW
21 Mar Johannes fs Antonii & Sara GRETTON
1719
26 Apr Anna fa Richardi & Maria MOOR
2 Apr Robertus fs Roberti & Ellena THACKER
2 Apr Samuel fs Johannis & Eliza. BELCHER
13 Apr Johannes fs Johannis & Maria BROWN
9 May Georgius fs Radulphi & Lydia TURNER
7 Jun Elizabetha fa Richardi & Maria WOOLLEY
23 Jun Josephus fs Samulelis & Ellena WOOLLEY
29 Jun Thomas fs Thoma & Ruth FINNEY
2 Jul Gulielmus fs Johannis & Maria SHERRATT
28 Jul Thomas fs Thoma & Elizabetha BLURTON
10 Aug Johannes fs Gulielmi & Elizabetha SAUNDERS natus nono die Augusti atq
       Renatus decimo
10 Aug Sampson fs Gulielmi & Dorothea BAYLY *[Bailey-BT]*
13 Sep Maria fa Guleilmi & Maria WARD Erraticor
16 Oct Thomas fs Thoma & Elizabetha RADFORD
2 Nov Thomas fs Thoma & Felicia WARD

19 Nov	Johannes fs Thoma & Eliz. RIGBEY
15 Dec	Rachel fa Josephi & Anna JOHNSON
17 Dec	Johannes fs Johannis & Catherina BRINDLEY
29 Dec	Anna fa Benjamini & Anna BELCHER
19 Jan	Elizabetha fa Simonis & Ellena BLOOR
21 Jan	Sherratt fs Gulielmi & Elizabetha HITCHCOCK
22 Jan	Johannes fs Johannis & Ellena SNAPE
28 Jan	Thomas fs Johannis & Sara JOHNSON
14 Feb	Maria fa illegitima Elizabetha BEVINS
12 Mar	Anna fa Antonii & Eliza. BROWN

1720

26 Apr	Johannes fs Nathanielis & Maria BLURTON
1 May	Gulielmus fs Jacobi & Dorothea MARSON
19 May	Edvardus fs Johannis & Elizabetha BELCHER
23 May	Elizabetha fa Thoma & Maria CLARK
23 May	Johannes & Maria gemelli fs & fa Roberti & Ellena TRYNLEY
30 May	Thomas & Elizabetha gemelli fs & fa Thoma & Anna HOLLINS
29 May	Elizabetha fa Gulielmi & Anna SHERRATT
6 Jun	Maria fa Georgii & Johanna WARD
10 Jun	Jana fa Roberti & Jana BEALEY
3 Jul	Thomas fs Johannis & Ellena RAWLINS
28 May	Sara fa Gulielmi & Johanna HOLLINS
17 Jul	Samuel fs Johannis & Anna STARTIN
1 Sep	Maria fa Job & Sara BYRD
24 Sep	Johannes fs Gulielmi & Maria JOHNSON
30 Oct	Philippus fs Philippi & Dorothea HOLLINS
3 Dec	Georgius fs Johannis & Elizabetha TURNER
22 Dec	Margareta fa Benjamini & Anna BELCHER
29 Dec	Thomas fs Roberti & Ellena HEATON
6 Jan	Johannes fs Thoma & Ruth FINNEY
15 Jan	Thomas fs Thoma & Elizabetha ADAMS
18 Jan	Francicscus fs Johannis & Elizabetha SHERRATT de Novâ Domo
5 Feb	Thomas fs Jonathanis & Maria TUNSTAL
6 Feb	Dorothea fa Gulielmi & Sara BAILEY
26 Feb	Johannes fs Johannis & Eliza. JACKSON
26 Feb	Thomas fs Thoma & Rebeck. FENTON
18 Mar	Antonius & Thomas fi gemelli Ludovici & Jodoca THACKER

1721

7 Apr	Josephus fs Georgii & Anna DEAKIN
11 Apr	Josephus fs Josephi & Anna JOHNSON
8 Jun	Thomas fs Johannis & Elizabetha ARMISHAW
8 Jun	Elizabetha fa Johannis & Elizabetha BELCHER
25 Jun	Gulielmus fs Antonii & Sara GRETTON
23 Jul	Johannes fs Samuel & Rachel HOLLINS
18 Aug	Sara fa Thoma & Maria ARMISHAW
2 Sep	Sara fa illegitima Dorothea CHAWNER
16 Sep	Radulphus fs Radulphi & Lidia TURNER
24 Sep	Edvardus fs Thoma & Elizabetha RADFORD
12 Oct	Maria fa Francisci & Anna HOWARD
12 Nov	Johannes fs Mosis & Sara JOHNSON
18 Nov	Josephus fs Francicsi & Elizabetha LOW

21 Nov   Johannes fs Johannis & Francisca STEEL
24 Nov   Georgius WARD fs Georgii & Joanna
3 Dec   Jana fa Francisci & Maria TUNSTAL
10 Dec   Elizabetha fa Thoma & Margaretta DAVIES
1 Jan   Jana fa Richardi & Maria MOOR
1 Feb   Thomas fs Isaaci & Maria BAILEY
1 Feb   Elizabetha fa Gulielmi & Sara RUSHION
6 Feb   Ellena fa Simonis & Ellena BLOOR
12 Feb   Theophilus fs Gulielmi & Elizabetha SAUNDERS natus 11 Feb atq Renatus 12 die eiusdem mensis
13 Feb   Maria fa Johannis & Elizabetha CARTWRIGHT & nata 11
17 Feb   Gulielmus fs Thoma & Felicia WARD
25 Feb   Thomas fs Thoma & Elizabetha RIGBY
1722
25 Mar   Josephus fs Gulielmi & Anna DANIEL
26 Mar   Alicia fa Gulielmi & Phebe DEAKIN
7 Apr   Georgius fs Edvardi & Dorothea TILL
29 Apr   Thomas fs Thoma & Ruth RUSHION
2 May   Robertus fs Roberti & Jana BAILEY
12 May   Johannes fs Johannes & Sara JOHNSON
17 May   Georgius fs Josephi & Ellena MASGRAVE
11 Jun   Johannes & Jacobus gemelli fi Roberti & Ellena TRUNLEY
2 Aug   Elizabetha fa Thoma & Elizabetha BLURTON
23 Aug   Gulielmus fs Johannis & Catherina BRINDLEY
29 Sep   Hanna fa Gulielmi & Joanna HOLLINS
2 Oct   Maria fa Thoma & Anna TOOTH
22 Nov   Elizabetha fa Nathanielis & Maria BLURTON
24 Nov   Marina fa Gulielmi & Dorothea BAILEY *[Bailye-BT]*
27 Nov   Hannah fa Jonathanis & Anna METE *[Meat-BT]*
19 Jan   Sara fa Thoma & Elizabetha ADAMS
21 Jan   Helena fa Johannis & Elizabetha TURNER
30 Dec   Mabel *[Mabella-BT]* TUNSTAL fa Francisci & Maria
15 Feb   Thomas fs Henrici & [ ] CHELL
17 Feb   Richardus fs Thoma & Maria WOOLLEY
28 Feb   Guleilmus fs Gulielmi & Helena FROST
7 Mar   Jodoca fa Georgii & Maria AYTKIN
18 Mar   Johannes fs Thoma & Dorothea COLLIER
16 Mar   Job fs Job & Sara BYRD
21 Mar   Johannes fs Johannis & Eliz. SHERRATT de Novâ Domo
22 Mar   Helen fa Richardi & Margaretta FENTON
1723
6 Apr   Samuel fs Johannis & Francisca STEEL
14 Apr   Eleonora fa Johannis & Elizabetha JACKSON
26 Apr   Anna fa illegitima Sara TURNER
26 Apr   Johannes fs Thoma & Anna HOLLINS
6 May   Gulielmus fs Gualteri & Maria HORDERN
11 May   Jana fa Radulphi & Lidia TURNER
12 May   Thomas fs Georgii & Johanna WARD
23 Jul   Elizabetha fa Johannis & Maria MEREDITH
18 Aug   Johanna fa Jacobi & Johanna BAILEY *[Bailye-BT]*
8 Sep   Maria fa Gulielmi & Maria KNIGHT

12 Oct	Sara fa illegitima Maria MELLOR
→ 5 Nov	Gulielmus fs Gulielmi & Elizabetha SAUNDERS
7 Nov	Thomas fs Edvardi & Anna TOOTH
19 Nov	Thomas fs Samuelis & Rach: HOLLINS
18 Nov	Maria fa Samuelis & Hanna POTTS
3 Jan	Anna fa Georgii & Elizabetha GARTEN
18 Jan	Sampson fs Samps. & Hanna WRIGHT
6 Feb	Josephus fs Josephi & Helena MASKREY *[MasgreaveBT]*
18 Feb	Johannes fs Roberti & Helena HEATON
27 Feb	Jodoca fa Jacobi & Dorothea MARSON *[Marston-BT]*
19 Mar	Edvardus fs Francisci & Anna HOWARD
21 Mar	*Josephs fs Robti & Helena TRUNLEY [BT]*
22 Mar	Johannes fs Thoma & Rebecca FENTON

1724

21 Apr	Gulielmus & Richardus fi Gulielmi & Sara RUSHTON
10 May	Gulielmus fs Roberti & [ ] TUNSTALL
26 May	Johannes fs Simonis & Helena BLEWER *[Blore-BT]*
28 May	Benjamin fs Benjamini & Anna BELCHER
29 Jun	Margaretta fa Richardi FENTON & Marg:
5 Jul	Johannes fs Henrici BAILEY *[Bailye-BT]* & ~~Anna~~ Margareta
5 Jul	Benjamin fs Gulielmi & Anna DANIEL
12 Jul	Robertus fs Gulielmi & Eliz: HYTCHCOTT *[Hitchcock-BT]*
19 Jul	Margaretta fa Johannis & Eliz: STRINGER
26 Jul	Martha fa Antonii & Eliz: BROWN *[Browne-BT]*
30 Aug	Thoma fs Thoma & Alicia HALL
28 Sep	Margaretta fa Thoma & Marg: DAVIS *[Davies-BT]*
18 Oct	Maria fa Josephi & Sara TURNER
27 Oct	Anna fa Josephi & Maria RATCLIFFE
23 Nov	Josephus fs Johannis & Eliz: TURNER
10 Dec	Maria fa illegitima Doroth: PARKER
13 Dec	Hanna fa Radulph: & Lid: TURNER
28 Dec	Johannes fs Johannis & Jana MIDDLETON
29 Dec	Franciscus fs Fran: & Helena TOWERS
4 Jan	Anna fa Richardi & Maria LYON
7 Jan	Francisca fa Francisci & Eliz: LOW
10 Jan	Carolus fs Roberti & Jane BAILEY *[Bailye-BT]*
17 Jan	Maria fa Georgii & Helena CLUIS *[Clowes-BT]*
17 Jan	Elizabetha fa Georgi & Jane WARD
25 Jan	Joshua fs Jos: & Maria PRESTICH de Gorton para: Manchester
4 Feb	Maria fa Josephi & Chris: HOLT para Lancaster
18 Feb	Sara fa illegitima Anna STARTIN
20 Feb	Maria fa Johannis & Eliz: SHERRAT *[Sherratt-BT]*
19 Mar	Anna fa Johannes & Francisca STEEL
21 Mar	Elizabetha fa Johannis & Sara JOHNSON

1725

26 Mar	Edvardus fs Thoma & Anne TOOTH
3 Apr	Maria fa Roberti & Maria ELSMORE
.. Apr	Sarah fa Thoma & Maria BLOUD nata est March 30 renata April
17 May	Maria fa Thoma & Elizabetha ADAMS
6 Jun	Anna fa Thoma & Elizabetha BLURTON
18 Jun	Anna fa Jonathani & Anna MEAT

24 Jun   Sarah fa Jobi & Sara BYRD
27 Jun   Maria fa Gulielmi & Sara RUSHTON
4 Jul   Anna fa Thoma & Maria CLARKE
18 Jul   Thomas fs Gulielmi & Helena FROST
1 Aug   Gulielmus fs illegitimus Gratia BAILYE
5 Sep   Jacobus fs Jacobi ASHENHURST de Parkhall Armiger & Hanna ux natus
      est Aug 29 Renatus Sep 5 in Congregationem admissus Sep 19
5 Dec   Josiah fs Johannis & Elizabetha COAKE [Cooke-BT]
6 Jan   Elizabetha fa Thoma & Ruth FINNY
6 Feb   Thomas fs illegitimus Thoma OSBORNE & Dorothea SHAWE
13 Feb   Gulielmus fs Mosis & Sara JOHNSON
20 Feb   Elizabetha fa Thoma & Sara HODIN
13 Mar   Rebekah fa Isaaci & Maria BAILYE
13 Mar   Elizabetha fa illegitima Debora PRITCHARD
20 Mar   Elizabetha fa Jacobi & Joanna RATCLIFFE
1726
27 Mar   Gulielmus fs Gulielmi & Dorothea BAILYE
11 Apr   Jacobus fs Joannis & Elizabetha BELCHER
16 Apr   Edvardus fs Edvardi & Lydia BLURTON
19 Apr   Sarah fa Samuelis & Hannah POTT
25 Apr   Samuel fs Michaelis WARD Rectoris Ecclesia de Leigh & Sara uxoris eius
      natus est April 6 Renatus 25
1 May   Helena fa Joannis & Hannah ALCOCK
5 May   Patientia fa Solomonis & Elizabetha SHAWE
15 May   Thomas fs Thoma & Dorothea COLLIER
22 May   Franciscus fs Henrici & Elizabetha COPE de Stafford
22 May   Anna fa Gulielmi & Margeria RATCLIFFE
5 Jun   Lucia fa illegitima Johannis LEWIS & Anna HILL
10 Jul   Joannes fs Thoma & Ruth RUSHTON
7 Aug   Maria fa Edvardi & Anna TOOTH
12 Aug   Thomas fs Samuelis & Anna BROWNE de Foale in Congregationem
      admissus est
14 Aug   Elizabetha fa Joannis & Maria TATTON
22 Aug   Ricardus fs Ricardi & Margaretta FENTON
28 Aug   Lucas fs Henrici & Anna BAILYE
26 Jun   Jacobus fs Thoma & Anna HOLLINS de Withington
26 Jun   Sarah fa Guleilmi & Maria GRIFFEN Parochia de Milsich
26 Jun   Elizabetha fa Ricardi & Sara BAILYE
2 Oct   Maria fa Samuelis & Rachel HOLLINS
16 Oct   Gamaliel fs Gulielmi & Elizabetha HITCHCOCK
1 Nov   Josephus fs Jobi & Elizabetha BULL
1 Nov   Josephus fs Edvardi & Dorothea TILL
13 Nov   Nathanael fs Gulielmi & Anna DANIEL
24 Nov   Elizabetha fa Georgii & Helena CLOWES
26 Nov   Robertus fs Roberti & Elizabetha HOLLINGWORTH
15 Dec   Hannah fa Jacobi & Dorothea MARSTON
25 Dec   Martha fa Gulielmi & Helena SHIPLEY
13 Jan   Joannes fs Antonii & Elizabetha THACKER
14 Jan   Gulielmus fs Gulielmi & Elizabetha BRERETON
23 Jan   Maria fa Edvardi & Anna SHERRAT Congregationem admissa Feb 24
30 Jan   Franciscus fs Joannis & Jana MIDDLETON

20 Feb Hannah fa Gulielmi & Hannah GOUGH
4 Dec Gulielmus fs Gulielmi & Elizabetha WRIGHT de Nobot

1727

5 Apr Anna fa Francisci & Anna HOWARD
8 Apr Maria fa Thoma & Elizabetha COPE
10 Sep Elizabetha fa Josephi & Sarah TURNER
28 Apr Dorothea & Martha fa gemela Philippi & Elizabetha HOLLINS
30 Apr Antonius fs Antonii & Elizabetha BROWNE
27 May Georgius fs Thoma & Elizabetha ADAMS
3 Jun Elizabetha fa Thoma & Maria WOOLLEY
4 Jun Sarah fa Thoma & Rebekah FENTON
15 Jun Anna fa Jonathanis & Anna MEAT
17 Jun Jana fa Francisci & Helena TOWERS
22 Jun Sarah fa Thoma & Sarah WETTON
25 Jun Gulielmus fs Joannis & Anna HIGGES
9 Jul Maria fa Roberti & Helena TRUNLEY
16 Jul Maria fa Francisci & Maria TUNSTAL
28 Jul Joannes fs Joannis SHILTON Ludimagistri de Leigh & Elizabetha ux in Congregationem admissus per Dr Dobson Sep 7
6 Aug Thomas fs Thoma & Ruth FINNY
12 Aug Maria fa Joannis & Catherina BRINDLEY
17 Sep Robertus fs Roberti & Helena HEATON de Leigh bapt per Magm Langley
24 Sep Elizabetha fa Georgii & Joanna WARD de Nobot bapt per Dr Hancock Jun & in Congregationem admissa Oct 30
1 Oct Theodorus fs Thoma & Margaretta DAVIS de Morrily Heath
8 Nov Jana fa Joannis & Lucia HOLLINS bapt per Magm Langley
26 Nov Edvardus fs Jacobi ASHENHURST de Park Hall Armiger & Hanna ux natus est Nov 23 Renatus Nov 26 in Congregationem admissus Dec 14
14 Dec Elizabetha fa Radulphi & Maria TURNER
26 Dec Philippus fs Philippi & Joanna HAWLEY de Checkeley Bank
11 Jan Jacobus fs Joannis & Elizabetha TURNER in Congregationem admissus Feb 10
12 Jan Thomas fs Thoma & Anna TOOTH
4 Feb Elizabetha fa illegitima Esthera HEELEY Vidua
17 Feb Anna fa Edvardi & Lydia BLURTON de Leigh Church
6 Mar Gulielmus fs Gulielmi & Sara RUSHTON
7 Mar Thomas fs Joannis & Elizabetha COOKE de Leigh
13 Mar Elizabetha fa Joannis & Maria BARKER

1728

22 Apr Leticia fila Jobi & Sara BIRD
4 May Catherina fa Thoma & Elizabetha BLURTON
29 May Elizabetha fa Samuellis & Hannah POTT
29 May Elizabetha fa Johannis SHERRATT de Hayes House nuner defuncti & Elizabetha ux
2 Jun Jana fa Joannis & Anna STRINGER
10 Jun Elizabetha fa Georgii & Helena CLOWES
28 Jul Maria fa Edvardi & Maria SPOONER
12 Aug Elizabetha fa Thoma & Elizabetha COPE bapt per Dr A. Fernyhough
8 Sep Joannes fs illegitimus Margaretta PODMORE de Leigh
12 Sep Thomas fs Michaelis WARD Rectoris Ecclesia de Leigh & Sara uxoris eius natus est Aug 7 & Renatus Sep 12

15 Sep	Gulielmus fs Thoma & Dorothea COLLIER bapt per Dr HANCOCK
23 Oct	Robertus fs Danielis & Rebekah WETTON de Aston juxta Stone
27 Oct	Radulphus fs Gulielmi WOOD de Foale Generosi & Francisca uxoris eius in Congregationem admissus Nov 28
3 Nov	Jacobus fs Henrici & Anna BAILYE
7 Nov	Sarah fa Edvardi & Elizabetha TONKES in congregationem admissa Nov 26
1 Dec	Thomas fs Joannis & Hannah ALCOCK
8 Dec	Joannes fs Samuelis & Jana TONKINSON de Leigh in Congregationem Admissus Dec 15
26 Dec	Maria fa Joannis & Sarah LEES
5 Jan	Maria fa Joannis & Lucia HOLLINS bapt per Dr HANCOCK
16 Jan	Elizabetha fa illegitima Elizabetha SNELSON
29 Jan	Joannes fs Gulielmi & Sarah PERKIN
30 Jan	Elizabetha fa Thoma & Helena TOOTH in Congregationem admissa Feb 27

1729

4 Apr	William s/o William & Elizabeth OADES
1 May	Anna d/o James ASHENHURST of Park Hall Esq. & Hannah his wife
5 Aug	Ralph s/o John & Elizabeth TURNER
11 Aug	Watson Robins s/o William & Elizabeth HITCHCOCK
31 Aug	Mary d/o Thomas & Sarah WETTON of Leigh
9 Sep	Thomas s/o Edward & Lydia BLURTON
13 Sep	Elizabeth d/o Thomas & Elizabeth COPE
13 Sep	Bridget d/o Thomas & Elizabeth NUTT
21 Sep	Mary d/o Joseph & Catherine RATCLIFFE
19 Oct	Mary d/o William & Prudence CHELL
5 Nov	Edward s/o Edward & Anne TOOTH
1 Jan	Charles s/o Charles & Bennett RICHARDSON of Hollington in the Parish of Checkley bapt at Leigh
3 Jan	Elizabeth d/o John & Mary HURT of Nobot privately
10 Jan	Ellen d/o John & Mary BAGNALL of Checkley Parish
25 Jan	Rushton the bastard s/o Thomas RUSHTON now under sentence of Transportation & Catherine BAILYE Jun. of Morrily Heath
1 Feb	Anne d/o John & Ursula MARTIN of With'ton
2 Feb	Elizabeth the bastard d/o Frances ARNOLD by William KNOWLES
8 Mar	John s/o Robert & Sarah BAILYE of Morrily Heath
21 Mar	John s/o John & Sarah STARTIN of the Hayes House privately

1730

30 Mar	Thomas s/o Thomas and Elizabeth HALL of Nobot
1 Apr	Elizabeth d/o Thomas & Elizabeth ADAMS privately & rec'd into the Congregation April 12
12 Apr	Frances d/o Francis & Mary TUNSTAL of Morrily Heath
16 Apr	Sarah d/o William & Anne DANIEL of With'ton
3 May	Elizabeth d/o John & Catherine BRINDLEY of Leigh privately at Leigh & rec'd into the Congregation May 19
17 May	Elizabeth d/o William & Dorothy BAILYE of Morrily Heath
21 Jun	Margaret d/o George & Joan WARD of Nobot
9 Jul	Mary d/o John & Mary KENT of Foale in the Parish of Checkley
20 Aug	John s/o Edward TONKS of Seighford & Elizabeth his wife
4 Oct	Anne d/o Thomas & Dorothy COLLIER of Middlet'n Green
11 Oct	Thomas s/o John LEES Jun & Sarah his wife
15 Oct	John s/o Phillip & Elizabeth HOLLINS of Buckhurst Farm

8 Nov	Thomas s/o George & Ellen CLOWES of Middleton Green
14 Dec	Jemima d/o Nicholas & Catherine BANISTER
27 Dec	Anne d/o Joseph BAILYE of Morrily Heath & Anne his Uncle's widow bapt at Leigh
28 Dec	Mary d/o Edward & Mary SPOONER of Checkley Bank
10 Feb	Thomas s/o Mr William WOOD of Foale & Frances his wife privately baptised
14 Feb	Elizabeth & John the twin children of William & Ellen FROST privately Elizabeth was rec'd into the Congregation March 7 by Mr Langley
21 Feb	Jane d/o John & Lucy HOLLINS of Dairy House
2 Mar	Thomas s/o Thomas & Elizabeth ALSOP of the Hayes House
7 Mar	John s/o Thomas & Elizabeth BLURTON of With'ton bapt by Mr Langley
16 Mar	Thomas s/o William & Sarah KEELING of Nobot
17 Mar	Jane d/o Thomas & Anne HOLLINS of With'ton Green
17 Mar	John s/o Edward & Margaret SHERRATT of Morrily Heath privately & rec'd into the Congregation March 26 1731

1731

2 May	Joseph s/o William & Anne CLAY of Morrily Heath
26 May	James s/o Samuel & Jane TONKINSON of Leigh privately & rec'd into the Congregation June 8
27 May	Bridget d/o Mrs Hannah ASHENHURST the Widow of James ASHENHURST Esqr late of Park Hall
7 Jun	Thomas s/o Thomas & Sarah MILLINGTON of Withington
18 Jul	William s/o Thomas & Mary WOOLLEY of Wood Leasows
27 Jul	John s/o Charles & Dorothy HART of Doddesley privately & rec'd into the Congregation Aug 12
3 Aug	Francis s/o Michael WARD Rector of Leigh & Sarah his wife was born & privately baptised at Leigh Aug 3 & rec'd into the Congregation afterwards by Mr Thomas Spateman Sept 12
8 Aug	Mary d/o William & Jane CARTER of Leigh
15 Aug	John s/o George & Mary SMITH of Nobot
22 Aug	Edward s/o Edward & Anne TOOTH of Field
9 Sep	John s/o Thomas & Elizabeth COPE
15 Sep	Richard s/o William & Elizabeth OADES privately by Mr Tho Spateman & rec'd into the Congregation the 19th by Mt John Ward Jun
20 Sep	Anne d/o Edward & Elizabeth DAVIS
30 Sep	John s/o Joshua & Anne PRESTON of Doddesley bapt by Mr Hancock
3 Oct	Richard s/o William & Dorothy BAILYE bapt by Mr Ashenhurst
3 Oct	William s/o Thomas & Elizabeth ADAMS bapt by Do.
5 Oct	Mary d/o Simon & Ellen BLORE bapt by Mr Hancock
10 Oct	Elizabeth d/o William & Prudence CHELL bapt by Mr Spencer
25 Oct	Susanna & Thomas the twin children of Richard & Susanna BAILYE of Morrily Heath privately
2 Nov	John s/o John & Elizabeth COOK of Leigh
2 Nov	James s/o John & Anne WALTER of Checkley
28 Nov	John s/o Luke & Elizabeth BILLING
5 Dec	Anne d/o John & Mary LOWE
9 Dec	James s/o James & Anne PAKEMAN of Nobot privately & rec'd into the Congregation Dec 12
29 Dec	James s/o Thomas & Rebekah FENTON of Middleton Green
10 Jan	Thomas s/o Solomon & Elizabeth SHAWE of Withington

2 Feb   Hannah d/o William BELCHER & Elizabeth SMITH of Field
10 Feb   Jacob s/o Jacob & Jane HOLLAND of Nobot
20 Feb   Anne d/o Sarah SNELSON of Withington Green bapt by Mr Adye
12 Mar   Margaret d/o George & Joane WARD of Nobot
16 Mar   John s/o Thomas & Dorothy OSBORNE of Withington
19 Mar   John s/o John & Ursula MARTIN of Withington
1732
25 Mar   John s/o Edward & Lydia BLURTON of Leigh Church
26 Mar   William s/o John & Anne STRINGER of Nobot
26 Mar   Thomas s/o Joseph & Catherine RATCLIFFE of Leigh Bank
26 Mar   Charles s/o John & Jane BLURTON of Field privately at Field
30 Mar   Margaret d/o Paul & Sarah SHERRATT of Field
10 Apr   Edward s/o William & Anne BRERETON of Leigh
16 Apr   Joseph s/o Robert & Ellen HEATON of Leigh
24 Apr   Mary d/o John & Elizabeth COLLIER of Middleton Green privately & Rec'd into the Congregation by Mr Hancock May 20
6 May   Elizabeth d/o Saml & Jane TONKINSON bapt by Mr Budworth
4 Jun   Mary d/o John & Sarah STARTIN of Hobb hill
13 Jul   Margaret d/o John & Prudence HODGKINS of Church Eyton
10 Aug   John s/o John & Mary TILL of Checkley Bank
12 Aug   Mary d/o Thomas & Mary AMERY of The Penelow Hill
20 Aug   William s/o William & Elizabeth HITCHCOCK of Withington
12 Sep   William s/o John LEES Jun & Sarah LEES his wife
2 Oct   Anne d/o James & Joan RATCLIFFE bapt privately by Mr Langley
22 Oct   Mary d/o William & Grace HOLLINS of Withington
8 Dec   Joseph s/o Charles & Dorothy HART bapt privately at Doddesley & rec'd into the Congregation Dec 27
14 Jan   Henry s/o Joseph & Anne BAILYE
9 Jan   Hannah d/o Francis & Mary TUNSTAL privately by Mr Hancocke & rec'd into the Congregation Jan 21
21 Jan   Dorothy d/o Thomas & Dorothy COLLIER
4 Feb   Mary d/o Thomas & Sarah MILLINGTON
21 Feb   Elizabeth d/o Richard & Susanna BAILYE
23 Feb   Joseph the bastard s/o Margaret SHERRATT
11 Mar   Mary d/o William & Sarah KEELING of Nobot
13 Mar   Mary d/o John & Hannah ALCOCK baptis'd privately. She was rec'd into the Congregation by Mr Langley April 8 1733
15 Mar   Thomas s/o John & Anne HIGGES privately by Mr Hancock
1733
26 Mar   Jeremiah s/o Edward & Elizabeth TONKES bapt by Mr Langley
27 Apr   Robert s/o William & Dorothy BELCHER bapt at Field & rec'd into the Congregation May 15
1 May   Mary d/o Robert & Isabel JOHNSON
29 May   Sarah d/o Thomas & Elizabeth NUTT
15 Jul   George s/o George & Ellen CLOWES of Middleton Green
18 Jul   Joseph s/o James & Joan RATCLIFFE bapt privately at Leigh Bank
12 Aug   Thomas s/o Edward & Margaret SHERRATT
13 Aug   Thomas s/o Thomas & Elizabeth TILL of Checkley Parish
14 Aug   Anne d/o Thomas & Anne SWAN of Fole
25 Sep   Elizabeth d/o William & Elizabeth DAVIES of Leigh privately & rec'd into the Congregation the 28th

27 Sep	Mary d/o John & Mary TONNYCLIFFE of Withington
30 Sep	Elizabeth d/o Thomas & Elizabeth ADAMS
6 Oct	William s/o Edward & Elizabeth DAVIES
1 Nov	William s/o William & Elizabeth BLOUD of Nobot
5 Nov	Thomas s/o Thomas & Elizabeth COPE
6 Nov	Mary the bastard d/o Dorothy PARKER of Withington Green privately & rec'd into the Congregation Nov 30
10 Nov	John s/o John & Jane BLURTON of Field
18 Nov	Jonathan s/o John & Sarah STARTIN
6 Dec	John s/o Thomas & Elizabeth TILL of Leigh
26 Dec	Thomas s/o Thomas & Elizabeth HOWE privately & rec'd into the Congregation Jan 8th following
29 Dec	Joseph s/o John & Elizabeth COLLIER of Middleton Green bapt by Mr Craven
8 Jan	Mary d/o John & Diana TURNER
10 Jan	Thomas s/o Widow Joan WARD of Nobot bapt by Mr Hancock
20 Jan	Martha d/o Edward & Anne TOOTH of Field bapt by Mr Craven
12 Feb	John & Jane the children of James & Anne PAKEMAN of Nobot were Baptiz'd privately
23 Feb	Thomas s/o William & Prudence CHELL of Leigh privately
3 Mar	Elizabeth d/o William & Elizabeth OADES
6 Mar	Thomas s/o Thomas & Sarah WETTON of Leigh privately

1734

31 Mar	Anne d/o Joseph & Catherine RATCLIFFE privately at Leigh Bank & rec'd into the Congregation April 15
15 Apr	Thomas s/o William & Anne CLAY
12 Apr	Mary d/o Thomas & Anne HOLLINS
5 May	William s/o Thomas & Anne RUSHTON of Morrily Heath
21 May	William s/o George & Mary SMITH of Fole
29 Jun	Lydia d/o Edward & Lydia BLURTON of Leigh Church
19 Jun	Anne d/o William HOLLINS of Froddeswall was rec'd into the Congregation by Mr Craven July 14 having been privately baptiz'd at Froddeswall June 19
14 Jul	William s/o John & Elizabeth COOK of Leigh bapt by Mr Craven
15 Jul	Isaac s/o James & Joan RATCLIFFE of Leigh Bank privately & rec'd into the Congregation July 21
18 Jul	Sarah d/o John LEES & Sarah his wife
8 Aug	John s/o Walter & Alice BURTON of Nobot
28 Aug	William s/o Samuel & Elizabeth FENTON privately at Withington by Mr Craven
1 Sep	Jane d/o John & Ursula MARTIN of Withington bapt by Mr Craven
16 Sep	Jane d/o William & Dorothy BELCHER of Field privately & Rec'd into the Congregation by Mr Craven Oct 7
22 Sep	John s/o John & Mary LOWE of Leigh Church
22 Sep	William s/o John & Mary TILL of Checkley Bank
10 Nov	John s/o William & Dorothy BAILYE of Morrily Heath
27 Dec	Anne d/o Charles & Dorothy HART bapt by Mr Craven
30 Dec	Thomas s/o Thomas & Elizabeth TILL bapt by Mr Craven
5 Feb	William s/o William & Elizabeth DAVIES was bapt at Leigh privately by Mr Craven Feb 5 & rec'd into the Congregation Feb 9
8 Feb	Francis s/o William & Sarah KEELING of Nobot bapt by Mr Craven

[no date] Elizabeth d/o Solomon & Elizabeth SHAWE of Withington bapt by Mr
Craven

21 Feb   Jane d/o William & Sarah EBBE bapt by Mr Craven

2 Mar   Anne the bastard d/o Phebe SPENCER bapt by Mr Craven

2 Mar   Francis s/o Thomas & Elizabeth NUTT of Leigh Church bapt by Mr Craven

1735

1 May   William s/o John & Jane BLURTON bapt at Field by Mr Fernihough

15 May   William s/o Charles & Anne LIGHTWOOD was bapt privately at the Hayes
House May 15 & rec'd into the Congregation Jun 7

18 May   Thomas s/o John & Mary TONNYCLIFFE of Withington

22 Jun   Hannah d/o William & Prudence CHELL

22 Jun   Anne d/o Mary DYCHE & George WRIGHT, who married her & ran away
afterwards having a former wife

6 Jul   James s/o Joseph BAILYE by Anne his Uncle Henry's widow

4 Aug   Anne d/o Samuel & Jane TONKINSON was baptiz'd privately & rec'd into
the Congregation Aug 17

12 Aug   Thomas s/o Thomas & Mary BOX

19 Aug   Elizabeth d/o Thomas & Elizabeth HOWE

24 Aug   John s/o George & Ellen CLOWES of Middleton Green

14 Sep   Anne d/o John & Anne STRINGER of Nobot

28 Sep   Joseph s/o Joseph & Margaret GERARD of Field

29 Sep   Thomas s/o William & Ellen PHILLIPS of the Bank in the parish of Checkley
was baptiz'd at Leigh

5 Oct   Thomas s/o Thomas & Sarah MOORE of Leigh

19 Oct   Elizabeth d/o Thomas & Sarah WETTON

30 Oct   Thomas s/o John & Elizabeth COLLIER

30 Oct   Robert s/o Anthony & Elizabeth THACKER

16 Nov   Henry s/o Henry & Anne WOODWARD of Leigh

9 Dec   Ellen the bastard d/o Grace HOLLINS the younger of Dairy House was
baptiz'd by Mr Gould Curate of Checkley

1 Jan   Thomas s/o William & Elizabeth BLOUD of Fole

4 Jan   Jane d/o Francis & Mary TUNSTAL

16 Jan   Mary d/o Joseph & Mary BULLOCK was bapt at Withington privately Jan 16
& rec'd into the Congregation 8 Feb

17 Jan   Edward s/o Thomas & Elizabeth COPE

2 Feb   Samuel s/o Thomas & Elizabeth ADAMS

27 Feb   Elizabeth d/o Edward & Elizabeth DAVIES was baptiz'd privately & rec'd
into the Congregation March 21

1736

4 Apr   Elizabeth d/o William & Elizabeth ROBOTHAM

24 Apr   Mary d/o Thomas & Mary WOOLLEY of the Wood Leasowes

8 Aug   Lettice d/o David & Mary BAILYE of Morrily Heath was baptiz'd by Mr
Moses Gould Cur. of Checkley & rec'd into the Congregation Aug 29 by Mr
Ward

15 Aug   Charles s/o Charles & Dorothy HART of Doddesley was baptiz'd by Mr
Langley

22 Aug   Elizabeth d/o James & Elizabeth CLULOW

26 Sep   Sarah d/o William & Elizabeth OADES

30 Sep   Elizabeth d/o John & Elizabeth COOKE

1 Nov   John s/o Thomas & Elizabeth HOWE

5 Nov   Joseph s/o John LEES Jnr & Sarah his wife

7 Nov   Sarah d/o Robert & Isabel JOHNSON
28 Nov   John s/o William & Margaret HARGREAVES
29 Nov   William s/o William & Anne CLAY was privately baptiz'd & rec'd into the Congregation Dec 5
26 Dec   Thomas s/o John & Sarah STARTIN
1 Jan   John s/o Thomas & Sarah MILLINGTON of Withington
6 Jan   Elizabeth d/o Thomas & Elizabeth TILL
23 Jan   George s/o Edward & Anne TOOTH of Field
30 Jan   Mary d/o John & Jane BLURTON of Field was privately baptiz'd at Field & rec'd into the Congregation Feb 10
1 Feb   William s/o William & Dorothy BELCHER of Field was privately baptiz'd at Field & rec'd into the Congregation Feb 11
6 Feb   John s/o Mr Robert & Mrs Elizabeth WOOD of Field was privately baptiz'd & rec'd into the Congregation March 4
10 Feb   Henry s/o Michael & Mary GOODALL
14 Feb   Robert s/o Francis & Maru TUNSTAL of Morrily Heath was privately baptiz'd & rec'd into the Congregation by Mr Gould Feb 20
16 Feb   Mary d/o John & Margaret GILBERT was privately baptiz'd & rec'd into the Congregation Feb 26
20 Feb   Robert s/o John & Anne MOOR (who lay in at Middleton Green) was privately baptiz'd by Mr Gould & rec'd into the Congregation April 3 1737
24 Feb   John s/o James & Bridget DONE
10 Mar   Anne d/o John & Elizabeth BRIERHURST was privately bapt'd at Middleton Green & rec'd into the Congregation March 13
25 Mar   Josephus s/o William & Dorothy HITCHCOCK
10 Apr   George s/o John & Ursula MARTIN
12 Apr   John s/o John & Elizabeth HODGSON
20 Apr   Richard & Anne the twin children of William & Sarah KEELING of Nobot were privately baptiz'd
26 Apr   Sarah d/o Joseph & Margaret GERARD of Field
1 May   William s/o William & Elizabeth BARKER
1 May   John s/o Charles & Anne LIGHTWOOD of Nobot
8*May   John s/o John & Diana TURNER of Leigh Church [*3-BT]
16 May   Joseph s/o John & Mary GILL was privately baptiz'd at Nobot & rec'd into the Congregation May 29
8 Jun   Michael s/o Mr John SPATEMAN and Mary his wife was born & privately baptized at Leigh
3 Jul   Mary d/o Thomas & Elizabeth NUTT
27 Jul   Mary d/o Edward BLURTON of Leigh Church & Lydia his wife was privately baptiz'd & rec'd into the Congregation Aug 2
10*Sep   Felicia d/o John & Mary TONNYCLIFFE was privately baptiz'd & rec'd into the Congregation Sept 18 [*16-BT]
25 Sep   Mary d/o John & Mary LOWE of Withington Green
16 Oct   Hannah d/o George & Ellen CLOWES of Middleton Green
29 Oct   James s/o James & Grace BRASSINGTON
1 Nov   Samuel s/o Samuel & Jane TONKINSON
4 Dec   William s/o Thomas & Elizabeth COPE
4 Dec   William s/o Thomas & Sarah MOOR
18 Dec   Jane d/o John & Elizth DRAKEFIELD of Leigh Bank
21 Jan   Robert s/o Antony & Elizabeth THACKER
7 Feb   Thomas s/o Thomas & Mary WOOLLEY of Wood Leasowes

14 Feb   Anne d/o Thomas & Anne TOOTH was baptiz'd by Mr Gould
26 Feb   Margaret d/o John & Anne STRINGER of Nobot
12 Mar   Joseph s/o James & Joan RATCLIFFE of Leigh Bank
23 Mar   Thomas s/o William & Dorothy BAILYE of Morrily Heath privately & rec'd into the Congregation March 30 1738

1738
27 Mar   Richard s/o Thomas & Margaret RUSSELL
3 Apr   Mary d/o Mr John SPATEMAN & Mary his wife was born & privately baptized at Leigh
3 Apr   Dorothy d/o John & Sarah LEES
5 Apr   Mary d/o Immanuel & Mary PERKIN
12 Apr   William s/o William & Anne CLAY
15 Apr   Anne d/o William & Prudence CHELL
22 Apr   Mary d/o William & Elizabeth ROBOTHAM was privately baptiz'd & rec'd into the Congregation April 30
6 May   Elizabeth d/o Thomas & Hannah CHELL
11 May   Anne d/o Henry & Anne WOODWARD
13 May   Thomas s/o Mr William & Mrs Mary HILL of Withington privately & rec'd into the Congregation May 31
28 May   William s/o William & Mary JELLY of Leigh
9 Jun   Anne the bastard d/o Elizabeth HOLLINS
2 Jul   Lewis s/o Lewis & Sarah THACKER
16 Jul   Anne d/o Thomas & Elizabeth ADAMS
27 Aug   Dorothy d/o Charles & Dorothy HART
10 Sep   John s/o John & Elizabeth COLLIER
17 Sep   Mary d/o Solomon & Elizabeth SHAWE
11 Oct   Joseph s/o Thomas & Anne RUSHTON baptiz'd by Mr J. Ward
9 Nov   Michael s/o Michael & Mary GOODALL baptiz'd by Mr J. Ward
12 Nov   Elizabeth d/o George & Ellen COPE baptiz'd by Mr J. Ward
12 Nov   Alice d/o William & Margaret HARGRAVES baptiz'd by Mr J. Ward
30 Nov   Mary d/o Dorothy OSBORNE
17 Dec   Lydia d/o John & Elizabeth HODGSON privately bapiz'd by Mr J. Ward at Withington & rec'd into the Congregation by me Jan 21 1739
19 Feb   Hannah d/o William & Dorothy BELCHER bapt by Mr J. Ward
25 Feb   John s/o Thomas & Sarah PERKINS of Lichfield baptiz'd by Mr J. Ward
3 Mar   Frances d/o Thomas & Elizabeth TILL baptiz'd by Mr J. Ward

1739
5 Apr   Elizabeth d/o William & Sarah PARKER was privately baptiz'd at Withington by Mr J. Ward & rec'd into the Congregation 22 May by Mr. J. Ward
13 Apr   William s/o Widow Elizabeth OADES bapt by Mr J. Ward
15 Apr   Hannah the bastard d/o Anne STARTIN bapt by Mr J. Ward
16 Apr   Anne d/o John & Anne WALKER of Withington privately & rec'd into the Congregation June 3
28 Apr   Joseph s/o Joseph & Anne JACKSON
13 May   Anne d/o John & Diana TURNER
14 Jun   Joshuah s/o Joshuah & Anne PRESTON
17 Jun   George s/o Anthony & Elizabeth THACKER
24 Jun   Thomas s/o John & Ursula MARTIN
24 Jun   George s/o George & Mary WRIGHT
1 Jul   John s/o Thomas & Elizabeth NUTT
8 Jul   Mary d/o Thomas & Alice COLLIER

15 Jul   William s/o George & Ellen CLOWES
29 Jul   John s/o John & Sarah LEES
21 Aug   Richard s/o Thomas & Elizabeth HARRIS
30 Aug   Francis s/o James & Bridget DONE
27 Sep   Mary d/o George & Sarah JOHNSON
6 Oct   Mary d/o John & Mary TONNYCLIFFE
7 Oct   John s/o Thomas & Anne HOLLINS
21 Oct   John s/o Daniel & Sarah BURTON
22 Oct   Mary d/o Mr Robert & Mrs Joyce THACKER was privately baptiz'd & rec'd into the Congregation Nov 6
11 Nov   William s/o William & Sarah KEELING
25 Nov   Robert s/o Robert & Isabel JOHNSON
9 Dec   Mary d/o Charles & Anne LIGHTWOOD
21 Dec   Anne d/o Elizabeth SMITH
22 Jan   John s/o Thomas & Hannah TOMLINSON was privately baptized & rec'd into the Congregation by Mr Rowlands Feb 17
10 Feb   Elizabeth d/o Philip & Joan HAWLEY
17 Feb   Thomas s/o Lewis & Sarah THACKER baptized by Mr Rowlands
22 Feb   Jane d/o Mr Richard & Mrs Margaret MILWARD
22 Feb   Edward s/o Thomas & Elizabeth TILL
12 Mar   Mary d/o William & Elizabeth HALL
23 Mar   John s/o Samuel & Jane TONKINSON was privately baptized & rec'd into the Congregation April 6 1740

1740
10 Apr   Samuel s/o Thomas & Elizabeth COPE
20 Apr   James s/o George & Ellen COPE
23 Apr   Hannah & Mary the twin daughters of Joseph & Margaret GERARD were privately baptiz'd at Field & rec'd into the Congregation May 4
26 Apr   William s/o James & Anne BAILYE
27 Apr   Richard s/o John & Elizabeth COOKE
27 Apr   Richard s/o Thomas & Sarah MOORE
8 May   Anne d/o John & Jane BLURTON
26 May   James s/o John & Elizabeth BRIERHURST
8 Jun   John s/o Samuel & Jane LACEBY
15 Jun   Thomas s/o William & Dorothy HITCHCOCK
29 Jun   Anne d/o Edward & Anne TOOTH
29 Jun   Edward s/o John & Elizabeth DRAKEFIELD
14 Jul   Mary d/o John & Anne WALKER was privately baptized
27 Jul   Alice d/o William & Alice DEAKIN
17 Aug   Joseph s/o John & Mary LOWE
28 Aug   Elizabeth d/o Edward & Anne WORZEY
14 Sep   Mary d/o John & Mary GILL
14 Sep   Mary d/o John & Mary SNAPE was privately baptized at Bustomley & rec'd into the Congregation Oct 4
21 Sep   Dorothy d/o William & Elizabeth ROBOTHAM
2 Oct   Mary d/o Michael & Mary GOODALL
9 Oct   Elizabeth d/o Mr Edward & Mrs Lydia BLURTON was privately baptized & rec'd into the Congregation Nov 3
25 Nov   Hannah d/o David & Mary BAILYE
30 Nov   John s/o William & Mary JELLY
2 Dec   Edward s/o William & Prudence CHELL

4 Jan   John s/o Joseph & Sarah WOOLLEY
12 Jan   Elizabeth d/o Thomas & Lydia FORD
15 Feb   Mary d/o Thomas & Elizabeth HARRIS
20 Feb   Francis s/o Mary HOWARD was privately baptized
22 Feb   Jonathan s/o Francis & Mary TUNSTAL
5 Mar   Margaret d/o John & Mary HOWE
6 Mar   Samuel s/o William & Anne CLAY
8 Mar   George s/o John & Diana TURNER
8 Mar   Anne d/o John & Sarah LEES
20 Mar   Barbara d/o William & Anna PICKERING was privately baptized & rec'd into the Congregation March 29 1741

1741

16 Apr   Jane d/o William & Sarah KEELING
16 Apr   Sarah d/o John & Mary TONNYCLIFFE
16 Apr   John s/o John & Sarah STARTIN
23 Apr   Joseph s/o George & Sarah JOHNSON
3 May   Francis s/o Thomas & Anne RUSHTON was baptized by Mr Rowlands
10 May   Elizabeth d/o Mr Robert & Mrs Joyce THACKER was privately baptized at Leigh & rec'd into the Congregation May 19
10 May   Mary d/o Thomas & Hannah CHELL
23 May   Sarah d/o John & Lettice GORDIN
29 May   Richard s/o George & Elizabeth HODGSON
11 Jun   Sarah d/o Mt John SPATEMAN & Mary his wife bapt by Mr Rowlands. She was born May 26
11 Jun   Sarah d/o Matthew & Mary HODGKINSON
22 Jul   Edward s/o Edward & Mary BARKER was privately baptized at Leigh Church & rec'd into the Congregation Aug 21
18 Oct   James s/o George & Ellen CLOWES
27 Oct   Elizabeth d/o William & Anne PHILLIPS of Nobot was privately baptized & rec'd into the Congregation Nov 5
5 Nov   Hannah d/o James & Bridget DONE
8 Nov   Mary d/o William & Sarah PARKER
22 Nov   Anne d/o John & Anne BIRD
17 Dec   Elizabeth d/o John & Anne PHILLIPS
1 Jan   Sarah d/o Thomas & Sarah MILLINGTON
23 Jan   Robert s/o John & Jane BLURTON
31 Jan   Thomas s/o Thomas & Hannah TOMLINSON
3 Feb   Elizabeth d/o John & Mary BELCHER
14 Feb   Joseph the bastard s/o Elizabeth BROWNE
15 Feb   John the bastard s/o Dorothy OSBORNE
18 Feb   William s/o Widow Elizabeth DANIEL
21 Feb   Robert s/o Thomas & Elizabeth COPE
2 Mar   Francis s/o Thomas & Elizabeth TILL
21 Mar   Elizabeth d/o Robert & Isabel JOHNSON
21 Mar   Mary d/o Robert & Grace BEARDMORE

1742

28 Mar   Joseph s/o John & Ursula MARTIN bapt by Mr Ra. Turner
4 Apr   Catherine d/o Samuel & Jane LACEBY
4 Apr   Ralph s/o John & Anne WALKER was privately baptized & rec'd into the Congregation April 29
16 May   Simon s/o Simon & Elizabeth FOWLER

22 May   Joseph s/o Antony & Elizabeth THACKER
26 May   John s/o John & Margaret GILBERT
8 Jun   Ralph s/o Ralph & Anne TURNER of Over Teane
27 Jun   Hannah d/o John & Elizabeth DRAKEFIELD
8 Aug   Elizabeth d/o Richard & Dorothy TILL
22 Aug   John s/o John & Mary TONNYCLIFFE was baptized by Mr Rowlands
5 Sep   Mary d/o William & Mary JELLY
16 Sep   Lydia d/o George & Mary TURNER
12 Oct   Janes s/o Thomas & Elizabeth JOHNSON
2 Nov   Elizabeth d/o Thomas & Elizabeth HARRIS
11 Nov   John s/o Michael & Mary GOODALL
14 Jan   Edward s/o John & Mary HOWE
16 Jan   Dorothy d/o James & Elizabeth RATCLIFFE
23 Jan   Ralph s/o Thomas & Elizabeth COPE
23 Jan   Mary d/o John & Anne PHILLIPS
23 Jan   Charles the bastard s/o Anne WETTON
2 Feb   Elizabeth d/o Thomas & Alice COLLIER
2 Feb   Elizabeth d/o James & Anne BAILYE [Baylye-BT]
6 Feb   Ellen d/o William & Elizabeth ROBOTHAM
12 Feb   William s/o John & Diana TURNER
14 Feb   Jonathan s/o William & Angelous TUNSAL
15 Feb   Elizabeth d/o William & Alice DEAKIN of Middleton Green privately baptized
         by Mr Robinson & rec'd into the Congregation Feb 20
21 Feb   Thomas s/o William & Anne PHILLIPS privately baptized
13 Mar   Thomas s/o Edward & Anne TOOTH
24 Mar   Mary d/o George & Sarah JOHNSON
1743
25 Mar   Thomas s/o William & Anne PHILLIPS rec'd into the Congregation
10 Apr   John s/o Thomas & Sarah MOORF
15 Apr   Thomas s/o George & Ellen COPE was privately baptized
27 Apr   Thomas s/o Thomas & Elizabeth COLCLOUGH privately baptized
1 May   Thomas s/o George & Ellen COPE was rec'd into the Congregation
8 May   Thomas s/o Thomas & Elizabeth COLCLOUGH was rec'd into the
         Congregation
15 May   George s/o Thomas & Anne RUSHTON bapt by Mr Smith
22 May   John s/o William & Prudence CHELL
23 May   Elizabeth d/o George & Elizabeth HODGSON privately baptized & rec'd into
         the Congregation May 29
10 Jul   Martha d/o Joseph & Sarah WOOLLEY privately
14 Jul   John s/o John & Susanna JELLY privately baptized by Mr Rowlands & rec'd
         into the Congregation by Mr Ward July 17
4 Sep   Joseph the bastard s/o Elizabeth HURST
15 Oct   Mary d/o Sampson & Mary BAILYE [Baylye-BT]
16 Oct   Mary d/o John & Sarah LEES
31 Oct   Richard s/o Thomas & Anne WILLIAMSON
1 Nov   Diana d/o Mr Robert THACKER & Mrs Joyce THACKER
1 Nov   Sarah d/o Robert & Sarah ROGERS
13 Nov   John s/o John & Anne WALKER
5 Jan   John s/o Mr William & Anne TURNER
15 Jan   Jane d/o John & Mary JOHNSON privately baptiz'd & rec'd into the
         Congregation Feb 5

26 Feb Sarah d/o William & Sarah PARKER
2 Mar Edward s/o Richard & Dorothy TILL
9 Mar William s/o William & Elizabeth HALL
14 Mar Sarah d/o Thomas & Dorothy TRUNDLEY
1744
1 Apr Sarah d/o John & Elizabeth DRAKEFIELD
1 Apr William s/o John & Sarah STARTIN privately baptized by Mr Cockayne
    [Cokayne-BT] & rec'd into the Congregation April 8
15 Apr James s/o George & Ellen CLOWES
6 May John s/o John & Elizabeth BRIDGET
6 May Edward s/o John & Sarah HYDE
14 May Sarah d/o George & Mary TURNER
3 Jun Joyce d/o Lewis & Sarah THACKER
22 Jun Richard s/o Simon & Elizabeth FOWLER
8 Jul William s/o John & Ellen FENTON
8 Jul Anne d/o John & Mary TONNYCLIFFE
14 Jul John s/o Thomas & Hannah TOMLINSON privately baptiz'd & rec'd into the
    Congregation July 22 by Mr William Cokayne
9 Sep Sarah d/o Thomas & Elizabeth TILL
6 Oct William s/o Philip & Mary HOLLINS privately baptiz'd
7 Oct Benjamin s/o James & Anne BAILYE
18 Oct John s/o William & Anne CLAY
4 Nov Hannah d/o Thomas & Elizabeth COPE
5 Nov William s/o Philip & Mary HOLLINS rec'd into the Congregation
20 Nov Anne d/o William & Anne PHILLIPS baptized privately & rec'd into the
    Congregation Dec 8
8 Dec Joseph s/o Edward & Mary BARKER
16 Dec Samuel s/o William & Elizabeth BLOOD
26 Dec Ralph s/o John & Diana TURNER
26 Dec Edward s/o John & Jane BLURTON baptized privately & rec'd into the
    Congregation Jan 1
23 Jan Elizabeth d/o John & Margaret GILBERT baptized privately & rec'd into the
    Congregation Feb 23
24 Jan Edward s/o Edward & Elizabeth HOWARD baptized privately & rec'd into
    the Congregation Jan 30
17 Feb Ellis s/o Sampson & Mary BAYLEY
24 Feb Francis s/o William & Angelous TUNSTAL
26 Feb John s/o John & Mary HOWE
1 Mar Elizabeth d/o William & Elizabeth MARSTON
6 Mar Catherina d/o John & Anne WALKER
10 Mar Anne d/o Thomas & Elizabeth HARRIS
10 Mar Thomas the bastard s/o Sarah TILL
13 Mar Samuel s/o William & Mary JELLY
13 Mar John s/o John & Mary COLLIER
17 Mar Elizabeth d/o John & Sarah LEES
21 Mar Richard & James the sons of Thomas & Alice COLLIER baptized privately.
    Rec'd into the Congregation March 31
1745
20 Apr Sarah d/o John & Mary LOWE privately Rec'd into the Congregation May 12
21 Apr Sarah d/o James & Elizabeth RATCLIFFE
19 May Mary d/o George & Jane THORNIWELL

16 Jun Mary d/o Aaron & Mary BLOOD
23 Jun James s/o John & Hannah RAWLINS
4 Jul Anne d/o Mr John & Mrs Catherine BRINDLEY
7 Jul Mary d/o Richard & Dorothy TILL
28 Jul Sarah d/o George & Sarah JOHNSON
28 Jul Anne d/o George & Elizabeth HODGSON baptized privately. Rec'd into the
Congregation Aug 25
4 Aug George s/o George & Ellen COPE
18 Aug John s/o William & Elizabeth ROBOTHAM
8 Sep Hannah d/o William & Alice DEAKIN
19 Oct Elizabeth d/o Robert & Sarah ROGERS baptiz'd privately. Rec'd into the
Congregation Nov 5
19 Oct Edward s/o Thomas & Dorothy DAWSON baptiz'd privately. Rec'd into the
Congregation Nov 5
20 Oct Job s/o Thomas & Anne RUSHTON
26 Oct Hannah d/o Philip & Mary HOLLINS baptized privately. Rec'd into the
Congregation Nov 5
5 Nov Sarah d/o Matthew & Mary HODGKINSON
15 Dec Samuel s/o Samuel & Alice DEAKIN
1 Jan Robert s/o Mr Robert & Mrs Joyce THACKER
13 Jan Lucy d/o James & Anne BAYLYE
2 Feb Anne d/o Thomas & Sarah MOORE
9 Mar Thomas s/o John & Joyce MUCHEL
20 Mar William s/o Robert & Anne TOWERS
1746
11 Apr John s/o John & Anne PHILLIPS privately
13 Apr Elizabeth d/o Simon & Elizabeth FOWLER
20 Apr Margaret d/o Edward & Elizabeth HOWARD
27 Apr Thomas s/o William & Prudence CHELL
4 May John s/o Thomas & Elizabeth TILL
4 May Ralph s/o George & Mary TURNER
16 May William s/o John WALKER & Anne his wife bapt privately. Rec'd into the
Congregation May 22 by Mr Hancock
21 Jun Mary d/o Edward & Elizabeth HOLLINGWORTH
29 Jun John s/o John & Sarah HYDE
17 Jul Jane d/o George & Jane THORNIWELL
3 Aug William s/o Thomas & Hannah THOMLINSON
3 Aug William s/o Richard & Elizabeth CARTER baptized privately. Rec'd into the
Congregation Sept 28
21 Sep Mary d/o John & Ellen FENTON
15 Oct James s/o Thomas & Lettice TATTON baptized privately. Rec'd into the
Congregation Oct 19
9 Nov Elizabeth d/o William & Mary BAYLYE
23 Nov Dorothy d/o Francis & Mary MARSTON
8 Dec Elizabeth d/o Thomas & Elizabeth HARRIS
11 Jan Lewis s/o Lewis & Sarah THACKER
18 Jan Sarah d/o Thomas & Sarah MOTTERAM
23 Jan Catherine d/o Mr John & Mrs Catherine BRINDLEY
30 Jan John s/o Thomas & Elizabeth HALL baptized privately. Rec'd into the
Congregation Feb 14
8 Feb Margaret d/o Robert & Isabel JOHNSON

10 Feb   Elizabeth d/o John & Anne BIRD privately.   Rec'd into the Congregation March 27

11 Feb   James & Samuel sons of John & Diana TURNER baptized privately. Rec'd into the Congregation March 13

15 Feb   William s/o George & Ellen COPE

26 Feb   William s/o William & Alice DEAKIN

13 Mar   Hannah d/o Job & Alice BROWN

1747

27 Mar   Hannah d/o George & Sarah JOHNSON

3 Apr   Elizabeth d/o Thomas & Mary HOLLINS

5 Apr   Anne d/o Thomas & Elizabeth COPE

5 Apr   Anne d/o John & Mary COLLIER

29 Mar   William s/o John & Mary BELCHER baptized privately. Rec'd into the Congregation April 20

20 Apr   Sarah d/o Henry & Anne WOODWARD

22 Apr   William s/o William & Anne HOLLINS

10 May   Charles s/o William & Elizabeth ROBOTHAM

16 May   Mary d/o Mr William & Mrs Anne SHERRATT

18 May   Mary d/o Thomas & Elizabeth JOHNSON baptized privately. Rec'd into the Congregation June 29

23 May   Anne the bastard d/o Alice PYOTT

24 May   John s/o John & Anne PHILLIPS

14 Jun   Richard s/o Richard & Dorothy TILL

21 Jun   Anne d/o Samuel & Alice DEAKIN

17 Jul   William s/o John & Mary TUNNICLIFFE

21 Jul   Mary d/o John & Mary HOWE

26 Jul   Lydia d/o William & Mary JELLY

26 Jul   Sarah d/o John & Sarah STARTIN

7 Sep   John s/o Samuel & Mary SALT baptiz'd privately. Rec'd into the Congregation Oct 4

27 Sep   William s/o William & Elizabeth MARSTON

29 Sep   Elizabeth d/o John & Sarah HYDE

27 Oct   Margaret d/o William & Anne PHILLIPS baptized privately. Rec'd into the Congregation Nov 12

10 Nov   George s/o George & Mary TURNER

15 Nov   George s/o Sarah WOOLLEY

25 Dec   Elizabeth d/o Thomas & Dorothy DAWSON

1 Jan   Ellen d/o Mr Robert & Mrs Joyce THACKER

17 Jan   Mary d/o Edward & Elizabeth HOWARD

17 Jan   John s/o John & Elizabeth DRAKEFIELD

26 Jan   John s/o Thomas & ~~Mary~~ Elizabeth BELCHER

13 Mar   Judith d/o John & Elizabeth BRIERHURST

23 Mar   Anne the bastard d/o Anne BLORE

1748

29 Mar   Bridget d/o Thomas & Elizabeth RUSHTON baptiz'd privately

15 Apr   Thomas s/o Simon & Eliabeth FOWLER

17 Apr   Richard s/o Richard & Mary WOOD

24 Apr   Thomas s/o Thomas & Hannah TUNNICLIFFE

26 Apr   Katherine d/o John & Anne WALKER

26 Apr   Elizabeth d/o Aaron & Mary BLOOD

15 May   John s/o Mr John & Mrs Mary LOWE

26 May	Thomas s/o Thomas & Mary HOLLINS baptized privately. Rec'd into the Congregation May 30
30 May	Thomas s/o William & Sarah PARKER
25 Jun	Mary d/o Richard & Elizabeth CARTER baptiz'd privately. Rec'd into the Congregation July 17
26 Jun	Elizabeth d/o William & Margaret RAWLIN
23 Jul	Elizabeth d/o Mr William & Mrs Anne SHERRATT baptiz'd privately. Rec'd into the Congregation 5 Aug
31 Jul	Joseph s/o Thomas & Sarah MOORE
18 Aug	Mary d/o John & Sarah LEES
9 Sep	Anne d/o Edward & Elizabeth HOLLINGWORTH
14 Sep	David s/o Sampson & Mary BAYLYE
9 Oct	Charles s/o George & Jane THORNIWELL
13 Oct	Charles the bastard s/o Elizabeth [ ]
31 Oct	Joseph s/o George & Ellen COPE
8 Dec	Jane d/o John & Ellen FENTON
11 Dec	Susan d/o Willm & Mary BAYLYE *[Bayley-BT]*
13 Dec	Mary d/o Willm & Elizabeth ROBOTHAM baptized privately
3 Jan	Sarah d/o Thomas & Elizabeth HARRIS
14 Jan	Thomas s/o Richard & Dorothy TILL
16 Jan	Richard the bastard s/o Sarah MOTTERAM
22 Jan	Mary d/o Henry & Mary BUXTON
22 Jan	Elizabeth d/o Francis & Mary MARSTON
2 Feb	George s/o George & Sarah JOHNSON
2 Feb	Alice d/o Thomas & Elizabeth HALL
25 Feb	John s/o William & Mary SALT
3 Mar	Jane d/o Job & Alice BROWN
12 Mar	Hannah d/o James & Elizabeth RATCLIFFE
1749	
30 Mar	John s/o George & Jane DLURTON
13 Apr	Elizabeth d/o Thomas & Sarah MOTTERAM
7 May	Samuel s/o William & Anne HOLLINS
14 May	Joseph s/o John & Mary TUNNICLIFFE
21 May	Joseph s/o Samuel & Alice DEAKIN
24 May	Thomas s/o Thomas & Mary JERVIS
10 Jun	Thomas s/o John & Sarah HYDE
3 Aug	Sarah d/o John & Mary WHEELDON baptiz'd privately. Rec'd into the Congregation Aug 20
4 Aug	Anne d/o Robert & Anne LAKIN baptiz'd privately
20 Aug	Francis s/o Thomas & Elizabeth TILL
24 Aug	Frederick s/o Thomas & Anne RUSHTON
17 Sep	Anne d/o Mr William & Mrs Anne SHERRATT baptiz'd privately. Rec'd into the Congregation Sept 23
8 Oct	Samuel s/o John & Anne WALKER
8 Oct	George s/o William & Alice DEAKIN
31 Oct	John s/o William & Margaret RAWLINS
1 Nov	Abigail d/o William & Mary JELLY
5 Nov	George s/o John & Mary HOWE
5 Nov	Elizabeth d/o Richard & Elizabeth CARTER
12 Nov	Mary d/o John & Mary COLLIER
16 Nov	James s/o Thomas & Elizabeth BELCHER baptiz'd privately

~	3 Dec	Elliot s/o John & Anne BAYLYE
	17 Dec	Francis s/o Edward & Elizabeth HOWARD
	31 Dec	John s/o John & Anne BIRD
	28 Jan	Charles s/o Willm & Eliz: ROBOTHAM
	25 Feb	John s/o George & Ellen COPE
	24 Mar	Charles the bastard s/o Elizabeth SHAWE

1750

	19 Apr	Francis s/o Willm & Anne PHILLIPS
	27 Apr	Samuel s/o John & Sarah STARTIN
—	29 Apr	Elizabeth d/o Sarah the wife of Joseph WOOLLEY
	6 May	Jane d/o George & Jane BLURTON
	9 May	John s/o Francis & Sarah SHERRATT baptized privately. Rec'd into the Congregation May 12
	29 May	Lydia d/o Thomas & Elizabeth COPE
	17 Jun	Mary d/o Anne GERRARD
	6 Jul	Patience d/o Thos & Patience CARTWRIGHT baptiz'd privately. Rec'd into the Congregatn. Aug 5
⌣	29 Jul	George s/o John & Mary LOWE baptiz'd privately. Rec'd into the Congregatn. Aug 5
—	6 Sep	Sarah d/o Thos & Sarah MOORE baptiz'd privately. Rec'd into the Congregatn. Sept 16
—	9 Sep	Lydia d/o Luke & Dorothy BAYLYE *[Bayley-BT]*
—	30 Sep	Mary d/o James & Anne BAYLEY
	30 Sep	Elizabeth d/o Joseph & Mary WOODINGS
	4 Oct	Francis d/o Mr Willm & Mrs Anne SHERRATT
	6 Oct	Michael s/o Thos & Hannah TUNNICLIFFE
	21 Oct	Thomas s/o John & Elizabeth BRIERHURST
	26 Oct	Charles the bastard s/o Mary CLOWES baptiz'd privately. Rec'd into the Congregation Oct 28
—	8 Nov	William s/o William & Sarah PARKER
	17 Nov	Thomas s/o Mr John & Mrs Catherine BRINDLEY baptiz'd privately. Rec'd into the Congregatn Nov 30
	8 Dec	Margaret d/o George & Sarah JOHNSON
⌐16 Dec		William s/o Mr John & Mrs Mary LOWE
— 1 Jan		Richard s/o John & Joyce MUTCHEL
— 10 Jan		Edward s/o Edward & Rebekah WALKER
— 16 Jan		Anne d/o Thos & Elizabeth HALL privately
— 20 Jan		Dorothy d/o Willm & Mary BAYLEY
	2 Feb	John s/o Elizabeth JOHNSON
	3 Feb	Joseph s/o John & Elizabeth DRAKEFIELD
	3 Feb	William s/o Henry & Alice BUXTON
	19 Feb	Joyce d/o Mr Robert & Mrs Joyce THACKER
~	10 Mar	John s/o George & Mary TURNER
	10 Mar	George s/o George & Jane THORNIWELL
	21 Mar	Thomasine d/o Edward & Elizabeth HOLLINGWORTH

1751

	8 Apr	Margaret d/o Willm & Margaret RAWLIN
—	8 Apr	Thomas s/o John & Anne WALKER
	21 Apr	Francis s/o George & Ellen COPE
+	12 May	Alice d/o Willm & Mary POTT
~	9 Jun	William s/o Willm & Mary SALT

10 Jun Anne d/o Simon & Elizabeth FOWLER
5 Jul James HOLLINS bastard s/o Sarah MOTTERAM baptiz'd privately. Rec'd into the Congregn. July 25
21 Jul Hannah d/o Francis & Mary MARSTON
13 Sep William s/o John & Anne PHILLIPS baptized privately. Rec'd into the Congregation Oct 6
15 Sep John s/o Lewis & Sarah THACKER
15 Sep William s/o Thomas & Mary JERVIS
15 Sep John bastard s/o Elizabeth ALCOCK
20 Oct Margaret d/o Richd & Elizabeth CARTER
22 Oct Elizabeth d/o Mr Thomas & Mrs Elizabeth HOWE
27 Oct Thomas s/o William & Mary JELLY [Jelley-BT]
3 Nov Mary d/o Thomas & Elizabeth BRADDOCK
5 Dec Sarah d/o John & Anne BAYLEY
20 Dec Anne d/o Willm & Anne HOLLINS
1752
1 Jan Walter s/o Daniel & Sarah BURTON
1 Jan Sarah d/o Aaron & Mary BLOUD [Blood-BT]
6 Jan Mary d/o John & Mary WHEELDON
26 Jan Elizabeth d/o James & Elizabeth RATCLIFFE
2 Feb John s/o Edward & Elizabeth HOWARD
14 Feb Joseph s/o Tho: & Eliz: HALL
22 Mar Mary d/o John & Mary BARNETT
27 Mar Joseph s/o William & Alice DEAKIN
4 Apr William s/o John & Mary HOWE
12 Apr Elizabeth d/o Luke & Dorothy BAYLEY
10 May John s/o James & Elizabeth HOLLINS
8 Jun William s/o George & Anne WOOD baptized privately. Rec'd into the Congregatn Jun 25
14 Jun John s/o William & Sarah PARKER
22 Jun James s/o Thomas & Elizabeth BELCHER baptized privately. Rec'd into the Congreg'n June 27
8 Jul Joseph bastard s/o Elizth SHERRAT
13 Jul Nathaniel s/o Tho & Elizth WALTON
30 Jul Mary d/o Frans & Sarah SHERRAT
2 Aug Kitty d/o John & Joyce MUTCHEL
7 Aug Ann d/o John & Catherine HUNT
9 Aug Mary d/o Will & Elizth ROBOTHOM
9 Aug Elizabeth d/o Henry & Charity BAILEY [Bayley-BT]
10 Aug Esther bastard s/o Sarah WOOLLEY [Wooley-BT]
22 Sep James s/o Wm & Elizth MARSTON
8 Oct Margaret d/o Willm & Elizth WALKER
12 Nov John s/o John & Esther WALKER
23 Nov James s/o John & Ann WALKER bapt privately. Receiv'd into the Congregation Dec 1
26 Nov Elizabeth d/o Joseph & Bridget STOKES
17 Dec William s/o Thos & Hannah TUNNICLIFF
27 Dec William s/o Willm & Margaret RAWLINS
1753
18 Feb Ann d/o Thos & Elizth BRADDOCK
26 Feb Abigail d/o Edwd & Rebeccah WALKER

11 Mar	Sarah d/o Thos & Mary PHILLIPS
23 Mar	Sarah d/o Jno & Ann BLEWER
23 Mar	Joseph s/o Robt & Ann LAKIN bapt'd privately. Reciv'd into the Congregation Apr 23
30 Mar	Alice d/o Richert & Alice JOHNSON
14 Apr	Fanny d/o John & Mary LOWE
14 May	Mary d/o Gorge & Sarah JOHNSON
25 May	Elizabeth d/o Sampson & Mary BEALEY *[Bayley-BT]* bapt'd privately. Rec'd into the Congrn Jun1 1
3 Jun	Ann d/o Willim & Mary SALT
14 Jun	Barbeara d/o Nicholalas & Sarah MOTTERAM bapt'd privately. Recied into the Congregation July 12
16 Jun	Josaph s/o Gorge & Mary TURNER *[Turnner-BT]*
17 Jun	Mary the d/o Willm & Mary BEALY *[Bealey-BT]*
22 Jun	Charles s/o Jams & Elizabeth HOLLINGS *[Hollins-BT]*
30 Jun	Thomas s/o Thomas & Ann BERRISFORD
8 Jul	Robert s/o Thomas & Sarah MOORE
10 Jul	Sarah d/o Robert & Mary ROBOTHON *[Robothoam-BT]* bapt'd privatly. Reiev'd into the Congregation July 29
5 Aug	Margaret bastard d/o Anne ALSOP
6 Aug	John s/o John & Mary JOHNSON bapt'd privatly & Reciev'd into the Congregation Aug 21
12 Aug	Simon s/o Gorge & Ellen COPE
12 Aug	Elizabeth d/o Henry & Mary BUXTON
30 Aug	Samuel s/o John & Mary BENNETT bap'd privately. Rec'd into the Congregation Nov 18
3 Sep	John s/o Thomas & Elizabeth HOW bap'd privately & Rciev'd into the Congregation Sept 6
30 Sep	Adam s/o Thomas & Anne RUSHTON
27 Oct	Sarah d/o Thomas & Elizabeth BELCHER bap'd privately. Rec'd into the Congregation Nov 15
29 Oct	Sarah d/o Edward & Elizabeth HOLLINGWORTH
4 Nov	Luke s/o Henry & Charity BEALEY
11 Nov	Elizabeth d/o George & Jane THORNIWELL
8 Dec	Wiliam s/o Simon & Elizabeth FOWLER
30 Dec	Harvey s/o Wiliam & Honour LEES

1754

27 Jan	Ann d/o Thomas & Mary JARVES
8 Mar	Mary d/o Frances & Mary MARSON
10 Mar	Thomas s/o Edward & Elizabet HOWARD
20 Mar	John s/o John & Mary WHEELTON *[Wheeldon-BT]*
28 Apr	Wm the bastard s/o Ann PALMER
31 May	John & Sarah s&d/o Thomas & Elizabeth BRADDOCK bapt'd privately & both Rec'd July 7
2 Jun	Sarah d/o Mr Michael & Mrs Anne WARD bapt'd privately. Rec'd into the Congregation 14 June
7 Jul	Richard s/o John & Anne BAYLEY
9 Jul	Thomas s/o Thomas & Eliz. WALTON
27 Jul	Anne d/o Frances & Hannah TUNSTAL
2 Aug	Thomas s/o John & Anne PHILIPS bap'd pri'ly. Rec'd into the Congregation Aug 18

3 Sep	Benjamin s/o Benjamin & Hannah BURTON
12*Sep	Thomas s/o John & Elizabeth CARTAR bap'd privately. Rec'd into the Congregation Oct 11 [*2-BT]
15 Sep	Phebe d/o Wm & Alice DEAKIN
29 Sep	Phillip s/o James & Elizabeth HOLLONS
6 Oct	Lucy d/o Luke & Dorothy BAYLEY
7 Oct	George s/o John & Anne WALKER
20 Oct	James s/o Thomas & Elizabeth HALL
4 Nov	Samuel s/o Robert & Anne LAKIN
17 Nov	John s/o Richard & Eliz. CARTER
8 Dec	Joseph s/o Thomas & Ann BERRISFORD
30 Dec	Fanny the bastard d/o Sarah TILL bapt'd privately. Rec'd into the Congregation Jan 21

1755

9 Jan	Catherina the d/o Mr Thos & Mrs Eliz HOW
11 Jan	John s/o Mr Robert & Mrs Joyce THACKER
26 Jan	Dorothy the bastard d/o Sarah BLOOD
17 Feb	Mary d/o Thomas & Hannah TUNNICLIFF bap'd privately. Rec'd into the Congregation April 10
23 Feb	Thomas s/o John & Mary BARNET
1 Apr	Catharina d/o John & Catherine HUNT
26 Apr	Alice d/o George & Eliz DEAKIN bapt'd privately. Rec'd into the Congregation May 19
18 May	Thomas s/o George & Rachel LOVATT
26 Jun	James s/o Thomas & Hannah MARSON bap'd pri'ly. Rec'd into the Congregation June 29
29 Jun	John s/o John & Joyce MUTCHELL
29 Jun	William s/o Wm & Mary SALT
4 Jul	Thomas s/o John & Mary BLOWER
9 Jun	Anne d/o Mr Thomas & Mrs Eliz BELCHER bap'd privately by Mr Hancock. Rec onto the Congregation July 5
10 Aug	Mary d/o Joseph & Bridget STOAKES
10 Aug	Barbara d/o William & Mary BAYLEY
12 Sep	William s/o William & Elizabeth PARKER bapt'd privately. Recied into the Congregation Oct 12
29 Sep	Martha d/o James & Martha SAUNDERS
12 Oct	Mary bastard d/o Elizath BAYLEY
2 Nov	James s/o Thomas & Mary PHILIPS
3 Nov	Walter s/o Walter & Elizth HUNT
29 Dec	John s/o William & Honor LEES

1756

7 Jan	Sarah the d/o Thos & Elizth BRADDOCK
15 Jan	John s/o William & Margaret RAWLINS [Rawlin-BT]
1 Feb	Katherine d/o Hen'y & Alice BUXTON
9 Feb	Sarah d/o Thos & Mary LOWNDES bapt'd privately
19 Feb	Elizabeth the d/o Richard & Mary HOW
28 Feb	Sarah d/o Richard & Mary MOTTERAM bapt'd privately. Rec'd into the Congregation April 8
15 Mar	Edward s/o Edward & Elizabeth HOLLINGWORTH
28 Mar	John s/o Thos & Mary JARVIS
30 Mar	James s/o John & Ann WALKER privately

31 Mar	Mary d/o Robert & Dorrothy PHILLIPS bapt'd privately. Rec'd into the Congregation April 19
16 Apr	Hannah d/o Edward & Elizth HOWARD
23 Apr	Robert s/o Samuel & Mary BAYLEY
24 Apr	John s/o Phillip & Sarah HAWLEY
9 May	Ann d/o George & Ellin COPE
22 May	Mary d/o John & Ellin MILLINGTON
2 Jun	Arthur s/o Thos & Ann HARRISON bapt'd privately. Rec'd into the Congregation July 4
7 Jun	James s/o John & Elizth CARTER
20 Jun	Martha d/o George & Jane THORNIWELL
27 Jun	James s/o George & Mary TURNER
1 Jul	Elizabeth d/o Daniel & Sarah BURTON
5 Jul	Sarah d/o George & Eliz. DEAKIN
8 Aug	Israel s/o John & Mary WHEELDON
29 Aug	Mary d/o Thos & Sarah MOORE
5 Sep	Hannah d/o Wm & Elizth ROBOTHAM
21 Oct	Margaret d/o Simon & Elizth FOWLER bapt'd privately. Rec'd into the Congregation Nov 14
29 Oct	William s/o William & Sarah RUSHTON
5 Nov	John s/o Thos & Elizth BOX
14 Nov	Lydia dautr of Francis & Mary MARSTON
26 Dec	Henry s/o John & Ann BAYLEY

1757

16 Jan	John s/o Joseph & Mary TILL
10 Feb	Joseph s/o Thomas & Hannah TUNNICLIFF
20 Feb	Dorothy d/o Frans & Ann RATCLIFF
24 Feb	John s/o Thos & Mary LOWNDES
11 Mar	Francis s/o Francis & Elizth SHERRATT
13 Mar	Hannah bastard d/o Hannah BEECH
20 Apr	Ann d/o Luke & Dorothy BAYLEY bapt'd privately. Rec'd into the Congregation May 1
10 May	Jane d/o John & Elizth BAYLEY bapt'd privately. Rec'd into the Congregation May 29
17 May	Mary & Elizth ds/o Thos & Elizth SHERRATT bapt'd privately. Rec'd into the Congregation May 29
5 Jun	Joseph s/o John & Mary KIRK
4 Jul	Ann d/o Robt & Dorrithy PHILLIPS
8 Jul	Mary d/o Jas & Elizth HOLLINS
13 Jul	Ann d/o Ricd. & Alice JOHNSON
9 Aug	Thos bastard s/o Ann TURNER
4 Sep	Mary d/o George & Ellin COPE
29 Sep	Elizabeth d/o William & Elizth PARKES
29 Sep	John s/o William & Sarah BELCHER bapt'd privately. Rec'd into the Congregation October 14
7 Oct	Elizabeth d/o Mr Thos & Mrs Elizth BELCHER
30 Oct	Thomas s/o Philip & Sarah HAWLEY
30 Oct	Mary d/o Geo. & Rachael LOVATT
13 Nov	Jane d/o John & Jane CHARLSWORTH
4 Dec	Ann d/o Wm & Mary BAYLEY bapt by Mr NIXON
25 Dec	James s/o John & Ann LOWE

28 Dec Lydia d/o Wm. & Honour LEES
1758
8 Jan Mary d/o Wm. & Mary SALT
13 Feb William & Samuel sons of Edwd & Elizth HOWARD baptized privately
16 Feb Thomas s/o Henry & Elizth WOODWARD
5 Mar Joseph s/o Willm & Sarah RUSHTON
19 Mar Thomas s/o Thos & Mary PHILLIPS
28 Mar Francis s/o Frans & Elizth SHERRATT
3 Apr Sarah d/o John & Ellin MILLINGTON bapt'd privately. Rec'd into the Congregation April 15 by Mr Manifold
23 Apr Ann d/o John & Ellin FENTON
24 Apr Mary d/o Joseph & Mary TILL
16 May Thomas s/o Willm & Margaret RAWLIN
18 May Elizabeth d/o George & Elizabeth DEAKIN
9 Jul David s/o Theodorus & Jane DAVIS
14 Jul William s/o Nicholas & Sarah MOTTERAM bapt'd privately. Rec'd into the Congregation August 17
21 Jul Hannah & Sarah daurs of John & Mary CROSLEY bapt'd privately. Rec'd into the Congregation Aug 18
6 Aug James s/o William & Elizth JOHNSON
20 Aug John s/o William & Alice DEAKIN
27 Aug Mary the d/o Thos & Elizabth BOX
31 Aug Elizabeth the d/o Thos & Ann HILL bapt'd privately. Rec'd into the Congregation Sept 30
21 Sep Ann the d/o Edward & Jane BRERETON
24 Sep James s/o James & [ ] CLEWLOW
28 Sep Ann the d/o Sampson & Mary BAYLEY *[Bailey-BT]*
21 Sep Alice d/o John & Elizabeth CARTER bapt'd privately by Mr Hancock. Rec'd into the Congregatn Oct 30
5 Nov James s/o Willm & Mary JELLY
12 Nov Henry s/o Henry & Alice BUXTON
1759
7 Jan George s/o Thos & Ann HARRISON
7 Jan Hannah d/o Thos & Hannah MARSTON
18 Feb Mary d/o Sampson & Ann BEARDMORE
3 Mar Thomas s/o Robt. & Dorrothy PHILLIPS bapt'd privately. Rec'd into the Congregation May 8
19 Mar John s/o Henry & Elizabeth WOODWARD bapt'd privately. Rec'd into the Congregation April 6
20 Mar George s/o Edwd & Elizabeth HOLLINGWORTH
14 Apr Robert s/o William & Mary HARVEY
15 Apr Ann d/o Thos & Elizabth SHERRATT
18 May John s/o George & Jane THORNIWELL bapt'd privately. Rec'd into the Congregation June 10
27 May Ann d/o Francis & Ann RATCLIFF
4 Jun Mary d/o Thomas & Elizabeth BELCHER
24 Jun Ann d/o Thomas & Elizabeth TOOTH
1 Jul John s/o John & Anne BAILEY
29 Jul Anne d/o John & Mary WILDON
2 Aug Mary d/o William & Elizabeth MARSTON
16 Sep Thomas s/o William & Sarah ADAMS

21 Sep   Eleanor d/o John & Mary BLOORE
25 Sep   Richard s/o Sarah ARMITT
27 Sep   Dorothy d/o John & Anne HART privately baptized. Admitted into the
          Congregation Nov 5
12 Oct   Margaret d/o William & Sarah BELCHER
11 Nov   Hannah d/o George & Elizabeth ROEBOTHAM
11 Nov   William s/o John & Sarah TILL
1760
12 Jan   John & Thomas twin sons of John & Elizabeth JOHNSON privately bapt
21 Jan   Sarah d/o Richard & Alice JOHNSON
30 Jan   Betty *[Elizabeth-BT]* d/o Richard & Sarah SMITH
3 Feb   Hannah d/o John & Jane CHARLESWORTH
9 Feb   William s/o Thomas & Mary LOWNDES privately baptized. Admitted into
          the Congregation the 28th
10 Feb   William s/o William & Honor LEES
2 Mar   Anne d/o Edward & Elizabeth HOWARD
9 Mar   Thomas s/o Thomas & Elizabeth BOX
12 Mar   Ellen d/o Francis & Mary MARSTON
12 Mar   William s/o Anne WOODWARD
25 Mar   William s/o John & Ellen MILLINGTON privately baptized. Admitted into the
          Congregation April 19
13 Apr   Thomas s/o Ralph & Laetitia RUSHTON
24 May   Thomas s/o Thomas & Anne HILL privately baptized. Admitted into the
          Congregation June 1
25 May   Solomon s/o William & Mary SALT
8 Jun   Mary d/o William & Elizabeth BOTT
8 Jun   Lydia d/o Nicholas & Sarah MOTTERAM privately baptized. Admitted into
          the Congregation July 3
9 Jun   William s/o Robert & Dorothy PHILLIPS
6 Jul   Thomas s/o Thomas & Elizabeth BOLTON
27 Jul   Thomas s/o Joseph & Mary TILL
25 Jul   Thomas s/o Thomas & Elizabeth PERKIN
23 Aug   Elizabeth d/o William & Elizabeth JOHNSON
24 Aug   John s/o Mary KIRK
4 Oct   Richard s/o John & Eleanor FENTON
5 Oct   William s/o Thomas & Mary PHILIPS
16 Oct   Dorothy d/o William & Dorothy WRIGHT
30 Nov   John s/o Theodorus & Jane DAVIS
14 Dec   Jeremiah s/o Sampson & Anne BEARDMORE
19 Dec   John s/o John & Anne LOWE
1761
1 Jan   Samuel s/o George & Rachel LOVATT privately baptized. Admitted into the
          Cong'n Jan 12
18 Jan   Hannah d/o Mary CHELL
30 Jan   Sarah d/o John & Sarah HYDE
8 Feb   Hannah d/o Henry & Alice BUXTON
11 Feb   Sarah d/o Thomas & Mary CROSLEY privately bapt'd. Admitted into the
          Congregation Feb 21
22 Mar   Samuel s/o William & Elizabeth PARKES
27 Mar   Elizabeth d/o Henry & Elizabeth WOODWARD
30 Mar   Hannah d/o Thos & Anne HARRISON

9 Apr   John s/o John & Elizabeth JOHNSON priv. bapt'd. Received into the Congregation Apr 12

12 Apr   Martha d/o William & Mary BAILEY

11 May   Sampson s/o Sampson & Mary BAILEY

28 May   Elizabeth d/o Thomas & Elizabeth TOOTH

6 Jun   Elizabeth d/o Thomas & Sarah LEES

9 Jun or   *George s/o Thomas TUNNICLIFF & Hannah his wife

thereabouts *[note at bottom of page]* *the baptism above was informed in the presence of the Boy & his Mother on the 5th of August 1773 by me Sam: Tolland Curate

23 Jul   Ralph Gilbert s/o Mr Ralph & Mrs Mary WOOD of Fole privately

16 Aug   Elizabeth d/o Edward & Jane BRERETON

12 Sep   Alice d/o John & Ellen MILLINGTON

1 Nov   John s/o John & Mary GOODWIN

15 Nov   William s/o William & Sarah ADAMS

28 Nov   Anne d/o Mary SHAW privately baptized. Admitted into the Congregation Dec 20

8 Dec   Mary d/o John & Anne HART

20 Dec   Mary d/o George TURNER deceased & Mary his wife

22 Dec   Robert s/o Nicholas & Sarah MOTTERAM priv. baptiz'd. Admitted into the Congregation Jan 15 1762

1762

4 Jan   Sarah d/o Thomas & Sarah HOWE

31 Jan   Mary d/o Ralph & Lettice RUSHTON

11 Feb   Sarah d/o James & Elizabeth JOHNSON

1 Mar   Francis s/o Francis & Hannah TUNSTALL privately baptiz. Received into the Congregation April 4

30 Mar   Philip s/o Philip & Ellen CROSSBY *[Crosby-BT]* priv. baptized. Admitted into the Congregation May 1st

30 Mar   William s/o William & Sarah BELCHIER priv. baptized. Admitted into the Congregation June 1st

4 Apr   Mary d/o Joseph & Abigail HURST

12 Apr   Robert s/o Robert & Dorothy PHILIPS

18 Apr   Mary d/o John & Jane CHARLESWORTH

18 Apr   Elizabeth d/o Philip & Sarah HAWLEY

3 May   William s/o Joseph & Ann WEBB privately baptized. Admitted into the Congregation May 31st

9 May   Lydia d/o Thomas & Elizabeth SHERRARD

10 May   Joyce d/o Francis & Mary MARSTON

14 May   William s/o Richard & Sarah SMITH

22 Apr   Webb s/o Thomas & Elizabeth BELCHIER priv'ly baptiz'd

24 May   James s/o William & Alice DEAKIN privately baptized. Admitted into the Congregation June 6th

31 May   William s/o Margarett HOWE

1 Jun   Sarah d/o William & Mary SALT

6 Jun   +Feales d/o John & Ann BAILY + Phillis sed quare

27 Jun   Elizabeth d/o Anne ADAMS

4 Jul   Mary d/o John & Sarah TILL

11*Jul   Mary d/o Mary KIRK *[*14-BT]*

17 Jul   Thomas s/o Thomas & Mary FENTON

24 Jul   Mary d/o Thomas & Sarah BLOOD priv. baptiz. Admitted into the
Congregation Aug 29th

25 Jul   George s/o George & Elizabeth RUEBOTHAM

8 Aug   Elizabeth d/o Joseph & Mary TILL

6 Sep   Lydia d/o William & Honor LEES
[Rec'd into the Congregation Sep 10-BT]

17 Sep   Mary & Elizabeth twin daughters of Tho: & Mary HOPKINS privately
baptized. Received into the Congregation Octob 4th

18 Sep   Mary d/o Thomas & Elizabeth PERKIN

28 Oct   George s/o John & Alice PRESTON

7 Nov   William s/o Jonathan & Hannah TUNSTALL

20 Nov   Mary d/o Mr Michael WARD & Mary his wife, privately baptized. Admitted
into the Congregation Dec 27

19 Dec   John s/o Joseph & Mary EDGE

20 Dec   Thomas s/o John & Elizabeth COPE privately baptized. Received into the
Congregation Feb 26 1763

1763

5 Jan   Elizabeth d/o Thomas & Mary LOWNDES

9 Jan   William s/o Theodorus & Jane DAVIS

19 Jan   Mary d/o William & Elizabeth JOHNSON

30 Jan   Elizabeth d/o William & Mary SALT

6 Feb   Elizabeth d/o Martha MEAT

8 Apr   John s/o John & Mary CROSSLEY

1 May   John s/o Thomas & Sarah LEES

5 May   Isaac s/o Henry & Alice BUXTON

12 Jun   Elizabeth d/o James & Eleanor CARNEL

12 Jun   Elizabeth d/o Thomas & Elizabeth TOOTH

5 Jul   Eleanor d/o George & Rachael LOVATT

10 Jul   Sarah d/o Edward & Jane BRERETON

12 Jul   William s/o John & Elizabeth BIRD privately bapt. Admitted July 25

17 Jul   George s/o Martha WOOLLEY privately. Admitted [no date]

31 Jul   Sarah d/o John & Suz: JOHNSON priv: ad: Nov 1

4 Sep   Jane d/o John & Ellen FENTON

17 Sep   Elizabeth d/o Thomas & Mary CROSSLEY priv: ad: Nov 1

19 Oct   Richard s/o Richard & Sarah SMITH p. ad: Oct 30

13 Nov   Joseph s/o Joseph & Mary TILL

1764

29 Jan   Thomas s/o Thomas & Sarah BLOOD

12 Feb   Thomas s/o John & Elizabeth JENKINSON

19 Feb   Mary d/o Jonathan & Hannah TUNSTAL

27 Feb   Anne d/o John & Anne HART

8 Mar   Thomas s/o Thomas & Sarah HOWE

25 Mar   Robert s/o George & Jane THORNIWELL

25 Mar   William s/o William & Mary BAILY

4 Apr   Catherine d/o Robert & Mary WALKER

6 Apr   Anne the d/o Thomas & Elizabeth BUXTON

13 Apr   Henry s/o Henry & Elizabeth WOODWARD

20 Apr   Mary d/o Elizabeth CARTER Widow

22 Apr   Robert s/o Robert & Anne HOLLINS

15 Apr   Sarah d/o Nicholas & Sarah MOTTERAM

24 Apr   John s/o John & Anne BAILY

3 Jun	Thomas s/o John & Jane CHARLESWORTH
8 Jul	William s/o Thomas & Eliz. PERKIN
8 Jul	Joseph s/o John & Anne LOWE
15 Jul	Elizabeth d/o William & Honor LEES
29 Jul	Anne d/o Ralph & Latitia RUSHTON
31 Jul	Thomas s/o Mary SHAW
1 Aug	George s/o Robert & Dorothy PHILIPS priv. baptized. Admitted into the Congreg. Aug 11
12 Aug	John s/o John BILLINGS deceased & Mary his wife
19 Aug	Samuel s/o William & Sarah ADAMS
9 Sep	Anne d/o John & Jane TURNER
14 Sep	John s/o John & Eliz. COPE priv. baptized.
2 Sep	Ellen d/o John & Ellen MILLINGTON priv. bapt'd. Admitted into the Congregation Nov 5
24 Oct	John s/o John & Anne SHENTON
5 Nov	Dorothy d/o Thomas & Mary FENTON
5 Nov	Diana d/o Edward & Anne WOOLLEY
22 Nov	John s/o Thos & Mary HOPKINS
22 Dec	Elizabeth d/o Thomas & Sarah LEES

1765

1 Jan	Elizabeth d/o John & Eliz. HEATH was received into the Cong'n
30 Jan	Catherine d/o Thomas & Mary MARSTON
3 Feb	Hannah d/o William & Elizabeth JOHNSON
3 Feb	John s/o Thomas & Ann COLLIER
8 Feb	James s/o Thomas & Jane SHAW priv. baptized. Admitted into the Congregation Feb 24
18 Feb	Anne d/o James & Eleanor CARNEL
1 Mar	William s/o Thomas & Sarah FROST priv.baptized. Received into the Congregation March 11th
28 Mar	Elizabeth d/o Mary KIRK Widow priv. bap'd. Rec'd April 21
7 Apr	Ellen d/o Theodore & Jane DAVIES
7 Apr	William s/o Philip & Sarah HAWLEY
21 Apr	William s/o William & Mary MARTYN
21 Apr	Samuel s/o William & Mary SALT
16 Jun	Thomas s/o Richard & Sarah SMITH
23 Jun	Elizabeth d/o James & Elizabeth JOHNSON
7 Jul	Betty d/o Thomas & Elizabeth SHERRATT
14 Jul	John s/o Mary PHILIPS of Checkley Bank
28 Jul	Ann d/o John & Ann BAYLY
11 Aug	George s/o George & Ann TOOTH
18 Aug	Mary d/o William & Hannah OSBORNE
29 Sep	Elizabeth d/o John & Ellen FENTON
29 Sep	John s/o John & Sarah TILL
27 Oct	Dorothy d/o Joseph & Mary TILL
4 Nov	Elizabeth d/o George & Mary PHILIPS
5 Nov	John s/o Martha WOOLEY
8 Dec	John s/o John & Alice PRESTON

1766

12 Jan	Joyce d/o John &m Elizabeth MUTCHEL
19 Jan	Thomas s/o Mary SHENTON
2 Feb	Elizabeth d/o Benjamin & Mary HOLMES

24 Feb	Ann d/o Margaret HOWE *[How-BT]* of Leigh
28 Feb	George s/o Philip & Ellen CROSBY
29 Mar	Sarah d/o Hannah SMITH
30 Mar	Philip s/o Philip & Ellen TITLEY
6 Apr	Ralph s/o John & Jane CHARLSWORTH
11 May	Ellen d/o Elizabeth THACKER
11 May	Mary d/o John & Jane TURNER
27 Apr	Mary d/o John & Catharine ASTBURY priv'ly. bap.Rec' May 18
27 Jul	William s/o Matthew & Sarah SMITH
10 Aug	Ann d/o John & Ann SHENTON
12 Aug	Elizabeth d/o John & Ann HART
28 Sep	Margaret d/o Ellis & Anne BAILY
2 Nov	Elizabeth d/o Robert & Ann HOLLINS
4 Nov	Thomas s/o John & Ellen MILLINGTON
20 Nov	Joseph s/o Joseph & Anne WEBB
23 Nov	William s/o Thomas & Catherine THACKER
30 Nov	Thomas s/o Thomas & Mary CROSLEY
30 Nov	Elizabeth d/o Jonathan & Hannah TUNSTAL
3 Dec	John s/o William & Mary MARTIN priv. baptized. Rec'd Dec 14
26 Dec	Ann d/o John & Mary BLOORE

1767

15 Jan	Sarah d/o Richard & Sarah SMITH
26 Jan	Mary d/o George & Mary PHILIPS priv. baptized. Rec'd Feb 24
29 Jan	Jane Maria d/o Thomas & Sarah FROST
30 Jan	Elizabeth d/o John & Elizabeth JOHNSON privat'ly baptized
8 Feb	Mary d/o Edward & Ann WOOLEY
15 Feb	Joseph s/o Ralph &Lettice RUSHTON
22 Feb	John son John & Elizabeth JENKIN
24 Feb	John s/o William & Honor LEES
1 Mar	Ann d/o Samuel & Mary ALCOCK
4 Mar	George s/o John & Ann LOWE
6 Mar	William KENT s/o Alice DEAKIN
13 Mar	John s/o Mary HOWARD
15 Mar	James s/o James & Ellen CORNWAL
22 Mar	Elizabeth d/o Thomas & Elizabeth SALT
3 Apr	Samuel s/o Samuel & Elizabeth COPE
26 Apr	Hannah d/o John & Jane BAGNAL
10 May	Thomas son Edward & Mary BARKER
29 May	Ann d/o Elizabeth COOKE
8 Jun	Catharine d/o John & Catherine ASTBURY
8 Jun	John s/o Philip & Sarah HAWLEY
14 Jun	Robert s/o Robert & Ann HORNE
14 Jun	John s/o Thomas & Elizabeth PERKIN
28 Jun	Sarah d/o William & Sarah ADAMS
19 Jul	Elizabeth d/o Robert & Mary REEVES
19 Jul	Samuel WOODROFFE s/o Sarah EDGE
.. Jul	Catharine d/o William & Elizabeth JOHNSON
.. Aug	Richard s/o Richard & Mary FOWLER
.. Aug	Hannah d/o John & Mary BUXTON
9 Aug	Joseph s/o Thomas & Ann COLLIER pri'ly baptized. Rec'd [no date]
16 Aug	George s/o Philip & Eleanor CROSLY privately baptized. Rec' Oct 10

20 Sep Hannah d/o George & Ann TOOTH
27 Sep Sarah d/o John & Mary BARNET privately baptized. Rec'd Nov ..
11 Oct Elizabeth d/o Thos & Mary COPE
10 Nov James s/o Thomas & Mary FENTON baptized priv'ly. Rec'd Xmas Day
8 Nov Elizabeth d/o Theodore & Jane DAVIES
2- [?] Nov Elizabeth d/o Edward HOLLINGWORTH & Ann his wife
23 Nov Francis s/o Robert & Sarah PHILIPS baptiz'd. Rec'd Jan 6
20 Dec Edward s/o Edward HOWARD & Mary his wife

Matrimoniala

1705
18 Apr Thomas ALLEN Parochia de Abbots Bromly & Maria ADAMS huius Parochia
1 May Ricardus JACKSON de Uttoxeter & Elizabetha SHERRAT de Nobott
24 Jun Ricardus LYON Parochia de Pipe Ridware & Maria RIGHT [Wright-BT] Parochia de Leigh
5 Nov Thomas PYOTT Parochia de Stone & Jana JOHNSON huius Parochia
9 Nov Thomas GRIFFIN Parochia de Milwich & Elizabetha SHELLEY huius Parochia
22 Dec Johannis MARTIN Parochia de Dilhorn & Elizabetha STANFIELD Parochia eiusdem [Paroch de Dilhorne-BT]
1706
16 May Johannis DIKISON [Dickinson-BT] Parochia de Mavison Ridware & Diana SHERRATT huius Parochia
23 May Radulphus WALKER Parochia de Checkly & Catherina HILL huius Parochia
31 Aug Gulielmus SPENCER de Uttoxeter Anna HILL huius Parochia
19 Feb Thomas WOOD Parochia de Stone & Ellena ROBINSON de Doveridge in agro Derbiensi
1707
1 May Johannis LOW & Martha MOSS huius Parochia
5 Feb Thomas MOWLE Parochia de Stone & Anna AUSTIN huius Parochia
1708
11 Apr Thomas BEECH & Alicia BLURTON
1 May Edmund BENNIT [Bennitt-BT] Parochia de Pipe Ridware & Anna SAUNDERS huius Parochia
12 May Thomas WOODWARD [Woodruffe-BT] Parochia de Checkly & Anna KEEN huius Parochia
11 Jul Josephus DEAKIN & Joanna HARRIS
19 Feb Moses VISE & Maria MEAKIN
27 Feb Georgius ATKIN de Bromshelf & Maria HILL huius Parochia
1709
19 Dec Ricardus RICHLAND de Parochia de Bralsford in agro Derbiensis & Alicia PLIMMER Parochia de Sudbury
1710
22 Apr Thomas HILL & Martha SHERRATT Parochia de Leigh
31 Oct Gulielmus BIRD de Gratwich & Maria HILL de Withington in Paroch de Leigh
1711
9 Jul Job BIRD Parochia de Breerwood & Elizabetha SALT de Leigh
18 Feb Thomas ASBURY & Maria PERKIN de Leigh
24 Feb Antonius BROWN & Elizabetha JOHNSON

1712

21 Apr Thomas ADAMS & Sara RUSHTON

6 Jun Ricardus WOOTEN Parochia de Armitage & Margareta HILL Paroch de Leigh

10 Aug Henricus KYNNERSLEY Paroch de Uttoxeter & Elizabetha PEDLEY Paroch de Leigh

1713

6 Apr [BT] Lucas WETTON de Paroch Checkley et Catherina SHENTON Paroch de Leigh

3 Nov Thomas MELLOR et Anna PICKSTOCK

23 Jan Johns TURNER et Elizabetha SHERRATT de Paroch Leigh

1714

29 Mar Johns RAWLINS et Ellena HARRISON de Paroch Leigh

1715

2 Jun Radulphus HOLLINS & Catherina HARVEY uterqe de Paroch Abbots Bromley

25*Jul Gulielmus JOHNSON Paroch de Leigh & Maria CARTAR de Bromshall [*5-BT]

31 Oct Johannes MORRIS & Anna ARMISHAW uterqe de Paroch Leigh

1716

5 Apr Gulielmus KENDER Paroch de Scrapon in agro Derbiensi & Margaretta PHILLIPS Paroch de Church Broughton in Com pradicto

30 Apr Thomas MARROTT & Dorothy WOOD uterqe de Leigh Paroch

2 Jun Thomas HALL & Alicia PERCEFALL uterqe Paroch de Leigh

7 Jul Benjaminus BELCHER Paroch de Leigh & Anna LYEMAR Paroch de Cheadle

26 Jul Thomas WOOLEY & Maria WRIGHT uterqe de Paroch de Leigh

9 Aug Thomas KINNERSLEY Paroch de Stone & Anna LEAGH Paroch de Leigh

28 Nov Edvardus BLOUNT Paroch de Uttoxeter & Margaretta WARD Paroch de Leigh

24 Dec Thomas CLERK [Clark-BT] Paroch Leigh & Maria SMITH de Paroch Checkley

1717

13 Jun Thomas WARD & Felicia SIMNET uterqe de Paroch Leigh

13 Jun Thomas DAVIS & Margaretta DAVIS uterqe de Paroch Leigh

26 Nov Gulielmus SHERRATT & Anna MOOR uterqe de Paroch Leigh

1718

17 Apr Thomas GILLER de Paroch Uttoxeter & Eliz. BULLOCK Paroch de Leigh

2 May Johannes BROWN & Maria ARNOT uterqe de Proch Leigh

22 Jan Johannes BRINDLEY & Catherina PHILLIPPS uterqe de Parochia Leigh

27 Jan Thomas RIGBEY de Paroch Tatenhil & Elizabetha TILL Paroch de Leigh

5 Feb Johannes JOHNSON & Sara RUSHEN uterqe de Paroch Leigh

1719

30 Mar Thomas HOLLINS & Anna BEALEY [Bailey-BT] uterqe de Paroch Leigh

30 Mar Johannes SNAPE & Ellen SMITH uterqe de Paroch Leigh

9 Apr Nathaniel BLURTON & Maria ALSOPE uterqe de Paroch Leigh

15 Aug Franciscus HOWARD & Anna LARRENCE [Lawrence-BT] uterqe Paroch de Leigh

27 Aug Georgius WARD & Joanna HOLDING uterqe de Parochia Leigh

5 Sep Franciscus FERNS & Elizabetha COLLIER uterqe Parochia de Leigh

14 Nov   Josephus CLOWES Paroch de Uttoxeter & Dorothea WRIGHT Paroch de Leigh

1720

22 Dec   Johannes DUROSE Paroch de Uttoxeter & Margaretta ARMISHAW Paroch de Leigh

12 Feb   Gulielmus SNAPE Paroch Checkley & Maria LOW Paroch Uttoxeter

1721

12 Jun   Thomas COLLIER & Dorothea PLANT uterqe Paroch de Leigh

30 Oct   Robertus SPENCER & Sara PLANT uterqe de Paroch de Uttoxeter

24 Nov   Thomas WOOLLEY & Maria TOWNSEND uterqe de Paroch Leigh

30 Dec   Jonathan METE & Anna ONDERWOOD uterqe de Paroch Leigh

3 Feb   Johannes GRIME de Paroch Stow & Anna PHILLIPS de Paroch Leigh

1722

16 Oct   Startinus WOOD Generosi Parochia de Leigh & Magistra Eliz. WOOD Paroch de Uttoxeter

1723

9 Jan   Georgius CLOWES & Helena WRIGHT uterqe de Paroch Leigh

1724

12 Apr   Johannes MIDDLETON & Jana BULLOCK Paroch de Leigh

1725

2 Nov   Josephus HEELEY & Esthera LUKES huiusce Parochia

30 Jan   Gulielmus RATCLIFFE & Margeria COLCLOUGH

1726

22 Aug   Gulielmus GOUGH & Hannah DEAKIN Paroch de Draycot & huiusce Parochia

17 Nov   Joannes HIGGES & Anna STARTIN huiusce Parochia

1726/7

1 Jan   Georgius SMITH & Martha JUPP

7 Jan   Thomas NUTT Parochia de Gratwich & Elizabetha SWINSHEAD huiusce Parochia

9 Jan   Joannes EMERY Parochia de Stone & Bridgisa CARTWRIGHT huiusce Parochia

1727

27 Apr   Edvard SPOONER & Maria TILL huiusce Parochia

28 Jul   Joannes STRINGER huiusce Parochia & Anna BOSTON Parochia de Uttoxeter

1728

10 Jun   Joseph TARR Parochia de Ashbourn in Comitata Derbiensi & Maria RAWLIN huiusce Parochia

12 Nov   Gulielmus CLAY huiusce Parochia & Anna MOOREHOUSE de Winster in parochia de Youlgreave in Agro Derbiensi

17 Nov   Ricardus FLETCHER Parochia de Shenston & Dorothea GRETTON de Stone per Licentiam

12 Feb   Joannes COLLIER de Middleton Green & Elizabetha PARKES huiusce Parochia

1729

7 Apr   Anthony BAILYE of the Parish of Froddeswall & Sarah DAVIES of this Parish (His residence having been chiefly here of late they were asked in Church in this Parish only)

19 Sep   Edward SHERRATT of Middleton Green & Margaret DAVIES of Morrily Heath

27 Oct   John MILLES of the Parish of Uttoxeter & Elizabeth WALLIS of Nobot
1730
4 Jun   Mr Thomas LOVATT of Newcastle under Lyme & Elizabeth d/o Michael WARD Rector of Leigh by Elizabeth his former wife were married by Mr John Ward of Stoke by License
20 Jul   Henry WARRINGTON & Anne MEAT
1731
21 Apr   William HOLLINS & Grace STEVENSON
27 Apr   Paul SHERRATT of the Parish of Uttoxeter & Sarah COLLIER of Field
13 Sep   Simon BODIN Jun. & Martha LOWE married by Mr Tho. SPATEMAN
13 Nov   John TILL & Mary PHILIPS of Checkley Bank
8 Feb   Robert DEGGE of the Parish of Uttoxeter & Dorothy MIDDLETON
1732
7 May   Francis COOKE & Mary HART married by Mr Luke Budworth
27 Nov   William DAVIES & Elizabeth COPE
1733
28 Apr   Richard FENTON & Elizabeth TURNER
1 Oct   Robert PODMORE & Elizabeth SHERRATT
29 Dec   Mr Robert WOOD & Mrs Elizabeth NICHOLS of Field
31 Dec   John CLAY & Catherine BAILYE
1734
6 May   David BAILYE & Mary CLULOW
4 Aug   John YATES of Brewood & Margaret WRIGHT of Clayton in Stoke Parish were married by License
28 Aug   George WRIGHT & Mary DYCHE were married by Mr Craven
16 Sep   Charles LIGHTWOOD & Anne DYCHE were married by Mr Craven
3 Oct   Thomas BOX of Froddeswall & Mary DEAKIN
7 Oct   William MELLOR of Checkley Parish & Mary HOLLINS were married by Mr Craven
31 Oct   Thomas MOORE & Sarah BULLOCK were married by Mr Craven
3 Nov   John SNAPE of Bustomley & Mary SMITH
29 Dec   Henry WOODWARD & Anne DEAKIN
30 Dec   John BRIERHURST & Elizabeth LEES
6 Jan   Immanuel PERKIN & Mary SHERRATT were married by Mr Craven
20 Jan   John ELSMORE & Elizabeth CHALONER of Marchington by License
2 Feb   Mr Joshuah GODWIN of Abbots Bromley & Mrs Sarah BATEMAN of Leigh by License
1735
9 Jun   William BARNET & Ruth FINNY of this Parish
17 Jul   Mr Edward NICKLIN of Bromsgrove & Mrs Jane HORSEMAN of Loxly by License
22 Sep   William JOHNSON & Anne MOSSELEY of this Parish
18 Nov   Thomas WOOLLEY of Wood Leasowes & Mary HEATON
30 Nov   Mr John SPATEMAN and Mary d/o Michael WARD Rector of this Parish & Sarah his wife married by Mr Jno Ward
2 Jan   William HARGREAVES & Margaret SHERRATT
1736
6 Jun   James DONE & Bridget SWINSHEAD
30 Nov   Thomas CHELL & Hannah SMITH
1737
11 Apr   Ralph TURNER & Anne SHERRATT

9 Jun   Matthew SMITH of the Parish of Ilem & Elizabeth HOLLINS
31 Jan   George COPE & Ellen DANIEL
1738
10 Apr   Thomas COLLIER & Alice NIGHTAM
29 Apr   Thomas COLCLOUGH & Elizabeth PHILLIPS
17 Aug   Joseph JACKSON & Anne SMITH
1739
5 May   Thomas HARRIS & Elizabeth BROMLY married by Mr John Ward
1 Jun   John GORDIN & Lettice CLEWLOW of Morrily Heath
1740
31 Mar   Thomas WALL & Elizabeth ARCHER both of Cheadle Parish by License
25 Sep   James HITCHCOCK of the Parish of Gratwich & Dorothy RATCLIFFE of this Parish
21 Jan   William SMITH & Mary LOWE
1741
2 Apr   John PHILLIPS & Anne LEES
27 Jul   Robert BEARDMORE & Grace BRASSINGTON
24 Sep   Simon BOLDIN & Elizabeth RATCLIFFE
3 Nov   Mr William GALLIMORE & Mrs Elizabeth CARTWRIGHT
19 Nov   John GREENE & Hannah GOODALL
1 Mar   James BLORE & Jane LOWE
1742
19 Apr   John STRONGITHARM & Mary SHAWE
8 Jan   John COLLIER & Mary DANIEL were married by Mr Rowlands
13 Jan   John HYDE & Sarah HOLLINS
1743
21 May   James MORREY & Mary CLARKE
7 Jan   William MARSTON & Elizabeth TURNER
30 Jan   Thomas JOHNSON & Catharine RATCLIFF
5 Feb   Edward HOWARD & Elizabeth BROWN
1744
9 Sep   Thomas THACKER & Margaret SMITH
3 Nov   Thomas COLCLOUGH & Elizabeth GEE
5 Nov   John MUCHEL *[Mutchel-BT]* & Joyce ATKINS
8 Dec   James DONE & Elizabeth BILLINS
2 Feb   Richard WOOD of the Parish of Checkley & Mary DEAKIN of this Parish
1745
7 Jul   John BURTON & Anne REW both of Cheadle Parish married by License
29 Jul   Joseph TURNER & Sarah ADAMS
9 Jan   William MELLOR of Hanbury Parish & Anne THORLEY of Fulford married by License
3 Feb   Francis MARSTON & Mary BADDELEY
7 Feb   Thomas MOTTERAM & Sarah FENTON
1746
31 Mar   Thomas HOLLINS & Mary CARTWRIGHT
1 May   Thomas ROBINSON of the Parish of Uttoxeter & Anne BROWN of this Parish
17 May   John WRIGHT of the Parish of Dilhorne & Elizabeth HARVEY Widow of this Parish
28 Jul   Mr John CRUTCHLEY School-master of Leigh & Mrs Elizabeth HITCHCOCK
24 Aug   Job BROWN & Alice DEAKIN

2 Nov   Alexander PERKIN of the Parish of Checkley & Mary HOLLIN of this Parish
15 Dec   William MARSTON & Elizabeth WOOLLESCROFT
15 Jan   Edward HARPER & Hannah BROWN
1747
20 Apr   William STOKES of the Parish of Uttoxeter & Mary EVANS of this Parish
20 Apr   William RAWLINS & Margaret SMITH
29 Apr   John COPESTAKE of the Parish of Cubley & Elizabeth WOOLLEY of this Parish
3 Oct   Joseph JOHNSON of the Parish of Kingsley & Elizabeth RATCLIFFE of this Parish by License
7 Dec   John WHEELDON & Mary CLULOW
26 Jan   John WEBSTER & Rachel CLULOW
1748
10 Apr   Henry ROWLSTONE & Sarah POYNTON both of the Parish of Uttoxeter by License
16 May   William SALT & Mary WHEELTON
1749
3 Apr   Luke BAYLYE & Dorothy BANNISTER
20 Jun   Philip HOLLINS of the Parish of Chedle & Mary LEA
24 Oct   Joseph WOODINGS & Mary WRIGHT
26 Dec   John WOOD of the Parish of Checkley & Sarah WETTON
27 Dec   Abraham LEES & Sarah BAYLEY [Baylye-BT]
6 Jan   John BEECH of the Parish of Checkley & Mary GOODAL
1750
17 May   John WILD & Mary STRINGER
5 Jun   Henry BAYLEY [Baylye-BT] & Charity SMITH
20 Aug   John BARNETT & Mary SMITH
20 Sep   Thomas ALLEN & Mary DAVIS
23 Dec   Oliver LACEBY & Anne COLLIER
1751
24 Sep   Thomas WALTON & Elizabeth CLARKE
1752
31 Mar   Richard CARTER & Katherine BRIERLEY
22 Aug   Peter BEET & Esther VENABLES
29 Oct   Robert ROBOTHAM & Mary WETTON
1753
21 Jan   John HITCHCOCK of the Parish of Uttoxeter & Elizabeth OSBORN of Withington in this Parish by License
1 Feb   James SAUNDERS & Martha PRESTON
1754
1 Jan*   John HARRIS of this Parish & Dorithy FENTON of the Parish of Checkley by Licence [*27 Feb-BT]
27 Feb   John GOUGH & Ann COLLIER

Ann acct. of the Communion Money

1713	£	s	d
Whitsunday	00	08	09
Mics. Here I began to receive it	00	11	00
Christmas Com. 1713	00	11	00
Palm-Sunday Anno Dom 1714	00	03	06
Good-Friday Anno Dom 1714	00	05	07
Easter-day Anno Dom 1714	00	08	04
Whitsunday Anno Dom 1714	00	08	04
Mich. Communion Money 1714	00	12	05
Xmas Communion 1715	00	10	02
Palm Sunday Anno Dom 1715	01	05	03
Good-Friday Anno Dom 1715	00	06	02
Easter-day Anno Dom 1715	00	07	09
Whitsuntide Anno Dom 1715	00	07	06
Michaelmas Anno Dom 1715	00	07	06
Xmas Anno dom 1715/16	00	08	11
Palm-Sunday 1716	00	03	11
Good-Friday 1716	00	06	05
Easter-day 1716	00	08	05
Low-Sunday 1716 at a private communion	00	02	02
Whitsunday 1716	00	6	11
Michaelmas 1716	00	7	04
Xmas 1716/7	00	8	5
Palm-Sunday 1717	00	3	00
Good-Friday 1717	00	7	10
Easter-day 1717	00	6	4

G:S:R:
Delivered up to the churchwarden August 8th 1717
[?]:P:R

De Sepultus

1704
11 Feb   Ricardus fs Francisci DITCH
12 Feb   Margareta uxor & Johannis fs Ricardi EMBERY
7 Mar   Anna uxor Francicsi WALL
15 Mar   Thomas HEALY senex pauperimus
1705
23 Apr   Georgius fs Johannis SHERRAT
4 May   Cacilia COVIL
5 May   Laurentious AUSTIN
18 Jun   Thomas HEALY senex *[pauperinus-BT]*
25 Jun   Maria uxor Gulielmi HILL
3 Aug   Elizabetha fa Henrici HEATON
4 Sep   Sara uxor Thoma LEA
7 Sep   Andreas LEES
8 Oct   Robertus HOLLINS
14 Nov   Thomas FRADSLY alias SMITH
3 Dec   Elizabeth fa dilecta Antonii BYRD *[Bird-BT]* de Uttoxiter

15 Dec Elizabetha BIGGINS
12 Jan Jacobus EDWARDS fs Johannis
14 Feb Ludovicus BARNS

Exam P. Joh. Higges ....

1706
29 Mar Josephus fs Ricardi DYTCH
20 Aug Sara unica fa Simonis & Margeria BLOOD
 4 Nov [ ] *Jacobus [BT]* fs [ ] *R. [BT]* BAILIE de Morrily Heath
23 Dec Franciscus COATES
29 Jan Helena uxor Rogeri RICHARDSON
 6 Feb Ricardus fs Rogeri RICHARDSON
17 Feb Dorothea fa Thoma & Dorothea JOHNSON
18 Feb Ricardus fs Francisci OSBORNE
 8 Mar Gulielmus SHERRAT de Painly Hill *[Painslow Hill-BT]*
14 Mar Sara fa Roberti BAILIE *de Morrily Heath [BT]*
15 Mar Anna CHELL *vidua [BT]*
17 Mar Thomas fs Rogeri RICHARDSON
22 Mar Martha HILL de Field vidua
1707
23 May Johannis HARRIS
26 Aug Jana LOW *uxor Johannis [BT]*
14 Nov Thomas fs Johannis SHAW
28 Dec Joanna fa Francisci SWINSHEAD
17 Jan Anna WETTON
29 Feb Johannis RATCLIFFE
13 Mar Thomas HEATON de Fradsal
1708
11 Apr Maris WOOD de Field
25 Apr Dorothea fa Phillippi HOLLINS
25*May Edvardus BAILIE senex *[*24 May-BT]*
31 Jul Elizabetha LOW virgo
20 Aug Dorothea RUSHON vidua
13 Sep Maria RAWBONE
23 Sep Dorothea PHILLIPS
28 Nov Elizabetha fa Johannis HAMSON
28 Dec Maria fa Dorothea BAILIE
 1 Jan Anna [?] JOHNSON
14 Jan Nicholaus HILL
Ult Feb Rachaelis fa Francisci SWINSHEAD
 9 Mar Gulielmus JOHNSON
24 Mar Catherina BRAMALL *[Bramwell-BT]*
1709
31 Mar Maria WHITTERANCE
10 Apr Ricardi fs Ricardi MOORE
18 Apr Helena LOW vidua
14 May Anna fa Thoma TILL
17 Jun Maria COVIL
 1 Aug Robertus BATE
 1 Aug Gulielmus SMALLEY
29 Aug Alicia SWINSHEAD
24 Sep Maria HILL vidua

13 Oct Thomas VISE
21 Oct Jocosa TILSTON vidua
7 Nov Jana RICHARDSON
2 Dec Gulielmus SALT
5 Jan Catherina PHILLIPS [Phillipps-BT]
26 Jan Jana fa Francisci DYTCH
19 Feb Thomas COLLIER
2 Mar Johannes OSBOURNE
1710
15 Apr Sara fa erratica mullieris
18 Apr Elizabetha BAILIE
8 May Maria JOBBER
23 May Thomas BURTON
29 May Elizabetha BLURTON vidua
1 Jun Gulielmus fs Johannis HAMSON [Hampson-BT]
22 Jun Maria fa illegitima Jocosa HEATH & Ricardi HOLLAND
10 Aug Elizabetha LEES vidua
1 Oct Elizabetha LOW
16 Oct Sara fa Gulielmi TAYLOR
12 Dec Robertus fs Samuelis POTTS
2 Jan [ ] WHITTAKER vidua
3 Jan Johannes HIDE de Nobott
16 Jan Elizabetha THACKER
21 Jan [ ] fa erraticus mulieris
27 Jan Josias WOOLY
1711
26 Apr Johannes CHAPLIN
12 Jun Aron fs Josephi HEELEY
14 Jun Martinus LOW
18 Jun Maria fa Johannis HAMSON
3 Jul Ricardus fs Francisci LAKIN
5 Aug Anna SPENCER
28 Aug Maria DENNIS
30 Sep Gulielmus WHITEHURST
7 Feb Maria BIRCH vidua
28 Feb Robertus WRIGHT
6 Mar Walterus fs Edvardi BLURTON
20 Mar Maria uxor Georgii TURNER
1712
8 Apr Maria LAKIN
1 Jun Samuelis JOHNSON
8 Jul Johannis fs Francisci HARVY de Field
12 Jul Catherina fa Thoma SHERRATT de Nobott
25 Sep Sarah JAQUES
10 Oct Everardus BIRD Gen:
15 Nov Anna fa Thoma & Anna TILL
10 Jan Thomas HOW Pontificius reputatus motuus est
19 Jan Maria BAILEY uxor Joh: BAILEY Jun de Withington
5 Mar Sam ARNALL [Anna Arnold-BT]
7 Mar Dorothea COLCLOUGH
7 Mar Thomas MIDDLETON

1713
23 Apr Franciscus KEENde Field
2 May Maria HOWE Pontificia reputata Motua fuerat
26 May Antonius SAUNDERS
31 May Gualterus BLURTON
4 Jul Georgius fs Georgii et Maria ATKINS
23 Jul Eliz: fa Guilielmi TAYLER de Foale
30 Jul Margeria LOWE uxor Ricardi
3 Sep Thomas MIDDLETON Pontificus
6 Nov Magistra Jana WILLINGTON
9 Nov Joseph fs Guli. et Dor: WHILTON
17 Nov Anna fa Gul: et Dor: WHILTON
19 Jan Elizabeth fa Jon: et Jona DONE
28 Feb Maria SHERRATT fa *Johns [BT]*
4 Mar Rachel BARKER
28 Feb* Sarah ARNAT *[Arnold-BT]* jun. *[*1 Mar-BT]*
7 Mar Ricd. *[Raphs-BT]* BARKER
12*Mar Thom: et Eliz: MIDDLETON fs et fa Roberti *[*9 May-BT]*
1714
15*May Johns fs Guli HOLLINS *[*15 May-BT1, 23 May-BT2]*
23 May Alicia SMITH
30 Jan Anna fa Ric: DAVIES
2 Jul Ric'dus DAVIES
10 Jul Joseph THACKER
16 Aug Johns TILL
30 Aug Anna fa Sim BLUER
12 Sep Sim fs Sim BLUER
9 Nov Johns fs Guili [written over Tho] BUCKLEY
23*Nov Eliz: BAILEY *[*3 Nov-BT]*
14 Dec Maria uxor Guil: JOHNSON
16 Dec Mich'l. WHITEHURST
16 Jan Leah LAKIN
16 Feb Georgius HOWE Pontif reput: mort
11 Feb Guil: SHAWE de Leigh Church *Infant [BT]*
25 Mar Cath: JOHNSON Pontifia reputat mortua
1715
3 Apr Thos. HILL fili Tho. HILL infans
10 Jun Maria uxor Roberti HEATON
18 Jun Maria HEATON uxor Gulielmi
30 Jun Maria MEREDEW Pontifia reputat mortua
14 Jul Richardus BULLOCK
29 Sep Dorothea uxor Guli: BEALEY
29 Oct Elizabetha uxor Jobi BYRD
28 Dec Gulielmus SHERRATT calebs
6 Jan Anna ASHENHURST virgo generosa
18 Feb Thomas WRIGHT
7 Mar Margaretta BELCHER vidua
1716
22 Apr Robertus fs Roberti BEALEY *[Bailey-BT]* infans
24 May Thomas JOHNSON senex
5 Jun Elizabetha fa infans Rogeri RICHARDSON

4 Aug	Anna HOLLINS virgo
3 Oct	Josephus MEKIN
3 Nov	Tho: GENKINS
4 Nov	Robertus MOOR
16 Nov	Thomas CARTWRIGHT infans
6 Feb	Johannes SAUNDERS Rector novissimus de Leigh die mercurii, ex hac vira disussit secundo; nobis dilectissimus pater
8 Mar	Samuelis HOLLINS infans
12 Mar	Robertus HOLLINS Adolescens
24 Mar	Johannes TOMLINSON senex

1717

5 Apr	Anna JOHNSON vidua
16 Apr	Gulielmus TILL senex
20 Apr	Samuel LAKEN senex
28 Aug	Anna BEALEY infans
12 May	Edvardus NORRIS generosus
22 May	Josephus LOWE infans
23 May	Robertus BEALEY [Baily-BT] infans
25 May	Margeria HYDE vidua
17 Jun	Thomas COLCLOUGH senex
3 Jul	Mattheus JAMES senex
28 Aug	Johannes RICHARDSON infans
30 Aug	Georgius TURNER senex
6 Sep	Eliz: BELCHER infans
7 Mar	Eliz: ROYLEY

1718

13 May	Eliz. SPENCER
26 May	Catherina OSBOURNE pontificia reput
29 May	Johs. SHAW infans
14 Jul	Gulielmus fs Jacobi MARSON
23 Sep	Jana KEEN vidua
25 Sep	Gulielmus fs Simonis BOODEN
12 Dec	Maria uxor Roberti MIDDLETON
26 Dec	Gulielmus BEALEY [Bailey-BT]
27 Feb	Ellena AYTKIN vidua
12 Mar	Thomas BEALEY [Bailey-BT] junr
12 Mar	Dorothea MARSON infans

1719

4 Apr	Thomas HOLLINS infans
28 Apr	Sara HOLLINS virgo
9 May	Johannes GRETTON infans
27 May	Richardus SPENSER senex
8 Jun	Johannes BEARDMORE senex
21 Jun	Elizabetha MOOR vidua
23 Jun	Johannes BELCHER infans
13 Jul	Thomas FINNEY infans
15 Jul	Maria WOOLLEY uxor
18 Jul	Maria HARRISON uxor
7 Aug	Sara ADAMS uxor
13 Aug	Anna GELLEY uxor
12 Aug	Elizabetha JACQUES infans

15 Aug Aaron HILL *senex [BT]*
16 Aug Elizabetha KENT vidua
18 Aug Thomas PARKER senex
5 Sep Catherina MOUNTFORD virgo vetusta
11 Oct Elizabetha EDWARDS vidua
2 Nov Franciscus HARVEY senex
11 Nov Edvardus DAVIES senex
11 Nov Anna TOWNSEND virgo
17 Dec Rachel fa Josephi JOHNSON infans
25 Dec Richardus SHERRATT senex Patronus sive Fiduciarius Shole Leigh
25 Dec Maria JAUQUES pontificia reputata
21 Feb Maria BEVINS infans
10 Mar Elizabetha HITCHCOCK
1720
5 Apr Elizabetha HOLLAND virgo
6 Apr Richardus WOOLLEY juvenis
6 May Maria ALLKINS infans
10 Jun Johannes TRYNLEY infans
11 Jun Anna HURD vidua pontificia reputata
12 Jun Gynar BAYLEY infans
29 Jun Richardus CARTWRIGHT senex
3 Jul Maria CHELL uxor
10 Jul Edvardus LAWRENCE senex
25 Aug Anna HILL vidua pontificia reputata
29 Aug Elizabetha CHELL virgo
3 Sep Johannes KEELING senex
22 Sep Edvardus HOW pontificius reputatus
25 Oct Johannes JOHNSON infans
24 ... Valentinus HOW pontificius reputatus
Dorothea LOW Jurat de legitimâ sepultus Valent. HOW coram Edv. Taylor Cur.. 27 die Novembris 1720
15 Jan Richardus DYTCH senex
Jana DYTCH Jurat de legitimâ sepulturâ mortui coram Domm Ashenhurst Armig. Justiciam 21 die Januarii 1720. Jura temporis Affidavit fuit.
4 Feb Thomas THACKER
Joh. BOX Jurat. de legitimâ sepultus Tho. THACKER coram Johan. Latham de Milwich eadem die & tunc temp mihi traditum fuit.
7 Feb Dorothea BAILEY infans
Gratia BAILEY Jurat de legitimâ sepult Infantis mortua coram Johanne Latham de Milwich octavo die Febru. & Aff traditum fuit nono die eiusdem
17 Feb Anna HOYL
Anna DEAKIN Jurat de legitimâ sepulturâ pradicto coram Dom Ashenhurst Justit. ad Pacem 21 eiusdem die Affidavet mihi traditum
8 Mar Martha HILL uxor
Alicia BAGNOLL Jurat. de legitimâ sepulturâ mortua coram Dom: Ashenhurst Justit. .. die Martii Sequent. tunc temporis Affi.... traditum fuit.
13 Mar Johanes SHERRATT Coelebs Fiduciarius Schola de Leigh
Elizabetha DEAKIN Jurat de Legitima sepultura supranominati Joh. SHERRATT coram Dom Ashenhurst Justit. hac 14 die Martii sequent. & 10 die eiusdam mensis Affidavit mihi traditum fuit
23 Mar Susanna BOODEN uxor
Nullum Affidavit mihi allatum fuit de legitimâ sepulturâ supranominate Sus. BOODEN de quâre sub chirographo certiorem feli Franc. Low Ecclesia de Leigh Aconomum 31 die Martii anno 1721

1721

8 Apr Elizabetha WOOLLEY infans
Samuel POTT Jurat de legitimâ sepulturâ predict mortua infantis coram Dom Ashenhurst
Justit. Pac 11 die Aprillis anno 1721 eadem die Affidavit traditum fuit Dom Felthouse
eiusdem Ecclesia Rectori

14 Apr Oliver LEA senex pontificius reputatus
Maria LEA Jurat de legitimâ sepulturâ pradicti mortui coram Dom Ashenhurst Justit. Pac 19
die eiusdem mensis & Affidavit mihi traditum fuit 20 die

— Hen VERNON [written in margin]

21 May Aaron HEALEY infans
hor: quarto pomeridianâ
Maria TOOTH Jurat de legitimâ sepulturâ pradicti Infantis coram Georgio Hancock Rect'r
de Bromshall 25 die eiusdem mensis & Affidavit traditum fuit 26 die.

17 Jun Johannes RIGBIE infans
Maria SMALLWOOD Jurat de legitimâ sepulturâ supranominati Infantis coram Johanne
SAUNDERS Vic. de Buston 17 die Junii tunc temporis Affidavit mihi traditum fuit.

11 Jul Gulielmus GRETTON Infans
Maria HOYL Jurat. de legitimâ sepulturâ pradicti Infantis coram Dom Ashenhurst Justit.
Pac. 15 die Julii eadem die Affidavit ministro traditum fuit.

19 Jul Josephus JOHNSON infans
Maria JOHNSON Jurat de legitima sepulturâ pradicti Infantis coram Dom Ashenhurst
Justit. Pac. 23 die Julii & Affidavit ministro traditum fuit 24 die eiusdem mensis 1721

27 Aug Maria TILL infans
Thomas TILL Jurat de legitimâ sepulturâ pradicta Infantis coram Dom Ashenhurst Justit.
Pac. eadem die; tunc temporis Affidavit Ministro obtulit.

9 Sep Anna WOODWARD *uxor [BT]*
Nullum Affidavit Ministro oblatum fuit de legitimâ sepulturâ pradicta An. WOODWARD de
quâ re Literas Certificatorias Sub Chirographo milit ad Dom Ashenhurst Justit. Pac. alterum
ex occonomis Ecclesia de Leigh cirsilis [?] horam quintum temp. pomarid. 17 die
Septembris ann. predict

5 Oct Gulielmus CARTWRIGHT senex & Coelebs
Jana BULLOCK Jurat de legitima sepulturâ pradicti mortui coram Dom. Ashenhurst Justit.
Pac. nono die Octobris ann pradict eadem die Affidavit Ministro oblatum fuit.

12 Oct Ellena DANIEL vidua
Margaretta LAKIN Jurat de legitimâ sepulturâ pradicta mortua coram Dom. Ashenhurst
Justit. Pac. 14 die Octobris Ann. pradict eaden die Affidavit Ministro traditum fuit.

17 Oct Elizabetha PHILLIPPS de Field Vidua
Maria CHELL Jurat de legitimâ sepulturâ pradicta mortua coram Dom. Ashenhurst Justit.
Pac. 22 die eiusdem mensis Ann. pradict eadem die Affidavit Ministro oblatum fuit.

28 Nov Johannes STANDLY senex
Anna STANDLY Jurat de legitimâ sepulturâ pradicti mortui coram Dom. Ashenhurst Justit.
Pac. 28 die Novembris tunc temporis Affidavit Ministro traditum fuit.

8 Dec Catherina WALKER virgo
Maria AYTKIN Jurat de legitimâ sepulturâ pradicta mortua coram Dom. Ashenhurst Justit.
Pac. 15 die Decembris & Affidavit Ministro traditum fuit 16 die eiusdem mensis, circitar
horam primam, tunc Funeris Justis circitus horam quartam octavo diei Celebratis.

13 Dec Thomas HILL viduus
Dorothea HOLLINS Jurat. de legitimâ sepulturâ pradicti Mortui coram Dom. Ashenhurst
Justit. Pac. 16 die eiusdem mensis eadem die Affidavit Ministro oblatum fuit.

25 Dec Jana TUNSTALL infans
Hanna TUNSTAL Jurat. de legitimâ sepulturâ pradicta Infantis coram Dom. Ashenhurst
Justit. Pac. 29 die Decembris eadem die Affidavit Ministro oblatum fuit.

26 Dec Maria HITCHCOCK infans
Anna HARVEY Jurat. de legitimâ sepulturâ pradicta Infans coram Dom. Ashenhurst Justit.
Pac 29 die eiusdem Mensis; eadem die Affidavit Ministro oblatum fuit.

5 Jan Maria SHERRATT uxor Johannis
Jana BULLOCK Jurat. de legitimâ sepulturâ pradicta uxoris coram Dom. Ashenhurst Justit.
Pac. 9 die Januarii; eadem die Affidavit Ministro fuit.

8 Jan **Josephus WRIGHT senex**
Anna DEAKIN Jurat de legitimâ sepulturâ pradicti Senis coram Geo: Hancock Rec're de Bromshulfe 12 die eiusdem mensis & Affidavit Ministro traditum fuit 13 die.

18 Jan **Thomas BLURTON Infans**
Maria ATKINS Jurat. de legitimâ sepulturâ pradicti Infans coram J: Holbrooke Cler. 22 die Eiusdem Mensis & 23 die Affidavit Ministro traditum fuit.

13 Feb **Gulielmus CARTWRIGHT Coelebs**
Dorothea LOW Jurat. de legitimâ sepulturâ pradicta coelebs coram Dom. Ashenhurst Justit. Pac. 19 die Eiusdem mensis; eadem die Affidavit Ministro traditum fuit.

14 Feb **Johannes MIDDLETON, Puer**
Margaretta LAKIN Jurat. de legitimâ sepulturâ pradicti Pueri coram Dom. Ashenhurst Justit. Pac. 17 die Februarii & Affidavit Ministro traditum fuit 18 die euisdem Mensis.

28 Feb **Josephus DEAKIN Infans**
Maria AUSTIN Jurat. de legitimâ sepulturâ pradicti Infantis coram Georgio Hancock Rect: de Bromshulfe 6 die Martii et Affidavit Ministro traditum fuit 7 die eiusdem Mensis

9 Mar **Anna MOORCROFT Infans**
Maria SNAPE Jurat. de legitimâ sepulturâ pradicta Infantis coram Dom. Ashenhurst Justit. Pac. nono die Martii, & eiusdem die Affidavit Ministro traditum fuit.

16 Mar **Gulielmus BAILEY Juvenis**
Catherina BAILEY Jurat. de legitimâ sepulturâ pradicti Juvenis coram Dom. Ashenhurst Justit. Pac. 16 die Martii, eadem die Affidavit Ministro traditum fuit.

18 Mar **Jana MOORCROFT Infans**
Nullum affidavit ministro allatum fuit de legitimâ sepulturâ pradicta Infantis, quod sub chirographo certificum Dom. Ashenhurst Justit. Pac. & occonam Ecclesia Martii 27 die Ann. 1722. dixit autun quandam ...dit [?] coram de Juratam esse.

20 Mar **Maria JOHNSON Uxor provectâ Otate**
Jana DONE Jurat. de legit. Sepult. Predict. Muliatis coram Dom. Ashenhurst, Justit. Pac. 27 die Martii, & Affidavit Min oblatum fuit 28 die eiusdem Mensis, cilcitit horam Septimo temp. Matuxin.

1722

22 Apr **Johannes TOMLINSON infans**
Maria CHELL Jurat. de legit. sepult. Predict. Infantis coram Dom. Ashenhurst Justit. Pac. 28 die Aprilis, eadem die Affidavit Ministro traditum fuit.

1 May **Josephus JOHNSON senex**
Nullum Affidavit Ministro allatum fuit de legitimâ Sepulturâ pradicti Jos. JOHNSON de quâ re sub chirographo certiorem feci Dom. Ashenhurst Ecclesia de Leigh oecunem [?]. & Justit. Pac. 13 die Maii Ann. Predict.

16 Jun **Thomas RADFORD infans**
Margaretta LAKIN Jurat de legit. Sepult. pradicti Infantis coram Dom. Ashenhurst Justit. Pac. 20 die Junii; & Affidacit addutum fuit habitationi Ministro 24 die eiusdem mensis sub noctem.

12 Aug **Edvardus SHARPE Senex**
Jana SHARPE Jurat. de legit. Sepult. pradicti Senis coram Dom. Ashenhurst Justit. Pac. 12 die Augusti; & Affidavit ministro traditum fuit 19 die eiusdem Mensis.

25 Aug **Johannes HYDE Senex**
Sara HEATH Jurat. de legitimâ sepulturâ pradicti Senis coram Dom. Ashenhurst Justit. Pac. 27 die eiusdem mensis, eadem die Affidavit Ministro traditum fuit.

13 Oct **Maria HOLLINS virgo**
Elizabetha SHERRATT Jurat. de legitimâ sepulturâ predict virginis coram Dom. Ashenhurst Justit. Pac. 17 die Octobris, suo die Affidavit Ministro traditum fuit.

2 Dec **Gulielmus WARD infans**

10 Dec **Phoebe BRASSINGTON virgo**
Jana BULLOCK Jurat. de legit. Sepult. pradicta Virginis coram Dom. Ashenhurst Justit. Pac. 11 die Decembris; eadem die Affidavit Ministro traditum fuit.

6 Jan **Anna HALL virgo vetusta**
Maria LEA Jurat. de legit. Sepult. pradicta virginis coram Dom. Ashenhurst Justit. Pac. 12 die Januarii; eadem die Affidavit Ministro traditum fuit.

18 Jan   Josephus LOWE Infans
Jana BULLOCK Jurat. de legit. Sepult. predict. Infantis coram Dom. Ashenhurst Justit. pac.
20 die Januarii; & Affidavit Ministro traditum fuit 21 die eiudem mensis.

1 Feb   Mabel TUNSTAL Infans
Maria TUNSTAL Jurat. de legit. Sepult. pradicta Mabelis corum Geo: Hancock Rect. de
Bromshulfe 5 die Februarii, eadem die Affidavit Ministro traditum fuit.

18 Feb   Thomas CHELL Infans
Henricus CHELL Jurat. de legit sepult. pradicti Infantis coram Dom. Latham Curat. de
Milwich 21 die Febru. & Affidavit adductam fuit [?]Tem Minist 24 die eiusdem Mensis.

1723

31 Mar   Editha HEALEY virgo
Anna HARVEY Jurat. de legit. Sepult. pradicta virginis coram Dom. Ashenhurst Justit.
Prefect. 4 die Aprilis 1723. eadem die Affidavit Ministro fuit.

16 Apr   Isabella TOWNSEND Uxor
Maria BISHOP Jurat de legit. Sepult. pradicta Uxor coram Johanne Latham Curat. de
Fradsall 16 die Aprilis. Tunc temporis Affidavit Ministro traditum fuit.

2 May   Margaretta BAILEY Uxor
Eliz. RUSHTON Jurat de legit. Sepult. pradicta uxoris coram Johanne Latham Curat. de
Milwich 5 die Maii; eadem die Affidavit Ministro traditum fuit.

19 Aug   Johannes SHERRATT Senex
Ellena WRIGHT Jurat. de legit. Sepult. pradict Senis coram Dom. Ashenhurst Justit.
Prafect 20 Augusti & Affidavit Ministro oblatum fuit 21 die eiusdem Mensis.

21 Sep   Robertus THACKER Jun.
Rebecca FENTON Jurat de legit. Sepult. predict Rob. THACKER coram Dom.
ASHENHURST Justit. Prafect. 24 die Septembris, quo die Affidavit Ministro oblatum fuit.

25 Sep   Johannes BARKER Senex Eliz. RADFORD Jurat. de legit. Sepult. predict. Senis
coram Dom. Ashenhurst Justit. Prafect. 28 die Septembris & Affidavit Ministro traditum fuit
29 die eiusdem mensis.

27 Sep   Thomas AMSON Puer
Anna DEAKIN Jurat. de legit. Sepult. predict. Pueri coram Geo. Hancock de Bromshulfe
Rect. 2 die Octobris, eadem die Affidavit Ministro tradit.

17 Oct   Johannes SHERRATT Infans
Hcn. VERNON
Anna STARTIN Jurat de legit sepult predict Infantis coram Georg. Hancock de Bromshulfe
Rect. 25 die Octobris, eadem die Affidavit traditum fuit.

5 Dec   Josephus GREEN (Infans)
Jana DYTCH Jurat de legitimâ sepulturâ pradicti Infantis coram Gul. Saunders Rect. de
Norbury 5 die Decembris.

23 Dec   Johannes HEATON (Infans)
Susanna HEATON Jurat de legit. Sepult. pradicti Infantis coram Gul. Saunders Rect. de
Norbury 25 die Decembris

5 Jan   Anna GARTEN (Infans)
Maria TOOTH Jurat de legit. Sepult. pradicta Infantis coram Gul. Saunders Rect. de
Norbury 9 die Januarii Affidavit Ministro oblatum fuit.

23 Jan   Antonius HOYL *[Hoyle-BT]* (Senex)
Eliz. NELSON Jurat. de legit. Sepult. pradicti Senis coram Gul. Saunders Rect. de Norbury
23 die Januarii, & Affidavit Ministro traditum.

7 Feb   Maria TILL Infans
Sara TILL Jurat. de legil. Sepult. pradicta Infantis coram Gul. Sanders Rectore de Norbury
7 die Februarii, & Affidavit Ministro oblatum fuit.

3 Mar   Sampson WRIGHT (Infans)
Margaretta LAKIN Jurata fuit de legitimâ Sepulturâ pradicti Infantis coram Gul. Saunders
Rect're de Norbury terio die Martii & Affidavit ministro oblatum.

9 Mar   Jana BELCHER (Uxor) *uxor Robti [BT]*

1724

10 Apr   Elizabetha fa Georgii DEAKIN Affidavit

14 Apr   Jana fa Radulphi & Lidia TURNER Affidavit

---

1 May	Johannes ALCOCK Infans Affidavit
12 Jun	Gulielmus PHILIPS Senex Affidavit
12 Aug	Elizabetha WOOLEY (Uxor) Affidavit
14 Aug	Dyfield TOMLISON Vidua Affidavit
5 Sep	Jana HOLLINS Vidua Affidavit
8 Sep	Maria FINNEY [Finny-BT] vidua Affidavit
10 Sep	Jana CHAPLIN vidua Affidavit
11 Sep	Elizabetha WETTON paroch de Stone, Affid:
19 Sep	Susanna fa Henrici & Anna BAILEY [Bailye-BT] Affidav:
10 Oct	Anna fa Josephi & Dorothea SMITH Affidavit adductum
8 Nov	Robertus AUSTIN Anno Aet 86 affidavit adductum
8 Dec	Rose BAILEY [Rosa Bailye-BT] Affidavit adductum
19 Dec	Hanna fa Radulphi & Lidia TURNER
20 Dec	Samuel fs Johannis & Hannah MOOR
22 Dec	Franci WALL Anno Aet 94
25 Dec	Lidia TURNER
29 Dec	Georgius fs Johannis & Eliz: TURNER
30 Dec	Josephus HEALEY [Heeley-BT]
9 Feb	Gulielmus fs Moses & Sara JOHNSON
13 Feb	Benjamin fs Benjam: & Anna BELCHER
20 Feb	~~Johannes~~ Thomas fs Johannis BASSET & Lydia
1725	
5 May	Henricus BAILYE Grandavus
27 May	Franciscus fs Francisci & Helena TOWERS
20 Jun	Samuel fs Gulielmi & Joanna HOLLINS
28 Jul	Ludovicus THACKER de Morrily Heath
11 Aug	Samuel POTT Sen. de Birchwood Park
22 Sep	Margaretta Uxor Francisci SHERRATT de Leigh
12 Oct	Anna fa Jonathani & Anna MEAT (per Mag. J. Langley Rect. de Checkley)
16 Dec	Nathanael BYRD de Field Generosus
13 Jan	Hannah fa Anna HARVEY de Field
3 Feb	Josephus HEELEY de Withington Green
8 Feb	Anna PARKER de Withington Green
8 Feb	Margaretta fa Ricardi & Margaretta FENTON
18 Feb	Hannah HYDE de Nobot Vidua
25 Feb	Gulielmus fs Joannes & Elizabetha PHILIPS
1726	
1 Apr	Jacobus FENTON de Doddesley
3 Apr	Thomas WETTON de Nobot
12 Apr	Francisca fa Francisci & Elizabetha LOWE
19 Apr	Anna fa Josephi & Catherina RATCLIFFE
12 May	Margaretta fa Ricardi & Anna HOW [Howe-BT] Romano-Catholicerum
4 Jun	Thomas fs Thoma SHERRATT de Over Nobot
25 Jun	Lucia fa Joannes & Lydia BASSET de Meare
26 Jun	Isabella Uxor Gul'mi HOLLINS de Withington Green
3 Jul	Franciscus SWINSHEAD Senior de Leigh Church
6 Jul	Elizabetha fa Ricardi & Sara BAILYE
17 Jul	Thomas fs Georgii & Joanna WARD
28 Jul	Elizabetha Uxor & Margaretta fa Joannis STRINGER
14 Aug	Elizabetha fa Georgii & Joanna WARD
11 Oct	Joannes fs Joannis & Elizabetha COOK de Leigh

15 Oct   Robertus HOLLINS Senior
1 Nov   Joannes JOHNSON de Morrily Heath
12 Nov   Hannah SWINSHEAD Relicta Francisci Swd
19 Nov   Anna Uxor Isaaci RATCLIFFE
24 Nov   Franciscus DYCHE de Nobot
6 Dec   Elizabetha HYDE de Nobot
11 Dec   Henricus HEATH de Leigh
11 Feb   Maria fa Roberti & Helena TRUNLEY
20*Feb   Hannah Uxor Gulielmi GOUGH *[26 Feb-BT]*
24 Mar   Gulielmus SHIPLEY de Leigh
1727
8 Apr   Elizabetha fa Georgii & Helena CLOWES
21 Apr   Anna Relicta Rev'di Francisci ASHENHURST Archidiaconi Derbiensis &
            Mater Jacobi ASHENHURST de Park Hall Armiger
6 May   Elizabetha fa Thoma & Eliz Anna HOLLINS
5 Jun   Gulielmus HOLLINS de With'n Green A'o Et 87
27 Jun   Gulielmus BLOUD de Leigh Ann. Et. 87
12 Jul   Thomas SHERRATT de Field Anno Etat 71
8 Aug   Maria Uxor Henrici CHELL
20 Aug   Anna LAURENCE de Middleton Green Vidua, per Mag'ra Langley
24 Aug   Thomas AYRES peregrinus, per Mag'ra Langley
27 Aug   Ricard's BAILEY de Morrily Heath, per Mag'ra Langley
1 Sep   Maria DAVIS de Morrily Heath Vidua, per Mag'ra Langley
4 Sep   Joannes COPE de Woodhall Fields, per Mag'ra Langley
5 Sep   Gratia BAILYE de Morrily Heath Vidua, per Mag'ra Langley
6 Sep   Maria fa Josephi & Sara TURNER, per Mag'ra Langley
8 Sep   Anna PAKEMAN de Nobot, per Mag'ra Langley
13 Sep   Francisc's HOWARD de Blakely Lane, per Mag'ra Langley
18 Sep   Edvardus TILL de Leigh, per Mag'ra Langley
25 Sep   Robert's BELCHER de Field, per Dm Geo. HANCOCK Jun'r
28 Sep   Elizabetha WRIGHT de Nobot Vidua, per Mag'ra Langley
1 Oct   Gulielm's HILL de Uttoxeter
5 Oct   Thomas KEENE de Gratwich
6 Oct   Anna HOWARD de Leigh Vidua
8 Oct   Joannes DWARE peregrinus
11 Oct   Elizabetha HODIN de Nobot Vidua
14 Oct   Georgi's TOOTH de With'ton Green, per Mag'ra Daniel
31 Oct   Anna Relicta Gul'mi PHILIPS de Leigh, per Mag'ra Broales [?]
5 Nov   Catherina JENKINS de Leigh Vidua
17 Nov   Maria BEARDMORE Vidua
18 Nov   Elizabetha LAKIN de Withington
19 Nov   Jana fa Joannis & Lucia HOLLINS
22 Nov   Henricus HEATON, per Mag'ra Langley
23 Nov   Dorothea LOWE Vidua Romano-Catholica
26 Nov   Jacobus HYDE de Leigh
14 Dec   Maria fa Thoma & Elizabetha RIGBY
19 Dec   Elizabetha fa Radulphi & Maria TURNER de Foale
23 Jan   Helena fa Philippi & Dorothea HOLLINS
28 Jan   Joannes BAILYE Sen. de Withington
2 Feb   Elizabetha BAILYE de Morrily Heath Vidua

1728

26 Mar	Elizabetha fa Joannis & Maria BARKER
3 Apr	Robertus JOHNSON
9 Apr	Georgius fs Thoma & Elizabetha ADAMS
14 Apr	Margaretta fa illegitima Johannis PARNELL nup de Leigh & Sarah ROBINS
19 Apr	Maria fa Edvardi & Anna SHERRATT
18 May	Elizabetha fa Sarah JOHNSON
19 May	Johannes SHERRATT de Hayes House
21 May	Ricardus fs Ricardi & Margaretta FENTON
25 May	Elizabetha Uxor Gulielmi WRIGHT de Beamhurst in Parochia de Checkeley
13 Jun	Catharina fa Thoma & Elizabetha BLURTON
15 Jun	Elizabetha Relicta Johannis SHERRATT de Hayes House
18 Jun	Editha SHARPE de Doddesley, nonageneria major
2 Jul	Margaretta LAKIN de Withington
1 Aug	Brigitta ASHENHURST Soror Jacobi ASHENHURST de Park Hall Armigeri
9 Aug	Maria fa illegitima Dorothea PARKER de Withington Green & Thoma SHERRATT Jun de Nobot
11 Aug	Thomas CLARKE [Clerke-BT] de Brook Fields. Per Mag'ri Langley
20 Aug	Joannes HILL de Field, per Mag'ri Langley
24 Aug	Gulielmus HILL Sen de Withington
31 Aug	Jana BULLOCK de Doddesley
8 Sep	Joannes PAKEMAN de Nobot, per Mag'ri Langley
8 Sep	Radulphus fs Radulphi & Lydia TURNER de Foale, per M'ri Langley
14 Sep	Franciscus KEENE de Field
19 Sep	Ruth Uxor Thoma RUSHTON de Morrily Heath, per D'm Jac. Milne
2 Oct	Anna fa Jonathanis & Anna MEAT de Morrily Heath
15 Oct	Anna Uxor Thoma HARRIS de Withington Green
17 Oct	Anna fa Edvardi BLURTON Jun. & Lydia Ux
29 Oct	Robertus fs Danielis & Rebekah WETTON de Aston juxta Stone, per Mag'ri Langley
10 Nov	Guleilmus CLARKE de Brook-Fields
30 Nov	Anna HURT de Nobot Relicta Simonis HURT
27 Dec	Elizabetha fa Thoma & Elizabetha COPE
29 Dec	Gulielmus WRATHBONE de Leigh
20 Jan	Elizabetha fa illegitima Elizabetha SNELSON
29 Jan	Anna Uxor Edvardi SHERRATT de Middleton Green
29 Jan	Thomas SHERRATT de Middleton Green
1 Feb	Maria fa Ricardi & Maria HOYLE
2 Feb	Jana Relicta Thoma PYOTT de Morrily Heath
3 Feb	Franciscus SWINSHEAD de Leigh
9 Feb	Henricus fs Henrici & Margaretta BAILYE
10 Feb	Joannes LOWE de Leigh
10 Feb	Elizabetha fa Roberti BAILYE
11 Feb	Joannes DAVIS alias THROWER fs Maria DAVIS
16 Feb	Henricus BAILYE de Morrily Heath
17 Feb	Anna HILL de Withington
19 Feb	Joannes LOWE de Withington Green
24 Feb	Gulielmus fs Mosis & Sarah JOHNSON
20 Mar	Sarah fa Edvardi & Elizabetha TONKES
23 Mar	Thomas FINNY de Nobot
23 Mar	Jocosa fa Jacobi & Dorothea MARSTON

24 Mar	Jana Uxor Joannis MIDDLETON de Doddesley
1729	
28 Mar	Elizabeth the Wife of Thomas RIGBY of Heatly in the Parish of Abbots Bromley was buried at Leigh. Ann Affidavit was brought to prove her Burial in Woolen.
1 Apr	Thomas DAVIS of Morrily Heath was buried. An Affidavit brought.
7 Apr	William TUNSTAL of Morrily Heath was buried. An Affidavit brought.
8 Apr	Mary d/o John & Sarah LEES was buried. An Affidavit brought.
8 Apr	Edith SHARPE of Doddesley was buried. An Affidavit brought.
12 Apr	Lettice d/o William & Joan HOLLINS was buried from the Lea. Affid. Brought.
15 Apr	Jonathan MEAT of Morrily Heath was buried. Affidavit was made bef. Mr. Ash't Mag.
17 Apr	Richard s/o Thomas & Anne TILL of Fulford in the Parish of Stone was buried at Leigh. An Affidavit brought.
22 Apr	Elizabeth HILL of Field Widow of John HILL was buried by Mr. Hancock. Aff'd brought.
28 Apr	Widow Mary DAVIES of Morrily Heath was buried by Mr. Hancock. An Affidavit brought.
6 May	Frances d/o John & Mary CLAY of the Parish of Rugeley was buried at Leigh by Mr. Hancock
13 May	Mary d/o Mr John BRINDLEY & Catherine his wife was buried. Affid. made
14 May	Thomas s/o John & Jane DONE of With'ton was buried. An Affidavit brought.
1 Jun	Francis SHERRATT of Leigh Sen'r was buried by Mr. Hancock. An Affidavit brought.
2 Jun or therabt	Lettice PARKER of With'ton Green was buried.
3 Jun	John DONE of With'ton was buried. An Affidavit brought.
6 Jun	Joseph s/o William MARTEN *[Martin-BT]* of Rocester was buried
7 Jun	Ellen d/o Jane DONE of Withington was buried. An Affid't brought
16 Jul or therabt	Ellen d/o Rich'd & Marg't FENTON of Leigh was buried. An Affid't brought
15 Aug	Sarah d/o Samuel & Hannah POTT of Birchwood Park was buried. An Affidavit brought
3 Sep	Robert s/o Francis & Mary MIDDLETON of With'ton was buried. Affid't made
3 Sep	Edward PAKEMAN of Nobot was buried. An Affidavit brought.
8 Sep	Mr Robert THACKER of Leigh was buried. An Affidavit brought.
19 Sep	John s/o Samuel & Jane TONKINSON was buried. An Affidavit brought.
2 Oct	Dorothy the Wife of Joseph CLOWES was buried. An Affidavit brought.
6 Oct	Job BIRD of Leigh was buried. An Affidavit brought.
2 Nov	Thomas BAILYE of Withington was buried. An Affidavit brought.
29 Nov	Jane DAB a Vagrant was buried from Sam'l WOOLLEYS. An Affidavit brought.
25 Dec	Lawrence s/o Widow Ruth FINNY was buried. An Affidavit brought.
31 Dec	Margaret DAVIES alias THROWER d/o Margaret SHERRATT late the Wife of Thomas DAVIES alias THROWER was buried. Affidavit made.
3 Jan	John DAVIES alias THROWER s/o Margaret SHERRATT late the Wife of Thomas DAVIES alias THROWER was buried. Affidavit made.
13 Jan	Elizabeth d/o John & Mary HURT of Nobot was buried by Mr. Hancock

16 Jan Edward BLURTON Sen. of Leigh Church was buried. Affid't brought.

31 Jan Margaret the Wife of Richard FENTON of Leigh was buried. An Affidavit brought.

14 Feb Mary the Wife of Ralph TURNER of Foale was buried. An Affidavit brought.

19 Feb Mary d/o Edward & Mary SPOONER was buried. Affidavit made.

23 Feb Dorothy the Wife of Philip HOLLINS of With'ton Green was buried by Mr. Hancock. An Affid't made.

1730

25 Mar John s/o John & Sarah STARTIN was buried. Affidavit made.

16 Apr Elizabeth d/o Thomas & Elizabeth ADAMS was buried. An Affid't brought.

21 Apr William HOLLINS of With'ton was buried by Mr. Hancock. An Affidavit brought.

13 May John TURNER the Parish Clerk was buried. An Affidavit brought.

19 May Anne the wife of John LAKIN of Withington was buried. I certif'd John CARTWRIGHT Jun 3 that no Affidavit was brought for her.

25 May Thomas s/o Thomas & Mary ATWOOD of Foale was buried. An Affid't brought.

27 May Mr George LEA of Tenford in the Parish of Chedle was buried by Mr Langley. Affid't brought.

2 Jun Mary HARVEY of the Parish of Millwich was buried. Affidavit made.

10 Jun James s/o John & Elizabeth BELCHER of Field was buried. Affidavit made.

25 Jun Edward s/o Edward & Anne TOOTH of With'ton was buried by Mr Hancock. An Affidavit brought.

13 Aug Elizabeth d/o Thomas RIGBY of the Parish of Abbots Bromley was buried.

14 Aug Margaret d/o George & Joane WARD was buried by Mr Hancock. An Affid't brought.

14 Aug Matthew s/o Parents unknown was buried by Mr Hancock. An Affid't brought.

30 Sep Mrs Felice SHERRATT of Burton upon Trent was buried. An Affidavit brought.

29 Oct Elizabeth d/o William & Dorothy BAILYE was buried by Mr Langley. Affid't brought.

25 Nov William s/o William & Elizabeth OADES was buried by Mr Hancock. An Affid't brought.

12 Dec Mary the wife of John HURT of Nobot was buried.

8 Jan Francis MIDDLETON of Withington was buried.

11 Feb Sherrat s/o William & Elizabeth HITCHCOCK was buried from Beamhurst. Affid't brought.

27 Feb Richard HOYLE of Foale was buried by Mr Hancock. An Affidavit brought.

4 Mar John s/o William & Ellen FROST was buried. An Affidavit brought.

8 Mar Thomas s/o Mr William WOOD of Foale & Frances his wife was buried by Mr Langley.

20 Mar James ASHENHURST of Park Hall Esqr was buried.

1731

19 Apr Robert BAILYE Jun. of Morrily Heath was buried. An Affidavit brought.

30 Apr Widdow Hannah TUNSTAL of Morrily Heath was buried. An Affidavit brought.

8 May George DEAKIN of Nobot was buried. An Affidavit was brought.

28 Jul Bridget d/o Mrs ASHENHURST of Park Hall was buried. An Affid't brought.

3 Aug Mary the wife of Thomas WOOLLEY of Wood Leasowes was buried.

5 Aug   William s/o Thomas WOOLLEY of the Wood Leasowes was buried. An Affid't brought for both of these.

12 Aug   Ward Grey ASHENHURST Dr of Physick & Sen'r Fellow of Trinity College in Cambridge was buried. An Affidavit brought.

15 Aug   Thomas FERNES of Leigh was buried. An Affidavit brought.

5 Sep   Judith MIDDLETON of Withington was buried by Mr Allen of Lincolnsh.

17 Oct   Dorothy d/o Thomas & Rebekah FENTON of Middleton Green was buried. Aff't brought.

26 Oct   William s/o Mary MOOR of Leigh was buried. An Affidavit brought.

27 Oct   William RALIN of Doddesley was buried. An Affidavit brought.

4 Nov   Susanna & Thomas the twin children of Richard & Susanna BAILYE of Morrily Heath were buried. An Affidavit was brought for both.

18 Nov   John WRIGHT of Great Fenton was buried. An Affidavit brought.

24 Dec   James s/o Anne BAILYE of Morrily Heath was buried. An Affidavit brought.

6 Feb   Thomas s/o Solomon & Elizabeth SHAWE of Withington was buried. An Affid't brought.

10*Feb   Hannah d/o William BELCHER & Elizabeth SMITH of Field was buried by Mr Hancock. Affidavit made. *[*16 Feb-BT]*

22 Feb   Anne the wife of John GRIME of Hixon in the Parish of Stowe was buried.

14 Mar   Jacob s/o Jacob & Jane HOLLAND buried by Mr Hancock. Affid't brought.

1732

28 Mar   Valentine s/o the late Robt. BAILYE of Morrily Heath was buried. Affid't brought.

4 Apr   John s/o Thomas & Dorothy OSBORNE of Withington was buried. Affid't brought.

6 Apr   Charles s/o John & Jane BLURTON of Field was buried. An Affid't brought.

25 Apr   William s/o Thomas RUSHTON late of Morrily Heath was buried.

14 Jul   Mary d/o John & Sarah STARTIN of Hob Hill was buried.

11 Sep   Mary WOOD of Leigh was buried. An Affidavit brought.

12 Sep   Ellen the wife of William FROST of Leigh was buried. An Affidavit brought.

4 Oct   Anne d/o James & Joan RATCLIFFE was buried by Mr Langley.

19 Oct   Joseph s/o John & Elizabeth JAKES was buried by Mr Hancock. An Affid't brought.

9 Nov   Patience d/o Thomas FENTON Sen. was buried. An Affidavit brought.

14 Jan   Elizabeth RUSHTON of Millwich Parish was buried.

16 Jan   Widow Anne JOHNSON of Checkely Parish was buried. An Affidavit brought.

31 Jan   Grace BAILYE of Morrily Heath was buried.

1 Feb   Dorothy d/o William & Anne BRERETON was buried. An Affidavit brought.

24 Feb   Anthony s/o Anthony & Elizabeth BROWNE was buried. Affidavit made.

27 Feb   Thomas HYDE of Fole Bank in Checkley Parish was buried.

1733

17 Apr   James s/o James & Dorothy MARSTON was buried by Mr. Langley.

18 Apr   Hannah d/o Widow Joan HOLLINS of Withington was buried by Mr Hancock

21 Apr   Dorothy the wife of Thomas JOHNSON of Middleton Green was buried by Mr Langley

2 May   Luke BILLING of Leigh Church was buried. An Affidavit brought.

5 May   Jonathan KEELING of Doddesley was buried. An Affidavit brought.

10 May   Thomas OSBORNE of Withington was buried

16 May   Elizabeth the wife of William HITCHCOCK of Withington was buried.
Affidavit made.

30 May   George WARD of Nobot was buried. An Affidavit brought.

7 Jun   Elizabeth d/o Mary MOOR of Leigh was buried. An Affidavit brought.

26 Jun   John s/o Thomas & Anne HOLLINS of Withington Green was buried. Affid't brought.

1 Jul   John SHERRATT of Middleton Green was buried. An Affidavit brought.

19 Jul   Joseph s/o James & Joan RATCLIFFE of Leigh Bank was buried. Affidavit made.

21 Aug   Isaac RATCLIFFE of Leigh Bank was buried. An Affidavit brought.

13 Oct   Simon BLOUD of Leigh was buried. An Affidavit brought.

11 Jan   John s/o Thomas & Elizabeth TILL of Leigh was buried. An Affidavit brought.

27 Jan   Richard SNAPE of Bustomley was buried. An Affidavit brought.

6 Feb   Mrs Mary HOWE the sister of Mr Thomas HOWE of Leigh was buried. An Affidavit brought.

24 Feb   John & Jane the children of James & Anne PAKEMAN of Nobot were buried. An Affidavit brought.

1 Mar   Thomas s/o William & Prudence CHELL of Leigh was buried. An Affidavit brought.

12 Mar   Thomas s/o Thomas & Sarah WETTON of Leigh was buried. An Affidavit brought.

1734

9 Apr   Anne d/o Wid. Joan HOLLINS of Withington was buried. An Affidavit brought.

10 May   Jane the wife of Philip STEENSON of Heathy Close in the Parish of Stone was buried.

12 May   Thomas COOKE of Nobot was buried. An Affidavit brought.

23 May   Edward PEDLEY of Withington was buried. An Affidavit brought.

22 Jun   Grace the wife of William HOLLINS of Froddeswall was buried at Leigh by Mr Craven. An Affidavit brought.

26 Jul   Mary the bastard d/o Dorothy PARKER of Withington Green was buried. Affid't brought.

8 Aug   Robert s/o Thomas & Anne JOHNSON (a Londoner) was buried from Withington. Affidavit made.

25 Aug   Sarah the wife of John COLLIER of Field was buried by Mr Craven.

10 Sep   Ellen the wife of John SNAPE of Bustomley was buried. Affidavit made.

13 Sep   William s/o Samuel & Elizabeth FENTON was buried. An Affidavit brought.

14 Nov   John TILL of Checkley Bank was buried by Mr Craven. Affidavit made.

16 Nov   Thomas JOHNSON of Middleton Green was buried. Affidavit made.

25 Nov   Joshua WOOLLEY of Leigh was buried by Mr Hancock. Affidavit made.

3 Dec   Margery FERNES of Stone Parish was buried. Affidavit made.

7 Feb   William DANIEL of Withington was buried. Affidavit made.

10 Feb   Dorothy the wife of Thomas COLLIER of Middleton Green was buried. Affidavit made.

1735

18 Jun   Margaret HALL of Doddesley was buried. An Affidavit brought

7 Jul   Anne d/o Mary DYCHE & George WRIGHT, who married her & left her, having a former wife, was buried. An Affidavit brought.

19 Aug   Mary the wife of Mt John BREVITT of Cannock was buried. An Affidavit brought.

18 Sep William s/o John & Elizabeth COOK of Leigh was buried. An Affidavit brought.

18 Sep Ralph s/o Thomas & Anne RUSHTON of Morrily Heath was buried. Affid't brought.

4 Nov Elizabeth the wife of John CARTWRIGHT of Leigh was buried. An Affid't brought

1 Dec Sarah the wife of Thomas WETTON of Leigh was buried. (Affid't made) by *Mr Jno Ward [BT]*

3 Feb Jane d/o Francis & Mary TUNSTAL was buried. An Affidavit brought.

29 Feb Richard HILTON of Leigh was buried. An Affidavit brought.

14 Mar Robert s/o Anthony & Elizabeth THACKER was buried. I sent notice in writing to Mr Thacker ChWn by Tho. Tomlinson March 25 1736 that no Affidavit had been brought.

22 Mar Sarah the bastard d/o Elizabeth SMITH of Doddesley was buried. An Affid't brought.

1736

6 May Jane d/o Thomas and Elizabeth RADFORD was buried. Affid't brought.

19 Jun William s/o James & Joane RATCLIFFE was buried. An Affidavit brought.

23 Jun Elizabeth d/o Thomas WETTON was buried. An Affidavit brought.

27 Aug Anne d/o Mr John CARTWRIGHT was buried. Affid't made

11 Nov John s/o John MIDDLETON of Withington was buried. An Affid't brought.

1 Jan Jane the Relict of Thomas FERNES of Leigh was buried. An Affidavit brought.

17 Feb Henry WARRINGTON of Heathy Close in the Parish of Stone was buried. An Affid't

8 Mar Roger BOLTON was buried. An Affidavit brought.

1737

10 Apr William s/o William & Anne CLAY was buried. An Affidavit brought.

28 Apr Richard & Anne twin children of William & Sarah KEELING of Nobot were buried. Affid't bro't

10 May Mrs Susanna SLAUGHTER was buried here from *Uttox'r [BT]* An Affid't brought

2 Jun Widow Mary KEELING the Elder of Doddesley was buried. An Affidavit brought.

9 Jun Michael s/o Mr John SPATEMAN & Mary his wife was buried. An Affid't brought.

26 Jul John PHILLIPS of Leigh was buried. An Affidavit made.

30 Jul Mary WOOD of Gayton was buried by Mr Hancocke. An Affidavit made.

14 Aug Uriah SNELSON of Withington Green was buried. An Affidavit brought.

14 Aug Widow Jane DYCHE of Nobot was buried. An Affidavit brought.

8 Sep James TURNER of Leigh Church was buried. An Affidavit brought.

10 Oct John s/o Walter & Alice BURTON of Nobot was buried. An Affid't brought

3 Nov Mrs Mary MONGER of Cheadle was buried. An Affidavit brought.

13 Nov Richard HORDERNE of Field was buried. An Affidavit brought.

15 Nov Thomas s/o Joseph & Margaret GERARD was buried. An Affid't brought.

19 Nov Margaret d/o Antony & Elizabeth BROWNE was buried. Affid't ....

22 Nov Robert s/o Robert & Elizabeth BLURTON of Gayton was buried by Mr Gould Curate of Checkley. An Affidavit brought.

18 Dec James BRASSINGTON of the Parish of Checkley was buried. An Affidavit brought.

1 Jan Joseph RATCLIFFE of Leigh Bank was buried. An Affidavit brought.

19 17 Mar Widow Susanna RUSHTON of Morrily Heath was buried. Affidavit brought.
1738
2 Apr Joan the wife of James RATCLIFFE was buried. Affidavit brought.
4 Apr Mary d/o Mr John SPATEMAN & Mary his wife was buried. Affid't bro
28 Apr Mr John THACKER of Leigh was buried. An Affidavit brought.
18 May Felicia d/o John & Mary TONNYCLIFFE was buried. An Affid't brought.
8 Jun Robert s/o Francis & Mary TUNSTAL was buried. An Affidavit brought.
13 Jul Elizabeth the wife of Mr Thomas HOWE of Leigh was buried. An Affidavit brought.
14 Jul Hannah the Widow of John COPE late of Woodall Fields was buried. An Affid't brought.
16 Jul Elizabeth the wife of Edward DAVIES was buried. An Affid't brought.
23 Jul Mary d/o John & Mary TONNYCLIFFE was buried by Mr HancockE. An Affidavit brought.
28 Jul Hannah d/o George & Ellen CLOWES of Middleton Green was buried. An Affidavit brought.
24 Aug William OADES of Morrily Heath was buried. An Affidavit brought.
7 Sep Mr John KEELING of the Parish of St. James in Clerkenwell in the County of Middlesex was buried. An Affidavit brought.
11 Sep John BELCHER of Field was buried. An Affidavit brought.
30 Sep John s/o Thomas & Rebekah FENTON of Middleton Green was buried by Mr John Ward. (This boy was accidentally drowned in a Marl-Pit on the 27th) An Affidavit brought.
26 Dec Lewis s/o Lewis & Sarah THACKER was buried by Mr Jno Ward. Affidavit made.
24 Feb Moses JOHNSON the Parish Clerk was buried. Affidavit made.
2 Mar Thomas s/o William & Dorothy BAILYE was buried. Affidavit made.
12 Mar John DONE of Withington was buried. Affidavit made.
17 Mar Hannah d/o William & Dorothy BELCHER was buried. Affidavit made.
17 Mar Frances d/o Thomas & Elizabeth TILL was buried. Affid't made
1739
4 May Philip HOLLINS of Withington Green was buried. Affidavit made.
17 Jun Anne d/o John & Anne WALKER was buried. An Affidavit brought.
25 Jul Margaret the wife of Richard HEWITT *[Hewit-BT]* was buried. Affidavit made.
3 Aug John s/o John & Sarah LEES was buried. An Affidavit brought.
8 Dec William s/o William & Sarah KEELING was buried. An Affid't brought.
14 Dec Francis s/o William & Sarah KEELING was buried. An Affid't brought.
15 Feb Widow Margery BLOUD aged 87 was buried. An Affid't brought.
22 Mar Francis s/o Samp'n & Bridget DONE was buried. An Affid't brought.
1740
9 Apr Robert s/o Robert & Isabel JOHNSON was buried. An Affid't brought.
14 May Thomas s/o Edward & Anne TOOTH was buried. An Affid't brought.
22 May Elizabeth d/o William & Sarah PARKER was buried. An Affid't brought.
14 Jun Sampson WRIGHT of Checkley Bank was buried. An Affidavit brought.
29 Jun Philip s/o Mr Philip & Mrs Sarah BARRATT was buried. An Affid't brought.
19 Jul Mary d/o John & Anne WALKER was buried. Affid't made.
19 Jul Francis FERNES was buried. An Affidavit brought.
5 Aug Dorothy the wife of Charles HART was buried. An Affidavit brought.
1 Nov Thomas HITCHCOCK was buried. An Affidavit brought.
27 Nov Elizabeth WRIGHT of Field was buried. An Affidavit brought.

28 Nov   William s/o James & Jane BAKER was buried. An Affidavit brought.
30 Nov   Anne the wife of John STRINGER was buried. Ann Affidavit brought.
20 Jan   Widow Mary HOYLE of Fole was buried. I sent notice to Mr Will'm Sherratt
by John Turner in writing Feb 1 1740/1 that no Affidavit had been brought me
12 Mar   Dorothy the wife of Simon BODEN was buried. An Affidavit brought.
15 Mar   Nathanael s/o Widow DANIEL was buried. An Affidavit brought.

1741

19 Apr   Francis bastard s/o Mary HOWARD was buried. An Affidavit brought.
21 Apr   Hester d/o Mr Philip & Mrs Sarah BARRETT was buried. An Affid't brought.
6 May   Daniel MORRIS of Birchw'd Park was buried by Mr Rowl'ds. An Affid't
brought.
17 May   Thomas DAVIES was buried. An Affidavit brought.
18 May   William s/o Mr John & Mrs Catherine BRINDLEY was buried. An Affidavit
brought.
4 Jun   William MARTIN of the Shortwoods was buried. An Affidavit brought.
5 Jun   Widow Mary RALIN of Doddesley was buried. An Affidavit brought.
13 Jun   Jonathan s/o Francis & Mary TUNSTAL was buried. An Affid't brought.
15 Sep   Sarah d/o Matthew & Mary HODGKINSON was buried. An Affid't brought.
11 Oct   Mary d/o Thomas & Elizabeth HARRIS was buried. Aff't brought
25 Oct   Thomas CARTER of Withington was buried. An Affidavit brought.
2 Nov   Ellen d/o Simon & Ellen BLORE was buried. An Affid't brought.
8 Nov   John s/o Mr Robert & Mrs Elizabeth WOOD was buried. An Affid't brought.
17 Nov   George WRIGHT was buried. An Affidavit brought.
24 Nov   Widow Mary SNELSON of Withington Green was buried. An Affid't brought.
27 Nov   Widow Mary DYCHE of Nobot was buried. An Affidavit brought.
29 Nov   Anne d/o John & Anne BIRD was buried. An Affid't brought.
14 Dec   Mary & Joseph the children of George & Sarah JOHNSON were buried in
one grave. An Affidavit brought for both.
29 Dec   Dorothy wife of William WHEELTON was buried. An Affidavit brought.
5 Jan   Sarah d/o Thomas & Sarah MILLINGTON was buried. Affid't made
5 Jan   Thomas RALIN of Doddesley was buried. Affidavit made.
9 Jan   Simon BOLDIN of Withington Green was buried. An Affidavit brought.
18 Jan   John s/o Robert & Ellen TRUNLEY was buried. An Affidavit brought.
23 Jan   Robert HEATON of Leigh was buried. An Affidavit brought.
25 Jan   Hannah d/o Joseph & Margaret GERARD was buried. An Affid't brought.
30 Jan   Widow Anne DANIEL was buried. Affidavit made bef. Mr Rowlands.
31 Jan   Benjamin BOLDIN was buried. Affidavit made before Mr Jn WARD
18 Feb   Thomas JOHNSON of Leigh was buried. An Affidavit brought.
5 Mar   Widow Mary WETTON was buried. An Affidavit brought.
5 Mar   Robert s/o Thomas & Elizabeth COPE was buried. An Affidavit brought.
7 Mar   Mrs Catherine the wife of Mr John BRINDLEY was buried. Affid't made bef.
Mr Rowl'ds

1742

15 Apr   Mr Thomas HOWE of Leigh was buried. An Affidavit brought.
5 May   Catherine MIDDLETON of Withington was buried. An Affidavit brought.
9 May   Mary d/o Ralph TURNER was buried. An Affidavit brought.
24 May   Widow Elizabeth PHILLIPS of Field was buried. An Affidavit brought.
3 Jun   John BLURTON of Leigh Church was buried. An Affidavit brought.
16 Jul   Francis COVEL of Stoke Parish was buried aged 86. Affidavit made.
6 Aug   Widow Elizabeth FERNES was buried. An Affidavit brought.

25 Aug David s/o Widow Catherine BAILYE *[Baylye-BT]* was buried. An Affid't brought.

24 Sep John MARTIN of Nobot was buried by Mr Hancock. An Affid't brought.

15 Oct John SHAWE of Withington was buried. An Affidavit brought.

1 Jan John s/o Michael & Mary GOODALL was buried. An Affidavit brought.

2 Jan James s/o John & [ ] KEELING was buried. An Affid't brought.

15 Jan Widow Margaret SHERRATT was buried. An Affidavit brought.

21 Feb Elizabeth d/o James & Anne BAILYE *[Baylye-BT]* was buried. An Affidavit brought.

3 Mar Solomon SHAWE of Withington was buried. An Affidavit brought.

14 Mar Ralph s/o Thomas & Elizabeth COPE was buried. An Affidavit brought.

1743

10 Apr Anne d/o John & Anne HEELEY was buried. No Affidavit brought.

16 Apr Hannah d/o Anne STARTIN was buried. An Affidavit brought.

17 Apr Mary d/o William & Sarah PARKER was buried. An Affid't brought.
I sent notice in writing to Mr J. Brindley Church Warden by Geo. Proctor April 20 that no Affidavit had been brought for Anne HEELEY; & to J. Cope by Ra. Turner April 21.

21 Apr James s/o George & Ellen CLOWES was buried. An Affidavit brought.

22 Apr Hannah d/o John & Elizabeth DRAKEFIELD was buried. An Affid't brought.

24 Apr Mary d/o George & Sarah JOHNSON was buried. An Affid't brought.

27 Apr William MARTIN was buried. An Affidavit brought.

29 Apr Richard FENTON was buried. An Affidavit brought.

1 May John s/o Dorothy OSBORNE was buried. Affid't made before my son & me.

2 May Widow Elizabeth TILL was buried. An Affidavit brought.

8 May Elizabeth the wife of Thomas COLCLOUGH was buried. An Affidavit brought.

11 May William SHAWE was buried. An Affidavit brought.

20 May Master James ASHENHURST was buried. No Affidavit was brought.

29 May Elizabeth d/o Thomas & Elizabeth HARRIS was buried. Affid't made.

2 Jun Anne HOWARD of Stone Parish was buried. An Affidavit brought.
I sent notice in writing to Thomas Belcher & Joshua Preston Churchwardens by George Procter Jun 4 than no Affidavit had been brought for James ASHENHURST.

16 Jul Ralph TURNER s/o Elizabeth FENTON was buried. An Affidavit brought.

24 Jul Elizabeth FROST d/o William FROST was buried. An Affid't brought.

30 Jul Elizabeth NIXON was buried. An Affidavit brought.

5 Aug Mary the wife of George ATKINS was buried. An Affidavit brought.

12 Aug Esther the Relict of Joseph HEELEY was buried. An Affidavit brought.

18 Sep Susanna the Relict of Henry HEATON was buried. An Affidavit brought.

30 Sep Bridget the wife of James DONE was buried. An Affidavit brought.

2 Oct John s/o Mr Philip & Mrs Sarah BARRATT was buried. An Affid't brought.

16 Nov Mary d/o John & Sarah LEES was buried. Affid't made.

4 Dec Elizabeth BOLDIN was buried. An Affid't brought.

14 Dec Mary d/o William & Anne PHILLIPS was buried. Affid't made

27 Jan Mary d/o John & Mary HOWE was buried. Affid't made

5 Feb Elizabeth d/o Thomas & Alice COLLIER was buried. Affid't made

21 Mar Thomas s/o Thomas & Elizabeth COLCLOUGH was buried. Affid't made

1744

31 Mar John TOMLINSON s/o Thomas & Hannah TOMLINSON was buried. Affid't made

15 Apr James s/o James & Jane BLORE was buried. Affid't made
3 May Elizabeth HITCHCOCK was buried. Affid't made
16 May Elizabeth d/o Thomas & Elizabeth COPE was buried. Affid't made
23 May Mary d/o William & Elizabeth ROBOTHAM was buried. Affid't made
13 Jul Jane d/o James & Jane BAKER was buried. Affid't made
6 Nov Mary d/o William & Grace HOLLINS was buried. Aff't brought & made
— 27 Nov Benjamin s/o James & Anne BAYLYE was bur'd. Affid't brought
15 Dec Thomas TILL of the Parish of Chebsey was buried. Affid't brought
30 Jan Mrs Hannah DIXON Relict of Mr Edward DIXON was buried. Affid't brought
— 5 Mar Elizabeth MARSTON was buried. Affid't brought   J.H.
1745
9 Apr Edward s/o John & Jane BLURTON was buried. Affid't brought
7 Jul Rawden s/o Mr Joseph & Mrs Hester KEELING was buried. Affidavit brought
— 6 Aug Catherine d/o John & Anne WALKER was buried. Aff't brought
27 Aug Hester Elizabeth d/o Mr Philip & Mrs Sarah BARRETT was buried. Affid't brought   J:J-L
17 Oct Catherine WETTON was buried. Affid't brought
— 5 Dec William BAYLYE was buried. Affid't made
20 Jan Rebeccah KEELING was buried. Affid't brought
11 Feb John STRONGITHARM was buried. Affid't brought
13 Feb Thomas FENTON of Middleton Green was buried. An Affid't brought
16 Feb Hannah d/o William & Alice DEAKIN was buried. Affid't brought
21 Feb Dorothy TILL was buried. Affid't brought
1746
18 Apr Mrs Ellen THACKER Widow was buried. Affid't made
20 Apr John s/o John & Anne PHILLIPS was buried. Affid't made
— 28 Aug Mrs Cicely COVEL from London was buried. Affid't brought
24 Oct John RAWLIN the younger was buried. Affid't made
9 Nov Thomas ADAMS was buried. Affid't brought
3 Dec James s/o Thomas & Alice COLLIER was buried. Affid't brought
11 Jan Elizabeth FINNY was buried. Affid't brought
1 Feb Richard s/o Thomas & Alice COLLIER was buried. Affid't brought
7 Feb Mary BILLING was buried. Affid't brought
12 Feb Joseph SHERRAT was buried. Affid't brought
— 7 Mar Hannah MARSTON was buried. Affid't brought
1747
21 Apr Elizabeth the wife of Thomas NUTT was buried. Affid't brought
8 May Ellen HOLLINS was buried. Affid't brought
4 Jun Mrs Mary KEELING Relict of Mr John KEELING of the Parish of St. James Clerkenwell in the County of Middlesex was buried. Affid't Brought
8 Sep John BELCHER of field was buried. Affid't brought
2 Oct Charles s/o Charles & Dorothy HART was buried. Affid't brought
— 15 Nov Hannah WRIGHT of the Parish of Kinston Uttoxeter was bur'd. Affid't brought
26 Nov Hannah the wife of Richard ORME was bur'd. Affid't brought
6 Dec Ellen the wife of Francis TOWERS was buried
23 Jan Elizabeth d/o William & Mary BAYLEY was bur'd
31 Jan William s/o John & Anne WALKER was buried.
2 Feb Elizabeth COOKE was buried
1 Mar Marry d/o Thomas & Elizabeth JOHNSON was buried

1748

5 Apr	Bridget RUSHTON an Infant was buried
6 Apr	Charles ROBOTHAM an Infant was buried
14 Apr	George s/o George & Jane BLURTON was buried
27 Apr	Thomas SMITH was buried
7 May	Sarah d/o Mr Philip & Mrs Sarah BARRETT was buried
7 Jul	Thomas s/o Thomas & Mary HOLLINS was buried
12 Jul	Francis TILL was buried
7 Aug	Thomas s/o William &Sarah PARKER was buried
7 Sep	Katherine d/o John & Anne WALKER was buried
9 Sep	Henry CHELL was buried
22 Sep	William COLLIER was buried
14 Dec	Mary d/o Willm & Elizabeth ROBOTHAM was buried
9 Jan	Diana the wife of John TURNER was buried
11 Feb	Anthony BROWN was buried
13 Feb	Mary the Relict of Edward PEDLEY was buried
3 Mar	Anne TOWNSHEND Widow was buried

1749

4 May	Anne SHERRATT was buried
14 May	William RADFORD was buried
14 May	Rachel WEBSTER was buried
20 May	John s/o George & Jane BLURTON was buried
13 Jun	Thomas s/o John & Sarah HYDE was buried
13 Jun	Mr Francis LOWE was buried
15 Jul	Alice SHAWE was buried
17 Jul	Joseph DEAKIN was buried
26 Jul	Catharine HART was buried
29 Jul	Mrs Anne KEELING the wife of Mr John KEELING of the Parish of St. James Clerkenwell in the County of Middlesex was buried
31 Jul	Simon BLORE was buried
27 Aug	Anne d/o Robert & Anne LAKIN was buried
29 Sep	Alice d/o Tho: & Elizabeth HALL was buried
14 Oct	William SMITH was buried
18 Dec	Anne d/o Mr William & Mrs Anne SHERRATT was buried
25 Dec	James s/o Tho: & Eliz: BELCHER was buried
1 Mar	Anne TILL from Norbury Park was buried
4 Mar	Mary the wife of Francis TUNSTAL was buried

1750

14 Apr	John LEES senior was buried
18 Apr	Elizabeth the wife of Thos. JOHNSON was buried
21 Apr	The Reverend Mr Francis ASHENHURST was buried
6 May	Thomas WOOLLEY was buried
27 May	William s/o Daniel & Sarah BURTON was buried
21 Sep	John ALCOCK was buried
20 Nov	Mr John SHERRATT of Leigh was buried
14 Oct	Mrs Sarah the wife of Mr Thomas HUGHES of London was buried
6 Dec	Anne HARVEY Widow was buried
23 Dec	William ROBOTHAM junr. was buried
6 Jan	Elliot s/o John & Anne BAYLEY was buried
28 Jan	Thomas s/o Simon & Elizabeth FOWLER was buried
31 Jan	Anne d/o Thos. & Elizabeth HALL was buried

	13 Feb	Margaret BAYLEY Widow was buried
	20 Feb	Mary CHELL was buried
	22 Feb	Mrs Anne the Wife of Mr William SHERRATT was buried
	9 Mar	Francis MIDDLETON was buried
	24 Mar	John s/o Willm. & Margaret RAWLIN was bur'd

1751

	4 Apr	Anne d/o Willm. & Grace HOLLINS was bur'd
	16 Apr	William s/o Willm. & Sarah PARKER was bur'd
	18 Apr	Elizabeth BLURTON was buried
	18 May	Richard s/o John & Joyce MUTCHEL bur'd
	19 May	Alice the wife of Thomas FERNIHOUGH was bur'd
	23 May	Ellen HEATON Widow was buried
	30 May	Sarah CROSSBY Widow was buried
	14 Jun	Sarah the wife of William GOODAL was buried
	23 Jun	Joan HOLLINS Widow was buried
	15 Jul	Sarah PARKER Widow was buried
1 [BT]	Aug	Elizabeth d/o Edward & Elizabeth DAVIS was bur'd
	4 Aug	Joseph s/o Joseph & Joan DEAKIN was buried
	6 Aug	Dorothy the wife of Joseph SMITH was buried
	23 Oct	Margaret ORME Widow was buried
	4 Nov	Ralph TURNER was buried
	3 Dec	Sarah wife of Lewis THACKER was buried
	8 Dec	Thomas TOOTH was buried
	19 Dec	Samuel s/o William & Anne HOLLINS bur'd

1752

	11 Jan	Frances d/o Mr Willm. & Mrs Anne SHERRATT *[Sharratt-BT]* bur'd
	20 Jan	Mrs Phebe Relict of the Revd. Mr Francis ASHENHURST was buried
	7 Feb	Katherine WALKER Widow was buried
	11 Feb	William WHEELTON was buried
	15 Feb	Hannah DEAKIN was buried
	22 Feb	Joyce THACKER Widow
	18 Apr	Thomas s/o John & Anne WALKER bur'd
	26 May	Mary TILL buried
	29 May	William s/o Edward & Eliz: DAVIS
	31 May	Elizabeth BELCHER Widow buried
	22 Jun	William s/o William & Mary SALT bur'd
23 [BT]	Jul	Lydia daught'r of Mr Edwd & Mrs Lydia BLURTON bury'd
	16 Aug	Elizabeth daught'r of Henry & Charity BAILEY *[Bayley-BT]* bury'd
	25 Aug	Richard BAILEY *[Bayley-BT]* was buryed

1753

	9 Jan	Willm. FROST Sen'r was buryed
	28 Jan	Mr Joseph GREY was buryed from Birchw'd Park
	25 Apr	Judith THACKER Widow was bur'd aged 88
	15 May	Elizabeth DEKIN *[Deakin-BT]* Widow was bur'd
22 [BT]	May	Mrs Rebeccah LEE widow from Newcastle bur'd
	26 Jul	Mary the wife of John CARTER was buryed
	21 Aug	Mary the wife of John JOHNSON was bury'd
	18 Nov	Luke s/o Henry & Charity BAYLEY was bury'd
	29 Nov	Sarah the d/o John & Anne RIGHT was bury'd

1754

	16 Jan	Benjamin BELCHER was buried

28 Jan Thomas FENTON was buried aged 95
23 Mar Elizabeth d/o Mr Wiliam & Mrs Anne SHERRATT buried
11 Apr Hannah the wife of Thomas RIGHT was buried
25 May John HARRIS *[Harrias-BT]* was buried
16 Jun Thomas TILL was buried
22 Jun Hannah the wife of Eward [sic] Harper was buried
3 Aug Sarah d/o Mr Michael WARD & Anne his wife was buried
17 Aug Mary MIDDLETON Widow was buried aged 97
26 Sep John s/o Thomas & Elizabeth BRADDOCK buried
3 Oct Mary d/o Mr John & Mrs Jane BLURTON bury'd
7*Dec Eliz d/o Richard & Eliz LEE bur'd [*altered from 8]

1755
7 Jan Robert FRADLEY was buried
29 Jan Joan DEAKIN Widow was buried
13 Feb Wm JOHNSON was buried aged 94
25 Feb Mary d/o John & Diana TURNER buried
25 Apr Mary wife of Immanuael PERKINS buried
18 May Elizabeth the wife of Mr Thomas HOW *[Howe-BT]* was buried
27*May Anne the wife of Thomas LEES was buried [*altered from 24]
16 Jun Sarah the wife of John STRINGER was buried
21 Jun James s/o John & Anne WALKER was buried
26 Jun Wiliam DEAKIN Sen'r was buried
24 Sep John s/o John & Mary BEECH was buried
20 Dec Sarah the d/o Thos. & Elizth BRADDOCK was buried

1756
15 Jan Samuel WOOLEY was buried
1 Feb Anne d/o Thos & Mary PHILLIPS ws buried
23 Mar Sarah d/o Thos & Mary LOWNDES ws buried
24 Apr James s/o John & Ann WALKER ws buried
28 Apr John s/o Philip and Sarah HAULEY ws buried
5 May Susan BAYLEY was burried
27 May Ann BLOORE was burried
9 *[BT]* Aug Ellin d/o John & Hannah RAWLIN was bur'd
5 Oct Elizth SMITH was burried
29 Oct George THORNIWELL was burried
17 Nov Ellen WOOLLEY *[Wooley-BT]* was burried

1757
13 Jan James BAKER was buried
27 Jan John s/o Joseph & Mary TILL was buried
4 Feb Sarah JOHNSON widdow was buried
5 Feb Jane DONE widow was buried aged 92
12 Feb Mrs Elizth wife of Mr Robert WOOD of Uttoxeter was buried
13 Feb Phebe DEAKIN widow was buried
14 Feb William s/o William & Sarah RUSHTON was bur'd
24 Apr Francis s/o Fran. & Elizth SHERRATT was bur'd
14 Jun Elizth d/o Thos & Elizth SHERRATT ws burried
30 Jul Mary CLARK *[Clerk-BT]* Wid'w was burried
26 Aug Sarah TURNER Wid'w of Cheadle Parish was buried
11 Sep Mary d/o Geo: & Ellin COPE was burried
30 Oct Hannah d/o Benjamin & Hannah BURTON ws bur'd
14 Nov Robert s/o Samp'n & Mary BAYLEY ws bur'd

1758

14 Jan	Lidia d/o Wm & Honour LEES was burried
31 Jan	Sarah the wife of Edw'd DAVIS was burried
14 Feb	Thomas COPE of the Wood was buried
17 Feb	Wm. & Sam'l sons of Edw'd & Eliz'th HOWARD were burried
28 Feb	Thos s/o Henry & Elizth WOODWARD was buried
19 Mar	Ann RATCLIFF was buried
30 Mar	James HAWKINS was buried
10 May	Robert s/o Anthony & Elizabth THACKER was buried
3 Jun	William s/o Godfrey & Ann BUXTON was buried
27 Jun	John RAWLIN was buried
31 Jul	Thomas TILL of Norbury Park was bur'd
22 Oct	Joseph s/o Wm & Sarah RUSHTON was buried
24 Oct	Thomas KINDER was bur'd
1 Nov	Ann the wife of Jno BIRD waa bur'd
14 Dec	Walter BLURTON was burried aged 81

1759

20 Jan	Mary the wife of John JOHNSON was bur'd
9 Feb	Mary the wife of Godfrey BUXTON was bur'd
12 Feb	Mary d/o Willm ans Sarah RUSHTON was bur'd
12 Feb	Thomas s/o John & Ann PHILLIPS was burr'd
19 Feb	Elizabeth the wife of John COLLIER was burried
13 Mar	Hannah the wife of Saml WALKER was burried
18 May	John KEELING Esqr of the Parish of St. James Clerkenwell in the County of Middlesex was burr'd
28 May	Elizabeth wife of Thomas WALTON was buried
26 Jul	John HART was buried
13 Aug	John s/o William & Sarah PARKER was buried
26 Sep	Eleanor GRETTON Widow was buried
22 Oct	William GOODALL of Birchwood Park was buried
20 Dec	William RAWLIN of Leigh was buried
2 Dec	Robt BAILEY was buried

1760

1 Jan	Sarah BIRD was buried
13 Jan	[ ] s/o John BAILY [Bailey-BT] was buried
14 Jan	John & Thomas twin sons of John JOHNSON buried
24 Feb	John CARTER of Withington was buried
3 Apr	Mary RADFORD of Leigh was buried
5 Apr	Grace HOLLINS Widow, of the Dairy House, was buried
1 May	Elizabeth CLOWES was buried
2 May	William s/o John & Ellen MILLINGTON was buried
26 May	Thomas CROSSBY was buried
6 Jun	Elizabeth wife of Edward HOLLINGWORTH was buried
15 Jun	Thomasin wife of Thomas FENTON was buried
6 Jul	Anne the wife of Mr Michael WARD was buried
13 Jul	Anne WARRINGTON Widow was buried
27 Jul	Thomas s/o Joseph and Mary TILL was baptized
29 Jul	Mary d/o William & Elizabeth BOTT was buried
17 Aug	Hannah TUNNICLIFFE was buried
25 Sep	John s/o Mary KIRK was buried
13 Nov	Geo: CLOWES was buried

20 Nov   John STANLEY was buried
19 Dec   Thomas FERNYHOUGH was buried
29 Dec   Elizabeth BOTT was buried
1761
23 Apr   Thomas s/o Thomas & Mary HOPKINS was buried
10 May   George HOW *[Howe-BT]* was buried
29 May   Mary CHELL was buried
13 Jun   Thomas TOFT was buried
27 Jul   Hannah d/o Mary CHELL was buried
4 Aug   Ralph Gilbert s/o Mr Ralph WOOD of Fole & Mary his wife buried
12 Aug   Walter BURTON was buried
29 Aug   Elizabeth HOLLINS was buried
9 Sep   Harvey s/o William LEES was buried
16 Oct   Ursula MARTIN was buried
23 Oct   George TURNER
1762
6 Feb   John s/o Edward HOWARD
16 Feb   James RATCLIFFE was buried
18 Feb   John EATON was buried
2 Mar   William CHELL was buried
7 Mar   Thomas RAWLIN of Checkley was buried
17 Apr   Elizabeth d/o Thomas & Elizabeth TOOTH buried
10 May   Webb s/o Thomas & Elizabeth BELCHIER was buried
30 May   Elizabeth wife of Edward HOWARD was buried
11 Jul   Richard CARTER was buried
1 Aug   Elizabeth d/o Thomas & Sarah LEES was buried
11 Sep   Lydia d/o William & Honor LEES was buried
6 Oct   Mary d/o Thomas & Sarah BLOOD was buried
13 Nov   William s/o Jonathan & Hannah TUNSTALL was buried
31 Dec   Mary COPE was buried
1763
13 Feb   Thomas RUSHTON was buried. Affidavit brought
4 Mar   Grace THORLEY was buried. Notice given the 13th
9 Mar   Ann MOORE was buried. Affidit brought
11 Mar   Hannah DENT buried. Aff. brought
12 Mar   Anne the wife of John BLURTON of Stallington was buried. Afft. brought
1 Apr   Anne DEAKIN was buried. Affidt. brought
15 Apr   John LOWE was buried. Affidt. brought
23 Apr   William HOWE was buried. Aff. brought
8 May   Thomas HOWE was buried. Aff. brought
11 May   Solomon s/o William SALT was buried. Aff. brought
15 May   Mary d/o Thos & Eliz. PERKIN w. b. Aff. brought
19 May   Jane d/o John & Ellen FENTON was buried. Aff. brought
24 May   Elizabeth JOHNSON was buried. Aff. brought
25 May   John s/o Thomas & Sarah LEES was buried. Aff. brought
25 May   Thomas MILLINGTON was buried. Aff. brought
4 Jun   Edward HYDE was buried. Aff. brought
9 Jun   William s/o William & Sarah BELCHIER was buried. Aff. bt.
24 Jun   Mary d/o Thos & Mary HOPKINS was buried. Aff. bt.
21 Jul   Ann BAILY was buried. Aff. brought
28 Jul   George s/o Edwd *HOLLINGWORTH [BT]*

16 Aug   Elizabeth wife of John CRUTCHLEY was buried. Afft. bt.
28 Sep   William s/o John & *Elizth* HEATH *[BT]* was buried. Aff. bt.
18 *[BT]* Oct   Elizabeth d/o *Thos. & Mary* HOPKINS *was buried. Afft. Bt. [BT]*
15 Nov   John BAILY of Withington was buried. Aff. Bt.
17 Nov   Elizabeth EDGE was buried. Aff. Bt.
1764
2 Jan   Eleanor RAWLIN was buried. Afft. Bt.
3 Jan   Elizabeth COPE was buried. Afft. Bt.
18 *[BT]* Jan   Rebeccah FENTON was buried. Afft. Bt.
27 Feb   Margaret GILBERT was buried. Afft. Bt.
7 Mar   Mary d/o Mary KIRK was buried. Afft. Bt.
19 Mar   Ellen BLOOR was buried. Aff. Bt.
25 Mar   Joyce MUTCHEL was buried. Aff. Bt.
4 Apr   Samuel BELCHIER was buried. Aff. Bt.
8 Apr   John CARTWRIGHT was buried. Aff. Bt.
17 May   John s/o John & Anne BAILY was buried. Aff. Bt.
10 Jun   Edward BLURTON of the Woodleasow was buried. Af. b.
27 Sep   John BREREHURST was buried. Aff. Bt.
28 Sep   John s/o John & Eliz COPE was buried. Aff. B.
7 Oct   William PHILIPS of Nobot was buried. Aff. Bt.
4 Nov   Elizabeth FENTON Widow was buried. Aff. Bt.
1765
24 Jan   William s/o Thomas BLURTON of Barton was buried. Aff. Bt.
23 Feb   Thomas MILLS of Stramshall was buried. Aff. Bt.
25 Feb   Anne TOOTH Widow was buried. Aff. Bt.
10 Mar   Joseph TURNER was buried. Aff. Bt.
31 Mar   Dorothy wife of Robert PHILIPS was buried. Aff. Bt.
4 Apr   John BIRD was buried. Aff. Bt.
13 May   Edward HOWARD was buried. Aff. Bt.
24 May   William BERRISFORD was buried. Aff. Bt.
13 Jun   James SHAW was buried. Aff. Bt.
21 Jun   Mary WOOLEY was buried. Aff. Bt.
7 Aug   Sarah BALL was buried. Aff. Bt.
24 Aug   Thomas HYDE was buried. Aff. Bt.
8 Sep   Mary wife of Robert HORNE was buried. Aff. Bt.
11 Oct   Alice HALL was buried. Aff. Bt.
20 Oct   Joseph BARKER was buried. Aff. Bt.
20 Dec   Catharine WALKER was buried. Aff. Bt.
27 Dec   Mary SHAW was buried. Aff. Bt.
1766
6 Jan   Elizabeth wife of George DEAKIN was buried. Aff. Bt.
29 Jan   John CARTWRIGHT was buried. Aff. Bt.
10 Feb   Joseph TUNNICLEFFE was buried. Aff. Bt.
26 Mar   Thomas s/o John & Elizabeth COPE was buried. Aff. Bt.
2 Apr   Thomas s/o Thomas & Mary FENTON was buried. Aff. Bt.
12 Apr   Lydia wife of Edward BLURTON of Leigh Church was buried. Aff. Bt.
14 May   George CROSBY s/o Philip & Ellen was buried. Aff. Bt.
26 Jun   Thomas TUNNICLIFFE of Nobot was buried. Aff. Bt.
22 Aug   Elizabeth RADFORD was buried. Aff. Bt.
14 Sep   John BILLINGS was buried. Aff. Bt.
21 Apr   Elizabeth d/o Thos & Lydia BLURTON was buried. Aff. Bt.

6 Nov   Thomas LEES was buried. Aff. Bt.
16 Dec   William s/o William & Mary MARTIN was buried. Aff. Bt.
1767
10 Jan   William s/o John & Hannah HOLLINS was buried. Aff. Bt.
14 Jan   Thomas HOLLINS of Withington was buried. Aff. Bt.
3 Feb   Jane THORNIWELL was buried. Aff. Bt.
3 Feb   Elizabeth d/o Jno & Elizabeth JOHNSON was buried. Aff. Bt.
1 Apr   Mary KEELING was buried. Aff. Bt.
13 Apr   Ann SHENTON an Infant was buried. Aff. Bt.
14 Apr   Thomas MILLINGTON an infant was buried. Aff. Bt.
7 Jun   John COPE was buried. Aff. Bt.
16 Jun   Ann HOWE was buried. Aff. Bt.
30 Jun   Margaret BAILY d/o Ellis & Ann BAILY buried. Aff. Bt.
13 Jul   Widow Ann BELCHER was buried. Aff. Bt.
11 Aug   Richard MILWARD of Withington was buried. Aff. Bt.
14 Aug   Hannah BUXTON in Infant was buried. Aff. Bt.
20 Aug   Joseph COLLIER an infant was buried. Aff. Bt.
17 Oct   Susanna WRIGHT wife of Sampson WRIGHT was buried. Aff. Bt.
23 Dec   Mary d/o William BAILEY & Mary his wife was buried. Aff. Bt.

Leigh, Staffordshire, Parish Register,

1768 – 1812
Baptisms in the Parish of Leigh in the County of Stafford

1768

17 Jan	Edward s/o Joseph TILL & Mary his wife
7 Feb	William s/o Joseph EDGE & Mary his wife
14 Feb	Ellen d/o John TURNER & Jane his wife
17 Feb	Mary d/o William STARTIN & Hannah his wife
19 Feb	Elisabeth d/o John MILLINGTON & Ellen his wife
6 Mar	Francis illegitimate s/o Mary SLANEY
13 Mar	Thomas s/o Francis KEELING & Dorothy his wife
27 Mar	Robert s/o John BAILEY & Ann his wife
30 Mar	Elisabeth d/o Samuel TURNER & Elisabeth his wife
3 Apr	Thomas s/o Thomas SHAW & Jane his wife
12 Apr	John s/o John HART & Ann his wife
17 Apr	Hannah d/o William SALT & Mary his wife
21 Apr	Margaret d/o Job RUSHTON & Ann his wife
22 May	Thomas s/o John NUTT & Margaret his wife
22 May	Thomas s/o John SHENTON & Ann his wife
23 May	Ann d/o Thomas BLOOD & Sarah his wife
29 May	Mary d/o Robert HOLLINS & Ann his wife
29 May	Catharine d/o Mary KIRKE
12 Jun	Elisabeth illegitimate d/o Mary WALKER
7 Jul	Elisabeth d/o John COPE & Elisabeth his wife
18 Jul	James s/o Francis MARSTON & Mary his wife
7 Aug	Thomas s/o Ellis BAILEY & Ann his wife
16 Aug	Hannah & Susanna twin daughter s of Abigail HURST
19 Aug	William s/o William MARTIN & Mary his wife
4 Sep	John s/o Robert *EATON & Mary his wife *or HEATON
18 Sep	Ann d/o Samuel COPE & Elisabeth his wife
18 Sep	Robert s/o John CHARLESWORTH & Jane his wife
28 Sep	George s/o George PHILIPS & Mary his wife
28 Sep	Thomas s/o John HOWE & Ellen his wife
20 Oct	Samuel s/o John WALKER & Mary his wife
3 Nov	Hannah d/o Richard SMITH & Sarah his wife
20 Nov	Joseph s/o Edward BARKER & Mary his wife
26 Dec	Hannah d/o John TILL & Sarah his wife
27 Dec	Mary illegitimate d/o Hannah DENT

1769

17 Feb	Edward s/o Edward WOOLLEY & Ann his wife
19 Feb	Elisabeth illegitimate d/o Ann TATTON
26 Mar	Thomas s/o William STARTIN & Hannah his wife
26 Mar	Margarett d/o John TURNER & Jane his wife
26 Mar	James s/o Joseph THACKER & Elisabeth his wife
9 Apr	Mary d/o Thos COPE & Mary his wife
21 Apr	Edward s/o Thomas TOOTH & Prudence his wife
23 Apr	Margaret d/o Edward HOLLINGWORTH & Ann his wife
26 Mar	George s/o Thomas FROST & Sarah his wife
	N.B. this child was baptiz'd in his Fathers House by the Revd Mr Hancock Rector of Broomshelf

7 May   William s/o Richard FOWLER junr & Hannah his wife
15 May   James s/o Robert PHILIPS & Sarah his wife
11 Jun   Thomas s/o John ASTBURY & Catharine his wife
11 Jun   Thomas s/o John PEDLEY & Mary his wife
2 Jul   Hannah d/o Aaron MIERS & Ann his wife
16 Jul   Sarah d/o John HEATH & Elisabeth his wife
26 Aug   Thomas s/o John GILBERT junr & Hannah his wife
3 Sep   William s/o *James *CARLILE & Ellen his wife
     [note on opposite page *James *CORNWAL]
     Sarah d/o Philip CROSBY & Ellen his wife
24 Sep   Mary d/o James JOHNSON & Elisabeth his wife
8 Oct   Ann d/o Robert HOLLINS & Ann his wife
29 Oct   William s/o Jonathan TUNSTAL & Hannah his wife
     Elisabeth d/o Thomas PERKINS & Elisabeth PERKIN
1 Nov   Ellen d/o William JOHNSON & Elisabeth his wife
19 Nov   William s/o Ralph RUSHTON & Lettice his wife
3 Dec   John s/o George TOOTH & Ann his wife
     Ann d/o William LEES & Honor his wife
10 Dec   William s/o Samuel TURNER & Elisabeth his wife

1770

4 Feb   Elisabeth d/o Anthony RUSHTON & Sarah his wife
     Elisabeth d/o Robert HORN & Ann his wife
11 Feb   Joseph s/o William ADAMS & Mary his wife
18 Feb   John s/o John BURTON & Mary his wife
     Elisabeth d/o Thomas MIDDLETON of Fordswel & Ann his wife
24 Feb   John s/o George PHILLIPS & Mary his wife
     Ann d/o Joseph TILL & Mary his wife
     George s/o Richard FOWLER Senr: & Mary his wife
4 Mar   Sarah illegitimate d/o Elisabeth WOOLLEY
21 Mar   Thomas s/o Thomas BARKER & (Mary**) his wife **Sarah
23 Mar   Sarah d/o John CHARLESWORTH & Jane his wife
30 Mar   Joseph s/o William MARTIN & Mary his wife
6 Apr   Sarah d/o Edward HOWARD & Mary his wife
16 Apr   Elisabeth d/o James PIERS & Judith his wife
22 Apr   Mary d/o Philip TITLEY & Ellen his wife
     Edward illegitimate s/o Sarah LEES, Widow
6 May   Thomas s/o Theodorus DAVIES & Jane his wife
20 May   William s/o Edward BARKER & Mary his wife
3 Jun   Ann d/o John *MUCHALL & Elisabeth his wife *or MITCHELL
3 Jun   Thomas s/o Nathaniel HINCKLY & Catharine his wife
10 Jun   William s/o John PRESTON & Alice his wife
17 Jun   William illegitimate s/o Dorothy RATCLIFF
24 Jun   John s/o John NUTT & Margarett his wife
8 Jul   Elisabeth d/o Thomas FENTON & Mary his wife
12 Aug   Sarah d/o Thomas COLLIER & Ann his wife
19 Aug   Robert s/o Robert EATON & Mary his wife
19 Aug   John illegitimate s/o Margaret HOWE
9 Sep   William s/o John LOWE & Ann his wife
Sep 30   Ann d/o John ASTBURY & Catharine his wife
7 Oct   Jane d/o William & Sarah IBBS [*Ebbes-BT*]
14 Oct   Martha illegitimate d/o Mary THORNIWEL

21 Oct   Thomas s/o Thomas TOOTH & Prudence his wife
          John s/o John MILLINGTON & Ellen his wife
1771
1 Jan   Mary d/o Richard SMITH & Sarah [*Mary-BT*] his wife
7 Jan   Sarah d/o John HART & Ann his wife
26 Jan   Ann d/o Edward COPE & Elisabeth his wife
10 Feb   Elisabeth d/o George WOOLLEY & Mary his wife
15 Feb   Thomas s/o John BAGNETT & Jane his wife
3 Mar   William s/o John LOWE & Mary his wife
15 Mar   William s/o Thomas BLOOD & Sarah his wife
24 Mar   Sarah d/o Joseph EDGE & Mary his wife
17 Apr   Thomas s/o Hannah DONE privately baptiz'd. This child was received
          afterwards
21 Apr   Stephen s/o Ellis BAILEY & Ann his wife
21 Apr   John s/o Isaac ASH & Mary his wife
25 Apr   Samuel s/o Robert PHILLIPS & Sarah his wife
5 May   John s/o John BUXTON & Mary his wife
          Thomas s/o John PEDLEY & Mary his wife
20 May   John ROGERS s/o Dorothy MARSTON
21 May   William s/o Thomas CROSLEY [*Crossley-BT*] & Mary his wife.
5 Jun   Edith BANKS illegitimate d/o Elisabeth RAWLIN privately baptized. This
          child was sometime after received.
23 Jun   Sarah d/o Thomas WOODWARD & Elisabeth his wife
7 Jul   George s/o Charles BENTLEY & Ann his wife
25 Jul   Margaret d/o John GILBERT & Hannah his wife
28 Jul   Sarah d/o John TILL & Sarah his wife
18 Aug   Ann d/o Edward BARKER & Mary his wife
15 Sep   Lydia illegitimate d/o Esther WOOLLEY
          Joseph s/o Joseph THACKER & Elisabeth his wife
22 Sep   Mary d/o Joseph SMITH & Ann his wife
13 Oct   Nathaniel s/o Nathaniel HINCKLY & Catharine his wife
20 Oct   Luke illegitimate s/o Lydia BAILEY
27 Oct   William s/o Joshua PRESTON junr & Mary his wife
3 Nov   William s/o William STARTIN & Hannah his wife
1 Dec   Ann d/o Edward WOOLLEY & Ann his wife
25 Dec   Ann d/o Thomas COLLIER & Ann his wife
28 Dec   Ann d/o George PHILLIPS & Mary his wife
30 Dec   John s/o John HOLLINS & Hannah his wife
1772
12 Jan   Joseph s/o Aaron MYERS & Ann is wife
9 Feb   James s/o James PIERS & Judith his wife
23 Feb   James s/o Joseph COLLIER & Elisabeth his wife
20 Mar   William s/o John ASTBURY & Catharine his wife
          John s/o Edward HOWARD & Mary his wife
25 Mar   Catharina d/o John BELCHER & Elisabeth his wife
12 Apr   Susanna d/o John CHARLESWORTH & Jane his wife
19 Apr   Samuel s/o Samuel BLOWER & Mary his wife
          Edward s/o Thomas BARKER & Sarah his wife
20 Apr   John s/o Samuel TURNER & Elisabeth his wife
10 May   Elisabeth d/o Job RUSHTON & Ann his wife
9 Jun   Elisabeth d/o William COPE & Joyce his wife

21 Jun Betty d/o Ralph RUSHTON & Lettice his wife
       William s/o Philip TITLEY & Ellen his wife
24 Jun Samuel s/o John HALL & Mary his wife
26 Jul Samuel s/o John SHENTON & Ann his wife
2 Aug Joseph s/o Robert PHILLIPS & Sarah his wife
9 Aug Samuel s/o Frederick RUSHTON & Jane his wife
13 Sep James s/o James JOHNSON & Elisabeth his wife
20 Sep William s/o George TOOTH & Ann his wife
11 Oct Samuel s/o Theodorus DAVIES & Jane his wife
3 Oct Samuel s/o John COPE & Elisabeth his wife privately baptiz'd [& died
      before it was brough* to Church.-BT] [*sic]
1 Nov John s/o John HIGGS & Mary his wife
1 Nov George s/o William ADAMS & Mary his wife
8 Nov Hannah d/o William MARTIN & Mary his wife
8 Nov John s/o John WALKER & Sarah his wife
22 Nov Elisabeth d/o John SALT & Mary his wife
21 Dec James s/o John BAILEY & Ann his wife

1773
1 Jan Mary d/o Samuel BRAIN [Braine-BT] & Elisabeth his wife
25*Jan Thomas s/o William STARTIN & Hannah his wife [*15-BT]
30 Jan Margaret d/o Richard FOWLER [Senr.-BT] of Leigh & Mary his wife
14 Feb William s/o Edward WOOLLEY & Ann his wife
23 Feb Elisabeth RUSSEL illegitimate d/o Hannah JOHNSON
7 Mar Thomas s/o Isaac ASH & Mary his wife
19 Mar Sarah d/o James KIRK & Elisabeth his wife
23 Mar William s/o William WALKER & Hannah his wife
14 Apr Frances d/o John HART & Ann his wife
15 Apr Thomas s/o John MILLINGTON & Ellen his wife
2 May Ellen d/o Thomas TOOTH & Prudence his wife
9 May George s/o Joseph TILL & Mary his wife
23 May William s/o John NUTT & Margaret his wife
30 May Thomas s/o John JOHNSON* & Hannah his wife
       *John JOHNSON 1st Grandson of Thomas JOHNSON now living at
       Shortwoods.
       Lydia d/o John GILBERT junr & Hannah his wife
11 Jul Edward s/o Edward BARKER & Mary his wife
18 Jul John s/o Joseph THACKER & Elisabeth his wife
25 Jul Mary illegitimate d/o *Mary THORNIWELL [Thorniwel-BT]
       *Since married to Samuel SHENTON
22 Aug Ann d/o Joshua PRESTON junr & Mary his wife
5 Sep William s/o George PHILLIPS & Mary his wife
31 Oct George s/o Philip HAWLEY & Sarah his wife
5 Nov Elisabeth d/o Joseph COLLIER & Elisabeth his wife
5 Nov Thomas s/o Joseph SMITH & Ann his wife
5 Dec William s/o Thomas CHELL & Mary his wife
27 Dec Elisabeth d/o George JOHNSON & Sarah his wife

1774
1 Jan Ann d/o William COPE & Joyce his wife
9 Jan William s/o William JOHNSON & Elisabeth his wife
16 Jan Ellen d/o Thomas COPE & Ann his wife
25 Feb Thomas s/o William SALT & Mary his wife

6 Mar	William s/o John BUXTON & Mary his wife
13 Mar	William s/o William HIBBERD & Ann his wife
17 Apr	Sarah d/o William IBBES & Sarah his wife
24 Apr	Joseph s/o Richard SMITH & Mary his wife
10 Apr	Thomas s/o John MUCHAL & Elisabeth his wife privately bapt'd
8 May	George s/o John HIGGS & Mary his wife
22 May	Edward & Thomas sons of Edward COPE & Elisabeth his wife
22 May	John s/o Robert PHILLIPS [Philips-BT] & Sarah his wife
12 Jun	Ann d/o James PIERS & Judith his wife
24 Jun	Thomas s/o John CHARLESWORTH & Jane his wife
26 Jun	Ann d/o James JOHNSON & Elisabeth his wife
26 Jun	George & Joseph sons of Frederic RUSHTON & Jane his wife
10 Jul	Dinah d/o Thomas CROSLY & Mary his wife
24 Jul	Thomas s/o John WRIGHT & Mary his wife
31 Jul	Elisabeth d/o Joseph COPE & Mary his wife
7 Aug	Job s/o Joseph RUSHTON & Catharine his wife
14 Aug	Mary d/o Samuel TURNER & Elisabeth his wife
24 Aug	Elisabeth d/o John HALL & Mary his wife
28 Aug	Elisabeth d/o George TOOTH & Ann his wife
11 Sep	Thomas s/o Thomas COLLIER & Ann his wife
18 Sep	Lydia d/o John CARTER* & Lydia his wife *of Stone Heath
25 Sep	Elisabeth d/o John TURNER & Jane his wife
25 Sep	Mary illegitimate d/o Esther WOOLLEY
2 Oct	Elisabeth d/o William CARTER & Ellen his wife
30 Oct	Lucy d/o George RUSHTON & Sarah his wife
30 Oct	Joseph s/o Thomas BARKER & Sarah his wife
5 Nov	Jane d/o John HIDE junr & Mary his wife
6 Nov	Ann illegitimate d/o Elisabeth RAWLIN
29 Nov	John done s/o William WALKER & Hannah his wife
1775	
1 Jan	Elisabeth d/o Thomas WOODWARD & Elisabeth his wife
6 Jan	Joseph PEMBER illegitimate s/o Mary MORVAN
19 Feb	Catharine d/o Isaac ASH & Mary his wife
12 Mar	Elisabeth d/o Thomas CHELL & Mary his wife
12 Mar	James s/o John BAGNETT [Bagnelt-BT] & Jane his wife
19 Mar	John s/o Ralph RUSHTON & Latice his wife
25 Mar	Joseph s/o Joseph LYCETT & Elisabeth his wife
7 Apr	Dinah d/o George PHILLIPS & Mary his wife
7 Apr	Thomas s/o Richard FOWLER* & Hannah his wife *the younger [Junr.-BT]
9 Apr	Elisabeth d/o John GILBERT junr & Hannah his wife
23 Apr	Elisabeth d/o William STARTIN & Hannah his wife
23 Apr	Ann d/o William MARTIN & Mary his wife
23 Apr	Ann d/o Thomas TOOTH & Prudence his wife
30 Apr	Joseph s/o Joseph COLLIER & Elisabeth his wife
7 May	Hannah illegitimate d/o Sarah LEES, Widow
14 May	Edward s/o Joseph COPE & Mary his wife
14 May	Thomas s/o Joseph MOORE & Elisabeth his wife
4 Jun	William s/o William COPE & Joyce his wife
6 Jun	Charles s/o John HART & Ann his wife
10 Jun	Thomas s/o John SHERRATT & Jane his wife
25 Jun	John s/o David BAILEY [Baily-BT] & Elisabeth his wife

25 Jun George s/o Joseph EDGE & Mary his wife
⌐ 30 Jul Ralph s/o Edward WOOLLEY & Ann his wife
⌐ 10 Sep Ellen d/o John SALT & Mary his wife
⌐ 1 Oct Mary d/o John MUCHALL & (Mary) Elisabeth
1 Nov Margaret d/o Robert PHILLIPS & Sarah his wife
19 Nov John s/o Thomas SAUNDERS & Elisabeth his wife
19 Nov Peter s/o William HIBBERT & Ann his wife
19 Nov John s/o Jonathan TUNSTAL & Hannah his wife
19 Nov Elisabeth d/o George STEVENSON & Martha his wife
⌐ 3 Dec Mary d/o Thomas TOOTH & Elisabeth his wife
3 Dec George s/o Joseph COPE & Mary his wife
24 Dec Dinah d/o John SHENTON & Ann his wife
25 Dec John s/o William JOHNSON & Elisabeth his wife
31 Dec Francis s/o John NUTT & Margaret his wife
1776
⌐ 7 Jan Elizabeth Howe (illeg) d/o Elizabeth BAILEY *[Baily-BT]*
⌐ 28 Jan James s/o Samuel TURNER & Elizabeth his wife
⌐ 28 Jan Elizabeth d/o George HOWE & Elizabeth his wife
28 Jan Thomas s/o Samuel SHENTON & Mary his wife
2 Feb Frances d/o Edward HOLLINGWORTH & Ann his wife
5 Feb Sampson (illeg) s/o Hannah LOWNDES
⌐ 3 Mar James & William illegitimate sons of Margaret HOWE
10 Mar William s/o John MILLINGTON & Ellen his wife
18 Feb Alice d/o Philip TITLEY & Ellen his wife
22 Mar Richard s/o Joshua PRESTON & Mary his wife
22 Mar William s/o John JOHNSON & Hannah his wife
26 Apr Joseph s/o George JOHNSON & Sarah his wife
28 Apr William s/o Frederic RUSHTON & Jane his wife
12 May Moses s/o Adam RUSHTON & Elizabeth his wife
⌐ 30 May James s/o James & Hannah TURNER
26 Jun Ellen d/o Robert HEATON & Mary his wife
29 Jun John s/o Thomas CROSLY & Elizabeth his wife
7 Jul Elizabeth d/o Samuel BARNET & Hannah his wife
15 Jul George s/o Joseph THACKER & Elizabeth his wife
27 Jul Aaron Whigmore s/o Joseph RUSHTON & Catherine his wife
⌐ 3 Aug Lydia d/o John TURNER & Sarah his wife
1 Sep Fanny d/o John CHARLESWORTH & Jane his wife
28 Sep William s/o John & Mary HIGGS
14 Oct Hannah d/o James & Elizabeth JOHNSON
22 Oct Thomas s/o William & Sarah TATUM of Uttoxeter
⌐ 3 Nov Mary d/o John & Mary WRIGHT
10 Nov Mary d/o Judith PIERS, Widow
24 Nov William s/o Joseph & Ann SMITH
22 Dec Alice d/o David & Margaret *[Mary-BT]* SHEMILT
⌐ 25 Dec Kitty d/o William & Hannah WALKER
1777
6 Jan Ellen d/o John & Mary BUXTON
14 Jan Sarah d/o George & Sarah RUSHTON
24 Jan Mary d/o Benjamin & Elizabeth ALLEN
14 Feb Thomas s/o George & Mary PHILIPS
16 Feb Ellen d/o Thomas & Mary CHELL

22 Feb	Richard s/o Robert & Sarah PHILIPS
22 Feb	Mary d/o William & Joyce COPE
23 Feb	John s/o William & Jane HAYWOOD
9 Mar	Ann d/o William & Mary PHILIPS
31 Mar	James s/o Richard & Mary SMITH
3 Apr	Robert s/o John & Jane SHERRAT
5 Apr	Lydia d/o Joseph & Elizabeth COLLIER
13 Apr	Mary d/o William & Mary JOHNSON
18 Apr	George (illeg) s/o Fanny TILL
25 May	Thomas s/o William & Ellen CARTER
7 Jun	Thomas s/o George & Hannah TOOTH
15 Jun	Mary d/o Thomas & Ann TURNER
6 Jul	Mary d/o Thomas & Ann PHILIPS
3 Aug	Mary d/o John & Hannah GILBERT
15 Aug	Ann d/o Thomas & Elizabeth WOODWARD
31 Aug	Ann d/o Thomas & Sarah BARKER
2 Sep	Ann d/o Daniel & Hannah LOWNDES
29 Oct	Thomas s/o Thomas & Jane SAUNDERS
3 Nov	John s/o Thomas & Prudence TOOTH
4 Nov	Ann d/o Edward & Ann WOOLLEY
5 Nov	John s/o Robert & Elizabeth BULL
16 Nov	John s/o Thomas & Ann COPE
20 Nov	Thomas s/o John & Sarah HOWE
29 Nov	Ellen d/o John & Mary CHARLESWORTH
2 Dec	David s/o David & Elizabeth BAILEY
13 Dec	Joseph Dickenson s/o Joseph & Sarah HART
24 Dec	John s/o Edward & Elizabeth COPE
1778	
4 Jan	Thomas s/o Samuel & Hannah BARNET
13 Jan	Robert s/o William & Sarah TATUM
25 Jan	Mary d/o Luke & Elizabeth BILLINGS
3 Feb	Elizabeth d/o John & Mary ALLCOCK
5 Feb	Samuel s/o Tho: & Eliz: YOUNG of Stoke Parish baptized privately
8 Feb	Hannah d/o Middleton & Mary ROBOTHAM
18 Feb	John s/o James Hollins MOTRAM & Ann his wife
19 Feb	George s/o Samuel & Elizabeth TURNER
1 Mar	Elizabeth d/o Samuel & Elizabeth LAYKIN of the Parish of Trentham
15 Mar	John s/o William & Hannah STARTIN
22 Mar	Samuel s/o Samuel & Mary SHENTON
3 Apr	Ann (illeg) d/o Ann WRIGHT
12 Apr	Adam s/o Adam & Elizabeth RUSHTON
26 Apr	Mary d/o Lawrence & Elizabeth GREENSMITH
3 May	Elizabeth (illeg) d/o Alice JOHNSON
11 May	Ann d/o Joseph & Elizabeth MOOR
19 May	Margaret d/o George & Martha STEVENSON
31 May	James s/o John & Mary SALT
14 Jun	Hannah d/o James & Ann CARTER
17 Jun	Thomas s/o Frederic & Jane RUSHTON
30 Jun	Robert s/o John & Mary HIDE
2 Jul	Elizabeth d/o Robert & Sarah PHILIPS
12 Jul	Samuel s/o John & Margaret NUTT

10 Aug Elias s/o Elias & Ann BAILEY
12 Aug Jane (illeg) d/o Sarah LOWE
14 Aug George s/o Joshua & Mary PRESTON
16 Aug Betty d/o William & Mary PHILIPS
18 Oct Thomas s/o Thomas & Elizabeth TOOTH
15 Nov Hannah (illeg) d/o Hannah JOHNSON
6 Dec Samuel s/o George & Sarah JOHNSON
9 Dec John GILBERT the younger was appointed Parish Clerk by the Reverend Walter Bagot Rector
29 Dec Sarah d/o John & Jane SHERRAT

1779

3 Jan Thomas (illeg) s/o Elizabeth YATES was received into the Congregation. Thomas FALKNOR the supposed Father.
5 Jan Mary d/o Daniel & Hannah LOWNDES
25 Jan Isaiah s/o Joseph & Catherine RUSHTON
28 Jan Thomas (illeg) s/o Mary HOWARD
31 Jan Francis (illeg) s/o Hannah CHARLESWORTH
14 Feb Ann d/o Thomas & Ann COPE
21 Feb Elizabeth d/o Robert & Elizabeth BULL
21 Feb Mary d/o Joseph & Elizabeth THACKER
22 Feb Joseph s/o Robert & Mary HEATON
28 Feb Betty d/o George & Elizabeth WRIGHT
7 Mar George s/o William & Elizabeth JOHNSON
21 Mar Hannah d/o Thomas & Mary CHELL
23 Mar Kitty d/o John & Ann HART
27 Mar Millecent (illeg) d/o Catherine TILL
2 Apr Nanny d/o Luke & Elizabeth BILLINGS
4 Apr Joseph s/o Joseph & Mary EDGE
16 Apr John s/o William & Joyce COPE
16 May John s/o John & Elizabeth MELLOR
23 May Elizabeth d/o John & Sarah TURNER
29 May Ellen d/o William & Ann RAWLINS
5 Jun Maria d/o George & Mary PHILIPS
6 Jun Joseph s/o Joseph & Ann SMITH
20 Jun Elizabeth d/o John & Ellen ROBINSON
27 Jun Ann d/o John & Ann SHENTON
4 Jul Ann d/o John & Hannah GILBERT
4 Jul Samuel s/o Samuel & Hannah BARNET
15 Jul Elizabeth d/o Edward & Ann WARNER
1 Aug Elizabeth (illeg) d/o Sarah WALKER
15 Aug Elizabeth d/o John & Ann CHELL
25 Aug Edward s/o William & Hannah WALKER
4 Sep William s/o Edward & Elizabeth COPE
16 Sep Lydia d/o James & Lydia MARSTON
19 Sep Joseph s/o Thomas & Ann COLLIER
16 Oct Ralph s/o Joseph & Sarah HART
17 Oct John (illeg) s/o Sarah LEES
31 Oct John s/o Richard & Mary SMITH
1 Nov William s/o William & Hannah HARPER
10 Nov George s/o John & Mary TOMKINSON
1 Dec Ann d/o Edward & Sarah HOLLINGWORTH

28 Dec William s/o Thomas & Ann PHILIPS
31 Dec Kitty d/o Robert & Sarah PHILIPS
31 Dec John s/o John & Mary PLIMMER
1780
 1 Jan Henry s/o Thomas & Mary CROSSLEY
20 Jan Elizabeth d/o John & Sarah HOWE
23 Jan Thomas s/o William & Mary MARTIN
24 Jan Hannah d/o Joseph & Elizabeth COLLIER
25 Jan Richard s/o Thomas & Jane SAUNDERS
 4 Feb Sarah d/o Thomas & Sarah BARKER
19 Feb Edward s/o Thomas & Prudence TOOTH
27 Feb Hannah d/o John & Mary ALLCOCK
 3 Mar Nelly d/o George & Sarah RUSHTON
        Sarah d/o Isaac & Mary ASH was baptized privately by Dr Langley & received March 26th
12 Apr Mary d/o George & Abigail THORNEWORK
16 Apr George s/o Middleton & Mary ROBOTHAM
19 Apr Lydia d/o Philip & Ellen TITLEY
 5 May Stephen s/o Adam & Elizabeth RUSHTON
 7 May Mary d/o William & Mary PHILIPS
14 May Ann d/o Samuel & Eliz: TURNER
14 May William s/o John & Elizabeth GREEN
14 Jun David s/o Samuel & Mary ALLCOCK
18 Jun Henry s/o John & Mary BUXTON
 2 Jul Francis s/o John & Ellen MILLINGTON
27 Jul Richard s/o Daniel & Hannah LOWNDES
10 Sep Edward s/o Luke & Elizabeth BILLINGS
 5 Oct Ann d/o George & Hannah TOOTH
15 Oct John s/o John & Ann CHELL
21 Oct William (illeg) s/o Elizabeth BOULTON
29 Oct Job s/o Frederic & Jane RUSHTON
30 Oct Jonathan s/o William & Hannah STARTIN
31 Oct Thomas s/o Laurence & Elizabeth GREENSMITH
12 Nov Lydia d/o William & Joyce COPE
23 Nov Elizabeth d/o Francis & Sarah SHERRAT
10 Dec William son Samuel & Mary SHENTON
28 Dec Thomas s/o Edward & Sarah HOLLINGWORTH
31 Dec Thomas s/o Thomas & Mary CHELL
1781
14 Jan John s/o George & Edith WALKER
 4 Feb Ann (illeg) d/o Elizabeth BAILEY
 9 Feb Mary d/o John & Margaret NUTT
24 Feb Ellen d/o John & Catherine LOVATT
25 Feb Sarah d/o James Hollins MOTRAM & Ann his wife
 4 Mar George s/o Ralph & Dorothy KENT
 4 Mar Nelly d/o Thomas & Martha BRANDRICK
11 Mar Sarah d/o Thomas & Ann PHILIPS
11 Mar John s/o John & Hannah GILBERT
17 Mar John s/o William & Ellen CARTER
 7 Apr James s/o James & Lydia MARSTON
11 Apr William s/o Thomas & Ann BLADON

19 Apr   Thomas s/o William & Sarah TATUM
20 Apr   Nanny d/o William & Elizabeth JOHNSON
25 Apr   Kitty d/o John & Ann HUGHES
29 Apr   Sarah d/o Thomas & Ann COPE
4 May   Sarah d/o Robert & Sarah PHILIPS
12 May   Elizabeth d/o Thomas & Margaret CHELL
20 May   George s/o William & Hannah HARPER
23 May   Sarah d/o Samuel & Mary ALLCOCK
10 Jun   William s/o William & Ann RAWLINS
15 Jun   William s/o Robert & Elizabeth BULL
22 Jun   Thomas s/o Thomas & Mary WOODWARD
4 Jul   Hannah d/o Joseph & Elizabeth THACKER
8 Jul   Francis s/o William & Mary BEARDMORE
19 Jul   Mary d/o Joseph & Sarah HART
22 Jul   Henry s/o Thomas & Sarah BARKER
2 Aug   Mary d/o John & Sarah TURNER
3 Aug   Elizabeth d/o William & Mary HILL
4 Aug   Samuel s/o Edward & Elizabeth COPE
9 Aug   Hannah d/o James & Hannah TURNER
19 Aug   Hannah d/o Joseph & Elizabeth MOOR
27 Aug   William s/o George & Sarah JOHNSON
8 Nov   Mary d/o William & Hannah WALKER
29 Nov   Sarah d/o John & Sarah HOWE
16 Dec   William s/o Simon & Elizabeth COPE
22 Dec   John s/o Daniel & Hannah LOWNDES
1782
6 Jan   William s/o John & Elizabeth BLADON
18 Jan   John WETTON (illeg) s/o Elizabeth DEAKIN
20 Jan   Betty d/o Joseph & Ann SMITH
22 Jan   Sarah d/o George & Abigail THORNEWORK
22 Jan   Thomas s/o Edward & Ann WARNER
1 Feb   Alley d/o Joseph & Catherine RUSHTON
11 Feb   Thomas s/o Thomas & Margaret TUNNICLIFF
17 Feb   Hannah d/o Samuel & Hannah BARNETT
22 Feb   William s/o Joseph & Elizabeth COLLIER
25 Feb   Elizabeth d/o John & Elizabeth GREEN
7 Mar   Sarah & Mary twin d/o William & Sarah MILNER
10 Mar   Joseph s/o John & Ann CHELL
10 Mar   Ann d/o Richard & Mary SMITH
7 Apr   William (illeg) s/o Mary ROBOTHAM
14 Apr   Sarah d/o William & Mary PHILIPS
14 Apr   Hannah d/o Luke & Elizabeth BILLINGS
14 Apr   James s/o John & Ann LANDER
23 Apr   Samson s/o Samuel & Elizabeth TURNER
7 May   Benjamin WALTHOE (illeg) s/o Lydia SHENTON
9 May   Mary (illeg) d/o Elizabeth HOLLINS
12 May   Thomas s/o William & Joyce COPE
6 Jun   Sarah d/o Thomas & Alice FOSTER
23 Jun   George s/o George & Elizabeth WRIGHT
23 Jun   Elizabeth d/o Thomas & Prudence TOOTH
30 Jun   Every s/o Adam & Elizabeth RUSHTON

30 Jun John s/o John & Jane BAGNAL
21 Jul Charlotte (illeg) d/o Alice CARTER
25 Jul James s/o Thomas & Jane SAUNDERS
6 Aug Phabe [Phoebe-BT] d/o George & Sarah RUSHTON
25 Aug Sarah (illeg) d/o Jane LYNN
25 Aug Sarah d/o Middleton & Mary ROBOTHAM
27 Aug Sarah d/o Thomas & Martha BRANDRICK
1 Sep Charles s/o Charles & Hannah THORNEWORK
7 Sep John s/o Francis & Sarah SHERRAT
7 Sep Dolly d/o Robert & Sarah PHILIPS
22 Sep William s/o Robert & Mary HEATON
26 Sep George s/o George & Martha STEVENSON
17 Oct James s/o John & Ellen MILLINGTON
17 Nov Edward s/o William & Jane WALKER of Withington
24 Nov Joseph s/o John & Elizabeth MELLOR
29*Nov Samuel s/o Thomas & Ellen WILSHAW of Dilhorn parish [*27 Nov-BT]
7 Dec Mary d/o Robert & Mary ARNOLD
26 Dec John s/o Alexander & Ellen PERKIN
28 Dec Thomas s/o James & Mary MARSTON
1783
31 Jan Francis s/o Frederic & Jane RUSHTON
27 Jan William ASBURY s/o John ASBURY Junr & Sarah his wife
8 Mar Ann (illeg) d/o Ann COLLINS
17 Mar James s/o John & Ann JOHNSON
20 Apr Thomas s/o John & Ann HUGHES
27 Apr Henry s/o Thomas & Mary WOODWARD
2 May Edward s/o Thomas & Mary CHELL
4 May John s/o Thomas & Ann BLADON
4 May Robert s/o John & Hannah GILBERT
9 May Mary d/o William & Ellen CARTER
10 May Sarah d/o Joseph & Sarah HART
18 May Thomas s/o Ralph & Dorothy KENT
18 May John (illeg) s/o Ann TURNER
27 May Mary (illeg) d/o Mary BUXTON
4 Jun Thomas s/o William & Mary MELLOR
8 Jun John s/o Samuel & Mary SHENTON
6 Jul Samuel s/o George & Edith WALKER
8 Jul Dolly (illeg) d/o Mary HOLLINS
3 Aug Sarah d/o Joseph & Elizabeth MOOR
25 Aug William s/o Daniel & Hannah LOWNDES
7 Sep Thomas s/o William & Hannah HARPER
21 Sep [BT] Sarah d/o Lawrence & Elizabeth GREENSMITH was baptized privately
by Mr Langley & received September the 21st
18 Oct Edith d/o Joseph & Elizabeth COLLIER
30 Nov William s/o William & Mary HILL
25 Dec Susannah d/o George & Ann FLORENCE
1784
25 Jan Thomas s/o Thomas & Jane WILSON
29 Feb John s/o John & Sarah TURNER
1 Mar Mary d/o William & Hannah STARTIN
7 Mar Charlotte d/o William & Mary PHILIPS

1 Apr   Maria d/o Adam & Elizabeth RUSHTON (paupers)
11 Apr   Mary d/o John & Barbara HEATH (Leek)
11 Apr   Diana d/o Thomas & Hannah BARKER
18 Apr   Ann d/o James Hollins MOTRAM (pauper) & Ann his wife
2 May   John s/o Samuel & Hannah BARNETT
9 May   Sarah d/o Job & Elizabeth SMITH
17 May   Edward s/o Robert & Sarah PHILIPS
18 Jun   Richard s/o John & Sarah ASBURY
1 Jul [BT]   William s/o James & Lydia MARSTON was privately baptized by Mr WRIGHT & received into the Congregation July 1st
8 Jul   Margaret d/o William & Ann RAWLINS
11 Jul   Alexander s/o Alexander & Ellen PERKIN
11 Jul   William s/o George & Hannah NOAKES
18 Jul   William s/o John & Ann CHELL
1 Aug   Ann d/o John & Diana CARTER
1 Aug   Mary d/o James & Mary MARSTON
30 Sep   Hannah d/o William & Jane WALKER (Leigh)
10 Oct   John s/o Joseph & Dorothy DEAKIN
11 Oct   Edward s/o John & Mary HYDE
18 Oct   William s/o John & Ann LANDER
4 Nov   John s/o William & Hannah WALKER
5 Nov   Joseph s/o Thomas & Martha BRANDRICK
11 Nov   George s/o Thomas & Jane SAUNDERS
19 Nov   Jane d/o George & Sarah JOHNSON
12 Dec   Mary d/o John & Mary ALLCOCK
12 Dec   Jane d/o John & Mary ELSMORE *[Elsemore-BT]*
18 Dec   Thomas s/o John & Mary BUXTON (paup)
18 Dec   William s/o Robert & Mary ARNOLD
26 Dec   Elizabeth d/o Thomas & Mary CHELL (paup)
1785
16 Jan   Stephen s/o John & Ann SHENTON
23 Jan   Thomas s/o Thomas & Ann BROOKES
30 Jan   Mary d/o William & Elizabeth LAUGHTON
2 Feb   Thomas s/o Samuel & Elizabeth TURNER
13 Feb   William s/o Joseph & Elizabeth THACKER (paup)
7 Mar   Thomas s/o William & Margaret BAILEY (paup)
12 Mar   John s/o Mr Thomas & Mrs Joyce BRINDLEY
16 Mar   John s/o John & Ann TAYLOR
29 Mar   Samuel (illeg) s/o Hannah OFFLEY
1 Apr   Martha d/o Daniel & Hannah LOWNDES
25 Apr   John s/o Middleton & Mary ROBOTHAM
28 Apr   Charles s/o Joseph & Sarah HART
8 May   George s/o Thomas & Prudence TOOTH
29 May   Mary d/o Charles & Hannah THORNEYWORK (paup)
11 Jun   Elizabeth (illeg) d/o Mary HOWE (paup)
11 Jun   George s/o Simon & Elizabeth COPE
7 Jul   James s/o William & Margaret DEAKIN
21 Aug   Sarah d/o John & Elizabeth MELLOR
28 Aug   George s/o George & Sarah RUSHTON (paup)
29 Aug   Thomas & Mary son & d/o William & Mary HILL
4 Sep   James s/o James Hollins MOTRAM & Ann his wife (paup)

4 Sep   Margaret d/o John & Ann NICKLIN
11 Sep   Sarah d/o John & Jane BAGNAL
11 Sep   Elizabeth d/o William & Hannah HARPER
16 Sep   John s/o John & Ann HUGHES
6 Oct   Maria (illeg) d/o Lydia SHENTON (paup)
14 Oct   Charlotte d/o Adam & Elizabeth RUSHTON (paup)
30 Oct   Lydia d/o Thomas & Ann BLADON
30 Oct   James s/o Ralph & Dorothy KENT
31 Oct   James s/o James & Mary MARSON
10 Nov   William s/o Thomas & Margaret TUNNICLIFF
4 Dec   Martha d/o George & Martha STEVENSON
28 Dec   John Bridgwood s/o John & Mary ELSMORE
N.B. On Sunday the 16th of July 1786 Lewis, Bishop of Norwich preached in Leigh church.

1786
15 Jan   Edward s/o John & Ann CHELL (paup)
1 Feb   Sarah d/o Francis & Sarah SHERRATT [Sherrat-BT]
12 Feb   Diana d/o John & Hannah GILBERT
12 Mar   Mary d/o Richard & Mary SMITH (paup)
12 Mar   Lydia d/o William & Jane WALKER of Leigh
John s/o Joseph & Ann WOOLLEY (Checkley-bank) was baptized Privately by Mr Langley & received into the Congregation April 16th
16 Apr   Joseph s/o Joseph & Elizabeth MOOR (paup)
16 Apr   William s/o William & Ellen ADAMS
20 Apr   Robert s/o Daniel & Sarah BURTON
24 Apr   Dorothy d/o George & Hannah NOAKES (paup)
21 May   John s/o William & Margaret DEAKIN
28 May   Catherina d/o Mary PHILIPS, Widow (Field)
28 May   Thomas s/o Mr Thomas & Mrs Joyce BRINDLEY
8 Jun   Lawrence s/o Lawrence & Elizabeth GREENSMITH
23 Jun   Jenny d/o Robert & Elizabeth MOOR
24 Jun   James s/o William & Ann RAWLINS
11 Jul   Theophila d/o Robert & Ellen JACKSON
16 Jul   Joseph s/o Benjamin & Alice WARD
6 Aug   William (illeg) s/o Elizabeth PHILIPS (paup)
6 Aug   Ann d/o George & Edith WALKER (paup)
31 Aug   Martha d/o Thomas & Martha BRANDRICK
3 Sep   Ann d/o Thomas & Sarah BARKER (paup)
8 Oct   Ellen d/o Francis & Sarah WATSON
Eleanor d/o William & Elizabeth LAUGHTON was baptized privately by Mr Hilditch & received into the Congregation October 22
29 Oct   Samuel s/o William & Hannah STARTIN (paup)
29 Oct   Samson s/o Ellis & Ann BAILY [Bailey-BT] (paup)
Thomas s/o Thomas & Margaret BAILEY was baptized privately by Mr Jno Langley & received into the Congregation October 30th
26 Nov   John s/o Job & Elizabeth BAKER (of Stoke parish) baptized privately
15 Dec   John s/o John & Dorothy SMITH
28 Dec   Richard s/o William & Margaret BAILEY (paup)
1787
28 Jan   John s/o George & Abigail THORNEWORK (paup)
11 Feb   Thomas s/o Alexander & Ellen PERKIN

18 Feb   Sarah d/o John & Sarah TURNER
25 Feb   Fanny d/o Robert & Sarah PHILIPS
4 Mar   Sarah d/o Joseph & Ann SMITH (paup)
4 Mar   John s/o John & Diana CARTER
30 Mar   William s/o William & Mary MELLOR
2 Apr   Joseph s/o John & Ann LANDER was baptized by Mr Lewes
4 Apr   Ellen d/o John & Mary ALLCOCK
9 Apr   Rebekah d/o Robert & Mary ARNOLD
14 Apr   Mary d/o William & Alice WRIGHT
22 Apr   Job s/o Samuel & Hannah BARNETT
20 May   Terence s/o Adam & Elizabeth RUSHTON (paup)
17 Jun   Elizabeth d/o John & Olive HUSON
1 Jul   Thomas s/o Adam & Elizabeth BARLOW (Leek)
7 Jul   Robert s/o William & Mary HOLLINS
15 Jul   John s/o James & Elizabeth MORRIS (Warwickshire)
27 Jul   Catharina d/o Mr Thomas & Mrs Joyce BRINDLEY
29 Jul   Ann d/o William & Mary HILL
30 Jul   Sarah d/o William & Elizabeth SLATER
6 Aug   Elizabeth d/o William & Mary LOWNDES
16 Aug   Mary d/o Robert & Mary HEATON (pauper)
19 Aug   Elizabeth d/o Joseph & Elizabeth THACKER (paup)
27 Aug   John (illeg) s/o Elizabeth LOWNDES
29 Sep   Peggy d/o William & Margaret DEAKIN
23 Nov   Charles s/o Samuel & Elizabeth TURNER
29 Dec   Mary d/o Benjamin & Alice WARD
1788
3 Jan   Jarvis s/o James & Lydia MARSON
6 Jan   Thomas (illeg) s/o Elizabeth LEES (paup)
19 Jan   Sarah d/o John & Hannah GILBERT
27 Jan   Elizabeth d/o William & Ellen ADAMS
7 Feb   Mary d/o Francis & Sarah SHERRATT
17 Feb   Michael s/o William & Margaret BAILEY (paup)
24 Feb   Betty d/o John & Elizabeth MELLOR
21 Mar   Mary d/o Thomas & Mary CHELL (paup)
25 Mar   Thomas s/o William & Ann RAWLIN
28 Mar   Rachel (illeg) d/o Catharina JOHNSON
30 Mar   Betty d/o Middleton & Mary ROBOTHAM
11 Apr   Elizabeth d/o Thomas & Elizabeth HAWLEY
22 Apr   Hannah d/o James & Mary MARSON
27 Apr   Benjamin s/o James Hollins MOTRAM (paup) & Ann his wife
27 Apr   Sarah d/o George & [ ] PRESTON
11 May   Charles s/o Robert & Sarah PHILIPS
18 May   Charles s/o Thomas & Prudence TOOTH (paup)
25 May   Ann (illeg) d/o Catharina RATCLIFF (paup)
30 May   William & Francis twin s/o William & Mary HOLLINS
15 Jun   Thomas s/o John & Ann CHELL (paup)
17 Jun   Mary d/o Robert & Elizabeth MOOR
9 Jul   Simon s/o Simon & Elizabeth COPE
13 Jul   Ann d/o Charles & Elizabeth WALKER
13 Jul   Joseph s/o Thomas & Jane SAUNDERS
27 Jul   Maria (illeg) d/o Elizabeth TILL (paup)

27 Jul	Mary d/o John & Mary ELSMORE	
3 Aug	Hannah d/o William & Mary MELLOR	
10 Aug	Thomas s/o Thomas & Martha BRANDRICK	
10 Aug	William s/o John HUGHES & Ann his wife	
17 Aug	William s/o Lawrence & Elizabeth GREENSMITH	
17 Aug	William s/o Thomas & Elizabeth CARTER	
17 Aug	George s/o George & Elizabeth DEAKIN	
24 Aug	Jane d/o William & Elizabeth LAUGHTON	
24 Aug	Sarah (illeg) d/o Fanny BAILEY	
7 Sep	Charles s/o Ralph & Dorothy KENT	
28 Sep	Thomas s/o William & Elizabeth SLATER	
12 Oct	Mary d/o Thomas & Hannah PERKIN,	born 7th Oct
26 Nov	Phoebe d/o John & Phoebe STEANSON	
	Ellen d/o John & Martha MILLINGTON,	born 18th Nov
23 Dec	Mary d/o John & Elizabeth LEES,	born 19th Dec
1789		
2 Jan	Elizabeth d/o Adam & Elizabeth RUSHTON - P.	
17 Jan	William s/o Joseph & Elizabeth MOOR, - P.	born 13th Jan
	Charles s/o Elizabeth COPE, - B.B.	born 4th Jan
7 Feb	Ann d/o Mr Thomas & Mrs Joyce BRINDLEY	
	Jane d/o Robert & Ellen JACKSON,	born 11th Jan
8 Mar	William s/o Charles & Ann BENTLEY,	born 26th Jan
	Charlotte d/o John & Sarah TURNER,	born 28th Jan
9 Mar	Diana d/o Mary SMITH, Widow, - P.	born 14th Feb
17 Mar	Mary d/o Thomas & Hannah BARKER	
20 Mar	Hannah d/o George & Hannah NOAKES, - P.	born 15th Mar
14 Apr	John s/o Willm & Mary LOWNDES,	born 8th Feb
	Patience d/o Benjn & Alice WARD,	born 17th Feb
10 May	Mary d/o Jams: & Mary MARSON,	born 13th Apr
14 May	Eadith d/o Ann HOWE, B.B. - P.	born 26th Apr
17 May	Ann d/o Thos & Alice FOSTER,	born April 29th
14 Jun	Samuel s/o Willm: & Elizabeth WETTON,	born 20th May
8 Jul	Sarah d/o John & Jane BAGNEL	
12 Jul	John s/o John & Olive HUSON,	born 8th June
1 Aug	Charlotte d/o Geo: & Margt: WRIGHT, - P.	born 30th July
27 Aug	John s/o John & Mary BELCHER,	born 23rd Aug
30 Aug	James s/o George & Elizabeth DEAKIN,	born 22nd Aug
24 Sep	George s/o George & Eadith WALKER, - P.	born 8th Sep
4 Oct	Thomas s/o John & Dorothy SMITH	
25 Oct	Thomas s/o Mary BUXTON - B.B. - P.	
1 Nov	Mary d/o Jams: & Lydia MARSON,	born 30th Sep
8 Nov	Hannah d/o Wm: & Hannah STARTIN, P.	born 4th Nov
23 Nov	Charlotte d/o Geo: & Sarah RUSHTON, P.	born 16th Nov
3 Dec	William s/o Charles & Ann KENT	
25 Dec	William s/o Wm: & Ellen ADAMS,	born 1st Nov
1790		
1 Jan	James s/o Willm: & Ann RAWLINS,	born 15th Dec 1789
15 Feb	Jane d/o Willm: & Mary HILL,	born 28th Jan
7 Feb	John s/o John & Mary ALCOCK, P.	born 6th Jan
12 Feb	Samson s/o John & Mary ELSMORE	
23 Jan	Henry s/o John & Ann CHELL, - P.	born 18th Feb

25 Jan	Ann d/o Elizabeth PHILIPS, B.B.- P.	
28 Jan	William s/o Willm: & Sarah PERKIN,	born 12th Feb
19 Mar	John s/o Willm: & Mary HOLLINS,	born 18th Feb
28 Mar	Catharine d/o Geo: & Abigail THORNEWORK,	born 26th Feb
25 Apr	Richard s/o Joseph & Ann SMITH,	born 18th Apr
16 May	Sarah d/o [ ] & Hannah SALT,	born 13th May
30 May	Catharine d/o Saml: & Hannah BARNETT, - P.	born 6th May
19 Jun	Jones s/o Mr: Jones & Mrs: Ann Eliz: PANTON	
24 Jun	William s/o Joseph & Sarah HART,	born 19th Jun
27 Jun	Middleton s/o Middleton & My: ROWBOTHAM,	born 2nd Jun
4 Jul	Charles s/o Daniel & Sarah BURTON,	born 29th May
	John s/o John & Phoebe STEVENSON,	born 25th Jun
26 Jul	John s/o Mr. Thomas & Mrs. Joyce BRINDLEY	
16 Aug	Ellen d/o Francis & Sarah SHERRATT,	born 7th Aug
20 Aug	William s/o Lawrence & Eliz: GREENSMITH,	born 10 July
	Elizabeth d/o William & Eliz: SLATER	
22 Aug	Sarah d/o Wm: & Eliz: LAUGHTON,	born 9th Aug
9 Sep	Thomas s/o Henry & Sarah STOKES	
10 Oct	Mary d/o Thos: & Martha BRANDRICK,	born 15th Sep
17 Oct	Ellen d/o Jane TILL, born Octr 10th: P: B.B.	
	Joseph s/o John & Sarah TURNER,	born 27th Oct
3 Nov	John s/o John & Martha MILLINGTON,	born 25 Oct
11 Dec	Sarah d/o John & Eliz: ALCOCK,	born 9th Dec
21 Dec	Olive d/o Adam & Eliz: RUSHTON, - P.	born 25th Oct
26 Dec	Richard s/o Richd: & Mary HOWE,	born 25 Dec
27 Dec	John s/o Sampson & Ann HANLEY,	born 22nd Dec
	Elizabeth d/o Thos: & Hannah PERKIN,	born 16 Dec

1791

3 Jan	John s/o Willm: & Ann GREENOP,	born 1st Jan
10 Jan	John s/o Benjn: & Alice WARD,	born 25th Dec 1790
6 Feb	Thomas s/o Willm: & Mary MELLER,	born 15th Aug 1790
	Mary d/o Jams: & Ann MOTTERAM, - P.	born 26th Dec 1790
6 Mar	Samuel s/o John & Susanna NUTT,	born 2nd Mar
13 Mar	Thomas s/o Geo: & Sarah JOHNSON. P.	born 9th Mar
3 Apr	Lydia d/o Ralph & Dor: KENT,	born 26th Mar
	Elizabeth d/o Thos: & Jane SAUNDERS.	born 28th Mar
25 Apr	Ann d/o Willm: & My: LOWNDES,	born 27th Mar
9 May	Saml: & Fanny son & d/o Catharine JOHNSON	
2 Jun	Harriott d/o Ellen MILLINGTON	
10 Jul	Elizabeth d/o John & Ann HUGHES,	born 25th Jun
	Margaret d/o Thos: & Eliz: CARTER,	born 15th May
28 Jul	Mary d/o Willm: & Mary HOLLINS	
31 Jul	Hannah d/o Jos: & Ann SMITH, P.	born 25th July
21 Aug	Mary d/o John & Olive HUSON. The Regis'n certified Augt 22	born 31st May
4 Sep	Fanny d/o Thos: & Ann COPE,	born 23rd Aug
13 Sep	William s/o John & Hannah HOWE,	born 24th Aug
19 Sep	Richard s/o Robt: & Mary ARNOLD,	born 24th Aug
19 Sep [BT]	Sarah d/o Willm: & Sarah PERKIN,	born 10th Sep
16 Oct	Mary d/o Joice MITCHEL, P.	born 11th Oct
23 Oct	William s/o Willm: & Cath: HEATH,	born 8th Oct
30 Oct	Elizabeth d/o Thos: & Ann PHILLIPS P.	born 10th Sep

1 Nov	John s/o Willm: & Ann RAWLINS,	born 19th Oct
	Maria d/o Geo: & Hannah NOAKES, P.	born 25th Nov
6 Nov	William s/o Jams: & Mary MARSON,	born 26th Oct
6 Nov [BT]	Elizabeth d/o Jos: & Eliz: MOOR, P.	born 28th Oct
13 Nov	Robert s/o John & Eliz: MELLER [Mellow-BT],	born 9th Nov

1792

1 Jan	Samuel s/o Willm: & Ellen ADDAMS,	born Novr 27th 1791
24 Jan	Lydia d/o John & Ann CHELL, P.	born 22nd Jan
12 Feb	William s/o Saml: & Hannah BARNET [Barnett-BT], P.	born 4th Feb
4 Mar	John s/o Cha: & Ann KENT,	born 1st Mar
11 Mar	John s/o Edward & Ann TITLEY. P.	
18 Mar	Sarah d/o Willm: & Hannah STARTIN, P.	born 13th Mar
18 Mar [BT]	Mary d/o Eliz: WALKER,	born 9th Mar
18 Mar [BT]	Henry s/o Saml: & Eliz: TURNER,	born Mar 13th
23 Mar	Jacob Vale s/o John & Sarah ASTBURY,	born 19th Mar
10 Apr	Joyce d/o Mr Thomas & Mrs Joyce BRINDLEY	[Mar 19th-BT]
10 Apr [BT]	Elizabeth d/o Wm: & Eliz: WETTON,	born 17th Mar
10 Apr [BT]	James s/o John & Dorothy THOMPSON,	born 6th Mar
22 Apr	Sarah d/o Robt: & Ellen JACKSON,	born 28th Mar
20 May	Mary d/o Saml: & Eliz: ELLIOT,	born 23rd Apr
2 Jun	Mary d/o John & Mary BELCHER,	born11th May
3 Jun	Eliza d/o Adam & Eliz: RUSHTON,	born 29th Aprl
16 Jun	Stephen s/o Lydia BAILY. P.	[29th Apr-BT]
18 Jun	William s/o Saml: & Hannah SALT,	born16th Jun
24 Jun	Prudence d/o Geo: & Sarah RUSHTON, P.	born16th Jun
8 Jul	William s/o Geo: & Edith WALKER, P.	born 16th Jun
12 Aug	James s/o George & Ann PRESTON,	Born 16th July
12 Aug [BT]	George s/o George & Eliz: DEAKIN,	Born 30th July
24 Sep	Margaret dau of John & Sarah TURNER, P.	born 20th Sep
30 Sep	Ralph s/o Willm: & Hannah MARTIN,	born 29th Sep
30 Sep [BT]	Ann d/o John & Sarah PERKIN,	born 28th Sep
	[P. between these last two entries]	
5 Nov	John s/o Rich: & Mary HOWE,	born 31st Oct
23 Dec	Ellen d/o Thos: & Han: BARKER, P.	born 7th Dec

1793

29 Jan	John s/o Willm: & Mary HILL,	born 24th Nov 1792
11 Feb	John s/o Thos: & Mary BLOORE,	born 30th Jan
11 Feb [BT]	Charles s/o Chas: & Ann BROWNE,	born 8th Feb
24 Feb	Thomas s/o Eliz: TILL P.	born 17th Feb
10 Mar	James s/o Thos: & Martha BRANDRICK,	born 11th Feb
24 Mar	Dorothy d/o Thos: & Eliz: PLANT,	born in 1791
14 Apr	Willm: s/o Benj: & Alice WARD,	born 2nd Mar
14 Apr [BT]	Elizabeth d/o John & Eliz: ALCOCK,	born 2nd Apr
21 Apr	Elizabeth d/o Eliz: PHILLIPS,	born 28th Feb
28 Apr	Thomas s/o John & Martha MILLINGTON,	born 21st Apr
13 May	Ann d/o Robt: & Hannah HOLLINS,	born 11th May
16 May	Sarah d/o John & Mary ALCOCK [Allcock-BT],	born 5th May
19 May	George s/o Thos: & Alice FOSTER,	born 12th May
31 May	Thomas s/o Hannah SMITH	
3 Jun	Francis s/o Francis & Sarah SHERRET [Sherratt-BT]	born 26th May
16 Jun	Hannah d/o John & Ann CHELL, P.	born 4th Jun

28 Jul	Ann d/o Willm: & Mary HOLLINS,	born 27th Jun
11 Aug	William s/o Willm: & Eliza LAUGHTON,	born 6th July
1 Sep	Richard s/o Ann WALKER, P.	born 13th Aug
3 Sep	Thomas s/o Willm: & Sarah PERKIN,	born 1st Sep
15 Sep	Mary d/o Sarah BARNET *[Barnett-BT]*, P.	born 27th Aug
22 Sep	Elizabeth d/o Mary TILL, P.	born 6th Sep
22 Sep [BT]	Ann d/o Geo: & Abigail THORNEWORTH, P.	born 12th Sep
6 Oct	John s/o Willm: & Cath: HEATH,	born 23rd Sep
7 Nov	Ellen d/o Robt: & Ann THORNYWORK,	born 3rd Nov
9 Nov	Jane d/o Ralph & Dor: KENT	*[born 3rd Nov-BT]*
3 Dec	Edward s/o Willm: & Mary MELLER, P.	born 28th Nov
5 Dec	Robert s/o John & Olive HUSON,	born 24th Nov
29 Dec	Thomas s/o John & Sarah PERKIN,	born 21st Dec
29 Dec [BT]	James s/o Jams: & Ann MOTRAM, P	born 19th Dec.
	Mary d/o Edwd: & Kitty BABB	
1794		
26 Jan	Jane d/o Thos: & Jane SAUNDERS,	born 19th Jan
26 Jan [BT]	Agnas d/o Phil: & Cath: SAUNDERS,	born 21st Jan
9 Feb	John s/o Ann MITCHELL,	born 2nd Feb
9 Feb [BT]	Ellen daugr of Willm: & Ellen ADDAMS, P.	born 3rd Feb
10 Feb	Sarah daugr of Saml: & Eliz: ELLIOTT,	born 8th Feb
16 Feb	William s/o Geo: & Ann DEAKIN,	born 4th Feb
23 Feb	John HALL s/o Eliz: LEES,	born 16th Feb
1 Mar	William s/o Willm: & Mary LOWNDES	born 19th Nov 1793
23 Mar	Easther daugr of Saml: & Hannah BARNET *[Barnett-BT]*, P.	born 17th Mar
5 Apr	Thomas s/o Jams: & Lydia MARSON,	born 1st Apl
4 May	William s/o Jos: & Ann SMITH, P.	born 26th Apr
1 Jun	Ann d/o Mary SMITH, P.	born 28th May
16 Jun	Mary d/o Thomas & Mary HOWE,	born 12th Jun
16 Jun [BT]	Fanny d/o Robt: & Ellen JACKSON,	born 11th Apr
16 Jun [BT]	George s/o James & Mary MARSON,	born 6th May
30 Jun	Elizabeth d/o Thomas & Eliz: CARTER,	born 27th Jun
6 Jul	Sarah d/o Saml: & Ann SKRIGLEY,	born 9th Jun
6 Jul [BT]	Mary d/o Geo: & Eliz: DEAKIN,	born 21st Jun
9 Jul	Edward s/o Ann HOWE, P.	*[21st Jun-BT]*
20 Jul	Abigail d/o John & Eliz: GOSLING,	born 19th Jun
22 Jul	John s/o John & Sarah ASTBURY,	born 13th July
16 Aug	Anne d/o the Rev'd H. THOMAS & Mary his wife	*[13th July-BT]*
24 Aug	Joseph s/o John & Ann HUGHES,	born 1st Aug
16 Sep	James s/o Willm: & Ann CARNEL,	*[1st Aug-BT]*
26 Oct	William s/o Chas: & Ann KENT,	born 1st Oct
2 Nov	Benjamin s/o Benjn: & Alice WARDE *[Ward-BT]*	born 25th Oct
15 Nov	John s/o Simon & Elizabeth COPE	*[25th Oct-BT]*
18 Dec	Anne d/o John & Eliz: PRESTON	*[25th Oct-BT]*
28 Dec	George s/o John & Sarah TURNER,	born 23rd Oct
1795		
18 Jan	Margaret d/o John & Eliz: ALCOCK,	born 11th Jan
20 Jan	Thomas s/o Willm: & Mary HOLLINS,	born 16th Jan
23 Jan	Anne d/o Thomas & Mary WARDLE,	born 22nd Jan
1 Feb	Jane d/o Eliz: TURNER,	born 14th Jan
17 Feb	John s/o William & Sarah PERKIN	*[14th Jan-BT]*

28 Feb	Mary d/o John & Ann BURTON,	born 26th Feb
28 Feb	Anne d/o Edwd: & Cath: BABBE	[26th Feb-BT]
1 Mar	Mary d/o Cath: MARSON,	born 19th Feb
6 Apr	James s/o Jos: & Dorothy DEAKIN,	born 1st Mar
19 Apr	John Kent s/o Wm: & Eliz: LAUGHTON,	born 14th Mar
21 Jun	George s/o Richd: & Margt: HOWE,	born 21st May
28 Jun	Hannah d/o Geo: & Edith WALKER,	born 19th Jun
12 Jul	William s/o Willm: & Sarah FOWLER,	born 5th July
26 Jul	Thomas s/o Jno & Mary ALCOCK,	born 5th July
20 Sep	George s/o Mary COOKE,	born Sep
11 Oct	Samuel s/o Willm: & Cath: HEATH,	born14th Sep
25 Oct	John s/o John & Sarah PERKIN,	born 18th Oct
1 Nov	Josiah David s/o Wm: & My: HILL,	born 22nd Aug
3 Nov	Anne d/o Thos: & Lydia NUTT,	born 31st Oct
5 Nov	Thomas s/o Willm: & Mary LOWNDES,	born 21st Oct
13 Dec	Jane d/o Jos: & Sarah BALLANCE,	born 21st Nov
25 Dec	William s/o Willm: & Mary CARTER,	born 24th Nov
	Sophia d/o John & Mary BELCHER,	born 4th Mar

1796

24 Jan	Ellen d/o Geo: & Hannah NOAKES,	born 14th Jan
22 Mar	Mary d/o Edwd: & Cath: FENTON	
31 Mar	Henry s/o Willm: & Mary HOLLINS,	born 12th Mar
31 Mar	Mary d/o John & Eliz: PRESTON,	born 19th Mar
3 Apr	Jane d/o Geo: & Martha STEVENSON,	born 26th Feb
9 Apr	Elizabeth d/o Geo: & Anne DEAKIN,	born 6th Apr
17 Apr	Joseph s/o Thos: & Alice FOSTER,	born 5th Apr
17 Apr	William s/o John & Martha MILLINGTON,	born 11th Apl
25 Apr	William s/o Saml: & Eliz: PLATT,	born 24th Apr
30 Apr	Sarah d/o Thos: & Mary HOWE,	born 12th Apr
1 May	John s/o Joseph & Eliz: MOOR,	born 16th Apl
8 May	Elizabeth d/o Geo: & Eliz: DEAKIN,	born 15th Apl
15 May	Thomas s/o Saml: & Eliz: ELLIOT,	born 22nd Apr
23 May	James s/o Robt: & Anne THORNYWORK,	born 20th May
14 Jun	Richard s/o Joseph & Ellen SMITH	
28 Jun	Olive d/o John & Olive HUSON,	born 14th Jun
28 Jul	William s/o Willm: & Sarah BLURTON,	born 18th July
14 Aug	Richard s/o Dorothy SMITH,	born 24th July
28 Aug	Isabel d/o Wm: & Ellen ADAMS,	born 6th Apl
4 Sep	William s/o Ellen MILLINGTON,	born 23rd Aug
11 Sep	Rebecca d/o Ralph & Dorothy KENT,	born 5th Sep
17 Sep	Mary d/o Saml: & Hannah BARNET,	born 21st Aug
2 Oct	Elizabeth d/o Edwd: & Eliz: COPE,	born 27th Sep
23 Oct	Joseph s/o John & Sarah ASTBURY,	born 2nd Oct
5 Nov	Thomas s/o Thos: & Hannah PERKIN,	born 31st Oct
6 Nov	Hannah d/o Thomas & Eliz: CARTER,	born 25th Sep

1797

15 Jan	Hannah d/o Willm: & Hannah MARTIN,	born 1st Jan
19 Jan	William s/o Charles & Anne BROWNE	
20 Feb	Edward s/o Richd: & Mary HOWE,	born 18th Feb
	William s/o Thos: & Martha BRANDRICK,	born 15th Jan
23 Feb	Francis s/o Willm: & Sarah PERKIN,	born 20th Feb

19 Mar	John s/o James & Mary MARSON,	born 25th Feb
26 Mar	Anne d/o Jos: & Anne SMITH,	born 19th Mar
2 Apr	Mary d/o John & Eliz: ALCOCK,	born 24th Mar
7 May	Thomas s/o Mary TILL,	born 1st May
14 May	Anne d/o John & Anne BURTON,	born 3rd May
14 May	Honor d/o Chas: & Anne KENT,	born 31st Mar
18 May	John s/o James & Lydia MARSTON,	born 17th May
4 Jun	Margaret d/o Thos: & Jane SAUNDERS,	born 21st May
9 Jul	Lydia d/o John & Anne HUGHES,	born 15th Jun
11 Aug	Lydia d/o Willm: & Eadith HOLLINS,	born 31st July
13 Aug	Mary d/o Daniel & Sarah BURTON,	born 5th Jun
28 Aug	Elizabeth d/o Ellen RAWLIN,	born 15th Aug
29 Aug	Joyce d/o Thomas & Mary WARDLE,	born 28th Aug
9 Dec	Elizabeth d/o Eliz: & Richd: INGRAM,	born 6th Dec

1798

12 Jan	Thomas s/o Jans: & Anne MOTTRAM,	born 2nd Jan
12 Feb	Thomas s/o Thos: & Lydia NUTT,	born 10th Feb
13 Feb	Elizabeth d/o Thomas & Mary HOWE,	born 6th Feb
4 Mar	Betty d/o Willm: & Cath: HEATH,	born 19th Feb
	Frances s/o Frances & Anne NUTT,	born 1st Mar
23 Mar	Martha d/o Willm: & Eliz: LAUGHTON,	born 14th Mar
6 Apr	Mary d/o Wm: & Sarah ADDAMS.	born 20th Mar
8 Apr	Mary d/o Willm: & Sarah FOWLER,	born 15th Mar
8 Apr	Sarah d/o John & Anne CHELL,	born 4th Api
30 Apr	Mary d/o Willm: & Alice PRESTON,	born 29th Apl
30 Jun	Anne d/o Willm: & Eliz: RUSHTON,	born 20th Jun
29 Jul	William s/o Frans: & Betty TUNNICLIFF,	born 22nd July
19 Aug	Cicilia d/o Thos: & Hannah BARKER,	born 11th Aug
27 Aug	John s/o John & Eliz: PRESTON,	born 23rd Aug
4 Sep	Jane d/o Saml: & Eliz: PLATT,	born 3rd Sep
30 Sep	George s/o Thos: & Emma SMITH,	born 17 Sep
30 Sep	Sarah d/o Eliz: JOHNSON,	born 23rd Sep
30 Sep	Anne d/o Thos: & Eliz: ASH,	born 30th July
20 Nov	William s/o John & Mary BELCHER,	born 9th Nov
18 Nov	John s/o Jams: & Cath: SMITH,	born 5th Nov
18 Nov	Hannah d/o Geo: & Eliz: DEAKIN,	born 4th Nov
27 Nov	John s/o John & Eliz: ALCOCK,	born 24th Nov

1799

6 Jan	Fanny d/o Jos: & Sarah BALLANCE,	born 5th Dec 1798
10 Jan	Richard s/o John & Dor: DEAN,	born 18thOct 1798
27 Jan	Mary d/o Willm: & Sarah BLURTON,	born 20th Jan
3 Feb	Joseph s/o Ann MITCHEL,	born 26th Jan
21 Feb	Edith d/o Willm: & Edith HOLLINS,	born 9th Feb
3 Mar	Hannah d/o Thos: & Alice FOSTER,	born 18th Feb
18 Mar	Joseph s/o John & Martha MILLINGTON,	born 8th Mar
18 Mar	John s/o John & Ann BURTON,	born 22nd Feb
18 Mar	Mary d/o Ann PRESTON,	born 12th Mar
18 Mar	John s/o Edwd: & Eliz: COPE,	born 10th Mar
20 Mar	Thomas s/o Geo: & Ann DEAKIN,	born 16th Mar
26 Mar	Sarah d/o Thos: & Eliz: LOVETT,	born 25th Mar
28 Apr	Sarah d/o John & Anne TWIGGE,	born 18th Apr

9 May	James s/o John & Olive HUSON,	born 26th Apl
12 May	Thomas s/o Willm: & Sarah PHILIPS	
	Hannah d/o Joseph & Eliz: MOOR,	born 18th Apl
18 May	Joseph s/o Chas: & Anne BROWNE *[Brown-BT]*	
19 May	Elizabeth d/o Willm: & Sarah PERKIN,	born 13th Apr
23 May	William s/o Danl: & Sarah BURTON,	born 8th Mar
3 Jul	Francis s/o James & Mary MARSON,	born 2nd July
14 Jul	Anne d/o Thos: & Eliz: CARTER,	born 21st Jun
20 Aug	Catharine d/o Willm: & Catharine HEATH,	born 15th Aug
5 Sep	Samuel s/o John & Sarah ASTBURY,	born 29th Aug
15 Sep	Thomas illegitimate s/o Eliz: WALKER	
15 Oct	Sarah illegitimate d/o Sarah SMITH	
10 Nov	Charlotte illegitimate d/o Martha SHENTON	
24 Nov	Benjamin s/o Benjn: & Anne WARDE,	born 13th Nov
17 Nov	Mary d/o Thos: & Mary HOWE,	born 22nd Oct
1 Dec	Mary d/o John & Mary STURGES,	born 2nd Nov
4 Dec	Anne d/o Thos: & Anne TATTON,	born 2nd Dec
8 Dec	Harvey s/o Charles & Anne KENT,	born 9th Nov
15 Dec	Samuel s/o Ralph & Dorothy KENT,	born 8th Dec
1800		
1 Jan	Sarah d/o Sarah DEAKIN,	born 4th Dec 1799
26 Jan	John s/o Saml: & Margt: BARNET,	born 31st Dec
31 Jan	Sarah d/o John & Eliz: HAWLEY,	born 29th Jan
2 Mar	John s/o Richd: & Eliz: DEAN,	born 20th Jan
30 Mar	Susan illegitimate d/o Sarah SHEMELT	
4 Apr	Harriott illegitimate d/o Nelly BRANDRICK	
27 Apr	Anne illeg: d/o Anne MOOR *[Moore-BT]*,	born 20th Apl
	William illeg: s/o Hannah LEES,	born 20th Apl
4 May	Mary d/o Willm: & Mary CARTER,	born 12th Apl
	John s/o John & Lucy HAZELTON,	born 11th Apl
17 May	James s/o Jams: & Cath: FENTON	
18 May	Hannah illegitimate d/o Anne TILL	
25 May	Anne illegit: d/o Anne WALKER,	born 4th May
2 Jun	Betty d/o Jams: & Martha BELCHER,	born 11th Apl
18 Jun	Ralph s/o John & Anne HUGHES,	born 30th May
26 Jun	Samuel s/o Saml: & Eliz: PLATT,	born 23rd Jun
3 Aug	Sophia d/o Maria PHILLIPS,	born 25th July
5 Aug	John s/o Willm: & Mary TURNER,	born 28th Jun
6 Aug	Anne d/o Willm: & Edith HOLLINS,	born 1st Aug
17 Aug	Ellen d/o Thos: & Eliz: GARLAND,	born 16th Aug
31 Aug	Mary d/o John & Eliz: HOWFOT,	born 27th Aug
19 Oct	Thomas s/o Thos: & Ellen LEES,	born 4th Oct
3 Nov	Mary d/o Willm: & Mary LOWNDES,	born 21st Sep
16 Nov	Thomas s/o John & Alice TILL,	born 23rd Octr
22 Nov	George s/o Willm: & Lucy BENNET,	born 31stOct
23 Nov	Anne d/o Wm: & Hannah MARTIN,	born 15th Nov
	Sarah d/o Francis & Anne NUTT,	born 15th Nov
1801		
3 Jan	Charles s/o George & Anne BENTLEY	
6 Jan	Arabella d/o Mary THACKER	
8 Mar	Thomas s/o Willm: & Sarah FOWLER,	born 21st Feb

15 Mar	Hannah illegit: d/o M: SAUNDERS,	born 8th Mar
5 Apr	Fanny d/o John & Eliz: ALCOCK,	born 15th Mar
25 Apr	Anne d/o Willm: & Sarah PERKIN,	born 22nd Apl
	Sarah d/o John & Sarah PERKIN,	born 1st Apl
5 May	Anne d/o John M. & Eliz: FROST,	born 3rd May
10 May	Charles s/o Richd: & Dor: SMITH,	born 22nd Apl
	Jeffrey s/o Willm: & Jane PHILLIPS,	born 2nd May
6 Jul	Mary d/o John & Martha MILLINGTON	
12 Jul	Thomas s/o Tjhos: & Mary WARDLE,	born 10th July
16 Aug	Elizabeth d/o John & Eliz: PRESTON,	born 29th July
23 Oct	Thomas s/o Danl: & Sarah BURTON,	born 24th Sep
10 Nov	Thomas s/o Anne MARTIN,	born 8th Nov
15 Nov	Anne d/o John & Eliz: COOK,	born 4th Nov
29 Nov	Anne d/o John & Anne TWIGGE,	born 23rd Nov
1802		
14 Feb	Samuel s/o Geo: & Eliz: DEAKIN,	born 16th Jan
21 Feb	William s/o Thos: & Hannah PERKIN,	born 3rd Feb
7 Mar	William s/o Saml: & Margt BARNET [Barnett-BT]	born 27th Feb
21 Mar	Mary d/o Willm: & Hannah MARTIN,	born 14th Mar
25 Mar	Hannah d/o Thos: & Eliz: FORESTER	
10 Apr	Edward s/o John & Sarah ASTBURY,	born 27th Mar
4 May	Anne d/o Benjn: & Anne WARDE,	born 24th Apl
6 May	Thomas s/o Saml: & Eliz: PLATT	
23 May	Edward s/o Edwd: & M. A. ALCOCK,	born 28th Apl
5 Jun	John s/o John & Eliz: HAWLEY,	born 29th May
6 Jun	Margaret d/o Jos: & Eliz: MOOR,	born 4th Jun
14 Jun	Thomas s/o Thos: & Eliz: CARTER,	born 15th May
27 Jun	Anne d/o Edwd: & Eliz: COPE,	born 23rd Jun
2 Jul	John s/o Thos: & Eliz: LOVETT [Lovatt-BT],	born 27th Jun
19 Jul	Hannah d/o Jos: & Sarah BRASSINGTON,	born 6th July
25 Jul	Thomas s/o Thos: & Sarah MILLINGTON,	born 5th July
15 Aug	Hannah d/o Thos: & Sarah BAGNELL,	born 30th July
29 Aug	William s/o John & Dor: DEAN,	born 24th Aug
19 Sep	John s/o John & Eliz: ALCOCK	
3 Oct	Charles s/o Geo: & Hannah EDGE,	born 21st Sep
10 Oct	John Walthow s/o Richd: & Mary FENTON,	born 9th
1 Nov	William s/o John & Dorothy DEAN,	born 24th Aug
7 Nov	Frances d/o Thos: & Mary FORD,	born 20th Octr
12 Nov	Robert s/o Willm: & Mary LOWNDES,	born 9th Nov
	William s/o Thos: & Eliz: ASH,	born 29th Aug
1803		
2 Jan	Elizabeth d/o Willm: & Sarah FOWLER	
1 Feb	William s/o Willm: & Mary TURNER,	born 31st Jan
6 Feb	Thomas s/o Willm: & Cath: HEATH,	born 8th Jan
26 Feb	Joseph s/o Willm: & Sarah PERKIN,	born 23rd Feb
28 Feb	Cicely d/o Thos: & Eliz: GARLAND,	born 26th Feb
3 Apr	George s/o John & Anne SAUNDERS,	born 21st Mar
18 Apr	Sarah d/o John & Eliz: BURTON,	born 17th Apl
12 May	Jane d/o John & Eliz: COOK	
26 Jun	James illeg s/o Anne MITCHELL,	born 23rd Jun
15 Jul	Edward s/o John & Anne HUGHES,	born 2nd July

17 Jul	Elizabeth d/o Joseph & Sarah KIRK,	born 15th July
1 Aug	James s/o Saml: & Hannah BALL	
7 Aug	George s/o George & Anne DEAKIN,	born 4th Aug
8 Aug	Thomas s/o Benjn: & Anne WARD,	born 17th July
	Robert s/o Richd: & Eliz: PHILLIPS	
10 Aug	Mary Anne d/o Richd: & Mary HIDE,	born 9th Aug
26 Sep	Sarah d/o Jams: & Martha BELCHER,	born 23rd Sep
2 Oct	Matthew illeg s/o Charlotte SNAPE	
31 Oct	John s/o Ralph & Dor: KENT,	born 7th Oct
1 Nov	Mary d/o John & Lydia ROGERS,	born 30th Oct
20 Nov	Samuel s/o John & Eliz: ALCOCK,	born 15th Nov
	William illeg s/o Anne TILL,	born 14th Nov
25 Nov	Anne d/o Chas: & Anne BROWNE,	born 22nd Nov
18 Dec	Elizabeth d/o Willm: & Sarah BLURTON,	born 13th Dec
19 Dec	Joseph & Mary twin children of John & S. PERKIN	
25 Dec	Elizabeth d/o Thos: & Mary WARDLE,	born 17th Dec
26 Dec	Jane d/o Thos: & Eliz: FORRESTER	
29 Dec	William s/o Thos: & Eliz: LOVETT [Lovatt-BT],	born 19th Dec

1804

8 Jan	Sarah d/o John & Jane TILL,	born 12th Dec 1803
5 Feb	Anne d/o Thos: & Eliz: GARLAND,	born 3rd Feb
10 Feb	Joseph s/o John & Sarah BARNES,	born 7th Feb
25 Mar	Sarah d/o Thos: & Eliz: FORD,	born 12th Mar
7 Apr	Thomas s/o Willm: & Anne ASBURY,	born 2nd Apl
8 Apr	Mary Anne d/o Edwd: & Mary Anne ALCOCK,	born 18th Mar
26 Apr	Matilda d/o Jams: & Hannah WALKER,	born 20th Apl
28 Apr	John s/o Thos: & Eliz: CARTER,	born 26th Apr
	Susannah illeg d/o Hannah BARNET,	born 24 Apl
	Robt: Milward s/o Willm: & Jane PHILLIPS,	born 24 Apl
	Elizabeth d/o John & Eliz: HAWLEY,	born 11th Mar
6 May	Sarah d/o John & Eliz: PRESTON,	born 31st Mar
13 May	Anne illeg d/o Dor: NOAKES,	born 12th May
31 May	Mary d/o Thos: & Anne SMITH	
10 Jun	Elizabeth d/o Thos: & Lydia BIRCH,	born 30th Apl
17 Jun	George s/o John & Charlotte WETTON,	born 26th May
22 Jul	William s/o Geo: & Eliz: DEAKIN,	born 30th Jun
5 Aug	George s/o Anne TURNER,	born 27th July
9 Sep	David s/o Mary ALLEN,	born 17th Aug
9 Oct	Sarah d/o Danl: & Sarah BURTON,	born 2nd Octr
	Harriott d/o Francis & Sarah SHERRATT,	born 14th Jan
4 Nov	Thomas s/o Rich: & Eliz: PHILLIPS,	born 26th Oct
7 Dec	Thomas s/o Edw: & Eliz: COPE	
	Anne d/o Saml: & Eliz: CARR,	born 12th Oct
30 Dec	Sarah d/o John & Dor: DEAN,	born 13th Nov

1805

1 Jan	Thomas s/o Jams: & Cath: FENTON	
5 Jan	John s/o Thos: & Hannah PERKIN,	born 3rd Jan
9 Jan	James s/o John & Anne BURTON,	born 2nd Jan
19 Jan	Anne d/o John & Hannah TIDSWALL [Tidswell-BT]	born 14th Jan
17 Feb	Mary d/o Mary STARTIN,	born 13th Feb
24 Feb	Thomas s/o Saml: & Anne GRIFFIN,	born 20th Feb

3 Mar	Mary d/o Willm: & Sarah PERKIN,	born 28th Feb
10 Mar	Sarah d/o Hannah LEES,	born 28th Feb
18 Mar	Sarah d/o Willm: & Mary LOWNDES,	born 8th Mar
31 Mar	Charles s/o Thos: & Mary JOHNSON,	born 20th Mar
22 May	Mary d/o John & Sarah TATTON,	born 16th May
31 May	David s/o Alice PRESTON	
2 Jun	Mary d/o Willm: & Mary TURNER,	born 23rd May
11 Jun	John s/o Thos: & Sarah MILLINGTON,	born 21st May
28 Jul	Charles s/o Jos: & Sarah BRASSINGTON,	born 18th July
20 Aug	Elizabeth d/o Thos: & Mary HOLLINS	
2 Sep	James s/o Alexr: & Eliz: COPE,	born 28th Aug
8 Sep	Sarah d/o Willm: & Eliz: CHELL,	born 31st Aug
19 Oct	Anne d/o John & Eliz: ALCOCK,	born 4th Oct
12 Nov	Thomas s/o Saml: & Margt: BARNET [Barnett-BT]	
17 Nov	John s/o Saml: & Jane WALKER,	born 14th Nov
22 Dec	Simon s/o Willm: & Sarah FOWLER	
29 Dec	Mary d/o Thos: & Eliz: FORRESTER	
1806		
5 Jan	Helen d/o Thos: & Sarah BAGNAL [Bagnall-BT]	
7 Mar	Thomas Jackson s/o John & Sarah BARNES	
12 Mar	Jane d/o Thos: & Eliz: WILSON,	born 8th Mar
17 May	George s/o Edward & Mary ALCOCK,	born 7th May
22 May	Elizabeth d/o Luke & Sarah TURNER	
25 May	Mary d/o Willm: & Sarah BLURTON	
3 Jun	John s/o John & Sarah TATTON,	born 26th May
	Samuel s/o Willm: & Sarah COPE,	born 24th Apl
15 Jul	Charles illeg s/o Mary COOK,	born 4th July
21 Jul	William s/o Geo: & Hannah EDGE,	born 16th July
27 Jul	Edith d/o Jams: & Hannah WALKER,	born 19th July
31 Jul	William s/o John & Anne BURTON,	born 22nd July
3 Aug	Henry s/o Hellen ALCOCK,	born 29th July
9 Aug	Sarah d/o Eliz: BULL,	born 6th Aug
17 Aug	Joseph s/o Willm: & Hannah MARTIN,	born 4th Aug
19 Aug	Anne d/o Mary BAILY	
29 Aug	Richard s/o Richd: & Mary HIDE,	born 26th Aug
31 Aug	John s/o John & Charlotte TURNER	
7 Sep	Charles s/o Richd: & Eliz: PHILLIPS,	born 26th Aug
19 Sep	John DEAKIN s/o Maria RUSHTON,	born 15th Sep
23 Sep	Mary illeg d/o Hannah CHELL,	born 22nd Sep
1 Oct	John s/o Thos: & Mary WARDLE,	born 29th Sep
16 Oct	John s/o Saml: & Anne GRIFFIN,	born 10th Oct
19 Oct	William s/o John & Charlotte WETTON,	born 15th Oct
2 Nov	Alice d/o Thos: & Lydia BIRCH,	born 6th Oct
30 Nov	William illeg s/o Anne TURNER,	born 22 Nov
20 Dec	Hannah d/o Geo: & [ ] MIOTT	
21 Dec	Sarah d/o Willm: & Sarah PHILLIPS,	born 26th Sep
	Anne d/o Benjn: & Anne WARDE,	born 3rd Nov
1807		
13 Jan	Elizabeth d/o Willm: & M. [Mary-BT] TURNER	
1 Feb	Helen d/o John & Alice TILL,	born 29th Dec
19 Feb	Charles s/o Thos: & Eliz: GARLAND,	born 17th Feb

21 Feb	George s/o Willm: & Sarah PERKIN,	born 20th Feb
22 Mar	John s/o Geo: & Eliz: DEAKIN,	born 20th Feb
3 May	Jemima d/o W: & Mary CARTER,	born 12th Apl
7 Jun	Charles s/o Chas: & Eliz: RATCLIFFE,	born 1st May
20 Jun	William s/o Thomas & Mary HOLLINS	
28 Jun	Mary Anne d/o Thos: & Sarah STARTIN,	born 9th Jun
9 Jul	Anne d/o Thos: & Eliz: WILSON,	born 8th July
24 Jul	Margaret d/o Willm: & Mary LOWNDES,	born 20th July
9 Aug	Elizabeth d/o Geo: & Mary TOOTH,	born 1st Aug
30 Aug	Henry s/o John & Eliz: ALCOCK,	born 27th Aug
10 Sep	William s/o John & Sarah TATTON,	born 4th Sep
13 Sep	Christopher s/o Thos: & Mary JOHNSON,	born 21st Aug
20 Sep	William s/o Geo: & Eliz: COPE,	born 18th Sep
27 Sep	William s/o John & Sarah PERKIN,	born 31st Aug
28 Sep	Anne d/o John & Eliz: HUGHES,	born 26th Sep
11 Oct	Rachel d/o Thos: & Eliz: LOVETT [Lovatt-BT],	born 2nd Oct
15 Nov	William s/o Edwd: & Eliz: COPE,	born 8th Nov
	William s/o Saml: & Anne GRIFFIN,	born 10th Nov
25 Nov	William DUROSE s/o Lydia WALKER,	born 20th Nov
4 Dec	John s/o John & Hannah TIDSWELL,	born 23rd Nov
1808		
28 Jan	Thomas s/o Jos: [Joseph-BT] & Sarah BRASSINGTON	
15 Feb	Dorothy d/o Willm: & S. PHILLIPS,	born 10th Feb
8 Mar	John s/o Richd: & Mary HIDE,	born 5th Mar
8 Apr	John s/o Geo: & Sarah JACKSON,	born 5th Apl
18 Apr	William s/o Thos: & Sarah MILLINGTON,	born 14th Apl
24 Apr	Hannah d/o Ellen ATKIN,	born 11th Apl
1 May	Elizabeth d/o T. & E. FORRESTER,	born 4th Apl
8 May	Sarah d/o Saml: & Jane WALKER,	born 27th Apl
	Mary d/o Anne PHILLIPS	
22 May	Richard s/o Dor: SMITH,	born 5th May
26 Jun	Jane d/o Thos: & Lydia BIRCH,	born 25th May
13 Jul	Joseph s/o Willm: & Eliz: CHELL	
15 Jul	John s/o Thos: & Sarah COPE,	born 30th Jun
31 Jul	Elizabeth d/o John & Anne BURTON,	born 26th Jun
14 Aug	Anne d/o Wm: & Sarah FOWLER,	born 24th July
	Eleanor d/o Sarah FOSTER,	born 7th Aug
11 Sep	Sarah d/o John & Anne BLOOD,	born 13th Aug
25 Sep	Thomas s/o Thos: & Sarah STARTIN,	born 31st Aug
11 Nov	Hannah d/o Ellen CHELL,	born 3rd Nov
20 Nov	Sarah d/o Geo: & Hannah EDGE,	born 6th Nov
13 Dec	Peggy d/o Richd: & Eliz: PHILLIPS,	born 5th Dec
1809		
20 Jan	Thomas s/o Thos: & Mary HOLLINS,	born 18th Jan
5 Feb	Mary d/o Saml: & Anne GRIFFIN,	born 25th Jan
15 Feb	John s/o Geo: & Eliz: COPE,	born 12th Feb
15 Mar	Mary d/o Thos: & Eliz: WILSON,	born 12th Mar
15 Mar	Joseph s/o Chas: & Dor: HART,	born 13th Mar
3 Apr	Mary d/o John & Anne TWIGGE	born 30th Mar
11 Apr	Lydia d/o Sampson & Anne BAILEY	
24 Apr	Thomas s/o Willm: & Sarah PHILLIPS,	born 21st Apl

6 May	Thomas s/o Willm: & Sarah BLURTON,	born 3rd May
30 May	Hannah d/o Willm: & Sarah PERKIN,	born 28th May
2 Jun	Hannah d/o John & Hannah TIDSWELL,	born 26th May
4 Jun	Joseph s/o Chas: & Eliz: RATCLIFFE,	born 30th Apr
2 Jul	Hannah d/o Jams: & Han: WALKER,	born 24th Jun
9 Jul	Elizabeth d/o John & Eliz: HUGHES,	born 19th Jun
30 Jul	John s/o Jonathan & Mary STARTIN,	born 9th July
16 Aug	Cicily d/o John & Sarah TATTON,	born 11th Aug
20 Aug	Jane d/o John & Charlotte WETTON,	born 2nd Aug
7 Oct	Adam illeg s/o Olive RUSHTON	
8 Oct	Mary d/o Geo: & Mary TOOTH,	born 23rd Sep
28 Oct	Hannah d/o John & Eliz: ALCOCK,	born 23rd Oct
13 Nov	George s/o Hannah NOAKES,	born 31st Oct
19 Nov	Robert illeg s/o Mary BRANDRICK	
4 Dec	William illeg s/o Anne BARKER,	born 19th Nov
1810		
14 Jan	Anne d/o Willm: & Hannah MARTIN	
8 Feb	Rebecca duar of Willm: & Mary TURNER	
13 Mar	Mary Anne d/o Jos: & Sarah BRASSINGTON,	born 17th Feb
18 Mar	Charles illeg s/o Edith HOWE,	born 12th Mar
6 Apr	Elizabeth Anne illeg d/o Maria RUSHTON	
20 Apr	Dorothy d/o Thos: & Eliz: GARLAND,	born 15th Apl
13 May	Robert s/o Geo: & Hannah MYAT,	born 19th Apl
29 May	Anne illeg d/o Anne TURNER,	born 13th May
9 Jun	Baptist s/o Thos: & Mary BRINDLEY,	born 30th May
6 Jul	Francis s/o Francis & Anne YATES	
15 Jul	Anne d/o Thos: & Sarah COPE,	born 28th Jun
22 Jul	Margaret d/o Sarah MOOR,	born 21st July
9 Aug	Elizabeth d/o Thos: & Sarah STARTIN,	born 4th Aug
26 Aug	Charles s/o Edwd: & Eliz: COPE,	born 17th Aug
4 Sep	Walter PERKIN s/o Cicily BROWNE	
5 Sep	Elisa d/o Richd: & Margt: FENTON	
23 Sep	Thomas s/o Thos: & Louisa BRINDLEY	
4 Nov	Edward illeg s/o Diana BARKER	
	Samuel s/o Saml: & Jane WALKER,	born 9th Oct
23 Nov	John s/o Jams: & Lydia DUROSE,	born 19th Nov
25 Nov	Mary Anne d/o Will & Eliz CHELL,	born 24th Nov
9 Dec	Sarah d/o Francis & Eliz: ERDLEY,	born 1st Dec
24 Dec	Sarah d/o Thomas & Eliz WILSON,	born 22nd Dec
30 Dec	Dorothy d/o John & Sarah BURTON,	born 3rd Dec
1811		
20 Jan	Sarah d/o Thos: & Eliz: FOSTER,	born 7th Jan
23 Jan	Sarah d/o Dor: & Chas: HART,	born 19th Jan
4 Feb	Elizabeth d/o Willm: & Anne JOHNSON,	born 2nd Feb
23 Feb	Benjamin s/o John & Alice MYAT,	born 23rd Jan
3 Mar	Prudence d/o John & Mary TOOTH	
24 Mar	William s/o Willm: & Sarah FOWLER,	born 2nd Mar
31 Mar	Jane d/o John & Sarah HUGHES,	born 6th Mar
14 Apr	Sarah d/o Thos: & Sarah MILLINGTON.	born 4th Apl
28 Apr	Hannah d/o Geo: & Hanh: EDGE,	born 26th Mar
12 May	Mary d/o Thos: & Mary HOLLINS,	born 21st Apl

21 May	Robert s/o Willm: & Sarah PERKIN,	born 20th May
10 Jun	Thomas illeg s/o Eliz: CHELL,	born 6th June
24 Jun	John s/o Thos: & Esther ALCOCK,	born 3rd June
16 Jul	Thomas s/o Samson & Anne BAILEY,	born 14th July
7 Aug	Mary d/o Jos: & Hannah EDGE,	born 30th July
25 Aug	Hannah d/o Jon: & Mary STARTIN,	born 6th Aug
29 Aug	Thomas s/o John & Eliz: GADSBY,	born 26th Aug
1 Oct	Anne d/o Chas: & Dor: KENT,	born 10th Sep
	Jane d/o John & Sarah CLIFFE,	born 31st Aug
17 Nov	Sarah d/o Rich: & Eliz: PHILLIPS,	born 16th Feb
15 Dec	William s/o John & Eliz: ALCOCK,	born 7th Dec
1812		
5 Feb	Jane d/o Willm: & Sarah BLURTON,	born 30th Jan
9 Feb	John s/o Anne ARNOLD,	born 29th Jan
16 Feb	Thomas s/o Thos: & Lucy PHILLIPS,	born 23rd Jan
12 Apr	Anne d/o Richd: & Eliz: INGRAM	
	George s/o Thos: & Sarah STARTIN,	born 18th Mar
13 Apr	Richard s/o Thos: & Louisa BRINDLEY,	born 9th Apl
	George s/o Jos: & Sarah BRASSINGTON,	born 12th Mar
20 May	John s/o John & Sarah TATTON,	born 6th May
	Thomas s/o Geo: & Mary TOOTH,	born 30 Apl
21 May	Hannah d/o Willm: & Eliz: CHELL,	born 17th May
23 May	Maria d/o Thomas & Eliz: WILSON,	born 17th May
14 Jun	Anne d/o Mary PHILLIPS,	born 8th May
23 Jun	Anne d/o Richd: & Eliz: PHILLIPS	
28 Aug	Susannah d/o Michl: & Cath: BAILEY	born 17th Aug [7th-BT]
30 Aug	Sarah d/o Mary BRANDRICK,	born 4th Aug
4 Sep	Anne d/o James & Lydia DUROSE,	born 29th Aug
13 Sep	Robert s/o Willm: & Sarah PHILLIPS	
20 Sep	Charles s/o John & Mary TOOTH,	born 25th Aug
12 Oct	George s/o T. OSBOURNE Esqr: & Lydia his wife	born 9th Sep
18 Oct	Anne d/o John & Dor: CHELL,	born 15th Oct
24 Oct	Rupert s/o John & Hanh: TIDSWELL,	born 23rd Oct
29 Oct	Samuel OAKES s/o Diana SMITH,	born 26th Oct
18 Nov	Hannah d/o John & Anne BURTON,	born 8th Nov
1 Dec	William s/o Eliz: RUSHTON,	born 23rd Nov
3 Dec	George s/o Edward & Eliz: COPE,	born 25th Nov
22 Dec	John s/o Thos: & Ellen HARRIS,	born 15th Dec
23 Dec	Sarah d/o Chas: & Dor: HART,	born 20th Dec

Burials in the Parish of Leigh in the County of Stafford

1768

24 Jan	Timothy BALL of Dodsley
26 Jan	Elisabeth ATKINS
23 Mar	Ann illegitimiate d/o Elisabeth COOK
25 Mar	Ann wife of Edward TOOTH
15 Apr	John s/o William MARTIN & Mary his wife
19 Apr	Mary d/o William STARTIN & Hannah his wife
24 Apr	Alice d/o John MILLINGTON & Ellen his wife

28 Apr   Francis SHERRAT of Lower Leigh
3 May   Margaret wife of Mr William BLURTON of Milwich
13 May   Joseph SMITH of Dodsley, aged 87
26 Aug   John COLLIER Sent
1 Nov   Mary d/o Robert HOLLINS & Ann his wife
12 Nov   Ann wife of Henry WOODWARD. Aff. made before Mr Ward
15 Nov   James BAILEY the elder, aged 87
24 Nov   Thomas HOLLINS of Withington
18 Dec   John STRINGER
1769
19 Jan   Mary illegitimate d/o Hannah DENT
2 Feb   Thomas COLLIER
20 Feb   Edward s/o Joseph TILL & Mary his wife
9 Mar   Edward TOOTH
6 Apr   Dorothy wife of James MARSTON
21 Apr   Jane BAILEY
20 Jun   Mary wife of John BARKER
23 Jul   Sarah STARTIN
6 Sep   George ATKIN, aged 94
20 Sep   Elisabeth wife of John JOHNSON
26 Sep   Elisabeth wife of Francis SHERRATT
12 Nov   Thomas illegitimate s/o Sarah TURNER
22 Nov   Mary d/o Nathaniel BALL of Dovebridge & Elisabeth his wife
6 Dec   Sarah TURNER
28 Dec   Edward s/o Thomas TOOTH & Prudence his wife
1770
28 Jan   James s/o Mary TURNER, Widow
13 Feb   William ROBOTTAM
26 Feb   Sarah MILLINGTON, Widow
27 Mar   Lidia d/o Joseph & Hannah RATCLIFF
8 Apr   Elisabeth d/o William SALT & Mary his wife
13 Apr   Joseph s/o Joseph EDGE & Mary his wife
18 Apr   Mr John BRINDLEY of the Parish of Checkley
1 Jun   Mr William BELCHER the elder of Field
June the 19th. No Affidavit has been brought as directed by the Statute for Burying in Woollen, concerning the burial of Mr William BELCHER the elder of Field, of this neglect I gave Notice to the churchwarden of this Parish on the 18th of June 1770 – N.B. An Affidavit was brought on the 20th. Geo: Jolland Curate of Leigh.
5 Jun   Thomas MUCHALL or MITCHEL
23 Jun   Ellen d/o Richard JOHNSON & Alice his wife, aged 27
3 Aug   James s/o Joseph THACKER & Elisabeth his wife
5 Aug   Mary the wife of Thomas LOWNDS
16 or 18 ? Sep   John STARTIN
11 Oct   Ann wife of Joshua PRESTON Senr
14 Oct   Sarah the wife of Daniel BURTON
22 Nov   Ann wife of John HIGGS
1771
2 Jan   Margarett wife of Edward SHERRATT
27 Jan   Francis WOOLLEY
7 Feb   Ann wife of Robert HOLLINS
23 Feb   Mary BELCHER Widow of John BELCHER of Field
9 Apr   Thomas WETTON

10 May	Thomas s/o William STARTIN & Hannah his wife
——	Edward s/o Mary HOWE Widow, aged 13
	Edward s/o *John BEECH & Mary his wife *of Checkley Parish
1 Jul	Alice BURTON Widow
2 Jul	Thomas NUTT
4 Jul	Samuel WALKER
10 Jul	Sarah wife of George [John-BT] JOHNSON
17 Aug	Margaret HIDE [widow-BT] of Fole in the Parish of Checkley
31 Aug	Sarah wife of Richard SMITH
14 Sep	Edward DAVIES
29*Oct	Mary TOMLINSON [*19-BT]
15 Dec	John BIRD
22 Dec	Ann d/o Edward WOOLLEY [Wolley-BT] & Ann his wife
1772	
3 Jan	Mary d/o Thomas SHERRATT [Sherrat-BT] & Elisabeth his wife
14 Jan	John s/o John HOLLINS & Hannah his wife
2 Mar	Mary wife of Thomas COPE
18 Mar	Jane HARVEY
3 Apr	Elisabeth d/o George TOOTH & Ann his wife
7 May	Mary d/o Richard SMITH
27 May	Godfrey BUXTON
21 Jun	Sarah illegitimate d/o Elisabeth WOOLLEY
24 Jun	James DONE
3*Jul	Elisabeth KINDER of the Parish of Checkley, Widow [*23-BT]
16 Jul	Ellen wife of James CORNWAL
19 Jul	Samuel s/o John HALL & Mary his wife
10 Aug	Elisabeth HART
19 Aug	Stephen s/o Ellis BAILEY & Ann his wife
1 Sep	William TILL of Norbury Park in the Parish of Norbury
20*Oct	Samuel s/o John COPE & Elisabeth his wife [*26-BT]
3 Nov	Thomas s/o John CHARLESWORTH & Jane his wife
29 Nov	Francis s/o Francis TUNSTAL [Tunstall-BT] & Hannah his wife
26 Dec	Mrs Sarah BOULTON from Park Hall
1773	
16 Jan	Samuel s/o Frederick RUSHTON & Ann his wife
18 Jan	John HOWE
31 Jan	John s/o Edward HOWARD & Mary his wife
24 Feb	Ann wife of Joseph BAILEY
13 Mar	Lydia d/o Thomas SHERRATT [Sherrat-BT] & Elisabeth his wife
8 Apr	Jane CLARKE of Lillyshall* in Shropshire, See the Affid't. *the Parish of Newport
30 May	William s/o Theodorus DAVIES & Jane his wife
26 Jul	Mary wife of Thomas FENTON
10 Oct	Jane d/o John FENTON & Ellen his wife
29 Oct	Thomas BELCHER Brother of Mr William BELCHER see June 1st 1770
11 Dec	Robert BELCHER another brother of the same.
1774	
5 Jan	John FENTON
25 Jan	Allen s/o James KIRK & Elisabeth his wife
13 Mar	Edward s/o Edward BARKER & Mary his wife
10 Apr	Edward BRUERTON

3 May   Thomas s/o John MUTCHALL *[Muchall-BT]* & Elisabeth his wife
7 May   Eleanor Widow of John HOWE – see Jan'y the 18th 1773
15 May   John DONE
8 Jun   Benjamin WARD s/o Thomas WARD of Upper Leigh
10 Jul   Ellen d/o Thomas TOOTH & Prudence his wife
12 Jul   James RAWLIN of Fulford in this County
13 Jul   Elisabeth BROWN of Colton in the Parish of Milwich
31 Aug   Thomas illegitimate s/o Elisabeth THACKER
27 Sep   Margarett RAWLIN
15 Nov   Theodorus DAVIES
29 Dec   Ann wife of George TOOTH

1775
N.B. no burial in this Parish for six months G.J.
29 Mar   John s/o Ralph RUSHTON & Latice his wife
2 Apr   Thomas s/o William SALT & Mary his wife
23 Apr   Mrs Elisabeth CARTWRIGHT Widow
27*Oct   Hannah d/o Abigail HURST   *[*28-BT]*
5 Nov   Mr Ralph WOOD of Foal, late of Uttoxeter
9 Nov   John s/o Robert THACKER & Joyce his wife
9 Nov   George s/o John TURNER & Sarah his wife
16 Dec   *Ann wife of William BRUERTON *suppos'd to have been a Papist
23 Dec   Ann wife of John COOK

1776
8 Jan   Alice COLLIER
8 Jan   Sarah STARTIN
25 Jan   Richard HOWE
30 Jan   John HOLLINS
5 Feb   Jane IBBS infant
15 Feb   John COOK
17 Feb   Sarah wife of Willm IBBS
17 Feb   Sarah d/o Willm & Sarah IBBS
17 Feb   Elizabeth d/o George TOOTH
21 Feb   John Done WALKER s/o Wm. & Hannah WALKER
28 Feb   Dorothy PARKER
3 Mar   Henry WOODWARD
9 Mar   John BLURTON of Wolverhampton
24 Mar   John TUNNICLIFF
24 Mar   Mary JOHNSON
29 Mar   William SHENTON and Mary his wife were buried
5 Apr   James PIERS
20 Apr   Thomas RADFORD
22 Apr   Prudence CHELL
4 May   Mrs Lydia wife of Mr Thomas BLURTON
20 May   Hannah MILLS of the Parish of Stone
4 Jun   Hannah RUBOTHAM of the Parish of Uttoxeter
28 Jul   Mr William BLURTON of the Parish of Checkley
23 Aug   Dinah infant d/o Tho: & Eliz: CROSLY
18 Oct   Mary d/o John & Elizabeth MUCHAL *[Mitchel-BT]*
15 Nov   George LOVATT
23 Nov   William infant s/o George TOOTH
12 Dec   George infant s/o Joseph & Mary COPE

15 Dec   Hannah infant d/o Mary BLOOD
1777
4 Jan   John JOHNSON
14 Jan   William infant s/o Joseph & Ann SMITH
15 Jan   William infant s/o John & Mary BUXTON
20 Jan   Mary BROWN of the Parish of Milwich
20 Jan   Thomas infant s/o Ed & Eliz: COPE
21 Jan   Elizabeth LYNN infant
6 Feb   Robert & Thomas sons of William & Sarah TATUM
17 Feb   Joseph WOODWARD infant of the Parish of Checkley
19 Feb   Edward HOWE
23 Feb   Elizabeth BRIDGWOOD
21 Mar   Immanuel PERKIN
9 Apr   Mary JOHNSON
20 Apr   Charles HART
21 Apr   Elizabeth PERKIN
27 Apr   Thomas SALT Senr.
28 Apr   Joshua PRESTON Senr.
14 May   John PHILIPS
10 Jun   Edward s/o Edward & Mary HOWARD
10 Jul   Alice JOHNSON
15 Aug   Elizabeth HARRIS
24 Aug   Margaret HARGREAVE
29 Sep   Thomas MARSTON
10 Oct   Mr John BLURTON of the Parish of Penkridge
7*Nov   Ann WOLLEY [Wooley-BT] [*17 written & 1 erased]
22 Nov   Hannah POTTS
16*Dec   Elizabeth infant d/o John & Mary SALT [*6-BT]
1778
19 Jan   Elizabeth infant d/o Samuel & Hannah BARNET [Barnett-BT]
11 Feb   Ann HOLLINS
15 Mar   James MARSTON Senr.
18 Mar   Ellen infant d/o Robert & Mary HEATON
25 Mar   William HARRISON of the Parish of Checkley
27 Apr   Thomas PERKIN
17 May   Hannah ALLCOCK
25 Jul   Joseph JOHNSON infant
30 Sep   John TURNER Parish Clerk
7 Oct   Mary NICKLIN
15 Nov   John WRIGHT
22 Nov   Sampson WRIGHT of the Parish of Uttoxeter
7 Dec   Ruth BARNET
9 Dec   John LOWNDES of Birmingham
9 Dec   John GILBERT the younger was appointed Parish Clerk by the Reverend
          Walter Bagot Rector
17 Dec   Samuel BELCHER
18 Dec   Robert (infant) s/o John & Mary HIDE
1779
15 Jan   Robert HOLLINS
3 Mar   Mr John BLURTON the eldest [Senr.-BT]
6 Apr   Edward SPOONER

24 Apr Mary BERRESFORD
5 May Catherine BUXTON
29 May Mrs Margaret MILWARD
17 Jul George s/o William & Mary ADAMS
25 Sep James s/o Daniel BURTON *[James Burton Junr.-BT]*
29 Sep William FENTON of the Parish of Stone
29 Nov John MIDDLETON
10 Dec Ann infant d/o Edward HOLLINGWORTH Junr.
22 Dec Robert ROBOTHAM of the Parish of Uttoxeter
1780
1 Jan William (infant) s/o Thomas & Ann PHILIPS
31 Jan Elizabeth THACKER
26 Feb Sarah PARKER
19 Mar Ellen CLOWS
24 Mar James KIRK
28 Mar Joseph TURNER
22 Apr Mr John CRUTCHLEY, Schoolmaster
9 May Thomas JOHNSON of the Shortwoods
12 May Elizabeth HEWIT
27 May Nathaniel BELCHER
8 Jun Mary CHELL
16 Jun David infant s/o Samuel & Mary ALLCOCK
16 Jul William TUNSTAL
3 Aug John LEES
22 Sep Thomas infant s/o Frederic & Jane RUSHTON
22 Oct Elizabeth DONE
14 Nov John WILSON
21 Nov A travelling boy, name unknown, aged about 14 or 15
3 Dec David SHEMILT
24 Dec Anthony THACKER
25 Dec Elizabeth CARTER
1781
17 Jan Ralph infant s/o Joseph & Sarah HART
3 Feb Mary POTTS
14 Feb John COLLIER
13 Mar John BARKER
18 Apr Joseph Dickenson infant s/o Joseph & Sarah HART
22 Apr Mary CHARLESWORTH
27 Jun Thomas BROOKS infant of Uttoxeter
5 Aug Ann infant d/o George & Hannah TOOTH
12 Aug Betty infant d/o George & Elizabeth WRIGHT
5 Nov John BARNETT *[Barnet-BT]*
25 Nov Thomas HARRIS
25 Nov Samuel infant s/o John & Margaret NUTT
26 Nov Mary PERKIN
28 Nov George TOOTH
14 Dec Sarah DEAKIN
16 Dec Martha MOOR of the Parish of Checkley
1782
13 Jan William infant s/o John & Elizabeth BLADON
24 Jan Thomas PHILIPS

—	22 Feb	Dorothy WRIGHT of Uttoxeter Parish
	1 Mar	John CHARLESWORTH
	1 Mar	Edward SHERRAT
—	7 Mar	John MITCHEL
	8 Mar	John DENT
	9 Mar	Sarah & Mary [infant-BT] daurs of William & Sarah MILNER
—	29 Mar	William WRIGHT infant of Uttoxeter Parish
	12 Apr	Ann d/o Thomas & Ann COLLIER
	22 Apr	Edward COPE
	11 May	Joseph infant s/o Thomas & Ann COLLIER
	14 May	Elizabeth BARKER infant of Uttoxeter Parish
	9 Jun	Elizabeth BILLINGS
	8 Jul	Ann LYNN
	10 Jul	Mr Thomas BLURTON the Elder [Senr.-BT]
	28 Jul	John Wetton DEAKIN (infant)
	1 Aug	Mr Edward BLURTON the eldest [natu maximus-BT]
	13 Aug	Hannah infant d/o Luke BILLINGS
—	13 Sep	Hannah infant d/o Joseph & Elizabeth MOOR
	17 Oct	James [entry not completed & rubbed out]
	8 Dec	Mary BOX
	16 Dec	George COPE

1783

	28 Mar	Edward HOLLINGWORTH of Uttoxeter Parish
—	7 May	Elizabeth BENTLY of Bramshal Parish
—	17 May	Samuel POTT
	30 May	Simon FOWLER the elder
	13 Jun	Thomas infant s/o William & Mary MELLOR
	17 Jun	Edward infant s/o Thomas & Mary CHELL
—	25 Jun	Thomas infant s/o Ann TURNER
	29 Jun	Ellen COPE
	13 Jul	Mary HOWARD
	7 Aug	Mary SPOONER
	21 Sep	Ann COPE
	3 Oct	Henry BARKER infant
—	29 Oct	Ann BAILEY (pauper)
	20 Nov	Job RUSHTON

1784

—	6 Jan	Dorothy BAILEY (pauper)
	12 Feb	Mr William BELCHER [Gen.-BT]
—	17 Feb	Sarah LEES the elder
	10*Mar	Thomas FENTON of St. Mary's Parish in Stafford [*15-BT]
	21 Mar	Robert JOHNSON
	30 Mar	Dorothy DEGG
	30 Mar	Mary LOWNDES
—	5 Apr	Mary BAILEY pauper
—	27 Apr	Mary infant d/o William & Hannah WALKER
—	4 May	Sarah PARKER
	20 May	William ASTON
—	16 Jun	John BAILEY pauper
—	7 Aug	Ann HOWE (pauper) infant
	9 Sep	Samuel SHENTON (pauper)

19 Sep Peter MOOR of Checkley Parish
30 Sep Elizabeth JOHNSON of the Shortwoods
2 Nov Elizabeth CHELL (pauper) infant
20 Nov Elizabeth BARKER infant of Uttoxeter Parish
1785
15 Jan Ann infant d/o William SALT
9 Feb Henry BAILY of Checkley bank
16 Feb William (infant) s/o John & Ann LANDER
9 Mar Thomas (infant) s/o William & Margaret BAILY *[Bailey-BT]* (p)
14 Apr Mary TUNNICLIFF of Stone Parish
20 Apr Hannah (infant) d/o William & Jane WALKER of Leigh
24 Apr Ann (infant) d/o Thomas BARKER
2 Jun Alice TUNNICLIFF of Uttoxeter Parish
3 Jun Mary SMITH
4 Jul Samson WRIGHT of Uttoxeter Parish
6 Aug James infant s/o William & Margaret DEAKIN
15 Dec Elizabeth BATE
16 Dec Mary infant d/o Thomas & Ellen WILSHAW of Dilhorn Parish
18 Dec Elizabeth FOWLER
1786
1 Jan Thomas COLCLOUGH
8 Jan Lydia WARD of Checkley Parish
30 Jan William PHILIPS of Field
6 Feb Ann PHILIPS of Nobut
22 Feb John BEECH of Checkley Parish
28 Feb Thomas HOOD pauper
4 Mar Edward BELCHER
18 Mar John BELCHER of Uttoxeter
23 Mar William BREWERTON of Stone Parish
26 Mar Thomas RUSHTON pauper
23 May John infant s/o William & Margaret DEAKIN
8 Jun Hannah TOOTH (pauper)
13 Jun Mary HOLLINS
13 Aug Jane HAWLEY
27 Oct William BUXTON
29 Dec William BOTT pauper
1787
4 Jan Richard (infant) s/o William & Margaret BAILEY (paup)
14 Jan Francis TUNSTAL (pauper)
15 Feb Thomas TUNNICLIFF of Uttoxeter Parish
18 Mar William MARSON
1 Apr William infant s/o William & Mary MELLOR
29 May William SMITH
31 May John (infant) s/o Mr Thomas & Mrs Joyce BRINDLEY
1 Jul Thomas MOOR (pauper)
28 Aug John LOWNDES (infant)
8 Sep Aaron BLOOD (pauper)
27 Oct Jane BLURTON
11 Nov Mary BOTT (pauper)
27 Dec Elizabeth COLCLOUGH

1788

27 Feb	Alice SHIPLEY (pauper) infant
23 Mar	Mary CHELL (pauper)
25 Mar	Miss Mary WARD
9 Apr	Mr John BRINDLEY
24 Apr	Hannah infant d/o James & Mary MARSON
10 May	Rachel JOHNSON infant
1 Jul	Ann infant d/o George & Edith WALKER (paup)
11 Jul	Elizabeth WRIGHT (paup)
30 Jul	The Revd. Mr. Thos. BROWNE Curate
10 Aug	James (infant) s/o William & Ann RAWLIN
24 Aug	Richard SMITH (paup)
11 Sep	Sarah infant d/o John & Jane BAGNAL
20 Oct	James PHILLIPS, Labourer
28 Oct	George s/o George & Elizabeth DEAKIN, infant
18 Nov	Mary wife of John TUNNICLIFF
2 Dec	Mary d/o James & Mary MARSON, Inft.
12 Dec	Sarah TILL, Spinster
22 Dec	Ellen RADFORD, Widow
25 Dec	Rebecca d/o Robt. & Mary ARNOLD, infant

1789

21 Jan	Cicely BROWNE
	Francis SHERRATT
4 Mar	James s/o James & Ann MOTTERAM, inft. P.
17 Mar	William s/o Lawrence & Elizabeth GREENSMITH, infant
23 Mar	John TURNER, Labourer
31 Mar	Mary SALT
14 Apr	Charles s/o Robert & Sarah PHILLIPS, infant
13 May	Mary wife of John LOWE. P.
14 May	Charles s/o Elizabeth COPE, infant
14 Jun	Margaret WARD
	Sarah COPE
12 Jul	Jane BAGNAL
	Sarah BAGNAL, infant
14 Jul	George PHILLIPS
10 Sep	Thomas HOWE
7 Nov	John GILBERT Senr.
17 Dec	James PERKIN. P.

1790

28 Jan	Thomas WALTON
12 Feb	Simon COPE, infant. P.
14 Feb	Thomas TOOTH, Labourer. P.
6 Apr	William KENT, infant
4 May	Elizabeth wife of Robt. MOORE. P.
25 May	Mary d/o Robt: & Eliz: MOOR, infant. P.
20 Jun	George TURNER
27 Jun	Elizabeth SHERRATT
6 Aug	Robt: HEATON. P.
8 Aug	Thos: HOWE
18 Aug	Ann BARKER of Uttoxeter
3 Oct	Richard s/o Joseph & Ann SMITH, inft. P.

7 Nov   William PARKER
23 Nov   Sarah BREWERTON. P.
24 Nov   Mary HOWE
1791
19 Jan   Phillip HAWLEY
23 Mar   Mary BAILEY. P.
4 Apr   Elizabeth THACKER, infant. P.
15 May   Ann WILSHAW, infant
19 May   John HART
26 May   Samuel & Fanny JOHNSON, infants
31 May   Ann WALKER, P.
2 Jun   Joseph BAILEY, P.
7 Jun   Hannah TUNSTAL. P.
3 Jul   Avary RUSHTON, infant. P.
26 Jul   John LEES, infant
18 Aug   John WALKER, Senr. P.
8 Sep   Ann COLLINS. P.
16 Sep   Mary BARKER
28 Oct   Sarah HARRIS. P.
17 Nov   Sarah MOOR. P.
23 Nov   William WALKER
16 Dec   John HIGGS
1792
28 Jan   Sarah WILSON
10 Feb   Harriott MILLINGTON
28 Feb   Thomas LYNN
24 Mar   Joshua PRESTON
25 Mar   John LOWE. P.
15 Apr   William BARNET. P.
16 Apr   James BROWNE
22 Apr   Francis COPE
2 Sep   Job RUSHTON. P.
12 Sep   Judith PEARCE
24 Oct   Willm. BELCHER, infant
4 Nov   Mary DANIEL. P.
27 Nov   Alice BUXTON'S. P.
4 Dec   James BERRISFORD
1793
6 Jan   Benjamin HEALY. P.
31 Jan   William WHEELDON
3 Mar   Mary ASBURY
23 Mar   Ann PHILLIPS
6 Apr   John PRESTON
14 Apr   Samuel ADAMS, infant
6 May   Mary SHENTON. P.
24 May   Elizabeth BLACKDEN
2 Jun   Thomas SMITH, infant
4 Jun   John BUXTON. P.
1 Jul   Joseph ASBURY
          William FENTON
7 Jul   Mary ALCOCK, P.

10 Jul   Sarah SLATER
20 Jul   Jane GRIFFIN
22 Jul   Willm. TUNNICLIFFE
5 Nov   Sarah BELCHER
12 Nov   Richd. JOHNSON. P.
12 Dec   Edward MELLER, infant. P.
22 Dec   John SMITH. P.
30 Dec   Mary BABB, infant
1794
1 Jan   Isabella JOHNSON
22 Jan   Elizabeth MELLER
30 Mar   Ann HOLLINS, inft.
2 Apr   Eliz: RUSHTON. P.
6 Apr   Hannah RAWLIN *[Rawlins-BT]* P.
7 Jun   Mary MELLER. P.
30 Jun   Ellen COPE
10 Jul   Thos: TUNNICLIFFE
26 Jul   Rebecca ARNOLD
5 Sep   Hannah TUNNICLIFFE
20 Sep   Jane WILSON
28 Sep   Elizabeth FOWLER
2 Oct   George BLACKDEN
2 Dec   Willm: STARTIN
28 Dec   Maria NOAKES, infant
1795
26 Jan   Mary HIDE
27 Jan   Alice DEAKIN
4 Feb   William *[Thomas-BT]* LOWNDES
25 Feb   Hannah STARTIN, infant
14 Mar   Esther BARNET, infant
19 Mar   Alice PRESTON
31 Mar   Alice BURTON, inft.
4 Apr   Thos: BUXTONS, inft.
5 Apr   Lydia BAILY, infant
21 Apr   Mary HOWE, infant
10 May   Willm: HUGHES, infant
12 May   Geo: TURNER, infant
15 May   Edward WALKER
19 May   Willm: DEAKIN
28 May   Willm: JOHNSON
8 Jun   John RAWLIN, infant
20 Aug   Eliz: SHENTON
23 Aug   Mary ALCOCK
30 Sep   Alice BROWNE
20 Nov   Mary HOLLINS
25 Nov   George THORNEWORK
27 Nov   Josiah David HILL, infant
23 Dec   Willm: RAWLIN
25 Dec   Mary WARDE
1796
14 Feb   Anne RUSHTON, aged 101

13 Apr Peter GRIFFIN
20 Apr Elizabeth GRIFFIN
18 May Mary HOLLINS
20 May Thomas BROWNE, inft.
20 May Eliz: LEES
2 Jul Mary BURTON
7 Jul Anne WILSHAW
12 Sep Thomas WILSON
20 Sep Eliz: ROWBOTHAM
13 Oct Cath: BARKER
15 Oct Thos: GRIFFIN, infant
2 Nov John EDGE
6 Nov Thomas CHELL
26 Nov James MILLINGTON
6 Dec Michael WARDE
9 Dec Thomas WARDE
25 Dec Thomas COLLIER
        Bartholomew RUSHTON

1797
1 Jan Frederick RUSHTON
       Hannah CHELL
9 Mar Edward HANSON
19 Mar John WALKER
19 Mar Willm: MILLINGTON, infant
12 Apr Sarah HOWE
30 May Mary BEECH
13 Jul Mary BLOOD
9 Aug William FOWLER, infant
10 Aug Margt: WRIGHT
16 Aug Ellen THORNEWELL, infant
21 Oct Edwd: HOWE
21 Oct Thos: MITCHEL, inft.
28 Nov Henry BUXTON
31 Dec John s/o Thos: & Eliz: LOVETT
1798
2 Jan Jane SAUNDERS
18 Jan Saml: LOVETT
8 Mar Mrs. Joyce BRINDLEY
2 Apr Lydia HOLLINS, infant
23 Sep Francis MILLINGTON
5 Oct Daniel BURTON
24 Dec Hannah BAGNETT
1799
23 Feb Ellen FENTON
23 Mar Sarah JOHNSON, infant
29 Apr William ADDAMS
20 Jul Eliz: WILSON
21 Jul Jams: TURNER
28 Aug Helena THOMSON
10 Sep Lettice BIRD
- Nov William BAILY *[Bailey-BT]*

5 Dec Sarah SHERRATT
15 Dec Willm: THORNEWORK
27 Dec Eliz: WOODWARD
1800
25 Jan Jemima BYATT
3 Feb Francis BLURTON
2 Mar Thomas FENTON
4 Mar Eliz: CARTER
23 Mar John BLURTON
19 Apr Rachel LOVETT
28 May Saml: TURNER
14 Jun Thomas SALT
13 Jul Jane SHAW
1 Aug Hannah MYATT
19 Aug Catherine BRINDLEY
19 Oct Richd: BROWNE
1801
5 Jan Charles BENTLEY, infant
15 Jan Willm: WOODWARD
3 Feb Abigail HIRST
17 Feb Eliz: MITCHELL
24 Feb Geo: DEAKIN
18 Mar Anne MARTIN
27 Mar Mary CARTER
21 Apr Thos: BROOKS
17 May Frances JACKSON
 Margt: SHERRATT
27 May Mary ARNOLD, infant
17 Jun Anne NUTT
10 Jul Joseph BROWNE
31 Jul Joseph EDGE
16 Aug Margt: BELCHER
31 Aug Anne HUBBARD
15 Sep Willm: HOLLINS
26 Sep Thomas SHAW
21 Dec Willm: FROST
1802
10 Feb Eliz: BULL
 Margt: HOWE
14 Feb Willm: ADAMS
25 Feb Jos: *[Joseph-BT]* HART
28 Feb Jos: TILL
9 Mar Eliz: HEATON
13 Mar Arabella THACKER, infant
28 Apr John BRINDLEY
10 Jun Elizabeth INGLEBY
27 Jul Thos: PLATT, infant
16 Aug Eliz: DEAKIN, infant
21 Sep John ALCOCK, infant
4 Oct Edward BARNES
23 Oct Mary FENTON

18 Nov   Catharine SALE
 2 Dec   Edward HOWE, infant
 7 Dec   Mary BARNET
1803
23 Jan   John HART
 9 Mar   John BROWNE
10 Mar   Henry WOODWARD, infant
22 Mar   Sarah HART
 2 Apr   Eliz: BOX
 7 Apr   Eliz: COPE
25 Apr   Helen WHITEHALL
27 Apr   John JOHNSON
 3 May   John CHELL
         John TILL
24 May   Hannah BARNET
 2 Jun   John BLURTON
25 Jun   Richard SMITH, infant
 3 Jul   Elizabeth SLATER, infant
 9 Jul   James FENTON, infant
 4 Aug   Grace BELL
16 Oct   Adam RUSHTON
      No Funeral in this Parish in 7 months, from Octr 16th 1803 to 17th May 1804. H.T.
1804
17 May   Henry WOODWARD
25 May   Eliz: HAWLEY
 7 Nov   Thomas BRINDLEY
18 Nov   Eliz: PRESTON
 3 Dec   Job: BROWNE
 5 Dec   Thomas WOODWARD
19 Dec   Mary CARTER
1805
 7 Jan   Elizabeth BILLINS
27 Jan   Jane THORNEWELL
29 Jan   Geo: JOHNSON
10 Mar   Stephen ROBINSON
12 Mar   Anne RUSHTON
21 Mar   Anne PLATT
31 Mar   Eliz: *[Elizabeth-BT]* FROST
 2 Apr   J. *[John-BT]* MILLINGTON
 4 Apr   M. *[Mary-BT]* HICKLIN
 9 Apr   Mary BRIERHURST *[Briryhurst-BT]*
17 Apr   Jos: *[Joseph-BT]* MARTIN
 5 Jun   David PRESTON, infant
29 Jun   Mary TATTON, infant
19 Jul   Mary BLOOD
16 Sep   Robt: PHILIPS, infant
28 Sep   Charles BENTLEY
19 Oct   Charles BROWNE
 8 Dec   James SMITH
1806
11 Feb   Eliz: COLLIER

15 Feb	Anne SMITH
30 Mar	Joyce BRINDLEY
6 Apr	Hannah WOOLLEY
16 May	Thomas SHERRATT
22 May	Mrs: RHUDDE
13 Jun	Lydia SNAPE, infant
22 Jun	Thomas & William ASBURY, infants
31 Jul	Charles BENTLEY
10 Aug	John TATTON, infant
2 Sep	Willm: TURNER, infant
4 Sep	Charles HART
23 Sep	James BALL, infant
10 Oct	Dorothy KINNERSLEY *[Kynnersley-BT]*
17 Oct	Helen BROWNE *[Brown-BT]*
25 Oct	John GAUNT, infant
17 Dec	Willm: CARTER
20 Dec	Edward HOWE
21 Dec	Sarah BAGNELL

1807

14 Jan	Helen JACKSON
24 Jan	John BLOOR *[Bloore-BT]*
1 Apr	Edward RADFORD
9 Apr	Sarah PHILLIPS
12 Apr	John WARDLE, infant
24 May	Robt: PHILLIPS
28 May	Margt: CHELL
2 Jul	Anne MOTTERAM
2 Aug	William PHILLIPS
13 Oct	John BLURTON
16 Oct	Alice TILL
14 Nov	Elizabeth MARSTON

1808

8 Jan	William DANIEL
17 Jan	Sarah RUSHTON
	Mary PLANT
2 Mar	Mary HARRIS
16 Mar	Thomas KENT
4 Jun	Thomas MOTTERAM
15 Jun	Henry ALCOCK
26 Jun	John GROSVENOR
12 Jul	Thos: CHELL
19 Aug	Samuel ENGLAND
21 Aug	Anne CHELL
20 Sep	James MARSON
29 Sep	Thos: HOWE
11 Oct	Eliz: TOOTH, infant
17 Oct	Anne BAILEY, infant
1 Dec	John JACKSON, infant
5 Dec	Thomas MOOR *[Moore-BT]*

1809

26 Jan	Lydia CARTER

2 Mar   Mary JOHNSON
31 Mar   Robt: MELLOR
18 Apr   John BUXTON
1 May   Sarah JACKSON
16 Jun   Hannah LEES *[Leese-BT]*
14 Jul   Eliz: HUGHES
18 Sep   William BLURTON
22 Oct   Willm: LOWNDES
28 Oct   Mary RATCLIFFE
2 Nov   Adam RUSHTON, infant
29 Nov   John GILBERT
1810
14 Jan   Willm: ASBURY, infant
          Sarah CHELL, infant
22 Jan   Mary LOWNDES
24 Jan   Anne NOAKES
5 Feb   Willm: BARKER, infant
26 Feb   Willm: WALKER
12 Apr   Hannah WALKER
3 May   Henry WOODWARD
10 Jul   Benjamin MOTTRAM
11 Jul   Mary HOWE
26 Jul   Honor LEES *[Leese-BT]*
31 Jul   Mary HIGGS
3 Aug   Mary GOLDSROW
10 Aug   Elizabeth STARTIN, infant
5 Sep   James HOLLINS
25 Oct   Mary WARDLE
24 Nov   Anne ROCK
27 Dec   Sarah TURNER
1811
29 Jan   John LOWE
3 Feb   John EATON
7 Feb   Eliz: ALCOCK
17 Feb   Thos: MARTIN
26 Feb   Eliz: KENT
2 Mar   Mary ARNOLD
11 Mar   Hannah COPE
21 Mar   Eliz: LOVETT
28 Mar   Willm: WARDLE
20 Apr   Eliz: SHERRAT
13 May   Sarah BRADSHAW
24 Jun   Willm: TATTON, infant
20 Jul   Edward BARKER, infant
21 Aug   Anne BAILEY
2 Sep   Martha HIGGS
25 Sep   Mary HAWLEY
24 Nov   Thomas POWNER
30 Nov   Thomas BARKER
1812
19 Feb   Robert BULL

1 Mar	James MOTTRAM
3 Mar	Francis GOFF
	John BLOOD
18 Mar	Francis MILLINGTON
16 Jun	Robert MOOR
30 Jun	Anne JOHNSON
5 Jul	James SALE
	Jane BRUERTON [Brewerton-BT]
	Thomas TUNNICLIFFE
26 Jul	John MOTTRAM, infant
27 Jul	Hannah EDGE
15 Sep	William WILSON, infant
2 Oct	Eliz: DEAKIN
10 Oct	Mary MARSON
11 Oct	Anne BENTLEY
8 Nov	Sarah HART
17 Nov	Elizabeth COPE

A MARRIAGE REGISTER BOOK.
For the Parish of Leigh in the County of Stafford
Begun 17th April 1754.

N. T. Rector

The Revd. John Ward M.A. Curate

17 Apr 1754 Lic. No. 1	Thomas FROST Parish of Leigh, Husbandman, & Sarah HANCOCK of the Parish aforesaid, Spinster Off. Min.:- J. Ward, Curate Wit: William WALKER, John BLURTON
9 Jan 1755 Banns No. 2	Thomas MARSON P. of Leigh & Hannah WALKER P. of Leigh Banns published: 20 Jan 1754 and two other days appointed by John Ward Curate Wit: John TURNER, George TURNER Off. Min.:- John WARD Curate
29 May 1755 Lic. No. 3	Robert PHILLIPS P. of Leigh, Husbandman, & Dorothy HARRIS P. of Leigh, Widow. Off. Min.:- John Ward, Curate Wit: Charles HART, John TURNER
14 Jun 1755 Lic. No. 4	Thomas LOWNS [s. Lowndes] P. of Grindon, County of Stafford, Husbandman, & Mary BARKER, P. of Leigh, Spinster Off. Min.:- John Ward, Curate Wit: William WALKER, Joseph TURNER
23 Jun 1755 Banns No. 5	John GILBERT P. of College & Ann [x] LOW P. of Leigh Banns published: "three several Sundays" by John Ward, Curate Wit: John TURNER, Thomas GILBERT
17 Dec 1755 Lic. No. 6	Richard HOW otp & Mary [x] JOHNSON, Spinster Off. Min.:- John Taylor, Rector Wit: Wm WININGTON, John TURNER
27 Dec 1755 Lic. No. 7	John MILLINGTON otp, Husbandman, & Ellin [x] BLOOR otp Spinster Off. Min.:- John Ward, Curate Wit: John PROCTER, Phillip CROSBY
3 Jan 1756 Lic. No. 8	William BELCHER, otp, Husbandman, & Sarah HAWKINS, P. of Uttoxeter, Spinster Off. Min.:- John Ward, Curate Wit: John PROCTER, Thos BELCHER
6 Jan 1756 Banns No. 9	Thomas BOX, otp, Husbandman, & Elizabeth [x] MILNER, otp, Spinster Banns published: 30 Nov, 7 & 14 Dec 1755 Off. Min.:- John Ward, Curate Wit: William WALKER, John PROCTER
9 Feb 1756 Lic. No. 10	Francis SHERRATT [s. Sherrat], otp, Widdower, & Elizabeth BELCHER otp, Spinster Off. Min.:- John Ward, Curate Wit: John TURNER, John PROCTOR
23 Feb 1756 Banns No. 11	Joseph TILL, otp, & Mary COLLIER [s. Collor] otp, Spinster Banns published: 11, 18 & 25 Jan Off. Min.:- John Ward, Curate Wit: Joseph TURNER, John PROCTOR
23 Apr 1756 Lic. No. 12	George [x] ROBOTHAM, P. of Leigh, Husbandman, & Elizabeth [x] SHAW, otp, Spinster Off. Min.:- John Ward, Curate Wit: Thomas NUTT, John PROCTOR

5 Jul 1756 Banns No. 13	John SHERRATT P. of Leigh, Taylor, & Hannah [x] WHIELDON otp, Spinster Banns published: 16 May, 27 June & 4 July 1756 Off. Min.:- Samuel Langley Rector of Checkly Wit: William CLARK, John TURNER
	Banns of Marriage between John LOWE & Ann EDGE were published the 4th, 11th & 18th July 1756, by me, Jno. Taylor, Rector
31 Aug 1756 Lic. No. 14	James FENTON otp, Husbandman, & Alice [x] MILLINGTON, otp, Spinster Off. Min.:- John Ward, Curate Wit: John TURNER, John PROCTER
3 Jan 1757 Banns No. 15	Francis [x] RADCLIFF [Ratcliff-BT] & Anne [x] BAILEY otp Banns published: 21 Nov 1756 by Mr Hancock, 28 Nov by Mr Bill & 5 Dec by Mr Willott Off. Min.:- [marriage] Samuel Langley Rector of Checkley Wit: William WALKER, John TURNER
9 Jan 1757 Banns No. 16	Theodorus DAVIES otp, Husbandman, & Jane [x] BARNETT, otp Spinster Banns published: 19 & 26 Dec 1756 by Mr Ford, & 2 Jan 1757 by Mr Bill Off. Min.:- John Ward Curate Wit: Joseph TURNER, John PROCTOR
21 Feb 1757 Lic. No. 17	John [x] KIRK, P. of Sandon, Chimney Sweeper, & Mary [x] RATCLIFF, P. of Leigh, Spinster Off. Min.:- John Ward, Curate Wit: John TURNER, John PROCTOR
18 Oct 1757 Lic. No. 18	Mr John BLURTON, otp, & Miss Ann BLURTON, P. of Gayton, Spinster Off. Min.:- J. Bill, Rectr. of Draycot Wit: Elen BLURTON, Edward BLURTON Junior
1 Nov 1757* Banns No. 19	Edward BRERETON [s. Brewerton] otp, Shoemaker, & Jane [x] HOLLINS, otp, Spinster [*30 Oct crossed out] Banns published: 25 Sep, 2 & 9 Oct 1757 Off. Min.:- John Ward, Curate Wit: John PROCTOR, John TURNER
28 Nov 1757 Banns No. 20	Simon [x] HYLE P. of Uttoxeter, Husbandman, & Ann [x] PERKIN, otp, Spinster Banns published: 13, 20 & 27 Nov Off. Min.:- John Ward, Curate Wit: William RAWLINS, John PROCTOR
29 Nov 1757 Banns No. 21	John CROSLEY, otp, Husbandman, & Mary BLOOR [s. Bloore], otp, Spinster Banns published: 13, 20 & 27 Nov Off. Min.:- John Ward, Curate Wit: William WALKER, John PROCTOR
8 Jan 1758 Lic. No. 22	William JOHNSON, P. of Leigh, Husbandman, & Elizabeth [x] CHELL, otp, Spinster Off. Min.:- John Ward, Curate Wit: John PROCTOR, Joseph TURNER
17 Jan 1758 Lic. No. 23	Henry WOODWARD, P. of Leigh, Husbandman, & Elizabeth HOW, otp, Spinster Off. Min.:- John Ward, Curate Wit: John PROCTOR, Joseph TURNER

4 Apr 1758	John BAGNAL [s. Bagnall], P. of Ronton, Blacksmith, & Ann [x] TOOTH, otp, Spinster
Banns No. 24	Banns published: 12, 19 & 26 Mar 1758 Off. Min.:- John Ward, Curate Wit: John PROCTER, John TURNER
2 Oct 1758	John GOODWIN, P. of Stone, Blacksmith, & Mary [x] BRERETON, otp, Spinster
Banns No. 25	Banns published: 10, 17 & 24 Sep 1758 Off. Min.:- John Ward, Curate Wit: Jno. PROCTER, Joseph TURNER
5 Oct 1758 Lic. No. 26	William HARVEY, P. of Checkley [Cheadle-BT], Flaxdresser, & Mary [x] HOLLINS, otp, Spinster Off. Min.:- Francis Ward, Curate Wit: John PROCTER, Joseph TURNER of Alveton
6 Nov 1758 Lic. No. 27	The Rev'd John WARD Rector of Cheadle & Curate of this Parish, & Miss Ann [s. Anne] COLCLOUGH, P. of Cheadle Off. Min.:- Francis Ward, Curate of Alveton Wit: Henry MANIFOLD, Caesar Arden COLCOUGH
22 Jan 1759	Richard [x] SMITH, otp, Husbandman, & Sarah [x] BLOOD, otp, Spinster
Banns No. 28	Banns published: 7, 14 & 21 Jan Off. Min.:- John Ward, Curate Wit: John PROCTER, John DONE
5 Feb 1759*	James DAWSON, P. of Checkley, Gardener, & Elizabeth [x] DAVIL, Spinster [26 Feb-BT]
Banns No. 29	Banns published: 21 & 28 Jan & 4 Feb Off. Min.:- John Ward, Curate Wit: John PROCTER, Edward HOLLINGWORTH
26 Feb 1759	John [x] JOHNSON, otp Husbandman, & Elizabeth [x] BAYLEY, otp, Spinster
Banns No. 30	Banns published: 11, 18 & 25 Feb Off. Min.:- John Ward, Curate Wit: John PROCTER, John TURNER
15 Apr 1759 Banns No. 31	William ADAMS, otp, Taylor, & Sarah [x] JOHNSON, otp, Spinster Banns published: 25 Mar, 1 & 8 Apr Off. Min.:- John Ward, Curate Wit: John PROCTER, Joseph TURNER
16 Apr 1759	William [x] SHENSTON [s. Shenton], otp, Husbandman, Sarah [x] STANLEY, otp, Spinster
Banns No. 32	Banns published: 25 Mar, 1 & 8 Apr Off. Min.:- John Ward, Curate Wit: John TURNER, Joseph TURNER
17 Apr 1759 Banns No. 33	John PLANT, P. of Stone, Weaver, & Mary [x] SNAPE, otp, Spinster Banns published: 21 & 28 Jan & 4 Feb Off. Min.:- John Ward, Curate Wit: John DONE, Joseph TURNER
19 Jun 1759 Banns No. 34	Ralph [x] RUSHTON, otp, Taylor, & Lettice [x] BAYLEY, otp, Spinster Banns published: 4, 11 & 18 Mar Off. Min.:- John WARD, Rector of Cheadle Wit: John PROCTER, John TURNER
21 Aug 1759 Banns No. 35	John BIRD, otp, Bricklayer, & Elizabeth [x] DICKINS, otp, Spinster Banns published: 5, 12 & 19 Aug 1759 Off. Min.:- Ralph BARNES Curate Wit: John TURNER, John GILBERT

15 Oct 1759	George [x] HOW, Bricklayer, otp, & Mary [x] PERKINS, otp Spinster
Banns	Banns published: 30 Sep, 7 & 14 Oct
No. 36	Off. Min.:- Ralph BARNES, Curate
	Wit: Francis SHERRATT, John TURNER

1 Nov 1759	John COPE, otp, Farmer, & Elizabeth POTTS, otp, Spinster
Lic.	Off. Min.:- Ralph BARNES, Curate
No. 37	Wit: John TURNER, John COPE

31 Jan 1760	Thomas CROSSLEY, otp, Husbandman, & Mary NUTT otp Spinster
Banns	Banns published: 13, 20 & 27 Jan
No. 38	Off. Min.:- Ralph BARNES, Curate
	Wit: William WALKER, Joseph TURNER

6 Apr 1760	George [x] GOUGH, P. of Colwich, Husbandman, & Dorothy [x] LEES, otp, Spinster
Banns	Banns published: 27 Jan, 3 & 10 Feb
No. 39	Off. Min.:- Ralph BARNES, Curate
	Wit: John TURNER, Joseph TURNER

1 Apr 1760	William [x] BOTT, otp, & Elizabeth [x] SHERRATT, otp
Banns	Banns published: 16, 23 & 30 Mar
No. 40	Off. Min.:- Ralph BARNES, Curate
	Wit: John TURNER, Joseph TURNER

6 Apr 1760	Thomas HERVEY [s. Harvey], P. of Checkley, Farmer, & Ann [x] LEES, otp, Spinster
Banns	Banns published: 16, 23 & 30 Mar
No. 41	Off. Min.:- Ralph BARNES, Curate
	Wit: John TURNER, William WALKER

13 Apr 1760	Thomas [x] BOLTON, otp, Husbandman, & Elizabeth [x] ADAMS, otp, Spinster
Banns	Banns published: 23 & 30 Mar & 6 Apr
No. 42	Off. Min.:- Ralph BARNES, Curate
	Wit: William ADAMS, Joseph TURNER

15 Sep 1760	Thomas LYMER P. of Draycot, & Anne HART [s. Ann], otp, Spinster
Lic.	Off. Min.:- Ralph BARNES, Curate
No. 43	Wit: Joseph HART, Joseph TURNER

8 Jan 1761	Thomas [x] WOOLLEY, otp, Labourer, & Jane [x] THACKER, otp, Spinster
Banns	Banns published: 21 & 28 Dec & 4 Jan 1760-1
No. 44	Off. Min.:- Ralph BARNES, Curate
	Wit: Robert PHILLIPS, John TURNER

29 Jan 1761	Thomas HOWE, otp, Farmer & Widower, & Sarah GOODALL, otp, Spinster
Lic.	Off. Min.:- Ralph BARNES, Curate
No. 45	Wit: William WALKER, John TURNER

15 May 1761	Samuel HILL, P. of Alveton, Husbandman, & Anne [x] JUTSUN, otp, Spinster
Banns	Banns published: 16 Apr, 3 & 10 May
No. 46	Off. Min.:- Ralph BARNES, Curate
	Wit: John TURNER, Joseph TURNER

15 Oct 1761	Thomas FENTON, otp, Husbandman, & Mary [x] COLLIER, otp, Spinster
Banns	Banns published: 23 & 30 Aug, & 6 Sep
No. 47	Off. Min.:- Saml. Langley, Rcr. of Checkley
	Wit: John GILBERT, John TURNER

26 Oct 1761	Michael WARD, otp, Gentleman, & Mary CARTWRIGHT, P. of Yoxal, Spinster
Lic.	
No. 48	Off. Min.:- John WARD Rector of Cheadle
	Wit: Thos. WARD, John PROCTER

- Nov 1761	Thomas RUSHTON, otp, Husbandman & Sarah LEES otp Spinster
Banns	Banns published: 18 & 25 Oct & 1 Nov
No. 49	Off. Min.:- Ralph BARNES, Curate
	Wit: Joseph LEES, Joseph TURNER

10 Dec 1761	John PRESTON, otp, Husbandman, & Alice [x] HARGRAVES, otp, Spinster
Banns	Banns published: 15, 22 & 29 Nov
No. 50	Off. Min.:- Ralph BARNES, Curate
	Wit: John TURNER, Joseph TURNER

10 Jan 1762	James CARNEL, otp, Husbandman, & Ellen [x] RUEBOTHAM, otp, Spinster
Banns	Banns published: 20 & 27 Dec 1761 & 4 Jan 1762
No. 51	Off. Min.:- Ralph BARNES, Curate
	Wit: Nicolas MOTTERAM, John TURNER

6 Feb 1762	Joseph [x] EDGE, P.of Gratwich, & Mary [x] LOWE, otp
Banns	Banns published: 3, 10, & 17 Jan
No. 52	Off. Min.:- Geo: HANCOCK, Rtr. of Bromshall
	Wit: John TURNER, Joseph TURNER

13 Apr 1762	Thomas SHAW, otp, Husbandman, & Jane [x] STRINGER, otp, Spinster
Banns	Banns published: 21 & 28 Feb & 7 Mar
No. 53	Off. Min.:- Ralph BARNES, Curate
	Wit: William [x] STRINGER, Joseph TURNER

5 May 1762	Thomas GERRARD, P. of Uttoxeter, & Elizabeth [x] COPE, otp Spinster
Banns	Banns published: 18 & 25 Apr & 2 May
No. 54	Off. Min..- Ralph BARNES, Curate
	Wit: John TURNER, Mary SPOONER

10 May 1762	Jonathan [x] TUNSTALL, otp, & Hannah [x] BAILEY, otp, Spinster
Banns	Banns published: 25 Apr, 2 & 9 May
No. 55	Off. Min.:- Ralph BARNES, Curate
	Wit: John TURNER, John STEVENSON

23 Aug 1762	William [x] EVANS, otp, Husbandman, & Elizabeth BENNETT [s. Elizebeth Bennet], otp, Spinster
Banns	Banns published: 8, 15 & 22 Aug
No. 56	Off. Min.:- Ralph BARNES, Curate
	Wit: John TURNER, Joseph TURNER

2 Mar 1763	Robert HOLLINS, otp, Farmer, & Anne WOODWARD [s. Ann], otp, Spinster
Lic.	
No. 57	Off. Min.:- Ralph BARNES, Curate
	Wit: Henry WOODWARD, John TURNER

13 Apr 1763	Francis [x] FEARNES, P. of Stone, Husbandman, & Elizabeth [x] DAVIS, otp, Spinster
Banns	Banns published: 27 Mar, 3 & 10 Apr
No. 58	Off. Min.:- Saml. Langley, R'r of Checkley
	Wit: John DONE, Joseph TURNER

26 Dec 1763	Richard KENT, P. of Checkley, Carpenter, & Sarah NUTT, otp, Spinster
Banns	Banns published: 11, 18 & 25 Dec
No. 59	Off. Min.:- Ralph BARNES, Curate
	Wit: John KENT, John TURNER

26 Dec 1763	Edward WOOLLEY, otp, Husbandman, & Anne [x] TURNER, otp, Spinster
Banns	Banns published: 20 & 27 Nov, & 4 Dec
No. 60	Off. Min.:- Ralph BARNES, Curate
	Wit: John TURNER, William TURNER

2 Jan 1764	William [x] MARTIN, otp, Husbandman, & Mary [x] MANNATT, otp, Spinster
Banns	Banns published: 11, 19 & 25 Dec
No. 61	Off. Min.:- Ralph BARNES
	Wit: John [x] MARTIN, John TURNER

27 Feb 1764	Thomas [x] NICKLIN, otp, Shoemaker, & Anne [x] BUXTON, otp, Spinster
Banns	Banns published: 11, 19 & 26 Feb
No. 62	Off. Min.:- Ralph BARNES, Curate
	Wit: Joseph COLLIER, Thomas FENTON

29 Apr 1765	Richard [x] MORECRAFT, otp, Husbandman, & Elizabeth [x] GREEN, otp, Spinster
Banns	Banns published: 14, 21 & 28 Apr
No. 63	Off. Min.:- Saml. Langley, R'r of Checkley
	Wit: George GREEN, John TURNER

4 Jul 1765	William OSBORN [s. Osbourn], P. of Kingston, Husbandman, & Hannah [x] BLOOD, otp, Spinster
Lic.	Off. Min.:- Saml. Langley R'r of Checkley
No. 64	Wit: John LOWE, John TURNER

10 Sep 1765	George PHILLIPS, P. of Leigh, & Mary GILBERT
Lic.	Off. Min.:- Geo: HANCOCK, Rector
No. 65	Wit: Thos. BELCHER, John GILBERT Junior

~~23 Dec 1765~~	~~Samuel ALCOCK, Singleman, & Mary PHILLIPS, Spinster, botp~~
~~Banns~~	~~Banns published: 24 Nov, 1 & 16 Dec 1765 by Geo: Jolland, Cl.~~
	[Entry not signed or witnessed and crossed through]

23 Dec 1765	John [x] BAGNAL, otp, Singleman, & Jane [x] TUNNYCLIFF, otp, Spinster
Banns	Banns published: 1, 8 & 15 Dec 1765
No. 66	Off. Min.:- Geo: HANCOCK, R'r of Bromshall
	Wit: John TUNIECLEFF, Mary SPOONER

23 Dec 1765	Samuel ALLCOCK & Mary [x] PHILLIPS, botp
Banns.	Off. Min.:- Geo: HANCOCK, R'r of ....
No. 67	Wit: Philip TITLEY, John TURNER

30 Dec 1765	William RIDDELL, P. of Hanbury, Singleman, & Dorothy HART, otp, Spinster
Lic.	Off. Min.:- Geo: Jolland, Cl.
No. 68	Wit: John SHERRATT, John TURNER

26 Mar 1766	Richard HEWITT, otp, Widower, & Elisabeth [x] WOOD, otp, Widow
Banns	Banns published: 9, 16 & 23 Mar 1766
No. 69	Off. Min.:- Geo: Jolland, Curate
	Wit: John BRINDLEY, Simon FOWLER

14 Jul 1766	Ellis [x] BEALEY & Anne [x] MANIFOLD, botp
Banns	Off. Min.:- Edward SHAW
No. 70	Wit: John TURNER, Francis [x] TUNSTALL

11 Aug 1766	Thomas SALT, otp, Singleman, & Elisabeth [x] ROBOTHAM, otp, Widow
Banns	Banns published: 27 Jul, 3 & 10 Aug 1766
No. 71	Off. Min.:- Geo: Jolland, Curate
	Wit: Jane JORDAN, Ann BRINDLEY

28 Oct 1766	James [x] PERKIN, otp, Singleman, & Mary SPOONER, otp, Spinster
Banns	Banns published: 14, 21 & 28 Sep 1766
No. 72	Off. Min.:- Geo: Jolland, Curate
	Wit: Elizabeth GILBERT, John GILBERT

13 Jan 1767	Samuel COPE, otp, Singleman, & Elisabeth [x] HIDE, otp, Singlewoman
Banns	Banns published: 29 Dec 1766 & 4 & 11 Jan 1767
No. 73	Off. Min.:- Geo: Jolland, Curate
	Wit: Thomas HOLLINS, William COPE

19 Jan 1767	Robert [x] HORN otp, Widower & Ann [x] MILNER otp Singlewoman
Banns	Banns published: 28 Dec 1765 & 4 & 11 Jan 1767
No. 74	Off. Min.:- Geo: Jolland, Curate
	Wit: Joseph TURNER, Thomas WOODWARD

2 Feb 1767	Edward HOLLINGWORTH, otp, Farmer, & Ann [x] HOLLINS, otp, Singlewoman
Lic.	
No. 75	Off. Min.:- Geo: Jolland, Curate
	Wit: Robt. HOLLINGWORTH, William [x] WRIGHT

22 Feb 1767	Thomas CHELL, otp, Bachelor, & Margaret [x] JOHNSON, otp, Spinster
Banns	Banns published: 1, 8 & 15 Feb 1767
No. 76	Off. Min.:- Walter Bagot, Rector
	Wit: Thomas CHELL, Robert JOHNSON

20 Apr 1767	Edward [x] HOWARD, otp, Widower, & Mary [x] BILLINGS, otp, Widow
Banns	Banns published: 5, 12 & 19 Apr 1767
No. 77	Off. Min.:- Geo: Jolland, Curate
	Wit: Elizabeth GILBERT, Hannah DONE

26 May 1767	Peter MOOR, otp, Baker, & Martha [x] JOHNSON, otp, Spinster
Banns	Banns published: 3, 10 & 17 May 1767
No. 78	Off. Min.:- Thos. KEELING, Curate
	Wit: Joseph TURNER, Samuel COPE

20 Jul 1767	William WARRAM, Sojourner in this Parish, & Mary [x] BERRESFORD, otp, Spinster
Banns	Banns published: 5, 12 & 19 Jul 1767
No. 79	Off. Min.:- Geo: HANCOCK, Rector
	Wit: Joseph TURNER, John GILBERT

9 Nov 1767	John NUTT, otp, Singleman, & Margaret [x] DANIEL, otp, Spinster
Banns	Banns published: 16, 23 & 30 Aug 1767
No. 80	Off. Min.:- Geo: Jolland, Curate
	Wit: John [x] HEATON, John TURNER

| No. 81 | Banns of marriage between Thomas TURNER & Elisabeth ROBINSON, botp were published 4th, 11 th & 18th October 1767 |
| | By:- Geo: Jolland, Curate |

9 Nov 1767	Job [x] RUSHTON, otp, Singleman, & Ann SALT, otp, Spinster
Banns	Banns published: 25 Oct, 1 & 8 Nov
No. 82	Off. Min.:- Geo: Jolland, Curate
	Wit: Thomas COPE, John TURNER

14 Nov 1767	Robert PHILLIPS, otp Widower, & Sarah [x] HOUGHFORD, otp, Spinster
Lic.	
No. 83	Off. Min.:- Geo: Jolland, Curate
	Wit: John GILBERT, John TURNER

3 Dec 1767	Samuel TURNER, otp, Singleman, & Elisabeth [s. Ellizebth] HOLLINS
Lic.	
No. 84	Off. Min.:- Geo: Jolland, Curate
	Wit: Thomas HOLLINS, John TURNER

8 Dec 1767	John HOWE, otp, Singleman, & Ellen [x] TURNER, otp, Spinster
Banns	Banns published: 15, 22 & 29 Nov 1767
No. 85	Off. Min.:- Geo: Jolland, Curate
	Wit: John TURNER, William MARSON

16 Feb 1768	Thomas Wharton ORME, of Combridge in the P. of Rocester, &
Lic.	Mary BLURTON, otp, Spinster
No. 86	Off. Min.:- Geo: Jolland, Curate
	Wit: Edward BLURTON, Thos. BLURTON

16 Feb 1768	William DUMOLO, P. of Uttoxeter, Widower, & Elizabeth [x]
Lic.	PHILLIPS, otp, Spinster
No. 87	Off. Min.:- Geo: Jolland, Curate
	Wit: Thos. DAVIES, Thos. PHILLIPS

| No. 88 | Banns of Marriage between Simon FOWLER, otp, Singleman, & Jane WOOD, of P. of Checkley were published 17 & 24 Apr & 1 May 1768 |
| | By:- Geo: Jolland, Curate |

18 Jul 1768	Thomas TOOTH, otp, Singleman, & Prudence [x] TURNER, otp, Singlewoman
Banns	Banns published: 12, 19 & 26 Jun 1768
No. 89	Off. Min.:- Geo: Jolland, Curate
	Wit: Richard FOWLER, John TURNER

29 Jul 1768	Richard FOWLER, otp, Singleman, & Hannah MOORE, otp, Singlewoman
Banns	Banns published: 19 & 26 Jun, & 3 Jul
No. 90	Off. Min.:- Geo: Jolland, Curate
	Wit: Elizabeth GILBERT, Joseph TURNER

30 Sep 1768	John COLLIER, otp, Singleman, & Ellen BLURTON, otp, Widow
Lic.	Off. Min.:- Geo: Jolland, Curate
No. 91	Wit: Thos HOWE, Elisabeth JOLLAND

| No. 92 | Banns of Marriage between William FROST otp & Elisabeth MURRY of the P. of Checkley, were published 18 23 & 30 Oct 1768 |
| | By:- Geo: Jolland, Curate |

22 Dec 1768	John GILBERT Junr. otp Singleman & Hannah COPE otp, Spinster
Banns	Banns published: 4, 11 & 18 Dec 1768
No. 93	Off. Min.:- Geo: Jolland, Curate
	Wit: Wm. BELCHER, Edwd. COPE

26 Jan 1769	Edward COPE, otp, Singleman, & Elisabeth [x] MARSTON, otp, Spinster
Banns	Banns published: 18 & 25 Dec 1768 & 1 Jan 1769
No. 94	Off. Min.:- Geo: Jolland, Curate
	Wit: John GILBERT Junr., John TURNER

6 Feb 1769	Thomas STOKES, P. of Uttoxeter, Widower, & Mary BAILEY, otp, Widow
Banns	Banns published: 8, 15 & 22 Jan 1769
	[no signatures & entry crossed through]
	A certificate given

28 Jun 1769	James [x] PEERS, otp, Singleman, & Judith [x] BRIERHURST, otp, Spinster
Banns	Banns published: 11, 18 & 25 Jun 1769
No. 95	Off. Min.:- Geo: Jolland, Curate
	Wit: Thomas CHELL, John TURNER

1 Aug 1769	John [x] BURTON otp, Singleman, & Mary [x] DAYKIN, otp Spinster
Banns	Banns published: 16, 23 & 30 Jul 1769
No. 96	Off. Min.:- Geo: Jolland, Curate
	Wit: Joseph TURNER, Mary BELCHER, William EDG

No. 97	Banns of Marriage between John DOLPHIN of the P. of Uttoxeter, & Elisabeth BILLINGS otp, were published 18 & 25 Sep & 1 Oct 1769
	A certificate given
	By:- Geo: Jolland, Curate

23 Oct 1769 Banns No. 98	Thomas [x] ELKINS, P. of Milwich, Singleman, & Ann [x] SNAPE, otp, Spinster Banns published: 8, 15 & 22 Oct 1769 Off. Min.:- Geo: Jolland, Curate Wit: William [x] RAWLINS, Joseph TURNER
14 Nov 1769 Banns No. 99	John [x] SALT, P. of Dilhorne, Singleman, & Mary [x] SAUNDERS, otp, Spinster Banns published: 22 & 29 Oct, & 5 Nov 1769 Off. Min.:- Geo: Jolland, Curate Wit: John ROWBOTHAM, Joseph TURNER
No. 100	Banns of Marriage between Ralph TURNER otp, & Hannah HOLLINS, of the P. of Uttoxeter were published 12, 19 & 26 Nov 1769. A certificate granted July 1st 1770 By:- Geo: Jolland, Curate
30 Nov 1769 Banns No. 101	Thomas [x] WRIGHT, otp, Singleman, & Ann [x] PHILLIPS, otp, Spinster Banns published: 12, 19 & 26 Nov 1769 Off. Min.:- Geo: Jolland, Curate Wit: Hannah FOWLER, Joseph TURNER
28 Nov 1769 Banns No. 102	Thomas BARKER, otp, Singleman, & Sarah WOODWARD, otp, Spinster Banns published: 12, 19 & 26 Nov 1769 Off. Min.:- Geo: Jolland, Curate Wit: John TURNER, Josep TURNER
1 Dec 1769 Banns No. 103	Anthony RUSHTON, otp, Singleman, & Sarah [x] WOOLLEY, otp, Spinster Banns published: 12, 19 & 26 Nov 1769 Off. Min.:- Geo: Jolland, Curate Wit: Joseph WEBB, Joseph TURNER
No. 104	Banns of Marriage between William SMITH otp, & Ann SMITH, of the P. of Checkley, were published 26 Nov, 3 & 10 Dec 1769 A Certificate granted By:- Geo: Jolland, Curate
24 Dec 1769 Banns No. 105	Charles [x] BUDWORTH, P. of Uttoxeter, Singleman, & Martha [x] Woolley, otp, Spinster Banns published: 3, 10 & 17 Dec 1769 Off. Min.:- Geo: Jolland, Curate Wit: Joseph TURNER, George [x] WOOLLEY
29 Jan 1770 Banns No. 106	John [x] BAGNAL, otp, Singleman, & Sarah [x] RATCLIFFE, otp, Spinster Banns published: 7, 14 & 21 Jan 1770 Off. Min.:- Geo: Jolland, Curate Wit: John DONE, John TURNER
12 Feb 1770 Banns No. 107	John [x] HALL, otp, Singleman, & Elisabeth [x] PHILLIPS, otp, Spinster Banns published: 21 & 28 Jan & 11 Feb 1770 Off. Min.:- Geo: Jolland, Curate Wit: John DONE, Joseph TURNER
16 Apr 1770 Banns No. 108	Isaac ASH, P. of Kingsley, Singleman, & Mary HUNT, otp, Spinster Banns published: 1, 8 & 15 Apr 1770 Off. Min.:- Geo: Jolland, Curate Wit: Edward BURTON, Mary SMITH

10 Sep 1770	Matthew PORTER, otp, Singleman, & Jane [x] BRADBURY, otp, Singlewoman
Banns No. 109	Banns published: 26 Aug, 2 & 9 Sep 1770 Off. Min.:- Geo: Jolland, Curate Wit: Lydia COPE, John TURNER
8 Oct 1770	George WOOLLEY, otp, Singleman, & Mary [x] LEES, otp, Singlewoman
Banns No. 110	Banns published: 16, 23 & 30 Sep 1770 Off. Min.:- Geo: Jolland, Curate Wit: John [x] EATON, Elisabeth [x] WOOLLEY
18 Oct 1770	Thomas [x] LYNN, otp, Singleman, & Ann [x] SWINSON, otp, Singlewoman
Banns No. 111	Banns published: 30 Sep, 7 & 14 Oct 1770 Off. Min.:- Geo: Jolland, Curate Wit: Thomas WOODWARD, Joseph TURNER
No. 112	Banns of Marriage between William FROST otp, & Elisabeth HOLLINS of P. of Checkley, were published 28 Oct, 4 & 11 Nov Certificate was granted Nov 22 1770 By:- Geo: Jolland, Curate
No. 113	Banns of Marriage between Joshua PRESTON Junr. otp, & Mary LAUGHTON of P. of Bramshall were published 2, 9 & 16 Dec 1770 A Certificate was granted Dec 18 1770 By:- G.J.
7 Feb 1771 Lic. No. 114	William WHIELDON [s. Junr.], P. of Cheddleton, in Co., Stafford, Grasier, & Ann BLURTON, otp, Spinster Off. Min.:- Geo: Jolland Wit: John BLURTON Junr., Robert BLURTON Curate
12 Feb 1771	Joseph COLLIER, otp, Singleman, & Elisabeth MARSTON [s. Elizabeth], otp, Spinster
Banns No. 115	Banns published: 2, 9 & 16 Dec 1770 Off. Min.:- Geo: Jolland, Curate Wit: William MARSON, Joseph TURNER
1 Apr 1771	Charles [x] BENTELEY *[Bently-BT]*, P. of Uttoxeter, Singleman, & Ann HOLLINGWORTH, otp, Spinster
Banns No. 116	Banns published: 3, 10 & 17 Mar 1771 Off. Min.:- Geo: Jolland, Curate Wit: Edward HOLLINGWORTH, Thomasin HOLINDWERITH
1 May 1771	Thomas WOODWARD, otp, Singleman, & Elisabeth [x] LYNN, otp, Spinster
Banns No. 117	Banns published: 14, 21 & 28 Apr 1771 Off. Min.:- Geo: Jolland, Curate Wit: Elizabeth COOKE, Joseph TURNER
11 May 1771 Lic. No. 118	William WALKER, otp, Singleman, & Hannah DONE, otp, Spinster Off. Min.:- Geo: Jolland, Curate Wit: John DONE, Mary DONE
	Banns of Marriage between John MIDDLETON of P. of Colwich, Singleman, & Lydia COPE, otp, Spinster were published 21 & 28 Apr & 5 May 1771 By:- Geo: Jolland, Curate A certificate granted June 20 1771
	Banns of Marriage between John HIGGS otp, Widower, & Mary HUDSON, Widow of P. of Checkley, were published 9, 16 & 23 Jun 1771 By:- Geo: Jolland, Curate A Certificate granted June 23rd 1771

2 Jul 1771	William COPE, otp, & Joice [s. Joyce] THACKER, otp
Banns	Wit: Edwd. COPE, Myry MILWARD
No.119	Off. Min.:- Geo: HANCOCK, Rr

11 Aug 1771	Benjamin [x] MORETON, P. of Cheedle*, Singleman, & Mary [x] GOODALL, otp, Spinster
Banns	Banns published: 14, 21 & 28 Jul 1771
No. 120	Off. Min.:- Walter Bagot, Rector
	Wit: John POYSER, John TURNER
	*altered from Checkley to Cheedle

5 Oct 1771	John BELCHER, otp, Singleman, & Elisabeth JOLLAND, otp, Spinster
Lic.	
No. 121	Off. Min.:- Geo: Jolland, Curate
	Wit: Thos. BELCHER, Cath: JOLLAND

29 Oct 1771	John HALL, otp, Singleman, & Mary [x] BARNETT, otp, Spinster
Banns	Banns published: 13, 20 & 27 Oct 1771
No. 122	Off. Min.:- Geo: Jolland, Curate
	Wit: Charles [x] PAKEMAN, Joseph TURNER

18 Nov 1771	George NOAKE, otp, Singleman, & Hannah [x] WHILTON, otp, Spinster
Banns	Banns published: 27 Oct, 3 & 10 Nov 1771
No. 123	Off. Min.:- Geo: Jolland, Curate
	Wit: Ellen [x] ROBINSON, John TURNER

15 Dec 1771	John SALT, otp, Singleman, & Mary [x] TURNER, otp, Spinster
Banns	Banns published: 17 & 24 Nov & 1 Dec 1771
No. 124	Off. Min.:- Geo: Jolland, Curate
	Wit: Edward BREWERTON, Joseph TURNER

23 Dec 1771	Frederick [x] RUSHTON, otp, Singleman, & Jane [x] HOUGH, P. of Draycott, Spinster
Banns	Banns published: 30 Nov, 6 & 13 Dec 1771
No. 125	Off. Min.:- Geo: Jolland, Curate
	Wit: George [x] RUSHTON, James TURNER

4 Jan 1772	John BERKIN [s. Birkin], P. of Milwich, Singleman, & Hannah [x] MARSON or MARSTON, otp, Spinster
Lic.	
No. 126	Off. Min.:- Geo: Jolland, Curate
	Wit: Edward COPE, Joseph TURNER

26 Feb 1772	Ralph WALKER, P. of Alvington in this County, Singleman, & Dorothy MARSTON [s. Marson], otp, Spinster
Lic.	
No. 127	Off. Min.:- Geo: Jolland, Curate
	Wit: Tho MASON, John TURNER

	Banns of Marriage between Robert TUNNICLIFF otp, Singleman, & Elisabeth VICARSTAFF of P. of Alventon, Spinster, were published in this church 9, 18 & 23 Feb 1772
	By:- Geo: Jolland, Curate
	Certificate was given on 26 Feb 1772

	Banns of Marriage between Francis PHILLIPS, otp, Singleman, & Mary BLOOD, of P. of Checkley, were published 19 & 26 April & 3 May 1772
	By:- Geo: Jolland, Curate

12 Jul 1772	William HIBBERT [s. Hibberd] otp, Singleman, & Ann HAWLEY, otp, Spinster
Banns	Banns published: 25 & 28 June & 5 July 1772
No. 127 (sic)	Off. Min.:- Geo: Jolland, Curate
	Wit: Sarah BLOOD, Joseph TURNER

23 Jul 1772 Banns No. 128	Thomas COPE, otp, Widower, & Ann [x] TATTON, otp, Spinster Banns published: 5, 12 & 19 Jul 1772 Off. Min.:- Geo: Jolland, Curate Wit: John HOWE, John KEELING
27 Jul 1772 Banns No. 129	Thomas BUCKLEY, otp, Singleman, & Hannah [x] FEARNE, otp, Spinster Banns published: 5, 12 & 19 Jul 1772 Off. Min.:- Geo: Jolland, Curate Wit: John BARNES, Samuel BLORE
10 Aug 1772 Banns No. 130	William [x] HARPUR, P. of Uttoxeter, Widower, & Ann [x] PALMER, otp, Spinster Banns published: 26 Jul, 2 & 9 Aug 1772 Off. Min.:- Geo: Jolland, Curate Wit: Mrs KENDRICK, John HARPER
12 Oct 1772 Banns No. 131	John JOHNSON, otp, Singleman, & Hannah [x] RUSHTON, otp, Spinster Banns published: 26 Jul, 2 & 9 Aug 1772 Off. Min.:- Geo: Jolland, Curate Wit: John BELCHER, Joseph TURNER
	Banns of Marriage between William MARSTON Junr., & Sarah BEECH, were published 11, 18 & 25 Oct 1772 By:- Geo: Jolland, Curate Certificate was given on the 8 Nov 1772 for the Rector
4 Nov 1772 Lic. No. 133	Thomas LOWNDES, otp, Widower, & Mary [x] WALKER, otp, Spinster Off. Min.:- Geo: Jolland, Curate Wit: William WALKER, Hugh MELLOR
14 Nov 1772 Banns No. 134	William DUROSE, otp, Singleman, & Ann [x] RATCLIFFE, otp, Spinster Banns published: 25 Oct, 1 & 16 Nov 1772 Wit: Thomas LOWNDES, Hannah HOLLONS
No. 137	Banns of Marriage between Thomas PARKER otp & Mary HAWLEY, of P. of Checkley were published 8, 15 & 22 Nov 1772 Certificate was given on 22 Nov 1772 By:- Geo: Jolland, Curate
8 Dec 1772 Banns No. 138	George JOHNSON the Elder, otp, Widower, & Sarah [x] HOUGH, otp, Spinster Banns published: 15, 22 & 29 Nov 1772 Off. Min.:- Geo: Jolland, Curate Wit: Thomas CHELL, Joseph TURNER
No. 139	Banns of Marriage between Joseph DEWROSE & Margaret STRONGITHARM were published 3, 10 & 17 Jan 1773. By:- Geo: Jolland, Curate
14 Jul 1773 Banns No. 140	Samuel [x] SHENTON, otp, Singleman, & Mary [x] THORNIWELL otp, Spinster Banns published: 10, 17 & 24 Jan 1773 Off. Min.:- Geo: Jolland, Curate Wit: John DONE, Joseph TURNER
11 Apr 1773 Banns No. 141	John KEELING the younger, otp, Singleman, & Mary [x] COPE, otp, Spinster Banns published: 21 & 28 Mar, & 4 Apr 1773 Off. Min.:- Geo: Jolland, Curate Wit: Elisabeth [x] PERKIN, Joseph TURNER

19 Apr 1773 Lic. No. 142	George [x] ASTBURY, P. of Gayton in Co. Stafford, Singleman, & Mary LEES, otp, Spinster Off. Min.:- Geo: Jolland, Curate Wit: John TURNER, John LEES
No. 143	Banns of Marriage between George RUSHTON, otp, Singleman, & Sarah WRIGHT, Spinster, of the P. of Stone, were published 16, 23 & 30 May 1773 By:- Geo: Jolland, Curate A Certificate was granted on the 15th Sep 1773 G.J.
14 Jun 1773 Banns No. 144	Thomas CHELL, otp, Husbandman, [Singleman-BT], & Mary BARKER, Spinster, otp, of Checkley Banns published: 23 & 29 May & 6 Jun 1773 Off. Min.:- Saml. Langley, Rector Wit: John TURNER, Joseph TURNER
For the marriage of Saml. SHENTON & Mary THORNIWELL see back to 140	
16 Sep 1773 Banns No. 145	Joseph [x] BAILEY, otp, Widower, & Mary [x] BAILEY, otp, Widow Banns published: 15, 22 & 29 Aug 1773 Off. Min.:- Geo: Jolland, Curate Wit: Joseph TURNER, Ralph [x] RUSHTON
25 Oct 1773 Banns No. 146	George [x] HOWE, otp, Singleman, & Elisabeth [s. Elizabeth] WOOLLEY, P. of Checkley, Spinster Banns published: 26 Sep, 3 & 10 Oct 1773 Off. Min.:- Geo: Jolland, Curate Wit: Thomas CHELL, John TURNER
1 Nov 1773 Banns No. 147	Thomas FENTON, otp, Widower, & Mary [x] DAYKIN, otp, Widow Banns published: 10, 17 & 24 Oct 1773 Off. Min.:- Geo: Jolland, Curate Wit: Dorothy JACKSON, Thomas [x] MOTTERAM
No. 148	Banns of Marriage between John CARTER, p. of Stone, & Lucy BAILEY were published 10, 17 & 24 Nov 1773. By:- Geo: Jolland A Certificate granted on 27 Oct by me.. G.J. Curate

1 Nov 1773
 	
Banns
No. 149
	Elias SIMMS [s. Sims], otp, Singleman, & Mary [x] HARRISON, otp,
	Spinster
	Banns published: 17, 24 & 31 Oct 1773
	Off. Min.:- Geo: Jolland, Curate
	Wit: William JOHNSON, John TURNER
	    N.B. This couple came out of Darbyshire & resided at Thomas Phillips's in
	                this Parish, till they might be married in this
	                Church without offending against the Marriage Acts. G.J.

3 Nov 1773 Banns No. 150	William [x] CARTER, otp, Singleman, & Ellen [x] ROBINSON, otp, Spinster Banns published: 17, 24 & 31 Oct 1773 Off. Min.:- Geo: Jolland, Curate Wit: Elisabeth [x] DAYKIN, Phillip CROSBY
4 Nov 1773 Banns No. 151	Richard [x] SMITH, otp, Widower, & Mary [x] STOAKES, otp, Spinster Banns published: 17, 24 & 31 Oct 1773 Off. Min.:- Geo: Jolland, Curate Wit: Thomas CHELL, Joseph TURNER
13 Nov 1773 Lic. No. 152	John SHERRATT, otp, Singleman, & Jane MILWARD, otp, Spinster Off. Min.:- Geo: Jolland, Curate Wit: Thos. PHILLIPS, Margret PHILLIPS

No. 153	Banns of Marriage between John TURNER, P. of Stoke, Singleman, & Sarah ARMSTRONG, otp, Spinster, were published 12, 19 & 26 Dec 1773 By:- Geo: Jolland, Curate A Certificate was given on 31 Dec 1773 G.J.
No. 154	Banns of Marriage between Francis BYARD, Singleman, of the P. of Alveton, & Dorothy RATCLIFF, otp, Spinster, were published 19 & 26 Dec 1773 & 2 Jan 1774. By:- Geo: Jolland, Curate [whole entry crossed through]
19 May 1774 Lic. No. 155	Joseph [x] COPE, otp, Singleman, & Mary [x] BILLINGS, otp, Spinster Off. Min.:- Geo: Jolland, Curate Wit: John KEELING, Joseph TURNER
23 May 1774 Lic. No. 156	James TURNER, otp, Singleman, & Hannah [x] MARSTON, otp, Spinster Off. Min.:- Geo: Jolland, Curate Wit: James MARSON, Elisabeth [x] FOWLER
27 Jun 1774 Lic. No.157	Francis [x] BYARD, P. of Alveton, & Dorothy [x] RATCLIFF, otp Wit: Thomas PERKIN, John TURNER Off. Min.:- Geo: Jolland, Curate
17 Oct 1774 No. 158 See below	Joseph [x] MOORE, P. of Leigh, & Eliz: [x] BETTERNEY Off. Min.:- Geo: H'k, R'r: Bromshall Wit: John TURNER, Elizabeth SPOONER
17 Oct 1774 Banns No. 158	Joseph MOORE, otp, Singleman, & Elisabeth BETTERNEY, otp, Spinster Banns published: 25 Sep, 2 & 9 Oct 1774 Off. Min.:- Geo; HANCOCK, Rector of Bramshall Wit: John TURNER, Elisabeth SPOONER <div align="right">The entry above was transcribed on the 17th day of October 1774 by me Geo: Jolland Curate</div>
4 Nov 1774 Lic. No. 159	Thomas [x] SANDERS, P. of St. Mary in Stafford Draycot in this County, Singleman, & Jane [x] BAILEY, otp, Spinster Off. Min.:- Geo: Jolland, Curate Wit: James YATES, James TURNER
27 Dec 1774 Banns No. 160	William NUTT, P. of Checkley, Singleman, & Elisabeth [x] PERKIN, otp, Spinster Banns published: 20 & 27 Nov & 4 Dec 1774 Off. Min.:- Geo: Jolland, Curate Wit: Thomas JOHNSON, James TURNER
	Banns of Marriage between John FORRESTER, Singleman, & Sarah LEES, Widow, were published 18 & 25 Dec 1774 & 1 Jan 1775 By:- Geo: Jolland, Curate
23 Feb 1775 Lic. No. 161	Joseph LYCETT, P. of St. Mary in Stafford, Singleman, & Elisabeth BLURTON, otp, Spinster Off. Min.:- Geo: Jolland, Curate Wit: Thos. BLURTON, Lydia BLURTON
5 Jun 1775 Banns No. 162	George [x] STEVENSON, otp, Singleman, & Martha [x] THORNIWELL, otp, Spinster Banns published: 9, 16 & 23 Apr 1775 Off. Min.:- Geo: Jolland, Curate Wit: Dorothy [x] STEVENSON, James TURNER

	Banns of Marriage between John BAMFORD, of Draycot & Elisabeth RATCLIFFE, otp, were published 28 May, 4 & 11 Jun 1775. By:- Geo: Jolland, Curate
	Banns of Marriage between Joseph DAYKIN, otp, Singleman, & Dorothy ALLEN, P. of Checkly, Spinster, were published 29 Oct, 5 & 12 Nov 1775 By:- Geo: Jolland, Curate
	Banns of Marriage between William PHILIPS otp, & Mary TUNNICLIFF, P. of Rocester, were published 28 Jan, 4 & 11 Feb 1776 By:- Tho: Browne Curate
25 Mar 1776 Banns No. 163	Gervas SNAPE, P. of Checkley, Singleman, & Mary [x] ROBINSON, otp, Spinster Banns published: 10, 17 & 24 Mar 1776 Off. Min.:- Tho: Browne, Curate Wit: Thomas ROBINSON, James TURNER
15 Apr 1776 Banns No. 164	John [x] WHITEHURST, otp, Singleman, & Mary [x] SHEMILT, otp, Spinster Banns published: 31 Mar, 7 & 14 Apr 1776 Off. Min.:- Tho: Browne, Curate Wit: John SCOTT, Elizabeth THACKER
2 Jul 1776 Banns No. 165	George [x] WALKER, otp, Husbandman, & Ellen [x] HAWLEY, otp, Spinster Banns published: 16, 23 & 30 Jun 1776 Off. Min.:- Saml. Langley R'r of Checkley Wit: Joseph TURNER, Wm. TURNER
9 Aug 1776 Banns No. 166	George [x] TOOTH, otp, Widower, & Hannah [x] LOWNDES, otp, Spinster Banns published: 7, 14 & 21 Jul 1776 Off. Min.:- Tho: Browne, Curate Wit: John TURNER, James TURNER
15 Aug 1776 Banns No. 168	Benjamin [x] ALLEN, otp, Singleman, & Elizabeth [x] BURTON, otp, Spinster Banns published: 21 & 28 Jul, & 4 Aug 1776 Off. Min.:- Tho: Browne, Curate Wit: James TURNER, Joseph TURNER
9 Aug 1776 Lic. No. 167	John [x] BRADSHAW, P. of Yedleston in the County of Derby, Farmer, & Mary SMITH, otp, Spinster Off. Min.:- Tho: Browne, Curate Wit: Thomas SMITH, Ann SMITH
	Banns of Marriage between Samuel MIDDLETON & Mary GOODWIN, botp, were published 11, 18 & 25 Aug 1776. By:- Tho: Browne, Curate
	Banns of Marriage between Thomas ARNOT otp, & Elizabeth GIBSON P. of Cheadle were published 13, 20 & 27 Oct 1776. By:- Tho: Browne, Curate
15 Nov 1776 Lic. No. 168	William HAYWOOD, P. of Colwich, Farmer, & Jane [x] CHARLESWORTH, otp, Spinster & Minor, wco her Father Off. Min.:- Tho: Browne, Curate Wit: Francis CHAMBERLAIN, John CHARLESWORTH
18 Nov 1776 Li c. No. 169	John CHARLESWORTH, otp, Farmer, & Mary MILLINGTON, otp, Spinster Off. Min.:- Tho: Browne, Curate Wit: Thomas TUNNICLIFF, Sarah BLOORE

23 Dec 1776	Joseph [x] KIRK, otp, Singleman, & Ellen [x] HALL, o.t.p, Spinster
Banns	Banns published: 17 & 24 Nov & 1 Dec 1776
No. 171	Off. Min.:- Tho: Browne, Curate
	Wit: John TURNER, Joseph TURNER

23 Dec 1776	John [x] PHILIPS, P. of Checkley, Singleman, & Hannah [x] RATCLIFF, otp, Spinster
Banns	Banns published: 8, 15 & 22 Dec 1776
No. 170	Off. Min.:- Tho: Browne, Curate
	Wit: John TURNER, James TURNER

14 Jan 1777	Simon [x] COPE, P. of Gratwich, Singleman, & Elizabeth [x] EDGE, otp, Spinster
Banns	Banns published: 15, 22 & 29 Dec 1776
No. 173	Off. Min.:- Tho: Browne, Curate
	Wit: John BABB, John TURNER

6 Jan 1777	James Hollins [x] MOTRAM, otp, Singleman, & Ann [x] BRADSHAW, otp, Spinster
Banns	Banns published: 22 & 29 Dec 1776 & 5 Jan 1777
No. 172	Off. Min.:- Tho: Browne, Curate
	Wit: James CARTER, John TURNER

1 Mar 1777	John [x] HEATH, P. of Leek, & a Minor Singleman, & Barbara [x] BAILEY *[Baily-BT]*, otp, Spinster, wco his Father
Lic.	
No. 173	Off. Min.:- Tho: Browne, Curate
	Wit: John TURNER, John KEELING

3 Apr 1777	Thomas COPE, otp, Farmer, & Sarah BLOORE, otp, Spinster
Banns	Banns published: 16, 23 & 30 Mar 1777
No. 174	Off. Min.:- Tho: Browne, Curate
	Wit: John COPE, Ellen BLOORE

22 Apr 1777	John [x] ALLCOCK, otp, Singleman, & Mary HEATON, otp, Spinster
Banns	Banns published: 16, 23 & 30 Mar 1777
No. 176	Off. Min.:- Tho: Browne, Curate
	Wit: Charles ALLCOCK, Samuel ALLCOCK

15 Apr 1777	Joseph ASTBURY, otp, Widower, & Mary [x] HOWE, otp
Banns	Banns published: 16, 23 & 30 Mar 1777
No. 175	Off. Min.:- Tho: Browne, Curate
	Wit: James TURNER, Joseph TURNER

17 May 1777	Samuel LAKIN, otp, & Elizabeth RAWLINS, otp
Banns	Banns published: 6, 13 & 20 Apr 1777
No. 176	Off. Min.:- Tho: Browne, Curate
	Wit: John LOVATT, Mary LOVATT

7 Jun 1777	Robert BULL, P. of Checkley, Singleman, & Elizabeth COOK, otp, Spinster
Banns	Banns published: 18 & 25 May & 1 Jun 1777
No. 177	Off. Min.:- Tho: Browne, Curate
	Wit: John COPE, James TURNER

16 Jul 1777	Middleton [x] ROBOTHAM, otp, Singleman, & Mary [x] JOHNSON, otp, Spinster
Banns	Banns published: 25 May, 8 & 15 Jun 1777
No. 178	Off. Min.:- Tho: Browne, Curate
	Wit: John TURNER, George LAUGHTON

3 Jul 1777	John ROBINSON, P. of Draycot, Singleman, & Ellen [x] BRIDGEWOOD, otp, Spinster
Banns	Banns published: 15, 22 & 29 Jun 1777
No. 179	Off. Min.:- Tho: Browne, Curate
	Wit: Joseph TURNER, Thomas ROBINSON

3 Mar 1778	John BAMFORD, otp, Singleman, & Elizabeth [x] RATCLIFF, otp, Spinster
Banns No. 183	Banns published: 28 Sep, 5 & 12 Oct 1777 Off. Min.:- Tho: Browne, Curate Wit: Mary [x] BLOUD, James TURNER
4 Nov 1777	Joseph [x] TAFT, otp, Singleman, & Ann [x] WOOD, otp, Spinster
Banns No. 180	Banns published: 19 & 26 Oct & 2 Nov 1777 Off. Min.:- Tho: Browne, Curate Wit: Joseph WOOD, William YARDLEY
	Banns of Marriage between William CHARLESWORTH otp, & Sarah BIRCH of P. of Uttoxeter were published 9, 16 & 23 Nov 1777 By:- Tho: Browne, Curate
23 Dec 1777	George WALKER otp, Taylor, & Edith [x] BLOORE, otp, Spinster
Banns No. 181	Banns published: 7, 14 & 21 Dec 1777 Off. Min.:- Tho: Browne, Curate Wit: Thomas CARTER, Thomas LOWNDES
7 Feb 1778	Joseph [x] SMITH, otp, Widower, & Ann [x] HOWARD, otp, Spinster
Banns No. 183	Banns published: 11, 18 & 25 Jan 1778 Off. Min.:- Tho: Browne, Curate Wit: Thomas TOOTH, John TURNER
5 Feb 1778	John MELLOR [s. Meller], otp, Singleman, & Elizabeth [x] HOWE, otp, Spinster
Banns No. 182	Banns published: 18 & 25 Jan & 1 Feb 1778 Off. Min.:- Tho: Browne, Curate Wit: Thomas CHELL, James TURNER
4 Jun 1778	James CARTER, otp, Singleman, & Ann [x] SLANEY, otp, Spinster
Banns No. 184	Banns published: 18 & 25 Jan & 1 Feb 1778 Off. Min.:- Tho: Browne, Curate Wit: John TURNER, Joseph TURNER
20 Aug 1778	Thomas [x] BROOKE, otp, Singleman, & Ann [x] TUNSTAL, otp, Spinster
Banns No. 185	Banns published: 19 & 26 Jul & 2 Aug 1778 Off. Min.:- Tho: Browne, Curate Wit: John TURNER, Samale BROMLY
1 Sep 1778	Thomas HEATH, otp, Singleman, & Mary [x] BOX, otp, Spinster
Banns No. 186	Banns published: 9, 16 & 23 Aug 1778 Off. Min.:- Tho: Browne, Curate Wit: Joseph TURNER, Sampson PROCTER
19 Oct 1778	John [x] PLIMMER, otp, Singleman, & Mary Bailey [x] THACKER, otp, Spinster
Banns No. 187	Banns published: 4, 11 & 18 Oct 1778 Off. Min.:- Tho: Browne, Curate Wit: James TURNER, Thomas COPE
7 Dec 1778	Thomas [x] KENT, otp, Singleman, & Sarah [x] GOOSETREE, otp, Spinster
Lic. No. 188	Off. Min.:- Tho: Browne, Curate Wit: Richard HOWE, James TURNER
26 Dec 1778	William [x] RUSHTON, otp, Singleman, & Ellen [x] MIDDLETON, otp, Spinster
Banns No. 189	Banns published: 6, 13 & 20 Dec 1778 Off. Min.:- Tho: Browne, Curate Wit: Edwd. BLURTON, J. GILBERT
9 Dec 1778	John GILBERT the younger was nominated Parish Clerk by the Reverend Mr. Bagot Rector

7 Jan 1779 Lic. No. 190	Thomas TUNNICLIFT, otp, Farmer, & Margaret [s. Margret] PHILLIPS, otp, Spinster Off. Min.:- Tho: Browne, Curate Wit: Francis PHILLIPS, John GILBERT
14 Mar 1779 Banns No. 191	William RAWLINS, otp, Farmer, & Ann [x] BULL, P. of Checkley, Spinster Banns published: 7, 14 & 21 Feb 1779 Off. Min.:- Tho: Browne, Curate Wit: John GILBERT, John TUNNICLIFF
20 Jun 1779 Banns No. 192	Thomas BRUFF, P. of Cheadle, Singleman, & Elizabeth [x] BERRESFORD, otp, Spinster Banns published: 23 & 30 May & 6 Jun 1779 Off. Min.:- Tho: Browne, Curate Wit: John GILBERT, James BERRYSFORD
16 Nov 1779 Banns No. 193	William [x] RUSHTON, otp, Singleman, & Ann [x] BAILEY, otp, Spinster Banns published: 30 Oct, 7 & 14 Nov 1779 Off. Min.:- Tho: Browne, Curate Wit: John GILBERT, Thomas GILBERT
23 Nov 1779 Banns No. 194	Robert [x] REEVES, otp, Singleman, & Ellen [x] SHENTON, otp, Spinster Banns published: 7, 14 & 21 Nov 1779 Off. Min.:- Tho: Browne, Curate Wit: Thos. SHENTON, J. GILBERT
6 Mar 1780 Banns No. 195	George THORNEWORK, otp, Singleman, & Abigail [x] SHENTON, otp, Spinster Banns published: 20 & 27 Feb & 5 Mar 1780 Off. Min.:- Tho: Browne, Curate Wit: John GILBERT, Thomas GILBERT
6 Jul 1780 Lic. No. 196	Thomas WOODWARD, otp, Widower, & Mary [x] PHILLIPS, otp, Spinster Off. Min.:- Tho: Browne, Curate Wit: Thos. GRIFFIN, John GILBERT
17 Aug 1780 Lic No. 197.	John LOVATT, otp, Farmer, & Catherine [x] HOWE, otp, Spinster Off. Min.:- Tho: Browne, Curate Wit: Wm. MILNER, Sarah HOWE
7 Sep 1780 Banns No. 199	Francis SHERRAT [s. Sherratt], otp, Singleman, & Sarah [x] MILLINGTON, otp, Spinster Banns published: 13, 20 & 27 Aug 1780 Off. Min.:- Tho: Browne, Curate Wit: Thomas HAWLEY, John GILBERT
4 Sep 1780 Banns No. 198	Ralph KENT, otp, Singleman, Dorothy HOLMES, otp, Spinster Banns published: 20 & 27 Aug & 3 Sep 1780 Off. Min.:- Tho: Browne, Curate Wit: John GILBERT, Tho HOW [?]
25 Sep 1780 Banns No. 200	John HUGHES [s. Hues], otp, Singleman, & Ann [x] SHERRAT, otp, Spinster Banns published: 10, 17 & 24 Sep 1780 Off. Min.:- Tho: Browne, Curate Wit: John COATES, John GILBERT
30 Oct 1780 Banns No. 210	George [x] FLORENCE, otp, Singleman, & Ann [x] BAILEY, otp, Spinster Banns published: 15, 22 & 29 Oct 1780 Off. Min.:- Tho: Browne, Curate Wit: John GILBERT, Thomas CHELL

18 Dec 1780	Joseph NICKLIN, P. of Milwich, Singleman, & Sarah [x] MOORCROFT, otp, Spinster
Banns No. 202	Banns published: 6, 19 & 26 Nov 1780 Off. Min.:- Tho: Browne, Curate Wit: John GILBERT, Robert MOORECRAFT
	Banns of Marriage between William BEARDMORE otp, & Mary CRICHLEY of P. of Draycot were published 3, 10 & 17 Dec 1780 By:- Tho: Browne, Curate
1 Jan 1781	John [x] SWINSON, otp, Singleman, & Elizabeth [x] DEAKIN, o.t.p, Spinster
Banns No. 203	Banns published: 10, 17 & 24 Dec 1780 Off. Min.:- Tho: Browne, Curate Wit: John GILBERT, Thomas SWINSON
1 Jan 1781	John STEVENSON, otp, Singleman, & Phoebe [or Phabe] [x] DEAKIN, otp, Spinster
Banns No. 204	Banns published: 17, 24 & 31 Dec 1780 Off. Min.:- Tho: Browne, Curate Wit: John GILBERT, Marget MITHUS [?]
8 Feb 1781	John [x] BLADON, otp, Singleman, & Elizabeth [x] SALT, P. of Bramshall, Spinster
Banns No. 205	Banns published: 14, 21 & 28 Jan 1781 Off. Min.:- Tho: Browne, Curate Wit: William BLADON, John GILBERT
	Banns of Marriage between William MELLOR otp, & Mary TITLEY, of P. of Checkley were published 18 & 25 Mar & 1 Apr 1781 By:- Tho: Browne, Curate
24 Apr 1781	Benjamin [x] THORLEY, otp, Singleman, & Elizabeth [x] MITCHEL, otp, Spinster
Banns No. 206	Banns published: 25 Mar, 1 & 8 Apr 1781 Off. Min.:- Tho: Browne, Curate Wit: John GILBERT, Thos. TITLEY
14 May 1781	Thomas [x] PLANT, P. of Milwich, Singleman, & Elizabeth [x] BAILEY, otp, Spinster
Banns No. 209	Banns published: 1, 8 & 15 Apr 1781 Off. Min.:- Tho: Browne, Curate John GILBERT, Joseph [x] THACKER
13 May 1781	Thomas BARKER, otp, Widower, & Hannah [x] JOHNSON, otp, Widow
Banns No. 208	Banns published: 22 & 29 Apr & 6 May 1781 Off. Min.:- Tho: Browne, Curate Wit: Edwd. BLURTON. John GILBERT
10 May 1781	Thomas FOSTER, P. of Bramshal, Singleman, & Alice DEAKIN, [s. Eales Dekin], otp, Spinster
Banns No. 207	Banns published: 22 & 29 Apr & 6 May 1781 Off. Min.:- Tho: Browne, Curate Wit: John WETTON, John GILBERT
26 Aug 1781	Thomas WETTON, P. of Bramshal, Widower, & Fanny [x] TILL, otp
Banns No. 209	Off. Min.:- Tho: Browne, Curate Wit: Edwd. BLURTON, John GILBERT
	Banns of Marriage between George REDFEARN of P. of Alstonfield, & Jane BRUERTON, otp, were published 19 & 26 Aug & 2 Sep 1781 By:- Tho: Browne, Curate

8 Nov 1781 Lic. No. 210	William MILNER [s. Millner], P. of Checkley, Singleman, & Sarah HOWE, otp, Spinster Off. Min.:- Tho: Browne, Curate Wit: Thos. EMERY, William MERRY
21 Nov 1781 Lic. No. 211	Edward [x] WOOLLEY, otp, Widower, & Hannah [x] MARSTON, otp, Widow Off. Min.:- Tho: Browne, Curate Wit: John GILBERT, James BERRYSFORD
	Banns of Marriage between William DEAKIN, otp, & Margaret MATTHEWS, of P. of Abbots Bromley were published 9, 16 & 23 Dec 1781 By:- Tho: Browne, Curate
	Banns of Marriage between Thomas MYCOCK otp, & Elizabeth PARKER, of P. of Colwich, were published 16, 23 & 30 Dec 1781 By:- Tho: Browne, Curate
16 Jan 1782 Lic. No. 211	Thomas WILSHAW, P. of Dilhorn, Widower, & Ellen BLOORE, otp,, Spinster Off. Min.:- Tho: Browne, Curate Wit: Wm. MILNER, Samull WILLSHAW
	Banns of Marriage between James MARSTON otp, & Mary BLAKE of P. of Hamstal-Ridware were published 6, 13 & 20 Jan 1782 By:- Tho: Browne, Curate
	Banns of Marriage between John JOHNSON & Margaret SHEMILT botp, were published 13, 20 & 27 Jan 1782. By:- Tho: Browne, Curate
29 Jul 1782 Lic. No. 212	Alexander [x] PERKIN otp, Weaver, & Ellen [x] ROBINSON, otp, Widow Off. Min.:- Tho: Browne, Curate Wit: John GILBERT, William JOHNSON
2 Sep 1782 Lic. No. 213	George BOWRING, P. of Uttoxeter, Widower, & Mary FURBER, otp, Spinster Off. Min.:- Tho: Browne, Curate Wit: William HILL, Mary HILL
22 Sep 1782 Banns No. 214	Daniel TOMLINSON, P. of Barlaston, Farmer, & Mary [x] BAYLEY [Bailey-BT], otp, Spinster Banns published: 26 May, 2 & 9 Jun 1782 Off. Min.:- Walt. Bagot Rector Wit: Thomas TOMLINSON, John GILBERT
11 Oct 1782 Lic. No. 214	Ralph BAGNALL [Bagnal-BT] Gen., P. of Leek Widower, & Miss Ann BRINDLEY, otp, spinster Off. Min.:- Tho: Browne, Curate Wit: T. MILLS Junr. [?], John PHILIPS
21 Oct 1782 Banns No. 215	George [x] GRIFFITH, P. of Milwich, Singleman, & Lydia [x] BAILEY, otp, Spinster Banns published: 6, 13 & 20 Oct 1782 Off. Min.:- Tho: Browne, Curate Wit: John SIMMS, John GILBERT
27 Feb 1783 Lic. No. 216	John ASBURY, otp, Farmer & a Minor, & Sarah WILSHAW, otp, Spinster & a Minor, with consent of their parents Off. Min.:- Tho: Browne Wit: Catharina ASTBURY, James BELCHER Curate
	Banns of Marriage between Job BAKER of P. of Stone & Elizabeth BRUERTON otp, were published 16 & 23 Feb & 2 Mar 1783 By:- Tho: Browne, Curate

12 May 1783	William [x] BAILEY, otp, Singleman, & Margaret [x] SHEMILT, otp, Widow
Banns No. 217	Banns published: 27 Apr, 4 & 11 May 1783 Off. Min.:- Tho: Browne, Curate Wit: Thomas BROWNE, Sarah BROWNE
22 Jul 1783	Edward TITLEY, P. of Checkley, Widower, & Sarah [x] TURNER, otp, Widow
Banns No. 218	Banns published: 6, 13 & 20 Jul 1783 Off. Min.:- Tho: Browne, Curate John GILBERT, James TURNER
25 Sep 1783	Thomas [x] KENT, otp, Singleman, & Elizabeth SPOONER, otp, Spinster
Banns No. 219	Banns published: 24 & 31 Aug & 7 Sep 1783 Off. Min.:- Tho: Browne, Curate Wit: Thomas BROWNE, Thomas GILBERT
27 Dec 1783	Luke BILLINGS [s. Billins], otp, Widower, & Elizabeth [x] BLOOD, otp, Spinster
Banns No. 220	Banns published: 16, 23 & 30 Nov 1783 Off. Min.:- Tho: Browne, Curate Wit: John GILBERT, Honour LEES
19 Feb 1784	John ELSMORE [Elsemore-BT], Chapelry of Fradswall, Farmer, & Mary BRIDGWOOD, otp, Spinster
Banns No. 222	Banns published: 1, 8 & 15 Feb 1784 Off. Min.:- Tho: Browne, Curate Wit: Heny BAKEWELL, John GILBERT
18 Feb 1784	William [x] THORLEY, P. of Draycott, Singleman, & Elizabeth [x] MYOT, otp, Spinster
Lic. No. 221	Off. Min.:- Tho: Browne, Curate Wit: John JOHNSON, Ralph WHILOCKS
20 Apr 1784	William [x] ADAMS, otp, Farmer, & Ellen [x] PARKER, otp, Spinster
Banns No. 223	Banns published: 28 Mar, 4 & 11 Apr 1784 Off. Min.:- Tho: Browne, Curate Wit: John GILBERT, Margaret [x] CHELL
29 Apr 1784	John CARTER, otp, Husbandman, & Diana WOOLLEY, otp, Spinster
Banns No. 224	Banns published: 11, 18 & 25 Apr 1784 Off. Min.:- Tho: Browne, Curate Wit: Samuel TURNER, John GILBERT
1 Jun 1784	James DUROSE, P. of Bramshal, Farmer, & Elizabeth HAWLEY, otp, Spinster
Lic. No. 225	Off. Min.:- Tho: Browne, Curate Wit: Thomas HAWLEY, Sarah DUROSE
12 Aug 1784	John TAYLOR, otp, Husbandman, & Ann TURNER, otp, Spinster
Banns No. 226	Banns published: 25 Jul, 1 & 8 Aug 1784 Off. Min.:- Tho: Browne, Curate Wit: Richard FENTON, Mary TURNER
12 Sep 1784	Joseph [x] ASBURY, otp, Carpenter, & Lydia [x] BAILEY, otp, Spinster
Banns No. 227	Banns published: 1, 15 & 22 Aug 1784 Off. Min.:- Tho: Browne, Curate Wit: Thomas BROWNE, John GILBERT
15 Sep 1784	John HUSON, otp, Farmer, & Olive CARTER, otp, Spinster
Lic. No. 228	Off. Min.:- Tho: Browne, Curate Wit: John HYDE, Thomas HUSON

29 Nov 1784 Banns No. 229	John [x] NICKLIN, otp, Husbandman, & Ann [x] JOHNSON, otp, Spinster Banns published: 14, 21 & 28 Nov 1784 Off. Min.:- Tho: Browne, Curate Wit: William NICKLIN, John GILBERT
8 Dec 1784 Lic. No. 230	George VERNON, P. of Milwich, Gen. & Mrs Ellen COLLIER, otp, Widow Off. Min.:- Tho: Browne, Curate Wit: Thomas STUBBS, Mary LOVATT
16 Dec 1784 Banns No. 231	Daniel BURTON, otp, Cordwainer, & Sarah SALT, otp, Spinster Banns published: 28 Nov, 5 & 12 Dec 1784 Off. Min.:- Tho: Browne, Curate Wit: Hales [?] BURTON, John GILBERT
30 Dec 1784 Lic. No. 232	William COPE, P. of Draycott, Carpenter, & Hannah DENT, otp, Spinster Off. Min.:- Tho: Browne, Curate Wit: John COPE, Ann BLOORE
21 Jun 1785 Banns No. 233	Job [x] BAKER, otp, Cordwainer, & Elizabeth [x] BRUERTON, otp, Spinster Banns published: 22 & 29 May & 5 Jun 1785 Off. Min.:- Tho: Browne, Curate Wit: John GILBERT, John ALLCOCK
	Banns of Marriage between Richard SMITH, otp, & Margaret EVANS, of P. of Alvington were published 31 Jul, 7 & 14 Aug 1785 By:- Tho: Browne, Curate
4 Sep 1785 Banns No. 234	William [x] HARRIS, otp, Husbandman, & Jane [x] WOODWARD, otp, Spinster Banns published: 14, 21 & 28 Aug 1785 Off. Min.:- Tho: Browne, Curate Wit: Thomas CAPE, John GILBERT
8 Sep 1785 Lic. No. 235	Thomas BAILEY, otp, Farmer, & Margaret FOWLER, otp, Spinster Off. Min.:- Tho: Browne, Curate Wit: Ann FOWLER, Luke TURNER
4 Oct 1785 Banns No. 236	Robert JACKSON, otp, Widower, & Ellen DAVIS, otp, Spinster Banns published: 28 Aug, 4 & 11 Sep 1785 Off. Min.:- Tho: Browne, Curate Wit: Alexander PERKIN, Margaret GRIFFIS
6 Oct 1785 Banns No. 237	Samuel [x] SMITH, P. of Cheadle, Singleman, & Ann [x] WOOLLEY, otp, Spinster Banns published: 18 & 25 Sep, & 2 Oct 1785 Off. Min.:- Tho: Browne, Curate Wit: William ALLCOCK, John GILBERT
6 Feb 1786 Lic. No. 238	John [x] GRINDY, otp, Singleman, & Sarah [x] SMITH, otp, Spinster Off. Min.:- Tho: Browne, Curate Wit: Edwd. BLURTON, John WOODDISSY [?]
13 Feb 1786 Banns No. 239	John [x] TREEN, otp, Husbandman, & Ann BRUERTON [s. Brewerton], otp, spinster Banns published: 29 Jan, 5 & 12 Feb 1786 Off. Min.:- Tho: Browne, Curate Wit: James TURNER, John GILBERT
24 May 1786 Banns No. 240	John SMITH, otp, Husbandman, & Dorothy FENTON, otp, Spinster Banns published: 7, 14 & 21 May 1786 Off. Min.:- Tho: Browne, Curate Wit: John GILBERT, Mary LOVATT

	Banns of Marriage between John HARDEN of P. of Cannock, & Elizabeth THACKER otp, were published 11, 18 & 25 Jun 1786 By:- Tho: Browne, Curate
4 Sep 1786 Lic. No. 241	William HOLLINS, otp, Farmer, & Mary HAWTHORN, P. of Colwich, Spinster Off. Min.:- Tho: Browne, Curate Wit: Elisabeth HOLLINS, Thos. HOWE
3 Oct 1786 Lic. No. 242	Samuel [x] WRIGHT, P. of Dilhorn, Widower, & Lydia [x] SHENTON, otp, Spinster Off. Min.:- Tho: Browne, Curate Wit: James MARSON, John GILBERT
20 Nov 1786 Banns No. 243	William [x] SLATER, otp, Husbandman, & Elizabeth [x] SMITH, otp, Spinster Banns published: 5, 12 & 19 Nov 1786 Off. Min.:- Tho: Browne, Curate Wit: Margret CARTER, William SMITH
	Banns of Marriage between Isaac WRIGHT otp, & Elizabeth MERE of P. of Checkley were published 3, 10 & 17 Dec 1786 By:- Tho: Browne, Curate
24 Dec 1786 Banns No. 244	William [x] CLEWLEY, otp, Husbandman, & Alice [x] JOHNSON, otp, Spinster Banns published: 10, 17 & 24 Dec 1786 Off. Min.:- Tho: Browne, Curate Wit: John HYDE, John HUSON
19 Jan 1787 Lic. No. 245	William LOWNDES, otp, Farmer, & Mary CARTER, otp, Spinster Off. Min.:- Tho: Browne, Curate Wit: William PHILLIPS, John GILBERT
	Banns of Marriage between Anthony HAWLEY & Mary TURNER botp, were published 26 Aug, 2 & 9 Sep 1787. By:- Walt. Bagot Rector
16 Oct 1787 Banns No. 246	Richard FENTON, otp, Miller, & Mary [x] ROBINSON, otp, Spinster Banns published: 30 Sep, 7 & 14 Oct 1787 Off. Min.:- Tho: Browne, Curate Wit: William ROBINSON, Elizabeth FENTON
18 Oct 1787 Banns No. 247	George [x] DEAKIN, otp, Farmer, & Elizabeth TURNER, otp, Spinster Banns published: 30 Sep, 7 & 14 Oct 1787 Off. Min.:- Tho: Browne, Curate Wit: Elisabet WILLSHAW, George DEAKIN
29 Oct 1787 Lic. No. 248	Thomas CARTER, otp, Farmer, & Elizabeth [x] LOWNDES, otp, Spinster Off. Min.:- Tho: Browne, Curate Wit: George LAUGHTON, Bettey HOLLAND
12 Nov 1787 Lic. No. 249	William [x] GEE, P. of Kings Bromley, Farmer, & Mary [x] MARSON, otp, Spinster Off. Min.:- Tho: Browne, Curate Wit: Oliver CLARKE, Wm. WRIGHT
7 Jan 1788 Banns No. 250	Thomas PERKIN, P. of Stone, Butcher, & Hannah [x] JOHNSON, otp, Spinster Banns published: 9, 16 & 23 Dec 1787 Off. Min.:- Tho: Browne, Curate Wit: John JOHNSON, William PERKIN
22 Jan 1788 Lic. No. 251	William BOSWEL [s. Boswell], P. of Alverton [Alveton-BT], Farmer, & Betty BELCHER, otp, Spinster Off. Min.:- Tho: Browne, Curate Wit: William SAUNDERS, Mary BELCHER

31 Jan 1788 Lic. No. 252	Thomas HAWLEY, otp, Farmer, & Elizabeth [x] COPE, otp, Widow Off. Min.:- Tho: Browne, Curate Wit: James DUROSE, John GILBERT
3 Feb 1788 Lic. No. 253	Richard HOWE, P. of Cheadle, Farmer, & Mary [s. Maray] LOVATT, otp, Spinster Off. Min.:- Tho: Browne, Curate Wit: John EMERY, Ellen LOVARTT
22 Sep 1788 Banns No. 254	John [x] MILLINGTON Junr., otp, & Martha [x] ALLCOCK, otp Banns published: 10, 17 & 24 Aug 1788 Officiating Minister: John Langley Wit: John GILBERT, Francis SHERRATT
1 Sep 1788 Banns No. 255	George [x] WRIGHT, otp, & Margaret [x] NUTT, otp Banns published: 17, 24 & 31 Aug 1788 Officiating Minister: John Langley Wit: William MELLER, John GILBERT
	Banns of Marriage between William SALE otp, & Susannah WOODWARD, P. of Checkley, were published 24 & 31 Aug & 7 Sep 1788 By:- Rev'd Mr John Langley
4 Nov 1788 Banns No. 256	John LEES, otp, & Elixabeth [x] MILLINGTON, otp Banns published: 21 & 28 Sep & 5 Oct Off. Min.:- H. Thomas Curate Wit: Francis SHERRATT, Thos. GILBERT
21 Feb 1789 Banns No. 257	Thomas RAWLIN, otp, & Hannah KENT, otp Banns published: 1, 8 & 15 Feb Off. Min.:- H. Thomas Curate Wit: John KENT, John GILBERT
13 Apr 1789 Banns No. 258	Charles [x] KENT, otp, & Ann [x] LEES, otp Banns published: 1, 8 & 15 Mar 1789 Off. Min.:- H. Thomas Curate Wit: Wm. BIRD, John GILBERT
3 Dec 1789 Lic. No. 259	Robert TUNNICLIFFE [s. Tunnicliff], P. of Rocester, & Elizabeth PHILLIPS [s. Elisebeth Philips], otp Off. Min.:- H. Thomas Curate Wit: John ARNOLD, John GILBERT
12 Dec 1789 Lic. No. 260	Philip [x] SANDERS or SAUNDERS, P. of Draycott, & Catharine [x] KIRK, otp Off. Min.:- H. Thomas Curate Wit: Thomas BRANDRICK, William WILSHAW
16 Dec 1789 Lic. No. 261	William BYATT, otp, Batchelor, & Jemima [x] RUSHTON, otp, Spinster Off. Min.:- H. Thomas Curate Wit: John GILBERT, Thomas GILBERT
4 Feb 1790 Lic. No. 262	Michael BELCHER, P. of Gnosal, Batchelor, & Mary BELCHER, otp, Spinster Off. Min.:- E. Lewes, Curate Wit: Thomas WARNER, Thos. BELCHER
25 Jan 1790 Banns No. 263	John [x] BRANDRICK, otp, & Margaret [s. Margreat] TURNER Banns published: 10, 17 & 24 Jan 1790 Off. Min.:- H. Thomas Curate Wit: John GILBERT, Samuel ALLCOCK
	Banns of Marriage between Francis MILWARD, otp, & Mary TRUNDLEY, P. of Alveton, were published 24 & 31 Jan & 7 Feb 1790 By:- H. Thomas Curate

25 Mar 1790 Lic. No. 264	George BLACKDEN, P. of Uttoxeter, Batchelor, & Elizabeth BELCHER, otp, Spinster Off. Min.:- H. Thomas Curate Wit: M. BELCHER, John GILBERT
13 Jun 1790 Banns No. 265	John [x] NUTT, otp, & Susannah [x] HIRST, otp Banns published: 23 & 30 May & 6 Jun Off. Min.:- H. Thomas Curate Wit: John GILBERT, Thos. GILBERT
2 Aug 1790 Banns No. 266	Henry [x] STOKES, otp, Batchelor, & Sarah [x] CROSSLEY, otp, Spinster Banns published: 4, 11 & 18 Jul 1790 Off. Min.:- H. Thomas Curate Wit: John GILBERT, William CROSSLEY
22 Sep 1790 Lic. No. 267	Joseph VAUGHAN [s. Vaughn], P. of Blithfield, Batchelor, & Hannah BARNES, otp, Spinster Off. Min.:- H. Thomas Curate Wit: John GILBERT, Thos. GILBERT
2 Oct 1790 Banns No. 268	William ROCK, P. of Checkley, & Margaret [x] RUSHTON, otp Banns published: 22 & 29 Aug & 5 Sep Off. Min.:- H. Thomas Curate Wit: John GILBERT, Elizabeth [x] RUSHTON
	Banns of Marriage between Thos. SMITH [?], P. of St. Mary's Stafford, & Elizth. SHAW otp, were published 20 & 27 Mar & 3 Apr 1791 By:- H. Thomas Curate
19 May 1791 Lic. No. 269	John LOVATT, P. of Draycot, & Elizabeth WOOLDRIDGE, otp Wit: John GILBERT, Richd. STEELE Off. Min.:- H. Thomas Curate
18 Jul 1791 Banns No. 270	Richard SHELDON, otp, & Mary [x] BUXTON, otp Banns published: 3, 10 & 17 Jul Off. Min.:- H. Thomas Curate Wit: John GILBERT, William WOOD
14 May 1792 Banns	James BODIN, & Sarah [x] EDGE, botp Banns published: 22 & 29 Apr & 6 May Off. Min.:- Samuel Langley A.M. Rector of the neighbouring Church of Checkley Wit: John MANSFIELD, Jenny LOWE, John GILBERT
9 Jul 1792 Banns	Robert HOLLINS, otp, & Hannah [x] JOHNSON, otp Banns published: 24 Jun, 1 & 8 Jul 1792 Off. Min.:- H. Thomas Curate Wit: John GILBERT, Hannah GILBERT
30 Jul 1792 Banns	James BRYRIHURST [s. Beiryhurst] & Mary [x] BICKHORN botp Banns published: 15, 22 & 29 Jul 1792 Off. Min.:- H. Thomas Curate Wit: John GILBERT, Ann PEARSE
25 Oct 1792 Lic.	Thomas BLOORE, otp, & Mary WARD, P. of Checkley Wit: Benjamin WARD, Ann BLOORE Off. Min.:- H. Thomas Curate
19 Nov 1792 Banns	John TUNNICLIFF & Mary [x] MELLO, botp Banns published: 4, 11 & 18 Nov 1792 Off. Min.:- H. Thomas Curate Wit: John GILBERT, John [x] ALLCOCK
24 Dec 1792 Banns	Thomas NUTT & Lydia [x] BAILEY, botp Banns published: 29 Jan, 5 & 12 Feb 1792 Off. Min.:- H. Thomas Curate Wit: Mary ALLCOCK, John GILBERT

20 May 1793 Banns	Thos. [x] HEATH & Mary [x] SHAW, botp Banns published: 17 & 24 Feb & 3 Mar 1793 Off. Min.:- H. Thomas Curate Wit: Walter HALDEN, Jno. GILBERT
17 Jun 1793 Banns	Thos. ARNOLD & Ann PLATT, botp Banns published: 26 May, 2 & 9 Jun 1793 Off. Min.:- H. Thomas Curate Wit: Joseph HART, John GILBERT
20 Jun 1793 Banns	George DEAKIN & Ann COPE, botp Banns published: 2, 9 & 16 Jun 1793 Off. Min.:- H. Thomas Curate Wit: John COPE, John GILBERT
4 Jul 1793 Lic.	Edward BABB, P. of Gratwich, Batchelor, & Kitty WALKER, otp, Spinster Off. Min.:- H. Thomas Curate Wit: John SHIPLEY, John GILBERT
30 Dec 1793 Banns	Edwd. [x] GRAVENOR, P. of Lapley, & Mary or Eliz.* [x] ALCOCK Banns published: 1, 8 & 15 Dec 1793 Off. Min.:- H. Thomas Curate Wit: John COPE, Saml. TURNER [*Name written as Mary at top of entry, but as Eliz. Adjacent to her mark, *Mary-BT*]
14 Jan 1794 Lic.	Gilbert [x] HALL, P. of Kingsley, Widower, & Jane [x] TILL, Widow Wit: Wm. HALL, John GILBERT Off. Min.:- H. Thomas Curate
9 Jul 1794 Lic.	John [x] PRESTON, otp, & Elizabeth GREENSMITH, otp Wit: John COPE, Robert GILBERT Off. Min.:- H. Thomas Curate
20 Jul 1794 Banns	Isaac [x] GRIFFIN & Eliz. [x] RUSHTON, botp Banns published: 8, 15 & 22 Jun 1794 Off. Min.:- H. Thomas Curate Wit: William ROCK, John GILBERT
14 May 1795 Lic.	Joseph SHAW, P. of Milwich, & Elizabeth FENTON, otp Wit: John SHAW, John GILBERT Off. Min.:- H. Thomas Curate
1 Oct 1795 Lic.	Samuel PLATT, otp, & Elisabeth WILSHAW [s. Willshaw], otp Wit: Elizabeth BOWEN, John GILBERT Off. Min.:- H. Thomas Curate
12 Oct 1795 Lic.	Thomas BLORE, P. of Waterfall, & Ann GREENSMITH, otp Wit: Margaret GILBERT, William BOULD Off. Min.:- H. Thomas Curate
26 Oct 1795 Banns	William MELLER & Jane LOWE, botp Banns published: 11, 18 & 25 Oct 1795 Off. Min.:- H. Thomas Curate Wit: John GILBERT, Hannah [x] BAGNAL
7 Dec 1795 Banns	Richard HALL & Mary [x] HORNE, botp Banns published: 22 & 29 Nov & 6 Dec 1795 Off. Min.:- H. Thomas Curate Wit: Richd. KEYS, John GILBERT
13 Jun 1796 Banns	Edward [x] COPE & Elizabeth TURNER, botp Banns published: 29 May, 5 & 12 Jun 1796 Off. Min.:- H. Thomas Curate Wit: Thomas FOWLER, John GILBERT
3 Oct 1796 Banns	John ASH & Sarah CHARLESWORTH, botp Banns published: 18 & 25 Sep & 2 Oct 1796 Off. Min.:- H. Thomas Curate Wit: John GILBERT, John MELLER

11 May 1797 Banns	Saml. [x] ALCOCK & Eliz: [x] DAVIES *[Davis-BT]*, botp Banns published: 9, 16 & 23 Apr 1797 Off. Min.:- H. Thomas Curate Wit: John GILBERT, John GILBERT Junr
25 Jun 1797 Banns	William PRESTON & Alice [x] SHERRATT botp Banns published: 11, 18 & 25 Jun 1797 Off. Min.:- H. Thomas Curate Wit: John GILBERT, John GILBERT Junr
26 Jul 1797 Banns	Richd. [x] INGRAM & Elizth. [x] PERKIN botp Banns published: 25 Jun 2 & 9 Jul 1797 Off. Min.:- H. Thomas Curate Wit: Thos. PERKIN, John GILBERT
27 Sep 1797 Lic.	Francis [x] NUTT P. of Leigh & Anne [x] HOWE of the same Wit: John SHERRATT, Thomas BOX Off. Min.:- H. Thomas Curate
14 Dec 1797 Banns	John BULL & Martha [x] BLURTON botp Banns published: 26 Nov, 3 & 10 Dec 1797 Off. Min.:- H. Thomas Curate Wit: Thos. BULL, John GILBERT
28 Dec 1797 Banns	John DEAN & Dorothy TILL botp Banns published: 10, 17 & 24 Dec 1797 Off. Min.:- H. Thomas Curate Wit: Rucherd *[Richard-BT]* DEAN, Robert GILBERT
16 May 1798 Banns	Robt. [x] THACKER & Hannah [x] SMITH botp Banns published: 15 & 22 Apr & 1 May 1798 Off. Min.:- H. Thomas Curate Wit: William LEES, Thos. GILBERT
15 Nov 1798 Lic.	James BELCHER otp & Martha ACTON P. of Gnosall Off. Min.:- H. Thomas Curate Wit: William ONLEY, A. *[Ann-BT]* BELCHER
24 Dec 1798 Banns	James JOHNSON & Mary [x] STANSLEY, botp Banns published: 11, 18 & 25 Nov 1798 Off. Min.:- H. Thomas Curate Wit: John GILBERT, William DANIEL
26 Dec 1798 Banns	John HAWLEY & Elizabeth LAUGHTON botp Banns published: 9, 16 & 23 Dec 1798 Off. Min.:- H. Thomas Curate Wit: Thos. HAWLEY, Mary WALTHO
31 Jan 1799 Banns	Richard DEAN & Elizabeth [x] CARTER botp Banns published: 13, 20 & 27 Jan 1799 Off. Min.:- H. Thomas Curate Wit: John DEAN, John GILBERT
19 Nov 1799 Banns	Saml. [x] BARNET & Margt. [x] WILSON botp Banns published: 3, 10 & 17 Nov 1799 Off. Min.:- H. Thomas Curate Wit: Samuel MOSTYN, John GILBERT
20 Nov 1799 Banns	Thos. [x] LEES & Ellen [x] BALLANCE botp Banns published: 3, 10 & 17 Nov 1799 Off. Min.:- H. Thomas Curate Wit: John GILBERT, Hannah [x] VENESON
27 Mar 1800 Banns	Thomas GARLAND & Elizabeth [x] COPE botp Banns published: 9, 16 & 23 Mar 1800 Off. Min.:- H. Thomas Curate Wit: Thomas BROWN, John GILBERT
15 Apr 1800 Banns	Willm. [x] ALCOCK otp & Mary [x] TURNER P. of Colwich Banns published: 23 & 30 Mar & 6 Apr 1800 Off. Min.:- H. Thomas Curate Wit: John GILBERT, Robt. GILBERT

1 2 Jul 1800 Banns	Samuel [x] ROBINSON otp & Catharine [x] FOWER, otp Banns published: 15, 22 & 29 Jun 1800 Off. Min.:- John Langley Officiating Minister Wit: John GILBERT, William WARDLE
19 Aug 1800 Lic.	John COOKE P. of Gayton & Elizabeth COLLINS otp Off. Min.:- John Langley Officiating Minister Wit: William HILL, Mary HILL
17 Nov 1800 Lic.	John Massey FROST P. of Doveridge & Elizabeth WARNER otp Off. Min.:- H. Thomas Curate Wit: Roger WARNER, Margaret GILBERT [this entry repeated and crossed out]
28 Jan 1801 Lic.	Joseph BRASSINGTON P. of Caverswall & Sarah [x] COPE otp Off. Min.:- H. Thomas Curate Wit: William SMITH, Ann TURNER
6 Apr 1801 Banns	Thomas MOTTRAM P. of Stoke upon Trent & Mary [x] GRIFFIN otp Banns published: 22 & 29 Mar & 5 Apr 1801 Off. Min.:- H. Thomas Curate Wit: Moses MOTTERAM, John GILBERT
21 May 1801 Lic.	Richard FENTON otp & Mary WALTHOW [s. Waltho] otp Off. Min.:- H. Thomas Curate Wit: George ATKINS, Ann PRINCE
8 May 1802 Banns	Thomas BAGNALL & Sarah [x] BARKER botp Banns published: 18 & 25 Apr & 2 May 1802 Off. Min.:- H. Thomas Curate Wit: John BAGNALL, John GILBERT
10 Jul 1802 Banns	George EDGE & Hannah [x] LEES botp Banns published: 20 & 27 Jun & 4 Jul 1802 Off. Min.:- H. Thomas Curate Wit: Joseph TATTON, Robt. GILBERT
20 Oct 1802 Banns	Willm. TITTENSOR & Mary [x] THACKER botp Banns published: 22 & 29 Aug & 5 Sep 1802 Off. Min.:- H. Thomas Curate Wit: John GILBERT, Joseph [x] THACKER
31 Jan 1803 Banns	Richard PHILLIPS & Elizabeth CHELL botp Banns published: 16, 23 & 30 Jan 1803 Off. Min.:- H. Thomas Curate Wit: William PHILLIPS, Ellen BLURTON
23 Mar 1803 Lic.	John ROGERS P. of Stone & Lydia MARSTON, Spinster, otp Off. Min.:- John Langley Officiating Minister Wit: James MARSON, Mary HOWE
16 May 1803 Banns	John [x] WETTON P. of Checkley & Charlotte [x] TILL otp Banns published: 24 Apr, 1 & 8 May 1803 Off. Min.:- H. Thomas Curate Wit: John BEECH, John GILBERT
26 May 1803 Lic.	William STUBBS P. of Stone & Edith COLLIER otp Off. Min.:- H. Thomas Curate Wit: John HAYES, Hannah COLLIER
18 Jul 1803 Lic.	Robt. BALLINTON P. of Mayfield & Mary GREENSMITH otp Off. Min.:- H. Thomas Curate Wit: George GREEN, Sarah GREENSMITH
15 Aug 1803 Lic.	Edward COPE, Bachelor, otp & Ruth [x] SUTTON, Widow, P. of Hanbury, Staffordshire Off. Min.:- Saml. Langley AM Rector of Checkley in Staffordshire Wit: John GILBERT, John COPE

10 Nov 1803 Lic.	Thomas SMITH, Bachelor, & Ann BLOORE, Spinster, both aged 21 years & upwards & botp Off. Min.:- Saml. Langley AM Rector of Checkley Wit: Charles BROWNE, Elizabeth COPE
19 Jan 1804 Banns	Samuel GRIFFIN & Anne [x] BILLINS botp Banns published: 1, 8 & 15 Jan 1804 Off. Min.:- H. Thomas Curate Wit: William BROWN, John GILBERT Senr.
23 Jan 1804 Lic.	John GOODWIN P. of Stone & Anne [x] WOOLLEY otp Off. Min.:- H. Thomas Curate Wit: Edward WOOLLEY, John GILBERT
9 Feb 1804 Lic.	William ASBURY otp & Anne [s. Ann] WILSON otp Off. Min.:- H. Thomas Curate Wit: Richard ASBURY, Elizabeth ASBURY
13 Feb 1804 Banns	Joseph TATTON & Helen [x] BAKEWELL botp Banns published: 29 Jan, 5 & 11 Feb 1804 Off. Min.:- H. Thomas Curate Wit: George EDGE, John GILBERT
30 Apr 1804 Banns	William CHELL & Eliz: [x] BAILEY botp Banns published: 15, 22 & 29 Apr 1804 Off. Min.:- H. Thomas Curate Wit: John CHELL, John GILBERT
22 May 1804 Banns	Willm. [x] WILSON P. of Checkley & Ellen RAWLIN otp Banns published: 15, 22 & 29 Apr 1804 Off. Min.:- H. Thomas Curate Wit: Chas. BROWN, John GILBERT
27 Aug 1804 Lic.	Robt: PORTER P. of Draycot, & Mary THOMAS P. of Leigh Off. Min.:- John DAVEY Curate of Capesthorne in Cheshire Wit: Jane THOMAS, John GILBERT
13 Nov 1804 Banns	Willm: [x] BROWNE & Lydia [x] NICKLIN botp Banns published: 28 Oct, 4 & 11 Nov 1804 Off. Min.:- H. Thomas Curate Wit: John GILBERT, Thos. MEARS
22 Dec 1804 Banns	Jos. [x] WETTON & Anne [x] MITCHELL botp Banns published: 24 Jun. 1 & 8 Jul 1804 Off. Min.:- H. Thomas Curate Wit: John GILBERT, John [x] WETTON, E. BLURTON
15 Apr 1805 Banns	John TATTON & Sarah HICKINBOTHAM botp Banns published: 31 Mar, 7 & 14 Apr 1805 Off. Min.:- H. Thomas Curate Wit: Joseph TATTON, Cicily HICKINBOTHAM
25 Apr 1805 Banns	Thos. [x] HOLLINS & Mary [x] CARTER botp Banns published: 31 Mar, 7 & 14 Apr 1805 Off. Min.:- H. Thomas Curate Wit: John GILBERT, Willm. [x] CARTER
11 Aug 1805 Banns	John TURNER & Charlotte CARTER botp Banns published: 11, 18 & 25 Aug 1805 Off. Min.:- H. Thomas Curate Wit: John GILBERT, Jane PHILIPS
26 Dec 1805 Banns	Thomas [x] SHINGLER & Jane SAUNDERS botp Banns published: 6, 13 & 20 Oct 1805 Off. Min.:- Samuel Langley AM Rector of neighbouring Parish of Checkley Wit: Samuel GRIFFIN, John GILBERT
13 Feb 1806 Banns	Saml. [x] LOWNDES, P. of Milwich, & Sarah [x] RUSHTON, otp Banns published: 12, 19 & 26 Jan 1806 Off. Min.:- H. Thomas Curate Wit: John GILBERT, George [x] GRIFFIN

26 Apr 1806 Lic.	John CLIFF, P. of Stone, & Sarah SHERRATT, otp Off. Min.:- H. Thomas Curate Wit: Thomas SHERRATT, Mary CLIFFE
6 May 1806 Lic.	Stephen ARNOLD otp & Mary Nield YATES otp Off. Min.:- H. Thomas Curate Wit: Ann HARVEY, Robt. ARNOLD Junr.
28 Aug 1806 Lic.	James MARSON otp & Mary HART otp Off. Min.:- H. Thomas Curate Wit: John GILBERT Junr., Dorothy RIDDELL
19 Dec 1806 Lic.	Edward [x] ADAMS P. of Norton & Margt. [x] JOHNSON otp Off. Min.:- H. Thomas Curate Wit: Robt. ARNOLD Junr., John GILBERT.
29 Dec 1806 Banns	John [x] HUGHES & Elizabeth [x] WRIGHT, botp Banns published: 16, 23 & 30 Nov 1806 Off. Min.:- H. Thomas Curate Wit: Isaiah [x] RUSHTON, John GILBERT
12 Jan 1807 Banns	William SHIRLEY & Hannah STONE, botp Banns published: 28 Dec 1806 & 4 & 11 Jan 1807 Off. Min.:- H. Thomas Curate Wit: William TURNER, John GILBERT
19 Jan 1807 Lic.	William PHILLIPS, otp, & Sarah ANSELL [s. Ancell], P. of Milwich Off. Min.:- H. Thomas Curate Richard PHILLIPS, Elizabeth PHILLIPS
30 Mar 1807 Banns	George TOOTH & Mary [x] SMITH, botp Banns published: 15, 22 & 29 Mar 1807 Off. Min.:- H. Thomas Curate Wit: Elizebeth COPE, John GILBERT
14 Apr 1807 Lic.	Walter TITLEY, P. of Eccleshall, & Peggy DEAKIN, otp Off. Min.:- H. Thomas Curate Wit: John TITLEY, Eliz. MILNER
28 Apr 1807 Banns	Chas. [x] HARRISON & Mary [x] PHILLIPS, botp Banns published: 5, 12 & 19 Apr 1807 Off. Min.:- H. Thomas Curate Wit: Elizabeth BENTLY, John GREEN
4 May 1807 Lic.	Michael GOODALL, P. of Marston Montgomery, & Sarah PHILLIPS [s. Phillip] otp Off. Min.:- H. Thomas Curate Wit: Thos. LOWNDES, Catherine PHILLIPS
8 Jun 1807 Banns	George COPE & Elizabeth MELLOR [s. Mellow], botp Banns published: 10, 17 & 24 May 1807 Off. Min.:- H. Thomas Curate Wit: Thos. COLLIER, John GILBERT
4 5 Oct 1807 Lic.	Thomas COPE, otp, & Elizabeth HUSON, otp Off. Min.:- H. Thomas Curate Wit: John HUSON, Elizabeth HAWLEY
13 Oct 1807 Banns	Francis ASH & Hannah [x] ORGAN, botp Banns published: 13, 20 & 27 Sep 1807 Off. Min.:- H. Thomas Curate Wit: Joseph WARD, John GILBERT
5 Nov 1807 Lic.	Thomas HALL, P. of Abbots Bromley, & Mary ARNOLD, otp Off. Min.:- H. Thomas Curate Wit: John HEATHCOTE, Martha SAVILE
24 Jan 1808 Lic.	Thomas [x] COPE, otp, & Sarah [x] SMITH, otp Off. Min.:- H. Thomas Curate Wit: John [x] SMITH, John GILBERT

25 Feb 1808 Lic.	Thomas CLEWLEY, P. of Uttoxeter, & Catharine BRINDLEY, otp Off. Min.:- H. Thomas Curate Wit: Thomas BRINDLEY, E. *[Edward-BT]* BLURTON
25 Apr 1808 Lic.	John [x] BLOOD, otp, & Ann PHILLIPS, otp Off. Min.:- H. Thomas Curate Wit: W. [x] SLATER, John GILBERT
20 Sep 1808 Banns	John DEAKIN & Mary [x] BAYLEY, botp Banns published: 4, 11 & 18 Sep 1808 Off. Min.:- H. Thomas Curate Wit: William CHELL, John GILBERT
31 Oct 1808 Lic.	Richard MELLER [s. Mallar], P. of Leek, & Cath: [x] HUGHES, otp Off. Min.:- H. Thomas Curate Wit: J. [x] HUGHES, Charles BURTON
26 Nov 1808 Banns	Sampson BAILEY & Anne [x] FOWER, botp Banns published: 23 & 30 Oct & 6 Nov 1808 Off. Min.:- H. Thomas Curate Wit: John HILL, William HEATON
13 Feb 1809 Lic.	Luke TURNER otp, & Elizabeth FENTON, otp Off. Min.:- H. Thomas Curate Wit: Sarah RAWLINS, William ONLEY
22 Jun 1809 Lic.	Thomas SMITH, otp, & Lydia COLLIER, otp Off. Min.:- H. Thomas Curate Wit: Thomas WILSON, Elizabeth COLLIER
27 Jun 1809 Lic.	John GREEN, P. of Cheadle, & Charlotte PHILLIPS, otp Off. Min.:- H. Thomas Curate Wit: John GILBERT, Philip DUROSE
4 Jul 1809 Banns	John HAMMERSLEY, P. of Dilhorne, & Helen [x] CHELL, otp Off. Min.:- H. Thomas Curate Wit: John GILBERT, William SALE
30 Nov 1809 Banns	Thomas [x] BRINDLEY, otp, & Mary [x] BARKER, otp Off. Min.:- H. Thomas Curate Wit: Saml. [x] STARTIN, Hannah [x] CHELL.

The Register of Marriages Solemnized in the Parish of Leigh, Staffordshire, & begun 28th Decr. 1809

The Honble: Rev'd Rich'd Bagot, Rector

28 Dec 1809 Banns	Willm: COPE & Anne [x] PHILLIPS, botp Wit: James ATKIN, Charles BURTON Off. Min.:- H. Thomas Curate
23 Apr 1810 Banns	John [x] THARME, otp, & Mary [x] MELLOR, P. of Uttoxeter Wit: John MELLER, Samuel ATKIN Off. Min.:- H. Thomas Curate
1 May 1810 Banns	James DUROSE & Lydia [x] WALKER, botp Wit: Willm. PERKIN Junr., Mary HUSON Off. Min.:- H. Thomas Curate
21 May 1810 Lic.	Francis EARDLEY P. of Abbots Bromley, & Elizabeth HAWLEY, otp Wit: George HAWLEY, Ann DEAKIN Off. Min.:- H. Thomas Curate
21 Jan 1811 Banns	Thomas [x] CARTERITE Bachelor & Ann [x] PROCTER Spinster botp Banns published: 6, 13 & 20 Jan 1811 Wit: D Richard SMITH, M. HILL, Saml. ATKIN Off. Min.:- Saml. Langley, A.M. Rector of Checkley
31 Jan 1811 Banns	Joseph [x] EDGE & Han: [x] BALLANCE, otp Wit: George EDGE, Saml. ATKIN Off. Min.:- H. Thomas Curate
31 Jan 1811 Banns	Thomas GURNEY & Mary [x] TILL, otp Wit: Saml. ATKIN, William MELLER Off. Min.:- H. Thomas Curate
5 Mar 1811 Banns	James BENTLEY & Elizabeth HOWE, botp Wit: Sarah PERKIN, Gallimor WHELOCK Off. Min.:- H. Thomas Curate
7 Mar 1811 Lic.	William Henry HOLMES, P. of Sudbury, & Elizabeth ASBURY, otp Wit: Rich. ASBURY, Elizabeth HILDITCH Off. Min.:- H. Thomas Curate
29 Apr 1811 Banns	Jams: [x] BAILEY & Pru: [x] RUSHTON, botp Wit: John [x] BOND, Saml. ATKIN Off. Min.:- H. Thomas Curate
21 Jul 1811 Banns	John [x] ALCOCK & Eliz: [x] RATCLIFFE, botp Wit: Sam. ATKIN, Saml. [x] STARTIN, Off. Min.:- H. Thomas Curate
10 Nov 1811 Banns	Geo: [x] MOOR & Eliz: [x] MADELEY, botp Wit: Mary FENTON, Sam. ATKIN Off. Min.:- H. Thomas Curate
2 Dec 1811 Banns	Thos. [x] PRITCHARD & Sarah ROGERS, botp Wit: Geo. [x] MIATT, Saml. ATKIN Off. Min.:- H. Thomas Curate
9 Dec 1811 Banns	William BROWN & Ellen BLURTON, botp Wit: Cicely BROWN, Joseph JENKINSON Off. Min.:- H. Thomas Curate
25 Dec 1811 Banns	John CHELL & Dor: [x] DUROSE, botp Wit: Thomas CHELL, Saml. ATKIN Off. Min.:- H. Thomas Curate
25 Dec 1811 Banns	Rob: [x] MOODY & Martha [x] OAKES, botp Wit: John WILLSON, Saml. ATKIN Off. Min.:- H. Thomas Curate

2 Jan 1812 Lic.	Laurence GREENSMITH, Bachelor, & Cicely BROWN, Spinster, botp, & also each being of the age of 21 years & upwards Wit: Thomas BROWN, Sarah GREENSMITH, Saml. ATKIN Off. Min.:- Samuel Langley, A.M. Rector of Checkley
7 Jan 1812 Banns	Geo: [x] DUROUSE & Mary [x] MARSON, otp Wit: Mary SALE, Samuel ATKIN Off. Min.:- H. Thomas Curate
1 Feb 1812 Lic.	Thos: BAKEWELL, P. of St. Mary's Birmingham, & Anne [s. Ann] HILL, otp Wit: William HILL, Mary HILL Off. Min.:- H. Thomas Curate
30 Apr 1812 Banns	Willm: [x] DEG & Mary BARNES [s. Marries Barns], otp Wit: Charles BURTON, Saml. ATKIN Off. Min.:- H. Thomas Curate
13 Jul 1812 Lic.	John COX, P. of Armitage, & Hannah [x] WARDLE otp Wit: Ann PICKFORD, Daniel KNOTT Off. Min.:- H. Thomas Curate
9 Sep 1812 Lic.	John BURNETT [s. Jhn Burnet] p. of Grindon, & Mary CARTER otp Wit: William CARTER, Ann BURNET Off. Min.:- H. Thomas Curate
7 Dec 1812 Lic.	Jams: ATKIN & Francis ENGLAND, otp Wit: Thomas BROWN, Harriot ENGLAND Off. Min.:- H. Thomas Curate
20 Dec 1812 Banns	Geo: [x] DEAKIN & Joyce [x] MITCHELL otp Wit: Mary ALLCOCK, Saml. ATKIN Off. Min.:- H. Thomas Curate
30 Dec 1812 Banns	William BYATT & Elizabeth ALCOCK otp Wit: Saml. ATKIN, Charles BURTON Off. Min.:- H. Thomas Curate

Leigh, Staffordshire, Baptism Register
1813-1841

1813

3 Jan	George s/o Thomas & Elizabeth FOSTER, Nobot, Labourer	HT
17 Jan	Charles s/o Ann SMITH, Withington, Servant	HT
31 Jan	Frances d/o Margt. RAWLIN, Leigh, Servant	HT
28 Mar	Jane d/o Samuel & Jane WALKER, Withington, Labourer	HT
29 Mar	Robert s/o Anne ARNOLD, Over Leigh, Servant	HT
18 Apr	William s/o Hannah NOAKES, Leigh, Servant	HT
12 May	John s/o John & Mary BURNETT, Nobot, Farmer	HT
16 May	Charles s/o Charles & Dor. KENT, Leigh, Labourer	HT
16 May	Elizabeth d/o Henry & Mary TURNER, Leigh, Butcher	HT
18 May	Charles s/o James & Eliz. BENTLEY, Leigh, Publican	HT
13 Jul	James s/o James & Frances ATKIN, Withington, Butcher	HT
14 Sep	Stephen s/o Samson & Anne BAILEY, Leigh, Labourer	HT
2 Oct	George s/o Willm: & Anne JOHNSON, Over Leigh, Labourer	HT
29 Oct	John s/o Thomas & Louisa BRINDLEY, Leigh, Gentleman	HT
13 Nov	Elisa d/o Elisa RUSHTON, Morley Heath, Servant	HT
3 Dec	Thomas s/o Thomas & Mary BRINDLEY, Leigh, Labourer	HT
5 Dec	Sarah d/o George & Hannah MYAT, Middleton Green, Labourer	HT

1814

8 Jan	William s/o Charles & Sarah BROWNE, The Wood, Farmer	HT
24 Jan	John s/o Joseph & Sarah BRASSINGTON, Over Leigh Labourer	HT
13 Feb	Charles s/o Thomas & Mary HOLLINS, Leigh Bank, Labourer	HT
27 Feb	Betty d/o James & Anne JOHNSON, Morley Heath, Labourer	HT
27 Feb	Sarah d/o William & Sarah FOWLER, Withington, Mason	HT
10 Apr	Sarah d/o Joseph & Hannah EDGE, Withington, Labourer	HT
3 May	Elizabeth d/o Thomas & Lydia OSBOURNE, Birchwood Park, Gentleman	HT
21 May	Francis s/o Thomas & Sarah MILLINGTON, Dodsley, Labourer	HT
29 May	John s/o Joseph & Eliz: TILL, Middleton Green, Labourer	HT
6 Jun	Susannah d/o Francis & Ellen PHILLIPS, Dodsley, Labourer	HT
15 Jul	James s/o Thomas & Harriet MARSON, Middleton Green Farmer	HT
27 Jul	Charles s/o Charles & Dorothy HART, Dodsley, Farmer	HT
1 Aug	Tomason d/o George & Mary WILLIAMS, Church Leigh, Farmer	HT
20 Aug	Sarah d/o William & Eliz: CHELL, Dodsley, Labourer	HT
28 Aug	Joseph s/o John & Sarah TATTON, Withington, Farmer	HT
4 Sep	William s/o Mary FOSTER, Leigh Bank, Servant	HT
21 Sep	Henry s/o Thomas & Ellen CHELL, Over Leigh, Labourer	HT
30 Oct	Hannah d/o John & Eliz: ALCOCK, Withington, Labourer	HT
6 Nov	Hannah d/o James & Lydia DUROSE, Leigh, Wheelwright	HT
6 Nov	James s/o Mary BRANDRICK, Leigh, Servant	HT
4 Dec	Charles s/o James & Prudence BAILEY, Withington, Labourer	HT
26 Dec	Anne d/o John & Mary BURNETT, Nobot, Farmer	HT

1815

8 Jan	Mary d/o Robert & Anne ARNOLD, Upper Leigh, Farmer	HT
15 Jan	William Arthur s/o William & Anne DEAKIN, Withington, Farmer	HT
15 Feb	Margaret d/o Thomas & Sarah PRITCHETT, Middleton Green, Labourer	HT
5 Feb	Elizabeth d/o Thomas & Hester ALCOCK, Upper Leigh Labourer	HT
12 Feb	Thomas s/o John & Mary TOOTH, Nobot, Labourer	HT
12 Feb	Anne d/o Thomas & Elizabeth FOSTER, Nobot, Shoemaker	HT

26 Mar	Mary d/o James & Elizabeth BENTLEY, Lower Leigh, Publican	HT
1 May	John s/o John & Dorothy CHELL, Dodsley, Mason	HT
7 May	James s/o Edward & Elizabeth COPE, Leigh, Shoemaker	HT
16 May	Elizabeth d/o Mary MITCHELL, Withington Green, Servant	HT
28 May	John Durouse s/o Hannah NOAKES, Church Leigh, Servant	HT
9 Jun	Robert s/o Richard & Elizabeth PHILLIPS, Dodsley, Farmer	HT
11 Jun	Philip s/o John & Alice MYAT [Myatt-BT], Morley Heath Labourer	HT
28 Jun	Louisa d/o Thomas & Louisa BRINDLEY, Leigh, Gentleman	HT
3 Jul	Sarah d/o Elizabeth RUSHTON, Morley Heath, Servant	HT
10 Jul	Hannah d/o Thomas & Lucy PHILLIPS, Withington, Labourer	HT
24 Jul	George s/o George & Mary TOOTH, Dodsley, Labourer	HT
6 Aug	Sophia d/o Thomas & Sarah STARTIN, Nobot, Blacksmith	HT
20 Aug	Charles s/o Michl: & Elizabeth BAILEY, Morley Heath, Pauper	HT
1 Oct	Mary d/o Joseph & Dorothy BIDDULPH, Upper Leigh, Maltster	HT
13 Oct	Mary d/o Thomas & Elizabeth BIRCH, Withington, Labourer	HT
26 Oct	Samuel s/o James & Frances ATKIN, Headland, Butcher	HT
31 Oct	Mary d/o Henry & Mary TURNER, Church Leigh, Publican	HT
5 Nov	William s/o John & Mary WETTON, Field, Labourer	HT
28 Nov	Francis s/o Francis & Mary SHERRATT, Benter, Labourer	HT
2 Dec	Eliza d/o John & Hannah TIDSWELL, Fole Hall, Farmer	HT
1816		
21 Jan	George s/o Willm: & Anne BULL, Birchwood Park, Labourer	HT
18 Feb	Mary Anne d/o Samuel & Jane WALKER, Withington, Labourer	HT
25 Feb	Joseph s/o Joseph & Sarah BRASSINGTON, Upper Leigh, Labourer	HT
14 Mar	Anne Prince d/o John Prince & Ellen ROBINSON, Middleton Green, Joiner	HT
17 Mar	Mary d/o Thomas & Mary HOWE, Upper Leigh, Maltster	HT
24 Mar	Gervase s/o Thomas & Harriet MARSON, Middleton Green, Farmer	HT
29 Mar	Thomas s/o Thomas & Elizabeth WILSON, Fole, Farmer	HT
6 Apr	Anne Olive d/o John & Elizabeth HUSON, Withington, Farmer	HT
9 Apr	William s/o Charles & Dorothy HART, Dodsley, Farmer	HT
14 Apr	Samuel s/o John & Mary HOLLINS, Leigh Bank, Labourer	HT
24 Apr	Sarah d/o Francis & Ellen PHILLIPS, Withington, Labourer	HT
8 May	Mary d/o Thomas & Mary MILLINGTON, Leigh Bank, Labourer	HT
19 May	Thomas s/o James & Anne JOHNSON, Morley Heath, Labourer	HT
16 Jun	Martha d/o Elizabeth MOOR, Withington, Servant	HT
3 Jul	William s/o Thos: & Ann BAKEWELL, Birmingham, Schoolmaster	HT
10 Jul	James s/o Joseph & Mary BRANDRICK, Leigh Bank, Labourer	HT
28 Jul	John s/o John & Sarah HUGHES, Morley Heath, Labourer	HT
4 Aug	Thomas s/o Thomas & Ellen JOHNSON, Lower Leigh, Labourer	HT
29 Sep	William s/o John & Mary RAWLIN, Middleton Green, Farmer	HT
5 Nov	William s/o Joseph & Hannah ELLERTON, Bents, Labourer	HT
24 Nov	George s/o Edward & Anne HOWE, Middleton Green, Labourer	HT
31 Dec	James s/o James & Lydia DUROSE, Upper Leigh, Wheelwright	HT
1817		
3 Jan	John s/o Joseph & Hannah EDGE, Withington, Labourer	HT
8 Jan	George s/o James & Eliz: BENTLEY, Lower Leigh, Publican	HT
9 Feb	James s/o Thomas & Prudence BAILEY, Withington Green, Labourer	HT
18 Feb	William s/o William & Elizabeth CHELL, Godstone, Labourer	HT
9 Mar	Eliza d/o Sampson & Anne BAILEY, Lower Leigh, Labourer	HT
9 Mar	Charles s/o Charles & Sarah BROWNE [Brown-BT], Park Hall, Farmer	HT

19 Mar	James s/o John & Mary BURNETT, Nobott, Farmer	HT
28 Mar	Anne d/o Thomas & Lydia OSBOURNE, Birchwood Park, Gentleman	HT
30 Mar	Anne d/o Mary PRESTON, Wood-side, Servant	HT
13 Apr	Mary d/o Thomas & Esther ALCOCK, Upper Leigh, Labourer	HT
4 May	Anne d/o William & Diana BURTON, Lower Leigh, Labourer	HT
20 May	William s/o Hannah JOHNSON, Work-House, Servant	HT
26 May	Elizabeth d/o Benjamin & Mary TOOTH, Birchwood Park, Labourer	HT
8 Jun	Eliza d/o John & Anne BURTON, Bents, Farmer	HT
25 Jun	Kitty d/o Saml: & Eliz: NOBS, Morley Heath, Labourer	HT
24 Jul	Sarah d/o John & Dorothy CHELL, Dodsley, Mason	HT
9 Aug	William s/o Joseph & Jane DEAKIN, Ivy House, Labourer	HT
10 Aug	Mary d/o Thomas & Mary SAUNDERS, Bent-House, Farmer	HT
24 Aug	Thomas s/o Thomas & Eliz: FOSTER, Nobot, Shoe-maker	HT
24 Aug	Mary d/o Thomas & Harriet MARSON, Middleton Green, Farmer	HT
1 Sep	Dorothy s/o Charles & Dorothy HART, Dodsley, Farmer	HT
21 Sep	Anne d/o George & Mary EDGE, Withington, Labourer	HT
11 Oct	William s/o William & Cecily GREENSMITH Wood Farm, Farmer	HT
17 Oct	Elizabeth d/o Thomas & Sarah STARTIN, Nobot, Blacksmith	HT
26 Oct	Elizabeth d/o John & Mary TOOTH, Withington, Labourer	HT
4 Nov	Stephen s/o Robert & Anne ARNOLD, Over Leigh, Farmer	HT
16 Nov	Thomas s/o Thomas & Mary HOWE, Upper Leigh, Maltster	HT
20 Nov	Mary d/o Thomas & Sarah MILLINGTON, Dodsley, Labourer	HT
28 Nov	George s/o Henry & Mary TURNER, Church Leigh, Publican	HT
28 Nov	William s/o William & Mary HOWE, Lower Leigh, Farmer	HT
30 Dec	Jane d/o Thomas & Charlotte BAGNALL, Nobot, Labourer	HT
1818		
9 Feb	John Prince s/o John Prince & Ellen ROBINSON, Lower Leigh, Joiner	HT
20 Feb	Anne d/o Stephen & Jane BAILEY, Lower Leigh, Labourer	HT
21 Feb	Mary d/o James & Frances ATKIN, Headlands, Butcher	HT
20 Mar	Joseph s/o Joseph & Jane DEAN, Middleton Green, Shoemaker	HT
22 Mar	John s/o Sarah FOSTER, Work-House, Servant	HT
22 Mar	Anne d/o Thomas & Sarah PARKER, Withington, Labourer	HT
5 Apr	Anne d/o John & Mary RAWLIN, Morley Heath, Labourer	HT
19 Apr	James s/o John & Eliz: HUSON, Withington, Farmer	HT
26 Apr	James s/o Thomas & Hannah RUSHTON, Upper Leigh, Labourer	HT
26 Apr	Hannah d/o Prudence TUNSTAL *[Tunstall-BT]* Dodsley Servant	HT
10 May	Ellen d/o Edward & Eliz: COPE, Church Leigh, Shoemaker	HT
27 May	John s/o Francis & Mary SHERRATT, Hob-Hill, Labourer	HT
5 Jun	Emma d/o Thomas & Louisa BRINDLEY, Leigh, Gentleman	HT
6 Jun	William s/o Ellen NOAKES, Upper Leigh, Servant	HT
8 Jun	Joseph & Mary Twins of Edward & Maria CHELL, Church Leigh, Labourer	HT
14 Jun	Elizabeth d/o Joseph & Elizabeth JENKINSON, Leigh, Wheelwright	HT
19 Jul	Mary d/o Thomas & Mary SMITH, Upper Leigh, Butcher	HT
24 Sep	Griffith s/o John & Mary TOOTH, Withington, Labourer	HT
2 Nov	Robert s/o Willm: & Anne JOHNSON, Upper Leigh, Labourer	HT
29 Nov	Sarah d/o Willm: & Sarah TILL, Nobot, Labourer	HT
2 Dec	John s/o George & Hannah SMITH, Withington, Labourer	HT
5 Dec	Laurence s/o William & Cicily GREENSMITH, Wood-Farm, Farmer	HT
9 Dec	Elizabeth d/o Thomas & Mary HOWE, Upper Leigh, Maltster	HT
23 Dec	John s/o Thomas & Lucy PHILLIPS, Withington, Labourer	HT

1819

24 Jan	Elizabeth d/o Charles & Elizabeth KENT, Dodsley, Labourer	HT
26 Feb	Rosannah d/o Sampson & Anne BAILEY, Lower Leigh, Coal Carrier	HT
26 Feb	Mary d/o Mary MITCHELL, Withington, Servant	HT
3 Mar	William s/o William & Mary PLANT, Morley Heath, Labourer	HT
21 Mar	James s/o George & Mary TOOTH, Church Leigh, Labourer	HT
21 Mar	John s/o Thomas & Ellen JOHNSON, Lower Leigh, Labourer	HT
4 Apr	Mary d/o Hannah JOHNSON, Dodsley, Servant	HT
15 Apr	Thomas s/o Thomas & Harriet MARSON, Middleton Green, Farmer	HT
22 Apr	William s/o William & Elizabeth BYATT, Withington, Labourer	HT
26 Apr	Sarah d/o John & Mary BURNETT, Nobot, Farmer	HT
10 May	Ellen d/o Thomas & Mary HOLLINS, Checkley Bank, Labourer	HT
13 May	Richard s/o Richard & Elizabeth PHILLIPS, Dodsley, Farmer	HT
17 May	Sarah d/o James & Prudence BAILEY, Withington, Labourer	HT
22 May	Jane d/o James & Lydia DUROSE, Upper Leigh, Wheelwright	HT
29 May	James s/o James & Anne BAGSHAW, Lower Leigh, Labourer	HT
6 Jun	Robert s/o John & Sarah HUGHES, Morley Heath, Labourer	HT
13 Jul	Thomas s/o John & Elizabeth PHILLIPS, Withington, Labourer	HT
18 Jul	John s/o John & Anne TORTERSHELL, Nobot, Farmer	HT
28 Aug	Sarah d/o Edward & Anne DUROSE, Field, Shoemaker	HT
21 Sep	Elizabeth d/o Charles & Sarah BROWNE, Park Hall, Farmer	HT
22 Sep	William s/o John & Dorothy CHELL, Upper Leigh, Mason	HT
10 Oct	James s/o George & Anne BOLTON, Morley Heath, Labourer	HT
10 Oct	Catherine d/o Charles & Elizabeth LOWE, Morley Heath, Labourer	HT
28 Nov	Betty d/o Saml: & Betty NOBS, Morley Heath, Labourer	HT

1820

16 Feb	Dorothy d/o James & Jane DEAKIN, Ivy-House, Labourer	HT
20 Feb	Thomas s/o Edith HOWE, Lower Leigh, Servant	HT
25 Feb	Stephen s/o Joseph & Hannah EDGE, Withington, Labourer	HT
28 Feb	Mary d/o Francis & Ellen PHILLIPS, Over-Leigh, Labourer	HT
5 Mar	Henry s/o Henry & Mary TURNER, Church Leigh, Publican	HT
26 Mar	Luke s/o Thomas & Sarah STARTIN, Nobott, Blacksmith	HT
26 Mar	Prudence d/o Anne COPE, Church Leigh, Servant	HT
1 Apr	Joseph & Mary Twin children of George & Mary EDGE, Withington, Labourer	HT
7 Apr	Margaretta d/o Thomas & Mary HOWE, Upper Leigh, Maltster	HT
16 Apr	George s/o John & Charlotte TURNER, Upper Leigh, Labourer	HT
16 Apr	Elizabeth d/o Thomas & Mary SMITH, Upper Leigh, Butcher	HT
16 Apr	Hannah d/o Mary FOSTER, Nobot, Servant	HT
21 Apr	Thomas s/o Saml: & Sarah ADDISON, Field Hall, Farmer	HT
2 May	Henry s/o William & Elizabeth CHELL, Godstone, Labourer	HT
9 May	John Harvey s/o Thomas & Elizabeth WILSON, Fole, Farmer	HT
13 May	Henry s/o William & Mary HOWE, Leigh Lane, Farmer	HT
9 Jun	Edith d/o John & Edith HOLLINS, Dairy House, Farmer	HT
18 Jun	George s/o William & Sarah FOWLER, Bents, Mason	HT
13 Aug	Thomas s/o William & Mary GRUNDY, Bent-Lane, Labourer	HT
30 Aug	Clementina d/o Sarah BARNES, Field, Servant	HT
12 Sep	James s/o James & Catharine DEAKIN, Dodsley, Labourer	HT
15 Oct	Joseph s/o Joseph & Elizabeth JENKINSON, Upper Leigh, Wheelwright	HT
18 Oct	John s/o James & Francis ATKIN, Head-lands, Butcher	HT
23 Oct	Sampson s/o Sampson & Anne BAILEY, Lower-Leigh, Labourer	HT

31 Oct	Thomas s/o William & Cicely GREENSMITH, The Wood, Farmer	HT
27 Nov	William s/o William & Anne COPE, Leigh, Butcher	HT
27 Nov	Henry s/o Sarah ALCOCK, Upper Leigh, Servant	HT
24 Dec	George s/o Charles & Elizabeth KENT, Church Leigh, Labourer	HT

1821

4 Jan	John s/o John & Mary RAWLIN, Morley-Heath, Labourer	HT
11 Feb	John s/o John & Sarah LEES [Leese-BT], Short-wood, Labourer	HT
13 Feb	Eliza d/o John & Elizabeth PHILLIPS, Lower Leigh, Labourer	HT
24 Feb	Mary d/o James & Anne SHENTON, Withington, Labourer	HT
23 Mar	Thomas s/o Saml: & Eliz: FELTHOUSE, Withington, Labourer	HT
25 Mar	Harriet d/o Elizabeth PHILLIPS, Leigh Bank, Servant	HT
30 Mar	Jane d/o John & Mary HOLLINS, Leigh Bank, Labourer	HT
9 Apr	John s/o Thomas & Mary MILLINGTON, Upper-Leigh, Labourer	HT
23 Apr	Samuel s/o William & Mary PLANT, Morley-Heath, Labourer	HT
28 Apr	Edward s/o Edward & Maria CHELL, Lower Leigh, Labourer	HT
2 May	Emma d/o James & Prudence BAILEY, Bitterns-dale, Labourer	HT
6 May	William s/o Jane BAILEY, Dodsley, Servant	HT
10 May	John s/o Matilda WALKER, Withington, Servant	HT
19 May	Olive d/o James & Lydia DUROSE, Upper Leigh, Wheelwright	HT
5 Jun	Thomas s/o Thomas & Mary TOOTH, Withington, Labourer	HT
8 Jun	Elizabeth d/o George & Hannah MIATT, Dodsley, Labourer	HT
8 Jun	Richard s/o Edward & Anne HOWE, Dodsley, Labourer	HT
10 Jun	Eliza d/o Thomas & Jane LEES [Leese-BT], Middleton Green, Labourer	HT
17 Jun	Emma d/o Margaret ALCOCK, Withington, Servant	HT
4 Jul	Thomas s/o Thomas & Lucy BROWNE, Morley-Heath, Labourer	HT
29 Jul	Thomas s/o Thomas & Mary SMITH, Leigh Lane, Butcher	HT
3 Aug	Joseph s/o Francis & Mary JOHNSON, Over-Leigh, Labourer	HT
31 Aug	Frederick s/o John & Hannah TIDSWELL, Fole-Hall, Farmer	HT
12 Aug	John s/o William & Anne STEVENSON, Bents, Labourer	HT
19 Aug	George s/o Mary MITCHELL, Withington, Servant	HT
26 Aug	Thomas s/o Robert & Anne ARNOLD, Upper-Leigh, Farmer	HT
29 Aug	George s/o Mary FOSTER, Godstone, Servant	HT
23 Sep	Thomas s/o John & Mary BURNET [Burnett-BT], Nobot, Farmer	HT
23 Sep	Lydia d/o Thomas & Harriet MARSON, Middleton Green, Farmer	HT
30 Sep	Joseph s/o Joseph & Anne WOODSON, Morley Heath, Labourer	HT
30 Sep	Charles s/o Charles & Sarah WARD, Withington, Labourer	HT
3 Oct	John s/o John & Edith HOLLINS, Dairy House, Farmer	HT
15 Oct	Mary Anne d/o Anne JOHNSON, Upper Leigh, Servant	HT
23 Oct	George s/o George & Anne DAWSON, Dodsley, Farmer	HT
30 Oct	Jane d/o Hannah TILL, Lower Leigh, Servant	HT
25 Nov	Mary d/o Joseph & Hellen GENT, Withington, Labourer	HT
2 Dec	Mary d/o Edith HOWE, Church Leigh, Servant	HT

1822

6 Jan	Lydia d/o Saml: & Elizth: NOBBS, Nobot, Labourer	HT
6 Jan	Thomas s/o Charles & Sarah BROWNE, Park Hall, Farmer	HT
13 Jan	John s/o John & Elizabeth RAWLIN, Morley Heath, Labourer	HT
18 Jan	Mary d/o William & Anne JOHNSON, Upper Leigh, Labourer	HT
3 Feb	Sarah & Ellen dau's of John & Anne TOTERSHALL, Nobot, Farmer	HT
16 Feb	George s/o George & Anne TILL, Church-Leigh, Labourer	HT
17 Feb	Mary d/o Joseph & Elizth: JENKINSON Upper Leigh Wheelwright	HT
23 Feb	John s/o George & Mary TOOTH, Church Leigh, Labourer	HT

23 Feb	William s/o William & Mary HOWE, Upper Leigh, Farmer	HT
8 Apr	Hester d/o William & Sarah MELLER, Lower Leigh, Labourer	HT
14 Apr	Thomas s/o Francis & Mary SHERRETT, Benter, Labourer	HT
23 Apr	Thomas s/o George & Hannah SMITH, Lower Leigh, Labourer	HT
27 Apr	Thomas s/o Henry & Mary TURNER, Church Leigh, Publican	HT
3 May	Edward s/o Edward & Anne DUROSE, Field, Shoemaker	HT
13 May	George s/o Thomas & Mary HOLLINS, Leigh Bank, Labourer	HT
26 May	Sarah d/o Michael & Catherine BAILEY, Stone Heath, Mendicant	HT
9 Jun	Thomas s/o Elizabeth NICKLIN, Checkley Bank, Servant	HT
7 Jul	William s/o Thomas & Hester ALCOCK, Upper Leigh, Labourer	HT
7 Jul	Harriet d/o John & Sarah LEESE, Short-woods, Labourer	HT
18 Jul	George s/o Sarah BURTON, Bents, Servant	HT
1 Aug	John s/o John & Elizabeth BURTON, Withington, Butcher	HT
4 Aug	Eliza Murray d/o Charlotte SHENTON, Middleton Green, Servant	HT
17 Aug	Mary d/o John & Charlotte TURNER, Morley Heath, Sawyer	HT
19 Sep	Jane d/o John & Mary TOOTH, Withington, Labourer	HT
20 Sep	Elizabeth d/o John & Elizabeth STOKES, Middleton Green, Labourer	HT
29 Sep	Elizabeth d/o Francis & Ellen PHILLIPS, Dodsley, Labourer	HT
9 Oct	Louisa d/o John & Louisa ASBURY, Painly Hill, Farmer	HT
18 Oct	William s/o Richard & Elizabeth PHILLIPS, Dodsley, Farmer	HT
5 Nov	Mary d/o) Thomas & Anne SHERRAT *[Sherratt-BT]*,	HT
5 Nov	Sarah d/o) Hay House, Farmer. Received into the Congregation	HT
11 Nov	Robert s/o William & Cicily GREENSMITH, Wood-Farm, Farmer	HT
24 Nov	Emma d/o Thomas & Sarah STARTIN, Nobot, Blacksmith	HT
3 Dec	Sarah Fenton d/o Thomas & Mary TILL, Middleton Green, Labourer	HT
8 Dec	Samuel s/o Elizabeth TILL, Church Leigh, Servant	HT
11 Dec	William s/o William & Anne STEVENSON, The Fields, Farmer	HT
31 Dec	Patience d/o George & Anne DAWSON, Dodsley, Farmer	HT
1823		
19 Jan	John s/o Charles & Anne HIGGINBOTHAM, Withington, Blacksmith	HT
17 Feb	Mary d/o John & Edith HOLLINS, Dairy House, Farmer	HT
9 Mar	John s/o John & Hannah CARR, Checkley Bank, Labourer	HT
30 Mar	Henry s/o Jane BAILEY, Dodsley, Servant	HT
6 Apr	Thomason d/o Charles & Elizabeth KENT, Church Leigh, Labourer	HT
7 Jul	Elizabeth d/o Francis & Mary JOHNSON Church Leigh Labourer	HT
27 Jul	Caroline d/o William & Anne DEAKIN, Field, Farmer	HT
17 Aug	Charles s/o James & Lydia DUROSE, Upper Leigh, Wheelwright	HT
24 Aug	William s/o John & Mary BURNET *[Burnett-BT]*, Nobot, Farmer	HT
24 Aug	Cicely d/o James & Prudence BAILEY, Ivey-House, Labourer	HT
4 Sep	John s/o Thomas & Rebecca KENT, Upper Leigh, Labourer	HT
14 Sep	Catherine d/o Thomas & Louisa BRINDLEY, Upper Leigh, Gentleman	HT
28 Sep	Thomas s/o Mary FOSTER, Withington Green, Servant	HT
2 Oct	John s/o Richard & Elizabeth PRESTON Morley-Heath Labourer	HT
24 Oct	Maria d/o William & Charlotte MEAKIN, Withington, Labourer	HT
2 Nov	Jane d/o John & Anne TOTERSHAL, Nobot, Farmer	HT
2 Nov	Anne d/o James & Sarah WALKER, Withington, Labourer	HT
6 Nov	Edward s/o Edward & Sarah BAILEY, Over-Leigh, Labourer	HT
16 Nov	Ellen d/o Saml: & Elizabeth FELTHOUSE, Withington, Farmer	HT
1824		
11 Jan	Joseph & Mary Twins of John & Prudence HAWKINS, Morley-Heath, Farmer	HT

15 Jan	Thomas s/o Sampson & Anne BAILEY, Nobot, Labourer	HT
1 Feb	Mary d/o Sarah RATCLIFFE, Withington, Servant	HT
10 Feb	William & Elizabeth Twins Elizabeth POTTS, Widow, Withington Green, Servant	HT
22 Feb	Margaret d/o William & Mary PLANT, Church Leigh, Labourer	HT
6 Mar	Joseph s/o Charles & Sarah BROWNE, Park Hall, Farmer	HT
	Received into the Congregation July 11th 1830 by James Beaven, Curate	
6 Mar	Thomas s/o Joseph & Elizabeth JENKINSON, Upper Leigh, Wheelwright	HT
7 Mar	James s/o Thomas & Hester ALCOCK, Upper Leigh, Labourer	HT
9 Mar	Jane d/o Thomas & Jane LEESE, Middleton Green, Labourer	HT
30 Mar	Susannah d/o Samuel & Elizabeth NOBBS, Morley Heath, Labourer	HT
2 Apr	Elizabeth d/o William & Elizabeth BYATT, Withington, Labourer	HT
8 Apr	Sarah d/o Thomas & Anne SHERRATT, Hay-House, Farmer	HT
21 Apr	Mary Anne d/o George & Anne TILL, Church Leigh, Labourer	HT
22 Apr	Thomas s/o William & Hannah BARNET [Burnett-BT], Field, Labourer	HT
14 May	Henry s/o Lydia MILWARD, Leigh Bank, Servant	HT
22 May	Mary d/o William & Sarah ARNOLD, Lower Leigh, Labourer	HT
6 Jun	William s/o John & Elizabeth BURTON, Withington Green, Butcher	HT
11 Jul	Edward s/o Henry & Mary TURNER, Church Leigh, Publican	HT
25 Jul	Thomas s/o John & Mary RAWLIN, Morley Heath, Labourer	HT
29 Jul	Walter Samuel s/o Thomas & Harriet MARSON, The Fields, Farmer	HT
20 Aug	William s/o William & Anne JOHNSON, Over Leigh, Labourer	HT
22 Aug	Frederick s/o Richard & Joanna ASBURY, Painly Hill, Farmer	HT
24 Aug	Mary Anne d/o Thomas & Mary MOUNTFORT, Lower Leigh, Shoemaker	HT
12 Sep	James s/o James & Jane DEAKIN, Blakely House, Labourer	HT
2 Oct	Henry s/o Edward & Maria CHELL, Lower Leigh, Labourer	HT
3 Oct	Eliza d/o Sarah BURTON, Bents, Servant	HT
24 Oct	Edward s/o John & Sarah LEES [Leese-BT], Shortwoods, Labourer	HT
28 Nov	Thomas s/o William & Anne STEVENSON, Lower Leigh, Farmer	HT
19 Dec	Charles s/o John & Charlotte SPENCER, Withington Green, Blacksmith	HT
1825		
3 Jan	Mary Anne d/o Michael & Catharine BAILEY, Stone Heath, Pauper	HT
3 Jan	Hannah d/o George & Anne DAWSON, Dodsley ~~Withington~~, Farmer	HT
16 Jan	Dorothy d/o Thomas & Mary SMITH, Over Leigh, Butcher	HT
17 Jan	Jane d/o Charles & Elizabeth KENT, Church Leigh, Labourer	HT
2 Feb	Thomas s/o John & Edith HOLLINS, Dairy House, Farmer	HT
15 Feb	Mary d/o Samuel & Frances BRIDGEWOOD, Field, Labourer	HT
20 Feb	John s/o John & Elizabeth WRIGHT, Withington, Wheelwright	HT
24 Feb	Eliza d/o Robert & Anne ARNOLD, Over Leigh, Farmer	HT
	Received into the Congregation Oct 31 1830 by me James Beaven Curate	
28 Feb	Mary d/o William & Hannah WATERHOUSE, Over Leigh, Labourer	HT
3 Apr	Charles s/o George & Mary TOOTH, Bents, Labourer	HT
3 Apr	Emma d/o Sarah BURTON, Nobot, Servant	HT
10 Apr	Emma d/o James & Sarah WALKER, Withington, Labourer	HT
22 Apr	Charles John s/o William & Cecily GREENSMITH, Wood-Farm, Farmer	HT
15 May	Hannah d/o Thomas & Mary HOLLINS, Checkley Bank, Labourer	HT
29 May	Rachel d/o Joseph & Jane GOODISON, Nobot, Labourer	HT
30 May	Mary d/o Richard & Elizabeth PHILLIPS, Dodsley, Farmer	SL
12 Jun	Sarah d/o Charles & Anne BEDSON, Lower Leigh, Wheelwright	SL
19 Jun	Joseph s/o Joseph & Hannah EDGE, Withington Green, Labourer	SL
26 Jun	Mary Anne d/o Thomas & Mary TILL, Middleton Green, Labourer	HT

24 Jul	William s/o Thomas & Mary MILLINGTON, Upper Leigh, Labourer	HT
29 Jul	John s/o Joseph & Hannah KID, Withington, Labourer	HT
7 Aug	Jane d/o Thomas & Rebecca PHILLIPS, Over Leigh, Labourer	HT
11 Aug	Elizabeth d/o Thomas & Anne WATSON, Withington, Labourer	HT
21 Aug	Maria d/o George & Mary EDGE, Park Hall Lodge, Labourer	HT
5 Oct	Charles s/o John & Anne DEAKIN, Dodsley, Farmer	HT
9 Oct	Emma d/o Mary STARTIN, Nobot, Servant	HT
16 Oct	Lydia d/o James & Lydia DUROSE, Over Leigh, Wheelwright	HT
29 Oct	William Robert Mountfort s/o William & Margaret BLURTON, Field Hall, Gentleman	HT
30 Oct	Henry s/o Joseph & Elizabeth JENKINSON, Upper Leigh, Wheelwright	HT
1 Nov	John s/o Thomas & Anne SHERRATT, Hays House, Farmer	SL
6 Nov	Harriet d/o Sarah BILLINGS, Work-house, Servant	HT
12 Dec	Anne d/o Joseph & Mary DENT, Morley Heath, Farmer	HT
18 Dec	Anne d/o John & Elizabeth BURTON, Withington, Butcher	HT

1826

24 Jan	Samuel & Edward Twins of Samuel & Elizabeth NOBBS, Morley-Heath, Labourer	HT
24 Jan	John s/o John & Elizabeth FLUER, Middleton Green, Labourer	HT
9 Feb	Jesse s/o William & Hannah BARNET *[Burnett-BT]*, Field, Labourer	HT
19 Feb	George s/o James & Prudence BAILEY, Ivy House, Farmer	HT
19 Feb	Thomas s/o Barnabas & Sarah BAILEY, Church Leigh, Labourer	HT
23 Feb	George s/o William & Anne DEAKIN, Field, Farmer	HT
28 Feb	Anne d/o Thomas & Hester ALCOCK, Over Leigh, Labourer	HT
19 Mar	Hannah d/o Mary MITCHELL, Withington, Servant	HT
13 Apr	Thomas s/o Francis & Ellen PHILIPS, Dodsley, Labourer	HT
2 Jun	George s/o James & Sarah LEES *[Leese-BT]*, Short-woods, Labourer	HT
11 Jun	John s/o Thomas & Mary MOUNTFORT Lower Leigh Shoemaker	HT
11 Jun	Anne d/o Sarah TILL, Nobot, Servant	HT
2 Jul	Richard s/o Charles & Sarah BROWNE, Park Hall, Farmer Received into the Congregation July 11th 1830 by James Beaven Curate	HT
8 Jul	Henry s/o Edward & Sarah BAILEY, Upper Leigh, Labourer	HT
28 Jul	William s/o Thomas & Harriet MARSON, The Fields, Farmer	HT
20 Aug	Elizabeth d/o Clement & Hannah COTTERIL, Birchwood Park, Farmer	HT
22 Aug	William s/o Mr Thomas & Louisa BRINDLEY, Upper Leigh, privately Gentleman Received into the Congregation July 1 1830 by me James Beaven Curate	HT
29 Aug	William s/o George & Anne DAWSON, Dodsley, Farmer	HT
30 Aug	Sarah d/o Henry & Mary TURNER, Church Leigh, Publican	HT
3 Sep	Thomas s/o Hannah SMITH, Work-house, Servant	HT
8 Oct	Elizabeth d/o Edward & Maria CHELL, Lower Leigh, Labourer	HT
30 Oct	Alice d/o Mary FOSTER, Withington, Servant	HT
30 Oct	William s/o William & Anne RATCLIFFE, Withington, Labourer	HT
10 Dec	Eliza *[Elizabeth-BT]* d/o Elizabeth FOWLER, Bents, Servant	HT
24 Dec	Thomas s/o Luke & Diana PARKER, Withington, Labourer	HT

1827

14 Jan	Mary d/o Charles & Sarah WARD, Field, Labourer	HT
19 Jan	John Waltho s/o John Waltho & Mary FENTON, Hay-House, Farmer	HT
26 Jan	William s/o John & Edith HOLLINS, Dairy House, Farmer	HT
24 Feb	William s/o William & Sarah ARNOLD, Lower Leigh, Labourer	HT
26 Feb	Mary d/o Charles & Elizabeth KENT, Church Leigh, Labourer	HT

4 Mar	Eliza d/o James & Sarah WALKER, Withington, Labourer		HT
11 Mar	Jane d/o John & Mary RAWLIN, Morley Heath, Labourer		HT
15 Mar	James s/o William & Anne STEVENSON, Lower Leigh, Labourer		HT
17 Mar	Jane d/o John & Anne STARTIN, Church Leigh, Labourer		HT
21 Mar	James s/o James & Mary TOWERS, Church Leigh, Labourer		HT
24 Mar	George s/o Sarah LEES [Leese-BT], Work-house, Servant		HT
5 Apr	Mary d/o Matilda WALKER, Withington Green, Servant		HT
8 Apr	Thomas s/o James & Jane DEAKIN, Blakeley House, Shoemaker		HT
22 Apr	Charles s/o William & Charlotte MAKIN, Withington, Labourer		HT
21 May	Mary d/o Francis & Mary SHERRATT, Withington, Labourer		HT
28 May	Anne d/o Luke & Anne TURNER, Wood-Leasow, Farmer		HT
3 Jun	William s/o Joseph & Mary-Upton COPE, Middleton Green, Farmer		HT
4 Jun	Hannah d/o Thomas & Mary DOLMAN, Withington, Basketmaker		HT
9 Jun	Mary d/o Francis & Mary JOHNSON, Church Leigh, Labourer		HT
17 Jun	Hannah d/o Thomas & Mary MELLER, Upper Leigh, Labourer		HT
30 Jun	Thomas s/o Joseph & Hannah KID, Withington, Labourer		HT
6 Jul	John s/o John & Anne MARSON, Middleton Green, Farmer		HT
27 Jul	Eliza d/o John & Anne DEAKIN, Dodsley, Farmer		HT
19 Aug	Caroline d/o Thomas & Sarah STARTIN, Nobot, Blacksmith		HT
23 Aug	William s/o Thomas & Anne WATSON, Field, Labourer		HT
2 Sep	Frances d/o James & Charlotte POYSOR, Middleton Green, Labourer		HT
12 Sep	Catharina d/o Thomas & Hannah CLARK, Withington, Labourer		HT
13 Sep	William s/o John & Julia MARSON, Lower Leigh, Labourer		HT
24 Sep	Samuel s/o John & Elizabeth BURTON, Withington, Butcher		HT
13 Oct	William s/o Joseph & Hannah EDGE, Withington, Labourer		HT
26 Oct	Caroline d/o Thomas & Mary TILL, Middleton Green, Labourer		HT
25 Nov	Margaret d/o William & Hannah BARNET [Barnett-BT], Field, Labourer		HT
9 Dec	Charles s/o William & Anne BROWNE [Brown-BT], Dodsley, Brickmaker		HT
26 Dec	Elizabeth d/o Matthew & Elizabeth SNAPE, Church Leigh, Labourer		HT

1828

10 Jan	John s/o William & Elizabeth BYATT, Withington, Labourer	HT
	Received into the Congregation Oct 31st 1830 by me James Beaven Curate	
26 Jan	Henry s/o Clement & Hannah COTTERIL [Cotterill-BT], Birchwood Park,	HT
	Farmer	
27 Jan	Mary d/o John & Sarah HUGHES, Morley Heath, Shoemaker	HT
10 Feb	James s/o William & Elizabeth BENTLEY, Birchwood Park, Labourer HT	
22 Feb	Richard s/o Joseph & Elizabeth JENKINSON, Over Leigh, Wheelwright	HT
16 Mar	Rosanna d/o Michael & Anne LOVETT, Nobot, Labourer	HT
23 Mar	Thomas s/o Charles & Anne DEAN, Lower Leigh, Labourer	HT
28 Apr	Harriet d/o Thomas & Harriet MARSON, The Fields, Farmer	HT
28 Apr	George s/o Anne MIATT, Bents, Dressmaker	HT
	Received into the Congregation June 2nd 1833 by me James Beaven Curate	
12 May	Joseph s/o Edward & Millington TATTON, Nobot, Labourer	HT
12 May	George s/o Edith WALKER, Withington, Servant	HT
13 May	Louisa d/o Saml: & Elizabeth NOBBS, Morley Heath, Labourer	HT
14 May	Anne d/o George & Anne DAWSON, Dodsley, Farmer	HT
17 Jul	Lydia d/o John & Edith HOLLINS, Dairy House, Farmer	HT
22 Jul	Anne d/o William & Francis HOLLINS, Middleton Green, Farmer	HT
3 Aug	Thomas s/o Michl: & Elizth: BAILEY, Stone Heath, Pauper	HT
3 Aug	Emma d/o James & Prudence BAILEY, Ivey House, Labourer	HT
17 Aug	William s/o William & Sarah GRIFFITHS, Withington, Miller	HT

9 Sep	James s/o Joseph & Mary UPTON, Middleton Green, Farmer	HT
25 Sep	Gervase s/o John & Anne MARSON, Middleton Green, Farmer	HT
2 Oct	Elizabeth d/o William & Anne STEVENSON, Lower Leigh, Labourer	HT
9 Oct	Elizabeth d/o Thomas & Mary MILLINGTON, Middleton Green, Labourer	HT
11 Oct	Richard s/o Mr Thomas & Louisa BRINDLEY, Over Leigh Gentleman	HT
	Received into the Congregation July 1 1830 by me James Beaven Curate	
12 Oct	Mary d/o John & Mary DEAN, Middleton Green, Labourer	HT
19 Oct	Eliza d/o Barnaby & Sarah BAILEY, Withington, Labourer	HT
28 Oct	Mary Anne d/o John Waltho & Mary FENTON, Field, Farmer	HT
5 Nov	Samuel James s/o Mary ODLE, Withington, Servant	HT
9 Nov	Jane d/o George & Mary DEAKIN, Bentes House, Labourer	HT
27 Nov	John s/o Sampson & Mary SMITH, Hobs-Hill *[Holl Hill-BT]*, Tailer	HT
9 Dec	William s/o Ellen MILLINGTON, Painly Hill, Servant	HT

1829

3 Jan	Charles s/o Charles & Elizabeth KENT, Church Leigh, Labourer	HT
9 Jan	John s/o John & Anne DUROSE, Withington, Shoemaker	HT
19 Jan	Hannah d/o Edward & Sarah BAILEY, Upper Leigh, Labourer	RP
25 Jan	Jane d/o James & Sarah WALKER, Withington, Labourer	HT
8 Mar	Thomas s/o Thomas & Sarah HEATH, Park Hall Lodge, Labourer	HT
12 Apr	James s/o Thomas & Anne WATSON, Field, Labourer	H
12 Apr	Charles s/o Matilda WALKER, Work-house, Servant	H
24 Apr	Anne d/o Thomas & Mary SMITH, Over Leigh, Butcher	HT
4 May	Caleb s/o Clement & Hannah COTTERIL, Birchwood Park, Farmer	HT
12 May	Sarah d/o Luke & Anne TURNER, Wood Leasow, Farmer	HT
18 May	Joseph s/o James & Lydia DUROSE, Upper Leigh, Wheelwright	HT
	Received into the Congregation Nov 1st 1835 by me James Beaven Curate	
14 Jun	Mary d/o Francis & Hellen COPE, Withington, Labourer	HT
20 Jun	Elizabeth d/o John & Dorothy CARTER, Withington, Farmer	HT
5 Jul	Emma d/o John & Anne STARTIN, Church Leigh, Labourer	HT
16 Aug	John s/o James & Jane DEAKIN, Blakeley House, Shoemaker	CBC
23 Aug	Catherine d/o John & Elizabeth BURTON, Withington Green, Butcher	CBC
30 Aug	John s/o Samuel & Francis BRIDGWOOD, Field, Labourer	CBC
30 Aug	Hannah d/o Edward & Maria CHELL, Lower Leigh, Labourer	CBC
30 Aug	Martha d/o John & Jane SMITH, Withington, Labourer	CBC
6 Sep	Hugh s/o Matthew & Elizabeth SNAPE, Withington, Labourer	CBC
17 Sep	Eleanor Sarah d/o Thomas & Harriet MARSON, Upper Leigh, Farmer	CBC
17 Sep	Thomas s/o William & Anne ADAMS, Church Leigh, Labourer	CBC
17 Sep	Sarah d/o Rachel BILLINGS, Church Leigh, Servant	CBC
26 Sep	Mary d/o Rebecca & John BUXTON, Withington, Wheelwright	JH
27 Sep	Harriet d/o John & Mary RAWLIN, Morley Heath, Labourer	CBC
	Received into the Congregation August 10th 1835 by me James Beaven Curate	
28 Sep	Mary d/o William & Elizabeth TURNER, Leigh Bank, Butcher. According to the Certificate of the Rev's Samuel Langley Rector of Checkley, transmitted to me, this day	CBC
25 Oct	Emma d/o John & Anne DEAKIN, Dodsley, Farmer	CBC
	Received into the Congregation Oct 31st by me James Beaven Curate	
1 Nov	Emma d/o William & Hannah BARNETT, Field, Labourer	CBC
11 Nov	Joseph s/o Joseph & Mary UPTON, Bustomly House, Farmer. According to the Certificate of the Rev'd R.B. Baker, transmitted to me this day	CBC

15 Nov	William s/o William & Anne BROWN, Dodsley, Brickmaker	CBC
26 Nov	Anne d/o Thomas & Elizabeth KENT, Fole, Farmer	CBC
	According to the Certificate of the Rev's Samuel Langley Rector of Checkley, transmitted to me the same day. CBC	
25 Dec	John s/o Henry & Mary TURNER, Church Leigh, Butcher	CBC
25 Dec	Samson s/o Henry & Mary TURNER, Church Leigh, Butcher	CBC

1830

10 Jan	Elizabeth d/o Thomas & Mary TILL, Middleton Green, Labourer	GH
14 Feb	Thomas s/o Joseph & Mary BECK, Withington, Brickmaker	CBC
21 Feb	Elizabeth d/o Charles & Elizabeth PHILLIPS, Dodsly, Farmer, privately	CBC
	Received into the Congregation Sep 26 1830 by me James Beaven Curate	
14 Mar	John s/o Ellen TILL, Nobut, Servant	CBC
11 Apr	George s/o Catherine LOWE, Dodsley, Servant	CBC
25 Apr	Catherine Middleton d/o Mary MITCHEL, Withington Green, Servant	CBC
9 May	James s/o John & Olive SMITH, Lower Leigh, Labourer	CBC
21 Jun	William s/o Thomas & Mary SMITH, Leigh Lane, Butcher	CBC
27 Jun	Charles s/o Charles & Anne DEAN, Upper Leigh, Labourer	CBC
11 Jul	John s/o Joseph & Sarah MEDDENS, Withington, Labourer	JB
30 Jun	Hannah d/o John & Dorothy TURNER, Church Leigh, Victualler, privately.	JB
	According to the Certificate of the Rev'd Samuel Langley Rector of Checkley, transmitted to me 18th July	
25 Jul	George base born s/o Hannah EDGE, Park Hall Lodge, Servant	JB
	(John RUSHTON reputed father)	
29 Aug	Harriet d/o James & Charlotte POYSER, Middleton Green, Labourer	JB
5 Sep*	Mary d/o Edward & Margaret HUGHES, Morrilow Heath, Labourer *privately	JB
5 Sep*	Elizabeth d/o Edward & Margaret HUGHES, Morrilow Heath, Labourer *privately	JB
24 Sep	Eliza d/o Samuel & Sarah BETTS, Upper Nobut, Labourer, privately.	JB
	Received into the Congregation Oct 31st by me James Beaven Curate	
26 Sep	Sarah d/o John Waltho & Mary FENTON, Field Mill, Farmer	JB
24 Oct	Hannah d/o Charles & Sarah WARD, Field, Labourer	JB
31 Oct	Thomas s/o William & Cicely PERKIN, Withington Green Tailor	JB
27 Nov	William s/o John & Ann MARSON, Middleton Green, Farmer	JB
5 Dec	Hannah d/o George & Mary DEAKIN, Withington Green Labourer	JB
20 Dec	William Smith s/o Susannah SHEMELT, Birchwood Park, Servant, privately. (William SMITH reputed father)	JB

1831

9 Jan	William s/o Sarah LEES, Chekley Bank, Servant	JB
	(John WRIGHT reputed father)	
16 Jan	Ann d/o John & Mary LOVATT, Upper Leigh, Farmer	JB
20 Feb	Sarah Ann d/o Clement & Ann COTTERIL [Cotterill-BT], Birchwood Park, Farmer	JB
20 Feb	Ann d/o John & Mary DEAN, Morrilow Heath, Labourer	JB
27 Feb	William s/o Samuel & Mary ALCOCK, Church Leigh, Labourer	JB
6 Mar	Mary Ann d/o Ann SMITH, Withington, Servant	JB
6 Mar	Elizabeth d/o Ann MYATT, Withington, Dressmaker	JB
	(Charles RATCLIFFE reputed father)	
13 Mar	George s/o William & Ann STEVENSON, Lower Leigh, Labourer	JB
20 Mar	Sarah d/o Thomas & Amelia TATTON, Lower Nobut, Labourer	JB
17 Apr	Sarah d/o John & Edith HOLLINS, Dairy House, Farmer	JB

17 Apr	William s/o Thomas & Sarah HEATH, Morrilow Heath, Labourer	JB
5 Jun	James s/o James & Sarah WALKER, Withington, Green Labourer	CBC
5 Jun	Thomas s/o Thomas & Mary MILLINGTON, Upper Leigh, Labourer	CBC
12 Jun	Elizabeth d/o William & Sarah GRIFFIN, Leigh, Shoemaker	CBC
3 Jul	John s/o Charles & Elizabeth KENT, Leigh, Labourer	CBC
31 Jul	William s/o John & Rebecca BUXTON, Withington, Wheelwright	JB
14 Aug	William s/o ~~John~~ Joseph & Hannah KIDD, Withington, Labourer	JB
4 Sep	John s/o William & Anne ADAMS, Church Leigh, Labourer	JB
11 Sep	Sarah illegit: d/o Ellen TILL, Lower Nobut, Servant	JB
	(Daniel KIRKLAND reputed father)	
11 Sep	Mary Ann d/o John & Dorothy CARTER, Withington, Farmer, privately	JB
28 Aug	Thomas s/o William & Ann BROWN, Dodsleigh, Labourer, privately	WM
	Received into the Congregation Sept 18th by me James Beaven Curate	
25 Sep	Thomas s/o Elizabeth JOHNSON, Lower Leigh, Servant,	JB
	([ ] reputed father)	
2 Oct	Ann d/o Edward & Sarah BAILEY, Upper Leigh, Labourer	JB
6 Oct	William s/o John & Ann STARTIN, Checkley Bank, Labourer	SL
16 Oct	Jane d/o James & Jane DEAKIN, Blakely House, Labourer	JB
6 Nov	Edward s/o Francis & Ellen COPE, Withington, Labourer	JB
27 Nov	William s/o Charles & Elizabeth PHILIPS, Dodsley, Labourer	JB
Xmas day	Edith d/o Thomas & Esther ALCOCK, Upper Leigh, Labourer	JB

1832

15 Jan	Mary Ann d/o William & Esther WALKER, Withington Green, privately Labourer	JB
	Received into the Congregation Apr 22 by me James Beaven Curate	
26 Jan	Mary d/o John & Sarah AULT, Upper Nobut, Labourer privately	JB
29 Jan	Blanche d/o James & Elizabeth Speed BEAVEN, Leigh Parsonage, Born Dec 16 1831. Clergyman	JB
5 Feb	Edwin s/o Matthew & Elizabeth SNAPE, Withington, Labourer	JB
5 Feb	Sarah Ann d/o Dorothy GARLAND, Withington Green, Servant	JB
5 Feb	Catherine d/o William & Hannah BARNETT, Patch Hall, Labourer	JB
22 Feb	Harriet d/o James & Prudence BAILY, Ivy-House, Labourer, privately. Received into the Congregation March 18	JB
12 Feb	John s/o William & Hannah EDGE, Field, Labourer	JB
21 Mar	James s/o Clement & Hannah COTTERIL, Birchwood Park, Farming Bailiff. Privately. Received into the Congregation Nov 8.	JB
25 Mar	Mary d/o George & Mary WILSON, Fole, Farmer	JB
29 Mar	Anne d/o Webb & Mary GRETTON, Upper Nobut, Labourer. Privately. Received into the Congregation April 8th	JB
22 Apr	Mary Ann d/o John & Mary RAWLINGS, Morrilow Heath, Labourer	JB
22 Apr	Thomas s/o John & Julia MARSON Upper Leigh Labourer Privately. Received into the Congregation March 8th 1835 by me JB	JB
29 Apr	John s/o John & Mary LOVATT, Upper Leigh, Farmer	JB
29 Apr	Mina d/o William & Elizabeth BYATT, Withington, Labourer	JB
29 Apr	John s/o John & Mary ALCOCK, Church Leigh, Shoemaker	JB
3 Jun	Edward s/o John & Edith HOLLINS, Dairy House, Farmer	JB
12 Jun	Sophia Louisa d/o John & Sophia BARNES, Field, Farmer	JB
25 Jun	Thomas s/o Edward & Ann DUROSE, Withington, Shoemaker	JB
19 Jun	Thomas s/o Thomas & Mary TILL, Middleton Green, Husbandman Privately. Received into the Congregation May 28th 1833 by me JB	JB
	Omitted in the proper place JB	

15 Jul Elizabeth d/o Thomas & Mary TOOTH, Withington Green, Labourer. JB
Privately. Received into the Congregation Nov 4
15 Jul Elizabeth d/o John & Anne BRAIN, Morrilow Heath, Labourer JB
22 Jul William s/o John & Dorothy TURNER, Church Leigh, Victualler JB
22 Jul Enoch s/o Charles & Anne DEAN, Upper Leigh, Labourer JB
19 Aug William s/o Thomas & Catharine GAUNT, Church Leigh, Tailor JB
19 Aug William s/o James & Elizabeth BRANDRICK Pickly Bank Farmer JB
9 Sep Sarah d/o Sarah & Barnaby BAILEY, Field, Labourer JB
16 Sep Ann d/o Thomas & Mary TOOTH, Field, Labourer JB
30 Sep Rosanna d/o Sarah BULL, Upper Tean, Spinster JB
(Thomas COPE reputed father)
16 Dec William s/o Michael & Ann LOVATT, Lower Leigh, Labourer JB
29 Dec William Thomas s/o Thomas & Frances PHILIPS, Dodsley, Farmer. JB
Privately. Received into the Congregation April 5th by me JB
1833
13 Jan Louisa d/o Samuel & Mary ALCOCK, Church Leigh, Labourer JB
27 Jan Elizabeth d/o John & Ann STARTIN, Upper Leigh, Labourer JB
28 Jan John s/o William & Cicely PERKIN, Withington Green, Tailor. Privately. JB
Received into the Congregation May 26th by me JB
3 Mar Harriet d/o Wiliam & Ann BROWN, Godstones, Brickmaker JB
8 Mar Joseph s/o Joseph & Mary UPTON, Middleton Green, Grocer. Privately. JB
Received into the Congregation May 28th by me JB
9 Mar Ann d/o William & Sarah GRIFFIN, Moore Lane, Shoemaker. Privately. JB
Received into the Congregation March 17th by me JB
18 Mar Jane d/o William & Esther WALKER, Withington Green, Labourer. JB
Privately. Received into the Congregation April 7th by me JB
28 Apr James s/o James & Charlotte POYSER, Middleton Green, Labourer JB
28 Apr John s/o William & Jane BURTON, Field, Labourer JB
12 May Dorothy d/o Charles & Elizabeth KENT, Church Leigh, Labourer JB
12 May Elizabeth d/o Ellen WHITEHALL, Carry Copse, Spinster. (Charles JB
GARLAND reputed father)
26 May Isaac s/o William & Ann STEPHENSON, The Bents, Labourer JB
7 Jul Charles s/o Ann MYATT, Withington Green, Servant. (Charles JB
RATCLIFF reputed father)
7 Jul Thomas s/o Thomas & Millicent TATTON, Lower Nobut, Labourer JB
14 Jul Charlotte d/o [Charles d/o-BT] Thomas & Catherine
BLACKBURN, Castle, Labourer JB
2 Aug Alice d/o Thomas & Alice HOLLINS, Bitternsdale, Farmer. Privately. CBC
Received into the Congregation Nov 3 by me JB
2 Aug Mary d/o Thomas & Alice HOLLINS, Bittersdale, Farmer. Privately. CBC
~~Received into the Congregation Nov 3 by me JB~~
4 Aug William s/o William & Ann ADAMS, Church Leigh, Labourer CBC
18 Aug Hannah d/o Clement & Hannah COTTRELL, Birchwood Park, Farmer CBC
15 Sep Ann d/o Francis & Ellen COPE, Dodsley Brickkiln, Labourer. Privately. JB
Received into the Congregation October 6th
12 Oct Maria d/o Edward & Maria CHELL, Lower Leigh, Labourer privately JB
24 Oct Hannah d/o William & Sarah MYATT, Dodsley, Labourer. Privately. JB
Received into the Congregation Nov 3 by me JB
29 Oct Edward William s/o James & Elizabeth Speed BEAVEN, Leigh JB
Parsonage, privately. Clergyman
Received into the Congregation November 9th by me JB

3 Nov	Mary Anne d/o John & Dorothy CARTER, Withington, Farmer	JB
3 Nov	Hannah d/o Joseph & Hannah KIDD, Withington, Labourer	JB
10 Nov	Thomas s/o Elizabeth RUSHTON, The Work-house, Spinster	JB
17 Nov	Thomas s/o George & Mary WILSON, Fole, Farmer	JB
24 Nov	Ann d/o William & Hannah EDGE, Field, Labourer	JB
15 Dec	Margaret d/o Charles & Elizabeth PHILIPS, Dodsley, Labourer	JB
15 Dec	Joseph s/o Thomas & Ann WATSON, Field, Labourer	JB
15 Dec	William s/o William & Elizabeth BENTLEY, Birchwood Park, Labourer	JB

1834

12 Jan	Emma d/o William & Elizabeth TURNER Checkley Bank Brewers Servant	JB
19 Jan	Amelia d/o Thomas & Mary STARTIN, Fole, Blacksmith	JB
16 9 Feb	George s/o George & Mary DEAKIN, Withington Green, Labourer	JB
11 Feb	Ellen d/o James & Jane DEAKIN, Blakeley House, Shoemaker. Privately. Received into the Congregation March 9th	JB
16 Feb	Ann d/o Joseph & Mary RATCLIFFE, Lower Leigh, Labourer	JB
22 Feb	William s/o Charles & Ellen GARLAND, Withington Green, Wheelwright. Privately. Received into the Congregation March 23rd by me JB	JB
23 Feb	John s/o James & Elizabeth BRANDRICK, Pickly Bank, Farmer	JB
23 Feb	Frederick s/o William & Frances HOLLINS, Upper Leigh, Labourer	JB
2 Mar	Hannah d/o James & Prudence BAILEY, Ivy House, Labourer	JB
9 Mar	Thomas s/o John & Hannah TIDSWELL, Fole Hall, Farmer	JB
9 Mar	Anne d/o John & Catherine TIDSWELL, Bradley, Farmer	JB
9 Mar	William s/o Charles & Sarah WARD, Field, Labourer	JB
6 Apr	Eliza d/o William & Hannah BARNET, Patch Hall, Labourer	JB
13 Apr	Jane d/o Charles & Susannah YATES, Middleton Green, Labourer	JB
19 Apr	Edward s/o Eliza RUSHTON, Upper Leigh, Servant. Privately.	JB
25 May	Anne d/o John & Edith HOLLINS, Dairy House, Farmer	JB
8 Jun	Mary d/o Jonathan & Mary FINNEY, Lower Leigh, Farmer	JB
27 Jun	John s/o Matthew & Elizabeth SNAPE, Withington, Coal-dealer privately	JB
13 Jul	Ann d/o Thomas & Sarah BARNES, Withington, Farmer	JB
13 Jul	George s/o James & Sarah WALKER, Withington Green, Labourer	JB
18 Jul	Dorothy d/o Thomas & Jane PHILIPS, Withington, Labourer. Privately. Received into the Congregation Nov 1st 1835 by me JB	JB
27 Jul	Ann d/o Joseph & Sarah BROWN, Wood-Leasowes, Farmer	JB
10 Aug	George s/o John & Mary RAWLINGS, Morrilow Heath, Labourer	JB
24 Aug	Joseph s/o Joseph & Maria HARRISON, Upper Nobut, Labourer	JB
24 Aug	Mary d/o John & Ann MARSON, Middleton Green, Farmer	JB
21 Sep	George s/o Thomas & Maria BUCKSTONE, Lower Nobut, Labourer	JB
5 Oct	William s/o Ann SMITH, Withington, Servant. (Robert PHILIPS reputed father)	JB
11 Oct	Mary d/o James & Jane DAVIS. Travelling to Oathampton beyond Uttoxeter. The man was a Soldier but died at Milford. Privately.	JB
2 Nov	Elizabeth d/o Edward & Sarah BAILEY, Upper Leigh, Labourer	JB
2 Nov	George s/o George & Mary EDGE, Park-Hall Lodge, Labourer	JB
2 Nov	Ann d/o Edward & Ann DUROSE, Withington, Shoemaker	JB
9 Nov	Charles s/o Thomas & Sarah HEATH, Wood-side, Labourer	JB
9 Nov	Mary Harriet d/o James & Elizabeth Speed BEAVEN, Church Leigh, Curate of this Parish	JB
16 Nov	George s/o George & Sarah STARTIN, Lower Nobut, Blacksmith	JB
21 Nov	Mary d/o John & Julia MARSON, Lower Leigh, Labourer. Privately. Received into the Congregation March 8th 1835 by me JB.	JB

28 Nov   Hannah d/o Joseph & Ann MARTIN, Sawyer, Upper Nobut. Privately.   JB
         Received into the Congregation Decr 25th by me JB

— 30 Nov   Emma d/o William & Anne NOKES, Lower Nobut, Labourer   JB

28 Dec   Ruth d/o Clement & Hannah COTTERIL Birchwood Park, Farmer   JB

1835

11 Jan   Edward s/o Michael & Ann LOVATT, Lower Leigh, Labourer   JB

18 Jan   Thomas s/o Thomas & Alice HOLLINS, Bittersdale, Farmer   JB

18 Jan   Charles s/o Hannah ALCOCK, Church Leigh, Servant.   JB
                           (Thomas TURNER reputed father)

— 8 Feb   Emily d/o Thomas & Mary TOOTH, Birchwood Park, Labourer   JB

14 Feb   Charles s/o ~~James &~~ Sarah ~~WALKER~~ TAYLOR, Withington Green,   JB
         ~~Labourer~~ Servant. Privately.
         Received into the Congregation Sept 26 1847 by me LFB Rector
         This last entry was corrected from a manuscript memorandum made at
         the time of baptising by me JB

15 Feb   Henry s/o Samuel & Mary ALCOCK, Church Leigh, Labourer   JB

8 Mar   Samuel s/o William & Mary ALCOCK, Morrilow Heath, Labourer   JB

15 Mar   Lydia d/o Charles & Elizabeth KENT, Church Leigh, Pig jobber. Privately.   JB

20 Mar   Ann d/o Mary ROWBOTHAM, Church Leigh, Servant. Privately.   JB

— 22 Mar   Hannah d/o Elizabeth TURNER, Withington, Servant   JB

22 Mar   Mary d/o William & Sarah GRIFFIN, Moor Lane, Shoemaker   JB

12 Apr   William s/o William & Sarah MYATT, Dodsley, Labourer   JB

24 May   Charles s/o Charles & ~~Elizabeth~~ Ellen GARLAND, Withington Green,   JB
                                 Wheelwright.

24 May   Mary d/o Elizabeth JOHNSON, Lower Leigh, Servant   JB

— 2 Aug   George s/o Barnabas & Sarah BAILEY, Field, Labourer   JB

— 16 Aug   William s/o William & Esther WALKER, Withington Green, Labourer   JB

23 Aug   John s/o William & Beatrice LYMER, Upper Leigh, Labourer   JB

30 Aug   Elizabeth d/o William & Jane BURTON, Godstones, Labourer   JB

6 Sep   Mary d/o Charles & Susannah YATES, Middleton Green, Labourer.   JB
         Privately.   Received into the Congregation Dec 27 by me. BSB

3 Oct   George s/o George & Mary WILSON, Fole, Farmer. Privately. Received   JB
         into the Congregation Octr 25th by me.   JB

11 Oct   Robert s/o James & Charlotte POYSER, Middleton Green, Labourer   JB

11 Oct   Joseph s/o James & Elizabeth BRANDRICK, Pickly Bank, Farmer   JB

11 Oct   John Phillips s/o John & Dorothy CARTER, Withington, Farmer   JB

11 Oct   John Bakewell s/o Thomas & Frances PHILLIPS, Dodsley, Farmer   JB

12 Oct   Henry s/o Thomas & Jane PHILLIPS, Withington Green Labourer   JB
         Privately.   Received into the Congregation Nov 1st 1835 by me. JB.

18 Oct   Ann d/o William & Ann STEVENSON, The Bents, Labourer   JB

1 Nov   Ann d/o Samuel & Hannah ROBINSON, Church Leigh, Labourer   JB

22 Nov   Matthew s/o Matthew & Elizabeth SNAPE, Withington, Coal-dealer   JB

12 Dec   William s/o Joseph & Martha HARRISON, Lower Nobut, Labourer. Priv.   JB

27 Dec   Thomas s/o Thomas & Mary STARTIN Lower Leigh Blacksmith   BSB

1836

— 17 Jan   Ann d/o Joseph & Mary GREEN, Checkley Bank, Labourer   JB

7 Feb   William d/o William & Hannah EDGE, Field, Labourer   JB

7 Feb   Robert s/o James & Elizabeth Speed BEAVEN, Leigh Parsonage,   JB
         privately Curate of this Parish
                 Received into the Congregation March 27th by me. JB

14 Feb   Sarah d/o Joseph & Hannah KIDD, Withington, Labourer   JB

         © Staffordshire Parish Registers Society

3 Apr	Sarah d/o George & Mary RAWLING, Morrilow Heath, Labourer — JB
17 Apr	Cicely d/o Joseph & Sarah BROWN, Wood Leasowes, Farmer — JB
1 May	Maria Hannah d/o William & Dorothy CHELL, Upper Leigh, Labourer — JB
15 May	Judith d/o Jonathan & Judith FINNEY, Lower Leigh, Farmer — JB
29 May	Ann d/o Thomas & Sarah BARNES, Withington, Farmer — JB
5 Jun	William s/o William & Hannah BARNETT, Lower Leigh, Sawyer — CBC
9 Jun	George s/o Jane BRIDGEWOOD, Field, ~~Labourer~~ Servant. Privately. — JB
	Received into the Congregation June 19th by me JB
19 Jun	Elizabeth d/o John & Edith HOLLINS, Dairy House, Farmer — JB
19 Jun	George s/o William & Sarah MYATT, Dodsley, Labourer — JB
26 Jun	Ann d/o Mary EDGE, Park-hall Lodge, Servant — JB
26 Jun	William s/o Charles & Elizabeth KENT, Church Leigh, Pig-dealer — JB
3 Jul	Caroline d/o Thomas & Millicent TATTON Lower Nobut Labourer — JB
5 Jul	Elizabeth d/o James & Jane DEAKIN Blakely House, Shoemaker. — JB
	Privately. Received into the Congregation July 10th 1836 by me. JB.
7 Aug	Elizabeth d/o Charles & Ellen GARLAND, Withington, Wheelwright — CBC
7 Aug	John s/o Mary JOHNSON, Upper Leigh, Servant — CBC
7 Aug	John s/o Joseph & Mary RATCLIFFE, Lower Leigh, Farmer — CBC
14 Aug	Ann d/o Elizabeth RUSHTON, Work-house, Servant — JB
21 Aug	Edward James s/o Thomas & Catherine GAUNT, Church Leigh, Tailor. — JB
26 Aug	John Augustus Jackson s/o John & Sophia BARNES, Field, Farmer. Priv. — JB
	Received into the Congregation Novr 13th 1836 by me JB
11 Sep	Edmund s/o Thomas & Margaret ARNOLD, Dodsley, Farmer — JB
30 Oct	Clement s/o Clement & Hannah COTTERILL, Birchwood Park, Farmer — JB
20 Nov	Sarah d/o James & Prudence HAWKINS, Nobut Brickkiln, Butcher. — JB
	NB Rec'd into the Congregation at the same time, being privately
	baptized at Uttoxeter by the Rev, John Dashwood, Elizabeth & John,
	children of the same parents, by me JB
20 Nov	William s/o John & Lydia CAPEWELL, Morrilow Heath, Labourer — JB
4 Dec	Mary d/o Thomas & Alice HOLLINS, Bittersdale, Farmer — JB
11 Dec	Frederick s/o William & Hannah BOTTOMER alias BOTHAM, Fole Hall, — JB
	Tailor
17 Dec	Elizabeth d/o Luke & Anne TURNER, Field, Farmer. Privately. — JB
	Received into the Congregation Novr 1st 1837 by me JB
18 Dec	George* s/o George & Mary WILSON, Fole, Farmer — JB
	*The true name is John. James Beaven August 27th 1837.
	This alteration was made in the presence of me George WILSON.
1837	
29 Jan	Sarah d/o John & Ann RAY, Godstones, Husbandman — JB
	(N.B. This entry was made with hands almost frozen. J.B.)
29 Jan	Charles s/o Samuel & Mary ALCOCK, Church Leigh, Labourer — JB
5 Feb	Mary d/o Margaret LOVET, ~~Morrilow Heath~~ Upper Leigh, Spinster — BSB
5 Feb	Edward s/o William & Alice POOL, Morrilow Heath, Labourer — BSB
12 Feb	John s/o Hannah NICKLING, Morrilow Heath, Spinster — JB
14 Feb	Hannah d/o William & Ann PERKIN, Weston, Shoemaker. Privately. — JB
	Received into the Congregation March 12th by me JB
26 Feb	Robert s/o Robert & Sarah MYATT, Dodsley, Labourer — JB
16 Apr	Hannah d/o William & Susannah TURNER, Withington, Farmer — JB
7 May	Myra *[Mira-BT]* d/o ~~George~~ Charles & Ann MOORE, Dodsley, Farmer's — JB
	son. Privately.
	Received into the Congregation June 3rd 1838 by me JB

14 May	Clara d/o Benjamin & Mary Ann PRESTON, Upper Leigh, Labourer.	JB
	Privately. Received into the Congregation July 9th by me JB	
31 May	John s/o Benjamin & Charlotte WILD, Broad Oak, Farmer. Privately.	JB
	Received into the Congregation Novr 19th by me JB	
11 Jun	Joseph s/o Edward & Sarah BAILEY, Upper Leigh, Labourer	JB
11 Jun	William Collier s/o Sarah WARD, Windy Fields, Dressmaker	JB
30 Jul	Sarah d/o William & Hannah BRIDGEWOOD Withington Green Labourer	JB
10 Aug	Charles s/o Charles & Frances BAILEY, Middleton Green, Labourer.	JB
	Privately. Received into the Congregation Aug 20th by me JB	
3 Sep	Sarah d/o William & Sarah GRIFFIN, Dodsley, Shoemaker	JB
10 Sep	Sarah d/o Walter & Mary BROWN, Withington, Wheelwright	JB
24 Sep	William s/o George & Mary PERKIN, Headlands, Farmer	JB
15 Oct	Joseph s/o Joseph & Ann MARTIN, Nobut, Sawyer	JB
29 Oct	Alfred s/o John & Sophia BARNES, Field, Farmer	JB
5 Nov	Alfred s/o William & Frances HOLLINS, Upper Leigh, Labourer	JB
19 Nov	Emma d/o George & Mary DEAKIN, Withington Green, Labourer	JB
25 Dec	Joseph s/o William & Dorothy CHELL, Upper Leigh, Labourer	JB
31 Dec	Thomas Wardle s/o Mary PHILLIPS, Church Leigh, Servant	JB

1838

7 Jan	Sarah d/o David & Charlotte ALLEN Morrilow Heath Husbandman	JB
12 Jan	Richard s/o James & Sarah BRANDRICK, Pickly Bank, Farmer. Privately.	JB
14 Jan	Thomas s/o Robert & Ann PHILLIPS, Withington, Farmer	JB
28 Jan	Sarah Ann d/o John & Dorothy CARTER, Withington, Farmer	JB
18 Feb	Sarah d/o William & Sarah MYATT, Dodsley, Mole-catcher	JB
25 Feb	Francis Shaw s/o Joseph & Ann PERKIN, Field, Farmer	JB
4 Mar	Elizabeth d/o John & Mary RAWLING, Morrilow Heath, Labourer	JB
4 Mar	Ann d/o William & Jane BURTON, Godstones, Labourer	JB
4 Mar	Elizabeth d/o William Jane DUROSE, Upper Leigh, Servant	JB
13 Mar	William s/o Thomas & Mary GAUNT, Dodsley Lane, Labourer. Privately	JB
	Received into the Congregation March 26th by me. JB	
18 Mar	George s/o Sampson & Elizabeth BAILEY, Morrilow Heath, Labourer	JB
11 Apr	Thomas s/o Thomas & Frances PHILLIPS, Dodsley, Farmer. Privately.	JB
	Received into the Congregation May the 23rd by me. JB	
22 Apr	Charles s/o William & Ann STEVENSON, The Bents, Labourer	JB
25 Apr	Thomas s/o Ann WALKER, Checkley Bank, Servant. Privately.	JB
	Received into the Congregation Octr Novr 4th by me JB	
25 Apr	John s/o John & Elizabeth CHELL, Lower Leigh, Bricklayer. Privately.	JB
	Received into the Congregation April 29th by me JB	
13 May	Aaron s/o William & Esther WALKER, Withington Green, Labourer	JB
20 May	William s/o Thomas & Alice HOLLINS, Bitternsdale, Farmer	JB
20 May	Barnabas s/o Barnabas & Sarah BAILEY, Field, Labourer	JB
27 May	John s/o William & Cicely PERKIN, Withington Green, Tailor	JB
27 May	Mary d/o Thomas & Mary MILLINGTON, Upper Leigh, Labourer	JB
24 Jun	Henry s/o George & Sarah STARTIN, Birchwood Park, Blacksmith	JB
24 Jun	Charles s/o Joseph & Sarah BROWN, Wood Leasowes, Farmer	JB
1 Jul	George s/o William & Susannah TURNER, Withington, Farmer	JB
8 Jul	Emma d/o Thomas & Sarah EARDLEY, Withington, Butcher	JB
29 Jul	Mary d/o Joseph & Mary GREEN, Fole, Labourer	JB
12 Aug	Charlotte d/o James & Mary BEARDMORE, Lower Leigh, Blacksmith	JB
19 Aug	Ann d/o Joseph & Martha HARRISON, Lower Nobut, Labourer.	JB
	N.B. This child was born Decr 15th 1836 JB	

19 Aug	Arthur s/o Joseph & Martha HARRISON, Lower Nobut, Labourer	JB
9 Sep	Thomas Jackson s/o Thomas Jackson & Sarah BARNES, Withington, Farmer	JB
30 Sep	Mary Ann d/o Charles & Ann MOORE, Dodsley, Farmer	JB
14 Oct	Sarah d/o William & Sarah COLLIER, Windy Fields, Farmer	BSB
24 Sep	Sarah Ann d/o Benjamin & Mary Ann PRESTON, Upper Leigh, Labourer. Privately. Received into the Congregation Novr 4th by me JB. This entry is made from a Certificate given at the time of baptism JB	JB
11 Nov	Richard s/o Joseph & Sarah GINNIS, Withington, Farmer	JB
8 Dec	Joseph s/o Joseph & Hannah KIDD, Withington Green, Labourer. Privately. Received into the Congregation Aug 6 1848 L. Bagot, Rector	JB

1839

13 Jan	Thomas s/o Henry & Elizabeth BENTLEY Hob Hill, Husbandman Mary d/o the same parents baptized by the Rev. J. Dashwood, received into the Congregation at the same time.	JB
13 Jan	Henry s/o James & Jane DEAKIN, Blakely House, Shoemaker	JB
20 Jan	Ann d/o Joseph & Ann MARTIN, Nobut, Sawyer	HS
21 Apr	Robert s/o Benjamin & Charlotte WILD, Broad Oak, Farmer	JB
21 Apr	James s/o Edward & Ann DUROSE Withington Green Shoemaker	JB
19 May	Mary d/o Luke & Anne TURNER, Field, Farmer	JB
19 May	Mary d/o Sampson & Elizabeth BAILEY, Morrilow Heath, Labourer	JB
19 May	Mary d/o John & Anne RAY, Godstone, Husbandman	JB
26 May	Jane d/o James & Prudence HAWKINS, Lower Nobut, Jobbing Butcher	JB
25 Jun	Francis twin s/o Charles & Elizabeth KENT, Church Leigh, Pig-dealer. Privately. Received into the Congregation July 7th by me JB	JB
7 Jul	Fanny Emily d/o John & Sophia BARNES, Field, Farmer	JB
7 Jul	Thomas twin s/o Charles & Elizabeth KENT, Church Leigh, Pig-dealer	JB
4 Aug	Charles s/o Walter & Mary BROWN, Withington, Wheelwright	JB
22 Sep	Thomas s/o William & Hannah EDGE, Field, Labourer	JB
12 Oct	Edwin s/o Jane DUROSE, Upper Leigh, Servant privately	JB
13 Oct	Thomas s/o Thomas & Anne WATSON, Nobut Brick kiln, Husbandman	JB
3 Nov	Emma d/o William & Sarah GRIFFIN, Dodsley, Shoemaker	JB
3 Nov	Robert s/o Robert & Ann PHILLIPS, Withington, Farmer	JB
24 Nov	Sarah d/o Thomas & Sarah KENT Withington Green Wheelwright	JB
8 Dec	Sarah Jane d/o Joseph & Anne PERKIN, Field, Farmer	JB
15 Dec	William Henry s/o Thomas & Frances PHILLIPS, Dodsley, Farmer	JB
15 Dec	John s/o Sarah PHILLIPS, Church Leigh, Servant. Privately.	JB

1840

5 Jan	Frederick s/o Thomas & Catharine GAUNT, Church Leigh. Tailor	JB
12 Jan	John s/o Thomas & Alice HOLLINS, Bittern's Dale, Farmer	JB
19 Jan	Mary d/o James & Mary BEARDMORE, Lower Leigh, Blacksmith Received into the Congregation Feby 9th by me JB	WH
25 Jan	Thomas Cope s/o Eliza TIDSWELL, Fole, Spinster. Privately.	JB
1 Feb Mar	Elizabeth d/o James & Elizabeth BRANDRICK, Pickly Bank, Farmer	JB
8 Mar	Mary d/o William & Susannah TURNER, Withington, Farmer	JB
19 Apr Easter Day	Fanny Louisa twin d/o John & Dorothy CARTER, Withington, Farmer	JB
19 Apr Easter Day	Thomas William twin s/o John & Dorothy CARTER, Withington, Farmer	JB
26 Apr	James s/o James & Hannah DEAKIN, Church Lane, Labourer	JB
3 May	Joseph Luke s/o Joseph & Sarah BROWN, Woodleasow, Farmer	ECSK

3 May	Richard s/o Robert & Frances SPENCER, Nobut, Farmer	ECSK
17 May	Elizabeth d/o Edward & Sarah BAYLEY, Upper Leigh, Labourer	TPB
24 May	Rachel d/o ~~John &~~ Margaret LOVATT, Servant, Upper Leigh	JB
24 May	Mary d/o Samuel & Mary ALCOCK, Labourer, Church Leigh	JB
24 May	Joseph s/o ~~William & Ann~~ Benjamin ~~STEVENSON~~ DUROSE, Labourer, ~~Patch Hall Withington~~	JB

This entry is erroneous JB

[The whole entry above is crossed out in addition to those names which have been struck through]

24 May	Joseph s/o William & Ann STEVENSON, Labourer, Patch Hall	JB
24 May	Thomas s/o Benjamin & Ellen DUROSE, Withington, Labourer. Privately.	JB

Received into the Congregation June 7th 1840 by me JB.

31 May	Elizabeth d/o Henry & Charlotte JOHNSON, Leigh Lanes, Labourer	JB
21 Jun	Sarah Ann d/o Thomas & Mary STARTIN, Lower Leigh, Blacksmith	JB
12 Jul	Elizabeth d/o Charles & Mary BATES, Upper Leigh, Labourer	JB
19 Jul	James s/o Thomas & Elizabeth SNAPE, , Morrilow Heath, Labourer	JB
19 Jul	Samuel s/o Thomas & Ann BAGNALL, Birchwood Park, Labourer	JB
26 Jul	Ellen Mahala d/o Thomas & Sarah EARDLEY, The Bents, Butcher	JB
9 Aug	John s/o Eliza LEESE, Middleton Green, Servant	JB
16 Aug	Samuel s/o William & Hannah BARNET, Lower Leigh, Sawyer	JB
4 Oct	Sarah d/o Joseph & Sarah GINNIS, Withington, Farmer. Born Augst 30th	JB
11 Oct	William s/o Joseph & Ann MARTIN, Nobut, Sawyer	JB
18 Oct	John s/o James & Mary SMITH, Bustomley, Farmer	JB
1 Nov	Hannah d/o William & Esther WALKER, Withington, Labourer	JB
1 Nov	Frances Louisa d/o Thomas & Sarah BARNES, Withington, Farmer	JB
22 Nov	Elizabeth d/o Joseph & Eliza CHELL, Lower Leigh, Labourer	JB
29 Nov	Maria d/o John & Elizabeth BALANCE, Nobut Brick Kiln, Tailor	JB

1841

3 Jan	Matilda d/o George & Frances WILSON, Fole, Farmer	JB
10 Jan	Frederick s/o George & Harriet RATCLIFF, Park Hall Lodge, Labourer	JB
17 Jan	Ann d/o William& Hannah BATES, Headlands, Labourer	JB
14 Feb	Susannah Campbell SIVIS d/o Archibald & Mary SIVIS, Birchwood Park, Labourer	JB
21 Mar	William s/o William & Cicely PERKIN, Withington Green, Tailor	JB
11 Apr	Charles s/o James & Jane DEAKIN, Leigh Lanes, Shoe maker	JB
13 Jun	Louisa d/o William & Hannah BRIDGEWOOD, Field, Labourer	JB
4 Jul	Sarah d/o Thomas & Alice HOLLINS, Bittern's dale, Farmer	JB

The proportion of Males to Females baptized between Dec 1820 and Jan 1831, both exclusive, is as 13 to 12.

The average number of baptisms in each of those years is 30.

The proportion of Males to Females baptized in the ten years ending 1840, is as 19½ to 18 nearly, or 19.5 to 17.875.

The average number of baptisms in each of those years is 29 4/5.

Important note for demographer

Leigh, Staffordshire, Burial Register
1813-1860
Transcribed here to 1837

1813

11 Jan	Thomas BLOOR	Litley Parish of Cheadle	59	HT
18 Jan	Mary HOWARD	Dodsley	86	HT
28 Feb	Thomas ALLEN	Radford Nr. Stafford	41	HT
29 Mar	Francis PERKIN	Leigh	16	HT
5 Apr	Geo: WALKER	Withington	23	HT
11 Jun	John COPE	Uttoxeter	82	HT
4 Jul	Anne HART	Derby	80	HT
4 Aug	Geo: RUSHTON	Morley-Heath	70	HT
31 Aug	Jane SHERRATT	Hay-House	74	HT
28 Sep	Eliz: BAILEY	Morley-Heath	81	HT
29 Oct	Sarah TILL	Nobot	80	HT
12 Nov	Anne BERRESFORD	Leigh Bank	70	HT
19 Dec	Charles KENT	Leigh	7 mths	HT
29 Dec	Sarah RUSHTON	Morley Heath	66	HT
31 Dec	John TUNNICLIFFE	Leigh	71	HT

1814

24 Jan	Mary ROBOTHAM	Leigh Work-house	62	HT
26 Jan	Robert HUSON	Withington	20	HT
5 Mar	Alice FOSTER	Leigh Bank	61	HT
17 Apr	Ellen ENGLAND	Fulford	28	HT
19 Apr	Dor: KENT	Leigh	31	HT
10 May	Robt: PHILLIPS	Dodsley	18 mths	HT
25 Sep	Thos: CHELL	Lower-Leigh	71	HT
10 Nov	Thos: RUSHTON	Dagdale	77	HT

1815

17 Jan	Joseph TURNER	Upper Leigh	24	HT
7 Feb	Edward HOWARD	Dodsley	92	HT
17 Feb	Jane DAVIES	Morley-Heath	84	HT
24 Feb	Mary FARLEY	Lower Leigh	15	HT
18 Mar	Olive HUSON	Withington	18	HT
27 Apr	Mary BENTLEY	Lower-Leigh	5 wks	HT
11 Jun	Elizabeth TURNER	Field	52	HT
1 Aug	Martin ROCK	Uttoxeter	5	HT
10 Sep	Saml: STARTIN	Cheadle	28	HT
17 Sep	Joseph TURNER	Over Leigh	3 mths	HT
25 Sep	William SUTTON	Field	65	HT
31 Oct	Mary HUSON	Withington	24	HT

1816

14 Jan	Thomas EATON	Leigh Workhouse	70	HT
27 Feb	John SHERRATT	Hays House	65	HT
16 May	Joseph PERKIN	Dodsley	67	HT
16 May	William FARLEY	Lower-Leigh	19	HT
28 May	Anthony RHUDDE, Esqr.	Uttoxeter	77	HT
9 Jun	Mary EDGE	Withington	78	HT
4 Jul	Anne PERKIN	Uttoxeter	23	HT
14 Jul	Sarah RUSHTON	Nobot	25	HT

19 Jul	Thomas COLLIER	Lower Leigh	29	HT
3 Sep	Samuel WARD	Uttoxeter	7	HT
4 Sep	Olive HUSON	Withington	57	HT
7 Sep	Martha MOOR	Bents	13 wks	HT
3 Nov	Hannah PERKIN	Over-Tean	57	HT
15 Nov	William HART	Dodsley	7 mths	HT
16 Nov	Elizabeth EARDLEY	Broom-Fields	7 mths	HT
		Parish of Abbots Bromley		
21 Nov	Thomas TILL	Leigh Work-House	56	HT
15 Dec	John BAGNALL	Checkley	75	HT
19 Dec	Hannah WALKER	Church-Leigh	21	HT
26 Dec	Thomas BLURTON	Longnor	63	HT
27 Dec	Helen WARD	Uttoxeter	4 mths	HT
1817				
18 Feb	Charles SHERRET *[Sherret-BT]*	Beamhurst	8 mths	HT
2 Mar	Margaret TUNNICLIFFE	Uttoxeter	69	HT
5 Mar	Anne GRIFFIN	Church Leigh	37	HT
20 Mar	Anne BLURTON	Field House near Eccleshall	59	HT
2 May	John MELLER	Bromshall	66	HT
3 May	Joseph COLLIER	Middleton Green	83	HT
11 May	Sarah LEES *[Leese-BT]*	Work House	83	HT
17 May	James HUSON	Withington	18	HT
29 Jun	Elizabeth HAWLEY	Nobot	13	HT
9 Jul	Mary BLORE	Cheadle	82	HT
10 Jul	Willm: Jams: SUTTON	Yoxall	42	HT
3 Oct	James HOWE	Workhouse	41	HT
7 Nov	Eliz: TOOTH	Withington	1 wk	HT
20 Dec	John LOWNDES	Withington	28	HT
28 Dec	Jams BRIDGWOOD	Draycott	77	HT
1818				
23 Jan	Saml: ALCOCK	Upper Leigh	70	HT
2 Feb	George PHILLIPS	Upper Leigh	53	HT
5 Feb	Edward WOOLLEY	Stone	85	HT
8 Feb	Willm, MARSTON	Lower Leigh	27	HT
17 Feb	Hannah NOAKES	Workhouse	63	HT
2 Mar	Ellen CHELL	Shortwoods	35	HT
24 Mar	Ellen WILSHAW	Nobot	80	HT
30 Mar	Susannah BAILEY	Stone-Heath	5	HT
13 Apr	Eliz: TWIGGE	Withington	9	HT
29 Apr	Eliz: TOOTH	Withington	82	HT
7 May	Mary MARSON	Middleton Green	8 mths	HT
9 Jun	Anne PHILLIPS	Uttoxeter	69	HT
15 Jul	John MIATT	Morley Heath	60	HT
23 Jul	Thomas MARTIN	Dodsley	16	HT
24 Jul	Anne MATTHEWS	Field-House	66	HT
31 Jul	John PHILLIPS	Withington	48	HT
17 Aug	Alice BLURTON	Mitton	76	HT
18 Oct	Willm: DEAKIN	Field-House	71	HT
13 Nov	John BAILEY	Morley-Heath	83	RP
16 Nov	Anne COPE	Brooke Houses near Cheadle	39	HT
25 Nov	James MARSON	Middleton-Green	66	HT

Date	Name	Place	Age	
27 Nov	Elias BAILEY	Workhouse	78	HT
20 Dec	Mary GOUGH	Dodsley	83	HT
1819				
18 Jan	Thomas JOHNSON	Workhouse	75	HT
21 Jan	Philip HAWLEY	Nobot	88	HT
7 Feb	Anne EDGE	Withington	15 mths	HT
14 Feb	John PHILLIPS	Withington	8 wks	HT
12 Mar	Sarah WARD	Uttoxeter	2 mths	HT
17 Mar	Hannah BARKER	Lower Leigh	69	HT
17 Mar	Jane PERKIN	Field	5	HT
23 Mar	Edward DEAKIN	Withington	6 mths	HT
30 Apr	John HOWE	Upper-Leigh	65	HT
30 Apr	Mary MITCHELL	Withington	10 wks	HT
30 May	Mary ENGLAND	Fulford	63	HT
30 May	John BELCHER	Godstone	72	HT
28 Jul	Martha MILLINGTON	Field	55	HT
1 Aug	Francis SHERRATT	Hob Hill	61	HT
14 Aug	Elizabeth HUSON	Gartside Green Parish of Stone	25	HT
16 Aug	Stephen BAILEY	Lower Leigh	27	HT
17 Aug	Edward ASBURY	Handford, Parish of Trentham	12	HT
17 Aug	Prudence TOOTH	Bents	72	HT
29 Aug	Thomas BAILEY	Lower Leigh	8	HT
29 Aug	Susannah BAILEY	Lower Leigh	8 mths	HT
2 Sep	Eliza BAILEY	Lower Leigh	2	HT
6 Nov	Ellen MILLINGTON	Dodsley	88	HT
2 Dec	Sarah TATTON	Withington Green	38	HT
1820				
12 Jan	John HUSON	Withington	59	HT
27 Feb	Sarah TWIGGE	Lower Leigh	81	HT
29 Mar	Anne ASBURY	Handford Parish of Trentham	39	HT
17 May	Mary THOMAS	Church Leigh	59	EL
20 May	Lawrence GREENSMITH	The Wood	80	HT
29 Jun	Mary DUMOLO	Uttoxeter	50	HT
4 Aug	Jane WILSON	Fole	14	CBC
19 Sep	James DEAKIN	Dodsley	5 days	HT
17 Nov	John ASBURY	Painly Hill	56	HT
18 Nov	Catharine WETTON	Church Leigh	8 wks	HT
1821				
7 Jan	John RAWLIN	Morley Heath	3 wks	HT
11 Jan	Richd: HOWE	Tean Ford	90	HT
18 Feb	Dorothy BURTON	Bents	10	HT
14 Mar	Geo: RUSHTON	Nobot	5 mths	HT
2 Apr	Jane HOLLINS	Leigh Bank	3 wks	HT
8 Apr	Joseph TILL	Workhouse	57	HT
18 Apr	Mary ALCOCK	Upper-Leigh	78	HT
12 May	John WALKER	Withington	3 days	HT
23 May	Willm: BAILEY	Dodsley	6 wks	HT
3 Jun	Lydia BLURTON	Church Leigh	69	HT
7 Jun	Mary BLURTON	Woodford Parish of Uttoxeter	29	HT
22 Jun	Chas: ENGLAND	Fulford	43	HT
29 Jun	Joseph EDGE	Withington	15 mths	HT

2 Jul	Thomas TWIGGE	Lower-Leigh	86	HT
17 Jul	Dor: DEAKIN	Blakely House	67	HT
31 Aug	Charles BAILEY	Stone Heath	6	HT
30 Sep	John FARLEY	Lower Leigh	19	HT
21 Oct	Sarah JOHNSON	Upper Leigh	77	HT
1 Nov	Jane TILL	Lower-Leigh	2 days	HT
23 Dec	Richd: SAUNDERS	Morley Heath	43	HT
1822				
7 May	Mary TILL	Workhouse	58	HT
6 Jun	Elizabeth JOHNSON	Middleton Green	87	HT
29 Jun	Sarah HAWLEY	Nobot	89	HT
4 Jul	Willm: BRANDRICK	Pinckley Bank	25	HT
28 Jul	Richd: FOWLER	Bents	78	HT
29 Jul	Sarah PERKIN	Field	54	HT
28 Aug	Mary TURNER	Morley Heath	3 days	HT
13 Oct	Joseph DEAKIN	Blakely House	70	HT
15 Nov	Sarah PHILLIPS	Morley Heath	43	HT
1823				
1 Jan	Anne RAWLIN	Morley Heath	4	HT
18 Jan	Harriet PHILLIPS	Leigh Bank	22 wks	HT
23 Jan	Thomas PHILLIPS	Dodsley	63	HT
25 Feb	Elizabeth HUBBARD	Work-House	68	HT
3 Apr	John LOWE	Morley-Heath	3 days	HT
14 Apr	Joseph RUSHTON	Work-House	47	HT
17 Apr	Joseph CHELL	Upper-Leigh	6 mths	HT
7 Jul	Anne HUSON	Nobot	24	HT
15 Jul	John PRESTON	Morley-Heath	23	HT
26 Sep	Catharine BRINDLEY	Upper Leigh	10 days	HT
7 Oct	Jane PHILLIPS	Lower-Leigh	66	HT
3 Dec	Sarah BAILEY	Stone Heath	18 mths	HT
14 Dec	William ALCOCK	Church-Leigh	55	HT
1824				
8 Jan	William HILL	Shooters Hill	79	HT
15 Jan	John COPE	Nobot	46	HT
8 Feb	Tommison KENT	Church Leigh	11 mths	HT
10 Feb	Ralph MARTIN	Lane-end	31	HT
24 Feb	Joseph MOOR *[Moore-BT]*	Bents	79	HT
27 Feb	Sarah ADDAMS	Lower-Leigh	86	HT
21 Mar	Martha WARDLE	Church Leigh	2	HT
26 Mar	Edwd: RATCLIFFE	Withington	15 mths	HT
26 Mar	Joseph BRIDGEWOOD	Field	18 mths	HT
8 Apr	Elizabeth HOWE	Over-Leigh	71	HT
15 Apr	Frederick RATCLIFFE	Withington	15 mths	HT
7 May	Mary PHILLIPS	Withington	86	HT
7 May	Dor Heath CORDON	Withington	2	HT
13 May	John BLURTON	Netherland Green Parish of Uttoxeter	48	HT
17 May	Henry MILWARD	Leigh Bank	2 days	HT
27 May	Thomas COPE	Dodsley	82	HT
21 Jun	Mary RATCLIFFE	Withington	5 mths	HT
8 Aug	John COPE	Dodsley	29	HT
18 Aug	Mary MOUNTFORT	Hilderston	25	HT

28 Sep	Elizabeth SLATER	Withington	65	HT
28 Oct	Saml. PLATT	Hopton	49	HT
30 Oct	Elizabeth ALCOCK	Withington Green	54	HT
30 Oct	Anne PHILLIPS	Over Leigh	80	HT
31 Oct	Elizabeth GREENSMITH	Wood-Farm	74	HT
19 Nov	Thomas PHILLIPS	Upper-Leigh	70	HT
27 Nov	Anne BLAGSHAW	Church Leigh	29	HT
30 Nov	Anne FALKNER	Bents	50	HT
6 Dec	Jams: JOHNSON	Middleton-Green	52	HT
29 Dec	Sarah ROBINSON	Brick Kiln Lodge	57	HT
30 Dec	Willm: WILSHAW	Painly-Hill	88	HT
1825				
8 Feb	Mary MILLINGTON	Over Leigh	8	HT
11 Feb	George NOAKES	Work-House	85	HT
4 Mar	Thomas SMITH	Over Leigh	3	HT
14 Mar	Anne WHEELDON	Woodgate Nr. Uttoxeter	84	HT
14 Mar	Mary PHILLIPS	Field	68	HT
18 Mar	John BARNES	Field	64	HT
1 Apr	Mary WATERHOUSE	Over Leigh	5 wks	HT
8 Apr	Anne WHITEHALL	Carry Lane	12	HT
22 Apr	Anne CHELL	Over Leigh	12	HT
13 May	Edward BAILEY	Over Leigh	18 mths	HT
2 Jun	William CHELL	Over Leigh	5	SL
1 Jul	Hannah WATERHOUSE	Over Leigh	32	HT
24 Aug	Hannah FOWLER	Bents	79	HT
15 Sep	Mary HOLLINS	Dairy House	57	HT
15 Sep	Thomas CARTER	Withington	72	HT
19 Sep	Henry CHELL	Over Leigh	11 wks	HT
24 Sep	Aaron PEPPER	Checkley Bank	16	HT
20 Nov	Mary MARTIN	Nobot	90	HT
2 Dec	Robt: BLURTON Esqr.	Nobot	84	HT
1826				
1 Jan	John MOOR	Bents	29	HT
2 Mar	Emma STARTIN	Church Leigh	6 mths	HT
20 May	Saml: ADAMS	Lower-Leigh	61	HT
22 Jun	John BURTON	Bents	79	HT
22 Aug	Joseph ADAMS	Lower Leigh	56	HT
31 Aug	Sarah PERKIN	Withington	56	HT
22 Sep	Mrs Catherine BRINDLEY	Uttoxeter	77	HT
11 Dec	Emma BAILEY	Ivey House	5	HT
1827				
7 Jan	Willm: TOMLINSON	Bents	2	HT
11 Jan	Margt: DEAKIN	Eccleshall	83	HT
27 Jan	Mary DEAN	Middleton Green	22	HT
20 Feb	Sarah BAILEY	Bitters Dale	7	HT
19 Mar	John GRIFFIN	Over Leigh	20	HT
25 Mar	Thomas YATES	Lower Leigh	55	HT
25 Mar	Jane STARTIN	Church Leigh	8 days	HT
19 Apr	Josh: BRANDRICK	Pickley-Bank	43	HT
23 Apr	Anne PHILLIPS	Uttoxeter	36	HT
16 Jun	James COLLIER	Windy Fields	52	HT

31 Aug	Elizabeth BURTON	Bents	19	HT
3 Sep	William WARD	Dillhorn Hall	45	HT
9 Sep	Sarah DEAKIN	Blakely-House	52	HT
29 Sep	Anne DEAKIN	Dodsley	12	HT
3 Oct	Willm: ADAMS	Withington	63	HT
13 Nov	George MIATT	Bents	26	HT
19 Nov	Willm: BALANCE	Field Hall	41	HT
5 Dec	Richd: FENTON	Field	67	HT
1828				
2 Jan	James FENTON	Middleton-Green	66	HT
30 Jan	Sarah HART	Litchfield	56	HT
15 Feb	Thos: BRANDRICK	Pickley Bank	39	HT
2 Mar	Hannah WALKER	Church Leigh	86	HT
4 Mar	James JOHNSON	Middleton Green	88	HT
6 Mar	Thomas WARDLE	Church Leigh	66	HT
13 Mar	John ALCOCK	Church Leigh	76	HT
5 Apr	Anne SMITH	Bents	70	HT
19 Apr	Henry PHILLIPS	Uttoxeter	12 mths	HT
24 Apr	Catharine FENTON	Middleton Green	60	HT
4 May	George TILL	Church Leigh	55	HT
4 May	Mary MARTIN	Nobot	26	HT
9 May	Anne BLURTON	Bradley	61	HT
19 May	Charles Edensor PHILLIPS	Uttoxeter	13 mths	HT
21 May	Geo'ge: LEES	Short-Woods	15 wks	HT
6 Jun	Anne BROWNE	Morley Heath	66	HT
14 Jun	Mary EVANS	Workhouse	40	HT
28 Jul	Martha BRANDRICK	Over Fole	74	HT
7 Aug	Thomas PHILLIPS	Uttoxeter	85	HT
3 Sep	Joseph BARNES	Field	24	HT
9 Sep	Mary INGRAM	Over Leigh	56	HT
10 Sep	Harriet BRANDRICK	Over Fole	27	HT
10 Sep	William ARNOLD	Over Leigh	18 mths	HT
12 Sep	Geo'ge: WALKER	Withington	4 mths	HT
15 Nov	Ann MOTTRAM	Benter House	73	HT
5 Dec	Elizth: TURNER	Church Leigh	85	H
31 Dec	Elizabeth PLATT	Hopton	61	HT
1829				
11 Feb	Anne COPE	Leigh	83	HT
11 Feb	Sarah MILLINGTON	Dodsley	17	HT
22 Mar	Mary HOWE	Tenford	72	HT
24 Apr	Robt: ARNOLD	Lower Leigh	86	L
8 May	Eliz: MYAT	Stone	70	HT
31 May	John Waltho FENTON	Field	2	HT
24 Jun	Henry Francis HOLLINS	Dairy House	41	HT
16 Jul	Rev'd Henry THOMAS	Church Leigh	74	CBC
[In margin]	Chas. B. CHARLEWOOD	Augt 2 1829		
26 Jul	Robert SHERRATT	Beamhurst Lane	52	CBC
4 Aug	John PLANT	Stone-Heath	94	*
	*Occasionally by Saml. Langley A.M. Rector of Checkley			
11 Aug	William COPE	Dodsley	72	GS
22 Sep	John HUGHES	Morley-Heath	77	*

Date	Name	Place	Age	Init
24 Sep	Luke BILLINS	Work-House	77	*
8 Oct	John BOX, a batchelor	Nobett	72	*
29 Nov	Lucy BROWN	Morley Heath	55	CBC
5 Dec	Thomas BROWN	Park Hall	73	CBC
1830				
19 Jan	Sampson BRIDGEWOOD	Field	12	*
14 Jun	Joseph TATTON	Nobut	2	CBC
28 Jun	Mary MARSON	Lower Leigh	72	CBC
3 Aug	John PRESTON	Woodside	65	JB
6 Aug	Mary Ann TILL	Middleton Green	5	JB
16 Aug	John MARSON	Middleton Green	28	JB
2 Sep	Hannah TURNER	Church Leigh	9 wks	JB
8 Sep	Sarah DEAKIN	Ivy House	30	JB
8 Sep	Mary HUGHES	Morrilow Heath	3 days	JB
14 Sep	Elizabeth HUGHES	Morrilow Heath	9 days	JB
31 Oct	Catherine LOVATT	Stafford	75	JB
15 Nov	Mary BUXTONS	Withington	14 mths	JB
1831				
2 Jan	Edward COPE	Garsall Green	53	JB
20 Jan	Joseph UPTON	Woodside	1	WH[1]
12 Apr	John SALISBURY	Dodsley	42	JB
10 May	Charles BROWN	Wood Leasowes	71	JB
19 May	Sarah BARNES	Field	65	JB
24 May	George EVANS	Church Leigh	81	JB
21 Feb	Ann BROWN	Wood Leasowes	68	JB
	Omitted from the proper place			
23 Jun	Mary HOWE	Upper Tean	72	CBC
26 Jun	Mary MOORE	Church Leigh	77	CBC
8 Jul	Edward John PHILLIPS	Upper Tean	36	JB
30 Jul	Edward BLURTON	Church Leigh	76	JB
4 Sep	Robert Richard HIDE	Withington	53	JB
9 Sep	William COPE	Draycot Waste	89	CBC
8 Oct	Jane HUGHES	Morrilow Heath	19	JB
27 Oct	Mary Ann CARTER	Withington	6 wks	JB
31 Dec	Sarah EDGE	Dodsley	88	WH[1]
1832				
1 Jan	Samuel BARNETT	Leigh	88	CBC
5 Jan	William STARTIN	Checkley Bank	3 mths	JB
15 Jan	Samuel WALKER	Beamhurst	21	JB
19 Jan	Mary BALANCE	Withington	3	JB
26 Jan	Elizabeth COLLIER	Upper Leigh	66	JB
8 Feb	John JOHNSON	Lower Leigh	6 mths	JB
16 Feb	William LOVATT	Upper Leigh	28	JB
15 Mar	Louisa BRINDLEY	Upper Leigh	44	JB
25 Mar	Thomas TILL	Middleton Green	36	JB
1 May	Thomas BOX	Lower Leigh	96	JB
7 Jun	Ellen LOVATT	Uttoxeter	5 mths	JB
9 Jun	George BLOOR	Withington	3 wks	JB
31 Jul	Mary LOVATT	Upper Leigh	28	CBC
15 Jul	Jane WALKER	Upper Leigh	91	JB
	Omitted in the proper place			

1 Aug	Sarah ALCOCK	Morrilow Heath	27	JB
4 Aug	Sir Robert GILBERT, Knight of St: Iveda [?] Waladimir	Ridgeway House, Repton, Derbyshire	49	JB
5 Sep	Hannah STARTIN	Lower Nobut	88	JB
18 Dec	John ALCOCK	Upper Leigh	66	JB
1833				
20 Jan	John WALKER	Withington Green	88	JB
29 Jan	Margaret BAILEY	Morrilow Heath	3 mths	JB
22 Feb	Thomas BRINDLEY	Upper Leigh	22	JB
3 Mar	Sarah ALCOCK	Morrilow Heath	9 mths	JB
4 Mar	Ann BENTLEY	Stafford	84	JB
18 Apr	William SHARP	Church Leigh	8	JB
1 May	George LOVATT	Lower Leigh	10	JB
2 May	Robert THORNIWELL	Middleton Green	69	JB
24 May	Thomas SLATER	Withington	43	JB
27 May	James DEAN	Middleton Green	2	JB
2 Jun	Sarah RATCLIFFE	Church Leigh	27	JB
27 Jun	Daniel BURTON	Fradswell	91	JB
13 Aug	Mary HOLLINS [surname changed from Holling]	Bitternsdale	Infant	TPB
5 Oct	Elizabeth RUSHTON	Church Leigh 80 & upwards		JB
5 Nov	Sarah Ann GARLAND	Withington Green	1	JB
6 Nov	James COTTERIL	Birchwood Park	1	JB
26 Dec	Ann HUGHES	Morrilow Heath	5	BSB
1834				
22 Jan	Sarah SLATER, Widow	Upper Leigh	84	JB
29 Jan	Hannah GILBERT, Widow	Church Leigh	89	TPB
14 Feb	Alice TATTON	Morrilow Heath	58	JD
10 Mar	Richard BRANDON	Upper Tean	54	JB
1 Apr	Elizabeth HEATH	Cheadle	68	JB
26 Apr	Edward RUSHTON	Upper Leigh	2 wks	JB
31 May	Dorothy KENT	Church Leigh	1	JB
5 Jun	Thomas LOVATT	Upper Leigh	79	JB
19 Jun	William HAWLEY	Nobut	68	WH[1]
30 Jun	Thomas TITLEY	Work-house	77	JB
6 Jul	Ann TURNER	Morrilow Heath	19	JB
3 Aug	John SNAPE	Withington	6 wks	JB
9 Aug	Edward SHARRATT	Beamhurst Lane in the Parish of Uttoxeter	18	JB
10 Sep	John PERKIN	Withington Green	1	JB
14 Sep	Henry ALCOCK	Upper Leigh	13	JB
1835				
22 Jan	Cicely SNOW, Widow of Thomas SNOW	The Knowles in the Parish of Milwich	69	JB
17 Mar	Ann MYATT, Widow of George MYATT	The Bents	26	JB
23 Mar	Mary Ann CARTER d/o John & Dorothy CARTER	Withington	1	JB
30 Mar	Ann BLOOD, Widow of John BLOOD	Bearsbrook	59	JB
14 Apr	Ann ROWBOTHAM illegitimate d/o Mary ROWBOTHAM	The Workhouse	7 wks	JB

Date	Name	Place	Age	Minister
23 Apr	Ellen COPE wife of Francis COPE	Godstone	36	JB
5 May	James DEAKIN illegitimate s/o Elizabeth DEAKIN	Withington Green	2	JB
19 Jun	Joyce DEAKIN wife of George DEAKIN	Withington Green	67	JB
21 Jun	Ann DEAKIN wife of John DEAKIN	Fole Farm	45	JB
12 Jul	Lydia KENT d/o Charles & Elizabeth KENT	Church Leigh	4 mths	JB
14 Aug	Elizabeth HUSON d/o John & Anne HUSON	Beamhurst	14	JB
10 Oct	Dorothy GARLAND d/o Thomas & Elizabeth GARLAND	Withington Green	25	JB
27 Oct	John HYDE, Widower Wetley Brooks in the Parish of Milwich		89	JB
25 Nov	Ann TATTON d/o Thomas & Millicent TATTON	Lower Nobut	10	JB
3 Dec	Thomas HUSON s/o John & Ellen HUSON	Madeley Farm in the Parish of Checkley	23 mths	JB
5 Dec	Mary SMITH d/o Thomas & Amy SMITH	The Workhouse Church Leigh	23	JB
15 Dec	William HARRISON s/o Joseph & Martha HARRISON	Lower Nobut	3 days	JB
25 Dec	John COLLIER, Widower	Lower Leigh	72	CBC
29 Dec	William s/o Charles & Ellen GARLAND	Withington	1 yr 9 mths	WH[1]
31 Dec	Joseph s/o Joseph & Mary UPTON	Middleton Green	3	WH[1]
1836				
1 Jan	George WILSON s/o George & Mary WILSON	~~Leigh~~ Fole	12 wks	CJP
3 Jan	Thomas TATTON s/o Thomas & Millicent TATTON	Lower Nobut	2	JB
20 Feb	Sarah TATTON d/o Thomas & Millicent TATTON	Lower Nobut	4	JB
23 Feb	George COPE s/o Elizabeth COPE widow of the late Edward COPE	Lower Leigh	23	JB
4 Mar	Margaret BAILEY Widow of William BAILEY	Morrilow Heath	Nearly 90	JB
5 Mar	Thomas PERKIN	Bromshall	75	JB
8 Apr	Anne RAWLINS Widow of William RAWLINS	Stoke upon Trent	81	JB
14 Apr	Mary Ann ALCOCK d/o Edward & Mary Ann ALCOCK	Morrilow Heath	32	JB
8 May	William RAWLINGS s/o John & Mary RAWLINGS	Morrilow Heath	19	JB
19 May	Thomas BUXTON	Nobett	52	*
	*S. Langley AM Rector of Checkley, then assisting here			
19 May	Rachel-Jane HUSON d/o John & Ellen HUSON	Madeley House in the Upper Tean	8	SL
22 May	John PERKIN, Widower		69	JB
23 Jul	Elizabeth RATCLIFFE wife of Charles RATCLIFFE	Withington Green	68	JB
31 Jul	Sarah BAILEY d/o Michael & [ ] BAILEY	Morrilow Heath	Infant	JB
9 Aug	Mary TURNER wife of William TURNER	Withington	62	JB

Date	Name	Place	Age	
13 Aug	Elizabeth HAWLEY wife of Thomas HAWLEY	Lower Nobut	87	JB
6 Sep	Lydia MARSON Widow of James MARSON	Middleton Green	76	CJP
6 Oct	George MYATT s/o William & Sarah MYATT	Dodsley	4 mths	JB
9 Oct	John DEAKIN, Widower	Fole	47	JB
11 Nov	William BUCKSTONES s/o the late Thomas BUXTON alias BUCKSTONES	Upper Tean	23	JB
15 Nov	Harriet POYSER d/o James & Charlotte POYSER	Middleton Green	6	JB
22 Dec	Joseph PERKIN s/o William & Cicely PERKIN	Withington Green	3 mths	JB
23 Dec	Charles BROWN	Park Hall	44	JB
25 Dec	John BATES s/o William & Ellen BATES	Field	21	JB
26 Dec	Joseph CHELL, Widower	Oakamoor	54	JB
1837				
4 Jan	Sarah BURTON widow of Daniel BURTON	Fradswell	73	JB
18 Jan	Sarah RAWLINGS d/o John & Mary RAWLINGS	Morrilow Heath	10 mths	JB
22 Jan	William RAWLINGS	Morrilow Heath	64	JB
27 Jan	Sarah PERKIN wife of William PERKIN	Hayes House	75	JB
1 Feb	James PYSER s/o James & Charlotte PYSER	Middleton Green	3 yrs 10 mths	CJP
6 Feb	Hannah MYATT wife of George MYATT	Dodsleigh	64	BSB
13 Feb	Mary ALLEN d/o David & Charlotte ALLEN	Morrilow Heath	2	JB
15 Feb	Hannah BENNISON	Upper Leigh	72	JB
26 Feb	William MARTIN, Parish Clerk	Nobut	68	JB
12 Mar	Martha BALL wife of John BALL	Leigh Lanes	61	JB
26 Mar	Ellen ADAMS widow of William ADAMS	Withington	81	JB
28 Apr	George MYATT, Widower	Dodsley	61	JB
15 May	Sarah DAVIES wife of David DAVIES	Morrilow Heath	76	JB
26 May	Mary WOODROFFE widow of Thomas WOODROFFE	Withington	81	JB
1 Jun	William Thomas PHILIPS s/o Thomas & [ ] PHILIPS	Dodsley	4	JB
28 Jun	Anne DEAKIN wife of George DEAKIN	The Shaw in the Parish of Stowe	66	JB
21 Jul	Richard ROWBOTHAM s/o Susanna ROWBOTHAM	the Workhouse	2	JB
2 Oct	Phebe BANKS wife of Samuel BANKS	Lower Leigh	59	JB
28 Oct	Mary COTTERILL d/o Clement & Hannah COTTERILL	Birchwood Park	13	JB
12 Nov	Hannah COTTERILL d/o Clement & Hannah COTTERILL	Birchwood park	4	JB

24 Nov	John SHEMELT	Morrilow Heath	65	JB
	s/o the late David & Margaret SHEMELT			
27 Nov	Mary HYDE	Withington	68	JB
	widow of Richard HYDE			

Leigh, Staffordshire, Marriages
1813-1842
[transcribed to 1837]

1813

29 Mar Thomas GREENSMITH otp & Mary LOVATT otp
Lic. Wit: Thomas LOVATT, Sa GREENSMITH
Off. Min.:- H. Thomas, Curate

25 Jul Charles GREEN otp & Frances [x] WEBBERLEY otp
Banns Wit: Thos GREEN, Saml ATKIN
Off. Min.:- H. Thomas, Curate

26 Aug Charles BROWNE [s. Brown] otp & Sarah GREENSMITH otp wco Parents
Lic. Wit: William GREENSMITH, Mary BALLINTON
Off. Min.:- H. Thomas, Curate

1814

20 Jan Edward [x] CHELL otp & Maria [x] STOKES P. of Ormarston
Banns Wit: William CHELL, Saml ATKIN
Off. Min.:- H. Thomas, Curate

3 Feb George HEALEY P. of Milwich & Sarah HOWE otp
Lic. Wit: Mary HEALEY, Thomas HOWE
Off. Min.:- H. Thomas, Curate

20 Mar Joseph [x] TILL & Eliz: [x] RUSHTON botp
Banns Wit: John [x] TAYLOR, Saml ATKIN
Off. Min.:- H. Thomas, Curate

14 Apr William DEAKIN P. of Stowe & Anne BARNES otp
Lic. Wit: Thomas PHILLIPS, Sarah BARNES
Off. Min.:- H. Thomas, Curate

16 May William PERKIN otp & Anne HOLLINS otp
Lic. Wit: Sarah PERKIN, William ROBINSON
Off. Min.:- H. Thomas, Curate

18 Jul Thomas CHELL otp & Ellen [x] IRELAND otp
Banns Wit: Joseph CHELL, Lydia FLINT
Off. Min.:- H. Thomas, Curate

24 Sep Robert ARNOLD otp & Anne [s. Ann] ARNOLD otp
Lic. Wit: May HALL, Sam PLATT __
Off. Min.:- H. Thomas, Curate

30 Nov John Prince ROBINSON P. of Checkley & Ellen SMITH otp
Lic. Wit: Joseph JENKINSON, Mary SMITH
Off. Min.:- H. Thomas, Curate
Groom signs as "Robbinso"

27 Dec Thomas [x] GAUNT otp & Hannah [x] CAPEWELL otp
Banns Wit: John [x] GAUNT, Anne [x] CAPEWELL
Off. Min.:- H. Thomas, Curate

31 Dec James KENT otp & Eliz. [x] TOOTH otp
Banns Wit: Charles KENT, Saml ATKIN
Off. Min.:- H. Thomas, Curate

1815

5 Jan Thomas BURNETT P. of Grindon in the County of Stafford & Hannah
Lic. CARTER otp
Wit: John CARR, Elizabeth CATER
Off. Min.:- H. Thomas, Curate

27 Apr Francis SHERRATT otp & Mary [x] MOTTRAM otp
Banns Wit: Saml ATKIN, Thos [x] FAULKNER
Off. Min.:- H. Thomas, Curate
Groom signs as "Sharratt"

1 May Joseph BRIDGEWOOD P. of Aston, Warwickshire, & Sarah GILBERT otp
Lic. Wit: John GILBERT, Diana GILBERT
Off. Min.:- H. Thomas, Curate
Groom signs as "Bridgwood"

11 Jul John WETTON otp & Mary WHITEHURST otp
Banns Wit: Samuel GREEN, Mary GREEN
Off. Min.:- H. Thomas, Curate

9 Aug Thomas BLAKEMAN P. of Stone & Mary SMITH otp
Banns Wit: William SMITH, Mary BLAKEMAN
Off. Min.:- H. Thomas, Curate

14 Aug Thomas [x] TURNER otp & Prudence [x] NICKLIN otp
Banns Wit: Saml ATKIN, Anne [x] NICKLIN
Off. Min.:- H. Thomas, Curate

14 Oct John MOOR otp & Maria BEARD otp
Lic. Wit: John WALKER, William MELLER
Off. Min.:- H. Thomas, Curate
Groom signs as "Moore"

6 Dec John HUSON otp & Elizabeth CARTER otp
Lic. Wit: James HUSON, Ann CARTER
Off. Min.:- H. Thomas, Curate

28 Dec Thomas [x] JOHNSON otp & Ellen [x] BARKER otp
Banns Wit: Thomas BAGNALL, Saml ATKIN
Off. Min.:- H. Thomas, Curate

1816

15 Feb Sampson CHALLINER P. of Milwich & Eliza [x] RUSHTON otp
Banns Wit: Thomas LYMER, Catherine STARTIN
Off. Min.:- H. Thomas, Curate
Groom signs as "Challennar"

7 Mar William SMITH, a Bachelor, P. of Millwich, and aged 21 years and
Lic. upwards, & Elizabeth COLLIER, a Spinster, otp of Leigh, and aged 21
years and upwards
Wit: Thomas SMITH, Hannah COLLIER, Saml ATKIN
Off. Min.:- Rev'd Samuel Langley, Rector of Checkley

14 Jul Edward [x] HOWE otp & Anne [x] MYATT otp
Banns Wit: Saml ATKIN, Willm MILLINGTON
Off. Min.:- H. Thomas, Curate

26 Oct Joseph [x] ELLERTON otp & Hannah [x] SMITH otp
Banns Wit: William MELLER, George WILLIAMS
Off. Min.:- H. Thomas, Curate

16 Dec Thomas RUSHTON otp & Hannah [x] NOAKES otp
Banns Wit: Saml ATKIN, William MELLER
Off. Min.:- H. Thomas, Curate

31 Dec William GREENSMITH otp & Cicely BROWNE [s. Brown] otp
Lic. Wit: Charles BROWN, Anna OAKDEN
Off. Min.:- H. Thomas, Curate

1817

24 Mar David [x] WHITEHURST otp Anne [x] BOULTON otp
Banns Wit: Saml ATKIN, John MARSON
Off. Min.:- H. Thomas, Curate

24 Mar John [x] HOLMES otp & Sarah [x] DUTTON otp
Banns Wit: Saml ATKIN, John MARSON
Off. Min.:- H. Thomas, Curate

6 Apr Samuel [x] NOBS otp & Elizabeth [x] HUGHES otp
Banns Wit: Saml ATKIN, Ann GAUNT
Off. Min.:- H. Thomas, Curate

15 May George EDGE otp & Mary [x] PERKIN otp
Banns Wit: Saml ATKIN, Jos [x] EDGE
Off. Min.:- H. Thomas, Curate

9 Jun William [x] RATCLIFFEotp & Anne [x] RUSHTON otp
Banns Wit: Robt ARNOLD, John MARSON
Off. Min.:- H. Thomas, Curate

18 Oct Thomas BAGNALL otp & Charlotte [x] SNAPE otp
Banns Wit: Saml ATKIN, Thos [x] JOHNSON
Off. Min.:- H. Thomas, Curate

4 Nov William CARTER otp & Jane BURNET P. of Grindon in
Lic. the County of Stafford
Wit: Thomas BURNET, Ellen BURNET
Off. Min.:- H. Thomas, Curate
Bride signs as "Burnett"

25 Dec John FOSTER otp & Eliz. [x] TILL otp
Banns Wit: John FOSTER, Catharine BRINDLEY
Off. Min.:- H. Thomas, Curate

1818

2 Jun James BLACKSHAW of Manchester & Anne [x] WARDLE otp
Banns Wit: Mary [x] WARDLE, Saml ATKIN
Off. Min.:- H. Thomas, Curate

15 Jun John HEATH otp & Catharine BRINDLEY otp
Banns Wit: Elizabeth CHALFIELD [Chatfield-BT], Mark MELLAR
Off. Min.:- H. Thomas, Curate

22 Jun John [x] PHILLIPS otp & Elizabeth [x] TWIGGE otp
Banns Wit: George WILLIAMS, Mary [x] TURNER, Saml ATKIN
Off. Min.:- H. Thomas, Curate

13 Jul George [x] SMITH otp & Hannah [x] MELLER otp
Banns Wit: Thomas MELLER, Saml ATKIN
Off. Min.:- H. Thomas, Curate

1819

17 May James COTTERILL otp & Elizabeth [x] COLLIER otp
Banns Wit: James [x] MEEHAM, Saml ATKIN
Off. Min.:- H. Thomas, Curate

27 Dec Thomas [x] PHILLIPS otp & Rebecca [x] KENT otp
Banns Wit: George PHILLIPS, Jane KENT
Off. Min.:- H. Thomas, Curate

30 Dec James [x] DEAKIN otp & Catharine [x] SMITH otp
Banns Wit: Mary SMITH, Saml ATKIN
Off. Min.:- H. Thomas, Curate

1820

3 Feb Charles [x] BOOTH otp & Lydia HUGHES otp
Banns Wit: Saml ATKIN, Joseph TABBERNOR
Off. Min.:- H. Thomas, Curate
Bride signs as "Lidia Hoas"

18 May Thomas TOOTH otp & Mary [x] BURTON otp
Banns Wit: Charles BURTON, Saml ATKIN
Off. Min.:- H. Thomas, Curate

19 Jun Thomas [x] HARDY otp & Maria [x] ALWOOD otp
Banns Wit: Saml ATKIN, Geo [x] SAMPSON
Off. Min.:- H. Thomas, Curate

19 Jun William [x] COPE o.t.p & Sarah [x] BURTON otp
Banns Wit: Saml ATKIN, Geo [x] SAMPSON
Off. Min.:- H. Thomas, Curate

21 Sep Thomas [x] YATES otp & Ann [x] TOOTH otp
Banns Wit: Charles TOOTH, Mary BURTON
Off. Min.:- Evan Lewes, Rector of Gratwich

5 Oct Richd. [x] LIMER P. of Stowe & Charlotte [x] MIDDLETON otp
Banns Wit: Mary ALCOCK, Samuel ATKIN
Off. Min.:- H. Thomas, Curate

2 Nov Benjamin PARR P of Colton in the County of Stafford & Sarah BARNES otp
Lic. Wit: John BARNES, Louisa BARNES
Off. Min.:- H. Thomas, Curate

[Next entry illegible – erased? & crossed through]

1821
6 Mar James WALLIS otp & Mary SMITH otp
Banns Wit: James [x] DEAKIN, Samuel ATKIN
Off. Min.:- H. Thomas, Curate

12 Mar John STOKES otp & Elizabeth [x] RUSHTON otp
Banns Wit: Thomas LYMER, Samuel ATKIN
Off. Min.:- H. Thomas, Curate

23 Apr Francis JOHNSON otp & Mary [x] ALCOCK otp
Banns Wit: John ALLCOCK, Samuel ATKIN
Off. Min.:- H. Thomas, Curate

12 May Benjamin [x] PRITCHARD otp & Anne GENT otp
Banns Wit: John [x] PRITCHARD, Samuel ATKIN
Off. Min.:- H. Thomas, Curate
Bride signs as "Ann"

9 Oct Joseph [x] GOODALL otp & Jane [x] SHIPTON otp
Banns Wit: Jonathan GOODALL, Samuel ATKIN
Off. Min.:- H. Thomas, Curate

4 Dec John BURTON otp & Elizabeth STEVENSON otp
Banns Wit: William STEVENSON, Ann BURTON
Off. Min.:- H. Thomas, Curate

31 Dec William [x] MELLER otp & Sarah [x] TWIGGE otp
Banns Wit: Samuel WETTON, C........... MELLER
Off. Min.:- H. Thomas, Curate

1822
28 Jan Samuel KENT otp & Elizabeth WHEAT otp
Banns Wit: Hannah FOSTER, William MELLER
Off. Min.:- H. Thomas, Curate

21 Mar Thomas FOSTER otp & Anne SHEMELT otp
Banns Wit: George SHEMILT, Hannah FOSTER
Off. Min.:- H. Thomas, Curate
Bride signs as "Shemilt"

29 Apr William [x] HOLLINS otp & Frances [x] ALCOCK otp
Banns Wit: John ALLCOCK, William MELLER
Off. Min.:- H. Thomas, Curate

29 Apr James WALKER otp & Sarah [x] TAYLER otp
Banns Wit: Willia WALKER, William MELLER
Off. Min.:- H. Thomas, Curate

27 May Thomas [x] TILL otp & Mary FENTON P. of Cheadle
Banns Wit: Thomas FENTON, Elizabeth TURNER
Off. Min.:- H. Thomas, Curate

10 Jun William [x] BARNET *[Barnett-BT]* otp & Hannah [x] DEAKIN P of Uttoxeter
Banns Wit: Samuel [x] DEAKIN, Samuel ATKIN
Off. Min.:- H. Thomas, Curate

20 Jun John ASBURY otp & Louisa BARNES otp
Lic. Wit: Joseph BARNES, Ellen ASBURY
Off. Min.:- H. Thomas, Curate

21 Oct William HILL otp & Hannah [x] MOOR *[Moore-BT]* otp
Banns Wit: George GRATWICH, Samuel ATKIN
Off. Min.:- H. Thomas, Curate

28 Oct Joseph [x] KIRKAM otp & Sarah [x] FOSTER otp
Banns Wit: George TILL, Samuel ATKIN
Off. Min.:- H. Thomas, Curate

1823

14 Apr Edward [x] BAILEY otp & Sarah [x] CHELL otp
Banns Wit: Hannah WORTENHOUSE, Samuel ATKIN
Off. Min.:- H. Thomas, Curate

5 May Samuel GRIFFIN otp & Margt. [x] BLOOD otp
Banns Wit: John COPE, Saml ATKIN
Off. Min.:- H. Thomas, Curate

5 May Francis [x] WRIGHT otp & Sarah [x] TUNSTAL otp
Banns Wit: George TILL, Saml ATKIN
Off. Min.:- H. Thomas, Curate

16 Jun Rupert [x] CALBERT otp & Elizabeth [x] PHILIPS *[Phillips-BT]*otp
Banns Wit: Charles KIRKLAND, Prudence FLEWELL
Off. Min.:- H. Thomas, Curate

1824

1 Mar John [x] BROCKLEHURST P. of Stoke-upon-Trent & Hannah MIATT otp
Banns Wit: S. MARCHINGTON, Saml ATKIN
Off. Min.:- H. Thomas, Curate
Bride signs as "Myatt"

24 May Edward WALKER otp & Harriet [x] REDFERN otp
Banns Wit: Michael REDFERN, Saml ATKIN
Off. Min.:- H. Thomas, Curate

30 May William PERKIN otp & Sarah KENDRICK P. of Weston-upon-Trent
Lic. Wit: Elizabeth PERKIN, Saml ATKIN
Off. Min.:- H. Thomas, Curate
Groom signs as "William Perkin Senior"

11 Oct Barnabas [x] BAILEY otp & Sarah [x] BRADBURY otp
Banns Wit: Joseph BRADBURY, Weller MELLER
Off. Min.:- H. Thomas, Curate

13 Dec Samuel [x] FLEWEL *[Flewell-BT]* otp & Elizabeth [x] PHILLIPS otp
Banns Wit: William MELLER, Mary INGRAM
Off. Min.:- H. Thomas, Curate

1825

27 Jan Joseph [x] KIDD otp & Hannah [x] BAGNELL otp
Banns Wit: William [x] KIDD, Samuel ATKIN
Off. Min.:- H. Thomas, Curate

13 Feb Thomas [x] WHITEHALL otp & Anne [x] BENTLEY otp
Banns Wit: Thomas MARSON, Samuel ATKINS
Off. Min.:- H. Thomas, Curate

16 Jul William ALCOCK otp & Catharine GADSBY otp
Banns Wit: John ALLCOCK, Elizabeth ALLCOCK
Off. Min.:- H. Thomas, Curate

15 Dec   Thomas GREEN P. of Gratwich & Catharine PHILLIPS otp
Lic.   Wit: Harriet GREEN, Samuel ATKIN
Off. Min.:- H. Thomas, Curate

28 Dec   John [x] WARD otp & Maria SMITH otp
Banns   Wit: Elizabeth SMITH, Samuel ATKIN
Off. Min.:- H. Thomas, Curate

1826

2 Jan   Matthew SNAPE otp & Elizabeth [x] GOUGH otp
Banns   Wit: Samuel ATKIN, Maria [x] COPE
Off. Min.:- H. Thomas, Curate

23 Jan   James BARNET P. of Leek & Elizabeth LOVATT otp
Lic.   Wit: Thomas LOVATT, Rachel LOVATT
Off. Min.:- H. Thomas, Curate

5 Jun   James TOWERS otp & Mary [x] WARDLE otp
Banns   Wit: William TURNER, Samuel ATKIN
Off. Min.:- H. Thomas, Curate

22 Aug   James BEARDMORE P. of Checkley & Anne PERKIN otp
Banns   Wit: John PERKIN, Sarah PERKIN
Off. Min.:- H. Thomas, Curate
Bride signs as "Ann Perkins"

14 Sep   Luke TURNER otp & Anne BROWNE otp
Lic.   Wit: Joseph BROWN, Eliza FENTON, Sam BROWN
Off. Min.:- H. Thomas, Curate
Bride signs as "Brown"

30 Oct   John MARSON otp & Anne BLOOR P. of Checkley
Lic.   Wit: James BEECH, Mary BLOOR
Off. Min.:- H. Thomas, Curate
Bride signs as "Ann"

1827

15 Jan   Joseph BECK otp & Mary [x] NICKSON otp
Banns   Wit: James NIXON, S. ATKIN
Off. Min.:- H. Thomas, Curate

22 Jan   Joseph NORRIS P. of Uttoxeter & Lydia BLURTON otp
Lic.   Wit: Thos. BLURTON, Anne BLURTON
Off. Min.:- H. Thomas, Curate

22 Feb   Joseph ELLSMOOR P. of Colwich & Eliza FENTON otp
Lic.   Wit: John Waltho FENTON, Elizabeth TURNER
Off. Min.:- H. Thomas, Curate

26 Feb   Thomas CHELL otp & Sarah [x] JOHNSON otp
Banns   Wit: Thomas JOHNSON, Phoebe STUBBS
Off. Min.:- H. Thomas, Curate

27 Apr   Joseph [x] MIDDENS otp & Sarah BURTON otp
Banns   Wit: John MEDDINGES, Elizabeth, S. ATKIN
Off. Min.:- H. Thomas, Curate

21 May   John MIDDENS otp & Anne LOVETT otp
Banns   Wit: Margaret LOVETT, Saml ATKIN
Off. Min.:- H. Thomas, Curate
Groom signs as "Meddinges"
Bride signs as "Lovatt"

24 Jul   George MIATT otp & Anne FOWLER otp
Banns   Wit: William MYATT, S. ATKIN
Off. Min.:- H. Thomas, Curate
Groom signs as "Myatt"

17 Sep   John [x] ASHTON otp & Eliza [x] BAILEY otp
Banns   Wit: William [x] FLEWEL, S. ATKIN
Off. Min.:- H. Thomas, Curate

31 Dec Thomas [x] EVANS otp & Sarah [x] WHITEHALL P. of Bromshall
Banns   Wit: William DUROSE, Lydia BEARDMORE
    Off. Min.:- H. Thomas, Curate

1828

14 Feb George [x] DEAKIN otp & Mary [x] TATTON otp
Banns   Wit: Samuel [x] DEAKIN, S. ATKIN
    Off. Min.:- H. Thomas, Curate

2 Jun John CARTER otp & Dorothy PHILLIPS otp
Lic.   Wit: Thomas PHILLIPS, Sarah LOWNDES
    Off. Min.:- H. Thomas, Curate

28 Jul Michael SALT otp & Elizabeth [x] TABERNER otp
Banns   Wit: Thos. MOUNTFORD, Marther [x] SHENTON
    Off. Min.:- H. Thomas, Curate

11 Sep Thomas HEATH otp & Sarah [x] EDGE otp
Banns   Wit: William EDGE, Catherine TURNER
    Off. Min.:- H. Thomas, Curate

6 Oct Samuel ALCOCK otp & Mary CARR P. of Cheadle
Banns   Wit: John ALCOCK, Ann CARR
    Off. Min.:- H. Thomas, Curate

20 Nov William ADAMS otp & Ann [x] TILL otp
Lic.   Wit: William MIDDLETON, Mary BEARD
    Off. Min.:- H. Thomas, Curate

18 Dec John BUXTON otp & Rebecca TURNER
Banns   Wit: John TURNER, Mary TURNER
    Off. Min.:- William Hutchinson
    Bride signs as "Rebecker"

1829

27 Jan William TURNER otp & Elizabeth HOLLINS otp
Banns   Wit: Thomas HOLLINS, Mary TOOTH
    Off. Min.:- H. Thomas, Curate

2 Mar John [x] SMITH otp & Edith WALKER otp
Banns   Wit: William WALKER, Samuel ATKIN
    Off. Min.:- H. Thomas, Curate

3 Aug Charles [x] ROBINSON, a Bachelor, P. of Burton-upon-Trent, & Matilda [x]
Banns   WALKER, a Spinster, otp
    Wit: John DUNN of Tatenhill, Samuel ATKIN
    By request, by me Saml Langley AM, Rector of Checkley

21 Sep John HEATH P. of Cheadle, Bachelor, & Elizabeth [x] JOHNSTONE. otp,
Lic.   Spinster
    Wit: E. BLURTON, S. ATKIN
    Off. Min.:- Rev'd C.B. Charleswood

29 Dec Samuel [x] DEAKIN otp & Anne [x] MOTTRAM otp
Banns   Wit: George MOTTERHAM, Samuel ATKIN
    Off. Min.:- Rev'd C.B. Charleswood

1830

8 Feb Thomas [x] FOWELL, Bachelor, otp & Mary [x] BAILEY, otp, Spinster
Banns   Wit: James TAFT, S. ATKIN
    Off. Min.:- Rev'd C.B. Charleswood

19 Apr John [x] SMITH, Bachelor, otp & Elizabeth [x] TUNSTALL, otp, Spinster
Banns   Wit: S. ATKIN, Ann ADAMS
    Off. Min.:- Rev'd C.B. Charleswood

26 Apr Thomas BARNES, Bachelor, P. of Shirley in the County of Derby, & Sarah
Lic.   LOWNDES, otp, Spinster
    Wit: Thomas LOWNDES, James WOODALL
    Off. Min.:- Rev'd C.B. Charleswood

26 Apr Charles WARD, Bachelor, P. of Cheadle in the county of Stafford, &
Lic. Margaret LOWNDES, Spinster, otp
Wit: James WOODALL, Thomas LOWNDES
Off. Min.:- Rev'd C.B. Charleswood

29 Apr William WALTERS, Bachelor, P. of Cheadle in County of Stafford, &
Lic. Elizabeth TURNER, Spinster, otp
Wit: George TURNER, Mary SMITH
Off. Min.:- Rev'd C.B. Charleswood

21 Jun William PERKIN, otp, Bachelor, & Cicely TATTON, otp, Spinster
Banns Wit: Thomas HADEN, Elizabeth PERKIN
Off. Min.:- Rev'd C.B. Charleswood

29 Aug William [x] BLOOR, otp, Bachelor, & Elizabeth [x] BOND, P. of Uttoxeter,
Banns Spinster
Wit: Richard PACKER, Sarah [x] MOTTRAM
Off. Min.:- James Beaven, Curate

19 Oct John LOVATT, otp, Bachelor, & Mary SMITH, otp, Spinster
Lic. Wit: James BEECH, Elizabeth WALTERS
Off. Min.:- James Beaven, Curate

11 Nov William GRIFFIN, otp, Bachelor, & Sarah ALCOCK, otp, Spinster
Banns Wit: Thomas GRIFFIN, Mary TOOTH
Off. Min.:- James Beaven, Curate

1831

12 Feb William EDGE, otp, Bachelor, & Hannah BATES, otp, Spinster
Banns Wit: Jane DEAKIN [?] [Lakin-BT], S. ATKIN
Off. Min.:- James Beaven, Curate

14 Feb John [x] HOUGH, otp, Bachelor, & Ellen [x] BAGNALL, otp, Spinster
Banns Wit: Daniel HOUGH, S. ATKIN
Off. Min.:- James Beaven, Curate

5 Apr William WALKER, otp, Bachelor, & Esther [x] GRIFFIN, otp, Spinster
Banns Wit: Simon FOWLER, Mary TUNNICLIFF
Off. Min.:- James Beaven, Curate

24 May Charles COPE, otp, Bachelor, & Sarah [x] CHELL, otp, Spinster
Banns Wit: Hannah CHELL, Samuel ATKIN
Off. Min.:- James Beaven, Curate

17 Oct William [x] WETTON, otp, Bachelor, & Ann [x] BUXTONS, otp Spinster
Banns Wit: William BUXTON, Samuel ATKIN
Off. Min.:- James Beaven, Curate

14 Nov George STUBBS, P. of Stone, Bachelor, & Rachel LOVATT, otp, Spinster
Lic. Wit: Thomas LOVATT, Hellen HUSON, John HUSON
Off. Min.:- James Beaven, Curate

1832

6 Mar Richard BRANDON, P. of Checkley, Widower, & Hannah COLLIER, otp,
Lic. Spinster
Wit: Joseph COLLIER, Edith STUBBS
Off. Min.:- James Beaven, Curate

22 Mar John [x] BLOOR, otp, Bachelor, & Sarah [x] LEES, otp Spinster
Banns Wit: William [x] BLOOR, Samuel [x] ATKIN
Off. Min.:- James Beaven, Curate

1 May John GILBERT, otp, Bachelor, & Anne LAWRANCE, otp, Widow
Lic. Wit: William BLURTON, Louisa BRINDLEY
Off. Min.:- James Beaven, Curate
Bride signs as "Lawrence"

11 Jun William BURTON, otp, Bachelor, & Jane DEAKIN, otp, Spinster
Banns Wit: John BURTON, Ann [x] DEAKIN
Off. Min.:- James Beaven, Curate

25 Jun Thomas [x] HILL, P. of Rocester, Bachelor, & Elizabeth [x] PRESTON, otp,
Banns Spinster
Wit: William [x] MANIFOLD, Samuel ATKIN
Off. Min.:- James Beaven, Curate

27 Sep John JOHNSON, P. of Colton, Bachelor, & Mary LOWNDES, otp, Spinster
Lic. Wit: Thomas LOWNDES, Samuel ATKIN
Off. Min.:- James Beaven, Curate

18 Oct William [x] KERLING *[Keeling-BT]*, otp, Bachelor, & Jane [X] FOSTER, otp,
Banns Spinster
Wit: Jhon PARKER, Samuel ATKIN
Off. Min.:- James Beaven, Curate

1833

22 Jan Thomas GRIFFIN, otp, Bachelor, & Mary TOOTH, otp, Spinster
Banns Wit: William GRIFFIN, Prudence TOOTH
Off. Min.:- James Beaven, Curate

26 Jan William [x] MYATT, otp, Bachelor, & Sarah [x] JOHNSON, otp, Spinster
Banns Wit: William MYATT, Sarah MYATT
Off. Min.:- James Beaven, Curate

20 May Thomas [x] BLACKBURN, P. of Castle, Bachelor, & Catharine [x] LOWE,
Lic. otp, Spinster
Wit: Ellenor MERY, James [x] TILL
Off. Min.:- James Beaven, Curate

22 Jun Charles YATES, P. of Abbot's Bromley, Bachelor, & Susannah PHILIPS,
Banns otp, Spinster
Wit: John MARTIN, Sarah PHILLIPS
Off. Min.:- James Beaven, Curate
Bride signs as "Phillips"

14 Oct Joseph BROWN, otp, Bachelor, & Sarah BLORE, otp, Spinster
Lic. Wit: John MORRIS, Ciselea BLOOR
Off. Min.:- James Beaven, Curate

4 Nov John COPE, P. of Checkley, Bachelor, & Hannah EDGE, otp, Spinster
Banns Wit: Samuel COPE, Mary HOLLINS
Off. Min.:- James Beaven, Curate

31 Dec James BOND, otp, & Mary [x] TAYLOR, otp
Banns Wit: William WALKER, Esther [x] WALKER
Off. Min.:- Bryan Sneyd Broughton

1834

18 Feb Charles YATES, P. of St. Mary's Stafford, Bachelor, & Ellen [x] TILL, otp,
Lic. Spinster
Wit: John [x] TILL, Samuel ATKIN
Off. Min.:- James Beaven, Curate

13 Mar Joseph WETTON, P. of Bramshall, Bachelor, & Sarah HAWLEY, otp,
Lic. Spinster
Wit: George HAWLEY, Elizabeth WETTON
Off. Min.:- James Beaven, Curate

18 Aug George STARTIN, otp, Bachelor, & Sarah EARDLEY, otp, Spinster
Banns Wit: Thomas EARDLEY, Elizebeth WILSON
Off. Min.:- James Beaven, Curate

27 Dec Thomas SHAW, otp, Bachelor, & Sarah EDGE, otp, Spinster
Banns Wit: John [x] SHAW, Mary [x] EDGE
Off. Min.:- James Beaven, Curate

1835

~~24 Feb Samuel TWIGG, P. of Uttoxeter, Bachelor, & Sarah [x] BRADBURY, otp,~~
~~Lic. Spinster~~
~~Wit: John FARMER, Sarah TWIGG~~
~~Off. Min.:- James Beaven, Curate~~

24 Feb John TWIGG, P. of Uttoxeter, Bachelor, & Sarah [x] BRADBURY, otp
Lic. Spinster
Wit: John FARMER, Sarah TWIGG
Off. Min.:- James Beaven, Curate

26 Feb John BLORE, P. of Leigh, Bachelor, & Margaret KEYS, P. of Cheadle,
Lic. Widow
Wit: John MELLOR, Cicelea BLOOR
Off. Min.:- James Beaven, Curate

10 Mar Joseph [x] GREEN, P. of Croxden, Bachelor, & Mary HOLLINS, otp
Banns Spinster
Wit: William HOLLINS, Ann PROCTOR
Off. Min.:- James Beaven, Curate

29 Apr Thomas TOMLINSON, P. of King's Bromley, Widower, & Hannah [x]
Banns DEAN, otp, Spinster
Wit: William TOMLINSON, Lydia [x] DEAN
Off. Min.:- James Beaven, Curate

6 Jun Benjamin WILD, otp, Bachelor, & Charlotte WALKER, P. of Uttoxeter,
Banns Spinster
Wit: Thomas WALKER, Edith WALKER
Off. Min.:- James Beaven, Curate

28 Jul Samuel ROBISON, otp, Bachelor, & Hannah [x] DUROSE, otp, Spinster
Banns Wit: Anne DUROSE, William DUROSE
Off. Min.:- James Beaven, Curate
Groom signs as "Robinson"

30 Jul Benjamin [x] PRESTON, otp, Bachelor, & Mary Ann [x] CHELL, otp, Spinster
Banns Wit: Thomas [x] BATES, William MARTIN
Off. Min.:- James Beaven, Curate

31 Dec John TURNER, P. of Stoke, & Elizabeth JACKSON, otp,
Banns Wit: Samuel KNOBBS, Elizabeth [x] KNOBBS
Off. Min.:- T.P. Browne, Rector of Gratwich

1836

11 Feb William [x] CHELL, otp, & Dorothy [x] HOLDEN, otp,
Banns Wit: William [x] BATES, Hannah [x] BATES
Off. Min.:- W. Higton, Perpetual Curate of Croxden

18 ~~Jul~~ Jeremiah [x] MAYER, P. of Draycot, Widower, & Mary TILL, otp, Widow
Aug Wit: John HARRIS, Charlotte [x] POYSER
Lic. Off. Min.:- James Beaven, Curate

29 Aug Charles [x] BAILEY, otp, Bachelor, & Frances SMITH, otp,Spinster
Banns Wit: James [x] BAILEY, William MARTIN
Off. Min.:- James Beaven, Curate

31 Oct Joseph PERKIN, otp, Bachelor, & Ann SHAW, otp, Spinster
Lic. Wit: Robert PERKIN, Ann BRIGHT, Jane SHAW, Robt. PERKIN Jn., Ann PERKINS,
William SHAW
Off. Min.:- James Beaven, Curate

3 Nov Thomas EARDLEY, otp, Bachelor, & Sarah MYATT, otp, Spinster
Banns Wit: George STARTIN, Sarah STARTIN
Off. Min.:- James Beaven, Curate

29 Dec Thomas [x] BAGNALL, otp, Bachelor, & Ann BAILEY, otp, Spinster
Banns Wit: Thomas [x] BLOOD, William MARTIN
Off. Min.:- James Beaven, Curate

1837

10 Apr Charles MOORE, otp, Bachelor, & Anne PHILIPS, otp, Spinster
Banns Wit: [?]J. MOORE, Caroline MOORE
Off. Min.:- James Beaven, Curate
Bride signs as "Phillips"

15 May John CHELL, otp, Bachelor, & Elizabeth GREEN, otp, Spinster
Banns   Wit: William RICHARDSON, Sarah CHELL
        Off. Min.:- James Beaven, Curate

8 Jun   Robert PHILIPS, otp, Bachelor, & Ann [x] SMITH, otp, Spinster
Banns   Wit: Thomas ADAMS, Frances POYSER
        Off. Min.:- James Beaven, Curate
        Groom signs as "Phillips"

The number of marriages from 1821 to 1830 both inclusive is 66, making the average between 6 & 7.

The number of marriages during the ten years ending 1840 is 50, making an average of 5.

Important note for demographer.

Signatures of Clergy and Churchwardens recorded in Leigh Bishops Transcripts
Between 1660 and 1854

1673	Edward Wood, Rich: Peercival	Churchwardens
1676	William [x] Salt, Francis Middleton	Churchwardens
1682	John Saunders	Rector
	William Bromwell, Thomas Hide	Churchwardens
1684	John Saunders	Rector
	Tho. Hide, Francis Keene	Churchwardens
1698	John Saunders	Rector
	Edward Wood, Thomas Townsend	Churchwardens
1701	John Saunders	Rector
	William Hill, Thomas Coleclough	Churchwardens
1705	John Saunders	Rector
	Thomas Fenton, William Hill	Churchwardens
1707	John Saunders	Rector
	Thomas Barnfield	
	John Sherratt, Thomas Hichcock	Churchwardens
1711	John Saunders	Rector
	Thomas Sherratt, Wm: Hill	Churchwardens
1714	Joh. Saunders	Rector
	George [x] Deakin	Churchwarden
1718	John Felthouse	Rector
	Sampson [x] Wright, Wm. [x] Wilton	Churchwardens
1722	John Felthouse	Rector
	J: Ashenhurst, [?] Carnells	Churchwardens
1726	Mi: Ward	Rector
	Edward Till, Simon Bloore	Churchwardens
1730	Mich: Ward	Rector
	John Preston, John Cartwright	
1732	Mich: Ward	Rector
	Moses Johnson	Churchwarden
1735	Mich: Ward	Rector of Leigh
	John Brindly, James Marson	Churchwardens
1738	Michl: Ward	Rector of Leigh
	Robert Wood, Ralph Turner	Churchwardens
1741	Michael Ward	Rector
	William Sherratt, John Hampson	Churchwardens
1744	Richard Woolley	Curate
	Thos. Belcher, Joshua [x] Preston	Churchwardens
1747	John Ward	Curate of Leigh
	Edwd. Blurton, Tho: Johnson	Churchwardens
1751	John Ward	Curate of Leigh
	Edward Blurton Jr, John Blurton	Churchwardens
1755	J. Ward	Curate of Leigh
	John Blurton, Hanry Woodward	Churchwardens
1758	J. Ward	Curate of Leigh
	John Brindly Junior, John Bloore	Churchwardens
1762	Ralph Barnes	Curate
	Thos: Hudson, Wm: Johnson	Churchwardens

1766	Waltr. Bagot	Rector of Leigh
	Robert Phillips, Philip Titley	Churchwardens
1773	Geo. Jolland	Curate of Leigh
	Thos. Belcher, John Blurton	
1776	Tho: Browne	Curate
	John Asbury, Thomas Tunnicliff	Churchwardens
1782	Tho: Browne	Curate
	Edward Blurton, Thomas Huson	Churchwardens
1786	Tho: Browne	Curate of Leigh
	John Hyde, James Sale	Churchwardens
1791	H. Thomas	Curate
	Thomas Brown, Richard Fenton	Churchwardens
1794	H. Thomas	Curate of Leigh
	William Wilshaw	
1800	H. Thomas	Curate
	Wm. Phillips	Churchwarden
1805	H. Thomas	Curate
	William Wilshaw	Churchwarden
1809	H. Thomas	Curate
	William Wilshaw	Churchwarden
1812	H. Thomas	Curate
	William Wilshaw	Churchwarden
1813-1828	H. Thomas	Curate
1813-1816	William Wilshaw	Churchwarden
1818-1819	William Marson	Churchwarden
1820-1830	E. Blurton	Churchwarden
1829	Chas. B. Charleswood	[Minister]
1830-1841	James Beaven	[Curate]
1831	Wm. Blurton	Churchwarden
1833	Wm. Blurton, Wm. Blurton Junr.	Churchwardens
1834-1846	Wm. Blurton	Churchwarden
1842-1845	Robert Haynes	Curate
1846-1854	Lewis Francis Bagot	Rector

Names of Clergy recorded in Leigh parish Registers
between 1813 and 1900

JA	John Anderson, Offg: Min.
FB	Frederick Bagot, Offg. Min.
LB or LFB	Lewis F. Bagot, Rector
Rev'd B	Rev'd Bagot, Off. Min.
TB	T. Barns, Vicar of Hilderstone
JB	James Beaven M.A. Oxon, Curate
WTB	W. T. Bennett, Officiating Minister
WB	W. Blathwayt, O.M.
or WTB	or Wynter Thos. Blathwayt, Curate (of Langridge, Somerset)
BSB	Bryan Sneyd Broughton, Off. Min.
TPB	T.P. Browne, Rector of Gratwich
CB	C. Bullivant, Curate of Checkley
AC	Algernon Capan, Offg. Min.
ESC	E. S. Carpenter
CBC	Rev'd C. B. Charleswood
FGC	Francis Grenville Cholmondeley, Curate (1880 – of Stoke on Trent)
RMC	R. M. Clark
HRC	Henry R. Coldham, Curate of Checkley
TC	Thomas Crossley, Curate
JC	J. Curtis Off. Min.
AD	A. Davy, Off. Minister
AHD	Arthur H. Drummond, Vicar of Mayne [?] Hill, Maidenhead
JHD	John H. Duck, Inct. of (Upper) Tean
DE	D. Edwardes
AF	Alb. Fosbrooke
SG	Sudlow Garratt
GH	Geo. Hake, Off. Minister
JH[1]	John Hamsted. Off. Min.
H or JH[2]	Rev'd Mr John Hand
RH	Robert Haynes, Curate
FAH	F. Aidan Hibbert, Denstone College
WH[1]	W. Higton, Perpetual Curate of Croxden
WTH	William T. Horton
LCH	L. C. Humfrey, Assist. Curate of Hollington
FWH	Frederick W. Humphreys, Curate of Tean
WH[2]	William Hutchinson, Off. Min. also signed as Rector of Checkley
TSH	Thomas Scott Huxley, Curate
JK	John Kinder, Offg. Min
RK or RCK	Richard C. Kirkpatrick, Curate
ECSK	E. C. Sneyd Kynnersley
EL	Ernald Lane, Rector (from March 1888 Archdeacon designate of Stoke on Trent)
SL or L	Rev'd Samuel Langley, Rector of (the neighbouring parish of) Checkley
WHL	W. Henry Leicester
ML or MAL	Morton A. Leicester, Curate
WGLJ	William Geo. Le Jeune, Curate

EL[2]	Evan Lewes, Rector of Gratwich
RL	Richd. Locker, Officiating Minister
JGL	John G. Lonsdale, Officg. Minister
HWL	H. W. Lowe, Chaplaine of Denstone College
PM	Pelham Maitland, Officiating Minister
GM	Geo. Mather, Inct. of Freehay
JTM	James Thomas May, Curate
WGM	William Gibbons Mayne M.A., Curate of Hollington & Croxden, later Vicar of Tean
HM	H. Meynell
WHFM	W. H. F. Meredith, Curate of Checkley
JHM	J. H. Moor, Offg. Min.
OM	Osbert Mordaunt, Off. Min.
WM	Rev'd W. Mould, Incumbent of Stowe
TLM	Thomas L. Murray, St. Chads Longton
WTN	W. T. Norton, Minister Offg.
RO	R. Oakden, Rector of Bramshall
EP	Edward Philips, Off. Min., Curate of Checkley 1868, Rector of Checkley 1884
JP	J. Picton A.M.
TMP	T. M. Pike, Offting Minister
CJP	C. J. Pinfold Rector of Bromshall
RP	Robt. Porter, Rector of Draycot
HWP	Henry William Pullen, Offic'g Minister
RR	R. Rawle, Rector of Cheadle
CRR	Chas. R. Round, Curate of Checkley
GTR	George T. Ryves, Vicar of Tean
GS[1]	Graham Smith, Off. Min., or Curate
HS	Henry Sneyd, Officiating Minister
GS[2]	Rev'd George Styche, Curate of Keel
HT	H. Thomas, Curate
GLT	G. Linton Thorp, Curate of Hampton Lucy
TWT	T. W. Tomlins, Curate of Checkley
GW or GWHW	G. W. H. Wanklyn, Curate of Checkley
BW	Bennett Williams, Rector of Bramshall

SURNAME INDEX

BAILEYE.......81
BAILIE.......30 66 103 107-112 153 154
BAILYE.......73 119 121-125 127 128 130 131
    148 149 161-166 169 171
BAKER.......114 170 172 175 192 242 244
BAKEWELL.......243 251 255 257
BALANCE.......274 280 281
BALD.......72
BALL.......5 6 17-19 27 49 57 67 178 202 206
    207 220 284
BALLANCE.......198 199 249 254
BALLE.......5 19 20 44
BALLINTON.......250 285
BAMFORD.......237 239
BANCKES, BANKS.......182 284
BANN.......60
BANNISTER, BANISTER.......67 122 151
BARBER.......61
BARKER.......11 31-33 36 38 59-61 64 68 69 86
    87 89 91 93 96 100-102 120 126 129
    131 145 155 160 163 178 180-184 186
    188 189 191 192 194 196 199 205 207
    208 211-215 217 221 223 231 235 241
    250 253 277 286
BARLOE, BARLOW.......193
BARLOUR.......114
BARNES, BARNS.......88 99 153 202 203 218
    225-228 234 247 255 259 267 269
    271-274 279-281 285 288 289 291
BARNET, BARNETT.......136 138 146 149 151
    185-187 189 191 193 195-198 200-203
    210 211 215 216 219 224 233 249
    262-265 267 269 271 274 281 289 290
BARRAT, BARRATT, BARRETT.......169-173
BARTLE.......71 79 80
BASFORD.......86
BASSET.......115 161
BATCOMBE.......59
BATEMAN.......149
BATES, BATE.......6 153 213 274 284 292 294
BATKYN.......7
BATMAN.......94
BAULL, BAULLE.......45 52
BEALEY.......114-116 137 147 155 156 228
BEALY.......137
BEARD.......286 291
BEARDEMOORE.......21 22
BEARDMOORE, BEARDMORE.......6 30 31 46
    56 129 140 141 150 156 162 189 241
    272 273 290 291
BEARDSLEY.......11
BEASTON.......67
BEAVEN.......267-270
BECK.......266 290
BEDSON.......262
BEE.......17 21 47
BEECH.......88 139 146 151 175 208 213 217
    234 250 290 292
BEELAND.......83
BEET.......151
BEETENSON.......7

BELCHER.......9 67 68 74 76 77 81-85 87 89 91
    93 96-98 104 105 109-116 118 119 123
    124 126 127 129 133 134 136-141 147
    155 156 160-162 165 166 169 172-174
    179 182 194 196 198-200 202 207 208
    210-213 215 216 218 223 228 230 233
    234 242 245-247 249 277
BELCHIER.......142 177 178
BELL.......219
BENNETT, BENNET.......7 27 137 200 227
BENNISON.......284
BENNIT.......146
BENTLEY, BENTELEY, BENTLY.......52 182
    194 200 212 218-220 222 232 252 254
    256 257 264 269 273 275 282 289
BERDMORE.......47
BERINGTON.......45
BERISFORD.......89
BERKIN.......233
BERRESFORD, BERRISFORD.......137 138 178
    211 215 229 240 275
BERRYSFORD.......240 242
BERWEEKE.......54
BETT, BETTS.......266
BETTERNEY.......236
BEVAN, BEVINS.......116 157
BICKHORN.......247
RIDDULPH.......257
BIGGEN, BIGGIN.......74 81
BIGGINS, BIGINS.......39 40 82 83 153
BIGINGS.......62
BILL, BILLE.......30 31
BILLING, BILLINGE.......9 122 166 172
BILLINGS.......144 178 186-189 212 229 230
    236 243 263 265
BILLINS.......150 219 251 281
BIRCH, BYRCH, BYRCHE.......6 8 13-15 21 23
    24 27-31 33 44 51 54-56 59 73 74 79
    81-83 87 154 202-204 239 257
BIRD, BYRD.......12 25 40-43 59 62 63 70 81 92
    95 98 112-117 119 120 129 133 135
    143 146 152 154 155 161 164 170 176
    178 208 217 225 246
BIRDE.......14 31 33 45 57 58
BISHOP.......160
BLACKBURN.......268 293
BLACKDEN.......215 216 247
BLACKMAN.......21 54
BLACKSHAW.......287
BLADEN, BLADON.......38 39 74-77 81 83 86
    188-190 192 211 241
BLAGSHAW.......279
BLAKE.......242
BLAKEMAN.......6 8 29 31 32 34 59 71 72 90-92
    286
BLAKMAN.......30 59
BLEWER.......118 137
BLOOD.......76 83 84 90 92 99 100 102 131-133
    138 143 153 177 180 182 204 210 213
    217 219 222 225 228 233 243 253 282
    289 294

141 143 145 176 179 182 184 185 188
190 191 194 208 210 211 213 215-217
221 228 247 265 267 281 283 284 291
292
BYARD.......236
BYATT.......218 246 255 259 262 264 267
BYLANDE.......8
BYLL, BYLLE.......8 27 28
BYLLINGE.......6 18-22
BYLLINGES.......22 47
BYLLINGS.......7 47
BYLLYNGE.......13 48 49 52 53
BYLLYNGES.......7 49 50
BYRD, BYRDE.......6 19 20 25 43 45-47 50 51 ⌐
53
BYRKE.......16 19 25 46 51
BYRKS, BYRKES.......20 44 49
BYRTCHE.......29

CADE.......48
CADMAN.......113
CALBERT.......289
CAN.........6
CANTRELL.......8 47
CAPE.......244
CAPEWELL.......271 285
CARNEL.......143 144 197 227
CARR.......202 261 286 291
CARTAR, CARTER.......5-7 9-11 13-18 24 33 45
47 50 57 61 62 103 104 108 112 113
122 132 134 136 138-140 143 147 151
170 174 176 177 184 186 188 190 191
193-195 197 198 200-202 204 211
218-220 235 238 239 243 245 249 251
255 265 267 269 270 272 273 279 281
282 286 287 291
CARTERITE.......254
CARTHWR.......67
CARTHWRIGHT.......76
CARTWRIGHT.......66 77 84-86 97 104 107-113
115 117 135 148 150 156-159 165 168
178 209 226
CATER.......286
CATERBANKE.......22 46 51
CAVNET.......15
CAWAP.......35
CAWAPP.......35
CEACRAP.......72
CHALFIELD.......287
CHALLENNER.......60
CHALLINER.......286
CHALONER.......149
CHAMBERLAIN.......237
CHAMBERLIN.......94
CHAPLAIN.......81
CHAPLIN.......38 39 41 42 87 95 104 154 161
CHAPMAN.......41-43
CHARLESWORTH.......141 142 144 180-182
184-187 208 211 212 237 239 248
CHARLEWOOD.......280
CHARLSWORTH.......139 145

CHARLTON.......63
CHAWLNER.......33
CHAWNER.......116
CHEDDLETON, CHEDULTON.......46
CHEL, CHELL....... 68 69 73-78 93 97-99 101
102 103 106 107 110 114 117 121 122
124 125 127-130 132 141 149 153
157-160 162 167 173 174 177 183-185
187-194 196 199 203-206 209 211-214
217 219-221 224 229 230 234 235 239
243 250 251 253 254 256-260 262 263
265 268 271 272 274-276 278 279 284
285 289 290 292 294 295
CHESSHIRE.......22
CHILD, CHILDE.......6
CHYLDE.......6
CLARK, CLARKE, CLEARKE, CLERK.......11 12
16-18 20 46 53 58 92 114-116 119 147
150 151 163 175 208 224 245 264
CLAY.......107 122 124 126 127 129 131 148
149 164 168
CLAYTON.......70 71 79
CLEWLOW.......140 150
CLEWLY, CLEWLEY.......245 253
CLIFF, CLIFFE.......206 252
CLOWES, CLOWS....... 74 119 120 122 123 125
126 128 129 131 135 148 162 164 169
171 176 211
CLUD, CLUDDE, CLUDE.......7 24-27 57 60
CLUIS.......118
CLULOW.......125 149 151
COAKE.......119
COAP.......101 104 105
COAPE.......66 69 80 86 90 92-94 96 97 100 106
COATE.......12 22
COATES.......7 21 22 24-27 45 47 48 50 54 70
72 73 81 89 153 240
COCLEHOUSE.......43
COKE.......23
COLCLOUGH.......74 95 130 148 150 154 156
171 213 225
COLCOUGH.......225
COLECLOUGH.......66 100 105 107
COLES.......35
COLLES.......35
COLLIER, COLIER, COLLYER.......9 23 26 27
29 33 60 63 64 66 69 73 74 76 77 79 80
82 88 95 97 98 100 101 103 106-109
111 117 119 121 123-125 127 130 131
133 134 144 145 147-151 154 167
171-173 176 179 181-184 186-190 207
209 211 212 217 219 223 226 228 230
232 244 250 252 253 273 276 279 281
283 286 287 292
COLLINS.......190 215 250
CONWAIE.......31
CONWAY.......18 30
CONWAYE.......8 19-22 26-28 30 54
CONWEY.......17
COOK, COOKE.......6 26 52 58 103 108 110 111
113 120 122 124 125 128 145 149 161

GOLDSROW.......221
GOODAL.......151 174
GOODALL.......126-128 130 150 171 176 226
233 252 288
GOODISON.......262
GOODWAINE.......35
GOODWIN, GODWIN, GOODWYN.......36 37
142 149 225 237 251
GOODWIND.......40
GOODWINE.......43
GOODWYND, GOODWYNDE.......40 60
GOODWYNE.......35-37 62
GOOSTREE, GOOSETREE.......239
GORDIN.......129 150
GOSLING.......197
GOUGH, GOFF.......37-39 62 86 100 120 148
151 162 222 226 277 290
GRAT..........72
GRATELEY.......81
GRATELEYE.......81
GRATLEY.......11
GRATWICH.......289
GRAVENOR.......248
GRAY.......12
GREATBACH, GREATBATCH,
GREATBATCHE.......12 31 32 34-36 59 60 67
81 83 87 88
GREEN, GREENE.......44 88 150 160 188 189
228 250 252 253 270 272 285 286 290
294 295
GREENEHOUGH, GREENEHOUGHE.......8 21
22 45 48 50 51
GREENOP.......195
GREENSMITH.......186 188 190 192 194 195
214 248 250 255 258 260-262 277 279
285 286
GREENWOOD.......91
GRENDON.......5
GRETTON.......114-116 148 156 158 176 267
GREY.......174
GRICE.......97
GRIFFIN, GRIFFEN.......119 146 202-204 216
217 240 248 250 251 267 268 270 272
273 276 279 289 292 293
GRIFFIS, GRIFFITH, GRIFFITHS.......242 244
264
GRIFFOLD.......12
GRIFFYN.......11
GRIME.......148 166
GRINDY.......244
GRIPHIN.......39
GROSVENOR.......220
GRUNDIE.......25-27 35 51 58
GRUNDY, GRUNDYE......10 24 27 35 59 60 259
GRYNDY.......11 60
GURNEY.......254

HADEN.......292
HAILES.......89
HAKIN, HAKINS.......95
HALDEN.......248

HALEY.......45
HALL........30-32 69 89 94 115 118 121 128 131
132 134-136 138 147 159 167 173 178
183 184 197 208 231 233 238 248 252
285
HALLEN.......60
HALLOM.......59
HAMBLETON.......56
HAMMERSLEY.......253
HAMPSON.......113-115
HAMSON.......110 111 153 154
HANCOCK.......121 162 223 227-229 233 236
HANCOCKES.......12
HANDY.......76 77 83-86
HANLEY.......45 195
HANSELL.......114
HANSON, HANSSON.......20 49 217
HARDEN.......12 88 245
HARDING, HARDINGE.......54
HARDY.......288
HARGRAVE, HARGREAVE, HARGREAVES....
126 149 210
HARGRAVES.......127 227
HARISON.......11
HARPER, HARPUR....151 187 189 190 192 234
HARRIS.......108-110 115 128-132 134 146 150
151 153 163 170 171 175 206 210 211
215 220 223 244 294
HARRISON, HARRYSON.......19-21 27 50 51 55
70 73 104 139-141 147 156 210 235
252 269 270 272 273 283
HART.......69 122-125 127 141-143 145 149 169
172 173 176 180 182-184 186 187
189-191 195 204-206 208 210 211 215
218-220 222 223 226 228 248 252
256-258 275 276 280
HARVEY, HARVIE, HARVY, HARVYE.......5-8
13-24 26-29 37 43-45 48-53 55 59 61 66
68 69 78 82 102 106-112 140 147 150
154 157 158 160 161 165 173 208 225
252
HASSALL.......63
HATHERINGS.......82
HATTOWE.......52
HAUGHTON.......15
HAULEY.......175
HAWCHARDE.......15
HAWKINS.......11 176 223 261 271 273
HAWLEY.......120 128 139 142 144 145 183 193
200-202 213 215 219 221 233 234 237
240 243 245 246 249 252 254 276-278
282 284 293
HAWTHORN.......245
HAYCOCK.......88
HAYES.......250
HAYWARD.......12
HAYWOOD.......186 237
HAZELTON.......200
HEALEY.......30 31 37 39 40 42 43 62 104 115
158 160 161 285
HEALIE.......29

HEALY.......36 42 60 63 64 66 68 77 87 89 92
 101 107-111 113 152 215
HEAPE.......17 19-24 26 29 48-50 55 57
HEATH, HEATHE.......44 70 85 88 90 93 95 99
 102 104 144 154 159 162 178 181 191
 195 197-201 238 239 248 265 267 269
 282 287 291
HEATHCOTE.......252
HEATON.......7 9 30 55 58 64 66-73 75 76 78 83
 88 90 91 93-102 106 107 109 114 116
 118 120 123 149 152 153 155 160 162
 170 171 174 180 185 187 190 193 210
 214 218 229 238 253
HEELEY.......70 73-75 79 80 100 102 120 148
 154 161 171
HEELEYE.......82
HEELY.......76 78 106 110
HEELYE.......72
HEILDRICH.......67
HEILEY.......28 44
HEIRES.......98
HEIRS.......67 96 99 101
HELE.......41
HELEY.......28 30 37 38
HELY.......37 38 41
HENSHAW.......94
HERNE.......13
HERRAT.......67
HERVEY.......13 226
HERVY.......60
HEWIT, HEWITT.......169 211 228
HEYLE.......14
HEYLEY.......28
HIBBERD.......184
HIBBERT.......185 233
HICHCOCK.......115
HICKCHOCK.......50
HICKINBOTHAM.......251
HICKLIN.......219
HIDE.......33 41 58 63 86 87 90 92 93 95 99 102
 104 154 184 186 202-204 208 210 216
 229 281
HIGGES.......120 123 148
HIGGINBOTHAM.......261
HIGGINS, HIGGENS.......45 75
HIGGS.......183-185 207 215 221 232
HILDITCH.......254
HILL, HILLE.......9-11 14 16 23 30-35 37-39 46
 57 59-64 69 71 73-76 78 81-86 88 90-92
 94 95 97 99 102-105 111-114 119 127
 140 141 146 147 152 153 155 157 158
 162-164 189-191 193 194 196 198 216
 226 242 250 253-255 278 289 293
HILTON.......94 168
HINCKLY.......181 182
HINLEY.......88
HIRST.......218 247
HITCHCOCK.......78 97 106 114 116 119 121
 123 126 128 150 151 157 158 165 167
 169 172
HIXON.......85

HOADE.......10
HODGEKYNSON.......51
HODGESON.......6 8 9 15 17 19 20 22 24 25 32
 33 44 46 48 50 53 54 56 58 103
HODGKIN, HODGKINS.......123
HODGKINSON.......129 132 170
HODGSON, HODSON.......9 11 34-36 40-42 62
 79 82 86 87 103 107 126 127 129 130
 132
HODIN.......119 162
HOILE.......103 104 107 109 111
HOLASTON.......16
HOLDEN.......294
HOLDING.......147
HOLINDWERITH.......232
HOLLAND.......66 107 109 123 154 157 166 245
HOLLANDE.......6
HOLLES.......44
HOLLIES.......46
HOLLIN.......151
HOLLINGS.......137
HOLLINGWORTH.......119 132 134 135 137 138
 140 146 176 177 180 185 187 188 211
 212 225 229 232
HOLLINS.......9 41-43 66 68 69 71 73 84 85
 88-90 94-96 99 101-104 106-125 127
 128 131-134 136 139 143 145 147
 149-153 155 156 158 159 161 162
 164-167 169 172-174 176 177 179-182
 189 190 193 195-200 203-205 207-210
 213 216-218 221 224 225 227 229 231
 232 245 247 251 256 257 259-264
 266-274 277 279 280 282 285 288 291
 293 294
HOLLONS.......138 234
HOLLTE.......19
HOLLYNS.......72 82
HOLMES.......144 240 254 287
HOLT, HOLTE.......6 11 13-18 38-40 42 48 53
 54 59 86 118
HOMERSLEY, HOMERSLY.......87 89
HOMES.......10
HOOD.......213
HOOE.......5 15 17 45
HOOFORD, HOOFORDE.......9 30 55 56
HOOMES.......59
HOOMS.......109
HOOWE.......33 58
HOPKINS.......143 144 177 178
HORDEN, HORDERN, HORDERNE.......8 55 74
 75 82 85 90 93 113 115 117 168
HORDORNE.......53
HORN, HORNE.......115 145 178 181 229 248
HORNEBYE.......6
HOROBBIN.......105
HORSEMAN.......149
HORTON.......88
HOUGH.......68 69 101 102 233 234 292
HOUGHFORD.......229
HOUGHTON.......10
HOULTE.......57

HOWARD.......116 118 120 129 131-133
        135-137 139-141 145-147 150 162 170
        171 176-178 181 182 187 208 210 212
        229 239 275
HOWE, HOW.......24 25 27 34 39-41 53 63 92
        93 95 99 105 124 125 129-131 133 134
        136-138 142 143 145 154 155 157 161
        167 169-171 175 177 179-181 185 186
        188 189 191 194-200 205 208-210 212
        214-221 223 224 226 229 230 234 235
        238-240 242 245 246 249 250 254
        257-261 276-278 280 281 285 286
HOWFOT.......200
HOYL.......87 92 94 95 157 158 160
HOYLE.......77 163 165 170
HUBBARD.......218 278
HUDSON.......64 232
HUGHES.......173 189 190 192 194 195 197
        199-201 204 205 216 221 240 252 253
        257 259 264 266 280-282 287
HULME.......9
HUNT.......136 138 231
HURD, HURDE.......7 157
HURDMAN.......7
HURST.......130 142 180 209
HURT.......121 163-165
HURTE.......22 23
HUSON.......193-195 197 198 200 243 245 252
        254 257 258 275-278 283 286 292
HYD, HYDE.......6-9 11 13 19 24 26 28-35 37-41
        43 52 55 56 58 60-62 64 69 73-77 79-82
        95 96 131-134 141 150 156 159 161
        162 166 173 177 178 191 243 245 283
        285
HYK.......81
HYLE.......224
HYLL.......5-7 15-20 23-28 45 46 48 52 54 97

HYLLE.......19 56
HYNCKS.......7
HYTCHCOTT.......118

IBBES, IBBS.......181 184 209
IBSON.......68 98 99
IGHT.......67
ILEM.......58
INGLEBY.......218
INGRAM.......199 206 249 280 289
INGRAMTHORP.......12
IPSO.......98
IPSON.......12 95 96
IRELAND.......285

JACKSON.......25 31 56 57 95 96 109 116 117
        127 146 150 192 194 196 197 204 218
        220 221 235 244 294
JACQUES.......156
JAKES.......97 166
JAMES.......87 156
JAQES, JAQUES, JAQUESS.......91 94 96 154
JARVES.......137

JARVIS.......138
JAUQUES.......157
JEFFREY, JEFFERY.......40
JEFFRIES.......76 77
JELLEY, JELLY.......89 99 127 128 130 131 133
        134 136 140
JENKIN.......145
JENKINS.......88 162
JENKINSON.......143 254 258-260 262-264 285
JERVIS.......134 136
JOBBER.......154
JOHNSON, JOHNSTONE, JONSON.......5 9
        16-21 33 34 39-43 45 47 49 57 58 67
        69-71 76-78 80 84-87 89-94 96-102
        104-106 112-119 123 126 128-130
        132-135 137 139-147 149-151 153-159
        161-163 166 167 169-177 179 181
        183-187 189-191 193 195 199 203-205
        207-217 219 221-225 229 234-236 238
        241-245 247 249 252 256-262 264 267
        270 271 274 277-281 286-288 290 291
        293
JOLLAND.......230 233
JOLLY, JOLLEY.......11
JORDAN.......228
JUMP.......68 98 99
JUPP.......148
JUTSUN.......226

KAY, KAYE.......50 53
KEALING, KEELING.......34 36 41-43 61 70-72
        76-78 83 87 88 91 122-124 126 128 129
        157 166 168 169 171-173 176 179 180
        229 234 236 238
KEEL.......73
KEELINGE.......7 11 13 14 16 17 21 23-28 30-34
        44-46 49 54 72 73 75 80
KEELYNGE.......43 52 53 55
KEEN, KEENE.......8 9 11 22 34 41 42 56 58 59
        64 71 75 77-79 83-86 90 98 113 115
        146 156 162 163
KEENS.......62
KENDER.......147
KENDRICK, KENDRICKE.......57 234 289
KENT.......121 145 157 188 190 192 194-200
        202 206 214 220 221 227 239 240 243
        246 256 259-263 265-268 270 271 273
        275 278 282 283 285 287 288
KERLING.......293
KEY, KEYE.......13 20-22 57 80 90
KEYLYNGE.......13
KEYNE.......23
KEYS.......248 294
KID, KIDD.......263 264 267 269 270 273 289
KINDER.......176 208
KINNERSLEY.......147 220
KIRCOME.......57
KIRK.......139 141 142 144 176 178 183 202 208
        211 224 238 246
KIRKAM.......289
KIRKE.......180

KIRKLAND.......267 289
KNIGHT.......66 100 107 117
KNOBBS.......294
KNOTT.......255
KNOWLES, KNOWLS.......110 111 121
KORNE.......12
KORTON.......79 80
KOTES.......59
KYNE.......23
KYNNERSLEY.......45 147
KYNSON.......8
KYRCAM, KYRKAM.......6 7 13 17-20 43 44 46
   48 50 52

LACEBY.......128 129 151
LACHIN.......110
LAKEIN.......102
LAKEN.......156
LAKIN.......66-69 77 78 83-85 88-90 92 95
   97-103 105-112 134 137 138 154 155
   158-160 162 163 165 173 238
LAKYN.......68 75 76 81
LANDOR, LANDER.......189 191 193 213
LAPLONE.......14
LARRENCE.......147
LATHBURY.......112
LATHEROP.......36
LATHEROPE.......10
LATHEROPP.......36 37 58
LATHROP.......37 43 70 74-78 83 84
LATHROPP.......10 37 60 61
LATHROPPE.......57
LAUGHTON.......191 192 194 195 197-199 232
   238 245 249
LAWRENCE, LAURENCE, LAWRANCE.......
   28-30 54 56 61 68 69 75 81 82 86 89 94
   96 98 102 103 108 157 162 292
LAWTON.......49
LAYKIN.......186
LAYTHROPPE.......55
LEADBITTER, LEADBEATER.......104
LEAGH.......147
LEAK, LEEKE.......27 53
LECESTER.......9
LEE, LEA, LEY.......13 14 18 21-23 25 28 35-38
   43 45 53 54 92 95 151 152 158 159 165
   174 175
LEES, LEESE, LEYES.......5-8 10 17 18 20-25
   29-31 35 39 40 42 46-49 52 53 55 57 62
   64 68-70 73 75-78 80 83 84 86 88 91-93
   95 96 98-100 102 104 106 110-112 121
   123-125 127-131 134 137 138 140-145
   149-152 154 164 169 171 173 175-177
   179 181 184 187 193 194 197 200 203
   211 212 215 217 221 226 227 232 235
   236 243 246 249 250 260-264 266 274
   276 280 292
LEEY.......21 22 49
LEICESTER.......80 81
LEIGH.......8 27
LEWIS.......12 119

LICESTER.......38 61
LIGHTWOOD.......125 126 128 149
LIMER.......288
LINY.......106
LOCKER.......114
LOOE.......46 48 49
LOTON.......12
LOVARTT.......246
LOVATT, LOVETT.......138 139 141 143 149
   188 199 201 202 204 209 217 218 221
   238 240 244 246 247 264 266-268 270
   274 281 282 285 290 292
LOVET.......271
LOWE, LOE, LOW.......5 8 9 13 14 16 17 19 21
   30-32 36 39-44 47 52 55 56 61 63 67 70
   72-74 80-83 85-91 95 104 111 114-116
   118 122 124 126 128 131 133 135 137
   139 141 144-146 148-150 153-157
   159-163 173 177 181 182 187 214 215
   221 223 224 227 228 247 248 259 266
   278 293
LOWNDES.......138 139 141 143 175 185-191
   193-195 197 198 200 201 203 204 210
   212 213 216 221 234 237 239 245 251
   252 276 291-293
LOWNDS.......207
LOWNS.......223
LUEL.......11
LUKES.......148
LYCET, LYCETT.......184 236
LYEMAR.......147
LYMER.......54 226 270 286 288
LYMYALLES.......48
LYNN.......190 210 212 215 232
LYNNALLES.......20 21
LYON.......110 118 146
LYRCAM.......5

MADELEY.......254
MAGIOR.......10
MAKIN.......264
MALKYN.......7 8
MALLER.......81
MALLOWE.......10
MANIFOLD.......10 225 228 293
MANNATT.......228
MANNERING.......33
MANSFIELD.......82 247
MARALL.......28 29
MARCHETT.......50
MARCHINGTON.......289
MARGEERAM.......23
MARGERAM.......7 23-26 50 63
MARGERISON.......55 58 59
MARGERUM.......7
MARLER.......104
MARRALL.......30 31
MARRET.......39
MARRETT.......39
MARROTT.......147
MARSON, MARSTON.......112 114-116 118 119

66-71 73 74 76 78 80 84-87 89 95-102
106 107 113 118-121 124 127 129 130
132-134 137 139-142 144 145 147 153
160 163 166 168 169 173 175-177
180-196 199 203 205 206 208 209
211-213 215-217 219-221 225 227 229
231 233-235 239 240 246-248 251 252
254 256-258 266 269 271 275 277 278
282 285-288
RUSSEL, RUSSELL.......5 6 44 49 127 183
RUSSON.......7
RUSTON.......72
RUTCHISON.......93
RYDER.......53

SALE.......219 222 246 253 255
SALISBURY.......281
SALSBURYE.......26
SALT, SALTE.......9 23 25 31-33 38-43 45 47 50
55 61-63 67 80 82 89 94 133-135 137
138 140-146 151 154 174 177 180 183
185 186 195 196 207 209 210 213 214
218 228 229 231 233 241 244 291
SAMMSON.......9
SAMPSON.......288
SANCT, SANCTE.......23 24
SANDERS.......79 96 236 246
SANT.......34
SAULT, SAULTE.......7 91
SAUNDERS.......69 70 77 78 82-87 89 90 92 94
95 98 100 102 103 106 109 115 117
118 138 146 151 155 156 158 185 186
188 190 191 193 195 197 199 201 217
231 245 246 251 258 278
SAUNT.......80
SAVAGE.......10
SAVILE.......252
SCILETO.......113
SCOT, SCOTT, SCOTTE.......8 11 237
SERGEANT.......88
SHARP, SHARPE.......42 72 73 77 80 82-84 86
159 163 164 282
SHARRAT, SHARRATT.......17 18 21 22 24-26
28 78 282
SHARRATTE.......22
SHAUKHURST.......95
SHAW, SHAWE.......6 10 50 76 78 83-85 87 88
97 106 109 110 113 115 119 122 125
127 135 142 144 150 153 155 156 166
171 173 178 180 218 223 227 228 247
248 293 294
SHELDON.......247
SHELLY, SHELLEY.......146
SHEMELT.......200 266 285 288
SHEMILT.......185 211 237 242 243 288
SHENTON, SHENSTON.......8 11 35 114 144
145 147 179 180 183 185-192 200 209
212 215 216 225 234 235 240 245 260
261 291
SHEPHARD, SHEPPARD.......10
SHEPPARDE.......44

SHERBROOK, SHERBROKE.......54
SHERET.......34 35
SHERETT.......34
SHERMAN.......74
SHERRARD.......31 142
SHERRARDE.......31 32
SHERRATT, SHERAT, SHERATT, SHERRAT,
SHERRET.......6-9 11-18 20-22 24 29 30 32 33
35-44 46-49 51-55 57 59-64 66-120 122
123 133-136 139 140 144 146-149
152-155 157-165 167 171-175 184
186-188 190 192 193 195 196 202 207
208 212 214 218 220 221 223 224 226
228 235 240 246 249 252 257 258
261-264 275-277 280 286
SHERRETT.......14 58 261
SHERWIN.......11
SHERWINE.......12
SHILTON.......120
SHINGLER.......251
SHIPLEY.......69 102 119 162 214 248
SHIPTON.......288
SHIRLY, SHIRLEY.......252
SHORT.......60
SIMMS.......235 242
SIMNET.......147
SIMSON.......96
SIVIS.......274
SKRIGLEY.......197
SKRIMSHER.......70 71
SKYDMOORE.......19
SLACK.......35
SLANEY.......180 239
SLATER.......193-195 216 219 245 253 279 282
SLAUGHTER.......168
SMALLEY.......153
SMALLWOOD.......158
SMITH, SMYTH, SMYTHE.......5 7 9-19 23-27
29 30 33-38 41 45 46 48 50-54 57 59 62
74 81 86 93 96 99 109 122-124 128
141-145 147-152 155 161 166 168
173-175 180 182-187 189 191-202 204
206-208 210 213-216 219 220 225 231
235 237 239 244 245 247 249-254 256
258-263 265 266 269 274 279 280 283
285-288 290-292 294 295
SNAPE.......68 78 94 96 97 99 101 102 104-106
110 116 128 147-149 159 167 202 220
225 231 237 264 265 267 269 270 274
282 287 290
SNELSON.......121 123 163 168 170
SNOW.......282
SOAMS.......10
SONT.......10 11 34 35 37 38 61 67 81 86 93
105
SONTE.......32 33 57 58
SPATEMAN.......126 127 129 149 168 169
SPENCER, SPENSER.......7 9-13 16-18 21
25-27 30-35 38-40 42 45-47 49-54
56-60 62 64 74 75 80-82 87 90 100 125
146 148 154 156 262 274

117-122 124 126-128 130 140 142-144 146 158 160 162 165 169 174 177 178 180-189 191 193 204-209 211 213 214 220 225 230 237 239 252 256-262 268 270 276 277 285 288 291-2

TORTERSHELL.......259

TOTERSHAL, TOTERSHALL.......260 261

TOWERS.......10 36 38 80 118 120 132 161 172 264 290

TOWNSEND.......9 97 98 104 148 157 160

TOWNSHEND.......173

TREEN.......244

TRUNDLEY.......131 246

TRUNLEY.......117 118 120 162 170

TRUNLY.......114

TRUSSILTE.......9

TRYNLEY.......116 157

TUCKETT.......24

TUNIECLEFF, TUNNICLEFFE.......178 228

TUNNICLIFF, TUNNICLIFFE.......133-136 138 139 142 176 178 189 192 199 209 213 214 216 222 233 237 240 246 247 275 276 292

TUNNICLIFT.......240

TUNNYCLIFF.......228

TUNSAL.......130

TUNSTAL, TUNSTALL....... 66 68 78 96 101 106 107 109 110 113 116-118 120 121 123 125 126 129 131 137 142 143 145 158 160 164 165 168-170 173 177 181 185 208 211 213 215 227 228 239 258 289 291

TUNSTLE.......98

TURNER.......5 8 9 22 57 93 96 98 99 111 113-118 120 121 124 126 127 129-133 135 137 139 142 144 145 147 149 150 154 156 160-163 165 168 170 171 173-175 177 178 180-182 184-191 193-197 200-203 205 207 209-212 214 216-218 220 221 223-239 243-246 248-253 256-259 261-266 268-273 275 278 280-283 286 287 289-292 294

TWIGG, TWIGGE.......199 201 204 276-278 287 288 293 294

TYBPER.......45

TYLSTONS.......58

TYTLEY.......18

UPPINGE.......39

UPTON.......265 268 281 283

UTTWARDE.......52

VAUGHAN.......247

VENABLES.......15 16 151

VENESON.......249

VERNON.......66 88 91 93 107 158 160 244

VICARSTAFF.......233

VISE.......111 146 154

WADE.......46 49

WAKEFIELD.......67 110 111

WAKLAT, WAKLET, WAKLETT.......34 35 58 59

WAKLIN.......12

WALCLATT, WALCLATTE.......18

WALKELAT, WALKELATE.......25 28 52

WALKER.......6 8 9 27 35-37 48 55 70 71 78 81 90 91 127-136 138 143 146 158 169 172-176 178 180 183-185 187-194 196-198 200 202-205 208 209 212-217 221 223 224 226 232-234 237 239 248 254 256 257 260-262 264 265 267-270 272 274-277 280-282 286 288 289 291-294

WALL.......7-9 30-33 40-42 46 48 57 69 84-86 90 91 93 94 99 101 150 152 161

WALLE.......7 19 44 56

WALLEY.......22

WALLIS.......149 288

WALLTON.......19

WALTER, WALTERS.......122 292

WALTHO, WALTHOE.......189 249

WALTHOW.......250

WALTON.......41 136 137 151 176 214

WARD, WARDE.......5-15 17-23 25-29 32-37 41 43 44 48 51 52 54 55 57-60 62 70-72 78 87 90 100 104 115-124 137 143 147 149 159 161 165 167 170 175 176 192-197 200-203 209 213 214 216 217 220 223 225 226 247 252 260 263 266 269 272 276 277 280 290 292

WARDLE.......68 101 197 199 201-203 220 221 250 255 278 280 287 290

WARNER.......27 187 189 246 250

WARRAM.......229

WARRINGTON.......149 168 176

WARTON.......41

WATERHOUSE.......262 279

WATSON.......9 14 18-21 31-35 37 40 44 45 48 53 59 76 79 82 89 93 99 192 263-265 269 273

WATTSON.......11 34 35 37 40 61

WAYDE.......16

WEBB, WEBBE.......54 88 142 145 231

WEBBERLEY.......285

WEBSTER.......151 173

WETERYNS.......14

WETTON.......33 34 70 72-76 81 86 87 89 90 97 100 103 108 110 120 121 124 125 130 147 151 153 161 163 167 168 170 172 189 194 196 202 203 205 207 241 250 251 257 277 286 288 292 293

WETTWOOD.......10

WEYDGEWOOD.......20

WEYTTON.......48

WHEAT.......288

WHEATLEY.......11

WHEELDON.......134 136 139 151 215 279

WHEELTON.......137 151 170 174

WHELOCK.......254

WHIELDON.......224 232

WHILOCKS.......243

WHILTON.......109-112 155 233

WHISTON.......78 102 106
WHISTONS.......69
WHITALL.......10 11 61
WHITBY, WHITBEY.......11 39
WHITCOME.......33
WHITE.......72
WHITEALL.......67 70-72
WHITEHAL.......76 77 80 81
WHITEHALL.......67 73 219 268 279 289 291
WHITEHURST.......79 80 154 155 237 286 287
WHITHERINGS.......88
WHITHOUSE.......10
WHITHURST.......40 43 64
WHITTAKER.......154
WHITTELL.......28 29
WHITTERANCE.......109 111 153
WHITWICKE.......11
WHYTEHURST.......7
WHYTTERYNS.......15
WIGSON.......11
WILD.......151 272 273 294
WILDON.......140
WILKES, WILKS.......69 101
WILKOPPE.......8
WILLIAMS.......256 286 287
WILLIAMSON.......10 130
WILLINGTON.......155
WILLOT, WILLOTT.......89
WILLOWES.......55
WILLSHAW.......242 245
WILSHAW.......190 213 215 217 242 246 248
  276 279
WILSON, WILLSON.......9 11 43 62 63 83 190
  203-206 211 215-217 222 249 251 253
  254 257 259 267 260 271 274 277 283
  293
WINDLE.......107
WININGTON.......223
WISTON.......108 109
WITHERINGS.......91
WITHRINGE.......30
WITTERANCE.......68 69 78 80 83 89 90 93 95
  97 98 100-103 106 107
WITTERANES.......80
WITTERANS.......31 74 76
WITTERING.......9 37
WITTERINGE.......11 12 35-39 57
WITTSNOLL.......10
WOD.......10
WOLLASTON.......15 34 35 45 46 52 53
WOLLE.......55
WOLLEY.......23 52 210
WOLLOSON, WOLLOSTON.......10 59
WOOD, WOODE.......6 9 10 13-18 24 36-39 46
  51-54 58 66 69-77 79-81 83 86 88 92 97
  101-103 105-109 121 122 126 133 136
  142 146-151 153 165 166 168 170 175

  177 209 228 230 239 247
WOODALL.......291 292
WOODDE.......5 44 46 48 50
WOODDISSY.......244
WOODINGS.......135 151
WOODROFFE.......145 284
WOODRUFF.......111
WOODSALL.......7
WOODSON.......260
WOODWARD.......86 89 125 127 133 140 141
  143 146 149 158 176 182 184 186 189
  190 207 209 210 218 219 221 224 227
  229 231 232 240 244 246
WOODWARDE.......78
WOOLASCROFT, WOOLLESCROFT.......151
WOOLDRIDGE.......247
WOOLLASTON.......33
WOOLLEY, WOOLEY.......57 58 89 114 115 117
  120 122 125 126 129 130 133 135 136
  143-145 147-149 151 156-158 161
  165-167 173 175 178 180-186 192 207
  208 220 226 227 231 232 235 242-244
  251 276
WOOLLEYS.......164
WOOLLY, WOOLY.......97 111 154
WOOTEN.......147
WORRILOW.......99
WORTENHOUSE.......289
WORZEY.......128
WOTTON.......8 43
WRATHBONE.......163
WRIGHT, WRIGHTE.......11-14 38 42 44 46 47
  49 56-58 66 68 80 90-92 95 98 106 109
  118 120 125 127 141 147-151 154 155
  159 160 162 163 166 167 169 170 172
  179 184-187 189 191 193 194 210-214
  217 229 231 235 245 246 252 262 266
  289
WULLASTON.......31 56
WYGGYN.......49
WYLDE.......25
WYTHERINGE.......28
WYTHERYNGES.......17
WYTHNALL.......5
WYTHRINGE.......27
WYTHRINS.......28
WYTTERANS.......5
WYTTERENS.......44
WYTTERINS.......29 55
WYTTRINGES.......52
WYTTRYNS.......6 47 49 51

YARDLEY.......239
YARDLY.......100
YATES.......12 59 88 149 187 205 236 252 269
  270 279 288 293
YOUNG.......186

STAFFORDSHIRE PARISH REGISTERS SOCIETY
List of Subscribers
(as of November 2008)

Mr. R. Ainsgough, Keyworth, Notts.
Mrs B. Allard, Bournville, West Midlands
Allen Library, Fort Wayne, Indiana, USA
Mr. B. Allerton, Stoke-on-Trent, Staffs.
Mrs E.B. Amphlett, Totnes, Devon
Mr. K. Askey, Heathfield, East Sussex
Mr. A. Aston, Stafford
Mr. R.J. Ault, Smethwick, West Mids
Mrs R.J. Ball, Oakamoor, Staffs
Mrs K. Barker, Weston Coyney, Staffs.
Mrs P. J. Barton, Walbottle, Staffs.
Mrs D.J. Bartram, Rushall, West Midlands
Mr. J. Baylis, Solihull, West Midlands
Mr. A.W. Bednall, Macclesfield, Cheshire
Mrs E. Beech, Stoke-on-Trent, Staffs.
Mrs J. Bell, Weybridge, Surrey
Mrs J. Bergwever, Erina, Australia
Mr. D. Berry, Ipstones, Staffs.
Mr. J. Bielwicz, Nanango, Australia
Mrs M. Billam, Deal, Kent
Birmingham Central Library, Birmingham
BMSGH, Birmingham
Blo(o)re Society, Audlam, Staffs.
Mr. J. Bloore, Kingswinford, West Midlands
Dr. P.D. Bloore, Hagley, West Midlands
Bodleian Library, Oxford
Mr. E.A. Bold, Whitchurch, Bristol
Ms. E. Bold, Whitchurch, Bristol
Mr. J.S. Booth, Stoke-on-Trent, Staffs.
Mrs D. Bouglas, Mottingham, London
Mr. C.J. Bowden, Skelton-in-Cleveland
Mr J.K. Bradley, DibdenPurlieu, Southampton
Mr. S.J. Bradley, Gawsworth, Cheshire
Mr. J.W. Bradshaw, Fareham, Hampshire
Mr. J. Brady, Whitefield, Manchester
Mrs L.J. Brailsford, Derby
Mr. R.A. Brassington, Werrington, Staffs.
Mr. I.D. Brindley, Newcastle-u-Lyme, Staffs.
Ms L. Brindley, South Woodford, London
The British Library, Boston Spa, W. Yorks.
Mr. A.T. Brookes, Cannock, Staffs.
Mr. W.R. Brough, Teignmouth, Devon
Mr. D. Brown, Wellington, Somerset
Mr. D.M. Bruce, Stafford, Staffs.
Mrs L.I. Bull, Littleover, Derbys
Mr. R. Burndred, Church Lawton, Staffs.
Burntwood FHS, Cannock, Staffs.
Mrs D.M. Camden, Ashley, Salop
Mr. D. Camm, Bradeley, Staffs.
Mrs S.J. Capewell, London
Mrs B.A. Carter, Stoke-on-Trent, Staffs.
Mr. C. Cawley, Campello, Spain
Mr. E. Chadwick, Stoke-on-Trent, Staffs.
Miss E.K. Charles, Leek, Staffs.
Mrs K. Christian, Wincham, Cheshire
Mr. P. Clark, Barton under Needwood, Staffs.
Mr. D. Cliffe, Trentham, Staffs.

Mr. S.W. Clives, Rhyl, Clwyd
Codsall & Bilbrook History Group, Codsall
Mr M Cole, Thropton, Northumberland
Mr. M.J. Coles, Sherborne, Dorset
Mrs M.W. Colling, Broompark, Durham
Mr. P.J. Collins, Upminster, Essex
Mr. B.V. Conduct, Havant, Hants.
Mrs H.R.B. Coney, Littleover, Derbys.
Mr. M.C. Cooper, Huntington, Staffs.
Mr. P. Coops, Wrexham
Mr. P. Cope, Ammanford, Carmarthenshire
Dr. R.J. Cope, Littleover, Derby
Mr. A.J. Corcoran, Longton, Staffs.
Mr. P. Cotterill, Willenhall, West Midlands
Prof. B. Cotton, Bassett, Southampton
Mr. J.D. Cotton, Carnforth, Lancs.
Ms P. Cotton, Stoke-on-Trent, Staffs.
Mr. B. Craddock, Penkridge, Staffs.
Mr. A. Craven, Bracknell, Berks.
Mrs J. Dagnall, Oliverburn, Perth
Mrs J. Davey, Saffron Walden, Essex
Mr. B. Davies, Tockington, Bristol
Mrs C. Davies, Fenton, Staffs.
Mrs J.A. Davies, Codsall, Wolverhampton
Ms P. Davies, Carshalton Beeches, Surrey
Mr. R.M. Degg, Bedale, N. Yorks.
Sir O. de Ville, Sonning-on-Thames, Surrey
Mrs W.J. Dobson, Cadeby, Doncaster
Mr. B.Y. Downing, Kingswinford, West Mids
Dudley Library, Dudley, West Midlands
Mr. A. Dunphy, Dinas Powys, S. Glamorgan
Mrs E.P. Durose, Caverswall, Staff Moorland
Mr. P. Eddowes, Lancaster
Mrs C.L. Edge, Kingswinford, West Midlands
Mrs B. Edwards, Stramshall, Staffs.
Mr. K.J. Edwards, Stramshall, Staffs.
Mrs P. Emmett, Kingsley Holt, Staffs.
Mr. E. Evans,Wolverhampton
Mr. R. Evans, Streetly, West Midlands
Ms S. Fish, Cambridge
Ms L. Flint, Southend-on-Sea, Essex
Mrs S. Gale, Esher, Surrey
Mrs V.A. Garvey, Tunbridge Wells, Kent
Mr. G.W. Gassor, Ongar, Essex
Ms M.E. Gassor, Stafford
Mr. M.J.E. Gater, Duston, Northants.
Ms M. Gennard, Adeje, Tennerife
Mr. P.H. Gibbons, Bewdley, Worcs.
Mrs S.M. Gill, Stone, Staffs.
Mr. C.J. Godwin, Walsall, West Midlands
Mr. A. Gough, Bristol
Mrs D.A. Grant, Newcastle, Staffs.
Mr. D.V. Gregory, Great Melton, Norfolk
Mr. J. Greasley, Stoke-on-Trent, staffs.
Ms K. Grehan, Newton-le-Willows
Mrs W. Grimmette, Paddock Wood, Kent
Guildhall Library, London

Mr.N. Hale, Helston, Cornawall
Mrs V.J. Hampton, Stourbridge, West Mids.
Dr. B. Haner, Claremont, USA
Hanley Library, Hanley, Staffs.
Mr. M. Harbach, Portsmouth
Mr. C.G. Harlow, Henley-on-Thames, Oxon.
Mr. J.E. Harper, Vaucluse, France
Mrs L. Harper, Meliden, Prestatyn
Mrs C. Harrison, Eastbourne, Sussex
Mr. W.J. Harrison, Norton-in Moors, Staffs
Harvard College Library, Cambridge, USA
Mrs B. Harvey, St. Albans, Herts.
Mr. J. Hawkins, Rudyard, Staffs.
Mr. A.E. Hayward, Stafford.
Mrs P.M. Hayward, Walsall, West Midlands
Mr. R. Hayward, Barlaston, Staffs.
Mr. H.R. Haywood, Cannock, Staffs.
Mrs V. Hepworth, Stoke Prior, Worcs.
Mrs D. Herbert, Endon, Staffs.
Mr. E. Hickenbottom, Pontefract, W. Yorks.
Mrs A. Hill, Stafford
Mrs C.A. Hodge, Willenhall, West Midlands
Mr. J.A. Hodgkiss, Alrewas, Staffs.
Mr. H. Hodson, Birmingham
Mr. J. Hodson, Reading, Berkshire
Mr. P.A. Holland, Hale, Cheshire
Mrs M.E. Hollis, Leighton Buzzard, Beds.
Mr. J. Holt, Rowley Regis, West Midlands
Mrs M. Horton, Deepcar, S. Yorks.
Mr. R.N. Hudson, Leece, Cumbria
Mr. J. Hughes, Tettenhall, West Midlands
Mrs K.J. Hughes, San Marcos, USA
Mrs L. Hughes, Southampton, Hants.
Mrs C. Hugill, Lydney, Gloucs.
Mrs A. Hunt, High Wycombe, Bucks.
Mrs C. Hunt, Leek, Staffs.
Mr. D. Hutt, Pershore, Worcs.
Mr. T. Inskip, Uttoxeter, Staffs.
Mrs C.L. Jackaman, Walsall, West Mids.
Mr. C.H. Jackson, Eastham, Merseyside
Ms. R. Jarvis, Market Harborough, Leics.
Mrs A.R. Jefferson, Derby
John Rylands Library, Manchester
Mrs E.M. Johnson, Market Drayton, Shrops.
Mrs S. Johnson, Stone, Staffs.
Mrs S.A. Johnson, Caerphilly, Glamorgan
Mrs G. Keeling, Doncaster, South Yorkshire
Mr. L.N. Kidd, Oldham, Lancs.
Landor Society, Rugeley, Staffs.
Mrs E.M. Lavender, Penn, West Midlands
Miss F.M. Lawrence, Acton Trussell, Staffs.
Miss D. Lawton, Kynpersley, Staffordshire
Ms. L. Lewis, Warwick
Lichfield Library, Lichfield, Staffs.
Lichfield Record Office, Lichfield, Staffs.
Mrs P. Lister, Malton, N. Yorks.
Mrs B. Lockett, Buxton, Derbys.
Mr. T. Lockett, Wellington, Shropshire
London Library, London
Mrs S. Lote, Brownhills, West Midlands
Mrs M. Lovatt, Biddulph, Staffs.

Mr. D.G. Lynall, Poole, Dorset
Mrs M. Maiden, Newport, Gwent
Mrs L. Marple, Bilston, West Midlands
Mr. A.E. Marshall, Crewe, Cheshire
Mr. S.D. Martin, Wigan, Lancs.
Mr. R. Mayer, Stoke-on-Trent, Staffs.
Ms E. McCoulloch, Tutbury, Staffs.
Mr. P.A. Mellor, Trentham, Staffs.
Mrs D. Merrett, Egremont, Cumbria
Mrs P. Miles, Wombourne, Staffs.
Mr. R.W. Minchin, Tutbury, Staffs.
Mr. K.L.A.C. Moore, Bromyard, Herefs.
Ms K. Morgan, Telford, Staffs.
Mr. F. Morlidge, Glasbury-on-Wye, Herefs.
Mr. R.F. Morton, Walton-on-the-Hill, Staffs.
Mr. C. Munday, Harpfields, Staffs.
Newberry Library, Chicago, USA
Newcastle Library, Newcastle, Staffs.
New England Genealogical Soc, Boston USA
Mrs E.B. North, Sedgley, West Midlands
North Cheshire Family History Society
Miss O. Nourse, Yate, South Gloucs.
Mr. F.J.A. Oakes, Halton, Lancs.
Miss C. Oakley, Willenhall, West Midlands
Ms E. Oakley, Nottingham
Mrs C. O'Neill, Wolverhampton, West Mids.
Ms L. Orritt, Delph Saddleworth, Yorks.
Mrs. J. Parker, Watford
Mrs S. Parkes, Willenhall, West Midlands
Dr. M.A. Patrick, Exeter, Devon
Mr. D.T. Pearsall, Dorridge, West Midlands
Mrs S. Pearson, Stourbridge, West Midlands
Mrs J.E. Penman, Hednesford, Staffs.
Mrs E.M. Phillips, Oulton, Staffs.
Ms. L. Phillips, Nuneaton, Warks.
Mr. J.R. Pickerell, Linton, Cambs.
Mrs M. Piper, Rugeley, Staffs.
Mr. G. Pitt, Walsall, West Midlands
Mr. S. Pitt, Stafford
Mrs E. Powell, Alsager, Staffs.
Mr. A.R. Pretty, Wadebridge, Cornwall
Mr. E. Pritchard, Willenhall, West Mids.
Mr. J. Proudlove, Darwen, Lancs.
Ms J. Rainsbury, Canterbury, Kent
Mr. W.J. Read, Stafford
Mrs F.M. Reeve, Derby
Ms. E. Roberts, Ludlow, Salop
Mr. J. Roberts, Blythe Bridge, Staffs.
Ms. P. Roberts, Tipton, West Midlands
Ms. S. Roberts, Telford, Salop
Ms M.W. Rogers, Kallaroo, Australia
Miss M.E.R. Rooke, Wombridge, Salop
Mrs M. Rosentritt, Bewdley, Worcs.
Mrs P.A. Ross, Tamworth-in-Arden, West Mid
Ms. J.M. Rowley, Birmingham
Mr. R.P. Rushton, Crewe, Cheshire
Mr. D. Salt, Baddeley Green, Staffs.
Mrs A. Satanow, Newcastle, Staffs.
Mr. D.R. Saunders, Chirk, Clwyd
Mrs S. Scargill, Ipstones, Staffs.
Mrs M. Schultz, Stockport

Mr. S.R. Scott, Betley, Staffs.
Mr. J. Shaw, Biddulph, Staffs.
Mr. P.R.B. Shotton, Belbroughton, Worcs.
Mr. G.A. Shufflebotham, Betley, Cheshire
Mrs A. Simcock, Amlwch, Anglesey
Mrs J.A. Simkins, Sutton Coalfiield, West Mid.
Dr. C.R. Sims, Royston, Herts.
Mr. J. Singer, Sandbach, Cheshire
Mr. M. Slaney, Creswell, Staffs.
Mr. A. Smith, Lightwood, Staffs.
Mrs E.A. Smith, Roughcote, Staffs.
Mr. J.C. Smith, Wednesfield, West Midlands
Mrs M. Smith, Stonehouse, Gloucs.
Mrs P. Smith, Coven, Staffs.
Society of Genealogists, London
Mrs C.A. Spink, Morley, W. Yorks.
Stafford County Library, Stafford
Staffs. County Record Office, Stafford
Staffordshire History, Stafford
Mr. J. Stead, Loughborough, Leics.
Mrs J. Steer, Allestree, Derby
Mr. M. Stevens, Les Aleuvenettes, France
Ms E. Summers Abbots Bromley, Staffs.
Mr. T. Sutton, Kingswinford, West Midlands
Mrs G. Swift, Lightwood, Staffs.
Col. I.S. Swinnerton, Longburton, Dorset
Ms. L. Tanner, Gosport, Hampshire
Miss J.M. Taylor, Biddulph, Staffs.
Mrs K. Taylor, Trentham, Staffs.
Dr. D. Thomas, Wolverhampton, West Mids
Mrs A.M. Thompson, Presteigne, Powys

Mr. D.A. Tomkinson, Crewe, Cheshire
Mrs S.M. Tonking, Abbots Bromley, Staffs.
Mr. N. Tooth, Ealing, London
Ms K.A. Twigg, Trentham, Staffs.
University of Keele, Keele, Staffs.
University of Lancaster, Lancaster
Major R. Unett, Bradford, W. Yorks.
Utah Genealogical Soc., Salt Lake City, USA
Mr. C.J. Vyse, London
Mr. I. Wallbank, Newcastle-u-Lyme, Staffs.
Ms. M. Walker, Uttoxeter, Staffs.
Walsall Central Library, Walsall, West Mids.
Ms P. Ward, Hadlow, Kent
Mrs W. Waterall, Loscoe, Derbys.
Mrs I. Wells, Crowle, South Humberside
Western Australia Geneal. Soc., Australia
Mr. D.G. Whalley, Newcastle-u-Lyme, Staffs.
Mr. G. Wilcox, Lichfield, Staffs.
Mr. R. Wilcox, Timperley, Cheshire
Mrs J.L. Wilkinson, Beccles, Suffolk
Ms. A. Willetts, Stourbridge, West Midlands
Mrs M. Williams, Aston, Flintshire
William Salt Library, Stafford
Wolverhampton Library, Wolverhampton
Mrs C. Wollaston, Walsall, West Midls.
Mr. B. Wood, Standish, Lancs.
Mrs M. Wood, Alsager, Staffs.
Ms A, Woolf, Waikerie, Australia
Mrs D. Wyers, Rolleston-on-Dove, Staffs.
Yale University, New Haven, USA